A *New History of*
SPANISH
AMERICAN
FICTION
Volume I

A New History of

SPANISH AMERICAN FICTION

by Kessel Schwartz

VOLUME I
*From Colonial Times
to the Mexican Revolution
and Beyond*

UNIVERSITY OF MIAMI PRESS
Coral Gables, Florida

TO BERTRAM D. LEWIN,
loving father-in-law, brilliant scholar

Contents

Preface

The primary intent of this work is to study the development of the Spanish American novel rather than the shorter fictional forms such as the novelette, the "relato," or the chronicle. The short story, especially, has unique narrative characteristics of thematic variety, brevity, conclusive action, and concise emotional and physical description. However, since some short story writers have had great influence in the development of the novel, and since most of the novelists also write short stories, some analysis of the short story (and similar forms) has been attempted from time to time although not on a completely consistent basis.

Many novelists write in a variety of styles and follow diverse literary schools in their individual production. Indeed, some writers combine various literary tendencies within the same novel. In these cases arbitrary judgments have been applied. Ignacio Manuel Altamirano exhibits both romantic and realistic aspects, but he has been included in the former category. Carlos Reyles has been treated in the chapter dealing with *criollismo*, even though he also wrote one of the most heralded modernist novels. Augusto d'Halmar, creator of imaginative and evocative fiction, has been placed with the modernists, although he wrote a fairly well-known naturalistic novel. Classification by generation, school or movement is at best a thankless task in the confused cultural context of Spanish American literature, and I have attempted, on the basis of available evidence and analysis of authors' works, to place them in the division which seems most nearly to reflect their proper niche in the luxuriant fiction of the continent.

No special critical point of view, formalist, archetypal, Marxist, or any other, has been attempted, but some novelists have been somewhat reinterpreted. It is difficult to separate literary history from personal literary criticism in a treatment of this scope, but I have, insofar as possible, attempted an objective treatment in presenting the logical development of fictional forces of the last 450 years in Spanish America. Discussions of generations, literary schools and movements, as they apply to fiction, have been included; an effort has been made to avoid a series of separate essays and to fuse the esthetic values with historical settings, hopefully conveying the common cultural attributes novelists in Spanish America have and at the same time showing their national identities. Rather than follow an exact chronology an attempt has been made to group authors by literary movements while at the same time emphasizing individual stylistic and aesthetic experiences. As Pedro Henríquez Ureña once said: "Noble deseo pero grave error cuando se quiere hacer historia es el que pretende recordar a todos los héroes. En la historia literaria el error lleva a la confusión." Although an effort has been made to include, for the most part, only authors of some significance either from a historical or an intrinsic point of view, the choice has not always been clear cut, and on occasion a kind of inventory of names and works has been included. Notes have been generously supplied, but hundreds of studies and background materials have been utilized beyond those footnoted. Every attempt has been made to read the novels discussed, but in a few cases this has not been possible.

Fictional traits may be cited from the *Cartas de relación* on through other chronicles and in a variety of novelistic sketches, although José Joaquín Fernández de Lizardi (1776–1827), a product of the Enlightenment, is often labeled the first "true Spanish American novelist." American romanticism served to loosen the literary strait jacket binding novelists to Europe, even though they were largely dependent on European culture. The historical novel, with varying elements of the historical and political, the sentimental novel, and the Indianist novel were among the romantic forms. Realistic novels reflected a given historical time, class distinctions, and society as a social entity, while naturalism, of brief duration in Spanish America, nonetheless generated the autochthonous elements of the *criollista* novel. Modernism concentrated on aesthetics, form, and the exaltation of the senses, combining cosmopolitanism with a search for remote American roots. The nineteenth-century novel of customs, whether romantic or realistic, had revealed a satirical, humorous, and *reformista* tendency, which later combined with historical determinism, a kind of positivism, and the poetic art of the modernist novelists.

Combining with naturalism, modernism created a novel dealing with man and nature in a total relationship and offered a new way to examine man and his values against a local background of jungle, river, or city. The fusion of previous movements, along with an attenuated *costumbrismo* and an insistence on a forceful natural background, an *ambiente* in which regional types such as the *huaso* and the *gaucho* acted, created what I have called criollismo, but quite often these novels concentrated in naturalistic fashion on people in urban environments. The tragic and catastrophic concern over the destiny of man, in all its pessimism and social degeneration, found one natural scapegoat in nature as a destructive and terror-inspiring force superior to man, who was usually portrayed as a symbolic counterforce of lesser proportions. Poetic and episodic narration tended toward the descriptive rather than the analytical, but novelists like Reyles and Barrios showed great insight concerning human motivations. The novelists seemed obsessed with landscape and the social problems of alienated remnants of their society such as the Indian or mestizo and voiced a continuing conviction about the triumph of civilization over barbarism. Whatever they lacked in dramatic force they replaced with vigor, color, and life. Eventually the essentially naturalistic orientation involving a malignant cosmic nature or social injustice became attenuated, but criollismo created a formidable flow of fiction.

The novels of the Mexican Revolution, with their episodic emphasis on local events, show nevertheless, in a general way, the conflict between the individual's personal morality and his commitment to the sociopolitical scene. The commitment to a common cause usurped values which in other contexts might have been treasured. The leaders of the revolution, demanding blind allegiance of their men, sought to superimpose on their established hierarchy of values an artificial pattern of motivations and thus ended by substituting one tyranny for another.

Many of the actors of the revolution were incapable of transcending the personal aspects of their conflict or of seeing their problems in the perspective of collective well-being. At times they turned from active involvement to sterile indignation, not so much in the initial fighting but in the political aftermath. The Mexican novelists provide us with a spectrum of emotion ranging from chronic despair to a childlike confidence in the efficiency and magic of revolution. In contrast with later neorealists they cannot convey the horror and compassion of the moment by humanizing abstract forms of social and economic tragedy through moving individual experiences, and they fail to stress the human dimension over the sociological implications of the characters' behavior. In their totality, nonetheless, these novels present an authentic effort at a kind of literary innovation and present us with a glowing and dramatic tapestry of historical events and the men who participated in them. They show us the revolutionary fervor of those men, their idealism and optimism along with their opportunism and pessimism, their sacrifices, as well as the illusions and moral anguish of those who saw their fondest hopes for a new kind of world defrauded by imperfect human beings who fell victim to their own greed and materialism at the expense of a noble idea.

A New History of
SPANISH
AMERICAN
FICTION
Volume I

1. The Beginnings

American writers like Pedro Henríquez Ureña claim that Columbus' *Diary* is the first Spanish American work. But it was not until the nineteenth century, when Juan Valera, Marcelino Menéndez y Pelayo, and Miguel de Unamuno were writing perceptively about Spanish America, that Spaniards began grudgingly to consider its literature as a unique and separate entity. Even Juan Valera and Menéndez y Pelayo, at times, considered Spanish American literature to be an aspect of Spanish literature. The different geographies (the plains of Argentina as opposed to the highlands of Bolivia) and racial and social entities (the gaucho in Argentina, where the ethnic background is largely European, the Indian in Ecuador, or the *roto* in Chile) in America impeded an evaluation of that continent's literature as a homogeneous whole, in spite of the superficially somewhat similar local color and spirit. Enrique Díez Canedo, Spanish critic, in his acceptance speech to the Royal Spanish Academy, partly recognized the special quality of the American spirit. Gradually many came to accept views such as that of Waldo Frank that the unity of Spanish America, the true melting pot, lay in its mestizo mixtures.

Today nobody questions the Spanish American novel as an entity, but a difference of opinion still exists as to when fiction first appeared in the New World. Many critics agree that it was not until the nineteenth century, but they can give no satisfactory explanation for the late arrival they postulate. The *Celestina*, picaresque novels, novels of chivalry, and *Don Quijote* were well known in America. One explanation, often given in the past was that the Spanish monarchs considered novels harmful to religion and good habits, a suggestion which like most of the other explanations does not really hold up. As early as 1506 King Ferdinand prohibited the sale of profane books "for the good government of the Indies," [1] and the wife of Charles V, the first of the Spanish "blue noses," succeeded in having a decree (4 April 1531) published prohibiting the exportation of works of fiction to the Indies. In spite of elaborations of the Royal Decree (14 July 1536 and 13 September 1543), these books, especially novels like *Amadís de Gaula* which the queen deemed detrimental to the moral health of the natives, found their way to the New World to be widely read there.[2] Charles V and Santa Teresa, among others in Spain, were quite fond of these novels, but in 1553 these "idle romances" were again prohibited from being printed, sold, or read in the New World. These decrees insisted that "libros de romances, de historias vanas o de profanidad como son de Amadís e otros desa calidad . . . es mal ejercicio para los indios, e cosa en que no es bien que se ocupen ni lean." The 1543 decree feared that the Indians might deduce from fictional accounts the false belief that the Bible and other such books were also fictional,[3] presaging the unfortunate transfer to the New World of European medieval institutions and values.

Gonzalo Fernández de Oviedo, in his *Historia general y natural de las Indias* (1535) calls novels of chivalry "nonsense." [4] Ironically, through his strong fictional approach to history (many of his incidents amount to short stories) and his novel *Claribalte,* which he wrote in America in 1514 and published in Madrid (1519), he may have produced the earliest novel of chivalry in America. *Claribalte* dealt with the adventures of don Félix, oldest son of the Duke Ponorio, brother and heir of Emperor Grifol of Constantinople and his wife Clariosa. At that time, Valdés, as he signed himself, thought his work was "obra gentil y nueva." Apparently, when the Royal Decree of 4 April 1531 appeared, forbidding profane books in America, he, as a faithful subject of Charles V, changed his mind. Perhaps the force of Erasmist arguments played a part in his decision, for men of the caliber of Pedro Mexía felt that to read "lying tales of Amadís and others is an offense against God."

Irving Leonard, elaborating a thesis by F. Rodríguez Marín, shows that in spite of all prohibitions these books circulated and were widely read in America, paradoxically, perhaps, since in the Peninsula itself idealistic and heroic fiction was then giving way to the anti-heroic picaresque novel. Cultural communication, both direct and indirect, was maintained through writers such as Guzmán de Alfarache, Tirso de Molina, and Lope de Vega. About 10,-000 copies of assorted novels were shipped on one boat in the sixteenth century, and one Antonio de Toro of Cartagena ordered one hundred copies *of Don Quijote de la Mancha* for Colombia.[5]

Printing presses existed in the New World as early as 1537 in Mexico City. John Cromberger, the son of Jacob Cromberger, a printer and bookdealer of Seville to whom the emperor granted a monopoly of the book trade with Mexico in 1525, printed the first American book, St. John Climacus' *La escala espiritual para subir al cielo* (1537), of which no copy exists. The oldest extant book, again a religious work, is *Breve compendio de la doctrina cristiana en lengua azteca y española* (1539). Pedro Ocharte, of French origin, established a second press in 1563; Pedro Balli another in 1574; and an Italian, Antonio Ricardo, another in Peru in 1577. More important than the repressive influence of the Holy Office in the failure to produce novels in the New World was "the commercial and economic pressure exerted by Peninsular dealers." [6] In America, presses were largely reserved for religious and theological works "to facilitate the work of evangelization by the Church among the Indians through printing the catechisms, dictionaries, grammars, and pietistic literature needed by the missionaries." [7] The king, probably deliberately, fostered the almost prohibitive, exorbitant costs of printing in the New World, for ". . . it is difficult to conceive of a more absolute jurisdiction than that which the kings of Spain exercised over all the ecclesiastical affairs of the Indies." [8] Thus, while the royal decrees were ineffectual in keeping books from entering the New World, the king's power, no doubt enthusiastically supported by Spanish businessmen, seemed equal to the task of forbidding the printing of such works on American presses.

George Lukács, among others, contends that fiction is born when society and culture reach the necessary maturity and realistic approach to life to support the novel, whose more original form is epic poetry. The unsettled life of the colonizers did not permit them to produce works of great length or to devote themselves to the philosophical meditation involved, but they could easily compose in fragmentary fashion, accounting, perhaps, in part for fictional elements in the early chronicles and histories. Although literature and the arts "were fostered by the universities and schools, by the convents, by the political and ecclesiastical authorities," [9] and even though a number of Indians learned Latin as well as Spanish, no large educated reading public existed. Novels of chivalry circulated freely, but the moral implications of the royal decrees lingered, even if the legalities involved were ignored, further hampering a developing sophistication and maturity and strengthening the persistent notion that novels were somehow immoral.

The increasing popularity of the Spanish theatrical productions of Lope de Vega and his circle offered an outlet, especially in the seventeenth century. With the fall in popularity of the novels of chivalry, especially after the publication of *Don Quijote*, writers devoted themselves to more historical events and to epic poetry, which lent itself to the description of heroic deeds. The new picaresque novels offered creative possibilities, but it was difficult for those who had been a part of the heroic conquest, so filled with famous figures, to accept the concept of the picaresque anti-hero. More than the lack of viable models for local writers to copy or the lack of complication in a simple frontier life, what hurt the novel was that real events far outstripped possible fictional elements. The public, apparently, found satisfactory reading material in deeds more fantastic than fiction itself. Juan Loveluck doubts that this explains the lack of fiction in the colonial period,[10] but Arturo Torres-Rioseco[11] and Luis Alberto Sánchez seem inclined to accept this theory, because "si todo era, en aquellos días, para los españoles en América, sorpresa, revelación, deslumbramiento, prodigio, a qué apelar a fábulas si la fábula era la atmósfera misma que respiraban, si lo maravilloso estaba en narrar lo acaeciente, en referir lo acaecido?" [12]

Although the culture of Spanish America in colonial times was a battle ground of political and moral ideas, the writers determined that "el mejor vehículo literario para el mensaje que propagaban no estaba en la de picarescas o pastoriles aventuras, sino en una prosa didáctica o en una poesía humorística . . ." [13] Since they had other ways of expressing themselves, they neglected the novel.

It follows, for some critics, that when Fernández de Lizardi was blocked from expressing himself journalistically, he wrote the "first" American novel, although the Cortes of Cádiz in 1812 removed the old printing press restrictions, allowing, for a brief time, freedom of expression which equally might account for his publication.[14]

Some hold that nature had a far greater effect on the conquistadores than did the human elements basic to fictional needs, that "el medio físico producía un impacto más profundo que el de la humanidad del salvaje, en la sensibilidad y en la inteligencia de los civilizados." [15] Pedro Grases states that the novelist needs a vast number of human types upon which to construct his own work, and that his spirit must be humanistic "para penetrar profunda y acertadamente en los actos de la historia del hombre"; but in America nature imposed itself so devastatingly and decisively on man that it delayed the novel, and when it finally succumbed to fictional pressures it had already forced the novel into a mold quite different from that of European fiction.[16] An opposing view holds that while "el ritmo vital de los países se ceñía por una sencilla tradición y una economía primitiva, la naturaleza continental no hacía sentir su existencia enemiga sobre los hombres . . ." [17]

It is not difficult to argue, in spite of the above theories, that fiction existed in the colonies. One must resist Fernando Alegría's conclusion that *none* of the early works of Latin American literature may be considered a novel and that "toda discusión al respecto es enteramente ociosa." [18] At the very least, many of these works contain the seeds of novels; indeed, Luis Alberto Sánchez qualifies *Los infortunios de Alonso Ramírez* as a novel, although he also believes that it is evident that "novela en su sentido más divulgado, no la hubo en la época colonial." [19] In our century, which has seen experiments with the stream of consciousness, interior monologues of various kinds, temporal destruction, and anti-novel novels, about the only definition of the novel we can give is that of E. M. Forster, who said, perhaps somewhat facetiously and tautologically, that it was "fiction in prose of no less than fifty thousand words." [20] Camilo José Cela, one of Spain's finest novelists, declares that a novel is "everything which, edited in the form of a book, admits, under the title and parenthetically, the word 'novel.' " [21] Labels and the limits of formerly fixed literary genres have become clouded and even disappeared. Cela feels that all attempts to limit or define the novel are useless. "Some day, with computers or with great patience and thousands of years, all novels might be written. Then one might have perhaps a vague conclusion as to what a novel is." [22] Indeed, some of Cela's travel books, as well as those of Juan Goytisolo and other contemporary Spanish novelists, have from time to time been called "narraciones" or even classified as novels. Luis Alberto Sánchez, also stressing the flexibility of the novel, calls it "agénero, la negación de los géneros. . . . Poema, ensayo, alegato . . . diagnóstico, narración, debate, pintura, coloquio, monólogo, libelo, pastoral, todo cabe en la novela; todo, estilos y personajes, asuntos y expresiones, clases sociales y tiempos históricos; realidad, posibilidad e imposibilidad." [23] Guillermo de Torre concurs that it is a "género sin límites. Todo cabe dentro de sus límites increíblemente elásticos . . ." [24] Some of the early candidates for the title of "first" Spanish American novel even seem to fit within the standard, if no longer germane, dictionary definition that a novel is a "fictitious prose tale of considerable length, in which characters and actions professing to represent those of real life are portrayed in a plot."

Chronicles and travel literature reflect the moral, theological, and philosophical concerns of the day. Francisco López de Gómara, in his history, after mentioning the great regard that the king should have for the welfare of the conquered, supports the "conquest and the conquerors." Early reports about the New World stress the peacefulness and timidity of the Indian, but the concept of the "noble savage" and the defense of evangelizers like Bartolomé de las Casas proved less effective than the works of Gonzalo Fernández de Oviedo and Juan Ginés de Sepúlveda, which justified the Spanish conquest on grounds of theology—theocratic assumptions of Indian inferiority and Spanish cultural superiority. Their "findings" gave a guise of intellectual respectability to what in essence was greed and injustice. The pleas of theologians to abolish the *repartimientos* (assigning of Indians to a Spanish landowner for free labor) went unheeded, and the *encomienda* system of Indian tribute to the conquerors became firmly established.

One may easily find novelistic traits in the *Cartas de Relación* of Hernán Cortés (1485–1547), five letters written to Charles V between 1519 and 1526. The first one, having been lost, was replaced by a letter from the Council of Veracruz. The authentic descriptions of the Indian civilization and the Spanish effect upon it, while sincere enough, contain some imaginative elements which seem factual because of the author's calm and sober style. The vivid descriptions of the capture of Tenochtitlán, various battles and historical expeditions, discoveries, and by now well-known historical events as told by one of the most cultured conquistadores include minute details of mountains, water systems, markets, and temples. Cortés shows sympathy for and understanding of Moctezuma and the Indian, but in spite of his struggle to "humanize" the conquest and his almost awelike admiration of Mexican civilization, he did not hesitate to destroy it. Bartolomé de las Casas (1474–1566), in *Brevísima relación de la destrucción de las Indias* (1552), includes episodic adventures and seminovelistic descriptions of characters, manners, and milieu as he pursues his theme of the genocide practiced by the Spaniards against the Indians. Among other marvelous accounts, filled with enumerations of physical details, not too different in their amorphous quality from some contemporary works but without any pretensions to a modern alienated consciousness, are the *Historia del reino de Quito* (1789) by Juan de Velasco (1727–1792), filled with adventures, legends, love affairs, and Amazons; and the two best-known historical narratives of this type, *La verdadera historia de la conquista de la Nueva España* (written around 1568 but not published until 1632) by Bernal Díaz del Castillo (1496–1584) and *Los comentarios reales* (1609, 1617) by Garcilaso de la Vega, Inca.

Bernal Díaz wrote his true history, of which unfortunately there are a number of "untrue" editions,[25] in order to refute the classic Renaissance one written by López de Gómara, private chaplain to Hernán Cortés in Spain. Bernal Díaz believed that the chaplain had praised Cortés to the exclusion of men of lesser rank who had fought nobly and well; so at the age of seventy-two this ex-soldier, who had been with Cortés in Mexico and later settled in Guatemala, where, it is said, he had the distinction of being the first man to plant oranges in America, decided to tell the "truth." He does not detract from Cortés' loyal service to the king, his sense of justice, his administrative ability in setting up the *ayuntamiento* or local government in Mexico. His impassioned personal account, while less cultured than that of Cortés, whose adroit psychology in dealing with the Indians Bernal Díaz admired, gives us more intimate views of the hopes and fears of the simple soldiers. He is overwhelmed by the buildings and plazas in Mexico and recalls the grandiose impression made by the New World on his fellow soldiers. Mexico recalls to his mind the marvels related in *Amadís* (was not California named for a mythical island in the *Amadís* sequel, *Las sergas de Esplandián*), and apparently he was one of the many in America who carefully read the novels of chivalry.[26] Unfortunately, the sophisticated Europeans, among them Montaigne, admired López de Gómara's work and ignored that of Bernal Díaz, for Europe "in general was slow to perceive the meaning of the discoveries." [27] Only with romanticism and the nineteenth century were the merits of the old soldier-writer recognized.

The Peruvian Garcilaso de la Vega Inca (1539–1616), America's first *criollo*, wrote *Los comentarios reales*, which, although technically history, used the Spanish novel as a model. His father, Sebastián Garci Lasso de la Vega Vargas, a disinherited second son related to the Marquis of Santillana, Jorge Manrique, and the famous pastoral poet, Garcilaso de la Vega, had gone to Mexico and from there had accompanied Pedro de Alvarado on his expedition to Peru. There he "married" the *palla*, princess, Chimpu Occlo, later christened Isabel, the niece of Huayna Capac and granddaughter of Tupac Yupanqui. José de la Riva Agüero somewhat stridently points out that "no fue sino manceba del orgulloso Garcilaso." [28] Their son, the Inca, learned the traditions of Peru and Ecuador from his mother's side of the family and his Spanish knowledge from his father. In inheriting two bloods and two cultures he became truly the first mestizo of America. He lived through the various conspiracies and attempts at power, including the reign of Gonzalo Pizarro, Francisco's brother, and at the age of twenty-one went to Spain to inquire about his inheritance. In Spain Lope García de Castro, using the text of Diego Fernández de Palencia (El Palentino), accused his father of having been a traitor for supposedly aiding Gonzalo Pizarro's escape. Garcilaso enlisted in the army, took part in the battle of Lepanto, and finally won his case.

La Florida del Inca (1605), based on reports of a companion of Hernando de Soto, Captain Gonzalo de Silvestre, and some written records, delineates heroic deeds in a fashion which make it almost a historical novel and book of chivalry combined. The fictional elements resemble greatly those of the Byzatine novels,[29] and the imaginary discussions, fantasies, and psychological analyses further the fictional impression. Garcilaso claimed he was writing fact and not fiction,[30] but in his Proemio he states, "Baste para que se crea que no escribimos ficciones." The titles of the chapters themselves, "Un castigo extraño," "Desafío singular," and the like contribute to the Inca's narrative techniques of heightened illusion and skillful presentation of reality.[31]

Garcilaso's most famous work, *Los comentarios reales*, consists of two volumes, the second of which was posthumously published. The first part of the *Historia general del Perú*, as the book was officially titled, deals with Peru before the arrival of the Spaniards. The latter suppressed the title, *Comentarios reales*, and prohibited the volume for a time because of its nostalgic and evocative description of the glorious empire of the Incas.[32] The second part includes an attack on Diego Fernández de Palencia, Garcilaso's father's enemy. In writing for both Spaniards and Indians, the Inca, hoping to give the former an understanding of his mother's people as well as to convince Spain of the mestizo's needs, combined apparently authentic history with legendary elements, folklore material, pleas for the dignity of man, a reflection of his humanistic idealism, and a firm belief in the need for mutual trust between the Indian and Spanish cultures. Fitzmaurice Kelly, rather slavishly emulating the pattern established by Ticknor, denied the historical veracity but admired the fictional qualities and local color in Garcilaso's work: "Su patriotismo y su credulidad han producido más bien novelas que historia." [33] Again the titles of the chapters convey the action: "Envía el Inca a conquistar los Quechuas," "Casaban al príncipe heredero con su propia hermana," "La fiesta principal del sol y como se preparaban para ello," and "La conquista de los Charcas y algunas batallas que indios y españoles tuvieron." The work contains insert stories such as the one about Pedro Serrano, the Spanish Robinson Crusoe, lyrical overtones, and flashes of humor, and is presented in a vivid but balanced manner. The *Comentarios reales*, which helped preserve Inca culture for Peru, may well have influenced writers like Marmontel and appears to have been the important European authority regarding the Incas until the nineteenth century. Another Peruvian, Pedro Pizarro (1514–1571), a cousin of Francisco, wrote *Relación del descubrimiento y conquista de los reinos del Perú* . . . (1571), which appears to be more novel than history. Some of the chroniclers, as well as the chronicles, seem to be of the stuff of fiction. Alonso de Góngora Marmoleja, for example, narrator of Pedro de Valdivia's sixteenth-century deeds in *Historia de Chile* (1575), was known as the "juez pesquisidor de hechiceros indígenas."

Many candidates have appeared to claim the title of first (chronologically speaking) Spanish American novelist. Diego Dávalos y Figueroa of Peru published *Miscelánea Austral* (1602), about unfortunate loves, heroic deeds, and an abiding admiration for the grandeur of America on the part of the hero, who had traveled there to recover from an unfortunate love affair. The work is marred by excessive Italian borrowings and Renaissance discussions of the human and divine. The Mexicans, more seriously, offer several candidates, of whom the first two are Bernardo de Balbuena (1561–1627), bishop of Puerto Rico, author of *Grandeza Mexicana* (1604), dedicated to Isabel de Tovar y Guzmán and in praise of famous deeds and passions, and *Bernardo o Victoria de Roncesvalles* (1624), an imaginative epic poem. His *El siglo de oro en las selvas de Erífile* (1608), a verse pastoral romance in the style of and based on the *Arcadia* of Sannazaro, to which Balbuena alludes in his preface—"agradable y rigurosa imitación del estilo pastoril de Teócrito, Virgilio y Sannazaro"—is filled with imaginative descriptions and an action into which the author intervenes; but it is no more entertaining than another pastoral, *Los sirgueros de la Virgen sin original pecado* (1620), written by Mexico's second candidate, Francisco Bramón (d. 1654?). Uslar Pietri feels that Balbuena's romance is "la más notable . . . escrita con refinado gusto . . . pero ajena por entero al mundo americano y a su literatura." [34]

Francisco Bramón, rector of the University of Mexico, had his work approved by the Church since its motive was "entretenerse honesta y sanamente, cosas que pocas veces se hallan juntas en una misma obra." It lacks the countless loves and magical encounters of many pastoral novels. The goldfinches of the title symbolize the shepherds who sing to the Virgin, and the author's purpose seems to have involved this praise in song. The work contains a description of a Mexican dance and many nature descriptions to accompany its symbolic conversations, along with a number of autobiographical elements as the author introduces himself into the story to write a theatrical piece. Marcilda, a beautiful shepherdess and a host of shepherds plan activities for the feast days in December and discuss the concept of original sin. Anfriso (Bramón) will write an auto sacramental, for he needs rest after having suffered a difficult examination at the university. Thus, the religious allegory with autobiographical details is also a pastoral novel whose author, within his own created work, writes still another one. Agustín Yáñez, who edited the work, feels that the auto included may not be the work of Bramón, but Anderson Imbert believes that it is.[35]

The clear fountain and sweet murmuring waters of Bramón's work are not echoed by that of a Colombian writer, Juan Rodríguez Freile (1568–1639), whose name also appears as Freire, Freyle, and Fresle. His work, *Conquista y descubrimiento del Nuevo Reino de Granada y de las Indias occidentales* (1636), popularly known as *El carnero*, was not printed until 1859. In the prologue, Felipe Pérez, the printer, insists it is a historical work, but others have called it a chronicle and also viewed it as "novelesco-anecdótico" and its author as "novelador de la historia colombiana." [36] Known as the first criollo writer of Colombian literature, Rodríguez Freile, son of a Spanish conquistador, was a farmer, warrior, and man of letters. His "scandalous chronicle," a semipicaresque narrative of Colombian lives, may have been influenced by *La Celestina* and certain picaresque novels.[37] Rodríguez Freile, priding himself on his culture, includes, along with his horror stories, literary debates, parts of Scripture, contributions by Church fathers, and Virgil. He mixes historical events (Bogotá's founding and Colombian civil wars), biographical notes, character analysis, portraits of conquistadors, and a host of intimate details of the Colombian society of his day. From this partly imagined chronicle we learn good and bad customs and hear gossip about love affairs, murders, and witchcraft. Attacking both Indian and Spaniard for avarice, alcoholism, and laziness, and in general excoriating those who take advantage of superstitious people, the author takes a highly moralistic tone. He is especially incensed by lying and sinful women, primary vessels of sin in the classical Eve tradition, their licentiousness often being responsible for the crimes of passion he portrays. As one critic says: "Parece existir en la obra una doble moral: con un criterio abstracto y fatalista se juzga al español, al hombre blanco; pero las acciones de los indios son juzgadas de manera muy diferente. Los indios, según el narrador, son metafísicamente malos, ladrones, perezosos . . ." [38] Rodríguez Freile calls his work a "discurso" but strives to make it pleasant (twenty-three of the episodes, such as "El indio dorado" and "El alcalde fratricida," are essentially intercalated short stories). He lacks a tightly structured style, to be sure, and the jokes and digressions as well as the moralizing tend to annoy a modern reader, who, on the other hand, remains fascinated by accounts of the murder of innocent victims and other such incidents which resemble, in a fragmented and curtailed fashion, the so-called nonfiction novel of Truman Capote *In Cold Blood*. Some critics consider *El carnero*—whose title may come from the fact that *carneros* were at the time common graves in churches—to be the ancestor of the *Tradiciones peruanas* of Ricardo Palma in its ability to delineate the experience of colonial life and, especially, in its malicious humor.

The Chilean seventeenth-century candidate for the title of first novelist is Francisco Núñez de Pineda y Bascuñán (1607–1682), whose *El cautiverio feliz o razón de las guerras dilatadas de Chile* (1673) was not printed until 1863. Núñez Pineda was the son of the Maestre de Campo Don Alvaro Núñez, known to the Indians (who, at least according to his son, had a fantastic admiration for his father) as Maltincampo. Named captain, the son decided to follow his father's advice and enlisted instead as a private at the age of sixteen. Six years later, in 1629, he was imprisoned by the Araucanian Indians. García Hurtado de Mendoza had suffered periodic rebellions against his forces from the region south of the river Bío-Bío. In these battles the Araucanians, given the to them familiar terrain off which they could live, had a decided advantage.[39] The Spaniards established a defensive line on the river, one which they violated for slave raids. These raids prompted Indian counterattacks, and it was in April 1629 during one such action that Núñez Pineda fell into the hands of Chief Maulicán and spent about six months, part of a winter and spring, with the Indians. Maulicán, respecting the father and hoping to protect the son from jealous rivals who wished to kill him, moved about from region to region.

The author narrates his chronicle, written twenty-one years after the events took place, in a fictional manner. He wanted to give a first hand account of the wars in Chile, in addition to denouncing the evil Christians among the Spaniards and lamenting the small recompense received by servants of the king. Yet his direct transcription of reality, tempered by his imagination, contains descriptions of nature, action, suspense, and real as well as invented events, including some elaborated from novels he remembered. Núñez Pineda's conceit is everywhere apparent. As a noble Spaniard, he faithfully keeps his word not to escape. He takes no part in the Indian fights or dances (he did a little drinking) and spends his time instructing Indians in Catholic prayers—he himself had a Jesuit education and had once dreamed of being a priest. For Christian reasons he rejects a variety of advances made upon his virginity, including one by Maulicán's young daughter to whom he was greatly attracted and who later, no doubt due to his teaching, became a Catholic. Yet his attacks on the Spaniards for their lack of courtesy and humility and his stress on the need for learning Indian languages seem sincere enough.

The variety of episodes, characters, and a maintained suspense make this chronicle more fiction than history. Although some of Núñez Pineda's portraits are too diffuse to be effective, such passages as the defense of his virtue against the charms of lovely Indian lasses who wished to share their favors with him (he triumphed over his baser instincts through works and prayers) or his descriptions of a river crossing in a storm, of quack doctors, fiestas, dances, and American nature are much more than a mere cataloguing of incidents. His portraits are often black and white, but he develops a number of his characters with sound psychological insight. Anderson Imbert feels that "this was the first chronicle in which an essentially novelistic element appears—the building up of suspense in the action . . . it is not always possible to distinguish between the literary embellishments of real-life scenes and pure episodic invention." [40]

Menéndez y Pelayo, José Toribio Medina, Mariano Latorre, and Arturo Torres-Rioseco support the candidacy of the Chilean Friar Juan de Barrenechea y Albis (d. 1707). His *Restauración de la Imperial y conversión de almas infieles* (1693), never published, relates the trials and tribulations of the Araucanian Indians, Spanish efforts to dominate them, and the love story of Rocamila and Cantabo. The romantic stereotyped Christian father who baptizes the Indian, the theme of love between the races, and various Indian types reveal a prophetic novelistic instinct about themes to become a commonplace in nineteenth-century Spanish America. Although the work passes for history, it is largely invention and a generally false picture of the times.

The Mexican Carlos de Sigüenza y Góngora (1645–1700), a baroque poet and prose writer friend of the famous poetess Sor Juana Inés de la Cruz, was considered by many to be the outstanding intellectual of his period. He served with distinction as geographer, historian, philosopher, and archeologist. In spite of his Jesuit training he wrote an article on how eclipses are produced, something a later Mexican novelist, Fernández de Lizardi, also attempted. His prose narrative, *Los infortunios que Alonso Ramírez padeció en poder de ingleses piratas* (1690), seems to be a biographical novel of a Puerto Rican who lived between 1662 and 1707. Ramírez relates the story of his life to the author, but Sigüenza invents and changes facts to suit his own conservative purposes in what may well be "el primer relato completamente novelable de América Española ..." [41] Ramírez in the first person narrates his adventures from the time of his early teens, and we learn not only of his mishaps but also of his hopes and despairs. He earns his living as a carpenter, is deceived in love, travels to a variety of places such as Havana, Mexico, and the Philippines, whose geography Sigüenza realistically describes, is captured by pirates, crosses the Indian Ocean, and is abandoned at the mouth of the Amazon River. Finally in Mexico, he visits Sigüenza y Góngora, who, touched by his story, not only helps him but writes down his adventures. The work at times evokes memories of the simple and unaffected *Lazarillo de Tormes*. In its adventures and pirate themes the novel also recalls a former Byzantine vogue.

The final serious candidate for novelistic honors is a product of a new period. Charles III expelled the Jesuits from Spanish soil in 1767 for alleged conspiracy. The ideas of the Enlightenment and new scientific knowledge were being disseminated in the New World through men like Jorge Juan (1712–1773), Antonio de Ulloa (1716–1795), and José Celestino Mutis (1732–1808). The anti-Spanish diatribes of visitors like the Abbot Guillaume Thomas Raynal in his six-volume *Histoire philosophique et politique de l'Establissement et du Commerce des Européens dans les deux Indes* (1771), documenting Spanish crimes against the Indians, influenced the intellectuals of the day. Americans, while still staunch

Catholics, refused to accept without question the existing order and stressed the role of logic and reason over theology, and natural law over divine law. The American Revolution and later the French Revolution were to give impetus to the wars of independence which the disorganized minority of the lower clergy would support against the wishes of the Catholic hierarchy of Spanish America, which supported the Spanish crown.[42] Young Americans also traveled to Europe to return with dangerous new ideas about liberty and social progress for the continent. A number of Creole writers, products of the Enlightenment, among them the Ecuadorian Francisco Eugenio de Santa Cruz y Espejo (1747–1795) helped prepare the way for the independence movement from Spain. His *Nuevo Luciano o despertador de ingenios* (1779), nine satirical and even bitter conversations in the manner of Lucian criticizing the status quo, show his awareness of the defects of colonial culture and the need of native reform.[43]

Lazarillo de ciegos caminantes . . . sacado de las memorias que hizo don Alonso Carrió de la Vandera . . . por Don Calixto Bustamante Carlos Inca, alias Concolorcorvo (1775) defends and attacks the Spaniard and defends the upper-class Creoles against the Indian and the Negro but in the final analysis chastises almost everybody who is not well-bred. The author was probably a government employee, Carrió de la Vandera (some believe the author to have been Fray Calixto de San José), who stated that the book, printed in Lima in 1775, had appeared in Gijón in 1773. Employed to reorganize the mail system and stagecoach stops between Buenos Aires and Lima, Carrió has Concolorcorvo relate the travel tale. The first person narrative, quite anticlerical in places, examines traditions, customs, jokes, and local color with a liberal lacing of picaresque flavor. The tone may be judged from a much quoted passage from the prologue which states: "Yo soy indio neto, salvo las trampas de mi madre, de que no salgo por fiador. Dos primas mías coyas conservan la virginidad, a su pesar, en un convento del Cuzco, en donde las mantiene el Rey nuestro señor." Concolorcorvo travels with Inspector Lavander on mule back, and he is careful to tell us about the origin of mules, their care and feeding. In a burlesque and mocking tone he describes primitive gauchos, religious superstitions, the slave trade, and women's clothes. The travelogue, for that is what it is, has been called "documento amenísimo," [44] but it is difficult to view it as a novel. Indeed, one is surprised that Fernando Alegría, while admitting its lack of plot, action, and true picaresque frame, states that it is the only work which has "cualidades novelescas" up to the publication of *El Periquillo Sarniento* in the nineteenth century.[45]

Aside from the works of Balbuena, Bramón, and Sigüenza y Góngora, Mexicans point to some titles of novels (the titles are often the only physical evidence left) before Fernández de Lizardi, such as the seventeenth-century *Sucesos de Fernando o La caída de Fernando* (1662) by Antonio de Ochoa and the eighteenth-century *El peregrino con guía y medicina universal del alma* by Marcos Reynel Hernández. Other proposed eighteenth-century novels are *Fabiano y Aurelia* (1760) by José González and *La portentosa vida de la Muerte* (1792), a philosophical, imaginative work by Fray Joaquín Bolaños.

Usually José Joaquín Fernández de Lizardi (1776–1827) is awarded the laurel as the first "true" Spanish American novelist. Known as El Pensador Mexicano, the name of his newspaper (1812–1814), he was one of the last purveyors of the picaresque novel. Fernández de Lizardi, the son of a second-class doctor at the Royal College in Tepotzotlán, about three miles from Mexico City, studied theology at a Jesuit seminary and at the University of Mexico but was much more interested in the Enlightenment and Rousseau and Feijoo than in theology. He was never really either antireligious or keenly interested in American independence, but he believed strongly in individual freedoms and the rule of reason, the absence of which he blamed partly on the Church and partly on the government. His own father, apparently, denounced him to the Inquisition in 1794 for having a deck of fortune telling cards in his possession.[46] Lizardi started his writing career as a poet with satirical verses in which he attacked the Church and aristocracy. By 1811 he had broadened his work to include popular dialogues, pamphlets, and satirical articles. In spite of his lack of strong feelings about independence, he aided José María Morelos when that revolutionary warrior priest entered Taxco in 1812. As a result Lizardi was imprisoned, the first of many such encounters with the law.

When the constitution proclaimed by the Cortes of Cádiz took effect in Mexico on 30 September 1812, with its guarantees of freedom of the press, Lizardi began publishing *El Pensador Mexicano*. In one of the issues he criticized Viceroy Venegas, was again arrested, and, so one story goes, was freed by the judge because he could not believe that the insignificant looking author could be "that terrible revolutionary." Lizardi tried unsuccessfully to start another newspaper and, finally, in order to escape the new censorship imposed by the reestablished autocratic Spanish monarch, Fernando VII, he decided to write a novel. When he started the first installment of his feuilleton novel, he was using that vehicle of expression only because he could not freely convey his ideas journalistically. *El Periquillo Sarniento*, consisting of three volumes, was not published in book form until 1816. The censor did not allow the publication of the fourth and final volume because "en que había sobre los negros, me parece . . . inoportuno, perjudicial en las circunstancias, e impolítico por dirigirse contra un comercio permitido por el rey." [47] A second edition of the first volume, with some changes, appeared in 1825, and the complete edition of the novel was published posthumously in five volumes in 1830–31. [48] Fernández de Lizardi published *Noches tristes y día alegre* in 1818, finished his third novel, *La Quijotita y su prima*, in 1819 (not published in complete form until after his death), and completed his last novel, *Don Catrín de la Fachenda*, in late 1819, although it, too, was not published until 1832. With the restoration of constitutional government in 1820, he abandoned the novel for journalism, his first love. He continued to fight the government authorities and the Church, which excommunicated him in 1822 for an article, "Defensa de los francmasones," but reinstated him the following year. He continued to have difficulties because of his attacks on hypocrisy, false pride, and greed and because of his increasingly poor physical condition brought about by a painful tuberculosis which finally killed him. He died a Catholic but refused even on his deathbed to accept a number of clerical concerns which he found to be mere superstitions.

El Periquillo Sarniento is supposedly written by an old *pícaro* who, as he lies dying, surrounded by his family, doctors, and a priest, tells his children he has written the story of his life to show them vices from which he suffered so that they may avoid similar ones. He states that "es sólo con la sana intención de que mis hijos se instruyan," but he also reminds them that all the events and vices are "ficción de mi fantasía." He warns that his work is not for wise men who do not need his poor lessons and apologizes for his "erro- res que no advertí," but evaluates his own novel as one whose defects "no quitaron el mérito que en sí tienen las máximas morales que incluye . . ." The novel, then, consists partly of a series of moral lessons about living, including attacks on foolish middle-class pride, especially that of indulgent mothers who spoil their chil- dren. He examines the defective educational system, the problem of the Indian and the Negro, corrupt justice, exaggerated mourn- ing, and matrimonial relationships. To include all these aspects of society the author indulges in a number of digressions which, for some, from an artistic point of view, detract from the total work.

With the *Periquillo* begins the tradition of literature as a kind of public service, an interest in social reform which was to continue to this day. Some may argue that El Pensador was not following an artistic creed,[49] since the author was seeking to bring about a transformation of society through political and social reform, but this criticism may be applied to all but a few of the most important Spanish American novels. The author combines shrewd criticism of the status quo[50] with *costumbrismo*, another standard aspect of Spanish American fiction, giving us moving portraits of Mexican colonial life with its types and customs, which for one critic were ". . . en calidad estética escenas costumbristas de plástico re- lieve." [51]

Fernández de Lizardi, a man of his age, knew Feijoo and Mura- tori well and apparently used his unindividualized protagonist to reflect his own philosophy. Some critics cast doubt on the novel's heritage as a late revival from Spanish picaresque sources, but most Mexican critics agree with Jefferson Rhea Spell, who devoted so much of his scholarship to this author, that "con su Periquillo me- jicano revivió Lizardi esta antigua y favorita forma literaria e inyectó en ella un nuevo contenido nacional . . . asió Lizardi el espíritu del México colonial y lo inmortalizó." [52] In any event, it is quite difficult to separate the patriot and social analyst from the pícaro.

One may argue as to whether the protagonist's bad luck comes from a silly mother, the defects of an undemocratic society, or the weakness of the hero himself. Poor little Periquillo (partly Lizardi himself)[53] received his name from his green jacket, yellow pants, and a bad case of the mange. Ill advised and easily influenced, he indulges in a feverish activity. After his education at a school where Rousseau's principles were followed, at a university, and at a theological seminary and monastery, he becomes a gambler, drunkard, friar, barber, quack doctor, sexton, and bandit. He learns lofty but temporary moral lessons from Don Antonio in jail and associates with a number of strange types including the rogue Chanfaina. After a host of misadventures of various kinds, he gives up his women and his other vices to repent, live an honorable life, and offer us his deathbed advice and funeral plans with which the novel ends. In spite of the many humorous episodes in the novel, the author may have wished to symbolize, in his protagonist, his country, which he hoped would abandon its "evil" ways for a more virtuous course. Mariano Azuela, himself a fine novelist, believes that this novel was designed exclusively for the public and that all in all "no es más que el primer balbuceo de la novela mexicana." [54] Alfonso Reyes, on the other hand, while admitting that the work has not always had critical acclaim, feels that it has come to be a historical symbol, that ". . . ha tenido estrella. Ha sido, desde la cuna, un libro simbólico, nacional." [55] Luis Alberto Sánchez, while at one point calling it "vano ensayo moralizante envuelto en inadecuado ropaje literario," [56] elsewhere admires its characters and sees it as a kind of tragicomic "especie de *Diablo Cojuelo* de México emancipado . . ." [57]

Lizardi's second novel and the only one he tried to polish and stylize, *Noches tristes, día alegre,* may well mark the beginning of romanticism in American prose. He admits in an introduction that it is based on the work of José Cadalso (*Noches lúgubres*) and that "propuse escribir otras tristes a su emulación y en efecto las escribí y las presento con las licencias necesarias." The novel relates the terrifying experiences of the virtuous and God-fearing Teófilo, tested by Providence for four nights. He is imprisoned, almost falls down a precipice, and sees a servant and a friend die and his wife's body in a cemetery. Returning home he is rewarded with a "día alegre dignamente aprovechado" (his wife did not die). Partly autobiographical, the novel is an apt presentation of psychological reactions during the wars of independence. The gloomy, melancholy nocturnal scenes include tirades against the rich and a statement about the moral values of justice and compassion. Preaching that it is always darkest before dawn and that fortune may follow misfortune, Lizardi nevertheless tries to modify the reality of his day and in so doing paints a negative picture of his society with no constructive ideas or immediate solutions.

La Quijotita y su prima, subtitled "The Education of Women," uses Rousseau's theories, which Lizardi knew so well, to discourse on parental authority and its limits. Two cousins, one the product of a corrupting education and the other of an approved environment, show the effects of the consequential processes. Pomposa, the "bad" one, known as Quijotita, ends badly, and Prudencia, the "good" one, triumphs. In his preface Lizardi states he is going to write "una historia verdadera que he presenciado y cuyos personajes Ud. conoce," fancying himself as a kind of utopian social idealist; but he succeeded only in creating a comic portrayal of odd types with odder names.

Lizardi's final novel, *Don Catrín de la Fachenda*, is about a vain, uneducated, haughty, boastful fop and bad son who represents the worst of his social class. This character is uninterested in abstractions or ideals and lives at the expense of the gullible. A dandy, exhibitionist, soldier, pimp, actor, cripple, prisoner, and sinner to the end, the protagonist escapes his creator's didactic intent. The other characters are more symbolic projections of social purpose, for Lizardi not only wanted to describe his tarnished society but to reform it. The novel has more than its share of humor and a number of grotesque and absurd situations, but the author apparently preferred it to *El Periquillo Sarniento*. He states, in his work, that it is "descargada de episodios inoportunos, de digresiones fastidiosas, de moralidades cansadas, y reducida a un solo tomito en octavo, se hará desde luego más apreciable y más legible." More tightly structured and optimistic than his first work, *Don Catrín de la Fachenda* cannot equal the moving Mexican spirit one finds in Lizardi's first work.

In summing up the novels of Fernández de Lizardi one is inclined to accept Azuela's contention that what attracts us primarily is "el mexicanismo que rezuman sus libros, lo auténticamente nacional," [58] even if we cannot completely accept his rejection of the literary values of Lizardi's fiction. Lizardi gave to Mexican literature "cuadros literarios de la vida mexicana," [59] complete and collective portraits of the times, and no one has surpassed him "in depicting the spirit of Mexican life, so that not only chronologically but from the viewpoint of national development he is the first Mexican novelist." [60]

2. Costumbrismo
and Romanticism

COSTUMBRISMO

Another constant characteristic of the Spanish American novel in the nineteenth and to a degree in the twentieth century is what we may loosely label *costumbrismo* or local color, which combined with the romantic, realistic, modernist, or naturalistic aspects of the novels in which it occurred. Costumbrismo had a long Spanish tradition, occurring as early as the sixteenth century in the works of Juan de Zabaleta and others. In its concern for customs and manners, it enjoyed great success in nineteenth-century Spain through the sketches of Mariano José de Larra and Ramón Mesonero Romanos. At times these were satirical or social commentaries, showing a reality shaped by a critical viewpoint (*artículo*); at others they were purely picturesque, stressing local color for its own sake (*cuadro*); sometimes they combined local color with social criticism. In its modern form it proved most popular from about 1830 on in Spain, continuing to be present in the regional novelists, at times to the exclusion of interest in the plot. While it is the costumbrismo of the Spanish American novel which concerns us, the cuadro or article which gave the form its popularity and which also existed since colonial times helped pave the way for its entry into fiction, at times awkwardly, and at times so smoothly fused with the action that the seams hardly showed. In dealing with customs, places, types, and the life of the times, these cuadros usually revealed picturesque and humorous overtones. Many of the realistic writers, more didactic in their portrayals and documentation because of their keen interest in the political, religious, and economic problems of the day, wove *reformismo* and custumbrismo into one cloth.

Although starting and ending dates for literary movements are also disputed in Spain, divisions from romanticism through regional and realistic fiction may be somewhat discerned and defined, but no easy chronology may be assigned in the New World. A concomitant difficulty involves not only the definition, classification, and isolation of literary trends and genres but also the role of "generations" in the ebb and flow of Spanish American fictional production. A number of different schemes have been offered by Luis Alberto Sánchez, Pedro Henríquez Ureña, Enrique Anderson Imbert, José Antonio Portuondo, and José Juan Arrom in determining generational limits, but the division by generations, whatever the method, offers no hard and fast rule for bringing order out of a complex and confused situation. Indeed, it may well be true that "toda tentativa de esclarecer una obra literaria por el grupo de hombres en que cronológicamente se inscribe el autor, ha de recibirse por lo menos con las mismas reservas que merecen las historias de la literatura concebidas por regiones o por razas." [1] Classic studies on this subject have been written by Wilhelm Dilthey and Julius Petersen and by the Spaniards José Ortega y Gasset, Segundo Serrano Poncela, Pedro Laín Entralgo, and Julián Marías. Its relationship to Spanish American fiction will be more fully explored in a later chapter.

Costumbristas in Spanish America, especially, between 1830 and 1880 wrote both sketches and fiction. Realistic portraits, vignettes, the mordant and the moralizing in both country and city were contributed by these writers of articles and novels "que trazan cuadros de tipos y modos de vida propios de la ciudad, con su rasgo y colorido local. Este género es relativamente el más abundante, porque el costumbrismo, de índole casi siempre satírica, es una rancia tradición en la literatura hispanoamericana, cultivada desde los tiempos del coloniaje." [2] Arturo Uslar Pietri believes that it is the unifying thread of the nineteenth-century novel, "la tendencia a concebir la novela como una sucesión de cuadros de costumbres, a buscar y destacar lo pintoresco, lo curioso, lo típico en la realidad. No toda la vida, no toda la realidad, sino la vida pintoresca, la realidad peculiar. A falta de mejor palabra y sacando el vocablo de su empleo genérico podríamos llamar este rasgo costumbrismo." [3]

Spanish American costumbristas concentrate less on city life than their Spanish counterparts, but their sketches include irony, good humor, observation of human nature, caricatures of native types, social criticism, and a deeply felt national reality. Some wrote character studies, some preferred philosophical pronouncements, but most confined themselves to regional descriptions of customs. Among the principal writers of this kind are: the Peruvians Manuel Ascencio Segura (1805–1871), who emphasized the historical and the national and taught Ricardo Palma, and Felipe Pardo y Aliaga (1806–1868), as conservative (really reactionary) as his countryman was liberal; the Mexicans Guillermo Prieto (1818–1897), who concentrated on the picturesque, and José Tomás de Cuéllar (1830–1894), who will be more fully discussed in a later chapter; the Venezuelans Juan Manuel Cagigal (1803–1856), Fermín Toro (1807–1865), a romantic of great culture who will be treated later, Rafael María Baralt (1810–1860), also a neoclassic poet, Daniel Mendoza (1823–1867), Arístides Rojas (1826–1894), known as the "cronista de Caracas," and Nicanor Bolet Peraza (1838–1906); the Guatemalan José Milla y Vidaurre (1822–1882), who used the pseudonym Salomé Jil; the Argentine Juan Bautista Alberdi (1810–1884), who signed himself Figarillo in obvious imitation of Larra; the Puerto Rican Manuel A. Alonso (1823–1890), the earliest commentator on national foibles, who called himself El Jíbaro; the Colombians José Manuel Groot (1800–1878), one of the first in his country to cultivate the sketch, Eugenio Díaz (1804–1865), more famous for his novel *Manuela* than as a sketch writer, José Caicedo Rojas (1806–1897), Juan de Dios Restrepo (1827–1897), better known as Emiro Kastos and for his apparently cynical search for truth, and José María Vergara y Vergara (1831–1872), whose sketch, "Las tres tazas," is one of the best known in Spanish America; the Chileans José Joaquín Vallejo (1811–1858), perhaps the most famous of all Spanish American costumbristas, under the pseudonym of Jotabeche, Daniel Riquelme (1857–1912), by some considered the first to use the *roto* as a literary figure, and Manuel J. Ortiz (1870–1945), whose "village letters" were well received; and finally the Cubans José María de Cárdenas y Rodríguez (1812–1882), who signed himself Jeremías Docaransa and was acclaimed as "el Mesonero Romanos de Cuba," [4] José Victoriano Betancourt (1813–1875), Francisco de Paula Gelabert (1834–1894), and Luis Victoriano Betancourt y Salgado (1842–1885). Like his compatriots, Betancourt wrote for a number of newspapers such as *El Patriota Americano* and *El Observador Habanero*, presenting scenes that the first important Spanish American costumbrista novelist, Cirilo Villaverde, had also presented. As has been stated, some of these American costumbristas were also novelists, and much of their fiction was first published in newspapers. Even their sketches, where plot is not a primary consideration, often have a short story framework or dialogue of some kind.

One of the first and perhaps most important Cuban novelists of his century was Cirilo Villaverde (1812–1894). José María Heredia (1803–1839), the Cuban poet (he had some hard criticisms to make about historical novels), had published some stories under the title *Cuentos orientales* as early as 1829; but the honor of putting Cuban fiction on the continental map belongs to Villaverde, teacher, newspaperman, and revolutionary. His early influences included his grandfather, who, he states in the prologue to *El penitente*, one of his successful novels, gave him its plot. In his youth he observed at first hand the horrible treatment of slaves in the sugar mills as well as the indifferent, pleasure-seeking upper classes, experiences which can be identified in his novels. An ardent supporter of Narciso López and Cuban independence, he was imprisoned a number of times for his activities and even condemned to death once, but he managed to escape to the United States to continue the struggle. He worked for the "Cause" on newspapers like *La Verdad* from 1849 on and *El Independiente* in 1853 and 1854. He went back to Cuba in 1858 for two years but finally returned to the United States, where he died.

Domingo Delmonte, whose *tertulias* Villaverde began to attend about 1834, along with José Antonio Echeverria, José María Cárdenas, and Anselmo Suárez y Romero, influenced the budding author. Villaverde, in addition to some early short stories he published under the title of *Miscelánea de útil y agradable recreo* (1837), wrote four novelettes of which two, *La peña blanca*, about incest, superstition, and violent death, and *La cueva de Taganana*, were encomiastically received, although the latter novelette is poorly developed. Some of his early fiction, classified at times as short stories and at others as novels, appeared in *El Album* in 1838. His works include *La joven de la flecha de oro* (1841), about a jealous husband who tortures his wife, *El penitente* (1844), a historical novel about eighteenth-century Havana which contains a careful description of customs, and *Dos amores* (1858)—which had first appeared as a serial in *El Farol Industrial* between 1842 and 1848 —a sentimental novelette about the love of a Cuban girl for a foreigner. The action occurs in 1836 and again the author includes significant costumbrista elements. These novels, influenced by Scott and Manzoni, who, the author admitted in *Cecilia Valdés*, his masterpiece, were his inspiration, offer the standard romantic themes of good versus evil, secret loves, frustrated vengeance, and violence.

The first two chapters of *Cecilia Valdés* were published in the pages of *La Siempreviva* in 1839 and later that same year the entire first part as a novel. Finally finished in 1879 but not published in its definitive edition until 1882 in New York, it carried the subtitle of "La loma del Ángel." It has been so popular in its reflection of Cuban customs that it was even adapted as a musical to the Cuban stage. The author dedicates his novel to the Cuban women, "reflejo del lado más bello de la Patria," perhaps an indication of his feeling about the symbolic value of the heroine of his novel. He explains the long delay in publication by his moving about to accept teaching positions, becoming engaged in other novels and newspaper work, and his agitated life and revolutionary activities. He had attempted to finish the novel in 1858, but again economic needs and politics prevented him from finishing it.

In spite of the influence of Scott and Manzoni, Villaverde considered himself to be a realistic novelist. In his prologue of 1879 he states that far from inventing or imagining characters and "escenas fantaseadas e inverosímiles, he llevado el realismo, según lo entiendo, hasta el punto de presentar los principales personajes de la novela con todos sus pelos y señales, vestidos con el traje que llevaron en la vida." He scrupulously tried to avoid the gross and ugly in his romantic tale with its realistic background, but not everybody is in agreement that he succeeded in his task.[5] The novel in its description and themes is basically costumbrista, but it might as easily be labeled historical, romantic, or anti-slavery fiction, as it gives us the social history of Cuba of yesteryear.

The plot itself is quite romantic. The Spaniard Cándido Gamboa, grown wealthy from the slave trade (by Villaverde's time carried on secretly), has an affair with the mestiza "Charo" Alarcón, a union which produces Cecilia Valdés, known for her beauty and color as "La virgencita de bronce." The author minutely describes her physical appearance and temperament. A paragon of passion and beauty, she falls in love with her half-brother Leonardo, Gamboa's legitimate son, and, unaware of their relationship, they become lovers. When Leonardo, a disagreeable and immature young man (for whom Villaverde surprisingly seems to have affection) is about to marry the wealthy Isabel Ilincheta, Cecilia asks her mulato friend, the musician-tailor José Dolores Pimienta, to kill Isabel, but he kills Leonardo instead. Gamboa's wife, jealous of her husband's affair, has Cecilia prosecuted as an accomplice to the crime and incarcerated in a hospital where her mother is also imprisoned as a mental recluse. Shortly before the mother dies she recovers her sanity and recognizes Cecilia Valdés as her daughter. Isabel, in the best tradition of the romantic novel, enters a convent.

The novel, in spite of its archaisms, digressions, and overwhelming detail, which adversely affect it structurally and aesthetically, is important to the modern reader for a number of reasons. The anti-slavery and patriotic themes are everywhere apparent. We see the various mental and physical tortures of the slaves, the excessive work, and the repressions of a despotic but ineffectual government. In addition to the anti-slavery theme, the novel traces the various relationships between the Spaniards and the *criollos* and the effects on the country of an outmoded educational system. Villaverde passionately rejects Spanish oppression, with a special hatred reserved for the military. Through a careful reading of this novel one can come to know fully the political, moral, and social status of Cuba between 1812 and 1831,[6] a political struggle party symbolized through the figure of father against son. But it is for its accurate evocation of nineteenth-century customs and types that the novel is primarily successful. The author describes all classes, professions of the day, and racial types in both city and country. Many of the secondary characters, black and white, are well drawn and reflect accurately the speech patterns of the different classes, especially the popular language and proverbs. Villaverde describes the carriages people used, their dress, their meals, the public buildings, churches, convents, hospitals, plazas, streets, markets, sugar and coffee plantations, the dances, fiestas, the religious holidays, even the children's games. The novel is a social document but is also artistically valid in its dramatic and live presentation of Cuban colonial life. The Cuban critics' assessment of the novel as "la mejor de nuestras novelas costumbristas de todos los tiempos," [7] and as the equal of "las grandes novelas hispanoamericanas del siglo XIX . . . *Amalia* de José Marmol tanto como . . . *María* de Jorge Isaacs," [8] is not an unreasonable one.

Other Cuban costumbrista novelists of the day include José Ramón Betancourt (1823–1890), who describes gambling, gangsterism and the general customs between 1835 and 1845 in his *Una feria de la caridad en 183* . . . (1858) which he labeled "cuento camagüeyano"; and Ramón de Palma (1812–1860), whom some believe to be the author of the first Cuban novel, *Matanzas y Yumurí* (1837), published in *Aguinaldo Habanero*. This "primer ensayo novelesco de escritor cubano" [9] apparently helped inspire Villaverde. Palma's other novelettes are *El cólera en la Habana* and *Pascua en San Marcos*, both published in *El Album* in 1838. The first deals with an epidemic of 1833 and the second with a don Juan type who comes to a bad end. In addition to the well-known poetess, Gertrudis Gómez de Avellaneda, whose novels we shall discuss in a different context, the only other Cuban costumbrista novelist worthy of mention is Anselmo Suárez y Romero (1818–1878), the author of *Francisco*, the first anti-slavery novel of Spanish America, written in 1838 but not published in complete form, because of Spanish censorship, until 1880. A member of Delmonte's tertulia, Suárez y Romero succumbed to his mentor's urging to write an abolitionist novel for the Englishman Richard Madden, who was publishing an anti-slavery collection. A fellow *tertuliano*, Antonio Zambrana (1812–1873), also undertook the task and produced a novel with a similar title, *El negro Francisco* (1875).

An amalgam of romantic, realistic, and propaganda elements, *Francisco*, set at a sugar mill, describes the tragic love of two slaves, Francisco and Dorotea, prevented by their masters from the realization of their desires. The theme of slaves pursued to their graves by a cruel and lascivious master is of less interest than the impressive descriptions of life at the mill, the Negro customs, the dances and songs. The mistress who mistreats her slaves considers herself to be a humanitarian, but the sugar mill manager's sadism, brutality, and cowardice are unrelieved by any such hypocritical pretensions. Francisco's resignation, his eternal love, and his docility are difficult for the modern reader to understand. Through his use of stereo-typed and lifeless characters, the author exaggerated "los perfiles virtuosos y delictivos de sus personajes, convirtiéndolos en seres unilaterales y por tanto inhumanos." [10]

Antonio José de Irisarri (1786–1868) of Guatemala, who used the pseudonyms Romualdo Villapedrosa and El Bachiller Hilario de Altagumea and was known as the "Central American Cervantes," was a newspaperman, politician, and philologist. In Chile he served Bernardo O'Higgins on a diplomatic mission, became a friend of Andrés Bello, and an active journalist in a number of countries such as Mexico, Colombia, and Peru whose customs he depicts. Considered by some to be a historical novelist and by Luis Alberto Sánchez as the originator of the American biographical novel,[11] Irisarri published his El cristiano errante (1847), an ironic and picaresque romantic autobiography which pictures colonial America in utopian terms, in Bogotá. He affirms that his purpose is to paint the customs of the day and reveal his own past, promising a second volume, further depicting his loves and travels, which never appeared. Of special fictional interest is the inserted episode of Dorila, a tragic and idyllic love story which seems to be a kind of incomplete precursor to Jorge Isaacs' sentimental novel, María. He also wrote a picaresque novel, Historia del perínclito Epaminondas del Cauca (1863), about Simón Rodríguez, Bolívar's teacher, which belies Irisarri's early conservatism, as it reflects his liberal ideology and combativeness in its corrosive and sarcastic attack on the cau-dillo system of the day. In his prologue he claims he has written a novel containing historical, political, and philosophical elements, but one critic denies that either of his works can really be called a novel.[12]

Another Guatemalan, José Milla y Vidaurre (1822–1882), pri-marily a historical novelist and to be treated as such later, was praised by Rubén Darío as "un gran novelista de costumbres, quizá y sin quizá el único verdadero novelista que ha tenido la América Central." [13] His costumbrista articles appeared as early as 1861 in a weekly La Hoja de Avisos, and at least two of his novels, Historia de un pepe (1882) and Memorias de un abogado (1876), in addition to their mystery and melodrama, emphasize costumbrista elements a great deal. Un viaje al otro mundo, pasan-do por otras partes (1875), an account of his travels and a kind of three-volume costumbrista novel, presents us with Juan Chapín, the representative of the Guatemalan middle class.

As we have seen, costumbrismo may combine with romantic or realistic elements in varying degrees. One of the best costumbrista novels with both romantic and realistic overtones is *Manuela* (1866) by Eugenio Díaz Castro (1804–1865), who, paraphrasing a statement by Fernán Caballero, stated that "los cuadros de costumbres no se inventan sino que se copian." His countryman, Rafael Maya, believes that Díaz "fue el iniciador, en Colombia, de un género literario que hoy se halla en plena vigencia, o sea la novela realista de carácter americano," [14] but others see the novel, together with *María*, as the culmination of the romantic period in Colombia.[15] The flimsy plot is romantic, but José María Vergara, to whose Mosaico circle the country author was first presented by Ricardo Carrasquilla, was correct in viewing the sketches of country and ranch life and the scenes of almost photographic intensity as a great costumbrista presentation of characters. He found the style to be original and warm, and he was happy to present the novel in installments in *El Mosaico* review, to which Jorge Isaacs, José Manuel Marroquín, and José María Samper also belonged and contributed. *Manuela*, subtitled "novela de costumbres colombianas," is set in the late 1850s. Díaz' purpose was to expose Colombian political chicanery. Demóstenes, a young liberal city politician, comes to live in Manuela's home and attempts to free her and the village from the tyrannical power of the hacendado Don Tadeo Candillo, whose advances the beautiful Manuela rejects. Demóstenes eventually defeats Tadeo but not before the latter sets fire to the church where Manuela, being married to a young villager, perishes in the flames. Díaz, a conservative, presents Demóstenes as a caricature, but the hacendado, the customs, dances, fiestas, and local politics are faithful portraits. Díaz effectively contrasts the beauties of nature with the material misery of the inhabitants. His other fiction such as *El rejo de enlazar* (1873) is now largely forgotten.

Juan Bautista Alberdi (1810–1884), known better for other activities and for his famous *Bases y puntos de partida para la organización política de la República Argentina* (1852), for obvious reasons called simply *Bases*, wrote *Peregrinación de Luz del Día* (1871), with the lengthy added title of "Viaje y aventuras de la Verdad en el Nuevo Mundo," a kind of allegorical-political novel on the order of the Puerto Rican Eugenio María de Hostos' *La peregrinación de Bayoán*. Alberdi's novel severely attacks American society and the even more hypocritical European one. He believed in determining American reality and solutions for humanity's problems along positivistic, scientific, and experimental lines. Truth or Daylight comes to the New World disguised as a woman but finds the same moral degeneration and hypocrisy she had abandoned in Europe and returns to that unhappy continent. Pessimistic and satirical, this work, labeled on its title page "Cuento publicado por A," has been called moral philosophy, history, and politics, as well as a good "fantastic story." [16] It is colorful and challenging, and its satirical pessimism in no way detracts from its fictional aspects.

To a degree almost all of the novels written in the nineteenth century can be called costumbrista works. Most of the Mexican novelists, for example Luis G. Inclán (1816–1875) and José Tomás de Cuéllar (1830–1894), while classified as romantic writers, rely heavily on costumbrismo. In Venezuela the costumbrista sketch and novel were also quite popular, costumbrismo having been born there at a moment in history when the towns and cities were "cobrando caracteres de complejidad. Viene a ser entonces como la historia viva de toda una inmensa sociedad en período de formación." [17] Daniel Mendoza (1823–1867) in *El llanero* (1845), subtitled "Estudio de sociología venezolana," gives us a complete description, in anecdotal fashion, of the plainsman's life and customs. Tulio Febres Cordero (1860–1938), the "Cronista de Mérida," historian and also author of fantastic stories, sketches, and pseudohistorical legends, provides us with a late sample of costumbrismo in *Don Quijote en América* (1905), the satirical study of progress in the rural village of Mapiche.

ROMANTICISM

It is not surprising, in the strange realistic-romantic literary chronology of Latin America, that it should be a romantic Argentine poet who produced the first realistic-costumbrista fiction in that country before the advent of most of the romantic fiction on the continent. Before discussing that poet, Esteban Echeverría, it will be necessary to examine romanticism in America.

In a sense one can say that Spanish literature has always been romantic. Golden Age dramatists had not bothered with the mythical unities of time, place, and action or other so-called classical niceties. Their interest in Spanish historical events was shared, it must be admitted, by the neoclassicists, who did much work on the Middle Ages and were as keenly nationalistic, despite romantic propaganda to the contrary. An emphasis on the Middle Ages, the popular, and the national was nevertheless one of the primary aspects of Spanish romanticism. Among other elements, by no means exclusively Spanish, are the revolt against neoclassicism, pessimism, doubt, passion, the distant in time and space, freedom of form, a somewhat pantheistic view of nature—at times seen as a direct inspiration and emotion as well as a reflection of subjective human states, often contemplated lyrically or seen in its wild and savage aspects—and an interest in the Christian as opposed to the pagan. In general the heart triumphed over the mind, often including a concern for the social outcast along with dreams of personal glory. Since the romantic considered himself as the center of the universe, he felt free to give way to his emotional impulses of inspiration.

In Spain Ramón López Soler, the Spanish Sir Walter Scott, Enrique Gil y Carrasco, Mariano José de Larra, Patricio de la Escosura, Espronceda, and many others contributed historical novels between 1830 and 1845. Since the sentimental novel emphasizing romantic melancholy had largely played itself out in Spain in the fifteenth and sixteenth centuries, the nineteenth-century fiction was largely concerned with the Middle Ages and national themes (perhaps a reaction away from French rationalism). The most prolific writer of these novels in Spain was Manuel Fernández y González; his and other novels of the day clearly reveal the influences of Victor Hugo, Manzoni, and especially Sir Walter Scott. As with other genres, many polemics existed over the role of the novel, as Martínez de la Rosa compared the ancient and the modern, Gil y Zárate defended the latter as more ingenious, and Serafín Estébanez Calderón considered historical fiction to be superior to history itself.

Early romantic trends in America can be seen in *Noches tristes, día alegre* and in the poetry of Andrés Bello, who, despite his conservative ideas and neoclassic form, extolled the pure fresh air of America, the concept of liberty, and the exaltation of American nature. He considered James Fenimore Cooper, whom he recommended to Americans everywhere, to be the New World's Sir Walter Scott. But Bello's role in America was much that of Alberto Lista in Spain. To counterbalance Bello's friendship with the romantic Blanco White and his translation of a Victor Hugo poem, we have his more traditional role in the Chilean polemics in the 1840s with José Joaquín de Mora and others. It must be remembered that José Victorino Lastarria, so important in the development of Chilean fiction, was a student of both men. José María Heredia, too, while revealing the influences of Cienfuegos, Quintana, and Meléndez Valdés, is at times clearly romantic. French romanticism, through Echeverría, arrived on the American scene. The Spanish romantics Espronceda, Zorrilla, and Bécquer later influenced Spanish American romanticism, which, whatever its uniqueness, definitely stems from a European source. As Emilio Carilla states: "El romanticismo en la América Hispánica sigue las líneas generales del romanticismo europeo. . . . Pero tiene, además, acentos propios . . . que surgieron . . . como algo consustancial a la tierra y al hombre de América." [18]

Among the differences which separate Spanish romanticism from that of the New World are a different view of religion and death and an emphasis on the concept of political freedom and activity, for "el romanticismo, en Hispanoamérica, coincide con el comienzo de la vida independiente de la mayoría de los países. Es en rigor el primer 'momento' literario de la vida de estas regiones." [19] Undoubtedly the movement in America served as a liberating force from the literary straitjackets to which American authors felt themselves tied. As in Spain, political tyranny caused the writers to equate public service and a social role with their literary aspirations. Since there were no Middle Ages in America, writers evoked the Indian in his natural surroundings as a noble and sorrowful figure to replace the legendary heroes of history. Paradoxically, these politically and socially active writers in a land where the ideas of the Enlightenment lingered on were incapable of seeing the true suffering of the Indian. Christianity, a concomitant and contributing factor to this blindness, seems omnipresent in Spanish American fiction. The Christian father appears to assuage doubts and fears, convincing only because of Indian resignation and a long missionary tradition. Finally, a remarkable geography became the strongest factor in the American romantic mode. American nature was by definition exotic in its strange, mysterious, and wild semblance, so American romantics did not have to search for far and distant lands as settings. The romantics, impressed by their continent's beauty, insisted more and more on the American aspects of their literature, the settings, the customs, the politics, the historical events, and, in essence, adapted European romanticism to the American scene in the hopes of creating a new and autochthonous literature.[20]

Some of the Spanish American romantic novels are largely costumbrista; a significant number deal with Indian themes; some are sentimental; some are political; some are abolitionist. The most representative romantic novel may have been historical, but most novels, exceptionally hard to classify, contain elements of many tendencies. Anderson Imbert, one of the more perceptive Spanish American critics, cites the difficulty of defining the historical novel but attempts, nonetheless, to categorize the themes and the novel chronologically from the discovery and conquest up to the recent past.[21] Marguerite Suárez-Murias attempts to delimit these novels as appearing between 1832 and 1888, but any specific limitation is difficult to defend.[22]

The historical romances of Sir Walter Scott were much translated and read. José Joaquín de Mora had translated Scott's works in Chile as early as 1825. François de Chateaubriand, whose *Atalá* was first translated into Spanish by Simón Rodríguez in 1801 (some cite Servanto Teresa de Mier as the translator), was quite popular in Chile by 1814. Bernardin de Saint-Pierre, author of *Paul et Virginie,* was also much admired. Andrés Bello, Vicente Fidel López, Bartolomé Mitre, and Domingo Faustino Sarmiento were ardent admirers of and propagandists for James Fenimore Cooper. Sue, Manzoni, Dumas, George Sand, and, later, Benito Pérez Galdós also influenced Spanish American fiction. Mexico became a center for Scott novels, but the whole continent, lacking the tradition of knighthood, substituted the Indian as the idyllic and thematic leitmotif for Americans, against a backdrop whose extravagant natural features and flora and fauna had been so falsely represented by Chateaubriand. Sarmiento's *Facundo* contributed a classic theme in Spanish American fiction, that of civilization versus barbarism, and in analyzing the gaucho, had an influence which transcended that of the developing historical novel.

The historical novel was the backbone of Spanish American romantic fiction, although a continuing conflict existed between invention and information. Many of the so-called historical novels had scanty historical factual material, and some were almost exclusively historical. According to Amado Alonso, in spite of their success, the historical novels were "en crisis desde su nacimiento." [23] Some novels treated the discovery and exploration of America; others were contemporary to the author, who could thus more clearly express his national, patriotic, and political preoccupations to the exclusion of character development and even authentic milieu. Vicente Fidel López, in the prologue to his novel *La novia del hereje*, written in 1840, praises the historical novel as a didactic instrument for awakening national pride in the past, achieving thereby a patriotic cohesion. A novelist shows the interactions of history with daily events and the lack of conflict between the recording of great events and replacing familiar ones with imagination to give the reader the whole truth: "... el novelista hábil puede reproducir con su imaginación la parte perdida creando libremente la vida familiar y sujetándose estrictamente a la vida histórica en las combinaciones que haga de una y otra para reproducir le verdad completa." A fairly simple definition of the historical novel, given by Antonio Castro Leal, states that it is a narrative which presents with adequate fidelity "el escenario de una época del pasado, en que aparecen algunas figuras históricas, en puntos que coinciden con la narración o como decoración de fondo para dar mayor realidad al cuadro, acomodando las acciones de los personajes reales o imaginarios a los acontecimientos y la sicología de la época en que se sitúa la novela." [24]

Pedro Henríquez Ureña believes that *Jicoténcal*, published in Philadelphia in 1826, is not only the earliest Spanish American historical romance but also the first real romanticism on the continent.[25] Anderson Imbert states that it is not clearly a romantic novel nor is he certain that it is of Mexican origin. Its criticism of Cortés and the conquest were general ideas of the Enlightenment rather than those of Mexican patriots.[26] Another critic, while finding the novel mediocre, points out "a pronounced similarity between the general trend of thought in parts of the novel and that of Voltaire's *L'Ingénu*." [27] Luis Leal agrees that it is the "primera novela histórica en castellano" but doubts the author was a Mexican, proposing as its author, instead, the Cuban Félix Varela (1788–1853).[28] He nevertheless justifies its inclusion as a Mexican historical novel because of the author's knowledge of local history. *Jicoténcal* antedates by two years historical novels written by Telesforo de Trueba y Cossío and Ramón López Soler in Spain. The theme must have been a fairly popular one, for in 1831 the Spaniard Salvador García Vahamonde also published a novel called *Xicoténcal, príncipe americano*, and *Jicoténcal* is also the title of a well-known poem by Diego Gabriel de la Concepción Valdés (1809–1844) of Cuba. The novel interprets the Mexican conquest, promotes an idealistic religion, along with abstract justice and the concept of the noble savage, and uncompromisingly attacks despots. Cortés, presented as a vile and tyrannical assassin of liberty, is opposed by its noble defender, Jicoténcal. Cortés forms an alliance with the Tlaxcaltecans. Jicoténcal, one of Moctezuma's senators, opposes it, as his enemy Magiscatzin and Cortés plot his death. Diego de Ordaz, Jicoténcal's friend and the only honorable Spaniard, rejects the advances of Doña Marina and falls in love with Teutila, Jicoténcal's wife. Teutila takes poison intended for the Spaniard and dies cursing Cortés.

Two Cubans were among the early romantic historical novelists of America, José Antonio Echeverría (1815–1885) and Gertrudis Gómez de Avellaneda (1814–1873). Echeverría, a Venezuelan by birth who had come to Cuba at a very early age and won a prize for his poetry as a teenager, was one of the founders, along with Ramón de Palma, of the *Aguinaldo Habanero* (1837) and *El Album* (1838). His one novel, *Antonelli*, first appeared in *La Cartera Cubana* in 1839; it was later published in 1855 under the pseudonym of Zacarías. Set in sixteenth-century Havana, the novel is filled with nocturnal walks, battles between good and evil, secret meetings, and excessive sentiment. Juan Bautista Antonelli, an Italian engineer, received from Philip II the commission to build Morro Castle and the fortifications of Havana. Antonelli, in love with the heroine, promotes her death and that of his rival through the jealousy of a vengeful criollo.

Gómez de Avellaneda, better known as a poet, dramatist, and writer of legends and short stories, was the daughter of a Spaniard and a lady of a well-known Cuban family. When her mother remarried, Gertrudis was quite unhappy, a factor, perhaps, in her well publicized love affairs with the Spanish poet Gabriel García Tassara and the Andalusian Ignacio de Cepeda. This eroticism and a feminine sentimentality can be discerned in her novels at the expense of the passion and tragedy so much a part of her historical and biblical dramatic productions. Her novels lack the imagination of her shorter works and in general "está muy por debajo de su lírica y de su teatro." [29] Yet, among the earliest of their kind, they have a certain historical importance.

Her first novel, *Sab* (1841), dedicated to that Spanish teacher of poets, Alberto Lista but set in Camagüey, Cuba, had been written, apparently, in 1838. In the prologue she says: "Tres años ha dormido esta novelita casi olvidada en el fondo de su papelera," and she admits that her absence from Cuba, the ensuing melancholy, and the need for distraction led her to write it. Although the novel deals with a slave of the Bellavista family and preceded *Uncle Tom's Cabin* by almost a dozen years, many question its anti-slavery sincerity.[30] Abolitionist feeling is implied, but the author takes an ambivalent position with regard to the Negro and mulatto and conveys a sentimental, maternal inclination toward the idealized Indian. The people of the time read it as anti-slavery, since the novel was prohibited for its "subversive doctrines," reading more into her message of love and dignity for all humanity than she intended. One explanation may be that she started the novel as an anti-slavery work but changed her mind to create what she hoped would be a psychological novel with a somewhat veiled autobiographical identification of herself as Carlota and Cepeda, her great love, as Enrique.[31] The Cuban customs and countryside, the tropical and exotic birds and flowers are realistic enough, but the idealized Sab, in his perfection, seems to represent a nostalgic recreation brought from the swamp of memory, and the other characters are all romantic stereotypes. In the disordered mosaic of the romantic frame, Sab, or Bernabé, Carlota's personal slave, saves Enrique, his mistress' fiancé, in a storm, wins a lottery, and in spite of his own love for Carlota, gives her his fortune, anonymously, so that she can marry Enrique, the man of her dreams. Teresa, Carlota's friend, who loves Sab, on his death enters a convent. Carlota, finally realizing the true heroism of her former slave, prays for his soul.

Halfway between a historical and costumbrista novel and her most original one,[32] *Sab*, apparently because its author thought little of it, was not even included in her complete works of 1869. In the prologue to *Dos mujeres* she exclaims: "Si la benévola acogida que el público de Madrid ha concedido a la novelita intitulada *Sab*, impusiese a su autora la obligación de presentarle otra obra de más estudio y profundidad, acaso no se atrevería a dar a la prensa su segundo ensayo en tan difícil género." Basically the work is a stylized imitation of European trends, with its romantically idealized "natural" Negro, but one senses the struggle between Avellaneda's undoubtedly sincere religious and human devotion and the beliefs of the social circles of which she was a member.[33]

Gómez de Avellaneda wrote two other major novels, *Espatolino* (1844) and *Guatimozín* (1846). The first is set in Italy in 1811, and its hero, a Robin Hood type Italian bandit, dies, which brings on the subsequent madness of his sweetheart. The standard romantic villain appears as do the concomitant diguises, betrayals, and vengeance. The author's protest against an unjust society which causes the hero's death and her comments on false virtue, human hypocrisy, the need for penal reforms, and the abolishing of capital punishment are refreshingly different from standard romantic fare. The second novel, closely following Sir Walter Scott, treats of Cortés, his loves, and that of Moctezuma's daughter for a noble Spaniard. Her sources, aside from the general ones of Scott and Chateaubriand, whom she considered to be "inmortal y divino," seem to have been Hernán Cortés and Bernal Díaz del Castillo.[34]

Dos mujeres (1842) incorporates her views on the psychology of women and their place in society, but she fails to live up to her promise in the prologue to "bosquejar caracteres verosímiles y pasiones naturales." *Dolores* (1851), which attacks marriages of convenience, is about a cruel mother who imprisons her daughter in order to destroy her love. *El cacique de Turmequé* (1854), considered by many to be a legend, is based on *El carnero* and deals with rivalries, conspiracies, and vengeance in sixteenth-century Bogotá. *El artista barquero* (1861) treats of the life of a French painter, Hubert Robert (1753–1808).

Esteban Echeverría (1805–1851), who had developed his romanticism in France from 1826 on, wrote what some consider to be the first romantic poem of America, *Elvira o la novia del Plata* (1832), and certainly the first of French inspiration. *Los consuelos* (1834), the first national poetry published in Argentina, and *Las rimas*

(1837) involve the romantic search for the exotic, the subjective, orientalism, liberty, landscape, local color, and rebellion against society. As part of his rebellion, Echeverría was instrumental in founding Joven Argentina in 1838. An outgrowth of the earlier Salón Literario under the leadership of the overly optimistic Marcos Sastre, who wanted to bring "new ideas" to the young generations, Joven Argentina was later baptized in 1846, by Echeverría himself, with its more popular title of Asociación de Mayo,[35] named after the 25 May 1810 uprising on behalf of the unworthy Spanish monarch Fernando VII. The organization dedicated itself to working for Argentina, and Echeverría hoped to divert it from the Federalist-Unitarian squabble so that the members might devote themselves to public good. Echeverría never fully realized his idealistic dreams because of his contradictory personality, his apparent ambivalence about the *pueblo*, and his difficulty in channeling his idealism into functional lines. One can find in him the great influence of Lamennais and Pierre Leroux, as well as a social Christian preoccupation.[36]

Echeverría believed firmly in the possibility of autochthonous literature based on local peculiarities, and romanticism for him meant not only beauty but liberty and independence from Europe. "La Cautiva," part of *Las rimas*, was the first national work that devoted itself poetically to the Argentine pampa and Indian and white frontier relationships. Although it may be true that the spiritual renovation of Argentine letters would have taken place without Echeverría, he is almost universally acknowledged as the progenitor, initiator, or renovator of his country's literature. Influenced by Chateaubriand, he discovered his native pampa and in the process introduced new liberal ideas that would be followed by members of his generation, being most authentically articulated by Sarmiento in his anti-traditional and anti-Spanish campaign.

Echeverría's *El Matadero*, short story, novelette, novelistic sketch, or chronicle,[37] chronologically the first Argentine fiction, was written about 1838 but not published until 1871 in the *Revista del Río de la Plata*, directed by Andrés Lamas and Vicente Fidel López. Juan María Gutiérrez found the manuscript, which for obvious reasons could not be published in Echeverría's lifetime, among his friend's papers. In his prologue to the work Gutiérrez calls it "una página histórica, un cuadro de costumbres y una protesta que nos honra," but he objects to the popular and vulgar language, a surprising reservation from a man who had been a political activist in the Asociación de Mayo and who as a novelist might have accepted it as matching and integrating the gross scenes of slaughter. In spite of certain romantic themes of fatality and good versus evil, the story is a precursor of the gaucho, realistic, and even perhaps naturalistic fiction of Spanish America. In its crude, fragmentary, but highly dramatic way, it undoubtedly pointed the way to Argentine literary themes.[38] In its mixture of grotesque and tragic elements to convey its symbolic social protest, and also in its impressionistic and pictorial style, it is a unique fictional work of the romantic period.

Set in the time of Rosas, the story reveals the power of the secret police, or Mazorca, using as its bloody background the slaughter house of Buenos Aires. The colorful, realistic scenes of grease and blood-spattered butchers, a beheaded child, hungry dogs, thieving rabble, a general hustle and bustle, and a grotesque humor involving investigations into the testicular makeup of one of the fifty steers sent in to feed the starving populace, offer the background for the death of the dignified *unitario*, insulted by his unworthy enemies. His death has been interpreted in a number of ways, even as an immolation and implied criticism of the alliance between the Catholic church and Rosas. The political implications of the slaughter house (Argentina) inhabited by cattle (deprived citizens) seem clear as does an implied, perhaps overly optimistic idealism about the possibility of a socially, intellectually, and morally free Argentine society. While for some it may be simply ". . . un cuadro de costumbres, cruda pintura realista de la plebe porteña de los suburbios," [39] the story directly attacks the Rosas government and, in addition to the vibrance and warmth of its narration, has tragic implications as a sadly historical spectacle, "la más vigorosa ejecutoria sobre los tiranos de ayer, de hoy, de mañana." [40]

Juan María Gutiérrez (1809–1875), poet and literary critic whom Menéndez y Pelayo considered one of the greatest, wrote *El hombre hormiga* (1838), a costumbrista sketch verging on fiction, and *El capitán de patricios* (1843), published in book form in 1874. The novel, set on a beautiful island in the year 1811, is filled with patriotism, sacrifice, romantic love, and the struggle between that idyllic love and duty. Although the inevitable convent reveals the

novel's romantic bent, it is "the first prose work in Argentine literature where the desire to tell a story is predominant, above and beyond political and social considerations, and which exhibits an
interplay of emotions and conflicts among several characters." [41]
Gutiérrez, the discoverer of Pedro de Oña's *El Arauco Domado*,
and the author of *Antología poética* (1846), the first anthology of
Spanish American poetry, was a firm believer in America and its
unifying force.

Bartolomé Mitre (1821–1906), poet, president, archeologist, and
historian, published *Soledad* (1847) when he was exiled in La Paz,
Bolivia, in *La Época*, a review he directed and which some consider
to be the first newspaper in Bolivia. In the prologue he makes clear
that he thinks the public in general is not mature enough to appreciate outstanding fiction and that "la América del Sud es la parte
del mundo más pobre en novelistas originales," a situation which
unfortunately his novel, of a contrived, trivial, and pretentious nature, did little to change. Soledad, after an unwanted marriage and
other misadventures, finds happiness and spiritual tranquility. Although Mitre is compassionate and fervently American, it is hard
to agree that his novel has "cierta significación de germen de una
novela genuina." [42] Mitre also wrote a slight fantasy, *Memorias de
un botón de rosa* (1848), about the memories of a once beautiful
but now withered bud in an album.

Miguel Cané (1812–1863), the father of an even better writer,
produced two novels in 1858, both of which have been largely forgotten. *Esther*, finished in 1851, resembles many modernist novels
written some four or five decades later. Written in Florence and
with its action in Italy, it is a sad tale of love and death. An Argentine hero, Eugenio Segry, saves the life of an unhappily married
and frustrated Englishwoman, Esther Wilson. They find spiritual
fulfillment in each other, travel through the country, discuss art
and literature, and she manages, in the end, to die in his arms. *La
familia de Sconner* contains the typically romantic theme about
the theft of an inheritance from two orphan brothers, and the
triumph of justice. More important than his lesson of Christian
charity is the author's description of a ranch and ranch life, the first,
"aunque rápidamente esbozada . . . estancia en la novela argentina." [43] Cané's short fiction is better left forgotten.

One of the outstanding historical novelists of the entire romantic

period was Vicente Fidel López (1815–1903), more famous to some
as a historian. Keenly interested in his country's history, he had
hoped, as he states in his enlightening prologue, to write "una serie
de novelas destinadas a resucitar el recuerdo de los viejos tiempos
. . . era una empresa digna de tentar el más puro patriotismo." He
hoped his fiction might awaken interest in Argentina's national
traditions but managed to write only two novels and three in outline form. We exist both as individuals and as components of a
society, and our individual actions may be called historical. What
we learn from historical documentation enables us to imagine
what we cannot know but may guess about human drama. The historical novel, then, saying what we know and what we can guess,
saves the past, and thus there can be no real conflict between fantasy and reality.

Whatever his views about the historical novel, Vicente Fidel
López, along with Sarmiento and Alberdi, helped stimulate the
growing Chilean romanticism (many believe they were its progeni-
tors). Vicente Fidel López started one of the early Chilean newspapers, *La Revista de Valparaíso* (1842), carried on polemics about
romanticism, and was Francisco Bilbao's favorite teacher, influ-
encing him with his analysis of the doctrines of Vico and Herder.
López stayed in Chile until 1848, then went to Montevideo, and
after the fall of Rosas returned to Argentina.[44]

La novia del hereje, written in 1840 but not published until
1854, is subtitled "La Inquisición de Lima." It is filled with light
and movement, contains picaresque and costumbrista as well as
romantic elements, and pictures rivalries between religious orders,
intrigues, spies, sacrifices, nocturnal encounters, the Inquisition
and its activities, pirates, priests, pharmacists, lawyers, prosecutors,
market places, restaurants, and, especially, against the colorful
tapestry of holiday scenes, the principal historical event, the expedition of Sir Francis Drake in 1578–79. Historical characters are sub-
ordinated to the fictional protagonists, the noble Protestant lieutenant Henderson and his beloved and beautiful Catholic María.
María, denounced to the Inquisition, is tortured, but an earthquake in Lima allows the English to free the prisoners. In this fast-
paced, occasionally humorous but impassioned and moving story,
Vicente Fidel López wished to explore the moral elements which
constituted American society of the time, Spanish reaction to the

new religious agitation of the day brought about by the Reformation, and the rise of England to world leadership. The author finds much good in English pirates and equates their success with the cause of criollo liberty in defying the tyrannical power of Spain, a somewhat frequent theme in nineteenth-century America. Vicente Fidel López takes pride in his documentation, and in spite of the digressions of a historical nature in the novel, its color, action, characters, and narrative merit the high praise bestowed upon it as "entre las principales novelas románticas de su especie escritas en castellano." [45]

López also wrote *La loca de la guardia* (1896), which he labeled "cuento histórico." It deals with the frontier activities between Argentina and Chile from 1813 to 1822. Teresa, the protagonist, goes mad because of her rape and the murder of her sweetheart, and the fictional drive is created through her monomaniacal desire for vengeance against the guilty and lecherous Spaniard, San Bruno. Other historical figures such as O'Higgins and San Martín come through the congeries of characters, but the themes of vengeance, madness, and patriotic fervor seem more perfunctory than persuasive. His epistolary novel, *La gran semana de 1810* (1909), is even less enduring.

The "Argentine George Sand," Juana Manuela Gorriti (1818–1892), married to a president of Bolivia, Manuel Isidoro Belzú, lived for thirty years in Peru, where Ricardo Palma was one of the most assiduous frequenters of her literary tertulia. Hating injustice and foreign tyranny, she was the first author to incorporate the Indian and his legends into Argentine fiction and one of the first to reflect the American spirit in all its mystery and humanity.[46] One of the original cultivators of romanticism, she was especially involved with the unknown, and her themes of love and jealousy are usually concerned with the force of destiny. Extremely popular in her time, she collected her legends, stories, and novels in two primary volumes, *Sueños y realidades* (1865) and *Panoramas de la vida* (1876). Her *La quena* (1845) is possibly the first short novel published by an Argentine novelist, although it was printed in Lima and treats of colonial Peru. *El tesoro de los Incas* reveals the evil machinations of Diego Maldonado to convince the daughter of the guardian of the treasure to betray her trust, and the family's choice of torture and death over betrayal. *El pozo del Yocci* (1869), a historical novel whose action occurs in 1814, shows with poetic justice the death of a criminal in the same well into which he had cast his victim.

Of all the romantic historical novels written in the nineteenth century, *Amalia* by José Mármol (1817–1871) stands out as the most popular and famous. Mármol, a sutdent of Vicente Fidel López, and a member of the Asociación de Mayo, managed to escape as had Sarmiento, Mitre, and Echeverría, in his case first to Montevideo and later to Rio de Janeiro. A poet, whose best known poetry is a bad imitation of Byron's *Childe Harold* called *Cantos del peregrino* (1844), and a dramatist, Mármol achieved permanent literary stature only through his novel. *Amalia* was published first in incomplete form as a literary supplement in *La Semana de Montevideo* in 1844, apparently planned as the first part of a trilogy, never completed. It appeared in book form in 1851, and the complete edition, containing a second part, was published in Buenos Aires in 1855. It may well be the first real Argentine novel by virtue of its book form, wide acceptance, and setting—"la primera verdadera novela hispanoamericana, aquella en que por primera vez los valores novelescos se sobreponen a las influencias y al simple costumbrismo." [47] The hatred, invective, and emotional and legal attack on Rosas that caused its early wide acceptance was also responsible for its publication delay. Mármol thought of his novel as an instrument of liberty and rather than simply record history or deal with abstraction and abstract ideals, he created a masterful picture not only of Rosas but of the entire contemporary atmosphere in all its horror, mystery, and psychological conflicts. *Amalia* fictionally represents one aspect of *Facundo*, Domingo Faustino Sarmiento's sociological essay, and Mármol's Rosas like Sarmiento's Facundo shows us a gaucho reaction to a European world. Although Mármol identifies Europe with good as opposed to the concrete Argentinian situation, he paradoxically represents an aesthetically false Europe. David Viñas, himself a twentieth-century novelist of some stature, sees the novel as an exemplification of Echeverría's thesis that Argentina's intellectual life should be both national and humanitarian, composed of progressive and yet traditional spiritual values of Argentine society. In his attempt Mármol develops his parallelism which "subyace y conforma la arquitectura del libro vinculado con la teoría inicial de la generación del 37: la síntesis entre lo americano y lo europeo." [48]

The novel begins with a struggle of Eduardo Belgrano and some of his friends against the *federales* during an attempted escape to Uruguay. The wounded Belgrano, saved by Daniel Bello, is taken to the house of Amalia Sáenz de Olabarrieta, the latter's widowed cousin. Eduardo and Amalia fall in love. Florencia Dupasquier, Daniel's fiancee, keeps him informed of the activities of the Mazorca. Eduardo, thanks to Amalia's loving care, recovers, and they plan to marry. Meanwhile, Rosas' sister-in-law, doña Josefa, has discovered their whereabouts. In an ensuing attack by secret police after the wedding, Eduardo is killed and Daniel's father, an influential citizen, arrives too late to save the rest.

Anderson Imbert considers the novel to be political and autobiographical rather than historical because Mármol shares aspects of both male protagonists, because the past is not really past, and because the author objectifies contemporary reality into historical form.[49] Mármol, in his preface, states that since the majority of the historical personages in his novel are still alive he has adopted the fiction of imagining he is writing the novel after several generations have elapsed to give it greater clarity and historical perspective. Even though the work is a social and political document of times through which the author himself lived, his telescopic projection of writing of a remote past rather than an immediate present seems to fall within the limits of historical narrative. He is unable to separate the enduring problems of mankind from circumstances in which he is is caught, but the knowledge of historical people and events, based on direct recollection, adds a creative if subjective force. Indeed, Mármol apparently used official documents to draw up an account about the tragic months between 4 May and 5 October 1840, when the Mazorca attempted to exterminate the so-called enemies of the State.

The fictional characters of this novel seem largely stereotypes. The few months in which the story takes place allow insufficient time for a full psychological development. The Unitarians are noble and idealistic and run the romantic gamut of sacrifice and death. Amalia is the perfect romantic heroine whom Mármol describes as a privileged creature who has inherited spiritual perfection both from heaven and earth. She may well have been an idealized portrait of his widowed aunt, María Mármol de Terrada, who gave him asylum. Florencia Dupasquier is a lifeless creation; Daniel Bello and Belgrano, reflecting the feelings of the author, are patriotic, bright, and virtuous beyond belief but without any real fire or even ashes of life. Fictional creations who have some substance are the grotesque friends of Bello, the school teacher Cándido Rodríguez and the go-between Doña Marcelina. The historical characters are something else again. Manuelita de Rosas y Escurra, Rosas' daughter, is a good girl badly used by her father; Doña María Josefa Escurra, the fanatical foe of unitarios, is clever, intelligent, and evil incarnate. Cuitiño, the bloody police chief, and especially Rosas, black, cruel, sadistic, and brutal tyrant, are other real people who help interweave and fuse historical events with invented ones.[50]

The novel is structurally defective, revealing the haste with which it was written. There are too many poetic descriptions of nature, lengthy and wordy digressions, tiresome details, and an inventory of districts, houses, streets, the river, and secret meetings, told by the author with an air of mystery and a constant sentimental exaggeration. Yet the novel has its symbolic touches, such as a glass of water transfused by the setting sun into the color of blood, and effective nature descriptions that reflect the intimate states of the characters. In general one finds the novel to have dimension, tragic breadth, color, and energy.[51] For the scholar, the implications of the work involving the relationship between Rosas and the Church,[52] and other historical tidbits, add interest to the dramatic description, the political documentation of tyranny, and its cost in degradation, terror, dirt, misery, and inhumanity.

Guatemala produced one outstanding romantic novelist in the nineteenth century, José Milla, whom we have already mentioned as a costumbrista,[53] considered to be also "el fundador de la novela guatemalteca . . . uno de los primeros autores de toda Hispanoamérica que cultivó sistemáticamente la novela histórica."[54] Milla wrote his novels under the pseudonym of Salomé Jil. *La hija del adelantado* (1866) comprises the period between 1539 and 1541—although previous events are alluded to—and presents a good study of Pedro de Alvarado, his daughter Leonor, and the princess Jicoténcal, along with the usual themes of an impossible love, tragic death, vengeance, and conspiracy. *Los nazarenos* (1867), about the conspiracy against the Conde de Santiago de Calimaya in the years between 1655 and 1657, treats of the rivalries of the Padilla and the Carranza families. In addition to "Los Nazarenos," the secret society of the first named family, again we are presented with the disguises, mystery, and terror so much a part of the fiction of this period, with the theme of adultery as well. *El visitador* (1868) is an unusually melodramatic work, about a son of Sir Francis Drake, with the usual run of noble hero, terrible villain, tragic loves (Milla is quite touchy about the differences between spiritual and carnal love), and miraculous escapes.[55] *Memorias de un abogado* (1876), more psychological and costumbrista than historical, paints apparently realistic scenes of nineteenth-century university life together with attacks on the legal profession. *Historia de un Pepe* (1882) treats of a foundling, Pepe Gabriel, the son of a highwayman, in the early nineteenth century. What is undoubtedly Milla's most intricately involved plot intensifies the highly romantic air, in spite of the author's desires, as Ramón Salazar states in the prologue to the 1936 edition, to write "una novela realista." [56]

Bolivia's Sebastian Dalenze's only claim to fame is that he supplemented the works of Argentine writers like Mitre and Gorriti by writing the first Bolivian novel, *Los misterios de Sucre* (1861), a fragmentary and mediocre imitation of Eugene Sue. Even this dubious distinction may have disappeared in 1969 with the rediscovery of Vicente Ballivián's *Claudio y Elena*, a short novel published in 1834. Novelists like Manuel María Caballero (1819–1866) and Félix Reyes Ortiz (1828–1882), whose novels about jealousy, passion, and death are historical relics, are even less known. Mariano Ricardo Terrazas (1833–1878) wrote *Misterios del corazón* (1869) and *Recuerdos de una prisión* (1899), only relatively better melodramatic novels in the style of Dumas, although Augusto Guzmán refers in a flattering fashion to the former work as "narración viva, matizada, ágil. Lirismo y patetismo." [57] The novel portrays the passion of the widow of a Peruvian viceroy for a young Spaniard, wrongfully imprisoned for twenty years. When he is freed, he becomes a priest, is called to a lady's bedside for her last rites, and discovers that she is the widow who had wronged him. Santiago Vaca Guzmán (1847–1896), a good literary critic, also produced several romantic novels: *Ayes del corazón* (1867), filled with melodramatic intrigues; *Días amargos* (1886), subtitled "Memorias de un pesimista," interesting for a psychological analysis of a suicide, a very early treatment of that theme; *Su Excelencia y su Ilustrísima* (1899), about colonial Paraguay in the sixteenth century and the enmity between the governor of Asunción and a bishop; and *Sin esperanza* (1891), about a priest who hopes to help a parishoner but is unable to prevent her murder by her husband.[58]

One novel of importance was produced in Bolivia in the nineteenth century. Nataniel Aguirre (1843–1888), in a sense the founder of the Bolivian novel, politician, playwright, and poet, and a blood relative of the Peruvian Manuel González Prada, published *Juan de la Rosa* (1885). When it first appeared in *El Heraldo de Cochabamba* in serial form, his name was not listed as author, perhaps because of the autobiographical aspects of the "Memorias del último soldado de la independencia," as its is subtitled. The author planned the volume as the first part of a tetralogy about the wars of independence, but the other titles, *Los porteños, Epopeya,* and *Los cochabambinos* were never published. The plot, with its good versus bad, mystery, and sentiment offers the usual melodrama, but Aguirre obtains a fresh insight by viewing the war through the eyes of a young orphan and his friends. He adds picturesque descriptions of the Cochabamba valley and colorful scenes such as that of the market women against the Spaniards. Juanito, the son of a Spaniard and a creole woman, is known as "de la Rosa," the name of the woman who cares for him when his mother dies. He is part of the activity of colonial times in Cochabamba, conveying the patriotic fervor of the period.

It might be argued that Narcisco Aréstegui (1824–1869) in his *El padre Horán* (1848), "Escenas de la vida del Cuzco," wrote the first Peruvian fiction. In spite of its *folletinesco* aspects and its theme of the Franciscan priest who kills a young girl, it is the first work which concerns itself with social circumstances and the unfortunate Peruvian Indian. As surprising that the first work of romantic fiction should have foreshadowed the *indigenista* novel of the next century is its theme of an assassin priest. His characters, an integral part of the social framework, are "apenas retocados, apenas idealizados." [59]

Usually the title of father of the Peruvian novel is awarded to Luis Benjamín Cisneros (1837–1904). An admirer of de Musset, he wrote two novels, *Julia, o escenas de la vida en Lima* (1860) and *Edgardo, o un joven de mi generación* (1864). The first is a sentimental novel about a middle-class family and an attack on gambling. The second novel, also sentimental, revolves around the theme of patriotic love of country. Cisneros also wrote two novelettes, *Amor de nido* (1864) and *Cecilia* (1865).

The most truculent of the early novelists and possibly the progenitor of the Peruvian social novel, Fernando Casós (1828–1882), wanted to create a literary revolution and describe the social deficiencies of his day. In a prologue to one of his novels, *Los amigos de Elena* (1874), a costumbrista effort, he writes: "Escribo la novela contemporánea porque estoy convencido que el maldito guano ha hecho nuestra sociedad tan insensible, que para nada ha de servir, sobre la generación presente, la crítica del pasado . . . yo divertiré al pueblo con los sueños más culminantes de mi época, los robos de los caminos de hierro, los negocios de guano, las crónicas de salón y los cuentos de los conventos." Treating of the political polemics which an increasing economic prosperity allowed, he adopts a strong anti-slavery position. *Los hombres de bien* (1874), a political attack written under the pseudonym of Segundo Provonena, also talks of Peruvian "men, deeds, institutions, and things." His *Romances históricos del Perú* (1848–73), through Alejandro Asecaux (his own pseudonym), reveal in a somewhat doctrinaire manner the institutional and political realities of the time.

Uruguayan romanticism found expression in *El Iniciador* (1838), founded by Andrés Lamas; but this magazine, although it saw its mentor in the Argentine Echeverría, followed French rather than American gods. Alejandro Magariños Cervantes (1825–1893), a poet, wrote *Caramurú* (1848), the story of a battle between Brazil and Uruguay which the latter won in 1827. The tale itself is typically romantic, with a kidnapping, love rivalries, a romantic heroine pure as the driven snow, and a protagonist who turns out to be a count's brother and marries his beautiful Lía. The author claimed in a prologue that he had no pretensions of writing a historical novel but that he hoped to excite his readers with noble sentiments and "bosquejar algunos rasgos del país, de la época y de los personajes que figuran en este libro." This he achieves in what some consider to be the first gaucho fiction, the first picture of rural life, the Charrúa Indian, and American and anti-Spanish spirit. Hugo D. Barbagelata denies that *Caramurú* is the first Uruguayan fiction, according that honor to the works of Manuel Acosta, *Los dos mayores rivales* (1856), and *La guerra civil entre los Incas*

(1861);[60] but Magariños Cervantes is usually credited with being the first to write novels in his country and "el primero también en cultivar el género en su forma histórica conforme la estética americanista de la época." [61] Alberto Zum Felde finds the plot arbitrary and even the title false, along with the characters and background of what he calls an "infeliz engendro folletinesco . . ." [62]

Other historical novelists of the day include Laurindo P. Lapuente (1835–1870), Florencio Escardó (1841–1898), and Antonio Díaz (1831–1911). By 1875 this first romantic generation had run its course. No real novels worthy of the name appeared before those of Acevedo Díaz, with the possible exception of *Cristina* (1885) by Daniel Muñoz (1849–1930), who wrote, under the Cervantine pseudonym of Sansón Carrasco, about Catholic and liberal polemics.

Jorge Isaacs (1837–1895),[63] a Colombian, wrote the greatest sentimental romantic novel, *María* (1867), which with *Amalia* forms the cornerstone of nineteenth-century Spanish American romantic fiction. Almost feverishly praised by local critics like Rafael Maya ("el código sentimental de una raza") and Baldomero Sanín Cano ("una de las creaciones literarias más hermosas y más cercanas de perfección que haya producido la literatura americana"), it has also been more universally accepted as "una flor del Cauca. . . . Es el *Pablo y Virginia* de nuestro mundo," [64] "el paradigma sentimental de un continente y de una época," [65] "la flor más pura e inmarcesible del romanticismo hispanoamericano," [66] and "sinfonía patética." [67] Even Unamuno, who read it in exile in Hendaya, states: "La sorbí como Efraín el agua clara de manos de María." [68] Isaacs, the son of a converted English Jew, spent his youth at the hacienda of El Paraíso, the "paternal house" of the novel on the banks of the Zabaletas, a small tributary of the Cauca on the western slopes of the central *cordillera*.[69] Isaacs' father lost his money, and young Isaacs planned a medical career which his military activities curtailed. He married, at the age of nineteen, Doña Felisa González, and they lived in Cali on the remnants of his father's estate. Forced to emigrate to Bogotá, the young poet became a member of El Mosaico group, impressing its members with his poetry and a number of plays. He wrote *María*, first conceived as a drama because of the popularity of costumbrista theater at the time, during a convalescent period after a malaria attack in 1864–65. José

María Vergara y Vergara convinced him to change it to a novel,[70] the first edition of which was five hundred copies. Isaacs, a friend of José Asunción Silva[71] and other well-known Colombia personalities, held a variety of positions from road inspector to teacher, but he had economic difficulties throughout his lifetime.

The simple, picturesque, charming, and sentimental tearjerker,[72] usually classified as an "idyllic romance," is similar in many ways to the sentimental novels written during the fifteenth and sixteenth centuries. The modern version of this kind of novel probably started with Rousseau's *La nouvelle Héloise* (1761) and was perfected by Bernardin de Saint-Pierre in his *Paul et Virginie* (1788) and to some degree later by Chateaubriand.[73] Largely autobiographical, Isaacs' novel deals with the love of Efraín and María, raised in their patriarchal home in the Cauca valley. The father wants Efraín to go to Europe to complete his studies. The girl becomes ill and dies before Efraín can return to her side. Undoubtedly Isaacs himself was Efraín and the mother and sister were Isaacs' own mother and sister. As for María (supposedly a distant cousin who had come from Jamaica, lived in the house, and died of epilepsy), she has been called Eloísa and identified as a number of women, among them, Julia Holguín, Felisa González, and Mercedes Cabal de Mallarino. When a painter, Alejandro Dorronsoro, painted an imaginary likeness of María, Isaacs wrote him a letter in 1880 telling him to modify the nose a bit in order to have a perfect copy.[74]

María, for all its sensitivity, freshness, tenderness, and a kind of provocative sensuality, is loaded with fatality, mystery, and a presentiment of impending tragedy symbolized by the sinister cawing crow. A vague exotic note of delicate touches and shadings is enhanced by the insert novel, so distant in time and place, about Nay, the daughter of a conquered African king, and Sinar, a slave. American nature, so familiar to Isaacs, hardly proved exotic enough for him. The novelist also loaded down his work with what Alfonso Reyes, who finds its voluptuousness intoxicating and almost suffocating, calls "un miniaturismo oriental, que no perdona detalle de las vestimentas . . . que . . . se recrea en las minucias del bordado y las labores domésticas." [75] Anderson Imbert thinks that Chateaubriand taught Isaacs to construct his vague eroticism in an aesthetic manner.[76] In spite of its romanticism, *María*, wherever elements do not directly bear on the protagonists' idyllic love, presents us with a series of costumbrista and realistic elements such as a tiger hunt, a wedding dance, a wake, and descriptions of Mayo, Efraín's dog, and a little fawn. Isaacs faithfully reproduces everyday life and authentic dialogue, especially of the Negro, with his music and marriage, dances, dwelling, dress, duties, superstitions, and death. The peasants and slaves are somewhat idealized and patronized in the patriarchal manner of Pereda. Isaacs constantly implies Efraín's sensual and sincere interest in a variety of mulatto women. Using these and other elements, Isaacs somehow fuses the regional and the romantic into a new American amalgam previously unknown.

The author dominates time by focusing most of the action on the house and garden. Through constant temporal references, direct and indirect, he allows the reader to savor the perfume of the roses, the evening prayers, the group readings of Chateaubriand, the singing, color, lights, and smells. Even more outstanding is the treatment of nature, which provides a sentimental background for human love.[77] The garden flowers which María cuts for her hair and for Efraín reflect their emotional states, fresh, when the humans are joyful, withered, when they are disconsolate. In addition to the rose bushes which reveal the sentimental, emotional, and physical states of the lovers, Isaacs attaches sensory and anthropomorphic projections to nature in his description of picturesque valleys, morning dew, silent forests, humid shadows, and perfumed branches. The poetic and aesthetic qualities and the lyric freshness give the tired themes a unique romantic flavor. A modern reader may find the pathos—verging on bathos—and the mouthings of the weak, sentimental, if charming, Jewish girl far removed from life. Yet *María*, as a kind of personal confession and intense discovery of love with which most people can identify, lives on.

Among other Colombian romantic novelists, Luis Segundo Silvestre (1838–1887), who used a variety of pseudonyms such as Hernán Pérez del Pulgar, wrote *Tránsito* (1886), a novel much admired by Juan Valera for its popular fiestas and passionate love,[78] and a kind of precursor, in its regionalistic realism, to the fiction of Tomás Carrasquilla. A colorful, romantic-realistic hybrid, it has been called "uno de los idilios más bellos que se hayan escrito en español." [79] Another novel which is still read is *El alférez real* (1886), a "crónica de Cali en el siglo xviii," by Eustaquio

Palacios (1830–1898). It contains the standard impossible love theme, the beautiful orphan, and a costumbrista wedding party. The author claims that although the story is imaginary, he used it as a vehicle to describe real people and events, customs and traditions. Daniel, a distant relative and secretary of the alférez real, wishes to marry Doña Inés de Lara, the beautiful orphan and a ward of the alférez. Daniel turns out to be wealthy after all, Inés reconsiders her decision to enter a convent, and all ends happily. The novel is saved from a standard romanticism by vivid descriptions of the city of Cali, its reading habits, the dances, the meals, and a rodeo, along with comments about Negro slavery.

A number of other Colombian novelists are worthy of at least a brief mention. José Joaquín Ortiz (1814–1892), a poet, is often credited with having started the Colombian romantic novel with his sentimental novelette, *María Dolores o la historia de mi casamiento* (1841). José Nieto (1804–1866) has a number of titles, including *Ingermina o la hija de Calamar* (1844) about the sixteenth-century conquest of Colombia. Felipe Pérez (1836–1891), a dramatist and poet, has a series of historical novels such as *Huayna Capac* (1856), *Atahualpa* (1856), *Los Pizarros* (1857), its sequel *Jilma* (1858), and *Los gigantes* (1875). José María Samper (1831–1888), a historian and husband of a better novelist, examines literary ideas in the 1870s in his *El poeta soldado* (1881) and shows a quaint mixture of love and humor in *Los claveles de Julia* (1881). His wife, Soledad Acosta de Samper (1833–1903), also a historian as well as a sociologist, has a variety of novels, collected in 1869 as *Novelas y cuadros de la vida suramericana*. She bases most of her novels on the works of Sir Walter Scott and Benito Pérez Galdós. Her best known fiction is probably *Los piratas en Cartagena* (1886), five historical scenes from the sixteenth to the eighteenth centuries. José Caicedo Rojas (1816–1898) also wrote a number of novels, but most of these as well as those of his contemporaries are today largely only historical curiosities.

Chile, home of American costumbrismo and the first important realistic novels, produced surprisingly few romantic ones. José Victorino Lastarria (1817–1888), famous costumbrista and literary critic, recalls in his *Recuerdos literarios* various novels published in the review *El Crepúsculo*, partly as a result of the famous polemic between Sarmiento and Bello in which he took part between

1842 and 1844. In that periodical he published in 1843 *El mendigo*, which he himself called "novela histórica," a frustrated love story involving the battle of Rancagua. Lastarria's narratives were later gathered under the title *Antaño y Ogaño. Novelas y cuentos de la vida hispanoamericana* (1885), including *Don Guillermo* (1860), a sarcastic, political novel and at least a precursor of Chilean realism, and *Mercedes* (1875). An observer of Chilean reality and popular life, Lastarria claims credit for the founding of Sociedad Literaria, one of the moving forces in the cultural development of Chile from 1842 on. *El Crepúsculo*, the monthly devoted to science and letters which he and some of his students had started, published some "novelettes" by Santiago Lindsay, Cristobal Valdés, and Lastarria himself. Manuel Bilbao (1827–1895), brother of the persecuted socialist-liberal, Francisco, wrote *El inquisidor mayor* (1852), and a sequel, *El hermano* (1852), set in Peru. Alberto Blest Gana, the founder of Chilean realistic fiction around 1860, may have been correct in lamenting that when he began writing no good Chilean novels existed. Chile's only good indianista novel, *Huincahual* (1888), by Alberto del Solar (1860–1921), was dedicated to José Toribio Medina (1852–1930), whose *Los aborígenes de Chile* (1882) Solar used as his source. In an Indian massacre the heroine María is carried off by Huincahual, son of the Indian cacique, and forcibly married to him. She names her resulting child Julián in memory of her murdered brother. Huincahual, truly in love but hating the Spaniards who have come to destroy Araucanian lands, saves some Spaniards from shipwreck. María is poisoned by a jealous rival, and Huincahual, pursuing María's captor, her former fiance, also dies. In addition to the romance, the novel delights in costumbrista descriptions of Indian life.

In Venezuela, Fermín Toro (1807–1865), one of his country's most cultured essayists, liberal politician, and defender of intuitive ideas, is probably the first romantic novelist, although Gonzalo Picón Febres rather cruelly stated that ". . . es evidente que sus novelas valen poco." [80] Many of his novelettes were published in the newspapers of the day such as *El Semanario*, some of them posthumously. *Los mártires* (1842), one of his better stories, is based on his English experiences and class rivalries. Some of his stories show his interest in Venezuelan costumbrismo, but most of them were based on French models. His fatalism seems ordinary enough, but he fills his works with light, color, movement, and occasional dynamic description. Juan Vicente González (1811–1866), a kind of Venezuelan Sarmiento, wrote *Biografía de José Félix Rivas*, which while not strictly fiction, influenced the development of the novel. Arturo Uslar Pietri, who believes that he may be the outstanding Venezuelan romantic, calls his biography "a ratos una gran novela romántica." [81]

More solidly entrenched as romantic novelists are Julio Calcaño (1840–1918), Juan Ramón Yépez (1822–1881), and Eduardo Blanco (1838–1912). Calcaño, the author of a treatise on Venezuelan Spanish, created a passable heroine in *Blanca de Torrestella* (1865), one of his half dozen novels. During the Renaissance in Florence, Blanca, the daughter of an official of Charles V, kills her lover's murderer with a poisoned ring and commits suicide—hardly original material. The rivalries between Francis I and the Spanish monarch are more creatively palatable. Juan Ramón Yépez published two brief *indianista* novels, *Anaida* (1860) and *Iguaraya* (1872), the first novels to describe the Venezuelan countryside and nature as a background for Indian activity. Among the usual indeterminate and almost impalpable cultural stereotypes, his Indian heroes, really rather seedy, show occasional humanity in their battles and legends. If Iguaraya foolishly goes mad at the erroneous impression that Taicu, her lover, had killed her father, Taicu, as the new chief, in fulfilling the prophecy shows nevertheless signs, at isolated moments to be sure, of sensibility and intelligence. Eduardo Blanco is best known for a collection of historical sketches, stories, and fantastic tales under the title of *Venezuela heroica* (1883), containing original descriptions of a series of battles.[82] His novel, *Una noche en Ferrara* (1875), whose action occurs there in 1769, offers only melodramatic duels, ruins, and cemeteries, but his *Zárate* (1882) has been called ". . . clara y definitivamente, la novela típicamente nacional." [83] Set in 1825, this historical novel, in spite of its obvious *afrancesamiento*, contains Venezuelan customs and types and the fabulous figure of José Antonio Páez, to whom the author was a devoted ally and personal friend. The bandit hero, José Oliveros (Zárate), is unwittingly destroyed by the very man he has befriended, a standard romantic device we have already seen in Gómez de Avellaneda's *Espatolino*.

Finally, José Gil Fortoul (1852–1943), author of the well-known

Historia constitucional de Venezuela (1907), published *¿Idilio?*
(1887) and, especially, *Julián* (1888), which he called "bosquejo de
un temperamento" in the manner of Paul Bourget. In a sense his
work is a challenge to the romantic novel, filled with tears and
tragedies.[84] In 1895 he published his last novel, *Pasiones*, which
like all his novels is romantic, realistic, impressionistic, and even
naturalistic to a degree. In almost every case they are simply vehicles for the expression of the author's pet ideas on literature, politics and justice, which for some might even make him a kind of
precursor of the criollista novel.

Mexican romanticism also dates from about 1830, first from
French and later from Spanish sources, but unlike Chile and Argentina, Mexico's literary situation precluded polemics between the
neoclassicists and the romantics. As in other countries the romantic
novel was tied to the tempestuous politics of the day as well as to a
desire for change, as the many revolutions of the times testify. Julio
Jiménez Rueda points out: "Cierto que la vida de estos escritores
está ligada íntimamente con la creación de sus obras. En lucha
constante con los hombres, en un medio hostil y perseguidos fre-
cuentemente por los enemigos en ideas ... y formando parte de los
partidos políticos en plena lucha, combatiendo a brazo partido con
la miseria, no es raro, pues, que trascienda a la obra el tinte obscuro
y tenebroso que sirve de fondo a su vida." [85] Typically, Juan Díaz
Covarrubias (1837–1859), a medical student who was executed at
the age of twenty-two for caring for some wounded, wrote *La clase
media* (1858), about a maiden's dishonor, and the better known *Gil
Gómez el insurgente* (1858), subtitled "La hija del médico," about
the wars of independence. The author relates the death of an innocent girl, reflects on an evil woman, and utilizes autobiographical, sentimental, and historical material. In a prologue the author
states that he is attempting to write a series dealing with the history
of Mexico in order to correct the derogatory opinion of Mexican
writers held by Europeans. Fernando Orozco y Berra (1822–1885),
author of the first novel in Mexico to concentrate on love as a
primary theme, expressed somewhat bitter-sweet feelings in *La
guerra de treinta años* (1850). He includes authentic and often poignant wartime experiences in his novel, but his conflicts and search
for happiness without destroying his idealism are amatory rather
than martial. Apparently most of the sensual and platonic loves he

describes from the age of seven on occurred, and "some of the women to whom allusions are made in the book devoted themselves to the difficult and costly task of removing copies from circulation; and for this reason, *The Thirty Years' War* has become a genuine bibliographical rarity." [86]

Justo Sierra O'Reilly (1814–1861), father of the famous essayist and historian, published *Un año en el hospital de San Lázaro*, his first fiction, in *El Registro Yucateco*, which he himself had founded. The work, planned as part of a longer one, appeared in 1841 and relates among other things the relationship of a leper with two harlots acting as nurses. He published his far better known *La hija del judío* (1848) in *El Fénix*, another of his journals, under the pseudonym or rather anagram of José Turrisa. The inquisitional intrigues to deprive a young girl of her fortune, conspiracies, a murder, and a ghost follow the flimsy fatality of many romantic novels, but it may be the first plot in Mexican fiction which combines harmoniously with its sub plots and is structurally ". . . superior to . . . all other Mexican novels published up to that time." [87]

One may mention minor romantics such as Florencio M. del Castillo (1828–1863), who attempted a rudimentary kind of psychological evaluation in his passionate conflicts between materialism and true love, within a framework of religion and the Catholic sacraments. For some critics he has social significance, but his pedantry and digressions make for heavy reading. His best known novel is *Hermana de los ángeles* (1854), about a woman's love for her blind husband, who has fallen from grace, and their reconciliation. Pedro Costera (1838–1906), a friend of Altamirano, was another minor romantic whose novel *Carmen* (1872), a Mexican *María*, went through a number of editions.

The major romantic Mexican novelists of the nineteenth century are Manuel Payno (1810–1894), Luis G. Inclán (1816–1875), José Tomás Cuéllar (1830–1894), Vicente Riva Palacio (1832–1896), and Ignacio Manuel Altamirano (1834–1893). Manuel Payno, newspaperman, diplomat, historian, poet, and dramatist, held various government positions and was jailed during the French intervention. His novels include *El hombre de la situación* (1861), an entertaining costumbrista novel, and his two best-known novels, *El fistol del diablo* (1845–46) and *Los bandidos de Río Frío* (1889–91). *El fistol del diablo*, a feuilleton production and the first full-length

Mexican novel after those of Lizardi, which it resembles, transfers the flavor of the chaotic world in which he lived, giving us almost a panoramic view of Mexican society. In the process of fulfilling his intention to "dar a conocer en cuanto sea posible las diversas clases de que se compone la sociedad mexicana," he had some critical things to say about the social irresponsibility of his society. His historical references are quite indirect, and he is not typically a historical novelist.[88] In *El fistol del diablo* Arturo undertakes a pact with Ruggiero, the devil, who gives him a charm to captivate women. Arturo meets a beautiful beggar girl, has a series of adventures and love affairs, and listens to the devil lecture on life and love. In the process Payno manages to discourse on cruel jailors, corrupt justice, and plead for jail reform to further the rehabilitation of mankind.

Payno wrote *Los bandidos de Río Frío*, subtitled "novela naturalista, humorística, de costumbres, de crímenes . . . ," during his second European stay, under the pseudonym of "Un ingenio de la Corte." The central plot is about Juan Yáñez, an aide of Santa Anna, and his accomplices, among whom is Evaristo, the son of a customs guard. Love affairs, attempted seductions, death sentences, and superstitions alternate with descriptions of customs, ranch life, gambling, and high and low society. His objective and authentic portrayal has the autobiographical ring of personal memoirs from time to time, but the overall perception and sensitivity are destroyed by a number of unrealistic characters, inept digressions, and often pointless dialogues. The meandering novel is saved by a series of interesting flashbacks, bandit action, gambling scenes, fights with soliders, an Indian attack, and a climactic battle at Río Frío worthy of a good movie scenario. Mariano Azuela feels that as a novel "vale bien poco y su valor se reduce a lo meramente documental. Las felices descripciones de una época de la vida nacional y de ciertos tipos sí tienen vital importancia para cuantos tengan amor o simplemente curiosidad por nuestro pasado." [89] Yet he finds in it a number of well-drawn characters and the vastest, most varied, and truthful panorama of customs already disappeared.

Luis Gonzaga Inclán's famous novel, *Astucia* (1865), as it is commonly called because its full title (*Astucia, jefe de los Hermanos de la Hoja o los Charros Contrabandistas de la Rama*) is a mouthful, has been highly praised by Rómulo Gallegos, Federico Gamboa,

Carlos González Peña, who devoted his entrance speech into the Mexican Academy to it,[90] and Mariano Azuela. In his prologue Inclán defends the contrabandists, "muy queridos, respetados y aun celebrados de cuantos los conocían." He is the first novelist to present the *charro* as a literary creation, but he knew the real charros well, had worked with them, and was concerned in their dangerous life. He describes the customs of the contrabandists, their popular dialect, and their humor. His intent is not direct social criticism, but the reformista tendency is strongly presented in his series of tales of dishonest lawyers, alchoholism, and police treachery. The novel is romantic, but as José de J. Núñez y Domínguez says in the prologue to the 1945 edition, "Causan verdadera sorpresa, cuando se lee esta novela, el colorido vernáculo, la fuerza en el trazo de los tipos, y la narración, la descripción vívida, el mexicanismo de su ambiente y su dramaticidad." Inclán's authentic descriptions of rancheros, their dreams, hopes, and fears, is an impressive and enlightening evocation which falls just short of a perfect wedding between style and subject. The title comes from Lorenzo's father who tells his son (the protagonist) to use *astucia* in his affairs. Lorenzo, later becoming the leader of the contrabandist band, adopts the name Astucia. Like the Periquillo of another day, Lorenzo was ruined by a permissive mother and took up with old school friends, one of whom was involved in tobacco contraband. Lorenzo is torn between duty to his father and to the band, but his father makes him keep his word. Good hearted, he is excessively generous to his enemies, even El Buldog, the police officer. The narrative also includes a series of cuadros of spendthrift youth, false women, and a seduction, as well as individual stories told by members of the band. Whatever its romantic European accoutrements, the novel, typically Mexican, is the "auténtico sucesor de Fernández de Lizardi ... por la verdad del ambiente, por la precisión de los procesos psicológicos, tales como aparecen en *Astucia*, esta novela no tiene rival en nuestras letras." [91]

José Tomás de Cuéllar, a newspaperman and dramatist, used the pseudonym "Facundo" in the twenty-four volumes he wrote from 1869 on and published under the general title of *La linterna mágica* (1889–92). He defines his purpose in the prologue to these humorous, moralistic, and often cruel novels and sketches: "Yo he copiado a mis personajes a la luz de mi linterna no en drama fantástico y descomunal, sino en plena comedia humana, en la vida real, sorprendiéndolos en el hogar, en la familia, en el taller, en el campo, en la cárcel, en todas partes . . . todo es mexicano, todo es nuestro que es lo que nos importa." [92] Primarily, his "novelas de costumbres mexicanas" (*El pecado del siglo*, 1869, is a historical novel about colonial times) deal with love affairs, dances, duels, and social customs of various kinds. Uncharitably, he has a surprising scorn for the Indian. Granting the Mexican qualities of style and spirit of stories like *Ensalada de pollos* (1869) and *Historia de Chucho el Ninfo* (1871), one must agree with Mariano Azuela that in general they are as passé as the society they describe but demur that Cuéllar represents real progress in the technique of novel writing, good dialogue, concise description, or "gracia al reproducir su medio . . . algunos toques de artista verdadero." [93]

Vicente Riva Palacio, poet, drama critic, and publisher of a satirical newspaper, wrote a number of short stories such as *Cuentos del general* (1896), among the earliest of their kind, but he is also known as the creator of the Mexican historical novel.[94] Among his titles are *La vuelta de los muertos* (1870) and *Un secreto que mata* (1917), but his three best are probably *Monja y casada, virgen y mártir* (1868) with the usual long subtitle of such novels, "Historia de los tiempos de la Inquisición," its sequel or second part, *Martín Garatuza* (1868), and *Los piratas del golfo* (1869). Of the three the first two deal with seventeenth-century New Spain and were supposedly based on documents of the Archivo General de la Nación, in his possession. In his prologue Riva Palacio states, "Los personajes y los episodios son históricos y he logrado encontrar precisos datos en la gran oscuridad que envuelve la historia de las costumbres de la época," but he shades the truth whenever it suits his purpose and prefers hair-raising adventures to historical fact. Published in installments, the first part and its more popular sequel contain almost every romantic cliché. Bachiller Martín Garatuza or Villavicencio y Salazar, a man of many roles and disguises, is the hero of a story which involves conspiracies, love affairs, the evil Inquisition, witchcraft, jealous women, a faithful and almost superhumanly strong Negro servant, a treacherous plot to steal an inheritance, a suicide, and a love between brother and sister. The noble Blanca, the faithful Teodoro, Esperanza, and the rest of the characters serve principally to reveal the discrimination against criollos, the generally corrupt and incompetent viceroyalty, and the role of the Inquisition in New Spain. *Los piratas del golfo,* supposedly based on the work of a man who had lived with pirates, includes kidnapping, various love relationships, revenge, and the inevitable inheritance and convent but is enlivened by good portraits of the pirate Morgan and by Spanish, French, and criollo rivalries. From his very first novel, *Calvario y Tabor* (1868), in which he depicts the struggle between liberals and conservatives, his great desire was to acquaint the Mexican people with their national history.

Ignacio Manuel Altamirano, poet, magazine editor, critic, politician, orator, professor, and patriot, inherited the mantle of Ignacio Ramírez (1818–1879), spiritual leader of the Reform. An Indian who did not learn Spanish until he was fourteen, Altamirano fought in the War of Reform and against the French under his fellow novelist, General Riva Palacio. Altamirano was the guide of an entire generation and the best writer of his day, and "from a strictly literary point of view, the first novelist that appears in the history of our literature . . ." [95] But the best of mediocre is obviously not great, and it is only in comparison with the digressive and stereotyped works of the day that he is a great novelist, at least in his concern for the technique of fiction, artistic plot construction, and the creation of real characters. Basically an interpreter of the Mexican landscape and people in a costumbrista and often realistic manner, Altamirano is nevertheless normally classified as a romantic, sentimental in nature. As Alfonso Reyes says, "Era romántico porque . . . hasta la llegada de Gutiérrez Nájera todo fue romanticismo en México." [96] An ardent nationalist and defender of the autochthonous, Altamirano lamented that his fellow Mexicans ignored their own history and legends, and he sought to enlighten them and at the same time promote patriotic, moral, and social precepts of honesty and obedience to the law.[97] He rejected the French novel and, although he admired Sir Walter Scott, Dumas, James Fenimore Cooper, and universal culture, wanted to create a nationalistic literature, presenting history in a manner his people could appreciate and understand. His often quoted statement in *Revistas literarias de México* (1868), which sums up the history of the Mexican novel, proclaims: "No negamos la gran utilidad de estudiar todas las escuelas literarias del mundo civilizado . . . pero

deseamos que se cree una literatura absolutamente nuestra." [98]
Clemencia (1869) first appeared in weekly installments in *El Rena-cimiento*. The dark, sensual, egotistical, aristocratic Clemencia, the blond and virginal Isabel, the stoic, proud, self sacrificing Fernando, and Enrique, his opposite in every way, are well drawn. Set at the end of 1863 and in early 1864 when the French under Maximilian were triumphant, the novel is romantic in its contrast of good and evil, the sacrifice of Fernando, and the resulting guilt feelings and entrance into a convent of Clemencia. Written at a time when the French invasion was still fresh in people's minds, the war and patriotic fervor, along with the local color were more impressive than the fervent love story. Although one may find in it imagination, artistry of a sort, and idealism, it is difficult to agree that "*Clemencia* es una de las obras maestras de la literatura romántica hispanoamericana." [99]

La navidad en las montañas (1871) is a sincere, idealistic, almost naïve little novelette. The rejected lover Pablo and his sweetheart Carmen find final happiness with the aid of a good, indeed, a perfect priest, an unusual portrait in Spanish American fiction, but the triumph of good over evil and true Christian service over religious fanaticism seem less important than the landscape, descriptions of Christmas dinner and carols, and army recruiting. *El Zarco*, written in 1888 but published posthumously in 1901, deals with episodes from Mexican life between 1861 and 1863. At the end of the War of Reform banditry was widespread, as was political rivalry. The *plateados*, so-called because of their silver ornaments, have as their leader the blue-eyed bandit, El Zarco. Manuela, the beautiful but avaricious girl, falls in love with him, scorning the good and honest blacksmith Nicolás. She learns too late about El Zarco's true character. The overly noble Nicolás who finally destroys El Zarco, the long suffering Pilar who loves Nicolás in silence, and the entire plot structure reflect an inept banality that detracts from his otherwise perceptive, compassionate, and critical study of the period of Mexican history through which he lived. His realistic descriptions of historical characters and psychological evaluation are also weakened by his obvious identification with Nicolás, his moral judgments, and his message that good will triumph over the glamorous.

Mexico was especially productive in novels which treated the Indian as a literary and historical figure.[100] Impossible loves, storms, noble savages, and a Christian father form the constant components of these works. Ireneo Paz (1836–1924) wrote *Amor y suplicio* (1873), about Moctezuma, *Doña Marina* (1883), and about a dozen other novels; José María Lafragua (1813–1875) wrote *Netzula* (1832), possibly the first Indianist novel; Juan Luis Tercero (1837–1905) offered *Nezahualpilli o el catolicismo en México* (1875). The two most important novelists of this kind may have been Eligio Ancona (1836–1893) and Crescencio Carrillo y Ancona (1836–1897). Eligio Ancona's *Los mártires del Anáhuac* (1870) may have been the first Mexican treatment of the conquest and "la novela más indianista del grupo romántico mexicano." [101] Ancona depends on the work of Bernal Díaz del Castillo but leaves to the historian detailed descriptions of battle scenes, content to say that the fighting lasted almost all day and that science "y la táctica triunfaron sobre el valor y sobre el número." [102] In the novel Tizoc loves Geliztli, Moctezuma's daughter, raped by Cortés and saved from a horrible death by Tizoc. Cortés' son is sacrificed, and later both lovers die. The novelist's anti-Spanish bias is omnipresent. Xicontencatl defends freedom against the ruthless Spaniard who so cleverly creates divisions among Indian tribes for his own advantage. The author also laments the ensuing tragic defeat and enslavement of a noble people, sacrificed to the cowardice of their king. Crescencio Carrillo y Ancona's *Historia de Welina* (1862) is a Yucatan legend based on events of 1541. An Indian maid and her husband Yiban, who decides to become a Christian, are captured in an uprising by the Mayas. About to be sacrificed, they are married and baptized by the noble Christian missionary, Father Diego, before that fateful event takes place. Supposedly this novel was much admired by the empress Carlota, who insisted that it be translated into French.

Juan León Mera (1832–1894) was the first important writer of *artículos de costumbres* in Ecuador in collections such as *Tijeretazos y plumadas* (1903). He also wrote a series of novelettes, among them *Los novios de una aldea* (1872) and *Porque soy cristiano* (1891), whose wicked soldier heroes achieve salvation; *Entre dos tías y un tío* (1889), in the *Revista Ecuatoriana*, a fairly realistic tale with romantic overtones about a wicked uncle and his niece's death by drowning; and *Un matrimonio inconveniente* (1893), about a man whose lack of Christian morality leads to his downfall in spite of the efforts of his good and virtuous wife. These were published together as *Novelitas ecuatorianas* (1909). Juan León Mera is primarily famous for having written what is probably the best of all Spanish American Indianist novels, *Cumandá, o un drama entre salvajes* (1879). Isaac J. Barrera states that *Cumandá* had an 1871 edition,[103] but it seems to have been finished not much before 1877 and first published two years later. He supposedly wrote the novel to be worthy of his appointment as Corresponding Member of the Spanish Royal Academy.[104] Conservative and even reactionary though he was, Mera had always been American oriented and keenly interested in Indian matters. In 1858 his *Melodías indígenas* had been poorly received because of its indigenous language, but he persevered and wrote an Indian legend, *La virgen del sol* (1861). In his *Ojeada histórico-crítica sobre la poesía ecuatoriana* (1868) Mera talks of "objetos brotados del seno de América, desarrollados al suave calor del sol americano, nutridos con sustancias especiales y ataviados con galas en nada semejantes a los que nos vienen de ultramar . . ." He hoped to write an original work, showing the beauties of American nature, because no study had ever been made of the virgin forests of the Oriente region. He seemed sincere in his desire for justice for the Indian, aware of his social problem and the crimes commited against him, as his direct address to the Indians in his novel testifies. A decade was to pass before Clorinda Matto de Turner of Peru fully treated this phase of Indian fiction with her *Aves sin nido* (1889). Mera's novel has more than its share of absurd and ridiculous romantic clichés, the standard idealized Indian, the melancholy nature, a storm, a Christian father, a girl captured by Indians and separated from her brother, their impossible potentially incestuous love, and the heroine's inevitable destruction. Mera's intention was to write a true history which, he said, had been narrated to him in part by Richard Spruce, an Englishman who had met Jívaro headhunters on his quinine-seeking expedition. Although the framing story is completely romantic, the customs are well drawn, and the nature descriptions are immediately recognizable by those who have lived in Ecuador. Pedro Antonio de Alarcón in the prologue to the 1891 edition notes this authenticity: "Los indios se palpan. Su obra es una fotografía de maravillosos cuentos." The plot tells of Cumandá who does not know who her parents are. Reared among the Jívaro Indians, she meets Carlos

Orozco, the son of a missionary, Padre José Domingo Orozco (he became a priest after fathering his son). Carlos wants to marry Cumandá, but her foster father, Tongana, offers her to the powerful chief Yahuarmaqui as his seventh wife. When the latter dies she is to be sacrificed, but she flees with Carlos. They are captured and to save his life she sacrifices herself. Domingo recognizes too late that she is really his daughter.

Juan Valera praised *Cumandá* highly as "lo más bello que como narración en prosa se ha escrito en la América española," but found it hard to believe that Cumandá, living among gross, dirty, and fierce Indians should preserve her purity or her beauty without any of the aids of civilized hygiene or cosmetics. Valera, furthermore, takes offense at what he claimed was an anti-Spanish attitude in the novel, something which hurt Mera deeply.[105] Juan León Mera admitted his debt to James Fenimore Cooper, Chateaubriand, and Bernardin de Saint-Pierre, but he also acknowledged the influence of Martínez de la Rosa and José Zorrilla. The novel has been highly praised by some American critics as ". . . la novela poemática más importante del grupo indianista," [106] and as "the first significant attempt to utilize for fictional purposes the Spanish American jungle." [107] Less charitably, Arturo Torres-Rioseco contends that the novel's fame was obtained through the aid of overly kind critics,[108] and Enrique Anderson Imbert, even more negatively, finds the novel false, absurd, and ridiculous, filled with overflowing sentimentalism and "weighing the reader down with heavy sentimental bundles, prepared, condensed, and wrapped with the trademarked ribbon of twaddling Romanticism." [109] Important in its poetic presentation of an American theme, the novel also foreshadows later indigenista trends.

The only other Ecuadorian of importance during this period in terms of purely fictional writing, was Carlos R. Tobar (1854–1920), who wrote two novels, *Timoleón Coloma* (1888), a satirical study of a student who wanted to be a man, and *Relación de un veterano del tiempo de la Independencia* (1895), considered by some to be the best Ecuadorian historical novel.[110] A critic and philologist, Tobar states in his dedication to *Timoleón Coloma* that he wanted to write not a novel but rather a series of "cuadritos de costumbres . . ." In his other novel, he interweaves history and fiction to present a beautiful firsthand account of the heroism and struggle of the times and an especially attractive examination of General Sucre.

Juan Montalvo (1832–1889), considered one of the great essayists of Spanish America, also attempted the novel in *Capítulos que se le olvidaron a Cervantes,* a rhetorical attempt to imitate that master. Some episodes inserted into other works such as *Siete tratados, Cosmopolita,* and *Geometría moral* also pass as romantic fiction. Included is the tale of the tragic passion of a priest for a young girl, another about a perfect parish priest who defends the poor, and one about Herculano, a paragon of virtue who manages to win Safira, a beautiful maiden. Montalvo once lamented that he lacked the gift of tears to be able to write a book he would entitle *El indio* to make the world cry,[111] but as we have seen, that task was to fall to Clorinda Matto de Turner—to be discussed in the second volume—the first to denounce directly the mistreatment of the Indian.

The best combination of historical novel, indianista, and indigenista themes may be found in the work of Manuel de Jesús Galván (1834–1910), from Santo Domingo, the author of *Enriquillo* (1879), published in a more complete edition in 1882. Although the author calls his novel a *leyenda,* he often interrupts the action and uses footnotes when a historical character speaks to show how accurate he is. He stresses, in the novel itself, that his work is "literally history," that to give color to a novel cannot justify inventing details—"No hemos de inventar . . . hemos de respetar la historia, aunque palidezca nuestro verídico relato." It is true that he used as his source materials the works of Bartolomé de las Casas, Juan de Castellanos, Fernández de Oviedo, and Washington Irving, copying passages from these works verbatim when it suited his purpose, but it is also true that he changed dates and events when they conflicted with his imagination. He fused the life, customs, problems, and politics of fictional and historical characters so that no seam appears. The plot, viewed telescopically, details events in Santo Domingo between 1503 and 1533. Mencía is the daughter of the princess Higuemota and the Spaniard Hernando de Guevara. Enriquillo or Guarocuyá is Higuemota's nephew. Don Diego Colón, having married María de Toledo, becomes viceroy and Mencía serves in their home. Enriquillo, adopted by Diego Velázquez, is also befriended by Bartolomé de las Casas. Meanwhile, Juan de Grijalva is in love with María de Cuéllar. Pedro Mojica, a villain who has attempted to steal Higuemota's inheritance, tries to obtain María for Andrés Valenzuela, the son of Enriquillo's protector, but she manages to delay the wedding for a year. Grijalva returns from an expedition, but his sweetheart dies on her wedding day, and so does he, shortly thereafter, in Nicaragua. Enriquillo marries his cousin Mencía, over Mojica's strenuous opposition, and when young Valenzuela attempts to seduce her, Enriquillo asks for justice. Despairing of obtaining it, he goes to the hills, unites the Indians in a thirteen-year revolt, and is finally pardoned by Charles V through the intervention of his good friend Bartolomé.

The neoclassical style of Jovellanos and Quintana shows through the romantic frame and vocabulary. Galván's romanticism lacks the melodrama and sugary sentiment of previous novels of this type. His fellow countryman, Max Henríquez Ureña, finds the work to be a "novela romántica, escrita por un espíritu dotado de serenidad clásica; todo en ella es admirable, el lenguaje castizo, la castigada sencillez del estilo, la ordenación y el método . . ." [112] *Enriquillo* elicited the admiration of José Martí, who was impressed by the characters, especially Enriquillo, for him a Christ figure, by the profound intention, and by the transparency of the scenes. Finding it tragic and epic, he exalted its "novísima y encantadora manera de escribir nuestra historia." [113] Enrique Anderson Imbert, not given to easy judgments, states that the novel, "leída ingenuamente . . . es tal vez la mejor novela histórica del siglo xix en toda la América española." [114]

Some difference of opinion exists as to the author's political motivation in writing the novel. Pedro Henríquez Ureña believes that Galván was objective and incapable of representing only one of two extremes of the conquest. Galván, he said, was a man who "había crecido, intelectualmente entre las ruinas de una cultura clásica y escolástica que tuvo asiento en las . . . universidades coloniales de Santo Domingo." [115] Enriquillo's rebellion may well have been deliberately chosen, not so much to condemn Spain as to point out the abuses of the "presidentes dominicanos en perjuicio de la masa humilde. Galván convirtió al padre Las Casas en el eje doctrinario de su novela. . . . Pero Galván no interpretó la prédica de Las Casas como una prueba de la bajeza moral de España, sino como un noble ejemplo que España ofreció al mundo." [116] If one examines the life and statements of the author, one may conclude that at times he believes in white supremacy; at others he pleads for national unity and progress and union of Indian and white, but his compassion is often tinged with criticism.

The Christian charity and the generosity and nobility of Enriquillo, an orphan respected by the Spaniards, with and off whom he lived, appears excessive. As he matured, he developed a social conscience and learned to love the Indian. In contrasting Enriquillo's forgiveness of Valenzuela with Tamayo's revenge on Mojica, the author has given us the key to the novel's dramatic tension that elevates it from a pedestrian endeavor. Galván himself rejected the label of "Indianophile." A Catholic conservative (the novel has an abundance of Biblical references), Galván sympathized with the forgotten and forlorn Indian, but he also insisted on an intelligible moral Catholic order. In the prologue to the first edition of the novel, José Joaquín Pérez (1845–1900), author of *Fantasías indígenas* (1877), sees Enriquillo as a symbol of the oppressed and a lesson for those who long for human freedom. In a note to the third edition Galván states that the episode of Enriquillo could be applied to current events in Santo Domingo. In conclusion, to interpret the work as a defense of the Indian and his freedom seems difficult in view of Galván's ambivalent attitude toward that unfortunate people; but Galván, as a man who suffered political persecution himself, may easily pass as a passionate defender of political and individual freedom.

Others writers from the Dominican Republic are Francisco Gregorio Billini (1844–1898), whose *Baní, o Engracia y Antoñita* (1892) is typical of the romantic costumbrista novel of the day; and Federico García Godoy (1867–1924), the author of a number of historical novels, especially a trilogy, *Rufinito* (1908), *Alma dominical* (1912), and *Guanuma* (1914), about the struggle against Spain and Haiti and the revolt of 1863. Also continuing the tradition of the historical novel, Max Henríquez Ureña (1885–1968), poet, literary critic, and historian, contributed the unromantic *Episodios dominicanos*, one of whose several titles is *La independencia efímera* (1938). His works show an even more passionate devotion to historical documentation at the expense of literature than *Enriquillo*.

Puerto Rico's Alejandro Tapia y Rivera (1826–1882), "el iniciador de la literatura en Puerto Rico," [117] wrote a number of works he himself labeled "leyendas," among them *La palma del cacique*

(1852), *La leyenda de los veinte años* (1874), and *Cofresí* (1876), but Eugenio María de Hostos (1839–1903), better known as a great educator and essayist, earned more lasting fame. His strange, symbolic novel, *La peregrinación de Bayoán* (1863) stresses his favorite theme, that of the union of the Antilles. A poetic, imaginative, effusive, voluptuous, passionate, and romantic novel, written in diary form, it is somewhat diluted by the allegorical and didactic intent, the objective moral judgment, and other peripheral nonfictional speculations involving the cause of justice and his country's freedom. Hostos, as the editor of the diary, intervenes in the plot where necessary, but he is more effusive than ignescent. Bayoán (Puerto Rico), a wanderer and lover of liberty like Hostos himself (in the chronicles Bayoán was the man who doubted that Spaniards were immortal), takes refuge in the home of Guarionex (Haiti). Guarionex, historically, was a Haitian chief during Columbus' time. Bayoán falls in love with his host's daughter, Marién (Cuba). Although absorbed by his virginal love, his patriotic fervor and concept of duty demand that he go to Spain to ask for Antillean liberty. Risking his personal happiness, he undertakes the pilgrimage. When Marién, eventually his wife, dies, Bayoán, kneeling, kisses her hand, as the novel ends. The editor, Hostos, finishes the work, and Bayoán goes back to America, which "está sufriendo, y tal vez su dolor calme los míos . . . si en una de esas repúblicas hay un lugar para un hombre que ama el bien . . ." He hopes for peace in one of the republics but, if he cannot find it, he will continue his peregrinations.

In discussing Spanish American romanticism, a special place must be reserved for the Peruvian writer Ricardo Palma (1833–1919), known as "el bibliotecario mendigo" for his efforts in rebuilding library holdings destroyed during the Guerra del Pacífico by begging books from friends all over the world. Although later in life he scoffed at the romantic frenzy, he always had a special love for the romantic past. Beginning as a poet in the 1860s, he soon created a special kind of picaresque, ironic, and anticlerical story which he called "tradición." They appeared in newspapers, but it was not until 1872 that he collected and published them in book form. He produced six series of *Tradiciones peruanas* between that date and 1883, later publishing other volumes under special titles. Palma, in a mocking, skeptical tone, mixes history, psychology, sociology, and truth and lies (his fantasies seem to have the authority of truth) in his tales of the Peruvian viceroys, their pecadillos and loves. Although his stories about viceroys are the best known, he has others on honor, pride, revenge, the Conquest, and the wars of independence. High and low, cloisters and convents, government men and pirates, superstition, theology, seductions, bullfights, cockfights, and duels provide a burlesque pageantry of color and action, a brilliant but at times almost grotesque panorama of his beloved native city, Lima, in colonial times. He utilizes historical documents, national archives, legends, gossip, and pure invention. Some of his stories are simple; others are quite complicated. He usually begins with a historical background, intersperses a tale, often with verse, abandons one story line for another, and at the end presents us with history and fiction neatly packaged. At times Palma surprises us with an ending which is pure O'Henry. Palma loved the past for its own sake, and his interest was largely archeological, but politicians of right and left have claimed him as their own. Mariátegui, so important in Peruvian culture, views Palma as a social and political leftist because of his satire of tradition, the Church, and aristocracy; but Palma's artistic gold nuggets transcend political theory to give us not only the spiritual essence of his country but a universally applicable format. As one historian says, "Palma tiene, en efecto, la intuición del pasado en su significación esencialmente humana. De este modo intuye y sublima el pasado que el historiador investiga y reconstruye." [118]

3. Realism, Naturalism, Modernism

REALISM

As previously stated, the application of European terminology to Latin American fictional movements involves, in the final analysis, an arbitrary decision. Realism appears in some countries before romanticism, and strange mixtures of these and other literary movements make a rigid classification difficult if not meaningless. As Luis Alberto Sánchez states: "No olvidemos que no existe una sola novela que pueda, con derecho, reclamarse sólo dentro de una categoría. Todas pueden pertenecer al mismo tiempo a varios casilleros, exactamente como la vida de los hombres, pueblos, colectividades o culturas que tratan de copiar e interpretar." [1] Few pure representatives of a given school or movement exist, and one must agree with Ángel Flores that "in Latin American prose fiction it is difficult if not impossible to categorize faithfully each movement." [2] In the twentieth century even more divisions and subdivisions can be made in an unending variety of designations such as indigenist, anti-imperialist, psychological, existential, magical realism, or anti-novel, terms which confuse as much as they clarify. Yet to bring order out of chaos some effort must be made at classification, however imperfect.

Many critics attempt the generational approach, a concept easily abused and overemphasized. In Spanish America the picture is complicated by authors like Alberto Blest Gana, who wrote a series of novels in the late 1850s and early 1860s, stopped writing for over thirty years, and began to write once more in the late 1890s. Literary generations do not always coincide with aesthetic tendencies and may even falsify developments. In the words of Torres-Rioseco, "Tenemos que reconocer este fenómeno: nuestra cultura no progresa por evolución constante sino por bruscos impulsos inconexos. No hay en nuestros valores culturales ese encadenamiento constante de causa a efecto que define una evolución progresiva." [3] In the 1860s Wilhelm Dilthey and Justin Drommel wrote perceptively on literary generations, but in the twentieth century the most persuasive thesis appears to be that of Julius Petersen. He specifies eight formative factors in the constitution of a literary generation, namely, inheritance, date of birth, homogeneous educational formation, personal relations, generational experiences, the presence of a leader, a peculiar language, and the paralysis of the previous generation.[4]

In Spain and Spanish America many have written on the concept of literary generations. Ortega y Gasset limits generational elements to identical chronological age, maintenance of a permanent vital contact, supervention of another generation, and possession of one's own spatial dimension. Ortega differentiates between *coetáneo* (to share the same age) and *contemporáneo* (to live at the same time). Coetaneousness is more important, but contemporaneousness must be taken into account, accepting the coexistence of several generations and also the possibility that certain writers born at the same time will not share the themes, thoughts, and moods of the same generation. Ortega believes that the concept of "generation" is basic to an understanding of history and "el gozne sobre que ésta ejecuta sus movimientos." [5] Pedro Laín Entralgo states that each generation has its own style, language, and mode of expression. How each author accepts and rejects from his world; what the creation, personal projects, and dreams of the group have in common; and the similarity in the individual manner of accepting, rejecting, creating, projecting, or dreaming are important.[6] Guillermo de Torre finds that the date of publication of the first work is decisive.[7]

It must be understood that however closely we define indeterminate terms such as "realism," they serve merely as approximations and not as rigidly enfolding matrices. Taine's definition of realism as a "methodical investigation of documents about human nature" has been amplified through the years. Fernando Alegría sees three types of realism in the Spanish American novel. The first, influenced by Stendhal, Flaubert, and Daudet, is characterized by minute descriptions and a simple style contrasting with the grandiloquence of romanticism; a second, dealing with types, customs, and, language, without limiting itself to the picturesque, explores social and intellectual conflicts; and finally we have that inspired by Zola and the Goncourt brothers.[8] It may be that there are as many types of realism as there are literary schools, "un realismo clásico con euritmia proporcional de formas; un realismo romántico como expresión de nuestra veracidad cordial; un realismo naturalista, como colorido análisis del mundo exterior; un realismo psicológico, queriendo llegar al fondo de las reacciones anímicas; un realismo modernista . . . y un realismo realista, en el que se integran los dos mundos, interior y exterior, con todas las complejas verificaciones del acontecer del hombre en lucha con los hombres, con las cosas y consigo mismo." [9]

To reflect a given historical time or reproduce a geographical space does not necessarily make a given work realistic, but "reproduce" and "reflect" serve as the key words whether the description is exterior costumbrismo or mirror image, as the novelist reacts to his reality, presumably with objectivity. As realists attempt to reflect the reality they see in its natural form, they may use minute description for incidental embellishment, to describe the relationship of man to his environment, social and intellectual conflicts, or "el ansia minuciosa de verdad, el instinto de observación y el empeño de realzar las bellezas latentes en los actos de la vida cotidiana . . ." [10] In general we can say that the realistic novel deals largely with commonplace details of ordinary people in everyday language, describes the environment of the characters, often with a somewhat limited psychological understanding of their materialistic motivations, often with symbolic implications. Some novelists wish to paint their total society; others search through their observation for more limited truths about humanity. Most nineteenth-century realists are better at viewing man from the outside, whether their object is local color or the promotion of a political or social thesis. One must also recognize that a basic theme of almost all Spanish American fiction, until very recent times, has been that of man overwhelmed by the cosmic forces of Nature and his attempts to acclimate himself to it and survive. In any event, efforts to reproduce, as exactly as possible, the surrounding world were by definition conditioned by the deforming eye of the novelist, however well intentioned, and could only evoke aspects of "reality" or the author's, and not real "reality."

Alberto Blest Gana (1830–1920), the father of the realistic and to a degree the sociological novel in Spanish America, and certainly in Chile,[11] was the son of an Irish doctor, William Cunningham Blest and María de la Luz Gana, a Chilean aristocrat. Alberto studied at the National Institute and after a five year stay in France returned to teach in a military school. He left the army in 1855 to devote himself completely to his writing. He tried his hand first at some poetry, a theatrical piece, and some *artículos de costumbres* under a variety of pseudonyms, publishing some as early as 1853 in *El Museo* and many others in 1859 and 1860 in *La Semana*. His fiction falls readily into three divisions: fairly romantic novels that largely antedate his study of Balzac; a group of realistic novels beginning in 1860 with *La aritmética en el amor* and running through 1864; and his final works, beginning with *Durante la reconquista* (1897).

His early novels include *Una escena social* (1853), published in *El Museo* and attacked by the Catholic press as immoral because it deals with seduction, suicide, and true love which compels the hero to care for the son of the woman he loved; *Los desposados* (1855), about a young revolutionary, his love, and their suicide published in the *Revista de Santiago*; *Engaños y desengaños* (1855), concerning frustrated love and a wrongfully suspected sweetheart; *El primer amor* (1858), about a poet's ruin through love for a married woman and the desire for vengeance by Manuela, his cousin, whose love he spurned; *La fascinación* (1858); and *Un drama en el campo* (1859), which first appeared in *La Semana*. Blest Gana realized his own deficiencies in his early attempts and in a letter to his friend Benjamín Vicuña Mackenna stated that "desde un día en que leyendo a Balzac hice un auto de fe en mi chimenea, condenando a las llamas las impresiones rimadas de mi adolescencia, juré ser novelista y abandonar el campo literario si las fuerzas no me alcanzaban para hacer algo que no fuesen triviales y pasajeras composiciones." [12]

He received his chance to incorporate what he learned from Balzac because of a contest sponsored by the university to help in the formation of a national novel. For the contest Blest Gana produced his first mature work, *La aritmética en el amor*, an authentic analysis of society life in Santiago, which while lacking a prose of translucent elegance and still showing a romantic overlay, conveys the flavor of the Chilean milieu. Fortunato Esperanzano, nephew of Anselmo Rocaleal, influenced by a cynical friend, Anastasio Bermúdez, decides it is as easy to fall in love with a rich girl as with a poor one. After he loses money gambling, he falsifies a document to save his true love's family from ruin but later repents of his ill-conceived actions. Love triumphs in the end, as his uncle's unfaithful wife is disinherited and he is given enough money for a happy life. Blest Gana falls short of his goal of writing a Chilean Comédie Humaine, but in his novels, beginning with this one, he conveys an almost encyclopedic picture of Santiago society. The total is much greater than the sum of his various works. The setting of his first mature novel is 1858, and Blest Gana takes a dim view of the new affluent and materialistic society of his country. His characters lack dramatic impact and tend to be types. Julia is the adulterous wife, Carlos Peñalta, her passionate lover, and Margarita Monteverde the rich heiress. His story of frustrated love and romantic reconciliation is unimportant when compared to his panoramic description of Chile, which proved that his country had fictional possibilities which he hoped sincerely to paint. José Victorino Lastarria, one of the judges in the national contest in 1860, in awarding the prize cited the novel's costumbrista aspects and its national spirit.[13] The characters, whatever their artificiality and lack of force, prove good representatives of the Chilean environment, which Blest Gana transcribes with reasonable fidelity.

Blest Gana believed in the novel of manners, maintaining that a novelist could generate interest if he showed color and life in his descriptions of everyday affairs. Unhappily, he could not fully carry out his desires in his next novel, *El pago de las deudas* (1861). Dedicated to José Victorino Lastarria, the novel is a muddled tale of selfish young Santiago society, a rich young widow, adultery, a thoroughly mixed-up love situation, and the suicide of the protagonist Luciano when he learns too late where true love and duty lie.

In 1862 Blest Gana published *Martín Rivas*, which first appeared in the daily *La Voz de Chile*. His most popular work, *Mar-*

tín Rivas is, along with *Durante la reconquista* and *El loco Estero*, his best fictional effort. It is easy to see in it reflections of Octave Feuillet's *Le Roman d'un Jeune Homme* (1858), but Raúl Silva Castro, who to date has written the most complete study on Blest Gana, sees in the novel the influence of Stendhal. In *Le Rouge et le Noir*, Julien Sorel, a boy from the provinces, is led astray by ambition; but Martín Rivas, the rigid puritan, lacks both the sensitivity and sudden rages of the Stendhal creation.[14] Many of the characters were somewhat distorted versions of real Chilean citizens of the day. In 1850 Martín Rivas comes from the provinces to live with the wealthy financier Dámaso Encina, who had cheated Martín's father out of a mine which eventually formed the basis for his great wealth. The energetic and intelligent Martín, a prospective law student in backwoods dress and ignorant of city ways, is at first mocked by those whom he in turn considers to have false values. He offers a sharp contrast to the empty-headed wife of Don Dámaso, Engracia, whose main concern seems to be for her little lap dog, and to Agustín, her son, a foppish, frivolous youth impressed with the power of money. As the novel progresses, Martín changes both inwardly and outwardly, as does the proud, beautiful, and headstrong daughter of the Encinas, Leonor. The social classes come to know and respect one another more, within the limitations of their heritage, and Leonor, finally realizing she loves Martín, helps free him from prison and the death sentence to which his activities in the 1851 rebellion had condemned him. They marry, thus uniting city and province. Many other threads weave in and out of the main story. Rafael San Luis, Martín's friend, loves Matilde, Leonor's cousin, but he seduces Adelaida, whose middle-class mother hopes to force Agustín, a frequent visitor to the house, to marry her daughter. Agustín, however, is saved from a fraudulent marriage through the efforts of the efficient Martín. Rafael, his impending marriage to Matilde ruined, becomes involved in La Sociedad de la Igualdad and is killed in the revolution. Edelmira, Adelaida's sister, in love with Martín, in the end sacrifices herself so that he may escape his death sentence.

The real protagonist of the story is the social body, which the author views as a moral entity qualitatively distinct from the individuals who comprise it. The historical and political happenings,[15] the struggle between province and city, and the power of money in a middle-class society are more important than the feuds and complex love affairs and help offset the occasional moralizing tone and patently false artificial solution of symbolic union of classes and province and city through the marriage of Martín and Leonor. The *siútico*, the representative of the infra-middle class of social climbers, is but one type of Chilean. Blest Gana in his other fictional efforts includes also the *roto*, member of the proletarian urban class, and the *huaso* or country peasant. In portraying the ordinary Chilean, aside from his tendency to overpraise the virtuous simple country life in contrast to city evils, Blest Gana is almost too detailed. Whatever the artificiality of Martín's overdone romantic rectitude, he represented thousands like him in Chile who also attempted to overcome caste prejudices. Since this was the first attempt to present the triumph over obstacles of the humble folk of Chile,[16] the author left no detail out which might promote the picture of that success. Fernando Alegría, who likes the novel for its creative force, human breath, and interpretation of Chile, sees it not as a realistic novel but rather as "una de las historias más bellas del romanticismo hispanoamericano."[17]

In 1862 Blest Gana wrote *La venganza*, about eighteenth-century Lima, and *Mariluán*, about the Araucanian Indians. His next important novel was *El ideal de un calavera* (1863), an even more complete social analysis than *Martín Rivas*. It is a somewhat romantic-costumbrista tale enlivened by comic scenes as well as the standard frustrated love and a woman's revenge—a romantic heritage Blest Gana could not overcome. The hero, possessed of dynamic, unchanneled energy, loses his life in the uprising in Quillota against Portales instead of triumphing as had Martín Rivas. Abelardo Manríquez, a spoiled only son, may be Blest Gana's best drawn male character. Candelaria Basquiñuelas, Abelardo's primitive and almost savage lover, is the author's best representation of "una mujer de medio pelo" in his entire gallery.

In 1864 the Chilean novelist ended his fictional output of that decade with *La flor de la higuera*, not to resume novel publication for the next thirty-three years. When one considers that Pérez Galdós did not publish *La Fontana de Oro* until 1870, one realizes the historical importance of Blest Gana. In these works up to 1864 he describes people, houses, and society, at times in indicative anecdotal language. His characters and social classes collide in unmotivated fashion, and stylistically these novels lack the subtle tension associated with a more mature technique. Uslar Pietri finds Blest Gana "frío y lento," but he also points out that the Chilean "sabrá suplir con su laboriosa observación y construcción las fallas de su don creador." [18]

Blest Gana began writing *Durante la reconquista* as early as 1864 but abandoned it. He later destroyed his first manuscript and, making a fresh start, finished the novel in 1888, publishing it in 1897. It begins with the battle of Rancagua in 1814 and ends in January 1817, but in an epilog or final chapter the author tells us what will happen in the remaining months leading up to independence. The efforts of Chilean patriots offer the background for the love story of young Abel Malsira and his cousin, Luisa Bustos, as well as that of his sister, Trinidad, for the Spanish colonel Laramonte. Abel becomes infatuated with a Spanish widow, Violante de Alarcón, but he finally realizes it is his cousin that he truly loves. Abel is guided by Manuel Rodríguez from political indifference to sacrifice for his country. Part of the action is related by Cámara, representative of the Chilean people. With him we can share the sad defeat after Rancagua, the fear, hate, terror, intrigues, and feuds between those who believed in the status quo and the revolutionaries, in all of which the wicked Captain San Bruno plays an active role. Abel and Luisa die, and San Bruno betrays Laramonte, but final victory belongs to the patriots. Blest Gana took his historical details from Diego Barros Arana's *Historia general de Chile* (1884–86),[19] but in describing his historical figures and all Chilean classes he reduces his commentary and his role as omniscient narrator to allow both his imaginary and historical creations some free will and growth. He wanted not only to write a history of individuals but to paint an entire age and the history of a people in their struggle for liberty.[20] Manuel Rodríguez, the patriot, immune to self-absorption and self-glorification is almost too perfect. The Spanish captain, Vicente San Bruno, is a standard villain. But Cámara, the roto,[21] is a brilliantly precise portrayal of a Chilean city criollo and a representative of Chilean fighting spirit, although his resourcefulness, glibness, and loyalty to his master reflect the picaresque and romantic more than the realistic.

Los trasplantados (1904) continues a detailed documentation of the effects of new nitrate riches in the transformation of Chilean society and the creation of a new wealthy class. In many cases these "nouveaux riches" went to Paris to live and hopefully to marry into French society. The Chilean family chosen as the stereotype by Blest Gana, the Canalejas family, appears to modern eyes to be almost a caricature, but Blest Gana's intent was not humor. He censors the rich criollos who live in Paris and waste their money, forgetting their nationality and seeking alliances with an empty nobility. Mercedes Canalejas, in spite of her real love for poor Patricio Fuentealba, is forced to marry an impoverished prince for his title, and sick in spirit and unable to struggle against the false allure of the French city, commits suicide. Alberto del Solar's *Rastaquouère* (1890) and Joaquín Edwards Bello's *Criollos en París* (1933) have a similar theme.

El loco Estero (1909), set partly in the 1830s, gives us many autobiographical details about the author's family and childhood. He shows us Chilean culture, the birth of romanticism, the discovery of silver mines, and a host of intimate glimpses of his country in what amounts to a personal history of nineteenth-century Chile. Don Julián Estero, an army captain considered mad by his family, was kept locked up in his room by his sister Manuela, who, although married, was carrying on a love affair with Major Justo Quintaverde. Another sister, Sinforosa, married to Agapito Linares, has a daughter, Deidamia, one of whose suitors, Carlos Díaz, is rejected by the family. To avenge himself, Carlos, with the aid of Matías, Manuela's husband, frees Julián, who wounds his sister and escapes. He later visits Manuela, and forgiveness ensues, but she dies. Deidamia marries Díaz, and Julián gives them the house as a present. *El loco Estero* adds a magnificent creation to Blest Gana's characters in the person of don Matías Cortázar, the betrayed husband. Deidamia is an adorable and tender girl. Major Quintaverde, the terror of timid husbands, is adequately portrayed, but Manuela, the repentant wife who enters a convent and dies, is a stock figure. Overall the novel has a freshness, simplicity, and clarity of style, as the author, seeing the past with the eyes of a child, recalls his youth and friends, adolescent love and jealousy. Alone states that *El loco Estero* is "la novela más liviana y entretenida de su autor, la más ligera y agil, y daría espléndido tema a una película." [22]

The last of Blest Gana's novels; *Gladys Fairfield* (1912), which he dedicated to the memory of his beloved wife, is a minor effort about high society in Switzerland, a Spanish American protagonist, and a flimsy love plot. As one reads the total production of Blest Gana, one learns about all the social classes of Chile, the power of money, the occupations, the customs, the psychology of individuals and groups. In this broad sweep of the entire nineteenth century, the author too often gives us an overly detailed study which is plagued by a monotonous style and a lack of psychological penetration and profundity. A romantic in a moment of transition to realism, Blest Gana assured his immortality in Chile at the cost of foreign critical acclaim by his "concienzuda y empecinada devoción a una especie de épico localismo, rico en materia histórica, observación de costumbres, caraterización de tipos autóctonos y diálogo regional." [23] Although most would deny that Blest Gana had a feeling for nature, Mariano Latorre claims that this is not "precisamente lo cierto . . . al describir aspectos de la vida rural su observación es aguda y seguro su dibujo." [24] In any event, Blest Gana, at least in Chile, is the progenitor who set the pattern for almost all future Chilean novelists, whose debt to him is usually acknowledged. His spontaneity, says Alone, was both his greatest charm and most serious drawback, but the Chilean critic insists that Blest Gana "es absolutamente, el más grande novelista y el más profundamente nacional." [25]

Daniel Barros Grez (1834–1904) held a variety of positions and wrote in a number of genres. Better known as a dramatist, he followed Blest Gana's realistic leadership in his somewhat melodramatic costumbrista works, which contained picaresque humor, biting satire, and a number of anti-clerical ideas. *Pipiolos y pelucones* (1876)[26] treats of real historical persons as well as imaginary ones, against the background of revolution and civil war. The plot, about the love of a liberal soldier for the daughter of a conservative, her kidnapping on her wedding day, and the happy ending, seems somewhat contrived. Although *El huérfano* (1881) is an obvious imitation of *Martín Rivas* and composed in a pseudo-Cervantine style, it is of interest as an indication of the opposition to Diego Portales and for its treatment of that period of Chilean history. His other type novel is best represented by *Primeras aventuras del maravilloso perro Cuatro Remos* (1898), a picaresque costumbrista effort.

The Colombian José Manuel Marroquín (1827–1908), known to his countrymen as "El castellano de Yerbabuena," gentleman farmer, founder of the Colombian Academy, and president of his country, wrote a number of costumbrista sketches (he was fond of pseudonyms such as Gonzalo González de la Gonzalera). He has several novels, among them *Blas Gil* (1896), the story of a rogue and an attack on the political and social deficiencies of Colombia; *Entre primos* (1897), a satire of the affectation inherent in tropical "gente de medio pelo"; and *Amores y leyes* (1898), a careful description of life in Bogotá. His one famous novel, *El moro* (1897), a typically regional novel in the manner of José Pereda, is the autobiography of a horse and a tale of human selfishness and evil. El moro, so-called because of his skin color, a Colombian Black Beauty, tells us about his change of masters, his youthful companions, stories he has heard from his friends, his teachers, and his life as an army and work horse. In the process he manages to give us a good insight into human life and experience.

Francisco de Paula Rendón (1855–1917), who used the pseudonym Jaime Valmar, wrote two short costumbrista novels, *Inocencia* (1904) and *Sol* (1919), the latter about a ten year old girl who is ostracized because of her poverty. *Inocencia*, his better known novel, deals with the beauties of Antioquia, its folklore, and superstition. Rendón recalls Pereda in his attachment to his land[27] as well as in his conservative politics. Inocencia, her father having died, falls in love with her mother's lover, Ángel, and dies on their wedding night. Rendón combines this bare plot outline with a love for the traditional values of the past and of the natural assets of his country, along with its "curas, curanderos, and caciques," to give us a good portrait of village and rural life and "sobre todo, . . . el corazón humano."[28]

Samuel Velázquez (1865–1942), whose *Madre* (1908) pleased Menéndez y Pelayo greatly because of its religious sentimentality, also shows the author's attachment to his native Colombia. The tale about a mother who manages to protect her daughter from seduction, overblown as it is, is superior to his other novels, *Al pie del Ruiz* (1898) and *Hija* (1904).

The Venezuelan Gonzalo Picón Febres (1869–1918), certainly a realist, might as easily be classified as a naturalistic or even possibly criollista novelist. He has a number of novels: *Fidelia* (1893), about a kind but abulic priest, his housekeeper, and a servant girl who becomes a politician's mistress; *Nieve y lodo* (1895), a satire of high society and one of the continent's earliest psychological novels; *Ya es hora* (1895); and *Flor* (1905). His most famous work, *El sargento Felipe*, which he wrote in jail, was first published in *El Cojo Ilustrado* in 1899. A historical novel based on a real episode in a revolution led by General Matías Salazar against Antonio Guzmán Blanco, it contains many scenes of country life, exuberant, colorful nature with its tropical flowers, and many costumbrista descriptions of meals, pulpería reunions, a rural wedding, a dance, houses, a religious pilgrimage, and a military parade. The author states that an artist can describe only what he sees. The invasion by Salazar from Colombia and his ensuing defeat in Tinaquillo are authentically realistic and historical, but the plot is overly romantic and moralizing. Felipe, an honorable small property owner, avenges that honor by killing his daughter's seducer and throwing himself off a cliff. Picón Febres interjects into his novel his negative feelings about the civil strife and the futility of war in general.

In Mexico the realistic novel as such did not enjoy the great vogue it had in Spain. With much less emphasis on regionalism, Mexican novelists largely followed in the fictional paths of Galdós and Pereda, and saw no significant differences between realism and naturalism.[29] Most of the novelists were given to exaggerated characterization and strong emphasis on humorous situations and language.

Emilio Rabasa (1856–1930), who used the pseudonym Sancho Polo, is generally credited with being the first of the Mexican realists and to some extent a precursor of the fiction of the Mexican Revolution.[30] A sociologist, lawyer, and expert on constitutional law, senator, professor, governor, and journalist, he published four novels, *La bola* (1887), *La gran ciencia* (1887), *El cuarto poder* (1888), and *Moneda falsa* (1888), which may be considered as one novel in four parts rather than a tetralogy. A thoughtful man,[31] as were most in his generation, he was influenced by positivism and theories of evolution. He saw a marvelous complication and contradiction in human nature and a capacity for change through the union of "las más fuertes oposiciones, lo repelente y lo hermoso, lo limitado y lo sin límites."[32] His novels, often filled with a gentle, picaresque, and self-effacing humor, resemble greatly those of

Galdós, "whom he followed in construction and style." [33] He analyzes the provincial cacique, the role of revolution, and the science,
and essentially counterfeit nature, of politics. In spite of the political corruption, amoral and ambitious politicians, and rampant
chauvinism he describes, Rabasa hopes for improvement in the
middle class and Mexico's eventual salvation.

La bola takes place in the imaginary town of San Martín de la
Piedra and concerns two rival caciques and armed peasants fighting
for the oppressed pueblo. Men change political parties as easily
as they change clothes and everyone pursues the *bola*. Juanito
Quiñones loves Remedios, the niece of one of the quarreling caciques, Mateo Cabezudo. Juanito helps the uncle and wins a battle
but loses the girl as the unmollified major exiles him from the village. In the next part, *La gran ciencia*, Quiñones has acquired a
small farm and continues his rivalry with Cabezudo. Betrayals and
counterbetrayals occur among contenders in the game of political
science, and Cabezudo, first a colonel and then a general, continues
to foil Quiñones' love for Remedios. In *El cuarto poder*, Sabas
Carrasco, an old acquaintance of Juan, encourages him to become
a newspaperman. Mateo is now a deputy. Juan writes for *El Cuarto
Poder*, the opposition paper, but his publisher changes sides as ill
fortune continues to pursue Juan in both his public and private
life. In the final novel, *Moneda falsa*, Juan, finally realizing that he
is incapable of fulfilling his political ambitions, really counterfeit
coin, returns to his village, as does Cabezudo, also out of favor, and
the lovers finally marry. Rabasa avoids many descriptive passages
involving nature, but he attempts to utilize costumbrismo and psychology to good effect in the scenes of violence and action in his
decadent society. His irony enlivens what otherwise might have
been a completely sordid portrayal of a vice-filled political system.
Yet, in spite of his presentation of rural scenes, he fails to capture
authentic Mexico or Mexicans. Among the other works of the
novelist, one may mention *La guerra de los tres años* (1891), which
deals with the power of the Church, tradition, and the difficulty of
progress and reform.

José López Portillo y Rojas (1850–1923), considered by the well-
known critic of Mexican literature Julio Jiménez Rueda to be the
outstanding realist of the group,[34] attempted to paint a broader
canvass than Rabasa, who largely confined his social criticism to

those years when he himself was politically active. A "pintor veraz de la vida mexicana," [35] he was Catholic and conservative but not without his own brand of idealism. His ideas about literature resemble those of Altamirano. In the prologue to one of his novels, *La parcela*, he states that he wants to maintain the orthodoxy of form and language of Spanish literature and tradition but also to exploit rich elements surrounding Mexicans, to "recogernos dentro de nosotros mismos y difundirnos menos en cosas extrañas." He defends the use of necessary regionalisms and customs and hopes to avoid refinements which are not Mexican. Yet his realism often verges on the romantic in his portrayal of good and evil and his stereotyped symbols. López Portillo lacked compassion for the poor and real understanding of their problems, at best treating them with paternalistic condescension. Azuela considers his characters and environment to be complete falsifications and denies that they are either realistic or Mexican.[36] López Portillo y Rojas has a number of stories and short novels, *Seis leyendas* (1885), *Novelas cortas* (1900), *Sucesos y novelas cortas* (1903), *Historias, historietas y cuentecillos* (1918), as well as a number of historical, philosophical, and travel books. His three full length novels are *La parcela* (1898), *Los precursores* (1909), and *Fuertes y débiles* (1919), which some see as related to the novels of the Mexican Revolution.[37]

La parcela concerns a quarrel between Pedro Ruiz, owner of a wooded land, Monte de los Pericos, and his friend Miguel Díaz, who also claims it. Pedro's son Gonzalo loves Miguel's daughter Ramona. After a series of clashes, court proceedings, crooked lawyers, and some criminal activity, the obvious solution occurs. The author indulges in minute descriptions of furniture, rooms, houses, people, and the customs of Jalisco, with satirical but usually pleasant humor. Among the well described types are the hacienda administrator, don Simón Oceguera, a giant centaur, and Chole, the ambitious town girl. *Los precursores* is a conservative statement about old Christian virtues and traditional values. Two orphans are brought up by the Sisters of Charity who are paragons of virtue. Under their loving care the orphans become model citizens and marry. Their sadness is shared by the author when the good Sisters are forced to move because of the anti-clerical laws of the Reform. This intruding religious sentiment overshadows what might otherwise have been an interesting view of classes and characters. *Fuertes y débiles* involves a peripheral treatment of the Mexican Revolution. A profligate and dissolute hacendado, Juan Nepumoceno, known as Cheno, unjustly uses the law to keep his peons in virtual slavery. He takes as his mistress the wife of one of them. He becomes involved in a plot against Madero, and his hacienda gradually deteriorates. When the agrarian revolt breaks out in the south, Cheno is captured, and the peon sent to seek clemency (the one whose wife he had stolen) arrives too late to "save" the hacendado. The novelist neither defends nor condemns the hacienda owners, but he adopts a moral Catholic tone. His orthodoxy, conservatism, and obvious bias overshadow his desire to write an honest novel.

Rafael Delgado (1853–1914), unlike Rabasa, avoided politics. A professor of literature, he led a rather lonely life, by all accounts, which may explain a melancholy note which intrudes in many of his novels. Aside from some theatrical works, poetry, and literary criticism, he wrote three novels, *La Calandria* (1891), *Angelina* (1893), *Los parientes ricos* (1903), and a novelette, *Historia vulgar* (1904). A kind of Mexican Pereda, he, like his Spanish counterpart, concentrates on the description of his native countryside. He projects a delicate poetic note in his pictures of the natural beauties of rural Mexico. His landscape is objectively painted and persuasive, but his simple themes do not offer a profound penetration into his characters or milieu but report only the surface of the hidden iceberg of reality. In his prologue to *Cuentos y notas* (1902) Delgado states that his stories are "meros apuntes de cosas vistas y de sucesos bien sabidos." Antonio Castro Leal, in a prologue to *Angelina*, says that Delgado is a fusion of French romanticism and Spanish realism; and his romantic overtones occur in all his fiction. Like Pereda he was extremely serious about his Catholicism and Christian relationships, a constant note in his novels. Delgado, a novelist of the provinces, has an excellent understanding of that society. In the prologue to *Angelina* he contends that he wants to write a simple history, more lived than imagined. Given his lack of outstanding invention or imagination, his decision to concentrate on everyday occurrences was wise.

La Calandria, his most popular novel, was first published in the *Revista Nacional de Letras y Ciencias* (1890). Carmen, or Calandria, loves Gabriel, the son of a woman who had befriended her mother. When Gabriel spurns her, she vengefully has an affair with another man, and finally, completely abandoned, takes poison. It is Gabriel, the carpenter, who makes her coffin. The novel, in spite of its quite romantic plot, abounds in the local color of Veracruz, the middle classes, and the relationships of the rich and the poor. *Angelina* is a somewhat sentimental novel and a weak imitation of *María*.[38] In the village of Villaverde, a fictionalized version of Córdoba, Rodolfo, educated through his aunts' sacrifice, falls in love with Angelina, an intelligent young girl living with them. Gossip causes him to accept a position at a hacienda where he meets the wealthy Gabriela, who eventually marries another. Angelina becomes a nun. Delgado brings to life the small town, its gossip, inertia, and false respectability, but he avoids attacking problems which would necessitate ugly descriptions. In the preface to *Los parientes ricos* he claims he wanted it to be "copia exacta de la vida mexicana," but his unlively scenes, fixed in time, seem musty museum pieces. A mother moves to Mexico City to live with her rich brother-in-law, who had ruined her husband. One of the sons of the house seduces her blind daughter, a situation to which the wealthy family is indifferent. The mother returns to her village, hoping to educate the girl's son and work out their own problems.

Most of Delgado's novels give us a good picture of different kinds of people. He writes pleasantly, simply, and soberly of a somehow sidetracked but not sordid society. In spite of his many defects and errors, he may be the greatest Mexican novelist of the nineteenth century[39]—"el primer escritor mexicano que arremete con el género novelístico, no sólo con dotes naturales de buen narrador y excelente descriptista, sino con preparación literaria y conocimientos, seguro de la técnica de este oficio."[40]

Ángel del Campo (1868–1908) used the pseudonym Tick-Tack for his newspaper articles and Micrós for his three volumes of short stories, *Ocios y apuntes* (1890), *Cosas vistas* (1894), and *Cartones* (1897). He wrote a novel, *La sombra de Medrano*, never published in complete form, and *La Rumba*, published as a folletín novel in *El Nacional*. His scanty production received surprisingly favorable critical acclaim, and he has been labeled, "uno de los precursores más notables del realismo moderno mexicano," [41] "tierno precursor de la trepidación revolucionaria," [42] and "un poeta, un moralista lleno de piedad para los seres débiles: niños, mujeres, animales." [43] María del Carmen Millán, the editor of his *Obras*

(Mexico, 1958), remarks, in the prologue, on the "fidelidad foto-gráfica del realismo, el cuidadoso análisis naturalista, y el sub-jetivismo dramático del romanticismo."

La Rumba exemplifies his identification with and pity for the unfortunate and sad victims of his society. He paints tellingly the frustration and miserable life of the pueblo in an environment of faded flowers and broken dishes. He is often ironic but also constantly tender. His human compassion shines through his delineation of the lives of the various types (some seem caricatures) who frequent La Rumba, a shop in an old, poor Mexican square, a district forgotten by citizens who were indifferent to its degradation. Remedios, a young seamstress born to poverty, is seduced by a salesman with whom she attempts to escape her environment. Unable to stand the sufferings and indignities at his hands, she finally murders him. Objects, too, come to life in this dull and dismal district, "como si todas estas cosas tuvieran vida propia." [44] Adding a personal note of authenticity and familiarity to his gentle satire and authentic portrait, Ángel del Campo saw a reality that "was the visible daily life of insignificant people. But to him this life was very meaningful, and he leaves his reader with an impression of the neighborhood rather than of individuals." [45]

Heriberto Frías (1870–1928), in some respects the most naturalistic of all the Mexican novelists,[46] was a newspaperman who fought against Porfirio Díaz and Victoriano Huerta, supported the Convention of Aguascalientes, and was quite possibly a direct precursor of the fiction of the Mexican Revolution. Grandiloquent and even vulgar at times, he exhibited a strong sense of justice and love of his country and people. His most famous novel, *Tomochic* (1894), is about a rebellion of an Indian mountain village in the Sierra Madre against the Porfirio Díaz regime. Frías, a lieutenant, took part in the military campaign to annihilate the village, a task accomplished with great difficulty not only because of fierce Indian resistance to the superior forces of civilization but also because of the ineptness of many of the army commanders. Manuel Mercado, the protagonist and Frías' alter ego, attacks the army and the government. He also gives us a description of Tomochic, the Indian chief; Cruz Chaves, the half-mad woman, the so-called Saint of Cabora who led them; the religious fanaticism; and the fierce fighting. The novel was published by *El Demócrata*, a newspaper opposed to the government, which caused its suspension and the arrest of Frías on the charge of treason and revealing military secrets. He was condemned to die, but his sentence was suspended and he was discharged from the army. Frías may have been "searching for symbols of security in his society, for durable elements upon which he could stand with faith." [47] Ernest Moore, who finds the novelist to be a "prophet of the Mexican Revolution," states that he "attacked evil as he understood it and preferred the simple life of primitive people close to the soil." [48] Frías' other important novel, *Águila o Sol* (1923), whose title means "heads or tails," charts the possible courses for a future viable Mexico. In a Mexico on the brink of revolution, Manuel Mercado encourages and leads a miner's strike in the village of Mixtlan. Two branches of the Ávila family, one Spanish and the other mestiza, live in the village. Gaudelia or Sol, the heroic, virtuous, and unselfish mestiza daughter of Juan Diego Ávila, a federalista, serves as an inspiration for Mercado. Among his other novels are: *El tiempo de Sancho Panza* (1911), a kind of sequel to *Tomochic* in which Manuel Mercado, now a journalist, attacks political corruption; *Naufragio* (1895), later revised and published as *El amor de las sirenas* (1908), about student life in Mexico City; and *El último duelo* (1896) about the evils of dueling.

Other Mexican novelists treated a variety of social and political problems of the day but with a caution they felt to be imperative during the dangerous days of Porfirio Díaz. These include Juan N. Cordero (1861–1915), author of *Inri* (1898); Porfirio Parra (1856–1912), author of *Pacotillas* (1900); Manuel H. San Juan (1864–1917), who wrote *El señor gobernador* (1901); Salvador Cordero (1876–1951), author of *Memorias de un juez de paz* (1913); Victoriano Salado (1867–1931), who wrote a number of realistic historical novels such as *La intervención y el imperio* (1903); Manuel Sánchez Mármol (1839–1912); Rafael Ceniceros y Villarreal (1855–1936); and Cayetano Rodríguez Beltrán (1866–1939).

The realistic period in Spanish America saw the production and popularity of many autobiographical, descriptive works, which for some readers lack fictional force. An early sample of this kind of work is *El llanero* (1845) by the Venezuelan Daniel Mendoza (1823–1867), to whom the work is usually attributed. His protagonist, Palmarote, is a remote ancestor of Gallegos' *llaneros*.

The outstanding representative of this kind of fiction and one of the most important works of the nineteenth century, *Una excursión a los indios Ranqueles* (1870), was written by the Argentine Lucio Victorio Mansilla (1831–1913), whose mother was a sister of the dictator Juan Manuel Rosas. Mansilla, who wrote other works and made several translations, was a kind of esthete and, according to some, a bon vivant. One of the unresolved problems of his time was that of the Indian population. In March 1869, Mansilla, a colonel, was named commander of the frontier under the orders of General Arredondo. President Sarmiento wished to recover the Indian lands along the river Quinto. The government had previously sent a number of futile expeditions against the Ranqueles, descendants of the Araucanian Indians who had emigrated to Paraguay. Without consulting his superiors, Mansilla worked out a peace treaty with the Indians, but his government was not too observant of its promises. To clarify matters Mansilla, unarmed and with but a few men, visited the cacique, Mariano, to convince him of his government's good intentions, an excursion he later called a "calaverada militar." The expedition lasted eighteen days, enough for him to produce a realistic picture of the Indians and the mestizos who lived among them. In his conversations with them Mansilla learned about captive women, each with her personal history, studied Indian ingenuity, their astonishing command of Spanish, their clothes, fiestas, homes, horses, gods, devils, funeral customs, and a complex of stories, anecdotes, and chronicles. Written in the form of letters to his friend Santiago Arcos, a Chilean writer, the book mocks the author's own role as narrator and ironically portrays a white civilization which he finds not at all superior to that of the Indian.

Filled with digressions, the work also evokes aspects of Mansilla's own youth, a period of political intrigues and ferocious factional disputes. Although he could not bring himself to attack his uncle violently, Mansilla, nonetheless, provides us with insight into himself and his society. Mansilla constantly describes the countryside, commenting at length on its beauty and aesthetic qualities, a deliberate subordination of action, plot, and characters to description. He utilizes nature, "la convierte en decorado y la adosa al plan general del relato. La naturaleza es su cómplice." [49] The work may be viewed as a kind of political justification of Mansilla together with his family and friends; but in its combination of virtues and defects[50] it is, along with *Facundo*, to whose philosophy it is diametrically opposed, and *Martín Fierro*, one of "las tres notas más originales de la literatura argentina del siglo XIX y notas peculiares de una literatura argentina en cualquier tiempo." [51]

William Henry Hudson (1841–1922), a naturalist born of North American parents in Argentina and later an English citizen, wrote in English and may, therefore, not properly belong in a discussion of Spanish American literature. Yet his works contain much information on the gauchos, their customs, the countryside, and historical events, and have had a marked influence on the development of Spanish American fiction. One of his works, a kind of travel book which may be considered a novel, *The Purple Land* (1885), in its original edition added the words "That England Lost." It is an evocation of Uruguayan history, its gauchos, whose primitive life he relished, the pampas, and nature in its various aspects. Several admirers of his works in Argentina feel that his novel—which presents the metamorphosis of Richard Lamb from scorn to passionate defense of Uruguayan civilization and his return, reborn in the natural American world, to the city—managed to sum up the national soul of Uruguay.[52] *El ombú* (1902) is a collection of four Argentine stories evaluating the gaucho in his poetic, fantastic, fatalistic, and bloody reality. *Far Away and Long Ago* (1918), his autobiography, gives us further insights into the man, his works, and his love for America. His most intriguing publication, *Green Mansions* (1904), is a beautiful description of tropical nature, a longing for lost beauty, and a version of an old Argentine legend about the bird woman or Kacuy. A keen observer, a lover of the simple life, he is interested in the good and the beautiful. His sincere, innocent view of a beautiful nature as a transcendental experience with which man can identify, his poetic feeling for the mysterious, strange jungle, is often contrasted with *La vorágine* by the Colombian novelist José Eustasio Rivera.

Another "foreign" Argentinian, Paul Groussac (1848–1929), a Frenchman who emigrated to Argentina in 1866, never became an Argentine citizen, but he experienced the life of farmers and gauchos as well as that of more sophisticated circles and came to love his adopted land and its people. The mentor of an entire generation, Groussac was an editor, historian (with special interest in psychology), a dramatist, literary critic (he may be the founder of Argentina's literary criticism), biographer, director of the national library, author of travel literature, and a novelist. Because he wrote in Spanish and because of his close identification with Argentina's national life, Groussac clearly belongs in a study of Spanish American literature. *Fruto vedado* (1884), his only full length novel, was first published in *Sud América*, a newspaper he and Lucio Vicente López founded. Partly autobiographical, the novel takes place first in Argentina, especially in the city of San José (his beloved Tucumán), and then on shipboard, in Brazil, and in Paris, where he makes full use of his knowledge of French by including many expressions in that language. The principal theme concerns people in the throes of a fatal sexual passion, torn between love and sensual desire. Marcel Renault, whose engineering education had been interrupted by a student revolt in Paris, has an adulterous love for Andrea, whose sister is in love with him. He betrays both her and her blind husband but atones for his fall from grace by dying bravely on a French expedition to Africa. The novel, subtitled "novela de costumbres argentinas," shows us political intrigues, landscape, and people. Although he later attacked Rubén Darío and the modernists, his dynamic prose reveals romantic, realistic, and modernist elements. In 1922 he published a collection of novelettes, *Relatos argentinos*.

One of the most important literary generations of Argentina, the so-called Generation of 1880, included among its realistic novelists Eduardo Wilde, Lucio Vicente López, Eugenio Cambaceres, and Miguel Cané, the son. The generation and their immediate followers in Argentina witnessed social changes, political transformations, and an ever increasing materialism. Foreign capital had been flowing into Argentina to help the growing prosperity of the country, and feverish economic activity was the order of the day. The economic boom was to give way to a market crash in 1890, with its concomitant bankruptcy, and provide material for some good naturalistic novels by other members of the generation. These writers believed in social progress, education, and religious agnosticism. In literature they were too thinly spread—through their travels, diplomatic careers, and club activities—to devote themselves fully to long sustained fiction.[53] Since the city of Buenos Aires became the capital of Argentina officially in 1880, and since their

principal interest lay in that city as a center for political and newspaper activity, the generation is aptly named. Many of them were
born outside of Argentina because their parents were refugees from
the Rosas dictatorship. Their membership in some of the leading
Argentine families (Mansilla is one example) conditioned their
condemnation of Argentine reality with a kind of unfounded optimism. Unlike Echeverría's generation, they did not have to fight
tyranny and suffer exile and hardships. This optimism, along with
a spiritual force, seems reflected "en el fondo de sus temas . . . un
deísmo, o al menos un espiritualismo difuso, al que casi ninguno
deja de prestar su respeto . . ." [54] This optimism can be confirmed
in the autobiographical pages of Eduardo Wilde's *Aguas abajo* and
Tiempo perdido—"en la descripción sencilla y melancólica de *La
gran aldea* de López; y hasta en los momentos más naturalistas de
Eugenio Cambaceres, vemos una luz de optimismo espiritual que
no está de acuerdo, de ninguna manera, con la etiqueta positivista
con que aparecen señalados los escritores de esta generación." [55]

Eduardo Wilde (1844–1913), whose companions generally considered him to be the most talented member of his generation, both
as a narrator and as a humorist, was born in Bolivia near the Argentine border of parents who had fled the Rosas tyranny. The
family returned to Buenos Aires, and Wilde became a doctor, politician, diplomat, and world traveler, observing the scene in Argentina and abroad with satire, irony, and a kind of self-mockery and
laughter, perhaps because "it hurt too much to cry." He regarded
literature more as a pastime than as a profession, and most of his
work is fragmentary. Wilde was something of a psychological mystery to himself and his friends. Strongly influenced by positivistic
thinking, he seemed in turn bitter, skeptical, ironic, humorous,
and tender. He loved Dickens and was the first Argentine to write
children's stories. Most of his work shows autobiographical tendencies, mixtures of the poetic and the romantic, and, at times, decidedly naturalistic traits. Whether he was cynical, insensible, cold,
sarcastic, scientific, poetic, tender, or compassionate depended on
the moment. His humor is not the result of an attempt to devalue
a disagreeable reality, for "Wilde parece haber amado el mundo
en que le tocó vivir y haberlo gozado con plenitud; la sonrisa y
cierto escepticismo en el juicio se explican mejor por la existencia

de una veta temperamental insobornable, cuanto por el usufructo de un clima de refinamiento espiritual, nuevo en la Argentina, propicio al desdén elegante y al ponderado descreimiento." [56] Wilde has a number of short story collections, *Prometeo y Cía* (1899), for example, but he is best known for *Aguas abajo* (1914), an autobiographical evocation of the past, his bohemian youth and escapades. He recalls an Andean village, Tupiza, the demagogues, the self-appointed professional defenders of the public, and dwells tenderly on the meadows, forests, mountains, and hills of that lost time and space. It is an autobiography, but it seems easily to meet the conditions of fiction and may well be the best autobiographical novel of its kind in Argentina.

Lucio Vicente López (1848–1894), the son of Vicente Fidel López, was a newspaperman, politician, and teacher who died tragically in a duel with Colonel Carlos Sarmiento at the age of forty-eight. His famous novel, *La gran aldea* (1884), subtitled "costumbres bonaerenses," reflects admirably the rapidly changing society of his time. First published in his *Sud América*, it shows the hasty composition resulting from his being forced to meet fixed deadlines. The title itself conveys the story of the transformation of Buenos Aires from a village to a cosmopolitan city, and the author, through his protagonist, obviously preferred the slower paced life of the good old days, when materialism and foreign capital were not so important. He recalls the 1860s and compares them to the hustle and bustle of the contemporary scene, the frenzied speculation, and the mercantile materialism. The plot is about a girl who marries for money and abandons her sweetheart, and the protagonist, Julio, who, impelled by fate and his own weakness, associates himself with shady stock speculations. The author in his preface admits that he admires "el robusto y valiente genio literario de Emile Zola," and Zum Felde labels it "novela de costumbres porteñas . . . dentro del un poco pesado objetivismo zoliano." [57] The novelist, however, seems more realistic than naturalistic in his often ironic documentation of the changes of his rustic village, his attacks on those Argentinians who aped foreign culture to the detriment of their own national spiritual and moral values, and his delineation of customs, gambling dens, the dissolute life, the power of money, and the get-rich-quick philosophy which ruled his society. The freshness of the novel and its picturesque qualities stem from its autobiographical form and the personal experiences of López, documental qualities which made the book successful.[58]

Miguel Cané (1851–1905), the son of the romantic novelist by the same name, was born in Montevideo where his parents had gone to escape from Rosas. He became a newspaperman, lawyer, politician, and diplomat, and as a member of the Generation of 1880, he wrote a great number of essays, memoirs, criticism, and travel literature. Most readers today remember him for one work, *Juvenilia* (1884), more autobiography than novel, which recalls his days at the Colegio Nacional of Buenos Aires—founded by Mitre—around 1870. Its series of memoirs, anecdotes, and stories of student life made the novel popular—"el éxito de fresca y ágil vitalidad . . . la han hecho una de las obras permanentes de nuestra literatura." [59] We learn about the food, the reading, the escapades, the director of studies, Amadeo Jacques, a student revolt, the author's expulsion and readmission, an epidemic, the founding of a newspaper, and a nostalgic return, years later, to the school.

Carlos María Ocantos (1860–1949), who at times exhibits naturalistic traits in his works, resembled more nearly Balzac and Galdós than he did Zola.[60] Ocantos, basing his novels on personal recall, attempted to write a comprehensive series about Argentina, even though he wrote mainly from Spain and Europe. Hardly the Argentine Galdós or Balzac, he presents in his twenty "novelas argentinas" the clash between aristocrats and immigrants and sketches types, atmosphere, and customs. At one time he was considered a "great" novelist, and he may have been the first true writer of realistic fiction, but time has not treated his profusion of titles kindly. The social analyses he attempted were unfortunately not matched by a corresponding artistic skill and novelistic technique. Yet his novels have many excellent qualities. He gives us a comprehensive and dramatic picture of Argentina—city and country—for which he conveys his warmth and love, with all the social classes, problems, conflicts, politics, parents, and children. *Entre las luces* (1892); *El candidato* (1893), a kind of sequel, about political corruption; *Tobi* (1896); *Promisión* (1897), about the adjustments and successes of Argentine immigrants and the disillusion of an idealistic sculptor; *Nebulosa* (1904), about unmarried women and their problems; *Victoria* (1922), whose protagonist is married to a madman and loved by two other married men, a problem she solves by moving to England; *El emboscado* (1928); and *Fray Judas* (1929) are representative novels, but his three best known ones are probably *León Zaldívar* (1888), *Quilito* (1891), and *Don Perfecto* (1902). *Leon Zaldívar*, the first of his *Novelas argentinas*, was originally called *León Saldívar*. When León's chosen love marries a thief, a French adventurer (her family's desire for a marriage of convenience matches León's), he consoles himself by marrying a poor orphan girl, Crucita. Love, for the superficial record, seems to triumph over materialism, but the motivations of most concerned are egotistical, a perfect reflection of Argentine society of his time. *Quilito* deals with the stock market crisis of 1890 and people caught by gambling fever. Quilito Vargas, the penniless protagonist, gambles with other people's money and then commits suicide. The author spares no one in his formidable flogging of reactionary elements, among which he includes a Jewish financier and a host of greedy Argentinians. Mr. Roberts, an industrious Englishman, voices the novelist's principal theme of a somewhat Victorian life and the value of virtue, hard work, and thrift as solutions to Argentina's problems. *Don Perfecto*'s protagonist, Juan de Dios, known as Perfecto to his friends, writes an autobiographical monologue about his unhappy childhood, the loss of his parents, his erring sister, and his jobs. In his own eyes, if not in those of his "friends" and the world at large, he is "perfect" because he neither smokes, nor drinks, nor has any other vices to speak of. In spite of Ocantos' obvious shortcomings, he has been called "a national novelist of notable merit and an important figure in the transition to the present century" [61]—an overly kind judgment about a novelist who primarily interests archeologists of fiction.

Cuban costumbristas continued to write novels and articles throughout the century, but few good realistic novels appeared. Ramón Meza (1861–1911), the most prolific novelist of his time, wrote a great number of novels such as *El duelo de mi vecino* (1886), *Flores y calabazas* (1886), *Carmela* (1877), and *Mi tío el empleado* (1887). The last named, his best work, is a howling, satirical, social commentary on life in the then Spanish colony, and the author joyfully views the various vices of Cuban classes and citizens, examining their relationships with the Spaniards or *gachupines*.

Nicolás Heredia (1852–1901), a Cuban born in Santo Domingo,

wrote literary articles under the pseudonym of César de Hinolia and political ones as Rodrigo Ruiz. He fought for Cuban independence and worked as a teacher, editor, and journalist. His *Un hombre de negocios* (1882), a costumbrista novel, lacks great importance, especially in comparison with his best novel, *Leonela*, written first in 1886 under the title of *Encarnadita* and published under its new one in 1893. In his introduction Heredia explains that the novel was based on a real event related to him by an old friend. An hacendado, Cosme Fernández Arencibia, shortly before the Revolution of 1868, is living in the town of Jarabacoa with his twin daughters, Leonela and Clara. Juan Valdespina, an engineer, involved in a mix-up of identities, seduces Clara, although he loves Leonela. When he refuses marriage, Clara commits suicide. The plot is trite, but some of the characters, as representatives of their class and occupation, are quite well done. Heredia indicates that sensualism may be one of the primary defects of Cuban society, as exemplified by the father's sexual relationship with a *guajiro*'s sweetheart. The novel, filled with costumbrista scenes,[62] contains much political and social commentary. The substitution, seduction, code of honor, and suicide are clearly romantic, but the total thrust of the novel would lead one to classify it under realism.

One of the outstanding novelists of the nineteenth century, the Uruguayan, Eduardo Acevedo Díaz (1851–1924), politician, revolutionary, journalist, and minister, whose identically named son achieved prize-winning fame as an Argentinian novelist, is considered by some to be a late romantic, by others to be a naturalist,[63] and by still another to be "the founder of the Uruguayan criollista novel." [64] Primarily a historical novelist (the line between romantic and realistic historical works is quite thin at times), he may have been the originator of that literary form in his country.[65] Francisco Espínola, in his prologue to the 1946 edition of *Ismael*, a novel by Acevedo Díaz, calls him "el iniciador y hasta hoy el insuperado novelista histórico de nuestro país." His concern for history was so basic that at times, says one critic, his apparently fictional endeavors appear to be not so much novels as "novelistic historical episodes united by a story line," [66] which is comparatively unimportant in the evaluation of his novels. Acevedo Díaz follows the pattern established by Vicente Fidel López in caring about the small and nameless protagonists of history, giving to major historical protagonists "el segundo plano, el de ambiente, el de fondo." [67] Although his characters are generic expressions of a determined historical period, they are also original personalities, each with unique traits. This combination of the universal and archetypal with the individual and exclusive is characteristic of much of Acevedo Díaz' fiction. In the introduction to his last novel, *Lanza y sable* (1914), he reaffirmed that in his judgment the novel was the best vehicle for an understanding of history because ". . . abre más campo a la observación atenta, a la investigación psicológica, al libre examen de los hombres descollantes y a la filosofía de los hechos."

Acevedo Díaz is also costumbrista and realistic in his descriptions of colonial Montevideo, the convents and friars, the estancias and rodeos, and the somewhat gruesome battle scenes, which he, as a soldier who had experienced army life, knew, as intimately, apparently, as he knew the life of the gaucho. His characters are attached to their local geography;[68] the author seeks causes and determining factors to explain the sacrifice and heroic deeds of fighters for the independence of his country but fills his novels with its nature and geography, its hills and rivers, its flora and fauna, a beautiful and natural setting from which its patriots launch their campaign for liberty and human dignity. Acevedo Díaz found great inspiration both in his country's traditions—which idealistically helped him to combat those negative political factors that held back progress—and in its natural beauties against and through which his humanity functioned. Acevedo Díaz knew women as well as men, and, as one of his admirers claims, "El mundo femenino bulle en la creación literaria de Acevedo Díaz en todas sus gamas de clase social y temperamental. Demuestra que si fue un gran conocedor de los hombres, igualmente lo fue de la mujer." [69] His novel, *Brenda* (1886), first appeared as a *folletín* in *La Nación* of Buenos Aires. Although it was an almost completely romantic tale of love and a tragic duel, it gave him a quick reputation among young writers. Alberto Zum Felde considers it to be an "ensayo juvenil" without any novelistic merit,[70] but Acevedo Díaz himself always maintained a special fondness for his first novel in spite of its lesser literary worth.[71]

Acevedo Díaz planned a cycle of novels about Uruguayan independence. His trilogy on the subject, *Ismael* (1888), first published in *La Tribuna Nacional*, *Nativa* (1890), and *Grito de gloria* (1893), starts its action in 1808, concentrates on the popular uprising of 1811 against the Spaniards in the first volume, and continues through the Brazilian invasion and the campaign of 1825 against Brazil in his next two novels. His plan was to present a gallery of types during the process of writing a kind of national prose epic.[72] He completed the cycle with *Lanza y sable*, which dealt with the civil wars in Uruguay. Of all these novels, *Ismael* is still probably his best. In it one finds descriptions of Montevideo, *tertulias*, the *cabildos*, *caudillos*, quarrels with the viceroy, and battles against the *godos*. Among the characters we find Fray Benito, pseudo patriot, General Artigas, the Vargas brothers, Lavalleja, and the fictional protagonist, Ismael Velarde, brave, taciturn, primitive, barbaric, rebellious, and sentimental gaucho. A vagabond, half *payador*, of unknown origin, he is more than life size. He is "el tupamaro clásico, el criollo puro, hijo del azar y de la libertad . . . y cuyo más gran placer es recorrer . . . las cuchillas del país . . . hundirse en los grandes montes impenetrables . . . siempre dispuesto a una pelea o a una fiesta . . . cantor por naturaleza, sobrio, sufrido y valiente." [73] Ismael joins the band of Venancio Benavides and Artigas while Almagro joins the Spaniards. Almagro accidently kills Felisa, Ismael's love, and he kills Almagro. Nature, customs, characters, and deeds are skillfully combined with authentic Indians, bandits, and soldiers, "arrancados a la realidad viva del medio, de una veracidad humana fiel a la observación y al documento, sin reflejo alguno foráneo." [74]

Nativa covers the years between 1821 and 1824 when Brazil and Uruguay were fighting, but the principal action occurs in 1824 during the Brazilian domination. Published first as a folletín in *La Opinión Pública* in 1889–90, it details the loves and adventures of Luis María Berón, an aristocrat turned lieutenant in the resistance forces of Uruguay against the Portuguese empire. Luciano Robledo, a patriotic criollo who even helps *gauchos malos*, leads an idyllic life on his ranch, in a typical *pago*, a rural district in the pampa, but the Uruguayan troops elsewhere suffer great hardships. Robledo has two daughters, Natalia and Dorila. The former and Berón are in love. Luis María had previously saved a lieutenant Souza of Lecor's army, part of whose troops attack the Robledo hacienda, and Souza spares his rescuer's life. Dorila drowns in the river, and the brave gaucho, Ismael Velarde, comes to the family's aid. Acevedo Díaz shows us an army united through its love of its native soil and stresses the feeling of solidarity among all the racial mixtures—a multi-racial native army which he views as the basis for a new integrated society.

In *Grito de gloria*, Lavalleja, a patriot, previously portrayed in the trilogy, raises troops and attacks the Brazilians. Ismael and Luis María join Lavalleja, as do Frutos Rivera and Manuel Oribe. Lecor, in command of Montevideo, seeks reinforcements. Various conspiracies occur. Souza dies in the fighting, and finally Luis María returns to the ranch where Natalia and her father are living, dies, and is buried next to Dorila. Zum Felde believes that the description of the battle of Sarandí, "la batalla gaucha por excelencia, es una de las páginas antológicas más culminantes de la literatura americana." [75]

Soledad (1894), a gaucho novel superior even to *Ismael*, is subtitled "Tradición de un pago." Pablo Luna, a simple man of nature, characterized as vague, mysterious, and desolate, sees his mother, and old witch, eaten by dogs. When the father of his one true love, Soledad, rejects and humiliates him, he burns the ranch down. His vengeance taken, he saves Soledad, and even though he is still a *gaucho matrero* and an outcast, he will be lonely no more. Pablo is a typical gaucho in his struggles against nature in which he shows a primitive love and instinct for freedom and the land. Aside from the psychological portrayal of his alienation from the world, highly poetic prose combined with gruesome scenes (in one he kisses his mother's dog-mutilated corpse) reflect an unusual combination and control of the pathetic and aesthetic.

Acevedo Díaz' other fiction includes *Minés* (1907) and the previously mentioned *Lanza y sable*, about Paula, the daughter of an estanciero during the civil war, Fructuoso Rivera, a caudillo, his daily living and his struggles with Oribe, and the love which a member of Oribe's forces, Abel, bears for Paula; also a short narrative, *El combate de la tapera* (1931), about the brave women who fight alongside their soldier men in the Uruguayan-Brazilian conflict.

A number of Ecuadorian novelists produced realistic fiction, but by far the best work of the first three decades of the twentieth century in Ecuador, and surely the best Ecuadorian novel since *Cumandá*, was *A la costa* (1904) by Luis A. Martínez (1869–1909).

This almost clinical study of the history of a single family contains some naturalistic elements, but Martínez refused to identify himself with any school: "No pertenezco a ninguna escuela, soy profundamente realista, y pinto la naturaleza como es y no como enseñan los convencionalismos." [76] The liberal revolution of 1895 which gave Ecuador one of its national heroes, Eloy Alfaro, marked the beginning of the first effort to rid the country of its feudal system. Martínez, a liberal, was highly in favor of such a reform. In a prologue to *A la costa*, Manuel J. Calle (1866–1918), himself the author of a realistic novel, *Carlota* (1900), and an ironic commentator in the newspapers *El Pensamiento*, *La Libertad*, and *El Diario de Avisos*, wrote that in backward and fanatical Ecuador (he ardently supported the liberal revolution of Eloy Alfaro) "hay uno que se atreve a hablar de nuestra sociedad, no pintando amores románticos sino vicios sociales en que el fraile y la beata andan siempre de por medio." [77]

Martínez, undoubtedly influenced by Europe's social novels in method, and the first to interest himself in sociological problems on any large scale, denounces the economic, social, and political conditions existing in Ecuador's coast and highlands and analyzes the sorrows of a sick society that includes in its structure corruption and injustices of all kinds. The novel, whose title comes from an immigration from the highlands to the coast in a futile search for a better life, talks of the evils of the Church, the anguish of the masses, the role of students in a revolution, and describes nature as a devouring force, an early fictional appearance of this theme. Salvador Ramírez' efforts to secure a government position, his long waits in the corridors of the government palace, his pleas to assistant secretaries, porters, and underlings, met with gross insults, are but one side of the coin. Quito is a city of convents where everyone belongs to a religious order or congregation under penalty of being labeled a heretic, losing his job, or being thrown into jail. While the priests live in luxury and corruption, poor workers starve and beggars fill the capital's streets. Salvador's attempt to escape by his trip to the coast, where he lives, struggles, and dies shows the novelist to be "un precursor de los novelistas freudianos," and the first revolutionary of the Ecuadorian realists.[78] Unquestionably, *A la costa*, not unmarked by naturalism, represents a great step forward in developing a novel which makes more than a superficial study of the ills of this nation.

Alfredo Baquerizo Moreno (1859–1951), diplomat, lawyer, and president, in addition to a volume of poetry, a book of essays, and a series of critical studies on Unamuno, Gabriela Mistral, and Montalvo, wrote six novels. The only one which need be mentioned here is *Tierra adentro* (1898), an objective study of the Montuvian. He deals at some length, considering the episodic character of the work, with the military caciques and the crooked elections, but his contribution is fragmentary in nature.

Roberto Andrade (1851–1938), better known as an historian and as a biographer of Juan Montalvo, is the author of two novels in which one critic finds qualities of "fecundidad, gracejo, espontaneidad, talento, estilo nervioso, deleitable." [79] Andrade, in *Pacho Villamar* (1900), deals with the moral hypocrisy of clerical education and its effects, especially on women. He gives fine pictures of Quito in the second half of the nineteenth century when the Jesuit tyranny was politically over but morally all-powerful, and of the connections between corrupt politicians and the even more corrupt clergy. The plot, dealing with a son abandoned by his mother to the Jesuits, shows how Jesuit education tries to subordinate all thought to the Jesuit Order. This concern with the clerical tyranny in Ecuadorian society marks Andrade, also, as a precursor of the contemporary social novelists. A mixture of romantic and naturalistic elements, the novel is "intensa por el realismo humano con que aparecen los personajes e intensa por la realidad del medio y del tiempo en que el autor supo interpretarlos." [80] His other novel, *La mujer y la guerra* (1926), deals with a small American republic whose women become legislators in order to prevent war. In addition to his bitter denunciation of war, Andrade anticipates the later Ecuadorian novelists in his plea for more culture, education, and a larger political role for women.

Lesser contributions include the works of José Antonio Campos (1868–1939), Eduardo Mera (1872–1926), and José Rafael Bustamante (1881–1961). Campos, often signing himself Jack the Ripper, satirizes national pastimes and gives us a series of sketches and short stories of Montuvian politics, customs, and humor and of a poor people victimized by its society. José Rafael Bustamante's *Para matar el gusano*, published in the review *Letras* in 1915 but not in book form until 1935, shows social conflict, symbolized by poor but honest Robert on the one hand and rich and arrogant George on the other. The novel evokes in chromatic fashion the country-side and telluric sense of the sierra, perhaps more important than his presentation of the *chulla* as the representative of the Ecuadorian lower classes.

NATURALISM

Although the Spanish realists Galdós and Pereda had an influence on the Spanish American novel, it was of fairly short duration. But even before their influence took full effect, French naturalism, Emile Zola's new realism, took hold in Spanish America. A kind of ultimate revolt against rampant romanticism, naturalism has in its ancestry the positivism of Auguste Comte, which excludes everything but natural phenomena or properties of knowable things, their relationships, and what Comte labeled the third of man's stages (the first two are theological and metaphysical), the positive or materialistic one. The nineteenth century, which gave birth to naturalism, involved struggles between science and religion, the philosophical and theological agonies and leap of faith of Kierkegaard, and the materialistic and fatalistic concept of history of Hippolyte Taine which held that history has to be what it is because of uncontrollable factors. Aside from his deterministic approach, he felt that literary works could be explained by the factors of race, environment, and period, a contention previously postulated by Madame de Staël and others but never as a rigid system. Claude Bernard's explorations of experimental medicine and physiology and Darwin's efforts to establish the scientific principles of evolution formed part of the background which led Emile Zola to think that other areas of human existence might also be treated in a scientific, experimental manner. Bernard's *L'Introduction a La Médécine Expérimentale* (1865) gave Zola his scientific method and the title, *Le Roman Expérimental*, for his literary experiments. He also adopted the physiological explanation for emotions proposed by Charles Le Tourneau in his *Physiologie des passions* (1868). Zola thus attempted to apply laboratory techniques to the novel, examining human beings as though he had them under a microscope, and dealing with factors such as heredity. He found that it was easier to handle the seamier side of life in showing the deterministic fatalism so inherently a part of these novels and much easier to pin down through observation and experience. Literary determinism, without rejecting the tenet that the causes behind each event limit man's choices and that his decision will be decided by natural or social forces, emphasizes more the instinctual drives or irrational feelings involved. Zola portrays social vices and tragic individuals, victims of the environment or of hereditary factors over which they have no control. Implicit in these novels is the assumption that a reform of society might lead to an alleviation of some of these problems, since man cannot save himself through his own efforts. The favorite material of these novels involved sexuality (quite prevalent in Spanish American naturalism), combined with primitive, brutal, or spineless characters who become alcoholics or victims of other social ills. Whereas realism treated all life, including pleasant and beautiful elements, the pseudo-scientific naturalism concentrated on crime and negative human histories. It must be understood, however, that nothing in the naturalistic models imposes the raw or sordid or the *feísmo* as an indispensable component.[81]

Naturalism caused controversy in Spanish America. The "obscenity," while proving successful with the public, was frowned on by critics who could not accept Zola's complete exclusion of the subjective element from literature. Spanish American novelists agreed with Zola that the novel is life or nature seen through a temperament and accepted Taine's theory of the effect of the milieu upon nations and individuals; impressed by the idea of agents which determine man's destiny, they sought to document a number of details and supposed scientific facts. Although they followed the techniques and form of Zola they could not countenance, because of their Catholic heritage, a complete determinism. Most Spanish Americans lacked the necessary objectivity and became impassioned participants in their laboratory experiments.

Naturalism, as a pure form, lasted but briefly in Spanish America, but it triggered a whole host of novels concerned with life among the poor and unfortunate, and naturalistic elements are easily found in the novels of Eduardo Barrios, Manuel Gálvez, or

Carlos Loveira, among many other twentieth-century novelists. Costumbrismo and romanticism continued to a degree, and a movement contemporary to naturalism, modernism, soon changed the direction of the developing novel; but naturalistic influence was generative in promoting autochthonous elements and furthering the development of criollismo. Arturo Uslar Pietri and Julián Padrón contend that "la literatura narrativa venezolana de valor cierto, nace al influjo del naturalismo francés y en especial de la lectura de Zola. El caso, con ligeras variantes, es análogo en todos los otros países americanos. Es sólo después de sentida la influencia del naturalismo que podemos hablar de una literatura criolla, de una expresión literaria propia de nuestra América." [82]

Both realists and naturalists belonged to the upper classes, but the latter introduced the lower classes as primary rather than secondary material. In studying people they came closer to reproducing the regional and national ambiance. To a greater degree than the realists, naturalists also involved themselves in the social remedies for the brutality they described. In conclusion, then, the objectivity and impassiveness, however imperfect, of the naturalists combined with the artistic preoccupations of form, expression, and reverent love of words of the modernists to become the dominant novelistic form for several decades. For want of a better label we shall call this phase criollismo and discuss it in the next chapter.

Naturalistic traits appeared in La gran aldea, but Juan Antonio Argerich (1862–1924) in Inocentes o culpables, a study of Italian immigrants, intensively applied the ideas of Zola. Other Argentine naturalistic novels are Ley social (1855) by Martín García Merou (1862–1905), Irresponsable (1889) by Manuel Podestá (1853–1920), and Libro extraño (1894) by Francisco A. Sicardi (1856–1927). Sicardi completed its fifth volume in 1902, and its characters include mystics, madmen, and murderers exposed to the author's strong sense of justice.

The outstanding Spanish American writer of naturalism, and the most important novelist to appear on the scene in Argentina after José Mármol, was Eugenio Cambaceres (1843–1888),[83] a man of wealth and of a distinguished family who, in spite of a somewhat aimless life of travel in the tradition of other members of the Generation of 1880, fought, as a member of Congress, for the separation of Church and State. He has been called conservative, liberal, moralist, aggressive, atheist, pessimistic, optimistic, intelligent, candid, daring, cynical, and bitter. Some critics, seeing sentiment and subjectivity in his autobiographical works, attribute it to the fact that he had a Spanish mother and a French father. They view him as a romantic or a modernist, claiming that subjective notes were forbidden to a true naturalist.[84] Others, less kindly, called him "cortesano de las pasiones bajas" and "manufacturer of aphrodisiac works."[85]

Originally Cambaceres intended the title *Potpourri* of his first novel as a general title. He then planned, under the heading of *Silbidos de un vago*, a tetralogy or four-part novel. Both *Potpourri* (1882) and his next novel *Música sentimental* (1884) carry "Silbidos de un vago" as a subtitle. His first novel is a first person monologue, full of digressions, but its diffuse plot contained a cynical and corrosive attack on the young ladies of high society, their education, their beliefs, their immorality, and the generally corrupt political Argentine scene. Sensing that his work might be in for adverse criticism, in the prologue he points out that he is writing about "fantastic things," but the book caused such a scandal, succeeding through its very truculence, that for a year he hesitated to admit that he was the author. *Música sentimental's* protagonist, Pablo, accompanies his friend, Cambaceres, to Paris. There Pablo gambles, has a duel, is wounded, and, nursed by Loulou, eventually dies. The author has warned Loulou of her lover's syphilitic condition, graphically described. After Pablo's death she again becomes a whore but visits his grave. The sordid love, sentimental prostitute, denunciation of Parisian life, direct description of the syphilitic hero, and somewhat detailed sexual experience and its aftermath, something much employed also by the angry young Argentine novelists of the 1950s, evoked the inevitable epithets, and his novel was called an "excusado cubierto de alfombras persas."[86]

Cambaceres' masterpiece, *Sin rumbo* (1885),[87] is a brutal, repugnant, pornographic, yet sentimental and religiously symbolic novel. Andrés, a man without faith, after raping Donata, a peasant girl who later dies, and becoming involved in a sordid scandal in Buenos Aires with a married actress, comes to consider Donata's daughter the raison d'être of his life. His bored, abulic condition changes, but when she dies at the age of two, he commits suicide by cutting open his abdomen in the sign of a cross, crucifying himself in a rejection of life and God and because of his own tragic weakness. Cambaceres describes the rich and the poor, the old and the new, the country and the city. His country setting is somewhat incidental to the novel, but he is credited with being the first Argentine writer to present "una visión realista de la vida del campo en su novela *Sin rumbo*," [88] and in his presentation of figures, scenes, and countryside, "iba a ser, pues, el primero en brindarnos una interpretación auténtica del campo porteño." [89] Enrique Anderson Imbert praises certain aspects of the novel highly and believes that Andrés "is one of the best delineated psychological studies in the Argentine novel." [90]

Cambaceres' final novel, *En la sangre* (1887), discourses on socialism, the effects of heredity, and the feelings of certain immigrants. Don Esteban's son, Genaro, a weakly offspring who takes after his idle Neopolitan father, is frustrated, timid and insecure. He wants to be accepted by Argentine society and forget his immigrant past. He seduces a rich girl, marries her, steals her money, mistreats her and his mother, and reveals, at the end, that he cannot escape his heredity.

The Argentine novelist's unpopularity, if that is what it was, stemmed, not from a lack of ability but from his overly honest and perhaps foolishly direct description of what he knew to be true. In the prologue to the third edition of *Potpourri* he finally defended himself against unwarranted attacks. His novels show the life and customs of his day, and what he lacks in artistry he makes up in force and daring. Martín García Merou, himself a novelist and Miguel Cané's secretary, said that Cambaceres was a true observer of reality and could not afford compassion. "Se dirá que es cruel algunas veces; que ante los ojos de su imaginación todos los objetos se deforman y afean. No lo culpemos demasiado; no olvidemos que todo verdadero observador carece de piedad." [91] To a modern reader his lack of compassion is not so apparent. He dared paint man and his environment accurately, and if to his contemporaries his view seemed implacable, their own false religion, stupidity, and hypocrisy was the raw material from which he worked. The members of the Generation of 1950 have revised upward critical opinion about Cambaceres' work, but not all critics in the twentieth century are ecstatic about him, even placed in his time. One such harsh judgment is that "el éxito de estas obras fue debido más que a su valor literario al escándalo que produjeron a causa de sus cuadros de subido color y las alusiones por demás claras y expresivas a la vida porteña de entonces," [92] certainly a minority opinion today. A more positive view, and probably closer to the truth, holds that one finds in Cambaceres ". . . desgarramiento sombrío . . . libertad en el idioma . . . desenfado . . . vigor en el retrato de sus personajes, en las descripciones." [93]

Another Argentine novel which made history in its treatment of the Stock Market crash of 1890, *La Bolsa* (1891), was written by José María Miró (1867–1896), better known by his pseudonym, Julián Martel. Miró, a business reporter for *La Nación* of Buenos Aires, which first published his novel as a folletín, labels his work "estudio social." Ostensibly the study of the rise and fall of a lawyer, it depicts an Argentina influenced by French culture, pursuing luxury and easy wealth, and suffering from the vices which this quest for material gain brings to society. More specifically it attacks the government and the economic fever and gambling madness which overrode moral values and love of family. Miró, unfortunately, a virulent anti-Semite, allows his feelings to overcome him in portraying the Jewish characters, Jacob Leony and Mr. Mackser. The novel treats sympathetically Dr. Glow, an ethical lawyer, perfect parent and husband, an angel among thieves, who is the victim of dishonest rascals. Ruined, he gambles to win back his losses, goes mad, and at the end views the Stock Exchange as a monster which will destroy the country. Myron I. Lichtblau believes that what is "outstanding in *La Bolsa* is the power of the written word to bring out and sustain the turbulent, nervous atmosphere of Buenos Aires . . ." [94] Ricardo Rojas, paladin of Argentine letters, states: "El autor de *La Bolsa* debe ser considerado como uno de los principales fundadores de la novela argentina . . . merece de la posteridad, si no la estatua, al menos una lectura más asidua . . ." [95]

Mercedes Cabello de Carbonera (1845–1909), a member of Juana María Gorriti's Peruvian tertulia and the most naturalistic Peruvian novelist, began as a sentimental, romantic writer. Perhaps the first real novel in Peru after those of Fernando Casós was the first edition of her *Sacrificio y recompensa* (1886). Apparently, the Guerra del Pacífico had severely damaged the creative impulses among Peruvian intellectuals. In the prologue to her novel the

Peruvian lady alludes to another novel, *Los amores de Hortensia* (1888), filled with sentimental protagonists, as her first work. Her third novel, *Eleodora* (1887), was also openly romantic. *Blanca Sol* (1889),[96] her first naturalistic novel, is also probably the beginning of Peruvian naturalism. Like her Spanish counterpart, Emilia Pardo Bazán, Mercedes Cabello also has the honor of having introduced Russian literature into her country. Although she published studies on Zola, in her novels she sometimes seems to struggle against the cold, scientific, and mechanical observation of the social and moral entity and the adaptation of the experimental novel and scientific theory to her positivistic philosophy.[97] Her doctor husband may have helped her with some of the precisely described anatomical matters in her novels.

Blanca Sol, a social novel which relies heavily on scientific theories, depicts an amoral and aristocratic family. The heroine, a Peruvian Madame Bovary, like most of Cabello's characters, comes to an immoral end. The protagonist was supposedly based on a real person, something which the author, in the prologue to the second edition of the novel, took great pains to disavow. The novel studies the education of Peruvian women, gambling, the curse of Peruvian high society, other vices which she also scathingly denounces, and the general social and moral degradation of that segment of Peruvian life. *Las consecuencias* (1890), set in a rural environment, again strongly attacks gambling and seems to be a naturalistic sequel to *Eleodora*. A high society woman rejects a marriage proposal in order to marry a gambler who destroys her fortune. *El conspirador* (1892), subtitled "Autobiografía de un hombre público," is about a young activist's experience with dirty politics. Jorge Bello, an orphan boy, a failure at seduction, joins some revolutionaries. Becoming disillusioned, he takes power from an old revolutionary leader, becomes a dishonest minister, and, defeated and deserted by his friends, is jailed. From his cell he writes the memoirs of his life. In one of the grotesque scenes of the novel, a woman who had become a prostitute to support him, lectures to him on her deathbed about political idealism. *El conspirador*, a forceful picture of the Peruvian political scene, incorporates biographical material of real people of the day (many were convinced that the novel was a political caricature of Nicolás de Piérola). The novelist's subjective denunciations seem to invalidate the scientific objectivism she claimed proved her social theories. Luis Alberto Sánchez sees in her style "algo de picante y cáustico. Sin alzar el tono, describía directamente y pintaba hechos cuya veracidad corría de boca en boca. Extraía sus temas de la realidad misma, sin perdonar aristocracias ni abolengos, sino más bien cebándose en ellos." [98] Her protests to the powerful were answered unworthily by scandalous personal attacks. Those who made her life miserable (one self-proclaimed wit named her Mierdeces Caballo de la Cabronera) are largely forgotten, but her place in the history of Peruvian fiction is assured.

Although the Puerto Rican Matías González García (1866–1936) wrote two novels, *Cosas* (1893) and *Ernesto* (1894), Manuel Zeno Gandía (1855–1930) is the progenitor of Puerto Rican fiction. After two unsuccesful novelettes, *Rosa de mármol* (1889) and *Piccola* (1890), he published *La charca* (1894), visualized as part of a series under the revealing title of *Crónicas de un mundo enfermo*. The characters of *La charca* reappear in his other novels, *Garduña* (1896)—apparently written but not published before *La charca*— *El negocio* (1922), and *Los redentores*, published in book form posthumously. Zeno Gandía, a physician, includes in his novels not only statements about medicine, but also orations on religion and economics. One receives an exact impression of the history of the times and all aspects of colonial life. Possessor of a social conscience, he hoped to dignify man through his narration of human and social conflicts, but his entirely naturalistic and scatological material about the effects of alcohol, the degenerative effects of mestizaje, the effects of heredity, and a host of degenerate characters, told in a language filled with expressions such as "putrid intestines" and "grams of vomit," remove the focus from his study of vice, hunger, and the human and social conflicts of his country. For the most part his characters lack life, becoming either villains (Deblas and Andújar), victims (Leandra and Silvina), or spectators (Juan del Salto and Father Esteban).[99]

La charca has a somewhat episodic and confused plot about promiscuous relationships, principally of Leandra and her daughter, Silvina. It also treats of a host of other characters in episodes of drunken revelry and murder. Juan del Salto, an abulic and idealistic theoretician, is a failure.[100] Most of the other characters end as victims of the unjust socioeconomic system in which, says Zeno Gandía, one may be either an idealist or an opportunist and oppressor. The novel is interesting for its use of a simple kind of flashback and interior monologue, along with time jumps (he may have been the first Spanish American novelist to use these techniques); but his oratorical prose, fondness for gerunds, constant use of the same figures of speech, overly metaphorical and poetic descriptions of nature, and a superabundance of types and moral judgments, all of them obviously the sincere but prejudiced view of the author, detract from the general worth.

The title of the second novel is based on a passage from Rabelais: "... a saber garduñas son unas bestias feroces, ... en *Gargantua y Pantagruel*, con tales uñas que nada que aprisionen sus garras puede escapar." [101] The novel, which takes place on mythical Paradise Island, shows us the useless fight of the peasants against the horrors of *latifundio* and *cañaveral*. The author condemns the avarice and immorality of a lawyer, Garduña, who makes himself indispensable by muddying the waters in cases where he is a participant, using his position to deprive Casilda, illegitimate daughter of a rich landowner, of her rightful inheritance. *El negocio*, a plea for freedom for Puerto Rico, analyzes the commerical life of his country, which he finds extremely dishonest, and reveals Spanish-criollo confrontations. *Los redentores* attacks the colonial administration of the United States. Cesáreo Rosa-Nieves patriotically praises these works whose "virtudes artísticas son tantas en las cuatro obras, que los argumentos nos agarran en suspenso y nos deleitan por veredas de buena lectura." [102]

Carlos Reyles, in his youthful *Por la vida*, may have rung the death knell for Uruguayan romanticism, but the originator of Uruguayan naturalism and an ardent disciple of Zola, Mateo Magariños Solsona (1867–1925), the son of Magariños Cervantes, created a sensation with his *Las hermanas Flammari* (1893). Less successful was *Valmar* (1896), also in the naturalistic vein. Probably his best novel, which has nothing to do with naturalism, is *Pasar* (1920),[103] a novel about rural and industrial problems and worker strikes. Vicente Salaverri finds him to be only "un discípulo discreto [of Zola] a quien no sedujo tanto lo crudo o pornográfico del pro-

cedimiento como el 'tipo compacto y formidable de novela' creado
por el maestro de Medan." [104]

Javier de Viana (1865–1926), basically a short story writer, wrote
one fairly well-known novel, *Gaucha* (1899). Among his short story
collections and novelettes in the naturalistic mode are *Campo*
(1896), whose contents Roxlo describes as costumbrista and political,[105] and *Gurí y otras novelas* (1901), about impotence, superstition, and the psychology of the gaucho. His stories abound in passion, violence, brutality, and sex but also give good insight into the
regional life of his country characters. Viana was especially interested in scientific method and psychiatry, which he tried to apply
in his brutal and pessimistic pictures of the rural proletariat. His
naturalism is also implicit in the inevitability of the fatal end for
his protagonists. As the first to pursue energetically the naturalistic tone in Uruguay, Viana had more followers than most fiction
writers: "Tuvo innumerables imitadores, al punto que puede
asegurarse que pocos han sido los escritores que no cayeron bajo
su influencia." [106]

There is nothing epic or heroic about Viana's gauchos. He describes them as miserable beings, victims of sexual promiscuity, idleness, brutality, and alcoholism. Ironically, he himself became an
alcoholic. He had been a medical student, sheepherder, cattleman,
contrabandist, revolutionary, and congressman, but he especially
considered himself to be a newspaperman, proud of the fact that
"nunca estuvo mi pluma al servicio de los prepotentes y sí al de los
oprimidos y desvalidos." [107] Most of his own life had been a harsh
struggle for survival, and some of the incidents he relates in his
stories, labeled *cuentos camperos, criollos,* or *costumbres del
campo,* reveal his own experiences. His reproduction in natural
dialogue of the simplistic desires of country folk shows his direct
knowledge of the environment; but it is difficult to accept at face
value the complete bigotry, hypocrisy, immorality, and crime he
sees there or his imposition of psychological analysis and "scientific
reasoning" on the novelistic structure.

In the prologue to *Gaucha,* Viana says he intended only a "humilde pintura de mi tierra, vista con cariño, sentida con pasión y
expresada con sinceridad," but it is nonetheless a brutal portrayal
of murder, rape, theft, and arson. Alberto Zum Felde, who knows

more about Uruguayan literature than most other literary historians, feels that in spite of the somber portraits of vice, ignorance, ugliness, and misery, Viana was "el pintor por excelencia de nuestra vida criolla; así como, por su procedimiento analítico y la crudeza moral de su pintura, ha de tenérsele como el primer representante del naturalismo zoliano en el Uruguay." [108] Around 1910, with the publication of *Macachines*, Viana began to produce criollo short stories, abandoning his outright naturalism. Other collections include *Leña seca* (1911), *Yuyos* (1912), *Abrojos* (1919), and *Biblia Gaucha* (1925). He was important, not only for his naturalism, but also as the principal link between the realism of the nineteenth century and "la nueva narrativa de tema criollo que surge hacia 1920 para dominar la literatura uruguaya hasta fines de la Segunda Guerra Mundial." [109]

In Mexico, *Perico* (1886) of Arcadio Zentella is often cited as that country's first naturalistic novel, but the outstanding naturalist of the day and one of the most important in Spanish America was Federico Gamboa (1864–1939), diplomat, lawyer, journalist, literary critic, and director of the Mexican Academy. He accepted, in theory, materialistic and deterministic philosophy, believing in the limitation of human moral responsibility in the grip of external forces. Zola and the Goncourt brothers influenced him, and his themes seem naturalistic enough (extreme alcoholism, prostitution, and the like); but he never followed their procedures faithfully. A romantic by nature, Gamboa found it difficult to be completely scientific and objective in spite of his avowed purpose of depicting "lo vivido, lo visto, lo que codeamos, lo que nos es familiar" [110] and managed to avoid detailed description or analysis. In spite of these inconsistencies, at least one critic of the Mexican scene believes that Gamboa "fue sin embargo el émulo más fervoroso y leal que a Zola le nació en el mundo hispanoamericano y en España." [111] Gamboa's works include a volume of short stories, *Del natural* (1889), and six novels, *Apariencias* (1892), *Suprema ley* (1896), *Metamorfosis* (1899), *Santa* (1903), *Reconquista* (1908), and *La llaga* (1910).

Apariencias discusses adultery in a small Mexican village and a husband's somewhat peculiar but effective vengeance. *Suprema ley*, violently naturalistic, concerns the morbid passion of a poverty stricken criminal judge's clerk, Julio Ortegal, for Clotilde Granada, a beauty accused of having killed her lover. Forgetting his wife and six children, Julio finally manages to make her his mistress but soon dies of tuberculosis. Clotilde, abandoning her perverse ways, takes up religion. The novelist realistically reproduces the strains involved in being a husband and father and the sexual passion to which we all may succumb. *Metamorfosis*, set in a country atmosphere, is about a school run by French nuns. Sor Noeline, one of the teaching nuns, is kidnapped by Rafael Bello (the father of one of her students), who has fallen in love with her. Sor Noeline recalls her love for a cousin, Gastón, who had abandoned her and caused her to seek shelter in the convent. Succumbing again to a biological urge, she is metamorphosized and agrees to marry her kidnapper.

Gamboa's masterpiece, *Santa*, was in its day one of the all-time best sellers among Spanish American novels. Gamboa discusses everything from bad women to bullfighters in his analysis of life in brothels and bordellos. Santa, an innocent country girl, is seduced and abandoned. She becomes a high-priced prostitute and subsequently is beset by personal tragedy—her family rejects her and her mother dies. For a time she takes up with a bullfighter, El Jarameño, but she gradually disintegrates and descends into the lowest levels, the victim of an incurable cancer. Hipólito, an ugly blind piano player who tells her of his own life in an orphanage, falls in love with her, pays for an operation to try to cure her, and mourns her when she dies, finally redeemed by his true love. In spite of some bestial and lascivious scenes, the novel is basically moral and is filled with religious references to the Virgin, churches, the Host, death, resurrection, and sin.

Although *Santa* and *Suprema ley* were somewhat autobiographical, his next novel, *Reconquista*, appears to be "little more than a novelized account of the great event which changed Gamboa's entire life, his reconversion to religious faith." [112] Salvador Arteaga, an agnostic and widowed painter, loses his teaching position, his two daughters, and his professional drive. Sick and lonely, he gradually returns to religion, marries the girl he had once seduced, and hopes for the future. His spiritual rehabilitation leads to artistic success, for he can discover the soul of Mexico and channel his own creativity, now that he has accepted Christ.

Gamboa's last novel, *La llaga*, is both the story of men in the San Juan de Ulúa prison and a general treatise on Mexican problems. Eulalio Viezca, imprisoned army officer who had strangled his wife, recalls his drunken father, his education, and his love affairs. Suffering both physically and psychologically from prison torture and his rejection by society, he tries to rediscover human dignity when he is released after eleven years in prison. Unable to find sexual relief because of the constantly intervening shadow of his dead wife, he finally meets Nieves, through whose love he may discover a key to regeneration. Gamboa relieves his strictures on the arrest of political prisoners, prison tortures, and the lack of hygiene with stories of various prisoners, among them Don Mariniano, the old philosopher who talks of past days, and special touches such as the birth of a litter of rats.

Mariano Azuela judges Gamboa somewhat harshly; he believes that *Suprema ley* and *Santa* are his best works and that *"Reconquista* marca su declinación como novelista y lo demás es literatura pura y sin vitalidad." [113] But Gamboa, like his Uruguayan counterpart, Javier de Viana, probably marks the transition from nineteenth-century naturalism to twentieth-century criollism, as the first modern Mexican novelist. He had a strong sense of compassion for the unfortunate, but his social criticism was circumscribed by his emotional and intellectual interest and his sentimental view of "amor en todas sus formas de sacrificio apasionado lo que sostiene el tinglado de la acción de todas las novelas . . ." [114] His works, contradictory at times and filled with didactic moralizing, can be spontaneous and colorful in their presentation of human scenes, especially in *Santa*, where authentic human needs, desires, and fears reveal the best and worst of humanity.

Minor figures of Mexican naturalism include Salvador Quevedo y Zubieta, whose *La camada* (1912) is a clear protest against injustice. In a variety of short stories and dramatic and historical works he covered a range of topics which include murder, alcoholism, as well as a group of neurotic and sickly characters. Carlos González Peña (1885–1955), better known as a literary historian and critic, wrote a variety of novels. His *La fuga de la Quimera* (1915) is definitely modernist in its aesthetic pretensions. Aside from this subjective exercise, González Peña also wrote a naturalistic novel, *La chiquilla* (1906), about a tenement house family, a fanatical mother, an irresponsible son, a sacrificing sister, and "la chiquilla," the youngest daughter. A victim of permissiveness and bad example, the girl is raped on the anniversary of Mexican Independence, a rather artificial and clumsy contrivance.

The Chilean Vicente Grez (1847–1909) wrote *El ideal de una esposa* (1887), about a jealous married woman, but his naturalism was less effective than that of Baldomero Lillo (1867–1923), a short story writer who resembles Zola in his description of the sufferings of workers in the coal mines, perhaps reflecting his own unhappy and illness-plagued life. Lillo had worked in the mines and knew the life of coal miners in Lota firsthand. His first collection, *Sub Terra* (1904), has been labeled a Chilean *Germinal*.[115] In part Lillo considered the miners victims of foreign capitalism, and he reiterated his theme in an unfinished novel, *La huelga*. His second collection, *Sub-Sole* (1907), is more clearly a combination of naturalistic, modernist, and criollo elements as well as a more positive expression of his faith in mankind. He was stimulated by the encouragement of Federico Gana and Augusto Thomson, whose literary tertulia he frequented,[116] and as a precursor of the criollista movement, he apparently had a great influence on following novelists.[117]

The Cuban teacher, newspaperman, and doctor, Miguel de Carrión (1875–1929), wrote largely about women, from society ladies to prostitutes. His pretense at psychoanalytic interpretation overshadows his costumbrismo, but his view of the political corruption, the wealthy sugar barons, the professional politicians, the Francophiles, the prigs, and the snobs, adds another dimension to his stories of sexual frustration. Carrión's first novel, *El milagro*, was written in 1896 but not published until 1903. Enrique José Varona was surprised by "la sutileza de su análisis psicológico unido a una extraordinaria firmeza de estilo." [118] The novel analyses a false religious vocation and morality and finds true love and tolerance more important than theology. Juan J. Remos believes the novel to be, technically, a copy of Blasco Ibáñez and "de Nietzsche en el pensamiento." [119] His last novel, *La esfinge*, never completely finished, was finally published in 1961. It tells about the moral scruples of a young married woman, scorned by her husband and surrounded by hypocrisy. Amada Jacob, finally having lost her virginity, dedicates herself to curing the sick and needy in a poor district.

In between these two novels Carrión produced his two major pieces of fiction, in a sense a two part novel, *Las honradas* (1918) and *Las impuras* (1919). In the first, a supposedly virtuous lady, Victoria, a Cuban Madame Bovary who had fallen victim to romantic novels and her own overactive imagination as well as to her Catholic education, is filled with the artificial values of her class. Married without love, she is finally brought to sexual satisfaction by a lover, with varying consequences. Finally realizing her lover's hypocrisy, she repentantly returns to her husband. Through her suffering and her daughter Adriana, she maintains some hope for the future. Remos, apparently overly impressed by Carrión's description of female genitalia, finds the novel to be "un monumento al naturalismo." [120] *Las impuras*, whose somewhat sarcastic title implies that the protagonist, a prostitute, is more pure than the "honorable" lady of the previous novel, contrasts the openness of Teresa about love with the frustrations of Victoria. More sentimental than *Las honradas*, it still supports modern woman in search of freedom. Women should have freedom of choice, if they are willing to pay the price. Carrión pretends to be scientific, but he does not really demonstrate that his "impuras" are any more honorable than his "honradas." His heroines indulge in a series of feminine monologues in an effort to explain their soul. All of his protagonists seem caught up in the web of destiny in a mechanistic universe which will not allow them free will. Victoria Fernández is trapped by ignorance and her childhood upbringing, Teresa Trebijo by a world she never made. Yet Carrión's scientific contribution to the novels consists largely of a superficial remedy, sexual education, and he generously manages to pardon most of his sinners.

A number of novelists comprise the "primera generación republicana" (1910–1939), among them, Emilio Bacardí Moreau (1844–1922), Raimundo Cabrera (1852–1923), a man of romantic dreams and a half-dozen novels largely on Cuba's struggle for independence, Alvaro de la Iglesia (1859–1940), and Luis Rodríguez Embil (1879–1954), most of them devoted to the historical novel. The social novel of this generation will be discussed in a later chapter. By far the outstanding figure of the day, Jesús Castellanos (1879–1912), viewed by some as a modernist,[121] by others as a naturalist,[122] and by still others as a criollista, belonged to the Sociedad de

Conferencias and the Cuba Contemporánea group, becoming president of the Academy of Arts and Letters of Havana of which he was a founding member. He wrote two short novels, *La conjura* (1908) and *La manigua sentimental* (1910), a number of short stories, and left an unfinished novel, *Los Argonautas*. In *La conjura*, through Augusto Román, we see his society's intimate thoughts and reactions. Román, an idealistic doctor, lives with his nurse, Antonia, a sensual girl who later turns out to be a whore. He is offered a hospital directorship by an uncle if he will break off his relationship. He cynically decides to live according to society's rules but feels persecuted. The sensual Antonia, the simple, innocent Román, doña Concha, an old procuress, and her criminal son are well drawn. The conspiracy or *conjura* is that of a selfish society which thinks more of its conventions than of a person's true value and will always try to destroy any man who wants to rise above its limited ideals. The novel also attacks the concept of making public decisions along political lines, analyzes the problems of professional jealousies, and examines the anguish of intellectuals at the surrounding decadence. The lesson that selfishness and indifference are the road to happiness and the description of the sordid, dirty, and chaotic atmosphere are clearly pessimistic; but Castellanos recognizes that man can, through his will power and intelligence, conquer an adverse fate. If man fights for his beliefs, he may eventually win, for dedication needs not succumb to public petulance and venom.

La manigua sentimental relates the affairs and adventures of a soldier who served under General Maceo during the Cuban fight for independence. Castellanos shows his love for and knowledge of the countryside and its peasants. Max Henríquez Ureña, impressed by the work, calls it perhaps the most beautiful evocation of Cuban life during that period and states that "como pintura de conjunto, está trazada de mano maestra." [123]

MODERNISM

The novelists of the nineteenth century who believed in science, reason, and progress also believed that literary realism was a positive and reasonable advance over romanticism, that naturalism was a scientific advance over realism, and that "la prosa modernista era un progreso de la ciencia del estilo sobre la prosa de la novela meramente naturalista." [124] Although the greatest impact of that movement generally known as modernism was primarily felt in poetry, it also affected rhetorical and structural changes and extended expressive possibilities in fiction. As a movement of artistic revival, it has countless definitions and explanations. Indeed, many deny it is a movement in the literary sense. Avoiding social and political realities, modernism's novelists concentrate on aesthetics, form, a refinement of technique, and a series of formal innovations including extended use of elements such as synesthesia and plastic arts. Modernism exalted the senses, emphasizing the rare, exotic, mysterious, subjective, amoral, intangible, aristocratic, evasive, and eccentric. Modernists held a largely pessimistic and melancholy view of man, delighting in dualisms such as life-death and soul-flesh.

The authors of this refined movement, in a sense an outgrowth of the very romanticism which it professed to attack, utilized archaisms, neologisms, and syntactical renovation to enrich their literary language. Considering themselves to be cosmopolitan skeptics, many of the writers sought to superimpose foreign importations onto an American base. The novel of the nineteenth century, largely a reflection of European ideas, lacked specifically American aesthetic, artistic, and stylistic elements. Combined with its foreign concerns, modernism, seeking its roots deep in the past, endeavored to introduce American literature into universal art, evolving at the same time until ". . . llegó a ser lo que debía ser: la expresión de la originalidad individual de los artistas y de los pueblos de América y el momento de la independencia del arte, como vehículo de belleza, con valor en sí mismo y como superación de la materia transfigurada en la belleza." [125]

With modernism Spanish American literature enters the universal stream, or, as one student says, "teníamos ya algo *propio que decir.*" [126] Critics tend to agree that modernism linked Spanish America with Europe, that it was perhaps the first great American literary movement, and that after its exotic excursion among the literatures of the world, it sought to define that which is American in an aesthetic and beautiful way. One of the most profound critics of modernism, Federico de Onís, defines it as the "forma hispánica de la crisis universal de las letras y del espíritu que inicia hasta 1885 la disolución del siglo 19 y que se había de manifestar en el arte, la ciencia, la religión y la política con todos los caracteres de un hondo cambio histórico cuyo proceso continúa hoy." [127] Onís also believes its essential attitude to be the search for and affirmation of the national through the universal.

In a sense Spanish American modernism is a conceited kind of movement, and its practioners felt that they were "different" from the middle class in its mediocre and commonplace cultural concepts. In their desire to prove this difference they often hunted the extremely old and new—"something borrowed and something blue"—to add to their aesthetic pool such as French symbolism, medieval poetry, eighteenth-century drawing-room matter, Hellenistic recreations, and Japanese and Chinese curios. In the final analysis, whatever its exotic pretenses, modernism aided the development of the Spanish American novel, and "novels such as *La vorágine, Doña Bárbara, Don Segundo Sombra, Los de abajo . . .* are beholden to the Modernist accomplishment in language and literary technique." [128]

Early exponents of the movement who use shorter paragraphs, supercharged prose full of adjectives, color, music, sadness, melancholy, and elegance include Manuel Gutiérrez Nájera (1859–1895). His very titles, *Cuentos color de humo* (1898–1901) and *Cuentos frágiles* (1883), perhaps the first modernist prose in Spanish America, reveal their gossamery form. His prose in the *Revista Azul* and elsewhere, filled with nostalgia, furthered the movement. He attempted only one novel, *La lancha de Lady Macbeth*, never finished. José Martí (1853–1895), a giant among Spanish American men of letters, may have written the first modernist novel, *Amistad funesta* (1885), which for all its romanticism, is an aesthetically modernist work.[129] First published in installments in the New York bimonthly *El Latino Americano* and in book form in 1911 under the pseudonym of Adelaida Ral, the novel, in later editions, bore the title *Lucía Jerez*, after its female protagonist, a lady jealous to the point of madness and murder and the most interesting of a number of female creations. The male protagonist, Juan Jerez, an idealistic poet and lover of nature (Martí, thinly disguised), is in constant doubt and despair over the future of his country. The prose is rhythmic and poetic, and the novel is filled with light and shadow and colors, especially modernist blue, as well as with a variety of American flora and fauna. Rubén Darío, too, in his stories in *Azul* (1888), helped set the tone for further fiction of this type, but it must be acknowledged that with one or two exceptions, no outstanding novels purely in the modernist vein were produced. Artistic and aesthetic preoccupations could not be completely divorced from content. Even though some of the Spanish American novelists resemble Pierre Louÿs, Oscar Wilde, D'Annunzio, or Barrès, their escapism often involves an attempt to define a new American sensibility, undoubtedly their most important contribution. As we shall see later, many writers not clearly modernists, such as Rufino Blanco Fombona, exhibit modernist and artistic prose in their works, even though they belong in a different classification.

Pedro César Dominici (1876–1954), greatly influenced by D'Annunzio, was a founding member in Venezuela of the literary review *Cosmópolis*, and also contributed to *El Cojo Ilustrado*. As a diplomat he traveled widely in Paris, Madrid, London, and Rome, which provided the setting of part of his fiction. His novels were but one aspect of his creativity, as he also wrote chronicles, literary criticism, theater, biography, and a political attack against Cipriano Castro, *Un sátrapa* (1901). His novel, *La tristeza voluptuosa* (1899), set in Paris, is about a self-centered pessimistic artist. Another, *El triunfo del ideal* (1901), takes place in an Italian Renaissance palace in Rome. Dominici called it a "poema novelado," but the theme of an Italian count interested in Greek art and aesthetics and a woman who commits suicide when she feels her spiritual love is no longer returned is trite. *Dionysos* (1904), a Parnassian reconstruction of ancient Greece in the age of Pericles and of Alexandrian eroticism, subtitled "Costumbres de la antigua Grecia," shows the definite influence of Pierre Louÿs' *Aphrodite*. The discussion of the theatre, the relative merits of Greek poets, the rivalry of the gods, the vengeance of one, and platonic love cannot completely counteract the art, beauty, color, harmony, and exoticism of the work which "es sin duda, la obra que mayor repercusión alcanzó entre las suyas." [130] In 1925 Dominici attempted a different kind of novel, *El cóndor*, about America in pre-Colombian times. The author called it a "novela de costumbres antiguas" and dedicated it "a mi América libre y a la España grande." In the prologue he explains that his life had been devoted to art and beauty but that he wanted to try his hand at an American novel (it took seven months and twenty days to write). Angol's loves, adventures, and enemies, the struggle between Huáscar and Atahualpa, the arrival of the Spaniards, and the love between Álvaro, a white prisoner, and Chaica, Angol's daughter, from which will spring the first Peruvian mestizo, are some of the themes. *Evocación* (1949) treats of the archeology of Caracas.

Enrique Gómez Carrillo (1873–1927), whose mother's name was Tible, used his father's two names because he considered them more euphonious and because of the pun involved in the authentic combination. Guatemala's "enfant terrible," he had an active and adventurous life, including an "understanding" with the dancer Mata Hari, and he incurred a number of enemies at his death for his unbelievable defense of the dictator Estrada Cabrera. He thought of himself as a disciple of the cult of beauty and an impressionistic searcher for sensations and brilliant elegance. Better known as a chronicler, essayist, short story writer, and author of travel books than as a novelist, Gómez Carrillo, to convey his message, produced in all his writings an attractively and harmoniously elaborated prose based on pure sensation. He succeeded, but, unfortunately, what he had in mind hardly merited saying. In some of his works he combines a decadent kind of sensualism and religion, examining with intellectual curiosity a number of perverse situations which he communicates at times almost as frivolous gossip. *Tres novelas inmorales* (1922), novels previously published separately, tell of love and sex in Paris. The first, *Bohemia sentimental* (1899), as the title implies, talks about bohemians, artists, spiritual and physical love (both legitimate and promiscuous), and renunciation. *Del amor, del dolor y del vicio* (1898) deals with a young girl married to an old man. Liliana, the protagonist, recalls her love life, both hetero— and homosexual, presented from her point of view. An abulic artist, a constant character in modernist fiction, is also presented. The third novel, *Maravillas* (1899), called *Pobre Clown* in a later version, discusses the theater. His best known novel and his own favorite was *El evangelio del amor* (1922), whose poetic qualities Blasco Ibáñez greatly admired in a prologue to the work. Set in Byzantium, it covers the invasion of Roger de Flor in 1311, the sacking of Thrace and Macedonia by the Catalonians, and the struggles of an ascetic to find religious purity. Finding love instead, he is stoned to death. The theme of the sensual versus the religious proved to be a favorite of the modernist writers. Gómez Carrillo was perhaps a better novelist than many thought. His individuals and their circumstances may not prove enduring, but he handled quite well, within his self-imposed limitations, the inevitable and universal relationships between men and women, which in the long run will ensure the fame of this self-styled "príncipe de los cronistas" as much as his color, fantasy, musicality, and pure sensation.

Ángel de Estrada (1872–1923), modernist poet, short story writer, and author of travel books, was, according to one critic, "el más calificado iniciador de esta tendencia en la Argentina," [131] and according to another the employer of more neologisms than any other modernist.[132] He and other Argentine writers, especially Payró and Lugones, were greatly influenced by Rubén Darío's visit to Buenos Aires in 1896. A solitary aristocrat, Estrada was an ardent follower of the theories of Théophile Gautier. In all his works he searches for beauty and art in a make-believe world that never was, putting into it a number of autobiographical elements which lend meat to the bones of his aesthetic, exotic, and refined landscapes. But in his chronicles or short stories, *El color y la piedra* (1900), *Cadoreto* (1914), a dramatic poem which is a kind of historical novel, and in his novels he describes better than he narrates, and his plots are but shadowy excuses for his descriptions.

Estrada's four novels are *Redención* (1906), *La ilusión* (1910), *Las tres gracias* (1916), and *El triunfo de las rosas* (1918). The first is a two part novel about France and Greece. Juan de Montfort and his love, Andrea, travel through the second country, and when she dies, he seeks solace in a regained religious faith and by building a school for lepers. *La ilusión* relates his experiences on board an ocean liner and then gives us a guided tour of France and Italy. *Las tres gracias* deals with a Renaissance artist, old Leone Landi, and the three symbolic women in his life. In his garden, the painter (Estrada himself) discourses on sixteenth-century painters and platonic and Christian love. His last novel brings us forward in time to modern Italy, the country of D'Annunzio, one of his heroes. Estrada's characters are not men and women of flesh and blood but rather "sombras sutiles fugitivas.

La acción es por veces lánguida, pues los héroes no la forjan con su propio infortunio, su amor o su esperanza sino el novelista la desenvuelve reflexivamente." [133] His reality is an exquisite, exotic, multicultural world of museums, art, and books.

A minor novelist, Martín Aldao (1876–1961), wrote two novels, *Criollismo aristocrático o la novela de Torcuato Méndez* (1912) and *La vida falsa* (1943), about the frivolous and elegant Argentine colony in Paris shortly after the First World War. But he is better known for his attack in 1913, under the pseudonym of Luis Vila y Chávez, against the modernist work of Enrique Larreta, not only the best Argentine modernist but probably the best writer of that type of fiction in America.

Enrique Rodríguez Larreta (1873–1961), historian, dramatist, and short story writer who wrote as Enrique Larreta, was wealthy enough to dedicate himself to literature, in whose pursuit he was encouraged by Paul Groussac. His first novel, *Artemis* (1896), appeared in Groussac's *La Biblioteca* and presaged his next and far greater work, *La gloria de don Ramiro*, in some of the themes. In *Artemis*, Dryas, an athlete, struggles against his sensual instincts and successfully resists the blandishments of Mircis. After this first effort, Larreta did not seriously dedicate himself to fiction again until December of 1903. He began an intensive five year study in libraries, cities, and towns which resulted in *La gloria de don Ramiro*, one of the most curious Spanish American novels, published in 1908. The novel, a historical reconstruction of the time of Phillip II, primarily about the city of Ávila, is so skilfully done that it appears to be a Spanish work of classic style. For some readers the novel's decadent sensual overlay and composite historical, antiquarian, half-poetic, half-archeological elements help show that Larreta from his geographically removed space and historically removed time was unable to come to grips with the true spirit of the period he was trying to evoke. In recreating the past, the novel served also as an escape from the tedium of the present, and his temporal excursion may well have been a search for secular and spiritual self-realization. As a kind of elegant man of the world, somewhat snobbishly imbued with a sense of the "good old days," Larreta recreates the kind of world in which he himself, far removed from the Argentine problems of the day, might have found himself at home. Larreta points out the impressionistic and autobiographical aspects of its construction: "Una mancha, una mancha lo más vaga y líquida que sea posible. En esta ocasión como buscando la más honda raíz, principié por el recuerdo de mi propia infancia." [134]

Amado Alonso criticized the novel's historical accuracy—which pained Larreta, a teacher of history who prided himself on his historical research. Whatever his motivation, Larreta had, indeed, steeped himself physically in the archives, tradition, spirit, and history of Toledo and Ávila. Although the fanatics and Spanish ladies and gentlemen in his work are no more real than his questionable Arabic, they convey, in their jealousy, religion, mysticism, and actions the reality of the moment. Larreta's sympathies seem to lie more with the sensual *moriscos* than with the intolerant and stiff-necked Catholics. The ornamentation, richness, light, shadow, and color (recalling the work of Azorín) are part of an artistic archaic style to match his recreation. Max Henríquez Ureña rejects the concept of Larreta's strict impressionism and contends that he used "a number of literary techniques in his attempts to be authentically archaic." [135]

Ramiro is the illegitimate son of a Moorish chief and a Catholic lady of high lineage whom the Moor had seduced. She later married a Spanish nobleman who died fighting in Flanders. Ramiro had dreamed of achieving personal glory in love and war, but, recruited as a spy to foil a Moorish plot, he falls in love with the voluptuous Moorish girl, Aixa, to the temporary exclusion of his duty. Plots and counterplots continue as Ramiro struggles to find a path between sensualism and true love for Beatriz. He finally betrays Aixa to the Inquisition and sees her burned alive. He becomes a hermit, meets a Moor (his father) who once saved his life, and learns of his birth. He goes to America, repents, dies, and is prayed over by the famous Santa Rosa de Lima, who places a flower on his breast.

Amado Alonso believes that the characters are drawn with a sure but perhaps limited stroke—the disloyal and passionate Ramiro, the sensual Aixa, or the giddy Beatriz being prime examples. Don Ramiro's world is represented "con abundancia de acontecimientos y personajes. Tales personajes y acontecimientos no guardan la armonía que pretenden representar." [136] Arturo Berenguer Carísomo considers the vocabulary, atmosphere, and history to be authentic and believes that Larreta's long study gave him a kind of plastic panoramic vision of Spain, "la comprensión de sus enigmas, el color de sus costumbres, las direcciones de su espíritu." [137] The novel may have a symbolic value which represents the entire complexity of the Spanish Christian tradition, but it is doubtful that "nunca, en las tierras jóvenes de América se habián escrito páginas que con más belleza de forma dijeran cosas tan graves y necesarias, desenvolvieran teoría más hermosa y honda de pensamientos." [138] One may doubt the historical and archeological authenticity, but the geography seems to be a first hand experience and exploration of old palaces and houses by Larreta. What is not so easily ascertained is the psychological penetration of the author. With modernism there occurred an intensification of interest in psychology, and Larreta tried to study the many facets of Ramiro's personality. Ramiro is no gentleman, either by birth, blood, or action. He dreams of fame and fortune but, instead of bearing himself as an honorable knight, proves to be a coward and a liar. He is temporarily awakened to pride by Lorenzo Vargas Orozco, of the Church of Ávila, who indoctrinates him with the *Summa Theologica* of Thomas Aquinas. Lorenzo, more soldier than monk, was not averse to female temptation or to turning Ramiro into a spy. Ramiro's glory lies neither in love nor in fame but in Christian repentance. He could not make a correct personal decision in the case of the sensual Aixa (considering the Spain of his day, theologically, if not ethically, his betrayal was in keeping with the tenets of Christianity), but he moved closer to salvation through eliciting the prayers for his soul by Santa Rosa de Lima. Unamuno found the work admirable for its combination of sixteenth- and twentieth-century language and was especially impressed by the characterization of the canónigo Lorenzo Vargas Orozco.[139] In the *Palabras preliminares* to Larreta's *Obras completas*, Enrique de Gandía states that *La gloria de Don Ramiro* is a profound psychological study, the expression of the most intimate conflict of the human soul, a constant struggle between ambition and renunciation, and a knowledge of human dreams "como si ellos fueran nuestros o los conociéramos, por arte de magia o de extraño poder, más a fondo que sus mismos poseedores." [140]

The poetic prose, filled with rich and involved, luxurious, and sonorous phrases, creates a beautiful, archaic atmosphere to help obscure the cracks in the concrete treatment of humanity. The abulic and adolescent protagonist is typically an exotic creation of an exquisite and excessively refined modernist, one who uses an archeological rather than human approach to history. Larreta has created a kind of "*Salambó* de la literatura criolla, lo arqueológico predomina sobre lo humano." [141] For this reason, even if one assumes the historical accuracy and research, the novel's somewhat musty museum atmosphere removes the author's fictional freedom to individualize the human cycle of universal experience. But it cannot be denied that *La gloria de Don Ramiro* is perhaps the most important work of its type and a monument to the impressionistic and artistic fiction of the time. Part of its success, whatever its intrinsic merits, may have stemmed from the fact that Buenos Aires was the center of modernism;[142] but the encomiums it has received, holding it to be not only the best contemporary work but ". . . la mejor novela escrita en castellano," [143] are exaggerated.

Zogoibi (1926) takes place in 1913 and 1914. Federico de Ahumada, like Boabdil, last king of Granada, is called Zogoibi or "the unfortunate one." He loves Lucía but falls under the spell of Zita, the mysterious and sensual wife of Mr. Wilburns, an American capitalist. One night, as he takes leave of Zita, he sees an intruder and kills him, only to discover that it is his disguised Lucía; so he commits suicide at her feet. In a later edition Lucía does not die, but Federico kills himself anyway. The protagonist conveys the pale reflection of Larreta himself, and Lucía seems more ideal than woman. In spite of Larreta's aristocratic viewpoint and the Frenchified characters like Federico, about whom he wrote, the novel is not necessarily false but well constructed. Its tragic end ". . . is ably arranged with convolutions in the plot, suggestive details, coincidences and forebodings. . . . The metaphors fuse the double experience of the Buenos Aires oligarchy: literary mannerism and the immediate knowledge of nature." [144]

Larreta first thought of setting the action in France but later decided on Argentina, subtitling his novel "El dolor de la tierra" to show us "la agonía de una Pampa que está desapareciendo." [145] In addition to portraying the effect of the city on the countryside, he hoped to reflect authentically the light, sounds, color, fragrance, flora, and fauna of the plains. In its contrast of the world of illusion and that of reality, his romantic tragedy of the gauchos' passions and dreams, *Zogoibi* has been interpreted as a "defensa del suelo patrio y de las virtudes de los moradores." [146] Juan Carlos Ghiano sees the novel as a "síntesis de la Pampa . . . una muestra peculiar del tono de las interpretaciones circunstanciales, tan distintas a las de los novelistas anteriores." [147] Others have criticized it as a "frustrado intento de profunda novela criolla," with a brusque and melodramatic denouement.[148] The same sensuality, sadness, and tragedy of *La gloria de don Ramiro*, this time in an Argentine setting, make *Zogoibi* almost a spiritual if less complicated twin of his first novel.

Larreta wrote several more volumes of prose. In a prologue to *La naranja* (1948), a book of ideas, memoirs, and meditations, Gregorio Marañón called it "autorretrato copiado . . . de su espejo. Este espejo es la soledad." This solitude can be found in *Orillas del Ebro* (1949), a novel which attempts to characterize Spanish traditions and twentieth-century Spain. Two young people, Máximo and Fernanda, fall in love and marry to their eventual sorrow, lack of communication, and lonely separation. The husband, recalling "El curioso impertinente," tests his wife's fidelity with resultant unhappiness, but they are eventually brought together by the tragic death of their son. Symbols of various kinds, authentic landscapes, and the interplay of popular tradition are important themes; but more important still is Larreta's ability as an architect of evocative words.

Gerardo o la torre de las damas (1953) has a second part, really a separate novel, *En la Pampa* (1955). These were published together as *El Gerardo* (1956). The first part is set in the Alhambra and is about an Argentine shortly after the Spanish Civil War. The second part takes place in Argentina. Gerardo, the hero, is a kind of frustrated don Juan whose six loves, some of them intellectual and some of them sensual, end in failure. The author, Gerardo himself, is in turn humorous, ironic, and bitter. Aside from the theme of woman's superiority over the victimized male, the novel examines the author's religious experience from tortured Christianity to a kind of pantheistic identification with the world. These novels again show the same beautiful language and apt metaphor of earlier works and also a knowledge of new fictional techniques. In the second part Larreta succeeds in portraying the pampa in all its profundity, something he had been unable fully to accomplish in *Zogoibi*. One ardent admirer of Larreta's novels states: "Yo me atrevería a decir que después de Hernández . . . y salvo el caso moderno de Benito Lynch . . . ninguno ha tenido de aquella (Pampa) una vivencia tan radical y profunda." [149]

A Venezuelan modernist, second in fame only to Larreta, Manuel Díaz Rodríguez (1871–1927), is considered by many to be the best stylist of his generation because of the musicality of his prose[150] and his aesthetic sense "inclined toward the appreciation of sound, shape and color. He was by nature indifferent to reality and to the ideas and principles back of appearances. As a writer he delighted in mere exquisiteness in form of expression." [151] Aesthetic preoccupations became so important to him that he grew intoxicated with words for their own sake and for their phonetic image, considering them as an end in themselves to the detriment of characters and content. He had a fine ear for sound, the picturesque, and especially the musical quality of words.[152]

Díaz Rodríguez wrote a number of volumes of travel literature —*Confidencias de Psiquis* (1896), *Sensaciones de viaje* (1897), and *De mis romerías* (1898)—about his trips through Rome, Paris, and Constantinople in which he seeks the eternal mystery of the human soul and recreates a magic world of beauty and art. His collection of short stories, *Cuentos de color* (1899), contains myths, legends, allegories, and a recurrent impressionism and parnassianism. His first novel, *Ídolos rotos* (1901), because of its pessimistic evaluation of his country, has been compared to *Todo un pueblo* (1899) by Miguel Eduardo Pardo, but the novels have little in common except the setting. The protagonist of *Ídolos rotos*, Alberto Soria, a typical abulic modernist hero, goes off to Paris to study sculpture. He is forced to return because of his father's illness but is not equipped to face a practical world. His one interest in life is art, which he sees as the moral justification for existence. He wants to bring a new aesthetic creed to Venezuela, but the unappreciative masses destroy his statues. Feeling as besmirched as the statues, he rejects his native land as barbarous and decides to return to Paris, the center of elegance, aestheticism, and intelligence, uttering, as he goes, his final damning words, "Finis Patriae." Alberto believes himself superior to his environment yet also its prisoner. Feeling that only through art and aesthetics can regeneration occur, he attempts to draw abstraction from experience while discarding experience itself; his dreams of artistic and political perfection, however, are impossible in our imperfect world. The novel also treats of sexual perversion and contains pagan and mystic elements.

Sangre patricia (1902), filled with discussions of aesthetics, painting, music, and philosophy, documents the defeat of a decadent aristocracy by the middle class. Tulio Arcos, an ancestor of Rómulo Gallegos' Reinaldo Solar, is the descendant of wealthy landowners. Instructed by his great aunt in family history, he feels almost like a ghost. He resents the middle classes for their lack of aesthetic preoccupations and, interested in social reform, joins a revolutionary movement, largely to carry on long conversations about religion, politics, and art. Arcos lacks the strength of the past and is typically a member of the current stagnant aristocracy, completely void of creative force. Belén Montenegro, seen as a vision, dream, and kind of illusion throughout the novel, is his middle-class bride who dies on her way to join him in Paris. Her death serves as a constant reproach for his abulic state. More and more he lives in a dream world, grows neurotic, finally becomes insane, and, lured by her image, drowns himself in the sea. Belén, in a sense, destroys the possibility of his revitalization and his ideal, but one may also argue that his thinning aristocratic blood contributed to his eventual death. Luis Monguió, examining Díaz Rodríguez' life as a participant and defender of dictatorship, sees his novels as an escape "del ambiente en que vivían su país y su grupo social."¹⁵³ The author's defense of a decadent aristocracy is a surprising anomaly in a time of its almost universal condemnation, but he seems also to be defending himself from his own guilty association with the forces of repression in Venezuela.¹⁵⁴ Some of the minor characters, the bitter traveler and deceived husband, Miguel Borja, or the musician, Alejandro Martí, are of interest; but Belén is superhuman in her miraculous, ethereal, colorful, mysterious, and bewitching beauty. In his description of her and of the sea (water symbolism is most significant in this novel), Díaz Rodríguez repeats a series of words such as green, blue, mermaids, and dream to give a special rhythm to his prose and a supernatural tinge to his sea imagery, typically artistic and elegant. His subconscious explorations, tactile hallucinations, and analysis of obsession with death, on the other hand, are done in surprisingly modern fashion and make him "un precursor del surrealismo y de la novela de interpretación psicológica e intención poética." [155] Indeed, some of Tulio's meanderings resemble psychedelic awareness.

Although Díaz Rodríguez never repudiated his definition of modernism as a return to nature combined with a tendency toward mysticism in the confrontation of the artist's soul with contemporary life, he eventually saw the necessity of defining the national soul. Overcome as he was by the visual beauty of his country, he, like Dominici, wanted to attempt a criolla novel which would more realistically show peasants of the region. His novel, *Peregrina o el pozo encantado* (1922), subtitled "Novela de relatos del valle de Caracas," is less a poetic breviary or personal confession. It is filled with nature description—the valley, the blue mountains, the weather—and these picturesque aspects and his artistic elegance are achieved only at the expense of human emotion. Two brothers are in love with the same girl. Bruno, the younger one, leaves her pregnant and refuses to marry her. She tries to commit suicide and is temporarily saved by the other brother, Amaro, but she dies anyway. At her death bed the two brothers, one representing real love and the other ardent passion, are reconciled, thus symbolizing the need for both to achieve completion. The projection of rural and regional themes makes the novel seem criollista at times, but the autochthonous plays a secondary role to the aesthetic. A number of Venezuelan critics have attempted to show its dramatic internal conflict not only as *nativismo* but even as naturalism.[156]

Augusto D'Halmar (1882–1950) of Chile, whose real name was Goemine Thomson (he later changed it to just Thomson) went to Calcutta in 1906 as consul general and for the next twenty-one years served in a variety of embassies in Madrid, Paris, London, Cairo, and Istambul and traveled around the world to exotic places, especially India and Arabia, about which he wrote many short stories. Apparently he had a mania for travel, and these sojourns in exotic climes certainly affected his novelistic production. It is difficult to know whether his travels were the cause or the result of his solitude and nostalgia for another time and another place. He was fond of a number of authors, among them Ibsen, Hans Christian Andersen, Pierre Loti, and especially Tolstoy, and was an intimate friend of Maeterlinck and Federico García Lorca, who called him his "confesor laico." With his friend and brother-in-law Fernando Santiván and with Julio Ortiz de Zárate, D'Halmar founded a Colonia Tolstoyana in 1904. He hoped to be able to read beautiful literature for the improvement of his soul, an experience of but brief duration. Apparently, direct contact with nature and work in a communal setting did nothing for his spiritual or mental health or, for that matter, for his sexual aberration, which may have been a factor in the establishment of the colony in the first place.[157]

D'Halmar's personal melancholy is constantly reflected in his fiction. Somewhat mysterious and with vague aspirations toward beauty, he was, as one biography of him states, "un hombre profundamente divorciado de la realidad." [158] One of the first professional writers of Chile, he was the first to receive the Premio Nacional de Literature in 1942. Fernando Alegría classifies him as "el representante más notable de la sensibilidad modernista en la prosa chilena," [159] but D'Halmar qualifies also as a naturalist. Many of his works, while poetic in form, are quite realistic and naturalistic in content. Mario Ferrero finds him to have "una estética vaporosa, de flotantes nebulosas melancólicas, vaga, sutil, con un imaginismo marinero siempre en trance de partir hacia ninguna parte." [160]

Part of the difficulty in classifying D'Halmar stems from the period itself. Two groups, the *imaginistas* and the *criollistas*, were contesting for supremacy in literature at the turn of the century. Augusto D'Halmar and Salvador Reyes belonged to the former, and Mariano Latorre eventually became the titular head of the second movement. The imaginistas rejected narrow regionalism and recognized no real geographical limitations.[161] The criollistas, although they had not yet achieved a complete elaboration of their theories, looked to the rural areas: "No había en él sino realidad, la sencilla actitud de la vida en función de la simplicidad de la naturaleza." [162] In spite of his leadership of the impressionistic group, D'Halmar's themes and techniques were also important in the development of Chilean criollismo, and, indeed, his work ". . . was the foundation of the mighty edifice of criollismo which was to dominate the Chilean literary horizon for many years." [163]

Although D'Halmar is clearly a modernist in most of his works, his *Juana Lucero* (1902), subtitled "Los vicios de Chile," in an earlier version called simply *La Lucero*, is a brutal, naturalistic novel of prostitution and the melodramatic story of the illegitimate child of a millionaire mistreated by an aunt. In addition to an obvious dependence on Zola, the author combines costumbrismo, social denunciation, and a close examination of brothel life with "la expresión más directa de la influencia de Tolstoy en Chile." [164] D'Halmar's descriptions of houses of prostitution easily equal those of Federico Gamboa and Joaquín Edwards Bello. With one exception his other fiction consists of short stories or novelettes. *La lámpara en el molino* (1912), a group of stories, is filled with light and shadows and deals with an abnormal relationship between a brother and sister. Other collections include *Los alucinados* (1917?) —four novelettes—*Amor cara o cruz* (1935), and *Cristián y yo* (1946). *Nirvana* (1918) describes trips to the west and east, Christmas Day at sea, and New Year's Day in London. *La sombra del humo en el espejo* (1924) is a series of impressionistic travel notes where it is hard to know the dividing line between the real and the imagined. It contains a Gide-like picture of an Arab lad, Zahir. Having gone to Peru to recover from an illness, D'Halmar met there Catalina, a kind of platonic Peruvian Lolita, who inspired his novelette, *Gatita*, which first appeared in the journal of "Los Diez" in 1916. Still another title is *Capitanes sin barco* (1934).

D'Halmar's best known novel, *Pasión y muerte del cura Deusto* (1924), is set in Seville in 1913. Ignacio Deusto, a Basque priest who is also a musician, takes over a Sevillian parish, San Juan de la Palma, and develops a three-year friendship with Pedro Miguel, a boy singer and dancer. The priest, aided primarily by his faithful servant, Mónica, attempts a variety of innovations. The village gossip has it that Pedro is Deusto's son. When Pedro attempts suicide the gossip increases and hints of homosexual attachments occur. Pedro runs off, and Deusto follows him, discovering to his horror that he sexually loves the boy. He commits suicide (death and suicide fascinated D'Halmar). Some feel that D'Halmar knew Seville and expressed its essence, types, countryside, light, color, religion, and bull fights better than did the Uruguayan Carlos Reyles in his famous *El embrujo de Sevilla* (1922). Whatever his shortcomings, there can be no doubt that D'Halmar has left "huellas perdurables en nuestra literatura." [165]

Pedro Prado (1886–1952), a fine poet and one of the first to use free verse in Chile, wrote a strange book of prose poems, supposedly a translation from the Persian Karez I Roshan (Prado himself). Antonio Castro Leal helped him write this literary spoof which appeared in 1922 but which was composed of fragments of early poetry. Prado wrote a number of other volumes of poetry, including an anthology in 1949. Stylistically he is a descendant of modernism as shown by his poetic essays in works like *La casa abandonada* (1912), filled with philosophical parables, pantheism, and a search for the beauty and meaning of quotidian events. Yet his *Flores de cardo* (1908) more or less marked the end of modernism in Chile, although the lines are somewhat blurred. As John Fein says, "the aesthetic conclusion of the movement came in 1908 with the publication of Pedro Prado's first book . . ." [166] Fernando Alegría lists Prado as a modernist but admits that he and members of his group "crean un regionalismo de impulso lírico." [167] Prado's *Andróvar* (1925), a tragedy in prose and a kind of dramatic poem, also reveals clearly his aesthetic sensibilities. Prado fits loosely into the criollista category, but his theories of art, his embellished style, his subjectivism and impressionism put him, with the exception of one of his novels, within the modernist ranks. Prado at times used the pseudonym "Los Diez" as well as that of "El hermano errante." The first name alluded to an association of nine (the tenth was the mythical Hermano Errante) musicians, painters, and writers he had founded around 1915, and his book by that same title makes clear his feelings about life and art. The artistic circle published a review in 1916, edited a series of books, and more or less dissolved in 1917, but the name continued to be used for years. "Los Diez" wanted to cultivate art with freedom and planned to erect a tower, a symbolic refuge from which they could publish their new art. The tower, to be on a cliff overlooking the sea, was never built, but the members of the group, Magallanes Moure (1878–1924), Armando Donoso (1886–1946), and later members like Eduardo Barrios and Augusto d'Halmar were all outstanding literary figures.

Prado's activities (architect, diplomat, farmer, director of the Museum of Fine Arts) limited his fictional production. His first novel, *La reina de Rapa Nui* (1914), a romantic fantasy, is set on a lost island of the South Pacific, specifically, Pascua. The author pretends that a friend left him a manuscript about the folklore of this island, known as Rapa Nui by its inhabitants. The editor of *El Heraldo* of Valparaíso visits the island, witnesses the dances and songs, and meets the island queen, Coemata Etú, a Dane, Adams, a French Crimean war veteran, Trou de Bornier, and some other inhabitants. The queen drinks poisoned water and dies. One may see the novel as an "exotic fantasy," a tour de force,[168] a series of stories, a psychological essay, or an aesthetic interpretation, in symbolic form, of legends and countryside;[169] but one may also easily view it as a glorification of the primitive life as opposed to the sorrows of civilization. Prado, who never visited the island, may have wanted both to evoke ancestral myths and arouse interest in his countrymen about their own beautiful geography, which he imaginatively embellished.

Alsino (1920), almost a symphonic poem, is the story of a young boy who wants to fly. Thinking that the can, he jumps from a tree, breaks his back, and sprouts wings. He flies above the world's ugliness, is mistaken for an angel, captured for display, and inadvertently blinded by Rosita, a girl who, desiring him, foolishly follows the prescription of a jealous local witch. People believe that Alsino possesses magic powers, but all persecute him. Abigail, the girl he loves, dies, and with her dies his only chance for happiness. After a bad fall, feverish and delirious, he commits suicide by flying toward the sun and falling to the earth as ashes. The book has lyrical outbursts, poetic imagery, songs, and rhymes; but Prado's beautiful descriptions of Chilean geography, based on his own voyages along the coast, are real enough. The multiplicity of details do not stem the narrative flow; instead they drown the soul of the reader in "un océano de sensaciones, emociones y presentimientos de la más pura calidad humana y estética." [170] The novel may be an allegory of man's freedom, of Daedalus breaking free from the world's labyrinth, a magical story, a poetic vision, a wish to be as one with nature and to be pure and free. We all dream dreams which are destroyed by the human executioners among us; but they cannot die completely, for a dream, the mystery of the world, along with man's search for God, will remain, as Alsino's ashes remain, diffused in the atmosphere, invisible but waiting to be evoked once more. The novel also contains social commentary, a satirical evocation of Yankee materialism, and pictures of everyday life in the country. Man may dream of ethereal flight, but he is also a victim of the world and all its problems. *Alsino* is a beautiful novel, surely one of the highpoints of continental fiction; but Raúl Silva Castro, seeing it as an allegory based on too much symbolism, finds the novel less than perfect in its combination of poetic prose and what he terms "fragmentos de burda naturalidad." [171]

Un juez rural (1924), an idealistic view of human existence, seems a strange combination of wisdom and naiveté. Partly autobiographical, it deals seriously and yet humoristically with moral and social problems and with human beings he knew. A series of scenes, customs, peasant frauds, and politics, the novel attempts to define the meaning of justice. Esteban Solaguren, an architect made a town judge, has a strong sense of justice but no legal training. He wants to cure the social ills affecting his country but soon realizes the impossibility of "hacer bien" or of living up to the best which man has within him. He renders a number of judgments but after two months realizes that law and justice have little in common and, unable to dispense perfect justice or weigh fully the consequences of his actions on fellow citizens, resigns. In a second short part Prado continues the story of Solaguren, his visit to a friend, and his hallucinatory encounter with his own mirror image. Prado gives us intimate details of the Chilean village and a wonderful description of a house abandoned by its builder, aspects which probably prompted Torres-Rioseco's claim that the novel is "la más pura interpretación del paisaje de América." [172]

Alfonso Hernández Catá (1885–1940) was born in Cuba but spent most of his productive career in Spain. Some might argue that he really does not belong in a history of the Spanish American novel, and, in truth, he fits no easy classification. Although he felt from time to time that he had to write Cuban patriotic material, he was not essentially a regionalist.[173] In a prologue to Hernández Catá's *Sus mejores cuentos* (1936), Eduardo Barrios cites the Cuban author as a master of language, thought, and vision in the best Spanish manner but with a sense of color and taste quite American and autochthonous. Cuban critics tend to find him quite Cuban, "en diversos libros, novela y cuentos . . . el tema cubano, el sabor insular . . .";[174] and "su cubanidad por devoción lo salvó del cosmopolitanismo de invernadero en que hubiera podido triunfar . . ." [175] Politically, his severe denunciation of Machado in *Un cementerio en las Antillas* (1933) endeared him to Cuban intellectuals. In his fiction, his themes of violence, guilt, psychiatry, the unconscious mind, deep passion, sexual perversion, and purification through suffering are more universal than regional. Pessimistic, anguished, gloomy, and decidedly aristocratic in his appeal, he shows modernist tendencies, "genuina prosa modernista ... trabajada con arte. Esa prosa castigada y elegante dio desde un principio realce a su producción." [176] His early work is somewhat melodramatic; irony, pain, and the theme of universal man characterize much of his later tragic vein.

A voluminous short story writer, he is at his best in the shorter fictional forms, especially in the novelette. His titles include *Cuentos pasionales* (1907), *Novela erótica* (1909), *Los frutos ácidos* (1915), *Fuegos fatuos* (1916); the short novels *La juventud de Aurelio Zaldívar* (1911), *Pelayo González* (1912), *Los siete pecados* (1918), *El placer de sufrir* (1920); and *La muerte nueva* (1922), probably his first long novel, about a protagonist who cannot adapt himself again to his native Spain after eleven years in England; *El bebedor de lágrimas* (1926), and *El ángel de Sodoma* (1928), a novel about a homesexual, José María Vélez Gómara, and his tragedy, not a usual theme in Spanish American fiction until the 1950s. Hernández Catá, in spite of his interest in psychology, has no talent for developing characters through an artistic maturation process, and most of them serve as mechanical proofs of his own philosophy and psychological acumen. Although his concern for form and his keen powers of observation are self-evident, what remains current is his special handling of fantasy and perverse sensuality along with a dynamic and exuberant style, characterized as "suntuoso, denso y ampliamente provisto, tanto en cuanto a elementos eufónicos como a sintácticos en su función de órgano verbal; en su aspecto ... de instrumento ideológico tiene toda la plasticidad y el colorido necesarios en estos empeños de evocación ajenos a otra mentalidad." [177]

Many lesser figures of modernism contributed interesting novels. José Asunción Silva (1865–1896) wrote *De Sobremesa* (1887–1896),[178] whose poet-protagonist José Fernández, lover of the abnormal and collector of art objects, is a typical modernist projection. Macedonio Fernández (1874–1952) of Argentina, an almost unclassifiable writer viewed by some as a criollista,[179] also exhibits decided existential and metaphysical traits in his search for the essence of his own being. He had a great influence on Jorge Luis Borges, with whom he edited the review *Proa* in 1922 and 1923, and other members of following generations. Yet his entire emphasis is on art and artistic creation as a product of irrational and intuitive experience. Humorous, ironic, he seeks the real moment in all its profundity, for his world is composed of elements which escape our direct perception but nevertheless form part of the phenomena we perceive. He was constantly preoccupied by death, insofar as one could make meaning out of his metaphysical, confused, illogical, strange, and absurd works. His titles include *No toda es vigilia la de los ojos abiertos* (1928), *Papeles de recién venido* (1930), *Una novela que comienza* (1941), and *Continuación de la Nada* (1945).

The Dominican Tulio Manuel Cestero (1877–1954) was greatly influenced by D'Annunzio, especially in his short stories. In addition to two novelettes, *Ciudad romántica* (1911) and *Sangre de primavera* (1908), he wrote a well-known novel, *La sangre* (1915), not typically modernist. Its hero is Antonio Portocarrero, a Quixotic teacher, and the novel treats of the assassination of the dictator Ulises Heureaux (Lilís) in 1899. The action takes place between 1899 and 1905. The protagonist mentally evokes the days of his childhood and life under the dictator, and the author skilfully fuses the two time zones. It may well be "una de las obras capitales de la literatura dominicana."[180]

Pedro Emilio Coll (1872–1947) of Venezuela, Amado Nervo (1870–1919) of Mexico, Froylán Turcios (1875–1943) of Honduras, José María Vargas Vila (1860–1933) of Colombia, Leopoldo Lugones (1874–1938) and Atilio Chiappori of Argentina, and the Peruvians Clemente Palma (1872–1946) and his sister Angélica Palma (1883–1935) are other names worthy of mention. Coll, a naturalistic writer at times, has a number of refined and pessimistic stories and literary essays. Probably his best known novel is *El castillo de Elsinor* (1901). Amado Nervo, who transcended at times the modernist trends of his work, has a number of fictional titles under the general heading of *Otras vidas*, such as *Pascual Aguilera* (1896), about the son of a hacendado who attempts to possess a peasant bride but finds satisfaction instead with his stepmother, and *El domador de almas* (1906). His best known short novel, *El bachiller* (1895), is filled with reminiscences of seminary life and sexual temptation, including that of a would-be priest who emasculates himself to save his purity. Abnormal psychology greately intrigued Nervo, and his stories of double personality, dream-life, and science fiction foreshadow the works of Horacio Quiroga and even those of Jorge Luis Borges. Froylán Turcios mixed politics and customs in his Poe-like stories and novels of which *Annabel Lee* (1906) and *El vampiro* (1910) are typical.

José María Vargas Vila, a kind of modernist-naturalist, wrote novels which seemed fairly pornographic. His generally iconoclastic position also made him enemies who considered him to be a blasphemer, something he enjoyed since he proudly acknowledged that he was an anticlerical atheist. "Provocative beyond any other Colombian novelist," [181] he encouraged the opinions of his fellow countrymen that held him to be a generally repugnant and impertinent clerophobe. Manuel Ugarte, somewhat of an egotist himself, exclaimed peevishly that "no hay ejemplo en ninguna literatura de vanidad tan estruendosa como la de José María Vargas Vila." [182] Vargas Vila wrote in all about sixty volumes, of which about twenty may be considered novels, often inarticulate, ungrammatical, originally orthographic, and almost paranoid in their fixation on beauty, art, and sex. He fills his novels with terms like "crueldad suprema," "piedad la más alta forma del amor," "amor exquisito del matiz," "pasión morbosa," "inexorabilidad fatal," and concentrates on the adventures of women possessed by an artist, by a frustrated priest, or by some other hedonistically inclined protagonist. The novels contain, along with a variety of sensual and perverse happenings, murders and odd suicides, all done in an extremely lyrical, if melodramatic, way. His production includes *Flor de fango* (1895), *Ibis*, his own favorite, published in 1900, *La caída del Cóndor* (1913), *María Magdalena* (1917), *El huerto del silencio* (1917), and *Salomé* (1918). From his first short novel, *Aura o las violetas* (1887), about animal pleasures and orgasms, to his latest one, like *La novena sinfonía* (1928), in which a countess, sex, a musicale, and a revolution form a witch-like brew, in novels like *El minotauro* (1919), about abortion, politics, and exile and with autobiographical elements of his youth, or in *Vuelo de cisnes* (1919), about murder, incest, sexual fantasies, and mythology, one finds the elements which made him, among Colombians, the "más popular fuera de las fronteras." [183]

Rafael Maya believes that Vargas Vila's youthful works are "irremediablemente cursis," but he finds his mature works to be "largas tiradas líricas," even though he contends that Vargas Vila "desconocía por completo el arte de novelar." [184] Possessed of great imagination, Vargas Vila made up for his humorless and stylistically inflated writing through his vivid creation of a kind of "spiritual autobiography."

Leopoldo Lugones, better known as one of the great poets of the continent, wrote a number of short stories on fantastic and science-fiction themes which predated those of Borges and Bioy-Casares, his fellow Argentines. Typical of these tales are the ironically burlesque ones in *Las fuerzas extrañas* (1906). *La guerra gaucha* (1905), a kind of historical novel in twenty-two episodes, is about the battle for independence in northern Argentina, perhaps "el más representativo intento de adaptación del modernismo al tema vernáculo . . . un modernismo americanizante." [185] His other fiction is *Cuentos fatales* (1924) and *El ángel de la sombra* (1926), a strange novel of passion. Atilio Chiappori in his short stories and in his novel *La eterna angustia* (1908) emphasized neuroses, hypersensitivity, and diabolical vengeance, reflecting the influence of Barbey D'Aurevilly, Poe, and D'Annunzio, among others.

In Peru the semi-pornographic novels of Felipe Sassone (1884–1954) were quite popular, but his importance is much less than that of Clemente Palma (1872–1946), friend of the short story writer Abraham Valdelomar and the son of Ricardo Palma, who brought to a head the Russian influence started by Cabello de Carbonera. He directed *El Iris* and *Prisma*, important modernist journals of Peru, although he expressed therein his reservations about certain aspects of modernism. Ironical and skeptical, he was nonetheless preoccupied with parapsychological manifestations and metaphysics, stressing also the magical and fictional properties of science. In 1904 he wrote *Cuentos malévolos*, to create the modern short story in Peru, and was instrumental in giving "Peruvian fiction of the turn of the century a more universal orientation." [186] *Mors en vita* (1922), a short novel, treats of the magic and the occult he loved so dearly, and *Historias malignas* (1924) reveals a continuing interest in fantasy and the macabre in the manner of his much admired Edgar Allen Poe. His one novel, *XYZ* (1935), is about a

North American scientist, Rolland Poe, who carries on experiments on an island in the hope of recreating human life. Hollywood exhibits his materializations, causing their destruction and his suicide.

Clemente's sister, Angélica, a modernist and periodic feminist, shared her father's interest in the colonial history of Peru and to an extent her brother's in psychology. *Vencida* (1918), written under the pseudonym of Marianela, *Por senda propia* (1921), her third novel and the first in which she used her real name, an examination of the changing customs from colony to independence, *Coloniaje romántico* (1923), *Tiempos de la patria vieja* (1926), and *Uno de tantos* (1926), considered to be her best novel, are among the ten she wrote. The last named is a psychological study of the spiritual frustration, political failure, and death due to drugs of a young student.

4. Criollismo

In the twentieth century, as we have previously stated, the student of the Spanish American scene may be tempted to classify novels as rural, city, naturalistic, *indigenista*, anti-imperialist, or psychological. Many of these novels, including some of the greatest produced in the first thirty years of the century, may be described under the broad banner of *criollismo*, which almost every writer on Spanish American literature has attempted to define in some way—among them José Juan Arrom, Arturo Uslar Pietri, Ricardo Latcham, Domingo Melfi, Milton Rossel, Mariano Latorre, Juan Carlos Álvarez, Félix Lizaso, Víctor Pérez Petit, Alberto Zum Felde, Luis Alberto Sánchez, Homero Castillo, and Pedro Henríquez Ureña. The word "criollo" was first used in the *Historia Natural y Moral de las Indias* by Padre José de Acosta in the late sixteenth century—"como allá llaman a los nacidos de españoles con indios" —and also by Garcilaso de la Vega, Inca, who states that the Spaniards "han introducido este nombre en su lenguaje para nombrar los nacidos allá." [1] A *criollo* is someone born in Spanish America, whether of foreign parents or of natives, although at one time it signified an American born of Spanish parents. Coming to be almost synonymous with native, the word was applied to almost anything national or vernacular, especially as something of local essence as opposed to the foreign. In a final evolution of a changing concept, the word as a literary expression "adquiere en nuestros días su pristino sentido de 'lo americano esencial.' " [2]

Luis Alberto Sánchez objects to the term "novela criolla" because the definition is so broad that it can include almost everything in it.[3] Nonetheless, by using this admittedly broad definition, one can avoid a number of classifications and subclassifications otherwise necessary and with categories so fragmented as to confuse the reader and render the labels meaningless. Criollismo varies according to one's concept of the artistic operation, and rigid definitions and dogmatic conclusions of any kind are questionable. But let us see if we cannot narrow the definition enough to make it useful.

Luis Alberto Sánchez himself differentiates criollismo from *costumbrismo*, with which some confuse it, stating that "el criollismo alcanza más, por cuanto se define, por su tono tanto como por su contenido. La costumbre es susceptible de caer en manos de un extranjero que puede ser anticriollista: el criollismo sólo cabe en el alma de un devoto de lo castizo." [4] Whether a novel is called *nativista* or indigenista (the term criollismo is extensively used only in Chile and Venezuela), the novelist attempts to present the New World, interpret its inhabitants in relation to the American cosmos, and give expression to authentic national spirit and aspirations. Arturo Torres-Rioseco believes that it was in "las llanuras del Uruguay y de la República Argentina donde adquirió prestigio de escuela literaria en su forma más especial de novela gauchesca. En el Uruguay lo cultiva Eduardo Acevedo Díaz, 'primer escritor nacionalista' de su patria." [5] Whether a novelist deals with country or city, sugar mill or rubber plantation, the *huaso* or the gaucho, psychology or sociology, man in relationship to nature or man in relationship to his fellowman, he is essentially trying to convey, beyond the picturesque, satirical, and critical, a total flavor of America, and more specifically of his own country. Criollismo is a Latin American form of realism or regionalism which stresses the people and their land. It may involve elements of costumbrismo, *reformismo*, the catastrophic and tragic elements of naturalism, social problems, nature as an external destructive force inimical to man, violence, love, hate, human passion, the anonymous, and the alienated. Two of the basic ingredients are the tragic and fatalistic elements of naturalism on the one hand, and the artistic legacy of modernism on the other. Uslar Pietri has pointed out that the apparently contradictory influences of modernist renovation and naturalistic fatalism combine and "pronto derivan hacia un realismo peculiar que llamaremos criollismo, donde estos elementos vienen a combinarse, en diversas formas, con otros que provienen de la tendencia artística." [6] Some writers, unsure of their own position about fiction, alternated in separate works between modernist flights of fancy and naturalistic novels. Among these writers were Pedro Prado, Carlos Reyles, and Eduardo Barrios, the first in *Alsino* and *El juez rural*; the second in *El embrujo de Sevilla* and *Beba*; and the third in *El hermano asno* and *Un perdido*. As we have already seen, this tendency develops in Díaz Rodríguez with his divergent novels, *Sangre patricia* and *Peregrina*. Guillermo de Torre has noted that "elementalismo y refinamiento mezclados constituyen pues, uno de los rasgos característicos más permanentes de buena parte de la literatura hispanoamericana." [7]

For some critics criollismo pertains only to the rural ambiance as opposed to city life, and especially reflects picturesque customs; but criollismo includes the entire environment of a region, applying as easily to the city in its artistic expression of the local soul or national spirit and in its examination of the social problems, the political motivation, or sexual habits. As with naturalism, where it was easier to examine specific segments of society, so with criollismo many novelists found they could best represent society through popular types. One can find, in the city, too, characters, conflicts, and problems typical of the region and its telluric and autochthonous elements. The city environment was obviously more European but only relatively rather than intrinsically. Pedro Henríquez Ureña has noted that "el movimiento criollista has existido en toda la América española con intermitencias, y ha aspirado a recoger las manifestaciones de la vida popular, urbana y campestre, con natural preferencia por el campo." [8] The criollo novel, then, while it is a descendant of old nativist forms, offers a new manner of examining man and his values, not only in the jungle, on the river, or on the plains but also in the city.

Often, universal aspects may be achieved through the regional and national, for in adapting or attempting to adapt to regional conditions, inevitably one must attempt to understand the new political and historical currents of the Western World in their conflict with traditional values. Yet these problems are almost always viewed in Spanish America from the local perspective and as a part of the local humanity, as "tipos, caracteres, sucesos, problemas, se definen y limitan en una zona de determinación nacional, regional, comprometiendo totalmente su universalidad específica en este sentido . . ." [9] Whether one calls it regionalism, nativism, or vernacularism, criollismo involves creation from and through the author's own personal experiences. By concentrating on one's own little corner, one may be better understood by the world, for "literariamente, la aldea bien descrita es la conquista de lo universal. Una cabaña puede contener el mundo." [10] The movement, if that is what it is, resembles, in its love of *paisaje*, the Generation of 1898 and Paul Valéry's analysis of relationships between the soul of nature and man.[11]

Pedro Grases, in a well-known essay which aroused the ire of a number of critics, somewhat arbitrarily and dogmatically decries the importance of man or the human factor and sees the only protagonist as Nature, with human types reduced to a kind of simple accident, their actions playing a subordinate role to geographic factors. For him nature will continue to be dominant, and anecdotal and regionally limited criollismo will give way to symbolic interpretations of natural events, "con evidente mengua de la participación humana." [12] Arturo Torres-Rioseco, objecting to Grases' definition of "human geography," considers that his thesis may have applied to past fiction but has little bearing on later novels;[13] and Anderson Imbert disputes that nature is necessarily dominant in a number of novels which deal with social injustice, urban and rural problems, or psychological ones.[14] An American phenomenon involving more than nature, criollismo reflects the social tragedy of the continent, "el latifundio, la gomera, la mina, la fábrica, el cañaveral, la pampa, la selva; tragedia protagonizada por indios, negros, cholos, zambos, rotos, mulatos. De ahí que muchas novelas y cuentos americanos encierren un germen revolucionario que, para el prestigio de nuestras letras, sólo excepcionalmente trasciende en expresiones de un inconformismo exaltado y desesperado." [15]

America, from its earliest moments a complete novelty to Europeans, was racially something neither European nor Indian. The American criollo differed appreciably from the Spaniard, and in a society in formation antagonisms between the two were common. With the passing years, differing views of American and European reality contributed to a growing dichotomy. Spanish

American fiction uniquely presented nature as a literary protagonist rather than as a mere backdrop, one of tragic dimensions
which inhibited man's progress. Literary mixtures combining the
mythic and the realistic, the epic and the psychological, the poetic
and the social, together with racial mixtures and an American love
for the baroque, the difficult, and the ornamental emphasized differing developments.[16] Although in general America was always
different in its search for new paths, until criollismo, with rare exceptions, novelists copied European experience and European
men and women. Even when they sought to reveal differing spiritual and temperamental factors, they elaborated a kind of folkloric-
costumbrista pastiche. The criollista, recognizing that peculiarly
local forms and models were needed, conceded the uniqueness of
each individual and tried to maintain his humanity while emphasizing the national aspects of his economic, social, and political
life. The growing American vernacular effort and its concomitant
withdrawal from European models, helped create the new autochthonous narrative which, as Homero Castillo points out, though
quite difficult to define specifically, is almost a tangible thing for
the reader: ". . . su caracterización se hace escurridiza e inapren-
sible hasta el extremo de ofrecer serios obstáculos al crítico que
desee individualizarla en abstracto con el fin de diferenciarla de
otros matices literarios o de realizar las categorías de contenido y
forma que ella involucra." [17] This difficulty is compounded by
the differing customs and racial mixtures within the same country,
which leads to a rapid and superficial examination at times instead of the complete and constant dedication needed to understand American man and his environment.

Criollismo reflects, as we have stated, a new kind of baroque
which, fusing with modernism in its search for beauty of expression and accepting from naturalism a tendency toward fatalism,
the cruelty of life, and an abnormal psychology, produced a new
primitive stylization of reality in landscape, characters, and action. After its early phase, especially in the second and third decades of the twentieth century, it emphasized symbolic, magic, and
mythical elements of man's struggle against his environment,
himself, and his society, and criollista novelists continued to use
fiction as an instrument of struggle for justice and reform.[18]
Criollismo, therefore, is more than a mere regionalism. It is au-

thentic Americanism, at times transposing and at others recording its often brutal, harsh, and violent environment. In his confrontation with American reality, the author who just indulges in a casual insistence on Americanism or depicts a few dialectal forms to produce local color is not a criollista. In its amalgam of impressionism, realism, and psychological, poetic, and sociological factors, and in its combination of naturalistic and modernist elements, the classical criollista novel allows for a more tightly controlled realistic and artistic portrayal of Creole life.

Undoubtedly the romantic *Zárate* (1882) and *Julián* (1888), the latter transfused with naturalistic elements, influenced the developing Venezuelan novel. Some readers believe it may even rival *Peonía* as the "first" criolla novel. Even more important was *Todo un pueblo* (1899) by the naturalistic writer Miguel Eduardo Pardo (1865–1905), a friend of Vargas Vila. The romantic story about a social reformer who kills the evil father of his sweetheart, a man who also undermined the morality of his widowed mother, is decidedly less important than its political, passionate, and crudely realistic and almost grotesque evocation of Villabrava (Caracas) and its customs and a world of phony politicians, revolutionaries, and a newly rich class. Generally, the first criollista novel and the first modern Venezuelan novel as well is considered to be *Peonía* (1890). Its author, Manuel Vicente Romero García (1865–1917), the son of a rich hacendado, traveled a good deal and became a newspaperman, which perhaps explains the partly journalistic tone of his novel. Strong attacks and defenses of the novel have occurred through the years; *Peonía* has been the cause of more than one impassioned polemic. Dillwyn F. Ratcliff feels that it is a half truth to say that criollismo began with *Peonía*,[19] but Hugo Barbagelata defends it vigorously as the beginning of Venezuelan criollismo and "dotada de envidiable visión de los hombres y de las cosas del terruño." [20] Rafael Angarita Arvelo, who called it "el primer intento meritorio de novela nacional," attacked Julio Planchart for his harsh evaluation of the novel,[21] prompting a long analysis and defense of his position by Planchart. The latter stated that *Peonía* was but a poor copy of *María*, that it was lacking in adequate nature description, proportion, taste, or unity, but grudgingly conceded that "con todo, *Peonía* era la materia informe de una buena novela." [22] The polemic continued to sputter among various writers for a number of years. Later evaluations more positively tend to view *Peonía* as the progenitor of Venezuelan fiction—"echa las bases de la novela venezolana al ofrecernos cuadros llenos de vida, saturados de paisaje, de gente, de pasiones nacionales." [23] Arturo Uslar Pietri, conceding that its hasty writing and improvisation make it not quite a novel, sees in it the convergence of spiritual and material circumstances "que iban a hacer posible y hasta necesaria la aparición y el desarrollo del género novelesco." [24]

The romantic story is about a young engineer, Carlos, exiled to the sugar plantation of his uncle. He falls in love with his cousin, Luisa, whose sister, Andrea, and stepmother, Carmelita, are having affairs with hacienda workers. Discovered, the two Negroes, Casiano and Bartolo, burn down the hacienda, and in the resultant fire Pedro, the uncle, and his daughter Luisa are killed. Since the author dedicated his novel to Jorge Isaacs and since the plot has some similarities, many saw in it a tighter connection to the Colombian novel than really exists. Mariano Picón-Salas, for example, claims that the author "quiso ser para la llanura venezolana el equivalente de la novela de Isaacs para la región del Cauca." [25] *Peonía* is the name of the plantation and not a woman. Carlos is exiled instead of going off to school, and Luisa manages to die in her sweetheart's arms. Beyond minor plot differences, the whole tone of *Peonía* is unlike that of *María*, even though costumbrista and romantic elements pervade both. Among *Peonía*'s scenes are a hunt, dances, music of various kinds, a wake, and other folkloric elements, including a rural witch who adds a dimension of mystery and superstition to the novel. These elements and the love story, however, although *Peonía* is subtitled "Seminovela y costumbres venezolanas," serve as background for an almost cynical and clinical analysis of Venezuelan reality, its essential nature, and it political life under Guzmán Blanco, for whom Casiano and Bartolo eventually become a general and a captain respectively. Romero García, in his *dedicatoria* to Jorge Isaacs, makes his intention quite clear: "*Peonía* tiende a fotografiar el estado social de mi patria: he querido que la Venezuela de Guzmán Blanco quede en perfil siquiera para enseñanza de las generaciones nuevas." A sociological and political disquisition, it contains the theme of *civilización y barbarie*, and progress versus tradition. Carlos represents the American spirit in his defense of the continent and in his pride in his Indian ancestry. His grandfather and his uncle, proud of their Spanish heritage, defend the old fashioned and traditional against Carlos' belief in progress. Beyond the vision of political, social, and economic reality which Romero García provides in his novel, Carlos and Luisa, whatever their defects, are eminently more believable and human than Efraín and María.

One of the earliest successful criollo novelists, Tomás Carrasquilla (1858–1940), a Colombian, received his nation's National Prize For Literature in 1936 at the age of seventy-eight. For years he had lived in comparative anonymity, possibly because his work appeared in small private editions, many of them published in Medellín, the capital of Antioquia. For a long time "los críticos han mostrado pocos deseos de ir más allá de breves frases de general y alta alabanza," [26] an esteem not always forthcoming in his early writings—during the height of modernism—which could not compete with those of Rubén Darío, José Asunción Silva, and Guillermo Valencia. Carrasquilla reacted against all formal schools and tendencies in his reaffirmation of local and American values. He rebelled against costumbrismo, at least in its picturesque aspects, rejected the fatalistic aspects of naturalism, proclaiming his faith in the dignity of man, and scorned the hermetic and exotic qualities of modernism. Antioquia, normally considered to be an extremely conservative and Catholic region, viewed by Carrasquilla with love and affection and reproduced in its popular regional flavor, is the scene for all his fiction. Cejador y Frauca viewed him as the first regional novelist of America—"El más vivo pintor de costumbres y el escritor más castizo, y allegado al habla popular, no sólo de su tierra antioqueña, sino, y por lo mismo, de cualquier región americana." [27] Many interpreted this to mean that Carrasquilla was an old fashioned nineteenth-century costumbrista writer, and some have continued to label him in this way.[28] Kurt Levy, however, for whom he is the "pioneer of Spanish stories," sees his American spirit: "Sus maiceros tienen sitio al lado de los gauchos, los llaneros, los cholos, los caucheros y demás especímenes nativos de América." [29] Federico de Onís, along with Mariano Latorre one of the first to recognize Carrasquilla's true stature, compared him to Benito Pérez Galdós and considered Carrasquilla to be an almost unique writer, a definite precursor of the modern world in its most genuine expression and in "la busca de lo propio," who has "más alcance y otra intención estética que el de los regionalistas, realistas y naturalistas europeos del siglo XIX y sus secuaces de América . . . la región no es . . . un resto rústico del pasado . . . es además la expresión más genuina del carácter original y distinto de América entera y de sus modalidades nacionales." [30] Carrasquilla was probably the only Spanish American novelist of his time who fully realized what his art and intentions were,[31] as well as "el primer novelista regional de Hispanoamérica . . . pocos prosistas contemporáneos igualan a Carrasquilla, y poquísimos lleguen a superarlo, ni como creador de personajes vivos e interesantes, ni como descriptor de costumbres y de paisajes reales . . ." [32] Carlos García Prada, who has written persuasively about Carrasquilla, insists that he "inició . . . entre nosotros el criollismo auténtico, al entrar de lleno y en firme en la entraña misma del pueblo y del ambiente americanos, y al utilizar el lenguaje popular como medio único y válido del quehacer novelístico autóctono y sincero." [33]

Carrasquilla attempted to reveal national character in artistic and aesthetically pleasing form. Although he rejected the artificial qualities of modernism and the fatalism of naturalism, he combined much of what he had learned from them to produce works not for a group of esoteric sycophants but for people everywhere. His novels have very little formal plot, but he pays great attention to characters, usually people of humble origin whom he found in the villages and cities of his region. These characters reflect the entire gamut of human emotion and endeavor, and one finds in his gallery the comic and the tragic, the greedy and the generous, the taciturn and the talkative, the dishonest and the honorable, and a variety of professions and callings, priests, farmers, doctors, servants, workers, and especially women and children, each with his own speech pattern, whether rustic or popular.[34] With color, variety, vigor, humor, sympathy, and truth, he treated the daily events and the legends and superstitions of their lives, and to a certain extent his own ("el elemento autobiográfico presente en mayor o menor grado en toda su obra"),[35] as he narrates almost exclusively in the first person.

Carrasquilla has four full length novels, *Frutos de mi tierra* (1896), *Grandeza* (1910), *La marquesa de Yolombó* (1928), and

Hace tiempos (1935). But he wrote also a number of novelettes or long short stories, among whose titles we find: *Blanca* (1897), *Salve Regina* (1903), *Entrañas de niño* (1906), a penetrating psychological examination, *Dimitas Arias* (1897), his most nostalgic story, saturated with memories, and *El zarco* (1922). Carrasquilla preferred *Salve Regina* above all his works, stating that it was the only one which pleased him completely.[36] In a psychologically sound manner, most of these short works seek to study the protagonist whose name heads the title and whose life affords the author an opportunity for autobiographical reminiscences of a popular or moral nature. Blanca is an innocent girl who provides spiritual force. The heroine of *Salve Regina*, more human and tormented, must choose between love and duty. Stressing the virtues of objectivity and humility, Carrasquilla seems to be saying in his fiction that overwhelming pride or obsession with material wealth or social status is always self-destructive.

One Colombian defined *Frutos de mi tierra* as "castiza, terrígena y humana." [37] Taken from nature and reality, it depicts the social classes of Antioquia and studies the obsession with material wealth and its consequences. Carrasquilla, conceding little artistic merit to his first novel, explains that he wrote it to fulfill an obligation to a literary circle he had joined. Carlos Restrepo, the leader of the group, decided to hold a discussion as to whether or not Antioquia contained material for fiction. With the exception of Restrepo and Carrasquilla, all felt that it did not. To prove his contention Carrasquilla wrote "un mamotreto allá en los reconditeces de mi cuartucho. No pensé tampoco en publicarlo: quería probar solamente que puede hacerse novela sobre el tema más vulgar y cotidiano . . ." [38] The Alzate family, of good origin, had become quite successful. When the mother, Mónica, died, the two older children, Filomena and Agustín, cheated the other two daughters out of their share, and refusing to face up to their own extravagances, blamed others for their difficulties. Agustín, shamed by a public whipping for slander, never recovers, and retires to the country. Filomena enlists the help of her nephew, César, who marries her for her money and absconds with it. She dies. Although the love of Martín Gala for Pepa Escandón, his difficulties, and final success enhance the positive moral virtues of the novel, the best characterization is that of the avaricious Filomena and her awakening to love.

Grandeza, in whose prologue Carrasquilla states that he wants to create characters but admits he has managed only types, discusses the disastrous effects of gossip and depicts high society in Antioquia, its fiestas, horse races, vanities, social pretensions, drinking, gambling, as well as various loves, and general social hypocrisy. Doña Juana Barraneda de Samudio has two daughters, Magdalena and María de Jesús, and one son, José Joaquín. María, known as Tutú, is superficial and as vain and socially conscious as her mother. Magdalena is quite intelligent. In spite of the financial difficulties in which she finds herself, Juana insists on giving a masked ball which all the finest families attend. To pay for it she pawns her jewels and a gift to Tutú from the rich Arturo Granda, known as Grandeza. Magdalena marries her cousin and with the help of her brother temporarily saves the family. Tutú marries Grandeza, who loses all his money as bad luck continues to plague the family.

Rafael Maya, in the prologue to the complete works (Madrid, 1952) of Carrasquilla, states that "la mejor novela de Carrasquilla, su obra maestra, es *La marquesa de Yolombó*." Few will deny that assertion, even though the novel was never popular.[39] In a prologue to the novel itself Carrasquilla traces the history of Yolombó, its ups and downs, its people, its solitude, its mines, and its churches. Even though he talks of people who have the same name as historical entities of Yolombó, he declares that "no es ésta, en ningún concepto, más que una conjetura sobre esa época y sus gentes..." In this historical novel about eighteenth-century Antioquia he changed facts and chronology "por tratarse, tan solamente, de evocar una faz de la colonia en estos minerales antioqueños." San Lorenzo de Yolombó, once half-desert but enriched through gold mining, numbered among its most important families that of Pedro Caballero, the town mayor, and that of José María Moreno, whose son Vicente marries Pedro's daughter, María. The other Caballero daughter is named Bárbara, a typical Carrasquilla heroine who falls in love with the wrong man and suffers the consequences. Bárbara is served by three ex-slaves whom she has freed and befriended. She teaches herself to read and write, founds schools, and seeks to better her region through a variety of charitable and educational activities. Because of her position and almost fanatical devotion to the Spanish throne she is given the title of "Marquesa" by Carlos IV. Her very success brings on tragedy, as she falls victim to Fernando de Orellano, a confidence man who marries and then deserts her. For a time Bárbara loses her sanity, as well as her title, as the ideas of the French Revolution prevail. Eventually she regains her reason and dies at a ripe old age. In addition to fine portraits of Rosalía, Pedro's wife, and her brother-in-law, Carrasquilla presents us with a variety of *chapetones* (a derogatory term for Spaniard) and physically and psychologically authentic Americans. He gives us a full-blown picture of the temporal and spatial coordinates (often with a keen sense of humor), the baptisms, the processions, the religious festivals, the mythology and superstition, the music, dances, social and economic factors, especially of the mining industry, and the daily experiences of Negroes, farmers, servants, Indians, and workers at work and at play.

Hace tiempos, his literary testament which seems more autobiography than novel, has three volumes. The first, *Por aguas y pedrejones*, describes, through Eloy Gamboa, his childhood, his friends, his parents, house, and street, together with the superstitions and social conditions of his region. *Por cumbres y cañadas* and *Del monte a la ciudad*, the second and third volumes, concern the struggles between conservatives and liberals, the educational system, the life of miners, their separation from the outside world, and the spiritual and intellectual growth of Eloy. Carrasquilla maintains his fine ear for dialogue, as he provides subtle and at times ironic observations about some 150 characters in the novel, which some consider his best work.[40]

Carrasquilla, who spent almost his entire life in Antioquia, which he once described as the "pueblo de tres efes—feo, frío y faldudo" but of a "quietud arcadiana," sought to express the soul of his region and its inhabitants. The living quality of his characters and theme allow the reader to penetrate to the deepest levels of what it means to be a man and an antioqueño. Rafael Maya, in the prologue to Carrasquilla's *Obras completas*, declares that his fellow Colombian is a conspicuous representative of his people and environment and that he "vale por antioqueño, y, más que todo todo por haber en cierto modo exagerado los valores humanos del antioqueño." His love of truth, his simplicity, and his "lealtad a la tierra en que vivió, y a sus gentes y modos de ser, sentir y obrar, a sus tradiciones, creencias y virtudes, y aun a sus vicios y supersticiones" [41] make him an almost unique entity in Colombian literature.

As we saw earlier, Miguel Cané (padre) in *La familia de Sconner* was already preoccupied with the gaucho as a child of nature on the wane. Later in the nineteenth century a number of writers, among them Domingo Faustino Sarmiento, Hilario Ascasubi, Estanislao del Campo, and José Hernández had established the gaucho as a literary figure and viewed him either as a barbaric, primitive victim of social injustice or as an idealization. A number of novelists, also, talked of the gaucho. *Amalia* contains a few fragmentary references to the gaucho. A series of minor novelists, among them Santiago Estrada (1841–1891), José Joaquín de Vedia (1877–1936), Bartolomé Mitre's brother-in-law, and Eduardo Gutiérrez (1851–1889), treated the gaucho more fully. Gutiérrez, especially, admired the gaucho and devoted several of his novels, among the thirty or so he wrote, to the gaucho theme. He also published, around 1880, some historical novels, *Juan Manuel de Rosas*, *La Mazorca* and detective stories such as *El asesinato de Alvárez*. *Santos Vega* (1880), *Juan Sin Patria* (1881), and *Juan Moreira* (1879), his most famous of all, are about the gaucho and his reaction to injustice which leads him into a vicious circle of crime and punishment. Juan Moreira, deceived by a justice of the peace who makes advances to his wife and by a merchant who refuses to repay a large loan, kills his false friend in a duel and becomes a hunted outlaw. His adventures involve vengeance, love, arrest, torture, and his eventual death.

Roberto J. Payró (1867–1928), probably accurately labeled "figura prócer de las letras argentinas," [42] while not explicitly a novelist of the gaucho, inherited and used the long tradition. His grandfather had been an immigrant, and perhaps this gave him his added insight and warm and human understanding so apparent in his treatment of Argentine society in transition and its difficult politics and rivalries between immigrants and established citizens. Payró was one of the earliest to have what Uslar Pietri has called "el sentido de los valores autóctonos." [43] Primarily a newspaper-

man and seeker of truth both in city and country, Payró founded
La Tribuna in Bahía Blanca in 1889, and in 1892 joined *La Nación*
of Buenos Aires where one of his good friends was Rubén Darío.
Earlier Payró had been befriended by Fray Mocho (José S. Álvarez), who saw his great promise. On *La Tribuna*, a liberal and progressive paper, Payró espoused socialist causes. *La Nación* helped
him travel around the country, and he gathered folkloric and
legendary material, some of which he incorporated into his travel
works. In his transcription of the transitional period in Argentine
life, he showed a strong social conscience but rarely lost his optimism or good humor; yet one must concur that his total work is a
protest against society and that "el propósito social de su arte es
claro; un propósito depurador, un afán de crítica." [44]

Payró's three major fictional pieces are a novelette, *El casamiento de Laucha* (1906), *Pago Chico* (1908), and the *Divertidas aventuras del nieto de Juan Moreira* (1910), but among his twenty
volumes he also has several chronicles, historical novels, plays,
literary criticism (some under the pseudonym of Magister Prunum),
and travel books. At the age of eighteen he wrote *Antígona* and
Entre amigos, consigned, with some justice, to obscurity. In 1887
he published *Scripta* and the following year *Novelas y fantasías*.
Of his two travel books, *La Australia Argentina* (1898) and *En las
tierras del Inti* (1909), the former, "excursión periodística a las
costas patagónicas," contains beautiful descriptions of local customs and essays on the realities and possibilities of southern Argentina; it has been called "libro trascendente para el porvenir
del país." [45]

His chronicles or historical novels treat largely of the conquest
of the Río de la Plata. *El falso Inca* (1905) and a posthumous edition (1930), labeled *Chamijo*, narrate the adventures of one Pedro
Chamijo, an Andalusian rascal who pretended to be a descendant
of the Incas. *El capitán Vergara* (1925), his best known chronicle,
is the story of Domingo Martínez de Irala, from Vergara, and the
Spaniards Pedro de Mendoza, the protagonist, and Alvar Núñez
Cabeza de Vaca. It contains political intrigues, conflicts with Spaniards, battles with Indians, and a number of love affairs. Captain
Vergara started as a private with Mendoza and became the ruler
of Paraguay. As his life impinges on others we see the conquistador's thirst for gold, the good and the bad in man, his hopes and

fears, and the racial mixtures during the conquest. *El mar dulce* (1927), "crónica romanesca del descubrimiento del Río de la Plata," has as its egotistical but noble protagonist Juan Díaz de Solís, a portrayal enlivened by the presence of the picaresque Paquillo. Germán García states that this novel is "la más perfecta obra literaria de Payró, donde se volcó el poeta que no pudo reflejar en versos prosaicos sus anhelos juveniles." [46] His posthumous publications include *Los tesoros del rey blanco* (1934) and *Por qué no fue descubierta la ciudad de los Césares* (1934). Payró planned a complete series of these chronicles but died before he could complete them.

El casamiento de Laucha, the tale of a gaucho pícaro, has timing, pace, and a great sense of the popular. Its more cynical and potentially cruel qualities set it somewhat apart from the normally tolerant and understanding position of the author; but the spontaneity, the humorous aspects of gaucho life, and the authentic gaucho speech of Payró's favorite place, Pago Chico, make this almost a short masterpiece. The novelette treats of Laucha, a criollo who loses one position after another. He comes to Pago Chico and works at a *pulpería* (a kind of country store) near there called La Polvadera, owned by an Italian widow, doña Carolina. She likes him and is willing to dispense him her favors but only as his wife. The equally picaresque priest gives Laucha a hand certificate, assuring him that he can tear it up if Carolina does not please him, and the priest does not enter the ceremony on the books. Through his gambling and the machinations of Barrabas, the political comisario, Laucha loses his money and his wife's pulpería. When she upbraids him, he tells her she is just his mistress, and as she rushes off to the church to verify her position, he disappears. Laucha is an anti-hero, "una excrecencia ciudadana que cae fortuitamente en la zona rural y que gracias a una feliz inspiración adquiere categoría estética . . ." [47]

Pago Chico, published as a book of short stories joined together in the form of a novel, is the generic image of provincial towns of the day—although it resembles clearly, and indeed is, Payró's own Bahía Blanca around 1886. A posthumously published collection, *Nuevos cuentos de Pago Chico* (1929), complemented the first volume. Payró satirizes the politics, the police, the social sores and classes. The village is subject to all kinds of political corruptions.

When the rival parties fall out over gambling control, the judge, Pedro Machado, is attacked by a rival, Domingo Luna, who uses as his vehicle the newspaper *El Justiciero*. But, as so often happens, the rivals become friends and the newspaper, the official organ. Viera (Payró), a young idealistic reformer, buys a newspaper, *La Pampa* (*La Tribuna*), in the hope of reforming Pago Chico, a semi-feudal area where a "free press" serves the political aims of the corrupt; but the hired assailants and political power structure prove to be too much for him. Payró evokes criollo life and types which largely disappeared some time ago in Argentina. He laments the absence of a will to work and of respect for the rights of others in Argentina and details thoroughly the exploitation of man by man, the ignorance, the speculation, the superstition, and the corruption. Pago Chico is a town filled with *pícaros* ready and able to deceive the ingenuous who visit the town.[48] Whether the work is a novel, short stories, or sketches of creole customs, it evokes and dissects that period of Argentine development when agriculture was gradually causing the disappearance of the gaucho.

Payró's love of progress and hatred of sham can best be seen in his *Divertidas aventuras del nieto de Juan Moreira*, whose ironic title reveals the inheritance left by Facundo and others of his type. Payró thoroughly documents Argentina's development, politics, and industrialization, from the fall of Rosas to the Stock Market crash of 1890. The protagonist, Maurico Gómez Herrera, who tells his tale in the form of memoirs, is in a sense still the "gaucho malo" of Eduardo Gutiérrez—cruel in a more penetrating way and without the poetry or romanticism of the legendary Juan Moreira. The "nieto" inherits his political role from his father, and, as the prototype of the successful Argentine politician, he exemplifies a complete barbarism and amorality covered over by the thinnest of civilized veneers. The new generation of rural bosses still scorn the central government and lack even the traditional virtues of their forefathers. Payró traces his early education in a picaresque manner. The boy is a gang leader, then a politician; he seduces and abandons his father's best friend's daughter and goes to Buenos Aires, betraying friend and foe, men and women. A young idealist writes a series of articles attacking Mauricio and uses the title of "Las divertidas aventuras del nieto de Juan Moreira," but he cannot recover from the shock when he learns that Mauricio, the really primitive, barbaric, and corrupt embodiment of evil, is his father. The superficially humorous tone hides a bitter vision: that of Argentine history and its collective soul. The implicit message seems clear; it is high time to forget about the gauchos, past and present, and, probing the national spirit, find a new dream of justice and political maturity.

Among other early criollo novels combining naturalism with modernism, politics, social reform, and regional description, one must note *Pax* (1907) by the Colombian Lorenzo Marroquín (1856–1918), the son of José Manuel Marroquín. He wrote the novel in collaboration with José María Rivas Groot (1863–1923), himself the author of two mediocre novels, *Resurrección* (1906) and *El triunfo de la vida* (1916). The first is a modernist novel about painting, music, religion, and the mystery of love and death. The second is about the redemption and spiritual purification of an unhappy and contradictory character. Like Payró, Marroquín is concerned about a society in transition, one swayed by currents from France and the United States and contending with criollo forces. Once again the struggle between "civilización" and "barbarie" takes place against the background of political maneuvering at the turn of the century and a civil war. *Pax*, usually defined as a naturalistic work and in reality a highly patriotic novel, was criticized by conservatives and aristocrats who considered the novel to be a *roman à clef* in which they were satirized. Although the novel is filled with descriptions of weddings, banquets, race tracks, funerals, and discussions of art and music, its author, an impassioned advocate of peace, decries the political intrigues and revolutionary activities of the day. He hated war and the needless sacrifice of youthful lives, and the ironic title of his novel clearly portrays his pessimism. At the end of the novel we see a vision of multiplying corpses, the crying of the wounded, and the silence of the dead.

The railroad of an unscrupulous speculator, Montellano, will be ruined if a canal along the Magdalena river is constructed. The canal had been proposed by the Frenchman Bellegart and approved by Roberto Ávila, Montellano's daughter's sweetheart. A series of political maneuverings takes place, some humorous, some deadly. Roberto, the idealist and progressive, loses out to the forces of evil, and most of the main characters die in the civil war.

The principal defect of *Pax* is the author's tendency to view good and evil romantically and his use of burlesque, to the point of caricature, in representing his actors. Among these is the poet Mata, a rather cruel portrait of the poet, José Asunción Silva. The novel's costumbrismo transcends the simple older type, "yendo más a fondo en su tema; aunque no tanto como los mexicanos que escribieron novelas de la revolución." [49] The novel is unrealistic in places, with unevenly treated characters and a faulty style, but "con todo, es obra representativa, nacional, reveladora de grande ingenio." [50]

Chile had a plethora of criollista novelists (to be examined shortly), but before a full-blown and obsessive criollismo found fruition, several novelists, belonging to the so-called generation of 1900, wrote in that manner. Inheriting the social conscience, if not the bitter humor, of Baldomero Lillo, Federico Gana (1867–1926) mixed simple yet poetic descriptions with stories of sad peasants, the victims of fate. Almost exclusively a short story writer, he is best represented by his collection *Días de campo* (1916). Alone called him "el primer criollista . . . pintó el campo chileno con realismo y belleza . . . ," [51] and Domingo Melfi, recognizing the new quality of Gana's work, stated that he gave "al cuento chileno una realidad y una sobriedad elegantes que eran desconocidas en nuestras letras." [52] His individualism and importance in the birth of criollismo, noted by other critics like Homero Castillo, have been succinctly expressed by Lautaro Yankas, who sees in his work "dos valores confluentes: el hombre moviéndose en su mundo y la creación que él entrega a los suyos, a su patria." [53]

Another of the early criollista writers, Luis Orrego Luco (1866–1948), classified often as a naturalist, is a transition figure, his works representing "el nexo entre el viejo realismo del siglo XIX y el criollismo del siglo XX." [54] Orrego was a diplomat, newspaperman, and professor of law, but his ambition was to write accurately of Chilean life and customs. In his novelistic themes, reminiscent of those of Blest Gana, he includes the role of the *siútico*, the power of money, and descriptions of the *roto*, the middle class, and especially the aristocrats whom he both warmly defended and energetically excoriated from time to time. The foibles of high society interested him, but he was more concerned with philosophical questions and problems such as materialism versus love and the importance of the concept of right over might.

Orrego started off with some short stories, *Páginas americanas* (1892), and in 1900 wrote his first novel, *Un idilio nuevo*, about love, insecurity, and the problems and privileges of empty-headed aristocrats. A kind of unsuccessful *Martín Rivas*, the novel treats of a young provincial who tries to recover social rank, is rejected by his cousin, takes money not belonging to him, and flees the country seeking for a new way of life. Orrego's other lesser novels include *En familia* (1912), about a doctor and events preceding the revolution of 1891, *El tronco herido* (1929), and some historical novels under the title of *Episodios nacionales de Chile. Memorias de un voluntario de la patria vieja* (1905), whose first volume bore the title *1810*, concerns the hatred of criollo for chapetón, rivalries among the patriots, and conspiracies during the period between 1810 and 1814. *Al través de la tempestad* (1914) is noteworthy for its character Apablaza, a lesser Cámara. *Playa negra* (1947) is about the Chile of 1876. It contains magnificent descriptions of the Maule River, but its romantic frame, which includes an earthquake and a suicide, seems somewhat overly melodramatic. Renato Vangirard, a Frenchman, becomes passionately involved with the wife of a Chilean millionaire, Rosita del Valle. The lady's seventeen-year old daughter, Silvia, also loves Renato. Upon discovering her mother's liason, she goes crazy. *Playa negra*, the final novel of what he conceived as a novelistic cycle, "Escenas de la vida en Chile. Recuerdos del tiempo viejo," is the most successful, if not the most famous, reproduction of one aspect of the some fifty years of Chilean history Orrego Luco managed to write about.

Casa grande (1908), a unique Chilean work,[55] also the study of a society in transformation, caused a great public outcry on its appearance and resulted, it is said, in duels being fought.[56] *Casa grande* is *Un idilio nuevo* reworked. Many novelists redid their works into a final form under a different title, a common practice for the twentieth-century Spanish novelist Ramón Sender and for some Spanish American ones, among others, Joaquín Edwards Bello, Alcides Arguedas, Carlos Reyles, and Ricardo Güiraldes. The tempest aroused by the novel stemmed largely from the author's castigation of Chilean aristocrats, their corrupt politics, champagne binges, and snobbishness. Social decomposition and a moral crisis caused in part by new customs from abroad and in part by newly rich families, made so by stock market speculation and the development of the saltpeter industry, preoccupied serious thinkers. Get-rich-quick fever struck the country, but almost nobody wanted to work or to make sacrifices of any kind.

In the story, set between the years 1905 and 1908, Orrego supplies his customary melodrama. Gabriela Sandoval, an aristocrat, is thwarted temporarily in her efforts to marry Ángel Heredia, of good but poor family. When her father, who had put her into a convent to avoid the marriage, dies, the marriage takes place. Their love soon cools and Gabriela leaves Ángel who goes off to Paris and to an affair with an American girl, Nelly. Receiving false information about his wife's infidelity with a former suitor, Ángel poisons her, but she lies about it to protect the family name. Gabriela, the melancholy and beautiful blond, hopes that love and spirituality will triumph over a frivolous society, personified by Magda. Ángel Heredia, whose sensual instincts are overpowering, represents, in his need for money and pleasure, the Chilean society of his day. They and minor characters such as the intelligent but immoral Senator Peñalver, are little more than puppets created by Orrego Luco to reflect his thesis.

Rufino Blanco Fombona (1874–1944), a Venezuelan newspaperman, diplomat, politician, poet, essayist, literary critic, political propagandist, historian, short story writer, and novelist, led a life filled with duels, gun fights, and imprisonment. He left Venezuela in 1910 for about twenty-five years, returning only with the death of the dictator, Juan Vicente Gómez. In Spain and France, through his publishing house, he helped introduce American literature to Europe. His feverish nonliterary activities consumed so much of his time that he had little of it left for polishing what he had written at fever pitch, accounting, in part, for the defects of development in his fictional creations.

After a youthful collection, *Cuentos de poeta* (1900), he wrote *Cuentos americanos* (1904) and *Dramas mínimos* (1920), short stories which reveal many of his religious and political ideas. He began as a writer under the aegis of modernism, which he adapted as a liberating artistic force to his interest in American reality, a combination which in turn produced a variety of criollismo. In one of his stories, "Idilio roto," apparently a favorite title among Spanish American novelists, animals are held to be superior to humans; "Gracia de Dios," another story, attacks the Venezuelan clergy; "Democracia criolla" examines the primitive concept of politics held by the peons as a kind of battle in which those who kill their rivals are immune, through their victory, from legal reprisals.

His first novel, *El hombre de hierro* (1907), is based on his short story, "Redentores de la patria," and is his most popular novel or *novelín*. Crispín Luz, the protagonist, a hardworking, honest bookeeper, is a victim of his society, of a wife who does not love him and betrays him with another, and of a mother who preferred his older cowardly and crooked brother Ramón. Crispín's monstrous child, melodramatically born during an earthquake, provides the only outlet for the love of the apparently insignificant little clerk. Revolution comes to Venezuela. Crispín, weakened by overwork, lies dying as an insensitive priest, indifferent to his suffering and gasping, insists on eliciting a confession. After his death (only one friend attend his funeral), his wife realizes that he was really a good man. The theme of an unappreciated and deserving person whose true value is only discovered after death appealed to Blanco Fombona. He wrote at least a part of the novel in jail in Ciudad Bolívar in 1905, and he could easily and emotionally identify with his creation. Blanco Fombona implied that Venezuela needed strength, will power, and energy. Lacking these qualities, Crispín was a failure in spite of his goodness; a quality which for the author was inevitably associated with weakness. Blanco Fombona wrathfully denounces the stupidity, evil, and cynicism he finds in humanity.

El hombre de oro (1916), set in the time of Cipriano Castro, recalls Pérez Galdós' *Torquemada* series. Miserly, dirty, ugly, grotesque but extremely rich Camilo Irurtia employs Cirilo Matamoros, a country curandero, for his ailments because he is shocked at doctor's fees (Blanco Fombona never misses an opportunity to display his feelings). Rosaura Agualonga and her two sisters have a spoiled, selfish but beautiful niece, Olga Emmerich, who plans to sacrifice her aunt and have her marry Camilo in order to further her own ambitions. To that end she enlists the aid of the opportunistic politician and general Aquiles Chicharra. Politically, Irurtia, the student, soon outstrips his teacher and becomes a minister and eventually president. Olga abandons her husband, Andrés Rata, and runs off with a bull fighter. The theme again is that the race belongs to the swift, and Blanco Fombona states in the prologue, "La Vida se burla de la Bondad y la arrastra por los suelos."

Blanco Fombona's other novels include *La máscara heroica* (1923), his most violent attack on the dictator Gómez and his Venezuelan supporters. He scolded his editor for calling it a novel, referring to it himself as "Escenas de una barbarocracia." *La mitra en la mano* (1927), through his protagonist, Federico Blandín, a vain provincial priest of Orotinto, attacks the compliant and complaisant clergy who work hand in glove with the dictator to oppress the people. The fiendish frocked don Juan, as a result of his activities, becomes a bishop and receives "la mitra en la mano." *La bella y la fiera* (1931), a kind of sequel, tells of the capture and torture of two revolutionaries and the activities of Griselda (the daughter of a nymphomaniac) who becomes the president's mistress. In 1933 Blanco Fombona published *El secreto de la felicidad.*

Blanco Fombona was a proud, passionate, violent, volatile, and belligerent person who believed that literature should serve a moral purpose. He used his novels to attack abject, cowardly, and evil men, and especially corrupt dictators. He reserved special scorn, also, for Venezuelans who took advantage of the poor and for what he called foreign capitalistic imperialism. A great patriot, he was conditioned by the dictatorships of Cipriano Castro and Juan Vicente Gómez under which he had lived and suffered. Indeed, he helped finance an abortive revolution to further his political beliefs. In the process of writing his novels he often failed to develop fully a number of his characters, but they are far from the caricatures or stereotypes some hold them to be. Better at moral judgments than at psychological analysis, he nonetheless created a gallery of types, if not outstanding and unique individuals, such as the miser, the priest, and the politician. One of the keys to his work is the spirit of Americanism, which he constantly defends. In his well-known study of modernism, Blanco Fombona refuted the theory that it was a product of French symbolism, viewing it as a native American occurrence and seeing among its traits, pessimism, verbal refinement, rebellious spirit, challenge to the old, sensuality, love of form, and a kind of moral indifference. Although he himself is somewhat cosmopolitan and impressionistic, his vision of things American is clearly realistic rather than modernist in spirit, in spite of its subjective personal judgments and aggressiveness. In his search for justice Blanco Fombona sought shocking effects. His hate quite frequently impeded his art, but he wrote with great force and vision. His novels are more than mere militancy but by dint of their very violence and temporality "han adquirido antes y después del libro ese hálito de barbarie americana y esa intemporalidad que condicionan a todo testimonio literario." [57] Arturo Uslar Pietri, admitting the novelistic defects of his fellow Venezuelan, claims that "nadie puede negarle a Blanco Fombona grandes virtudes de novelista . . . ninguna novela venezolana sobrepasa las suyas. Aun en sus defectos es un gran escritor, y tuvo aliento, visión, y fuerza creadora . . ." [58]

Luis Manuel Urbaneja Achelpohl (1874–1937), probably the initiator of the modern short story in Venezuela, also combined the artistic tenets of modernism with a naturalistic fatalism. Along with Romero García he is often called "padre del criollismo venezolano." [59] He started writing for *Cosmópolis* and later for *El Cojo Ilustrado*, one of the primary vehicles for the printing of modernist literature. Most of his novels revolve around romantic love in a rural setting and involve a simple, spontaneous, and natural description of the Creole soul and culture. Since he owned and worked a farm, he was quite familiar with the atmosphere he describes; his crude realism and occasional attacks on city life are raised to an artistic level by his fresh and spontaneous approach. He wrote a series of short stories about peasant loves, dances, murder, and the tropics. His three novels are *En este país* (1916), *El tuerto Miguel* (1932), and *La casa de las cuatro pencas* (1937). *En este país*, a prize winning novel, is the love story of a peasant, Paulo Guaramba, and the daughter of a rich hacendado who, as Paulo rises in station, blesses the marriage he had previously forbidden. Paulo is the descendant of a line of slaves of the Macapo family; in his marriage with Josefina Macapo he holds out hope for the future, for he represents the force of the common man and strong blood which the aristocrats have lost. The author has much to say, too, of progress versus tradition through his portrayal of

Gonzalo Rusiñol, the progressive hacendado and his rivalry with the Pichirre clan.

José Rafael Pocaterra (1888–1955), a social novelist interested in politics and Venezuelan city scenes, is also a criollista, though not in the rural vein of Urbaneja Achelpohl. Pocaterra, who held government, administrative, and diplomatic positions, was an "enfant terrible" and, like Blanco Fombona, was imprisoned several times, in 1907 for combating Cipriano Castro and later for fighting against that dictator's heir and betrayer, Juan Vicente Gómez. Pocaterra was briefly freed and again arrested, but he finally managed to escape from La Rotunda prison, going into exile from 1922 to 1935. With a bitterness for which one can hardly blame him, he relates the brutal prison tortures and life under a dictator in his *Memorias de un venezolano de la decadencia* (1927), not a novel but a work which has been called "una de las más significativas de la literatura venezolana y americana de este siglo." [60] Anderson Imbert labels Pocaterra's novels "irate and aggressive creolism." [61] Pocaterra, who states, "Yo escribo en venezolano, pienso y siento en venezolano," [62] analyses Venezuela's provincial society, at times humorously, at others almost poetically, but most often with a stinging satire and a realism verging on naturalism. His characters, a gallery of types, appear almost as caricatures or deformed puppets, but they are real enough, precursors of Reinaldo Solar, even more destructive, in an unscrupulous society in the process of moral and spiritual disintegration. Indeed, many of his novels were based on the activities of real persons and were often written as personal attacks in which he laid bare the quivering flesh of victims and society. He has a good ear for authentic dialogue and an ability to describe environments and people, if not to analyze them, giving us a panoramic social vision of his society.

Pocaterra is at his best in the short story, especially in the violent and crude mixture of realism and fantasy to be found in *Cuentos grotescos* (1922). Perhaps Venezuela's greatest writer of short stories, a popular form of publication in a country where life has been so tormented and frenzied, he is one of many in whom sensibility, intuition, and emotion predominate over reason and will— a further explanation why "muchos de los mejores escritores han dejado lo más valioso de su obra en cuentos." [63] Pocaterra's first novel, *Política feminista* (1912), was later republished as *El doctor Bebé* (1917). It is a social and political satire about end-of-the-century customs in Valencia, Venezuela. In his preface to the novel, Pocaterra notes that his characters, too, "piensan en venezolano, hablan en venezolano, obran en venezolano." Governor Bebé attempts to seduce Josefina Belzares with the help of his secretary, Pepito, who marries Josefina's sister and claims Bebé's child as his own. When Bebé falls from power, Pepito throws mother and child out. Pocaterra exposes a corrupt society run by unscrupulous political bosses, the inevitable sycophants of such a system and the ruin of a middle class which lends itself to the perpetuation of the status quo. *Vidas oscuras* (1916), about social revolution and the downfall of an agricultural society, documents the rivalry between ranch and city folk of Caracas, the inability of the ranch owner to adapt to a new way of life, and the triumph of opportunism and hypocrisy over sincerity and virtue. Crisóstomo Gárate, the old *llanero*, represents the best of traditional Venezuela. His brother Juan Antonio, by contrast, contaminated by a false civilization, can never be happy. Mariano Picón-Salas calls this novel an "especie de enorme cuadro de la existencia venezolana en sus dos planos de campo y ciudad, a comienzos del 900. . . . Frente al mundo puramente idílico o heroico de la vieja narración venezolana, Pocaterra levanta su gran tragicomedia . . ." [64] *Tierra del sol amada* (1919), his best known novel, describes the role of foreigners in Venezuela and specifically Maracaibo, its love affairs and the double standards its society exemplifies. Julio Planchart, quite ambivalent about the novel, states that it seems as though the novelist hated his own creations and that he feared that "el objeto de su sátira se le fuese a escapar de tal modo se apresura a atacarlo." [65] But Pocaterra, although he is sarcastic and attempts to deform reality, is never sly or malicious in his portrayal of characters. In 1946 Pocaterra published *La casa de los Ábila*, a political attack and caricature of Venezuelan oligarchies. He had written the novel originally in 1920 and 1921 during his stay at La Rotunda jail. In it he extols the merits of the rural over the urban, which imposes false foreign ideals on the native scene.

In Venezuela the so-called first literary generation, of which Blanco Fombona and Urbaneja Achelpohl were members, belonged to *El Cojo Ilustrado* and *Cosmópolis*. The generation of

1910, that of Rómulo Gallegos and José Rafael Pocaterra, centered around *La Alborada* and *Sagitario* reviews. *La Alborada*,[66] founded in 1909, had among its members Julio Planchart, Rómulo Gallegos, Julio Rosales, who cultivated the short story, and Henrique Soublette. This last named may well have furnished Gallegos with his model for Reinaldo Solar, in the novel by that name, a reflection of his association with university students from the above named group. Lowell Dunham traces other phases of Gallegos' association with literary journals, such as *Actualidades*, and also discusses at length his importance as an essayist. In any event, Rómulo Gallegos (1884–1969), who until the age of about twenty was subject to "inclinaciones místicas," [67] is the supreme example of a balanced use of modernism and realism in his treatment of all aspects of Venezuelan reality and geography in both an impressionistic and realistically detailed style. One student of his work finds it "la versión más amorosa y acertada del paisaje venezolano, y de las vicisitudes cordiales del hombre que dialoga con él." [68] A school administrator, teacher of literature, psychologist, minister of education, and president of his country, Gallegos, in all his work, preaches the Christian ethic, the avoidance of violence, a belief in justice, and the need for law and understanding—in spite of his own ten-year exile in Cuba and Mexico and the difficulties and imperfections of his Venezuelan countrymen in their involvement with civilization and barbarism. In 1959 a "Semana Galleguiana" was celebrated to honor his seventy-fifth birthday, and his *Obras completas* (10 volumes) were published to almost universal acclaim.

In 1913 Gallegos published his first fiction, a book of short stories, *Los aventureros*, which revealed modernist tendencies along with a compulsion toward social criticism and an interest in anti-social types. *La rebelión y otros cuentos* (1940) and *Cuentos venezolanos* (1949) are other collections. His first novel, *El último Solar* (1920), was reedited in a more definitive edition as *Reinaldo Solar* (1930). Gallegos depicts the frustration and failure of an entire generation and protests against the intellectual enslavement fostered by all dictatorships. Reinaldo Solar, an abulic and neurotic modernist hero, the son of a wealthy landowner, is indulged by an overly loving and religious mother, which partly accounts for his rebellion against orthodoxy as an adult. The boy suffers from mystic seizures. He decides to manage the hacienda because the caretaker is dishonest, tries to write a novel, and with former schoolmates discusses the founding of a new religion. His friend Ortigales comes to live with him. Reinaldo seduces a young lady whom Ortigales marries to protect her reputation. Reinaldo meets Manuel Alcor, a young writer from the provinces, and Antonio Menéndez, a law student. Meeting Rosaura Mendeville, an unhappily married pianist whom he calls La Gioconda, Reinaldo, for a time, seems to find himself. He founds an Asociación Civilista to help his country, but it, too, fails. Tiring of Rosaura and of his unproductive and useless existence, he becomes a revolutionary, fruitlessly, and dies of malaria. Alcor abandons writing and returns to his village to be a pharmacist. Menéndez marries and also abandons his profession. Reinaldo, a man who never found happiness, resembles the protagonist of *Idolos rotos* by Díaz Rodríguez. Through his central character Gallegos attempts to express his ideas about Venezuela and Venezuelans, and, in spite of an apparent pessimism, as in all his novels, he shows an optimistic hope for the future.

As if aware of the importance of the positive view, in his next novel, *La trepadora* (1925), which he wrote in six weeks, Gallegos notes that previous Venezuelan literature had been pessimistic and desperate. In the prologue he acknowledges his novel as "mi primer libro optimista. . . . *La trepadora* es ansia de mejoramiento y, por lo tanto implica confianza en el porvenir." In this story of a social climber, he describes the country life he knows so well, in this case that of high coffee lands shaded by tall trees. Jaimito Casal mismanages the hacienda, Cantarrama, one of the best on the river, but his half-brother, Hilario Guanipa, his father's illegitimate son through an affair with a peasant girl, has the force and energy his more aristocratic relative lacks. Hilario marries well but is unable to bridge the social barriers himself. He will triumph through his daughter, the lovely Victoria (Gallegos was fond of symbolic names, even in English, as can be seen by the ironic labeling of the childish Mr. Builder), who will marry into the nobility and thus finally fuse the two bloods which may well be the salvation of Venezuela. The symbolic ending and the heroine's victory resemble those of Benito Pérez Galdós, who also believed that through new blood and racial mixture the pueblo, uniting with an older aristocracy, might save his country. The characters here are no longer abulic. Hilario Guanipa, a man of overwhelming will power, seeks to impose his wishes on all around him, including his high society wife, Adelaida. Victoria inherits the same strong will, along with some of the sweet kindness of her mother. Success is not for the dreamers, especially the refined, egotistical ones, simply part of the raw material of a rotten society where cheap politicians rule. Not surprisingly, his friend, Julio Planchart, considered the work to be objective and impersonal and a good example of Gallegos' "imaginación objetiva fértil en recursos inventivos condicionales del novelista." [69]

Doña Bárbara, bearing the title *La coronela* in manuscript, first appeared in Barcelona in 1929. The following year, extensively revised, enlarged, and partly rewritten, another edition appeared, the second of about two dozen to date. The novel, based on an actual trip Gallegos made to the llanos in 1927, contains characters based on real people he met during the some eight days he spent at a hunter's paradise, the Candelaria ranch.[70] The constant references and geographical place names seem to place El Paso del Algarrobo as the Paso Arauca and the geographical range of the novel from San Fernando de Apure to the Río Orinoco and from Ciudad Bolívar to San Carlos de Río Negro. Gallegos himself admits that his novel was born in "un hato de Juan Vicente Gómez: el hato de La Candelaria. Allí asimilé ese olor a vacadas y a boñiga de que mi novela está llena. También sentí, a través del cuadro campesino, el hálito de la barbarie que afligía a mi patria." [71] The novel, interpreted as an attack on *gomecismo*, was written in the most tragic moments of the Gómez dictatorship and seemed to symbolize the whole weight of repression suffered by the Venezuelan people. As Mariano Picón-Salas says: "Por un como proceso de transferencia espiritual se vio en la diabólica varona, vengativa, cruel y oscura, la imagen de la tiranía." [72] Gómez, apparently, liked the novel anyway and for personal or political reasons named Gallegos a senator, a dubious honor which the latter managed to avoid by going off to Spain. In a sense, beyond political or symbolic messages, the plains themselves are the protagonist of *Doña Bárbara*, a magnificent natural background of what was to have been a cyclic series about the entire Venezuelan geography.

Jorge Añez, in a labored exercise, tries to show that Gallegos copied, or at least was deeply indebted to his reading of *La vorá-*

gine for inspiration—something which Gallegos and most others deny. Añez insists that Gallegos could not escape the powerful influence "que sobre él ejerció la producción de Rivera, influencia que motivó las múltiples y extrañas similtudes y coincidencias que existen entre estas famosas novelas." [73] *Doña Bárbara*, receiving early critical acclaim as a book filled with American color, bold exploration, and sincere human content, was acknowledged a masterpiece by critics like Jorge Mañach, Mariano Picón-Salas, and Jesús Semprum. [74]

The melodramatic plot is filled with action, color, and suspense. It lent itself beautifully to a film and even to an opera in 1967. Bárbara, a mestiza, is sold as a slave to a repulsive and filthy Syrian. She places her hope for freedom and all her love in young Asdrúbal. The crew kills him and rapes Bárbara, her first real introduction to the world of men. The pilot takes her with him to live among the Indians. She becomes the owner, through fraud, of a large hacienda to the north of the Orinoco, and each day her territories increase. As the present action begins, she is about forty years old. The neighboring Luzardo estate is the chief victim of her depradations, and she uses her body and murder to gain her ends. Among her victims is the pitiful Lorenzo Barquero, a relative of the Luzardos, whose lands she has stolen. He and Bárbara have a child, Marisela, whom the mother ignores and allows to live in misery. Santos Luzardo, having finished law school, takes charge of the hacienda. At first he tries honorable and legal means to succeed but soon learns that the law of the plains is violence. He is indifferent to Bárbara's allure but feels attracted to her half-savage daughter. At the end he wins, and Bárbara, knowing true love only for the second time in her life, triumphing over her baser instincts, cannot kill Marisela, her rival, to whom she gives her property, and mysteriously disappears.

Although many of the characters are based on real individuals, Santos Luzardo and Marisela are pure inventions to give the novel its optimistic coloration. [75] Antonio Sandoval, the most proficient llanero of them all, was Antonio José Torrealba Osto, who provided coplas for the work. Melquiades Gamarra, the brujeador and Bárbara's henchman and hired assassin, was supposedly Juan Ignacio Fuenmayor. Doña Bárbara herself was based on a real *hombruna* of the *hato* Mata el Totumo, one Doña Pancha, whom the author never met.[76] The characters in the large view represent social rather than individual conduct,[77] and Gallegos uses them to express his theme of civilization versus barbarism: Bárbara is barbaric, Santos Luzardo is saintly light, Mr. Danger is North American imperialism, the forward-looking hacienda of Luzardo is "Altamira," while that of Doña Bárbara is "El Miedo." But, in spite of everything, most of the characters, Santos Luzardo excluded, live also as unique individuals.[78] Santos is too good to be true. He is noble, idealistic, civilized, dedicated to the law and justice, and generous to a fault. He loves the plains, of which he himself is partly a product. Mr. Danger, the hunter and trapper, a sensual, hypocritical thief, represents the negative side of Americans everywhere. Pajarote, a typical cowboy and story teller par excellence, likes the plains and the ranch work at which he is so adept. Lorenzo Barquero, an unfortunate human being for whom one feels compassion, is alcoholic, abulic, and a victim of the llano whose telluric force he cannot resist. Mujiquita, unable to overcome his own listless personality, also succumbs to superior force and corruption, a sad, ill, melancholy victim of alcohol and malaria. Colonel Perñalete, the corrupt representative of the law, and Balbino Paiba, the boaster, criminal, and deceitful overseer, as well as others, seem more than symbols or types. Overshadowing them all is Doña Bárbara, like the plains she represents, a creature of impulse, superstitious, credulous, and yet shrewd, sensual and frigid, a woman whose dreams having been lost, allows her love to turn to hate and uses her beauty to destroy men. Her transformation occurs when, recognizing something of Asdrúbal in Santos, she dreams old dreams. In spite of her belief in her familiar, in herself as a witch, and in ghosts, she is also, in her way, quite religious. But at times she is completely negative, sadistic, self-sufficient, and bitter. As if aware of her contrasting and conflicting personality, Gallegos uses an inordinate number of epithets to describe her. She is in turn "la trágica guaricha," "la supersticiosa mujerona," "la bruja del Arauca," "la bonguera," "la mestiza," "una mujer terrible," "la devoradora de hombres," "la mujer insaciable," "la mujerona siniestra," "la barragana," and "la cacica del Arauca."

The novel marks a criollista high point with its episodic portrayal of man against nature and man against injustice, in its combination of modernism and naturalistic emphasis, and in its superstitions, fatalism, and folklore of the plains. The plainsmen believed that the spirit of an animal buried alive at the entrance to a corral when a hacienda was founded would watch over the land which imprisoned it. Doña Bárbara had once added a man to the customary bull or horse to be sacrificed. Juan Primo has his own mad fantasy, that of the *rebullones*, the birds who feed on blood and vinegar. The author presents the work of the llanos from the manufacture of cheese and the roundups to cattle rustlers and rural justice, each facet with poetic tenderness, psychological penetration, and full comprehension of both moral idealism and aesthetic appreciation. But overshadowing everything is the epic sweep of the plains, the rivers and their roaring currents, the voice of America itself, "el ritmo de nuestra tierra hecho belleza en la reproducción artística," [79] "extraordinario intérprete del paisaje americano," [80] "cargado de inmensidad americana." [81]

Doña Bárbara, for all its criollismo, uses modern stylistic techniques, and one can find symbolism, parallelism, metaphor, imagery, introspection, and a kind of interior monologue in the novel, along with a mosaic of subtle words, which prompted Ulrich Leo to say that "y se comprenden sus condiciones de eficacia solamente considerándose casi cada piedrecita por sí misma." [82] The novel's development depends on interaction among the principal characters who symbolize the forces in Venezuela, but by adopting some of the techniques "developed in stream of consciousness writing and combining them with more traditional novelistic techniques, Gallegos presents vividly the minds of the actors and gives the novel added depth and perspective." [83] The vivid and beautiful pictures of the plains, with its bronco busting and branding and the powerful and passionate Bárbara, convey a dramatic intensity which transcends the romantic, realistic fusion and the admittedly loose structure.

The plains, with their beauty, terror, color, and movement, display a social, political, and universal dimension which Gallegos fully analyzes. Man must fight his environment to survive. The plainsman is indolent and yet energetic, malicious but loyal, impulsive and sensual, and the man-made laws and corrupt cacique system thrive on the barbarity, violence, and compulsive *machismo* of the area. On the one hand, Bárbara, as barbarism, fights Santos Luzardo, the representative of civilization; but on the other, the novel shows the struggle of man against the evil within his own soul, not only against the exterior environment but against superstition and ignorance which exist everywhere, "even in the heart of the individual of whatever race or nation." [84] *Doña Bárbara* can share with *La vorágine* aspects of an Odyssey, and like the protagonist of Alejo Carpentier's *Los pasos perdidos,* Santos Luzardo returns to prehistory, "el civilizador Santos Luzardo," [85] to find himself but also to kill that part of the centaur which he knows is half beast.[86] Bárbara, the representative of the plains, can never be destroyed, although she may be temporarily suppressed. She, too, wants to find herself, reflecting and enhancing, in a dynamic interplay, the conflicts experienced by the male protagonist. One has the impression that Gallegos almost instinctively, regardless of political program, is drawn to Bárbara and that his artistic perception sensed her dramatic possibilities and the universal significance to be found in her soul.[87]

The novel, in addition to its universal significance, is also a part of Gallegos' effort to create a geographical atlas of his country.[88] Venezuela's mountains and rich resources, though beautiful and desirable, are also potentially deadly. In Doña Bárbara's time the population still succumbed to typhoid, hookworm, malaria, smallpox, and yellow fever. But a worthy human might always triumph over his geography. Santos, of course, had the advantage of an early life on the llanos, and as a "medio llanero . . . digno de aquella raza de hombres sin miedo que había dado más de un centauro a la epopeya," he could change the land into a "tierra abierta y tendida." Lorenzo Barquero, also a man of civilization and intelligence, lost to the llanos because he lacked the will power, idealism, and strong sense of law which Santos had in full measure. Barquero's failure adds realism to Gallegos' optimistic and perhaps ingenuous vision of the plains as a land of open horizons "donde una raza buena ama, sufre y espera." Gallegos' thesis is that the man of the plains, with the will to succeed and with proper education, will substitute law for superstition and win victory over his environment and himself. The author obviously favors Santos, the man of law and order, who holds his own view that human progress depends on respect for law based on justice. Even though in practice this rarely occured in his violent Venezuela, Gallegos endeavored to promote the Christian ideals in which he believed.

Cantaclaro (1934), which along with the following novel, *Canaima* (1935), he wrote in Spain, continues the story of the plains, "desde las galeras del Guárico hasta el fondo del Apure, desde el pie de los Andes hasta el Orinoco. ¡Y más allá! por todos estos llanos de bancos y palmares, mesas y morichales . . ." More lyrical than its predecessor, *Cantaclaro* has been acclaimed as fictionally superior to *Doña Bárbara* "por su uniformidad y armonía, por el timbre firme y suave que va desde la primera hasta la última página de *Cantaclaro*. Novela de técnica superior, de esbelta arquitectura . . ." [89] The novel, containing local color, folklore, superstitions, legends, archetypal conflicts, and using interior monologue to good effect, in a remote way is related to the mythic novels of Miguel Ángel Asturias and Alejo Carpentier, in its poetry, fantasy, and quest for the mythological bases of the country. The protagonist, Florentino Coronado, known as Quitapesares, undertakes his mysterious odyssey over the plains, crossing lonely and solitary rivers, having adventures, witnessing the conditions under which the plainsman lives, composing and singing at every turn, fighting for liberty, and risking all, including life itself, at every turn in the road.

Florentino's uncle, Manuel, has taken him and his brother José Luis to live with them. José Luis stays on the ranch, but Florentino sets out on his journey, finally arriving at Hato Viejo Payareño, owned by Dr. Payara, the Diablo de Cunaviche. Florentino falls ill, is treated by Payara and Juan Parao, a Negro, meets Juan el Veguero, whose land has been stolen by a corrupt politician and whose three children have died of snake bite and illness, and learns Payara's tragic history. Payara had hanged Carlos Jaramillo, owner of a neighboring ranch and member of a feuding family, because Jaramillo had deceived Ángela Rosa, seducing and abandoning her shortly before she was to marry the doctor. Payara marries her anyway, takes her to Hato Viejo, and cares for her daughter Rosángela as his own, when the mother dies—or was murdered, some said. Rosángela is terrified of Payara's potentially sensual interest in her and begs Florentino to take her away. He leaves her at his brother's ranch. Payara, meanwhile, refuses Martín Salcedo's request for help in the revolution, but Juan Parao leaves Payara's service to revolt against the government. José Luis and Florentino both love Rosángela, but Florentino gives way to his brother. The revolutionaries are first successful and then defeated. Florentino joins them and later, legend says, is carried off by the devil; but we never really know what has happened to Florentino (Cantaclaro).

Gallegos is again fascinated by the plains, but he has created some outstanding human beings in this novel. Dunham calls Juan Crisóstomo Payara "el más poderoso y quizá el mejor de los caracteres creados por Gallegos," and points out that he is a fictionalized version of a friend of Gallegos, Dr. Robert Vargas.[90] Payara has Calderonian traits. Frustrated in his desires to serve humanity, he has achieved a moderate success in his fight against the barbarous environment. Cantaclaro, symbolism aside, "tiene consistencia humana, su motivación parece cosa de la vida y sus peripecias y desarrollo interno aumentan armoniosamente sus relaciones con el mundo circundante." [91] Juan el Veguero, without either the love of life of Florentino or the moral skeletal framework of Payara, succumbs to the enervating circumstances imposed on him by his society and the immense and isolated surroundings. In a fit of madness he destroys what little property remains to him and kills the Jefe Civil, a symbol of his misfortune and degradation.

Again Gallegos explores the effect of violence on the Venezuelan soul, the fight against nature, the struggle between civilization and barbarism, and the struggle of man to find a moral code and meaningful human values. Payara acts through an imposed self-discipline to struggle against the effects of caudillismo and the dehumanizing effect of the llanos. Juan Parao, the idealistic dreamer, represents the difficult life of the poor Venezuelan Negro, his suffering and rebellion; but he does not achieve his goal. Martín Salcedo, the visionary student, finally realizes that armed revolt is not the answer to Venezuelan problems, that "por aquí no saldremos nunca de la barbarie. ¡Basta ya de correr en pos de la sombra siniestra del caudillo muerto!" The Venezuelan lacks clear purpose, but evolutionary processes may succeed where revolution has failed.

Canaima (1935) is a forceful, almost vehement, vigorous, and rich novel about the jungle with as much poetic insight and with fewer romantic overtones than *La vorágine*. Canaima, the Indian name for the forest god in the poverty-stricken region of Guayana, represents the face of evil; but few can resist him. It is this relationship between man and nature that Gallegos explores, as the characters attack, cajole, or surrender to the jungle deity. Gallegos did not know the jungle firsthand, but he heard stories from a Trinidad woman who tutored him in childhood and from his uncle who knew the jungle well. His apparently intimate familiarity with Venezuelan geography is deceptive; he spent his own youth around Caracas, and his knowledge of Zulia and other areas came from fairly brief stays or from electoral campaigns.[92]

Marcos Vargas, a generous, manly, and socially conscious native of Ciudad Bolívar, having heard tales of travels along the Orinoco, goes to the Yuruari where he meets a friend of his father. The friend, Manuel Ladera, sells Marcos a mule train so that he may compete for freight business with José Francisco Ardaván, a coward who hated Ladera because the latter had refused to allow him to marry his daughter, Maigualida. José Francisco had murdered one of her suitors, and the family leader and powerful political figure leaves his machine to a cousin Miguel instead of to the cowardly and destructive José Francisco. Marcos defeats Ardaván in a dice game and in securing customers, and Ardaván hires Cholo Parima to kill Manuel Ladera. Parima, or Pantoja, had also killed an innocent Negro, for political reasons, and the brother of Marcos Vargas. After Marcos kills Parima in self-defense, José Francisco destroys Marcos' wagon train. Vallorini, a rich merchant, gives Marcos a position as overseer of a group of balata gum workers in the jungle, partly to remove him from the company of his susceptible daughter, Aracelis. Marcos observes the slave-like existence of the workers, learns of Indian mythology, and overcome by the spell of the trees, goes temporarily native. José Francisco eventually kills Miguel, but he does not obtain the political power he craves, loses his money, and finally goes mad. Maigualida, meanwhile, marries Gabriel Ureña, the manager of the Ladera properties. Marcos returns to civilization briefly but, disgusted with its artificiality and corruption, returns to the jungle to marry an Indian girl. He arranges to have José Gregorio Ardaván, who had gone off into the forest with an Indian mistress and died, declared her husband so that she may inherit his holdings. Marcos himself reverts to a natural life, but he eventually sends his twelve year old son to Gabriel to be educated and to obtain the necessary tools to prevent future exploitation by adventurers.

The jungle and nature in general overshadow the other protagonists. To hear the roar of the Orinoco, witness the exuberant, violent, and tropical nature, which Gallegos describes in magnificent word pictures, cast its magic spell over man; to see an entity of mythical proportions test and temper its human antagonists, the good and the bad, the superior and the inferior, the criminal and the law-abiding, is to learn about mankind. Conde Giaffaro disappears, the American Mr. Davenport survives, and Marcos Vargas, the seeker, living with an Aymará girl, surrenders to the magic of the Indian god but is not destroyed. He faces the tropical storms and takes his own measure before the onslaughts of a cosmic nature which cannot defeat him. He is not a failure, but neither is he victorious, and only through his son may he achieve full success. The circle is complete, and Gallegos, as Güiraldes had stated earlier, seems to say that America needs both European influence, culture, and civilization and American natural man and resources —which if properly channeled into productive areas may mean a human and natural regeneration. One must seek native roots to find national identity; but Marcos' son, like Fabio Cáceres in *Don Segundo Sombra*, also needs civilization. If nature is to be used properly, so must human resources be properly treated. Marcos, a man with a social conscience but not an active social reformer, is not the man for Venezuela. His son, half Indian, may well be that man. He may end the exploitation of the Indian and the Negro and destroy the cacique system and the reign of tyranny which holds his country back. Through the Indian mythos and social organization, combined with the knowledge of Western culture, he may triumph over the duality within himself and achieve a true brotherhood of man. Ángel Valbuena Briones sees the tragedy of individualism as the central theme. Vargas failed because he allowed himself to be overwhelmed by the temptation "de ser el hombre macho que se impone a la naturaleza por el placer de la violencia." [93] *Canaima* can also be interpreted as an allegory of the choice between good and evil and the problem of free will.

Pobre Negro (1937), almost a historical and psychological essay, shows Gallegos' continued interest in the Negro. On the Alcorta plantation, Negro Malo rapes Ana María and escapes. Their offspring, Pedro Miguel Candelas, is brought up by a mulatto couple to whom Ana's brother, Fermín, has given him. Fermín's youngest daughter, Luisana, and her brother Cecilio are quite fond of Pedro

Miguel, who has a burning desire to free the slaves. Luisana falls in love with Pedro Miguel. When her brother contracts leprosy, Pedro agrees to manage the estate. When the leader of a roving band of marauders tries to possess her, Pedro realizes that he, too, loves her. She joins the liberals. The Alcorta property is attacked and Pedro Miguel is wounded. They board a ship for Trinidad, and Cecilio, seeing the new future, disappears. The novel is set in the 1850s, but the problem is contemporary. Pedro must fight to discover his own meaning as a man. He must learn to live with his hatred for the white; he must come to terms with his self-delusion, with his feelings of inferiority and betrayal. When Luisana and Pedro decide to make a life together, they help solve the struggle in Venezuela's soul. Through a racial integration and the infusion of new strength and blood into Venezuelan upper classes, his country may yet face the future unafraid.

El forastero, begun in 1921, rewritten and finally published in 1942, is as much political essay as novel. Usually this novel is regarded as Gallegos' weakest effort, but it impressed Alberto Zum Felde with its intensive attempt at psychological analysis and certain unusual character studies,[94] and it conveys a dramatic force in spite of its lack of sustained characterization. Filled with student revolt, political chicanery, and the ironfisted rule of a caudillo, the novel again shows us the tragedy of a land and people victimized by barbarism. The Guaviare family controls a Venezuelan city and uses public resources for private gain. The caudillo is prevailed upon to restore the river he had diverted, but he does so only for further personal profit at the expense of a better Venezuela. The novel may be a work of fundamental importance as an essay of political psychology about the transition from a dictatorship to a democracy; but in the process of making his point Gallegos has done mortal damage to his narrative.[95]

Sobre la misma tierra (1944) is the story of oil exploitation and the destruction of the agricultural land of the Indians. The title symbolizes the coexistence "on the same earth" of Yankee wealth and domestic misery. Demetrio Montiel seduces his brother's fiancée, becomes a smuggler, and amasses enough money to buy a boat, the *Arrepentida*. He seduces one of the Indian girls, Cantarelia, smuggles Indians as slaves, and, when his mistress dies, gives her daughter, Remota, to her aunts, Dorila and Palmira. Her father later abducts her, and a legend of her disappearance grows among the Indians. He tempers his incestuous desires and gives her to his sister, who takes her to New York and renames her Ludmila Weimar. Demetrio commits suicide. The oil company wishes to steal Venezuelan land; but one of the employees, a sympathetic and honest American, Mr. Hardman, tries to help Ludmila, who has returned to try to help her Indian countrymen. Her idealism and altruism contrast with the opportunism and selfishness which her father had exhibited, and she tries to elevate the Indians into a participation in their country's society.

Gallegos emphasizes the human and geographical contrasts between country and city. The semidesert Guajira down to Lake Maracaibo is a land of sand dunes, brush, and cactus, whose people, unable to raise their cattle, migrate to the outskirts of Maracaibo to eke out a miserable existence in search of oil-field jobs which do not materialize. For the most part the North American lives apart from the natives. But not all Americans are evil; Hardman, the Arizona Yankee, warns Remota of the dangers of foreign capital and of her own duties to her country and people. Unfortunately, not all are equally concerned for the essential human dignity of all men and tend to promote conflicts, but it is not only the Americans who are to blame. Adrián Gadea, the shrewd and rich landowner, also prospers, and his rapaciousness, at the expense of his own people, is undoubtedly the greater evil. A poetic and primitive view of foreign luck and national misery, *Sobre la misma tierra* is an aesthetic fusion of two worlds presented with cinematic and dramatic force.

Gallegos' last published novel (an announced one, *La brasa en el pico del cuervo*, has not appeared), *La brizna de paja en el viento* (1952), is about Cuba. The novel studies the revolutionary student movement at the University of Havana during the Machado dictatorship. Starting as a pure and spiritual renewal, symbolized by Rafael Trejo, the movement degenerated into one of rival gangster bands. In the "entrega" to the novel Gallegos comments on "la tragedia de la cultura que aquí comparto con ellos"; but in addition to student activities and the causes and cures for dictatorship, class rivalries and divisions, Gallegos complicates this work with Afro-Cuban magic rites and culture. He shows us the sugar plantations of Oriente, the tobacco plantations of Pinar del Río, different

Havana scenes, a variety of racial types, the voluptuous and tragic mulatto Clorinda, the mestizo Juan Luis Marino, the Spaniard Azcárate, a North American school teacher, and Justo Rigores, the *hombre macho*, young, strong student leader who betrays Juan Luis' youthful idealism. Probably Juan Luis, in love with Florencia Azcárate but separated by social status, tempted and buffeted by fate and the world but remaining true to himself throughout, best represents the Cuban people. In no other novel has Gallegos so clearly expressed the fundamental idea which has guided him "en su actitud hacia sus semejantes, así como su fe en la necesidad de una firme base moral." [96]

Rómulo Gallegos touched the cornerstone of the Venezuelan soul with all its convolutions and contradictions, its joys and sorrows. Himself an idealist and perhaps utopian dreamer, he visualized a new America of peace and freedom where all would work together (he believed miscegenation to be an imperative necessity) for human dignity. He had a strong faith in his country's ability to awaken the best in man and thus achieve social and individual salvation. He recognized that man is inherently subject to a series of temptations and that many people, while not themselves actively evil, offer an acquiescent silence in the face of injustice. A liberal spirit, Gallegos realized the implications of the struggle between tradition and progress and hoped for a fusion of the best of both worlds, a fusion to be brought about through dedication, strength, love, willpower, and, above all, education. Man has within him the spiritual resources to triumph over adversity, both natural and man-made, and if he can only harness these in the defense of liberty, justice, and dignity, he will triumph over both his physical and human impositions. Perhaps more impressive than even his corking good stories, mythology, characters, or even his thesis are the beautiful natural backgrounds Gallegos presents, the unforgettable canvases of the plains, jungles, and rivers of Venezuela, which, together with humanity, he treats with love and understanding.

Although criollismo stresses the American spirit, the apparent spiritual affinity existing between the Russian and Spanish American soul, what one critic calls "secreta afinidad de sensibilidad," [97] led to the great influence of Russian models on the Spanish American novel around the turn of the century. Chekhov, Gorki, and especially Andreyev were translated between 1906 and 1925. Indeed, Andreyev's novel, *Sashka Jigouleff*, portraying the death of a protector of the poor against oppression, was tearfully commented on by young idealists in Spanish America. Although Tolstoy, as we have seen, influenced authors like D'Halmar, among nineteenth-century Russian writers it was Dostoevski who most influenced the New World. Clemente Palma and Mercedes Cabello de Carbonera were early leaders of this "rusofilia" in the nineteenth century, but surprisingly enough Dostoevski had a far wider influence on budding socialist writers in the early 1920s. In spite of his opposition to socialists in general, he was viewed as a utopian idealist, a defender of the poor, and even as a precursor of the Russian Revolution.[98] Many Spanish American and U.S. critics have seen this relationship, among them George O. Schanzer, Luis Alberto Sánchez, Max Daireaux, Hugo Barbagelata, Mariano Latorre, Jefferson Rhea Spell, Alberto Zum Felde, Bayona Posada, Pedro Henríquez Ureña, and Torres-Rioseco.[99]

Among general points of contact and parallels between the fiction of the two countries, one may mention a kind of magic sense, mysticism, pantheism, interior fatalism, a love for the mysteries of the transcendent, a concern for the anonymous and the alienated, the exploitation of man by man, and the drawing of strength from solitude. References to Russia and things Russian are found in the novels themselves, as can be seen in Arguedas' *Raza de bronce*, Rómulo Gallego's *Reinaldo Solar*, and César Vallejo's *Tungsteno*. In many novels, *Criollos en París* and *El chileno en Madrid* by Joaquín Edwards Bello and *Raucho* by Ricardo Güiraldes, expatriates, intellectuals, poor and wealthy, suffering from what Blest Gana had called "Parisitis," not only resemble Russian emigrés but also associate with them and display contempt for their fatherland. In both civilizations novelists repudiated the present, protested against man's inhumanity with propagandistic fervor, and discussed uprooted classes or national types such as the *mujik* or the roto. Superstitions, cruel violence, hatred of foreigners, bitterness, and a messianic hope are other similarly constant themes. José Carlos Mariátegui wrote on the *mujikista* aspects of Spanish American literature, comparing indigenist problems, ". . . salvadas todas las diferencias de tiempo y de espacio al mujikismo de la literatura rusa prerevolucionaria."[100] In Russia the peasant suffered from the *knut* (whip) of the *pomeshchik* (landowner), the *pop* (minister), and the political authority. In Spanish America the *látigo*, the *gamonal*, and the *cura* were the American counterparts of peasant oppressors. The sexuality, illiteracy, dialect, superstition, and abulia in the naturalistic novels by Gamboa, in novels like *Nacha Regules* by Manuel Gálvez, *Raza de Caín* by Carlos Reyles, *La vorágine* by José Eustasio Rivera, or *Doña Bárbara* by Rómulo Gallegos, testify to a similarity of some duration.

Later, after the Russian Revolution, influences became more direct, and communism, at least as interpreted locally, influenced Peruvian authors like César Vallejo, César Falcón, Ernesto Reyna, and Juan Seoane and Ecuadorian novelists like Jorge Icaza, Demetrio Aguilera Malta, Alfredo Pareja Diezcanseco, Enrique Gil Gilbert, and Pedro Jorge Vera. These novelists, and some in other countries, dreamed utopian dreams of a new future as they read the works of Maxim Gorki and Ilya Ehrenburg, translated in journals such as *Amauta* and *Nosotros*, reprinted, usually, from French reviews like *Le Disque Vert*. Still later Russian writers like Sholokhov, Pilnyak, Gladkov, and Ivanov had a somewhat attenuated influence on Spanish American fiction.

Carlos Reyles (1868–1938) of Uruguay, whom some consider to be a naturalist (*Por la vida*, 1888, was the first naturalistic novel in Uruguay) and many others a modernist because of the obvious aesthetic and artistic elements in *El embrujo de Sevilla* (1922), seems, if one judges his total narrative, to fit most easily within the classification of criollista.[101] Reyles reveals more affinity for the Russian spirit than any Spanish American novelist of his time.[102] The son of a rich hacendado and a millionaire at eighteen (he later lost most of his fortune), Reyles lived on a hacienda, was a gentleman farmer, and also traveled through Europe and read Huysmans, D'Annunzio, and Dostoevski. This double inheritance can be seen in Reyles' attitude toward rural realism, for he largely views it from above, from a hacendado's point of view. The dichotomy in his own soul seems constantly reflected in his heroes, who look for meaning in a chaotic universe of violence and bloodshed, a meaning they seldom find. They search for a new set of values, unable to adjust to their society, some because they are too intellectual, others because they are too refined. Within the souls of many of his protagonists a constant struggle takes place between the intellectual, theorist, and inactive dreamer of European culture on the one hand, and the primitive American practical man of action on the other. Reyles hoped to become a novelist of souls, "pero no lo fue, si acaso pudo serlo, se lo impidió esa . . . manía de la tesis, que sustituye a la verdad; su arte quedó en aquella maestría de la objetividad ambiental, como la mayoría de sus congéneres." [103] Reyles' thesis of a Uruguay in the grip of disruptive changes—a struggle of industry against old traditions and methods, the need for agrarian reform—suggests his own lifelong attempt to raise cattle scientifically according to the laws of eugenics. His philosophical development, partly confirmed in his fiction, may be determined through reading his essays, *La muerte del cisne* (1910), *Diálogos olímpicos* (1918), *Panoramas del mundo actual* (1932), *Incitaciones* (1936), and *Ego sum* (1938).

Reyles' first novel, *Por la vida*, a fully naturalistic presentation, partly of his own life, has been called "audaz ataque contra la sociedad y la familia." [104] *Beba* (1894), acclaimed by Uruguayan critics as the beginning of a new period in the development of a national novel, shatters the public indifference which Reyles, in the novel itself, uses as one of the themes, that of the artist against society. The novel, filled with brutal and melodramatic scenes and Balzacian, Ibsenian, and Russian echoes, is somewhat damaged by the constant interjections of the author to promote his pet theories; but he was the first "en copiar de modo tan certero la vida del campo rioplatense." [105] In the novel, Gustavo Ribero (the author himself, perhaps), interested in scientific reforms, especially in horse breeding, becomes attracted to his somewhat romantic and rebellious niece, Isabel (Beba), married to an unworthy social butterfly in Montevideo, a city life Ribero cannot abide. Her canoe is swept away by a raging river (the appropriately named Río Negro where Reyles had spent his youth). Her uncle rescues her, but the two are stranded and discover their love for one another. She abandons her husband, but Ribero's business goes bad. They have a monstrous child (Reyles had pet theories on consanguine mating), for which he blames her, and she drowns herself. Ribero, the visionary and intellectual, will replace Rafael, the husband, an abulic parasite; but both are victimized by tragic destiny in the person of Beba. Reyles is neither subtle nor sophisticated in his symbolism as he presents pseudoscientific pathological states, agrarian reform, the evils of city social life, the rights of women, the beauties of nature, and the perils involved in consanguineous marriages. More importantly, *Beba* is a typical picture of *estancia* life in the 1890s. From this point of view it is the best novel Reyles wrote; he was in intimate contact with the land he was describing[105] when he composed it.

Between 1896 and 1898 Reyles wrote three short narratives which, under the general heading of *Academias,* he called "ensayos de modernismo." *Primitivo* (1896), *El extraño* (1897), and *El sueño de rapiña* (1898) are more modernist and aesthetically oriented than *Beba. Primitivo,* which Valera in his *Cartas Americanas* found unpleasantly pessimistic and naturalistic, was later reworked and expanded into a novel, *El terruño; El extraño,* into *La raza de Caín;* and only *El sueño de rapiña* was neither repeated nor amplified as fiction. Most of Reyles' novels are elaborated versions of previous novelettes or short stories. In his preface to *Primitivo,* Reyles states: "Me propongo escribir bajo el título de *Academias* una serie de novelas cortas, a modo de . . . ensayos de arte . . . un fruto que sea hijo legítimo de su tiempo." By examining these novelettes and some of his later *refundiciones,* one can see a change in Reyles himself from an intellectual attraction for neurotic nihilism to a more materialistic viewpoint of life.

La raza de Caín (1900), a kind of Uruguayan *Crime and Punishment,* is Reyles' first prose in which the artistic, naturalistic, and psychological analyses seem effortlessly joined. The novel studies the conflict between intellectuals and the middle class, one of Reyles' favorite themes. Here, in keeping with his thesis, the intellectuals are cowardly and immoral, and their opposite numbers morally sound and pragmatic; but this does not negate Reyles' penetrating psychological analysis of soul states and motivations— for the most part his complicated and tortured personalities are brilliantly conceived. Fond of Nietzsche's works, Reyles likes to think that willpower will dominate emotion and that the strong overcome the weak. The novel centers on the lives of Jacinto Cacio, the son of a tavern keeper, and the idealistic but neurotic Julio Guzmán (seen, in his portrayal in *El extraño,* at least by one critic, as a literary reflection of Julio Herrera y Reissig).[107]Cacio is abulic, cowardly, vain, ambitious, and cannot abide the happiness of others. Guzmán, Crooker's nephew, and thus of superior education, because of his excessive intellectual refinement is unable to cope with the materialism of the modern world. He indulges in a series of love affairs, for he feels completely unmanned by his parasitic dependence on his wife's money; he finally runs off with Sara Casares, one of his girl friends. They plan a suicide pact, but after killing her he cannot kill himself. Cacio, a victim of paranoid delusions, poisons Laura, his loved one and Crooker's niece, and blames her death on Arturo Crooker, her cousin, the man she loves and a member of the family he hates and envies. Arturo, in turn, loves Ana Menchaca, who, rejecting the pathetic and loyal love of her husband, abandons him, causing his alcoholism and madness. The novel deals with envy, hate, pride, and failure, but its principal theme relates to the evils of intellectualism in a modern world.

In *El terruño* (1916) puppet-like characters collide in unmotivated fashion in order to prove their creator's theories that intellectuals, dreamers, and metaphysical abstractions cannot provide what Uruguay needs, namely modern agriculture and practical men of action. The anti-intellectual tone is self-directed, a reflection of Reyles' life when he was a traveler, reader, and intellectual. Yet one critic finds the portrait of one of the characters, Pantaleón, the typical revolutionary caudillo, "la mejor cosa escrita por Reyles." [108] The outstanding character in the novel, Doña Ángela, affectionately called Mamagela, has a practical proverb for every occasion and is a "Sancho con faldas," as José Enrique Rodó calls her in his prologue to the novel. She is married to the *pulpero* Gregorio, or Goyo, and has two sons-in-law, Tocles and Primitivo. The latter, a somewhat simple gaucho, loses his wife to his brother, becomes a revolutionary, avenges himself, and commits suicide. Tocles, whose portrayal Rodó admired, a philosophy student and an overly idealistic and impractical dreamer like Don Quixote, is brought closer to the real world through Mamagela's practical advice and example and through her personification of the country spirit. Hard work and not dreams, says Reyles repeatedly, brings progress and happiness. In Tocles, the representative of the intellectual point of view, Reyles created almost a caricature, apparently not his intention since he seems to say that a civilizing force is necessary to exploit the national wealth and to dispel "la indolencia y la rutina de los rurales." [109] His double accent is on the "rural, vital, y utilitario por un lado, cosmopolita, filosófico y esteticista por otro." [110] As we have said, Reyles' thesis unfortunately seems to be so important to him that he turns his characters into cybernetic creations operated for the occasion or the moment.

El embrujo de Sevilla (1922), an elaboration of a short story, *Caprichos de Goya* (1902), is along with *La gloria de don Ramiro* the best American novel to describe a Spanish setting. Since Reyles' mother was an Andalusian, perhaps the spirit of Seville was indeed not foreign to him. The novel, the culmination of Reyles' sensual and pictorial style, and one of the outstanding modernist efforts, drew the applause of Spaniards of the caliber of Pérez de Ayala and Unamuno. The latter considered the work to be the best representation of the "alma sevillana." [111] Rich, vibrant, and above all sensual, Reyles' novel documents authentically the characters, customs, language and general atmosphere of Seville, even as it avoids Andalusian miseries and social inequities which seem completely to have escaped its author's attention. We hear the picturesque expressions of bull fighters and the local songs; we observe the flamenco dancers, gypsy psychology, and activities in the typical cafe, El Tronío. In its auditory, olfactory, and tactile imagery, in its beautifully elegant, aristocratic, and somewhat artificial prose, the novel clearly exemplifies the modernist spirit. It has its didactic moments, but the pageantry and artistry are more important. The city of Seville itself becomes the protagonist, and the novel closes with the pageantry of Holy Week and Easter with its religious brotherhoods, statues, and decorated city. Paco Quiñones, whose uncle's speculations had caused his financial ruin, becomes a daring bullfighter. Breaking his engagement with Pastora, the daughter of a rich cattle rancher, he meets Pura, a gypsy dancer, known as la Trianera, whom he had known in his youth. She sums up, in her beautiful, sensual dances, the grace of Seville itself. They become lovers, but her first love, Pitoche, a cafe singer, fights for her. Pura stabs her new lover in an impulsive moment but repents. Paco recuperates and marries Pastora. Pura leaves Seville with the painter Cuenca, who also loves her. Ángel Valbuena Briones believes the novel is a roman à clef and identifies Paco as Emilio Torres Reina and Cuenca as Ignacio Zuloaga.[112] In any event, the refined Cuenca is the spokesman for Reyles about philosophy, art, and life; he analyzes the Sevillian soul, smothered in passion, light, color, and thoroughly vibrant. *El embrujo de Sevilla* was to have become a movie with Rudolph Valentino playing the lead role.

Contracts had already been signed, but Valentino died before film-
ing could begin. The novel would have been a marvelous movie,
but it stands on its own merits as an almost unique work. Arturo
Torres-Rioseco said it best in his analysis of the work: *"El embrujo
de Sevilla* es un libro de maravillosos entusiasmos, de arduroso
sensualismo, de singular belleza plástica y lírica. . . . Del misticismo
de la voluptuosidad y de la muerte pudo haberse llamado esta
novela . . . con ser novela moderna, no es de vanguardia. No tiene
esa condescendencia obligada con el gusto imperante: no rinde
vasallaje a la moda. Aspira a ser novela de todos los tiempos, novela
con intriga y desenlace, destinada al intelectual que no se haya
olvidado de la vida en el ambiente formalista del cenáculo y al
humilde lector que sabe hallar placer allí donde hay intensidad de
pasión, realismo verdadero, entusiasmo, en una palabra, vida." [113]

El gaucho Florido (1932), subtitled "Novela de la estancia cima-
rrona y del gaucho crudo," is based on a short story Reyles wrote
in 1893 called "Mansilla." Reyles evokes estancia life, the fights, the
horse races, the love affairs, and gaucho honor. Although a number
of critics find the novel unconvincing,[114] it is a representative and
authentic reflection of the ambiance and psychology of the plains.
The hacienda "Tala Grande," apparently Reyles' own "Bellavista," is but one of many autobiographical elements in the novel.
The high point of the work is the striking scene in which Florido,
revenging himself on Ramón, spreader of false rumors (he had
caused Florido to cut off his sweetheart Mangacha's hair), cuts out
Ramon's tongue and pegs it to his wronged girl friend's door.
Mangacha is accidentally killed by a bullet destined for the protagonist. Florido finally avenges himself after a number of years
but rejects a possible happy life with Micaela who loves him. The
gaucho of Reyles' novel is not the guitar-playing idler but rather
a cowboy unable to cope with progress and mechanization. The
author's sympathetic portrayal of the gaucho seems a faulty memory exercise to recall the "good old days," but since life is illogical
and its climactic events are not chronologically arranged, the indeterminate ending itself creates a kind of greater realism. *A batalla de amor . . . campo de pluma* (1939), which he had worked on
for a number of years, appeared posthumously. A psychoanalysis of
Pepe Arbiza, his ex-wife, their friends and shared lovers, the novel
also attacks the idle rich of Buenos Aires.

Another Uruguayan, Otto Miguel Cione (1875–1945), published a short story collection, *Maula* (1902), which he labeled "bosquejo de novela nacional," and several others such as *Caraguatá y otros cuentos* (1920) and *Chola se casa* (1924). His novel about night life in Buenos Aires, *Luxuria* (1936), is comparatively unimportant, but his *Lauracha* (1906), about estancia life in the Río de la Plata region and dedicated to the memory of his daughter Myriam, who died tragically at seventeen years of age, is a good study of the psychology of a hysterical woman. The heroine, indifferent to several suitors, succumbs to Carlos, who scorns her, and commits suicide.

The Uruguayan Edgar Allen Poe, Horacio Quiroga (1878–1937), possibly Spanish America's outstanding short story writer, started off as a modernist with an artificial style and the exotic themes of sexual compulsions. His more lasting and mature work, objectively done, allowed him to place man and nature in proper perspective, and his fiction of this kind was "la más viva . . . la más ejemplar y de más perdurable huella." [115] Although his stories offer a kind of synthesis of various themes and styles, and he has been called everything from a nativist to a universal writer, he probably fits more correctly within the criollista category. As Seymour Menton states: "Horacio Quiroga fue uno de los iniciadores del criollismo en Hispanoamérica. Sus cuentos, en gran parte, presentan la derrota del hombre ante la barbarie de la naturaleza tropical, tema explotado por casi todos los criollistas." [116]

Quiroga's father was the Argentine consul in Salto, and as a result both Uruguay and Argentina have claimed the short story writer as their own. By all accounts Quiroga was a maladjusted and neurotic man who had a fairly miserable and unhappy life filled with spiritual torment. Befriended by Leopoldo Lugones, he also belonged to La Brasileña, a tertulia frequented by Payró. Quiroga wrote for a number of newspapers and magazines such as *Caras y Caretas*, *La Nación*, and *La Prensa* of Buenos Aires and held positions as a teacher and justice of the peace. He committed suicide, carrying on the tradition of violent and suddent deaths established in his family and among those dear to him.

In addition to Poe one may cite Maupassant, Kipling, Chekhov, and Conrad as having influenced Quiroga, although at times this influence is quite tenuous. Quiroga deals with objective reality but (like the novelists of the last two decades) seeks the hidden life within people and objects and often finds a world of magic realism and the mysterious within the commonplace. Almost all his stories are based on his own life incidents and in their emphasis on tragedy, death, the supernatural, and hallucinatory and abnormal mental states reveal the sadness of his life, one in which ". . . el horror y la dureza . . . ni respondían a indiferencia, a lujuria verbal, sino al auténtico horror que padeció el creador en su propia vida y que hechizó tantos momentos de su existir." [117] In some of his stories Quiroga reveals the primitive life and social problems of the farm worker; in others he portrays his own jungle experiences in Misiones and the Chaco region in northern Argentina. One of his constant themes is that of man surrounded by and struggling against a hostile nature where death awaits, where victory allows only a continuing fight, where a character defect is always fatal. Whether his stories are of fantasy, magic, the occult, or animal stories (he at times shows great tenderness towards animals and children), Quiroga's principal and only concern is humanity. He rejected "el arte deshumanizado o desvitalizado. Exige como materia primera e insustituible al hombre y su pasión; sus penas y alegrías, sus miserias y grandezas." [118] One can say, nonetheless, that Quiroga condemns the society of man and infinitely prefers the solitude of remote regions. Quiroga wrote only two passable novels, *Historia de un amor turbio* (1908), a psychological analysis of jealousy and an enlarged version of "Rea Silvia," a short story, and *Pasado amor* (1929), both based on his own love affairs. Rohán's love for the Elizalde sisters in the first novel and that of Morán for Magdalena are less than moving to a modern reader. Quiroga was unprepared for sustained and prolonged development of his characters and experiences; he is rightfully better known for his short story collections such as *El crimen del otro* (1904), *Cuentos de amor, de locura y de muerte* (1917), *El salvaje* (1920), *Anaconda* (1921), *El desierto* (1924), *Los desterrados* (1926), and *Más allá* (1935).

Also of Uruguay, Vicente A. Salaverri (1887–   ) started as a modernist, then wrote some "novelas de la ciudad," and finally novels of country life. He was one of the earliest Uruguayans to give importance to the novel of the city, although he is usually considered a devout and dedicated describer of rural scenes. Among his titles are *El corazón de María* (1918), *Este era un país* (1920), *El hijo del león* (1922), novels, and *El manantial y otros cuentos del campo* (1927), short stories. Salaverri is especially good at showing the relations of city with rural life. His ranges are no longer the limitless ones, and his peons are neither poetic nor heroic.

Adolfo Montiel Ballesteros (1888–   ) has written in many literary genres and styles, but, as a criollista, he mixes country scenes and telluric elements with a number of city happenings. His tone is often poetic, humorous, satirical, at times verging on burlesque. While living in Italy (he was the Uruguayan consul there) he wrote *Cuentos uruguayos* (1920) and *Alma nuestra* (1922), which show his deep sense of identification with Uruguay. Although patterned after the stories of Javier de Viana, they are more nostalgic and less violent and brutal. Montiel Ballesteros has produced a considerable number of other short story collections, *Los rostros pálidos* (1924), *Luz mala* (1926), *Fábulas* (1928), children's stories and legends, and *Querencia* (1941). Among his novelettes are *Montevideo y su cerro* (1928) and *La jubilación de Dios* (1951). His first novel, *La raza* (1925), studies a struggle between two gauchos who represent tradition versus progress and the old versus the young. His themes also include Spanish America as a mestizo continent, the effect of nature on man, the latter's struggles against an ugly world of corrupt and ignorant politicians, and the conflict between idealism and reality in which the author optimistically favors the former. *Castigo 'e Dios* (1930) is about Don Panta Carreno, his German and Catalán neighbors, and his daughter, Blanca, who commits suicide. *Pasión* (1935) uses flashbacks to relive the protagonist's introduction to sex and a marriage to avoid scandal. *Barrio* (1937), the social struggle of a suburb to avoid the encroachment of the city, *Mundo en ascuas* (1956), and *Don Quijote Grillo* (1961), written for children, are other novels. Throughout his works Montiel Ballesteros exudes optimism and extols the merits of virtue. In the prologue to *La jubilación de Dios* he states that he hopes his "modest literature" will contribute "a modificar el adusto gesto que nos ensombrece la máscara o nos la avinagra . . ."

One of Montiel Ballesteros' most interesting works is *Gaucho Tierra* (1948), apparently a story for children. Tico-Tico, the son of a bronco buster, in a kind of poetic fantasy, creates a gaucho from mud. Gaucho Tierra learns to be a bronco buster, acquiring a formal education in school and an informal one in contact with nature. In the end he returns to his basic elements, washed and fused by the rain into the land from which he came; but he has been a man and a gaucho and though he has disappeared he has left his mark and a hope for the future. Various similarities exist between this work and *Don Segundo Sombra*, and Tico-Tico, "la figura idealizada del 'gaucho' que llega a ser el resultado de una rica y policromática fantasía con raíz en la verdad histórica," recalls the imaginary creation of Fabio Cáceres in Güiraldes' novel.[119] Englekirk and Ramos consider Montiel's work to be "buena y original" and the author important "como fecundo cuentista de lo criollo en el extendido movimiento nativista del 20; como temprano narrador del renovado tema urbano . . . y por último, como uno de los primeros fabulistas que logra contribuir eficazmente a la creación de una auténtica 'mitología rústica' de la naturaleza y de la vida campera uruguayas." [120]

José Mármol had viewed the contemporary scene as the past in order to gain historical perspective; Galván promoted the concept of love of liberty and hatred of oppression in the present through the portrayal, in *Enriquillo*, of injustice in the past; Eduardo Acevedo Díaz realistically observed the wars of independence, fusing events skilfully with romantic invention to give extra color to his political ideas. A Uruguayan chronicleer who obtained unusual success in the biographical and historical novel was Justino Zavala Muniz (1897–   ), a grandson of General Muniz, a gaucho leader. Zavala wrote a political defense of his maternal grandfather, *Crónica de Muniz* (1921), really a historical novel of the bloody political struggles of the day; studied gaucho crime and the gaucho malo in *Crónica de un crimen* (1926), and pulpería and country life in *Crónica de la reja* (1930), probably his best work. These *crónicas*, a label he used because of its documentation of historical events, form a kind of fictional cycle in which one may see "una visión razonada y de profunda penetración psicológica de los núcleos de sociabilidad constituidos en nuestra campaña en las últimas décadas del siglo pasado y en las primeras del presente." [121] Luisa Luisi considers the three a gaucho trilogy of epic dimensions; his use of the modest title "crónica," she states, "desmiente el alto valor literario de la obra de un autor que merece figurar entre los mejores novelistas del país." [122]

Crónica de Muniz, coincidentally published the year that Acevedo Díaz died, is filled with dramatic and aesthetic evocations of the civil wars, authenticated either by direct documentation from his family or events and people he had heard about in his youth from friends and relatives. Muniz' Cortés, a vengeful *payador,* Garcilaso of the long locks, and others have their moments of hate and love, defeat and triumph. *Crónica de un crimen,* for all its dramatic scenes of rural living, is marred by a morbid fatalism. El Carancho, El Mellao, and Franco murder three women and are condemned to jail. The author ponders the meaning of it all and its relation to the destiny of Uruguay. *Crónica de la reja's* protagonist, Ricardo, an orphan, comes to the country to work and meets the gauchos of the *reja* (window grilles in front of the pulpería where the gauchos gathered to hold their *charlas*). Ricardo knows them all, good and bad, heroes and cowards, and learns of their love affairs and their superstitions. One of them, old Felipe, tells him stories of horror and bloodshed. The owner of the store, Don Manuel, envisions the day when the land will be fully settled and when gauchos will not wage constant war. Ricardo eventually becomes the owner of the pulpería, marries, becomes a judge, and eventually dies. The author's fictional style is reflected even in his historical work *La revolución de enero. Apuntes para una crónica* (1935), about revolution, class struggle, and exile to Brazil. Zavala Muniz analyzes reality with all its tragic implications in his three major crónicas, studying the psychology and human aspirations of the protagonists and the natural background against which they act. He has captured the folklore, the passion, the countryside, and the problems, and, without preaching, he has even managed to fight for social reform.

Juan José Morosoli (1899–1957), whom we shall consider the last Uruguayan representative of criollismo (Enrique Amorim and later writers will be discussed in the second volume), began as a poet. Largely a short story writer, he published *Hombres* (1932), *Hombres y mujeres* (1944), *Perico* (1945), *Tierra y tiempo* (1958), *El viaje hacia el mar* (1962), and one novel, *Muchachos* (1950). He announced another novel, *La estancia y el camino,* which he did not live to see published. A compassionate writer, Morosoli deals with the miserable victims of injustice, humble people, and a number of regional types, some of whom exhibit grotesque traits.

Muchachos, as he says in his prologue, was really the recreation of a natural and melancholy youth. His primary virtues are his concentration, sobriety, clean style, and his knowledge of Uruguayan psychology.[123] Mario Benedetti, who thinks quite highly of his compatriot, calls him "cronista de almas." [124]

As we have seen, the gaucho theme has a long ancestry in Spanish American poetry and also enjoyed a steady novelistic treatment in the works of Gutiérrez, Viana, Payró, and Reyles. One of the most consistent purveyors of gaucho themes in Argentina, Benito Lynch (1880–1951), between the ages of six and thirteen lived on his father's estancia. He learned about the gaucho, his traditions, his relationship to the hacendado, his frustrations, and especially his vernacular language. On "El Deseado" (his father's ranch) he tried to share the gaucho's stoicism and sadness, grew to love him, and later, in his novels, to mourn his passing. A follower of Payró, he nevertheless lacked the satirical sense of the man from Bahía Blanca but knew even more intimately the gaucho way of life and his hopes and fears. His novels are filled with their spicy rural language as well as with suspenseful action and concisely drawn landscapes and characters. But "el Hudson de nuestros días," [125] as a fellow Argentinian calls him, while giving a complete and authentic portrait of the semi-feudal *estanciero* and the harsh reality of gaucho life in rural Argentina between 1890 and 1915, at times allowed sentiment to influence his normally objective attitude, also tempered by a strong sense of humor and flavored by an occasional irony. Estela Canto, a novelist of some repute in Argentina, sees him as the most important Argentine novelist in certain respects, as "el único escritor argentino que ha tenido una visión europea de su país," and as the "único escritor nuestro que nos ha dado la amenidad y la inocencia." [126]

A strong criollista writer, Lynch was concerned with the tragic and passionate struggles of his protagonists against their environment, at times with universal implications. Directly or indirectly the theme of civilización and barbarie is characteristically a part of his novels. His gauchos are almost always tragic victims, both of the social and political system and of foreign elements. He stresses a psychological realism over stylistic nuances and is at his best with small and humble folk without "esa aristocracia rural de Don Segundo Sombra ni la exhuberancia lírica de Martín

Fierro. Pobres de ideas y de palabras, tres o cuatro principios guían sus vidas . . ." [127] Yet Lynch's spirit is closer to José Hernández than to William Henry Hudson.[128] A practicing journalist, he knew both country and city and the struggle between them—the thesis of his first novel, *Plata dorada* (1909), obviously an auto-biographical work. A strange mixture of the tender and the brutal, it tells of a country boy in Buenos Aires for his education who falls in love with a young girl living under the protection of an old Englishman. When the girl dies tragically, the boy kills her protector. Lynch, who had strong feelings against the English and an almost pathological fixation about interpolating English phrases into his works, presents us with a caricature; but the protagonist is adequately portrayed. In another early novel, *Los caranchos de la Florida* (1916), Don Francisco Suárez Oroño's son, Panchito, educated in Europe, falls in love with his father's mistress. When the father whips him, Panchito kills him and is in turn killed by Cosme, one of his father's workers. Mosca, a crazy peon, voices the theme of the novel, that the *caranchos* (vultures) are no more cruel than the gaucho owners of "La Florida," their hacienda. The novel faithfully reflects the reality of the times, the rivalry between the old gaucho of the countryside and the new, foreign culture. Ironic humor, melancholy, sadness, and, above all, violence and brutality characterize this novel, a painting in vivid colors of ranches, corrals, and gauchos. Don Panchito suffers from excessive pride and arrogance; Sandalio is insolent; Bibiano is servile; Eduardo, the kindly and democratic nephew, is irresponsible.

Lynch also wrote a number of short stories and novelettes, many of which first appeared in newspapers or magazines such as *La Nación*, *Atlántida*, and *El Día*, the last named a paper founded by his father. *Raquela* (1918), a rural tale, is lighter in tone and less pessimistic than his previous story. A young city man disguises himself as a peon to work on a hacienda and thus to achieve a change of pace from his literary endeavors. He falls in love with and is loved by the lovely Raquela. In addition to gaucho types, Lynch describes a fire, quite similar to one found in Acevedo Díaz' *Soledad*. Another novelette, *La evasión* (1922), treats of a strong and ruthless hero and his love. *Las mal calladas* (1923) offers a different approach in its treatment of city life but again contains autobiographical reminiscences as well as Lynch's philosophy of life. He concentrates on women in love, their evasions, and the consequences of their deceit. In the country the friendship of a peasant or that of nature can be won only with great effort, but its hostility and struggle are overshadowed by the hypocrisy, suffering, and pessimism of the city. In any event, the society of man is no comfort, and one may seek solace in the memory of "la campaña bonaerense, tercamente aferrado a la memoria, del cual no desea salir el autor, como si sólo allí pudiera plantar con seguridad sus figuras." [129] As a general rule Lynch's women are much nobler characters than his men, who are likely to be brutal and unfeeling. Other novelettes which point up Lynch's sharp observance and great memory are *El antojo de la patrona* (1925), about a frustrated woman and her unfeeling husband, and *Palo verde* (1925), about a noble gaucho who kills in order to save a woman's honor. *De los campos porteños* (1931), his best collection of short stories, contains the much anthologized "El potrillo ruano," about a boy and his colt, and presents us with a spontaneous, simple, and innocent view of Argentine life.

Lynch's masterpiece and the novel which most appealed to him, *El inglés de los güesos* (1924), may have been inspired by his reading of Darwin and Humboldt's voyages. The novel describes the life of the *puestero*, a kind of tenant farmer who lives on the land and produces while the owners preoccupy themselves with stock market deals. Near Puesto number three in the story, there exists a pre-Colombian fossil bed to which an Englishman, James Gray, a student of anthropology, comes to perform Indian excavations. On the estancia "La Estaca," where the puestero Juan Fuentes has to accept him on the boss's orders, the Englishman is given part of the kitchen as his room. Other members of the family include Fuentes' wife, Doña Casiana; his eighteen-year old daughter, Balbina, known as La Negra because of her black hair, black eyes and suntanned skin; and the youngest in the family, Bartolo. James is a ridiculous figure because of his eccentricities and broken Spanish, but he wins over most of the gauchos. After an initial dislike and some difficulties, Balbina learns to like and finally to love him, first when he nurses her and then when she helps him recover from a wound inflicted by Santos Telmo, her jealous suitor. Receiving a letter from the backer of the expedition asking him to return, the tall, slender, blond, and reserved Englishman, temporarily torn between love and duty, decides to return. Balbina hangs herself. The superstitions, folklore, the customs of the times, an occasional bit of philosophy about the indifference of the world to suffering, and the relationships of nature to the man of the pampas are not enough to insure the novel's success. To modern eyes, although Balbina's fluctuation between love and hate for Mr. Yemes (which he for all his wisdom cannot comprehend) is fairly well portrayed, the Englishman is a grotesque caricature of the *gringo*, and his motivation is less convincing than that of the simple and somewhat stupid Balbina, who immolates herself to her love.[130] Indeed, Lynch seems to have a special knack for penetrating the psychology of women and children, more individualized than his adult men, as he explores the hidden world of moral values, foreign to most egotistical males.

El romance de un gaucho (1933), a more spiritualized version of life on the plains, may well be "desde un punto de vista técnico la obra más acabada de Lynch."[131] Pantaleón Reyes, a young and pampered gaucho, becomes obsessed with love for Julia Fuentes, the wife of a drunkard who has come to the village. The boy takes up with bad companions, the Rosales brothers, and abandons his ranch, "La Blanquiada," forever. Julia, her husband dead, becomes an intimate of Doña Cruz, Pantaleón's mother. Pantaleón, the victim of an ever-growing madness, in an effort to return to the village when he hears that Julia's husband has died, kills his horse which can run no more. Hallucinating that its ghost is chasing him, Pantaleón dies. The Dr. Jekyll and Mr. Hyde transformation and madness remind one of Eduardo Barrios' psychological novels. The protagonists, far from being rural stereotypes, are complicated human beings, kind and cruel, scrupulous and unscrupulous; although Julia, a more complicated and sophisticated Balbina, appears too good and noble to be true. Pantaleón, tortured, unable to extract strength from solitude, filled with emotional needs he cannot express through rational statements, is perhaps Lynch's best drawn character. In his preface to the novel Lynch states that his work is thoroughly and essentially gaucho because he had the story from don Sixto, "un viejo gaucho porteño, fallecido hace muchos años, y a quien conocí allí en los dorados días de mi niñez campera . . . no puede ser más genuinamente gaucha, como que fue sentida, pensada y escrita por un gaucho."

Germán García believes that this novel can pass the closest scrutiny and that "los diálogos son de maestro y sobrios en la frase los personajes. . . . El realismo en la observación y en la descripción de tipos es característico de este extraordinario costumbrista." [132] One sees in Lynch the end of the gaucho of the epic pampas and the arrival of the sedentary one, themes of love, and the passions of the human heart.[133]

Many Argentine novelists, each in his own way, represent the criollista theme, man against nature, the immigrant's problems and conflicts with Argentines, or the industrialization of rural Argentina. Eduardo Acevedo Díaz, Jr. (1882–1959), won a national Argentine prize in 1932 with *Ramón Hazaña*, about life on the estancia "La Quinua" on the pampa near the frontier. The protagonist, Ramón Sandoval, nicknamed Hazaña, is a mestizo who vies with the loyal and hardworking gaucho Fausto for the love of Rosario. The author handles remarkably well the theme of the *china* (half-breed) as the victim of a society where sexual prowess is an alternative to celibacy, where she serves largely as an object of sexual fulfillment, and where the peon, even when he wants to, cannot marry. *Argentina te llamas* (1934), *Eternidad* (1937), which one Argentine critic labeled "magnífica novela. . . . Huxley, el celebrado autor de *Contrapunto*, no habría desdeñado firmarla," [134] and *Cancha larga* (1939), an evocation of the Argentine countryside from 1875 on, are his other novels. Through several generations of a gaucho family, Acevedo Díaz, Jr., in *Cancha larga*, treats thematically progress versus tradition and country versus the city and details the folklore and superstition of otherwise hardened gauchos.

Another representative of the Argentine plains must be mentioned here. Gustavo Martínez Zuviría (1883–1954), better known as Hugo Wast, was one of the most popular novelists of Argentina, but he has largely been ignored by critics. Wast emphasizes the sentimental, the historical, the social, and the national, and has written some warm and charming stories. A lawyer and later the director of the National Library, he unfortunately became the victim of anti-Semitic madness, becoming, for a time, the leading spokesman for that sickness in Argentina. Irrationally justifying the persecution of the Jews, he equated the cry of "muera el judío," with "viva la Patria." [135] Promoting the rawest and most repugnant racism, he and other extreme nationalists believed that they were offering an antidote for those novelists like Alberto Gerchunoff who exalted the role of the Jew in Argentine life. Hugo Wast, who had been educated by the Jesuits, used a twisted form of that upbringing to exalt what he thought was a fervent Catholicism and defense of religion.

Wast's first novel, *Alegre* (1906), is about the travels and heroic death of a Negro boy. Other novels include *Novia de vacaciones* (1907), about unrequited love; *Fuente sellada* (1914), the story of two sisters, their upbringing, intricate love affairs, and the role of provincial politics, in which the "bad" sister, María Teresa, finally becomes religious, and, when her husband is assassinated, Evangelina, the "good" one, marries her former sweetheart, Juan Manuel; *La casa de los cuervos* (1916), about the struggle against caudillismo, political ambition, and love between the brave Captain Insúa and the widow of the man he had killed during a revolutionary period in the province of Santa Fe in 1877; *Valle negro* (1918), a tragic tale of family feuds in Córdoba which won a Spanish Academy prize; *Ciudad turbulenta—ciudad alegre* (1919), a bitter analysis of social classes in Buenos Aires; *Los ojos vendados* (1921); and *Pata de zorra* (1924), fairly autobiographical, about a law student's attempt to pass a course by making love to the old maid sister of his professor. Wast wrote historical novels, *La corbata Celeste* (1924), about Rosas and a defense of the federales; *Myriam la conspiradora* (1926), about love versus duty in which devotion to the loyalist cause wins out; *Lucía Miranda* (1929), about an Indian-white love affair; utopian novels, *Juan Tabor* and *666*, both set in the year 2,000 and the latter of which fervently holds the position that Catholicism and the Church will be eternal; and among his more recent titles, *Morir con las botas puestas* (1952); *Los huesos del coronel* (1952); *Estrella de la borde* (1954), and *¿Le tiraría usted la primera piedra?* (1954).

Of all Wast's novels, those of provincial life, *Flor de durazno* (1911) and *Desierto de piedra* (1925), his own favorite, are his two best works. In the former, the mother of the heroine, Rina, had planted a peach tree on the day of her daughter's birth, thus tying her fortune, symbolically, to that of the tree. The struggles between city and country, the poor and the rich, seduction, flight, jealousy, illegitimate birth, romantic forgiveness, and the death of the principal protagonists, except for the blind Germán Castillo, Rina's father, and his granddaughter, add to the story of traditional prejudices and rural rivalries. Wast deals with everyday events, often involving a series of complicating relationships, love, exploitation, loneliness, and the seduction of a beautiful, good, but innocent girl at the hands of a rich young man, perhaps his favorite situation. *Desierto de piedra* is about Argentine ranch life, especially about one estancia in a remote mountain zone. Through his heroine, Marcela, the daughter of the nephew of the old ranch owner, we learn of the rugged virtues of country life, much as Cervantes through his own Marcela defended the concept of feminine virtue. Wast's novels make up in pace and sustained interest what they lack in profundity.

Alberto Gerchunoff (1883–1950) was born in Russia, but his family moved to Argentina in 1889 to the Jewish farm colony established there, aided by Baron Mauricio de Hirsch. Gerchunoff, a dedicated criollo, recalls the beauties of Argentine skies, country life, and the pampa, and in spite of the tragic death of his father at the hands of a drunk, the growing mutual respect between criollos and Jews. When the family moved to Buenos Aires he had a difficult time and to survive worked at a variety of manual labors. Gerchunoff states in *Entre Ríos, mi país,* his autobiography published posthumously in 1950: "Fue este trabajo el que me proporcionó los mayores sufrimientos y las más grandes humillaciones de mi vida."

Gerchunoff attended school and became the good friend of Leopoldo Lugones and especially of Roberto Payró. A steady contributor to *La Nación,* he also christened the famous literary magazine *Nosotros.* Most of his work is autobiographical and, in its treatment of the gaucho, manifests a European point of view. Throughout one can sense the great love for his adopted land, his sufferings, the relationships between the old and the new, conveyed at times poetically, at times sadly, and occasionally satirically. Baldomero Sanín Cano classified his style as "de un sabor clásico en que se nota la fuerza de Quevedo y de Saavedra Fajardo, preciosamente combinado con la suavidad de un Fray Luis de León y la sonora corriente de un Solís." [136]

Gerchunoff concentrated on the short story form, of which his most important collection is *Los gauchos judíos* (1910), an ironic and humorous treatment of the Jew in a free environment, his daily life as an integrated Argentine, and the beauty, poetry, and religion in Jewish life. *El hombre que habló en la Sorbona* (1926) is a caricature of South American intellectuals; *La clínica del doctor Mefistófeles* (1937), combining fantasy and myth, shows us a human, complaining, and quite tolerant Devil. His *Los amores de Baruj Spinoza* (1932) is a novelized biography of that philosopher. In his novel *El hombre importante* (1934) Gerchunoff deals with Spanish American politics, the incompetents who succeed, and the use of the big lie technique to keep power. His protagonist, Vespasiano Pardeche, is a modern version of Payró's Mauricio Gómez Herrera. By and large Gerchunoff's fiction portrays nature in all its pleasant and peaceful guises; because of this love of the land his extensively descriptive works develop quite slowly. He combines opulence and plastic imagery with philosophical, racial, social, and political concerns and psychological intuition, evident both in short stories like *Cuentos de ayer* (1919) and in his non-fiction, posthumous *El pino y la palmera* (1952). In him two different cultures became fused in a new way, and his knowledge and experience of Jews and things Jewish "hicieron de él un escritor de habla española absolutamente original." [137]

Alcides Greca (1896–   ) also writes of immigrant life on the Argentine plains. In *Viento norte* (1927) he shows us rural customs. In *La pampa gringa* (1936) he tells us about the problems of European immigrants, in this case Italian, modern agriculture, and the expulsion of criollos by gringos who in turn give way to an animal population. In César Hidalgo, teacher and utopian dreamer, we see Greca's hopes for a better society.

Miguel Ángel Correa (1880–1943), better known as Mateo Booz, was essentially the novelist of Sante Fe. Newspaperman, educator, dramatist, poet, and short story writer, he handles legends, superstitions, and politics of the Argentine people. Combining tenderness and satire, Booz is an "agudo y encariñado intérprete del alma vernacular." [138] Author of a well-known collection of short stories, *Santa Fe, mi país* (1934), he also wrote two short novels, *El agua de tu cisterna* (1919) and *La reparación* (1920), encouraged to do so by Hugo Wast, probably the first to recognize his fictional talent. Booz' novels include *La vuelta de Zamba* (1927), *El tropel* (1932), *Aleluyas del Brigadier Santa Fe* (1936), and *La ciudad cambió de voz* (1938). *El tropel* is a historical novel about the time of Rosas. More representative is *La ciudad cambió de voz*, which narrates the history of Rosario from 1870 on, its economic and social problems, its immigrants, and its growing pains. A Spanish family comes to Argentina, and the protagonist, as a result of an accidental death in which he is involved, flees to Rosario, marries, has three sons, and finally commits suicide. His life corresponds to the mercantile growth of an essentially rural area. Booz is undoubtedly at his best in short narratives,[139] which lend themselves better to his anecdotal, humorous, and ironic but tender tone. His typical protagonist is a provincial who seeks broader horizons in Buenos Aires and, disillusioned and defeated, comes once more to the land he knows and loves, removed from the false charity and hypocrisy of the big city.

Ricardo Güiraldes (1886–1927), an author whose vision and fantasy bring him close to the contemporary novel, carried the theme of the gaucho to its ultimate poetic conclusion. In his work the legendary gaucho, the victimized gaucho of *Martín Fierro*, the picaresque gaucho of Payró, and the realistic one of Lynch, give way to one whose very substance is the dream stuff of the Argentine soul. Born of well-to-do parents in Buenos Aires, Güiraldes and his family traveled to France. He studied law and architecture but from the age of fifteen on he knew he wanted to be a writer. He traveled abroad and lived in France, where he began his masterpiece, *Don Segundo Sombra*, and where later he returned to die (of Hodgkins disease). He himself reveals that his French experiences had great influence on him. In a long letter written to Guillermo de Torre on 27 June 1925 Güiraldes tells about an unfinished love novel he began at seventeen years of age, only to abandon it, and his interest in Flaubert, whom he saw as the progenitor of his work and a direct influence on his novel *Xaimaca*. States Güiraldes: "Creo que en mí fue Flaubert el propulsor . . ." [140]

Güiraldes had known real gauchos in his youth, but as an esthete and aristocrat his cultural heritage was also French. The dual aspect of his nature can be seen in *Raucho*, finished by 1912 but not published until 1917,[141] and in his short stories, *Cuentos de muerte y de sangre* (1915), which Güiraldes calls "anécdotas oídas y escritas por cariño a las cosas nuestras" and which reflect modernism, his trips to Europe and Asia, and local superstition. The conflict between his Argentine heritage and European culture was most completely modified and resolved in his masterpiece, where the author achieves a synthesis of sorts. He created a kind of narration which was at the same time "dentro de las corrientes más modernas y más antiguas. Güiraldes era el hombre argentino de educación europea, que conoció profundamente—por haber vivido en Francia —la literatura francesa, y también la inglesa, pero que sentía que, debajo de toda su cultura moderna, su verdadero ser estaba en aquello que él había vivido en su infancia y en su propia tierra: aquella vida en las estancias, junto a los gauchos que aun quedaban." [142] Güiraldes was one of the founders of the *Revista Proa*, which ran for twelve issues and had a profound influence on members of the *Martín Fierro* review, the instrument through which Argentina was to learn about new European literature, and whose members deliberately sought to shatter old Argentine values. But Güiraldes declined to confine himself to a limited concept of artistic creation. He used whatever literary devices and structures he could find, along with the local and the foreign, to express his feelings about life—too broad a canvass to be confined to literary convention and combinations. He hoped for a representative and partial symbolic reflection of the living process.[143]

Güiraldes began his published writing with a collection of poetry, *El cencerro de cristal* (1915), which shows his interest in both the material and the spiritual. *Cuentos de muerte y de sangre* (1915) contains stories about the pampa and the peons in their daily tasks, anecdotes that in part he had heard and written down; whatever his total viewpoint as esthete, European, hacendado, or poet, he manages to fuse geography, psychology, poetry, and history to reflect a real given time and space.

His first novel, *Raucho* (1917), a kind of autobiography he began in Granada when he was twenty-four, is a prototype or preliminary sketch novel of what will later be his masterpiece, much of whose emotional qualities and symbolism it manages to convey in its series of *cuadros*. The author admits that the work is autobiography of "un yo disminuido. Iba a llamarse algo así como 'Los impulsos de Ricardito' pretendiendo yo entonces que poseemos en nosotros un personaje a nuestra imagen, pero disminuido, que nos hace cometer todas nuestras tonterías. Después el libro evolucionó naturalmente hacia un personaje autónomo." [144] The first part of the novel takes place on "El Esparto," the hacienda of Leandro Galván, a widower who lives only for his son. The father's excessive concern and the ministrations of a German governess cause the son to rebel at his "sissy" existence. At the hacienda he comes to know the men and the countryside of Argentina, and the pampa, the light, the dawn, and other aspects of nature influence his spirit. Raucho goes off to Paris, throws away his money on wine, women, perfumes, bright lights, and alcohol, and suffers a nervous collapse. A friend finally helps him return home. Some of the characters, like Don Segundo Sombra and Fabián Caceres, the latter a kind of juvenile delinquent, changed in a number of ways, will become major characters in *Don Segundo Sombra*. Güiraldes, whatever he may have thought of the culture, found European life to be morally enervating when compared to the lure of the pampa and the rough life of the gaucho, whose honor and simplicity he contrasts with the artificial one of the city. But the gauchos are more than types, and as Ara points out, "Las faenas tienen en el libro la virtud de dejarnos imágenes como de una realidad actual y fascinante." [145]

Rosaura (1922), a novelette, is a sentimental, melancholy, nostalgic, and ironic work that the author says he wrote in twenty days for *El Cuento Ilustrado* of Horacio Quiroga: "Hice *Rosaura* en veinte días a capítulo por día. En esos momentos, Horacio Quiroga, que empezaba a lanzar una edición popular de novelas cortas, me pidió colaboración. Le mandé *Rosaura* a quien por motivos de venta se cambió el nombre, intitulándola, *Un idilio de estación*, 1916." [146] Rosaura Torres, a simple soul who represents the Argentine pueblo, sees a man (for whom she conceives a passion) on the platform of the Lobos station. He is Carlos Ramallo, the son of a rich hacendado. Her father owns a livery stable in Lobos. Carlos and Rosaura meet each other, but he goes off to England to study farming. On his return, she sees him at the station with his wife and throws herself under the wheels of a train. Lobos, a "tranquil town in the middle of the Pampa," whose monotony is relieved by the passage of two daily express trains, is where Rosaura and others dreamed dreams about the trains which led to another world. The train that stopped there afforded the local citizenry a glimpse of that other tempting, luxurious life, but at the same time dragged an innocent girl to her doom.

*Xaima*ca (1923), whose title is the poetic and original one for Jamaica, is a poetic travel book or novel, depending on one's point of view. Barbagelata calls it "la más completa de sus 'nouvelles' a la francesa," [147] but Adelina del Carril, Güiraldes' widow, in the foreword to its 1960 edition says that the work was "notas del viaje que hicimos el verano de 1916–17, con Alfredo González Garaño y su mujer Marietta Ayerza." She states that Güiraldes wrote it up in novel form to please Leopoldo Lugones. He finished it in 1919, and in 1923, the year of its publication, it sold only ninety copies. In the novel, Marcos jots down his impressions of a journey from Buenos Aires to Peru, Valparaíso, and eventually Jamaica; his encounters, adventures of various kinds, his love affair with Clara Ordóñez, its discovery by her brother, and Marcos' return. Most of the action occurs on the boat, a place of enchantment and the "subtle aroma of irreality," also an aspect of Jamaica where Marcos achieves the fulfillment of his love for woman and nature. The diary covers the period between 28 December 1916 and 10 March 1917. The poetic and at times almost mystic and impressionistic evocations of nature and the impressionistic view of the inner soul states of the protagonist clearly denote Güiraldes' exposure to French culture.

Don Segundo Sombra (1926), which makes use of characters and descriptive material the author had used in previous stories, was begun in Paris in 1919 where he wrote the first ten chapters. He also used material he gathered in his travels through Argentina in 1921 and 1922 when he saw a series of cock fights and visited the crab colonies of the crabflats. Don Segundo himself had appeared in one of the stories of *Cuentos de muerte y de sangre*. Although some controversy exists on this as well as on a number of other points concerning the novel, Don Segundo Sombra was based on a real prototype known to Güiraldes in his youth. Adelina del Carril states in the preface to the novel (Buenos Aires, 1952) that she heard her husband discuss Don Segundo Ramírez Sombra many times, even the night of their wedding, 20 October 1913.[148] The novel, finished at "La Porteña" in Buenos Aires, is dedicated to Don Segundo and to the memory of figures such as Don José Hernández, a number of gaucho friends, and above all "To the gaucho whom I carry within me sacredly as the monstrance carries the Host." His widow, in the same prologue, maintains that Güiraldes intended to disclose "the poetic-philosophical, musical and pictorial aspect of an inexpressed race."

The novel, which we are to assume was written by its young protagonist after he has acquired his European culture, views the gaucho from an aesthetic and nostalgic viewpoint but, in spite of its refinement, shows a profound knowledge of the popular and dialectal. Although some difference of opinion exists as to Güiraldes' position on the gaucho, one has to agree that the novel is written by a man whose culture was more European than American. A literate and cultured man, a product of a sophisticated European environment, Güiraldes somehow avoids the artificial in his aesthetic and poetic evocation of a time that was and in his prophecy for the unknown future. Autochthonous elements and authentic Argentine reality need not strike one as paradoxical, for Güiraldes, whatever his Parisian background, had also been an *estanciero*.

Don Segundo Sombra explores the relationship of man and nature. Erotic interest intrudes only incidentally to show the maturation process of the young hero in his fleeting contact with feminine wiles. Güiraldes presents the Argentine pampa, its superstitions, mysteries, pulperías, towns, estancias, dances, bronco busting, horse racing, and cock fights. The pampa, an extension of land and sky, a timeless sea of cosmic force, is a place where telluric forces strive for universal fusion, where animals and vegetables, the big and the small, the natural and the grotesque, the real and the unreal, sound and shape, movement and smell convey an emotional and spiritual impact almost by a process of osmosis. Güiraldes affirms things both in their temporality and physical aspects and as part of one vast reality. His heroes seem always to be in the process of becoming without ever fully arriving. Even in the case of young Fabio Cáceres, he only reaches another plateau from which he will continue his odyssey, as will the others who seek to understand, to exalt, or who seek salvation through a nature and a land in perfect harmony with its citizens.[149] The concept of the affinity between man and nature seems to have been a central thesis for Güiraldes; he uses figures of speech deliberately to convey this communion and harmony in *Don Segundo Sombra*. His purpose, at least in part, seems to have been to complete "de manera indirecta la visión de la pampa . . . una finalidad esencial de las comparaciones de *Don Segundo Sombra*," [150] and he fuses both nature and man to give an illusion as well as satisfaction of absolute freedom.[151]

Güiraldes uses a number of techniques in his novel, weaving personal sensation, impressionism, metaphors, the sensation and personification of the countryside, superstition, folklore, dreams, and symbols into an almost symetrically perfect structure. In its use of flashbacks, temporal flow, and symbolic representations such as water imagery, colors, stars, and night, the novel in some ways foreshadows later developments made by magic realism.[152] Güiraldes used, in addition to visual imagery and symbols, philosophical concepts, theosophic readings, and numerology and mystic numbers to symbolize the unending cycle of life (the past, present, and future are represented by Sombra, Fabio, and Raucho, respectively). One may find cosmic duality in the title of the novel itself,[153] whose "sombra" may also be the protective shadow of Don Segundo hovering over young Fabio Cáceres.[154]

The novel is divided into three equal parts of nine chapters each. The orphan boy of fourteen sees Segundo Sombra, becomes attached to him, and rides with him. This may be viewed as the apprenticeship and maturation process. In the second part five years have passed and the orphan boy has become a gaucho and has experienced gaucho life and customs and witnessed, too, the loneliness of man. The third part shows Fabio with Sombra for a time, his return to inherit his property, and his writing his experiences, which may be viewed as his liberty and fulfillment. The work has three sallies, much like those of Don Quijote, and Fabio, in his peripatetic examination of life on the plains, is a pícaro for whom the novel's cuadros serve as a picaresque framework.[155] The novel extracts the poetic quintessence of the native language and has a coherence and a central vision; however, some fault it for a lack of rhythmic unity in what is a boy's Odyssey along the path to his ultimate destiny.[156] It has extraneous material, to be sure, in its mixture of reality, memory, and invention; but its structure is quite symmetrical and is aesthetically arranged. More important than the structure is the profound lyric quality of some of its passages,[157] an artistic prose, and a vision that shows the influence of modernism. Güiraldes' impressionistic flair in describing the countryside does not veil the primitive epic quality of the novel, but the lyrical overtones are inescapable.[158]

Don Segundo Sombra has very little plot. Fabio Cáceres, the illegitimate son of a rich rancher, is sent to be educated in a small town. In the care of two maiden aunts the boy wastes his time until one day he meets Don Segundo Sombra. He goes to the ranch of Leandro Galván, sees the ranch life, the horse-breaking, at which Don Segundo is a past master, and the preparations for a round-up. Sombra and Fabio begin their five year association, wandering through the pampa, seeing the natural beauties, at times terrifying, of its flora and fauna, such as an enormous crab colony. They arrive at various ranches, and the boy sees knife fights, cock fights, gambling, a cattle stampede, and a Christmas dance and experiences tropical rainstorms and saddle sores. At the beginning of the second part, Pedro Barrales, a companion of his first roundup, evokes his memories in a kind of recapitulation of his experience. Don Segundo Sombra tells a number of stories as they sit around the camp fire,[159] and we hear further descriptions of pampa life, its beauties, trials, and tribulations. Finally Pedro Barrales brings him the letter from Galván about his inheritance of his father's ranch and name. Segundo Sombra stays on to help with one aspect of his education, while Raucho Galván undertakes to teach him about literature and culture. Don Segundo, his task completed, leaves, and the boy is prepared to take over his duties as a ranch owner and complete man.

In spite of his widow's statement as to the model used, many interpretations have been made about Güiraldes' own statement that Segundo Sombra is "more idea than being and more an idea than a man." Segundo Sombra seems to be the artistic presentation of an idealized figure, one that is an abstraction in the sense of combining the best characteristics of a series of gauchos to create a living one and yet one larger than life. T. B. Irving insists that the author created don Segundo "out of the whole cloth of his imagination, and perhaps out of his own misgivings" but sees in him qualities like those of any cowhand who ever lived. Sombra is thus both a symbol of Güiraldes' own escapism and yet a man with a code of ethics and a certain nobility.[160] Germán García sees the novel as a defense of tradition and a gaucho who is disappearing, one who at the same time is a figure in a timeless dimension, "desde que es esencia e idealización, no realidad de un instante." [161] One can say that in spite of Güiraldes' stated nostalgia about estancia life, his gaucho is an aesthetic recreation, a symbol of a life that never was except in the dreams of his creator, at least in the way in which events are presented.

Sombra is a mythical gaucho in his final evolution—but not the last one. Two decades later the Uruguayan Adolfo Montiel Ballesteros undertook a similar mythification process.[162] The gaucho in Güiraldes' novel then is a poetic projection of a moral and spiritual heritage, possessed of almost metaphysical qualities. He is but an impalpable shadow at the beginning and almost ghostlike in his fade-out at the end of the novel. He is portrayed as a kind of martyr willing to sacrifice himself for the new generations, for even though industrialization had conquered the gaucho, his traditional virtues were needed to help create a new Argentina in the face of the challenge of European civilization—hence Don Segundo's constant admonition to Fabio to "hacete duro." Sombra affirms the national personality and the necessary link to tradition;[163] Fabio learns from his fatalism, energy, and stoicism and feels his very life's blood draining away when his mentor leaves him. Torres-Rioseco compares Don Segundo to Don Quijote as a "knight of an ideal, an ideal of simple manliness and freedom . . . a legendary symbol of a heroic type that was." [164]

One may view the novel in a different light. His spiritual and physical perfection may make of Don Segundo "una imagen arbitraria del gaucho." [165] The hero is modest, unselfish, brave, calm, strong, noble, ethical, quiet, self-reliant, clever, a philosopher, story teller, bronco buster, cattle driver, and many other things. If he appears larger than life at times, he is also all too human as he travels the vast solitudes of the Argentine plains on his own voyage of discovery. Even if the prototype of this version of life's journey was real, Sombra represented a gaucho who had all but disappeared. In spite of the lyric qualities inherent in his portrayal, Sombra has been viewed as a real portrayal, as have been those around him, of real work and scenery, "una realidad de hombres que existieron." [166] For this type of reader the novel is "un documento social y psicológico. Dirá a las generaciones futuras como eran a principios de este siglo la pampa y su morador. Lo imaginado apenas cuenta." [167]

Philosophically, Güiraldes' central thesis is that the transformation of Argentina from a rural nation to a modern one holds inherent dangers, as Raucho's Parisian experiences testified. He also shows that the Argentine gaucho had traditional moral virtues not easily discarded or ignored, a dualism and interplay of realism and idealism which continues throughout the novel. Don Segundo's moral code and stoicism is as old as the nation itself, and he is both a traditional and transcendental symbol. He and a wiser and more mature Raucho have much to offer their country; but it is Fabio Cáceres, the product of a ranch owner's whim with a woman of the pueblo, who must assimilate the best of both worlds—the morality and vigor of the pampa, without its brutality, and the liberal culture of Raucho, without its dissipation. The mixture will be leavened by a new spirit of social equality implicit in his inheritance from his mother, representative of the Argentine people. Fabio starts his Odyssey in search of a heritage, slowly maturing and learning from Don Segundo, imitating him in every way. From him he acquires a philosophy of life, "fatalism, moral force, and his ascetic reluctance toward women and drink. When the boy acquires name and family, he carries within him still the lessons learned from Segundo . . ." [168] He also learns from his exposure to life on the plains, from Aurora and Paula, from his friends Antenor and Patrocinio, for it is only by facing life that one can live. His initiation into manhood represents that of the boy in Faulkner's *The Bear*. Finally, the boy learns from Raucho, his guide to European culture; but his education will never be complete because he will always have to try to assimilate the traditions of the Western world and yet "preserve sacramentally his pristine gaucho self although the freedom and joy will be his no more." [169] Raucho may represent the Argentine who is seeking wider horizons, while Fabio, the incarnation of conservatism and tradition, must accept Raucho's lesson and become a flexible, open-minded, progressive, and yet patriotic man. "During the process of evolution these two forces, conservatism and progress, will keep each other in balance." [170]

The natural vernacular, the animated tone, and the "sharp-toned pictures of certain strata of Argentine society" [171] are more impressive than character or plot development, as are the themes of the fusion of man with nature, the lyric tone, and the national

Argentine spirit in its temporal manifestations as represented by the protagonists. In spite of its positive qualities many have criticized the novel. Jorge Luis Borges found the novel to be a kind of obeisance to a mythical past, repeating Groussac's "el smoking sobre el chiripá," and the Boedo group's "La estancia vista por el hijo del patrón." [172] For them the novel is a completely false and elaborated dream, its gaucho a kind of slave seen from above by the master, and the so-called synthesis of a time that was, an Argentina now disappeared, a pure invention. Objecting strongly to the acclaim afforded the novel, one critic calls it an exaggerated product of "literatos extranjerizantes" who do not understand Argentina and thus stressed the mythical and poetic aspects of the novel. He believes that *Don Segundo Sombra* is the expression of a national class and that "podrá ser un bello poema, es un bello poema, pero también una atroz herejía." [173]

Viewed by one who is not an Argentine, the novel seems warm, rich, human, and vital, for all its romantic and nostalgic escapism in wanting to preserve a way of life gone beyond recall. It evokes the spiritual qualities of the protagonist, whatever his human defects, and dreams of a democratic, moral, and ideal nation, expressing the American spirit in a universal frame.[174]

Carlos B. Quiroga (1890–   ), a novelist of the Argentine north, has written much literary criticism. His novels are almost all set in the Catamarca area. *Cerro nativo* (1921) examines the evils of alcohol and sociological factors in what amounts to a largely pantheistic, almost religious, and nostalgic evocation of the beauties of Catamarca as a symbol of the American soul. *La montaña bárbara* (1926); *La imagen noroéstica* (1929); *La raza sufrida* (1929); *Los animalitos de Dios* (1930), a magical description of Catamarca and the role of the condor in American life, more a zoological study than novel; *Almas en la roca* (1938); *El tormento sublime* (1938); *Lirolay* (1939), labeled "Poema de la montaña," a fantasy about daily tasks on the estancia, the cattle horses, man in his natural milieu and the dreams of Lirolay, doña Pancha's daughter, in love with a shadowy, fantastic, and unreal mountain singer; *El lloradero de las piedras* (1941); and *Los deiterranos* (1957) are his other fictional productions. As a criollista he deals with pioneers and mountainsides, man in his struggles against nature, and man in his struggles against man. Usually his nature

ennobles rather than destroys man, but nonetheless his environment is a sad one. His best work is still *La raza sufrida*, a kind of
emotional monologue in diary form which shows his love of and
identification with nature in all its aspects, with the mule drivers,
hunters, and other types who inhabit it. Ventura Quinteros, an
intellectual dreamer, visits the "sea of rocks," a place of immense
solitude. He lives the sierra life in Catamarca, in the village of
Fiambolá, a place of dances, cock fights, misery, and beautiful
countryside. He falls in love with Alicia, his landlady's daughter.
Shaken from his spiritual lethargy, he resolves to climb the mountain and be worthy of his love. On his return Ventura learns that
Alicia has been seduced by Quipildor, but now restored in spirit
he can resist the turn of events. The reverse of Martín Rivas,
Ventura, a city man, challenges the mountain, triumphs, and returns to his urban environment a new man, leaving others to succumb to the mountain's spell.

Almas en la roca and its sequel, *El tormento sublime*, which the
author first wanted to call *Dios* and later *Tormento cósmico*, deal
with a different type of cosmic force. Jacinto Quijano, a priest,
seeks the mystic revelation of the origin of the world. His faith
lost, he moves to Buenos Aires, becomes a successful lawyer, and at
novel's end returns to the *montaña* to save his uncle's ranch. The
theme of a priest in search of divine love is not too common in
Spanish American fiction. *El lloradero de las piedras* contends that
man's political and social struggles will not change the eternal
land, a thesis often repeated in Quiroga in his search for both the
real and legendary Andes. In this novel a mestizo destroys the mine
which profanes the mountain tranquility.

The criollo resentment of and competition with foreigners and
the sturdy virtues of the native country show but one side of the
criollo novel. Many novelists recognized the abject misery in
which the Indian lived (naturally, these novels were prevalent in
those countries with large Indian populations). Most of these
novels, loosely labeled "indigenista," with their visions of under-
fed and underpaid cholos, Indians, and Negroes, victims of the
latifundio, the factories, the mines, the sugar fields, and the cotton
farms, will be discussed in a later chapter on the social novel.
Clorinda Matto de Turner started the vogue with her *Aves sin
nido* as early as 1889; but the most militant voice of all, albeit in

nonfictional tones, was that of Manuel González Prada (1848–1918), "el que dará carácter y fuerza expresiva al movimiento indigenista" [175] and at least "la nota precursora del indigenismo militante." [176] Later, many powerful novelists in Ecuador, Mexico, Peru, and Bolivia undertook the theme of the Indian as a victim of society, and at times, his defense and reformation.

Bolivia in the early twentieth century produced few important novelists. Demetrio Canelas (1881–   ) wrote *Aguas estancadas* (1911) containing many cuadros de costumbres about Cochabamba. A key novel which apparently referred to real people and events, it was the best known novel of its generation; but Augusto Guzmán, overly generous, declares that it can figure "entre las mejores novelas de ambiente, superando en ciertos aspectos a cuantas pudieran comparársele." [177]

The first competent defender of the Indian and one of the good novelists of America, Alcides Arguedas (1879–1946), was also a diplomat, historian, poet, and sociologist. He wrote but a few novels, *Pisagua* (1903), *Wuata-Wuara* (1904) often transcribed as *Wata-Wara*, *Vida criolla* (1905), subtitled "La novela de la ciudad," and *Raza de bronce* (1919), a reworked *Wuata Wuara*. One of his nonfictional works, *Pueblo enfermo* (1909), had presented a pessimistic study of the Bolivian Indian, his alcoholism, superstitions, misery, and strong and weak points. Arguedas compares him as a social factor to the gaucho and the roto as a victim of society. In Bolivia, as in other countries with heavy Indian populations, the Indians became vassals of a feudal lord; exploited in fields and mines, they lived agonized and meaningless lives. Dozens were crowded together in miserable housing; hundreds died of a variety of illnesses. Hacienda owners fought against educating their slave workers, indeed furthering their alcoholism to keep them subservient, a design in which they were aided and abetted by the priest and the law. A further and somewhat racist thesis that Bolivia was doomed because of the mestizo was not calculated to endear Arguedas to fellow Bolivian intellectuals such as Fernando Díez de Medina, although later Hugo Blym and a few others recognized the validity of "Arguedismo." [178] Unamuno found his remarks exciting and commented on a number of them.[179]

Pisagua treats of the War of the Pacific with Chile and an attack by Chilean forces on Pisagua. Julio Villarino, an idealistic young poet, is in love with the daughter of a cacique, but she comes to a tragic end. *Wuata-Wuara* tells the tale of the Indian girl by that name raped by the mayordomo, Troche, but whose child she miscarries. She marries Agiali, her Indian sweetheart, but violated by the son of the hacendado and some friends, she dies. The Indians burn the hacienda down. *Vida criolla*, as Julio César Valdés claimed in the prologue to the first edition, tore asunder the rosy veil which Bolivian fantasy had used to cover "las llagas que corroen el cuerpo social." Carlos Ramírez, a newspaperman, fails in a society where religious bigotry, ignorant caudillos, and empty-headed ladies are in command. Filled with intrigue, politics, civil war, revolution, a seduction, a love affair with a priest, jealousy, and murder, the novel was intended as the first volume of a trilogy which might have evolved from the pessimistic note of failure of the idealistic protagonist.

Arguedas' masterpiece, *Raza de bronce*, takes up the anguished lives of the miserable and exploited Aymará Indians. Arguedas presents a problem for which he has no real solution. He describes the degradation of the Indian, points out his difficulty in adapting rapidly to Western culture, and thinks that although miscegenation might be an eventual hope, the Indian would have had more success in life without the Spaniard. Arguedas portrays the Indian as part of his scenic countryside, from the high wastelands to the beautiful valleys and Andean cordillera. Against this poetic landscape he combines Indian customs, rites, witch doctors, dances, and fiestas with feudalism, sadism, and the sordid and cruel yoke applied by the dominant caste to a race once strong and powerful but now a remnant cruelly oppressed. Arguedas, as a professional, has a fine grasp of the sociology and psychology of the Indian in his relationship with the white man. The plot, essentially that of *Wuata-Wuara*, has two parts, "El valle" and "El yermo." The Indians go on a long, almost epic journey from the highland to the valley to sell their products and to buy seed for the landowner. In the second part we are given a detailed picture of the suffering and enslaving of the Indians at the hands of avaricious, brutal, and sensual whites. The priest deceives them, the boss skimps on the promised feast, and Maruja, Agustín's sweetheart, in spite of her pregnancy, is raped by the son of the terrateniente. An Indian uprising is put down by the army. Arguedas inserts an Indian legend into the novel. The young poet, Suárez, a modernist with a social conscience and a friend of Isaac Pantoja, in his "La justicia de Huayna Capak" lends a historical and legendary aspect to the story of the tortured and denigrated Indians.

Fernando Díez de Medina, who is not objective about Arguedas (he calls Arguedas "prejudiced" and a "gran resentido"), labels *Raza de bronce* a thesis novel, "realista y nativista simultáneamente, con brotes insospechados de poeta y talento pictórico reproductivo." [180] Whatever the Bolivians' feelings on the matter may be, it seems apparent that Arguedas wrote the first important Bolivian novel and was the first to attribute human dignity to an oppressed and subjugated race. Through his portrayal of a fatalistically resigned people, yet one composed of subjectively responsive individuals, Arguedas managed to fuse ideology with the emotions and experiences of human beings to give us a glimpse, however imperfect, into the soul of man.

Armando Chirveches Arrózpide (1881–1926), who began as a modernist, is with Arguedas one of the founders of Bolivian realism, the painter of his country's customs, its strengths and weaknesses, its people and their problems. He lived in Europe for a time but devoted himself rather consistently to awakening the conscience of the Bolivian power structure to the problems of his fellow citizens, although, as his suicide seems to show, he could not solve his own. Chirveches' first novel of consequence is *La candidatura de Rojas* (1909), which recalls Payró's ironic account of corrupt voting procedures and politics in the Argentine provinces. A first person narrative, it describes the vain and ambitious Enrique Rojas y Castilla, who persists in a fruitless political endeavor. Through the antics of this young lawyer and would-be deputy, we learn about *caciquismo* and rural customs. *Casa solariega* (1916) also treats of social problems. Subtitled "Novela de costumbres latinoamericanas," it describes the rich middle class of Sucre, a city of the colonial past. In the struggle between the liberal young student Gaspar on the one hand, and the conservative, reactionary Dorotea and the rascally Spaniard Juan Luque on the other, the evil forces, aided by the Church, triumph, and Gaspar commits suicide. *La virgen del lago* (1920), his most famous novel, contains a love story and a pilgrimage which are incidental to the archeological expedition that allows Chriveches to show off his knowledge of the past and give us some penetrating and ironic insights into the meaning of being an Aymará Indian. In spite of its essayistic manner nd contrived happy ending, it has been called, "por el tema, el ambiente, los paisajes, los personajes, tipos de pueblo, costumbres y la psicología del boliviano . . . una de las mejores novelas del estilo descriptivo realista-criollo que se ha escrito en Bolivia." [181] *Flor del trópico* (1926), about the Rio de Janeiro society Chirveches had encountered there on his diplomatic tour of duty, occurs on the night before Carnival with the concomitant unleashing of human passion. *A la vera del mar* (1926), written during an extended period of convalescence, is a historical and partly autobiographical novel about a Bolivian engineer rejected by a British girl.

The city of Buenos Aires, along with some other important cities, contributed its share of geographical background for criollista works. The novel (not criollista) that first presents Buenos Aires as a twentieth-century theme, *Stella* (1905), was written by Emma de la Barra de Llanos (1861–1947), better known as César Duayén. She attempted, through the portrait of a typical porteño family, to reveal the world of privileges, the tertulias, and the gossip centers of the Barrio Norte. Alejandra, Stella's older sister, cares for the invalid child who dies at the age of eight, but the psychological insight and synthesis of Argentine society transcend the plot. Her other novels, such as *Mecha Iturbe* (1906), were less successful.

Carlos Alberto Leumann (1888–1952) offers us another twentieth-century view of high society in Buenos Aires. A poet, dramatist, and newspaperman, and one of the early exponents of the European psychological novel, "se ahinca en novelar el ambiente refinado de la alta clase burguesa porteña . . ." [182] He wrote a half dozen novels among which we find *Adriana Zumarán* (1920), a dissection of the heart of an Argentine woman whose own hesitation in love causes her marriage to a man she does not want; *La vida victoriosa* (1922), about conjugal love, a search for happiness, and political and psychological observations; *El empresario del genio* (1926), which he kept rewriting in the hopes of producing "un grito, un llamamiento al genio aletargado del alma argentina"; and *Trasmundo* (1930), a fantastic novel about the land of dreams. Leumann also wrote *El país del relámpago*, short stories published in 1932, and *Los gauchos de a pie*, a novel, published in 1940. Leumann is a bridge between the Buenos Aires of Martel and that of Mujica Láinez and later twentieth-century novelists. He handled provincial and rural life also, as his last fiction shows, but not as well. A kind of romantic out of time and an idealist interested in the solitude of the soul, he recognized, nonetheless, the intellectual infirmities of his country.

As we have stated, the city as well as the country may serve the criollista in his search for indigenous material and the physical and spiritual essence of his people. City authors were often as sentimental and naturalistic as their rural counterparts, but a few showed greater sophistication in their psychological analyses. One of the major novelists of twentieth-century Argentina, Manuel Gálvez (1882–1962), whose most important note may well be "su vinculación a la capital del Río de la Plata," [183] wrote about thirty novels most of which fit into the naturalistic, realistic, criollista tradition. One of the few purely professional novelists of the continent during most of his career,[184] he spent his early years in the provincial capitals of Paraná and Santa Fe and attended religious institutions and the University of Buenos Aires. He combined his legal training with an interest in sociology for his doctoral dissertation, "Trata de blancas." Gálvez founded, together with Ricardo Olivella, a literary magazine, *Ideas,* whose contributors included Ricardo Rojas and Alberto Gerchunoff. He also traveled abroad, especially in Spain. After a stint as a law clerk Gálvez became an inspector for secondary schools, a position he held for a quarter of a century and whose impact may be seen in some of his novels. He also edited, in 1919, the first anthology of the Argentine short story.

Critics constantly comment on what they believe are Gálvez' defects, especially that superficial psychological assessment which results in a weak character portrayal. His strongest point is usually acknowledged to be his authentic recreation of the atmosphere in the provincial cities and in Buenos Aires, and he has given us one of the broadest portrayals of the entire Argentine *ambiente* up to the present time.[185] Gálvez' geographical and spiritual evaluation of his country included—increasing with age—a dislike of democracy, an ardent defense of Catholicism, a right-wing philosophy, and a perhaps overly stringent belief in law and order. His social criticisms at times elicited an overly negative critical reaction such as that of time having already done its duty in eliminating much of Gálvez' production because it lacks passion, humanity, or even *paisaje* and because "las novelas resultan ahora plenas de artificialidad cuando debiera haber hondura, y alegato abogadil en vez de libre juego de instintos, caracteres o pasión." [186] But whatever his bias, excessive melodrama, abundance of details, or exaggerated psychology, Gálvez' great love for his country always shines through. He fought for tradition and against a growing materialism, as "not only a good novelist but a truly patriotic citizen." [187]

Gálvez' first prose, *El diario de Gabriel Quiroga* (1910), an ardent defense of Catholicism and a refutation of an earlier more liberal period, is essential for an understanding of his later works.[188] In 1913, in *El solar de la raza*, Gálvez' best-known volume of essays, he defended the Spanish cultural heritage of his country and adopted a position akin to that of Unamuno on the essential aspects of things Spanish. He evokes the Generation of '98 and, as they do, expresses his admiration for El Greco, on whom he later wrote a complete study. In writing his novels Gálvez hoped to examine current reality in terms of a historical past so as to analyze its permanent value. Many of his characters repeat from novel to novel in major or minor roles; but Gálvez believed that the essential quality of a novelist was his total vision of life. He contended that the novelist had to view things from above, "en su conjunto y en sus detalles. Ha de percibir los acontecimientos desarrollándose, el hilo que los une, la manera como unos y otros se encadenan y se mezclan. Ha de saber hallar lo dramático del momento que pasa, las tragedias encerradas en el fondo de las almas. Ha de ser un poco filósofo, y puesto que está por encima de todas las cosas, estudiarlas con amor, pero sin tomar partido por ninguna de ellas. Y ha de ser también artista y poeta." [189]

In his analysis of Argentine life Gálvez reverses Sarmiento's thesis, finding spiritual values in the provinces which contrast with the materialistic relationships of Buenos Aires. He also rejects the easy world of Europe. He was interested in both the spiritual and the physical aspects of his country and its characters. Although his novels lack the telluric feeling of many others that analyze the pampa or the gaucho (his one novel on this theme, *La pampa y su pasión* [1926], is similar to *Zogoibi* in many ways), Gálvez was, for all his European cultural contacts, a regional novelist of his country's high and low society, the rich and the poor, the strong and the weak, and especially criminals, prostitutes, and intellectuals. His frozen sections of Argentine life are more historically criollista than the country views of many other more authentically autochthonous novelists. In his examination of the political, social, economic, and spiritual resources of Argentina, Gálvez hoped to convey the anguish and faith hidden beneath the surface reality of his countrymen. Although his early visions of the future may not easily be equated with his later reinterpretations of the past, in his own way Gálvez has shown a steadfast optimism which places him at an enormous temporal distance from modern existential geography. Yet, among his galaxy of heroes and heroines who act in the social, political, and economic life of his country, we often find some who foreshadow the existential anguish of later novelistic heroes of fellow fiction writers like Eduardo Mallea.

Gálvez' first novel, *La maestra normal* (1914), is a somewhat naturalistic and detailed analysis of life in a small Argentine town, La Rioja, whose beauty, soul, solitude, melancholy, and surrounding mountains he describes. The novel evokes, albeit sentimentally, the character and personality of the static and sleepy provincial town. Gálvez believed that he had created a "true" and "human" work, evoking an entire society, a novel of "ambiente" rather than of characters, and essentially, "una novela social." [190] La Rioja is a drowsy, sad, melancholy town of neglected streets and fragrant orange trees. Doña Críspula's pensión offers us gossip, and Don Numeraldo's drug store tertulia enlightens us about town politics and sex. Gálvez shows his special liking, transcending political views, for the unfortunate. His characters are the victims of stresses and spiritual strains and of an outmoded provincial educational system. Julio Solís, a teacher from Buenos Aires who has come to La Rioja for his health, meets Raselda Gómez, a fellow teacher who has innocent and timid dreams of a perfect love. The school director, carrying on his own affair with a teacher, accuses Julio and Raselda of the same thing. Julio eventually seduces Raselda and abandons her. After an abortion she loses her position because she rejects the school inspector's advances. A teachers' revolt is thwarted, and Raselda, now dedicated to her religious beliefs, becomes a village school teacher. Julio, the city slicker and professional ladies' man, ends his days as a tubercular drunkard in Buenos Aires. The solitude and sadness, dreams, hates, loves, envy, and prejudices, the portrayal of the vernacular, the countryside, and a host of accumulated details of this "dolorosa y terrible novela," as Unamuno called it,[191] give us a perfect insight into its total ambiance and more than counterbalance any technical shortcomings Gálvez may exhibit in his first novel.

El mal metafísico (1916), the first of a series of novels about Buenos Aires that included *Nacha Regules, Historia de un arrabal,* and *El cántico espiritual,* has, like the others, an impractical and idealistic dreamer for a protagonist. Carlos Riga, a law student (Gálvez himself), boards at the house of the Regules. A timid, unrealistic visionary, he unsuccessfully undertakes an intellectual review, *La Idea Moderna,* is rejected by the aristocratic family of Lita, the girl he loves, and becomes a drunkard, supported by the landlady's daughter, Nacha, who had become a prostitute. Learning that his sweetheart is to marry, he cannot survive the final blow to his spirit. Gálvez portrays the bohemian life of Buenos Aires at the turn of the century, exhaustively studies the physical and spiritual composition thereof, and includes descriptions of many well-known literary figures of the day as well as what he himself called "la lucha heroica" of his own generation. The protagonist is spiritually defeated by the public disdain for literature, a frustration in love, and his own neurotic temperament—his *mal metafísico* or sickness of soul (Gálvez defines it as "de crear, de soñar, de contemplar"), resulting from being exposed to the stupidity and banality of Buenos Aires life. More important than his presentation of Gerchunoff, Almafuerte, or José Ingenieros is his empathic identification with the intellectual ambitions of the students of the day, their disillusion and anguish.

Nacha Regules (1919), which for Gálvez summed up the hopes and suffering of the pueblo, has as its major protagonist a minor character from the previous novel. His description of the lowest strata of Buenos Aires society, the prostitutes, the gigolos, and the alcoholics, allows the author to dwell on man's inhumanity to man in what is Gálvez' most impassioned defense of social values and noble ideals, especially as related to the poor. His portrayal of "Pampa" Arvedo, the bully, is again tempered by a kind of romantic identification with Fernando Monsalvat, the socialistic idealist who attempts to rescue Nacha from her unfortunate profession, as he also compassionately defends other such ladies. Monsalvat mortgages his property to help poor tenants and eventually loses all his money. Nacha, who had told him about her life since the death of Riga and her frustrated resolve to reform, cannot return his spiritual love. Yet, when her mother dies, she marries the by now almost blind and destitute Monsalvat and reopens the boarding house. Gálvez somehow manages to blame the British speculators for the miseries of Nacha and Argentina; his case histories of prostitutes, borrowed from his doctoral dissertation, are quite authentic. In his analysis of the intellectual struggles of his characters with their circumstances, he stresses that love and spirit transcend defeat and disillusion.

Historia de arrabal (1922) again treats of houses of prostitution and the lower depths, specifically in the Boca de Riachuelo district, and shows less interest in social problems than in his study of a case history. Rosalinda Corrales has a step-brother, El Chino, an evil man who exerts a hypnotic power over her and forces her into a life of prostitution. She refuses to marry Daniel Forti, an honest young Italian mason in love with her, but finds happiness with him for a time. El Chino rediscovers her, forces her to stab Daniel to death, and once more makes her the tool of his malignant influence. Gálvez again gives society a choice between good and evil, but Rosalinda is much less capable than Nacha of transcending the sensual to choose the spiritual. In *El cántico espiritual* (1923), a young artist, Mauricio Sandoval, falls in love with a married woman but rejects her for his concept of a beautiful statue, "el cántico espiritual."

Another provincial capital, Córdoba, which Gálvez lovingly describes, is the setting for *La sombra del convento* (1917), a novel about the conflict between the traditional and Catholic ideology of that university city and youthful ideas of progress. Gálvez, who in the prologue asserts that his purpose is not to preach a thesis but to analyze the spiritual development of his protagonist, describes many of the religious customs which play such a large part in the city's daily life, the life of the servant class, and the search for new freedoms among the young people. José Alberto Flores, back from ten years in Europe, finds the Cordoban priests to be positively medieval. He loves his cousin, Teresa Balderraín, whose father, an ultraconservative man, objects to her suitor's liberal ideas. When the bigoted father dies, José marries Teresa and apparently returns to his Catholic faith. Gálvez, admitting the influence of Pío Baroja, once stated that "Baroja . . . me ha enseñado a ver el paisaje de ciudad y a buscar lo típico en cada individuo," [192] something Gálvez does well in this novel despite its overdone symbolism and lack of dramatic tension, style, or dynamic characters.

Gálvez also tried his hand at more purely psychological novels such as *La tragedia de un hombre fuerte* (1922), which he said was not precisely a novel. Through his existential protagonist, Víctor Urgel, the author studies the pious, imaginative, and obstinate Argentine women, the meaning of love, and the spiritual aspects of his land. A much better novel, *Miércoles Santo* (1930), is filled with inner conflicts and the hidden vices of mankind, as revealed by the confessions to Eudosio Solanas, a priest apparently based on a real model. Sick and fat in the torturous and narrow confines of the confessional, the priest, too, is a victim of the anguish, frustrations, and problems of the modern world. As the most popular priest of Buenos Aires, on this night before Holy Wednesday, he pays for that popularity and for a sexual transgression as a young man. His faith weakened by a doubter, seen by him as a devil, he permits an abortion, thus heightening his feeling of sin. Each sinner represents a different transgression. The priest, as he assigns his penances, suffers, agonizes, and finally dies. *Hombres en soledad* (1938) is about wealthy Ezequiel Toledo and his family, members of the Buenos Aires society of 1930. Provincials, frustrated writers, and foreigners help represent the vain, banal, and materialistic society, the political corruption, and the European-oriented folk like Claraval, who consider Argentine ills to be beyond remedy. Claraval toys with the concept of the purging aspects of war, gradually learns that Europe is also ill, and finally realizes that he must choose between spiritual dislocation and a gross materialistic world. Gálvez seems to say that if Argentinians would only turn to their inward sources of spiritual strength rather than relying on materialism or European culture, they might triumph over their environment. The general tone is pessimistic, and the protagonists, for all their pejorative attitude toward the gaucho, are timid, fearful, and solitary. A kind of sequel, *El uno y la multitud* (1955), deals with Buenos Aires life during World War II. *El mal metafísico, Hom-*

bres en soledad, and *El uno y la multitud* form an analysis (some would say archeological document) of the Argentine malaise, its causes, and its cure.

Gálvez wrote many biographies on figures like Miranda, Hipólito Irogoyen, Sarmiento, Rosas, and García Moreno as well as a dozen historical novels, about half of them on Rosas. Criticizing Vicente Fidel López and other liberal historians, Gálvez sought to rehabilitate the dictator and to portray him as an Argentine patriot against foreign imperialists, especially the British. Gálvez, conservative, Catholic, and chauvinistic, believed that Rosas was good for Argentina because he maintained law and order. Under the title *La época de Rosas* he began, with *El gaucho de los cerillos* (1931), a series of novels about that period. The other volumes are *El general Quiroga* (1932), whose hidden protagonist, in spite of the title, is Rosas, a man whose honesty contrasts with the dissipated life of Quiroga; *La ciudad pintada de rojo* (1948); *Tiempo de odio y angustia* (1951); *Han tocado a degüello* (1951); *Bajo la garra anglofrancesa* (1953); and *Y así cayó don Juan Manuel* (1954). The first volume deals with the years 1828–1829, the second with the period up to 1835, the third with the years between 1835 and 1839, the fourth with the action-packed years of 1839 and 1840, and so on up to 1852. He paints the period in all its color and, in the *advertencia* to *Han tocado a degüello*, prides himself on his portrayal of what he calls "ambiente histórico" as opposed to history. He justifies the regime, even when it seems that no justification can be given, and weakly excuses the inexcusable on the grounds that the times were abnormal. Nonetheless, as one of his perceptive critics has maintained, "the completion of the series . . . represents a noteworthy accomplishment of Gálvez' . . . fictional production . . ." [193]

The most powerful and evocative novels among his historical works (and those which have drawn the most critical attention)[194] belong to his trilogy *Escenas de la guerra del Paraguay,* whose three parts are *Los caminos de la muerte* (1928), *Humaitá* (1929), and *Jornadas de agonía* (1929). Gálvez worked on his trilogy in the Jockey Club library and prides himself on his historical accuracy, claiming that he made only insignificant changes which in no way affected the historical veracity of his novels.[195] Francisco Solana López, succeeding his dictator father and angered at Argentina's refusal to grant him permission to cross its territory to attack Brazil and Uruguay, seized two gunboats near Corrientes and occupied the city. In his first novel, set in 1865, Gálvez describes that city, the emotional tensions involved, and the first seven months of the war. *Humaitá*, set in 1866, reproduces a famous cholera march, the capture of Humaitá, where López took refuge, and the politics, terror, and battles. The final novel, which takes place between 1868 and 1870, describes the capture of Asunción and the pursuit of the murdering López. Gálvez builds a mosaic of minute detail to reproduce the atmosphere but overindulges in many digressions, including superfluous matter, "de tal modo que el lector, a veces fatigado y confundido, pierde el hilo de la narración . . ."[196] Although Gálvez gives us few clues to the internal conflicts and emotions of many of his characters for whom he speaks,[197] his description of the adulation of the masses, Elisa Lynch, the dictator's mistress, the ever-increasing loss of mental stability and fear of assassination of the dictator, and his final death take on a Hitlerian perspective and remind one of that tragic period of human history. In spite of the digressions, excessive detail, and historical inaccuracies, which elicited adverse criticism, Gálvez, in his novel, manages to convey the terror of tyranny, the sordid aspects of the war, and the misery of defeat and to mix beautifully the historical and the fictional. Various narrative threads of dramatic intensity include those of Evaristo Sauce, an Argentine soldier in love with a Brazilian nurse and finally killed by a jealous rival; Damasceno Fragoso, in search of his wife, Joaninha, who has been isolated by the war; and the family feud of the three Cienfuegos boys of Paraguay, divided by the war, one of whom becomes a fratricide. The carrion in the street, the torture of prisoners, the dictator's condemnation of his own mother, and the final scenes are perhaps more impressive today than they were when Gálvez wrote them, for one can recognize the universality of the dialogue between man and his world and the tragic implications of being human protagonists and victims of history.

Among Gálvez' final works is *Las dos vidas del pobre Napoleón* (1954), an excursion into the world of the the subconscious in which the author existentially seeks the meaning of life and the essence of the individual. A middle-aged man takes on a fictional life which he cannot separate from reality and which eventually leads to his madness. Reminding us at times of Maximiliano Rubín of *Fortu-*

nata y Jacinta, the protagonist, who seeks escape through his "limit-less thought," may be Gálvez' attempt at a moral answer to the existentialists. *Tránsito Guzmán* (1956) is the story of the persecution of the Catholic church in 1954 and 1955. Gálvez attacks the anti-Catholicism of certain Peronistas. *Perdido en su noche* (1958) is a portrayal of a kind of modern Doña Perfecta, Graciana Mirabel, and the struggles in the soul of an honest Jesuit who finally abandons his order. *Me mataron entre todos* (1962), published a month before his death, also has a fantastic science fiction atmosphere. According to Gálvez he and Eduardo Barrios had the idea for a novel of this type at about the same time, as early as 1921, but Barrios never finished his. In the novel, Segismundo Cuenca, a philosophy professor, learns to read the minds of others and comes to think of reality as a dream world. With the help of a psychiatrist he manges to rid himself of his unwanted gift and is prepared to return to reality from the mental institution.

Throughout his novels Gálvez stresses the power of love as a spiritual and physical part of the Argentine soul, which he views sentimentally, intellectually, philosophically, metaphysically, and almost always optimistically rather than in terms of anguish. But as we have already stated, some of his characters presage the arrival of the existential beings of Mallea and others, and although Gálvez' concern for reality overshadows his thrust for technique and form, his deceptively uncomplicated style contributes a subtle aesthetic dividend not found among any but the greatest novelists.

Eduardo Barrios (1884–1963) of Chile, one of the best psychological novelists of the continent,[198] had as his best friend in Peru (his mother was Peruvian) Ventura García Calderón (1886–1959), who himself was to write passionate short stories of violence, death, and superstition. Barrios abandoned thoughts of a military career to which his grandfather had dedicated him and spent some time as a merchant, circus strong man, and typist. He became a member of "Los Diez," to which Pedro Prado and other young intellectuals belonged, and served twice as director of the National Library and also a term as minister of education. As with most of the Spanish American novelists we have thus far examined, differences of opinion exist about Barrios' fictional classification. As one article on his work states, "La figura de Barrios, aunque por lo general se lo coloque entre los representantes del criollismo literario, escapa en cierto modo de esta clasificación." [199] Hernán Díaz Arrieta sees Barrios as occupying a middle ground between the *imaginistas* and the *criollistas,*[200] and Torres-Rioseco believes that though Barrios is not a criollista, "toda su obra es de raigambre americana . . ." [201] Whatever his classification, Barrios' primary characteristic is his concern for psychological knowledge about human beings. Raúl Silva Castro points out that Barrios is the novelist of Santiago but also a novelist of souls with all their complexities, "y cuando se trata de aquellos pliegues íntimos que forman la persona humana, toda atención le parece poco a fin de establecer lo que cree significativo." [202]

Barrios, an excellent dramatist, produced some of the finest works of the Chilean theater, as Gabriela Mistral points out in the prologue to *Y la vida sigue.* But it is as a writer of prose fiction that he made his primary contribution, beginning with *Del natural* (1907), a naturalistic collection of short stories about provincial life. The collection also included *Tirana ley,* a novelette about a love affair between a painter and a widow. Barrios' first novel, *El niño que enloqueció de amor* (1915), is done in the form of a diary of a neurasthenic boy. The author would have us believe that the story is partly autobiographical (he identifies emotionally with the protagonist) and based on "un episodio de mi vida cuando apenas contaba yo nueve años," [203] but the autobiography is external and not psychological. In the prologue he states that he knew the boy involved, "a bird that sang in the night and had no tomorrow." The boy has a neurotic fixation on and cannot control the passion he feels for Angélica, a lady friend of his mother who kissed him one day. He feels happy only in her presence, and his obsession finally drives him mad. Barrios pretends, as he intervenes at the end, that he received the diary from a friend who asked him to see the sick lad. The language of the novel, although quite simple, is poetically beautiful and creates a perfect balance between the human content and the literary expression. Indeed, the first page is a "verdadero poema . . . de tal belleza expresiva, que bien se puede situar entre las clásicas de nuestra literatura." [204] Barrios, in his delicate touch and fine shading in the autopsy of a human soul, reveals a total vision of man's heart and the chaotic disintegration ending in madness which may beset us all. Included with this work is a story, "Pobre feo," about an ugly man ridiculed by the girl he loves.

Un perdido (1917), called in a prologue by Manuel Gálvez "quizá la mejor novela producida por un hispanoamericano," is, according to him, an essentially realistic novel, something with which Torres-Rioseco disagrees.[205] A naturalistic and psychological study, again in part autobiographical, it tells of the life of Lucho or Luis Bernales, a boy who suffers from a profound inferiority complex. Born late in the life of a harsh military father who takes him to whorehouses and sends him to military school, the boy, an abulic dreamer, cannot surmount his environment. His one happy recollection, about a brief period of his childhood, is marred by the deaths of his mother and grandparents. Lucho has a series of adventures with a variety of prostitutes, one of whom, understanding and ethical, refuses to contaminate the boy she feels sorry for. He tries unsuccessfully to find love through his compassion for an unfortunate girl but ends up supported by a rich sister, pitied by friends, and an alcoholic and sodden lost soul. As Barrios piles detail on detail in his mosaic, analyzing the hates, loves, tensions, and anxieties of the boy, the family that surrounds him, the adulterous father, the understanding grandfather, the protective mother, and the surrogate father, Lieutenant Blanco, he provides us with a gallery of social classes and occupations to give us a detailed view of Chilean life. Many profess to see in the novel the influence of Flaubert, but *Un perdido* is not a simple reflection of French or other foreign models.[206]

In 1922 Barrios produced what most critics consider to be his masterpiece, *El hermano asno*, a work which fully reveals his understanding of the human soul and his technical brilliance and poetic style. The title is taken from Saint Francis' definition of man's sexual instincts, and the author spent some time in a Franciscan monastery in Santiago to absorb the atmosphere and some of the raw material for his characters. The psychological struggle, presented in aesthetic, lyric, and impressionistic form (Gabriela Mistral in the prologue to *Y la vida sigue* called it "una especie de franciscanismo artístico"), touches on the sexual urge, which man, however spiritual he may be, must still cope with as a human animal. Done in the form of a diary of Fray Lázaro, perhaps Barrios himself, the novel tells of his seven-year stay in the Franciscan monastery. He had become a friar when his girl friend, Gracia, had married a pianist. The other protagonist, Fray Rufino, having obtained the reputation of a saint, mortifies and tortures himself constantly to avoid his sexual instinct or "hermano asno." In a final rapturous attempt at Christian humility, Rufino, apparently, attempts to rape María Mercedes, Gracia's sister. The girl had always been in love with Lázaro, who also had to struggle to control his own feelings for her. Rufino dies, and the prior, knowing the truth, in order to preserve the saintly legend and the order's reputation sends Lázaro to a province to live out his days, consoling himself spiritually with the thought that he is saving Lázaro from sinful temptation. As for Lázaro, he agrees to his exile and silence. As he hears the church bells ringing and the bustle of visitors coming to kiss the Saint's feet, he hopes that God will accept his sacrifice and make him a better priest in the process.

The novel, which recalls the flavor of Anatole France, poses a number of questions about the protagonists. Rufino may have had a normal mind at one time, but he suffers from a progressive deterioration brought on not only by his desire for martyrdom but by isolation, frustration, and the constant surfacing of a sexual drive in his struggle with pride. The two priests are also symbolic projections—Lázaro of the intellectual and reasonable approach, and Rufino of mystic emotion and intuitive and instinctive reassertion of faith. María Mercedes, sexual passion personified, represents for Lázaro a heavenly test in his desire for redemption, and he elevates himself through his intellect. Rufino "unconsciously transforms the sexual conflict into a battle against his pride." [207] Both men try to fulfill the requirements of obedience and chastity; but we cannot know if Rufino's attempt at rape represents lust, the desire for humility, an attempt to save his friend, Lázaro, from his own temptation, or a simple mental breakdown.[208] Lázaro, too, faces spiritual testing and, in his reaction to María Mercedes and his acceptance of Rufino's guilt as his own, may be closer to saintliness than Rufino, who worked so hard to achieve it.[209] Barrios, although deliberately dealing with the dualism of soul versus body, treats the novel as an aesthetic and psychological exercise; but the spiritual elements are overpowering. Carlos Hamilton has compared the novel to an El Greco painting, "The Burial of the Count of Orgas." Like El Greco, Barrios "ha exagerado las figuras principales, las ha estirado, estilizado. No hasta deshumanizarlas, pero al menos hasta arrancarlas del plano de la lógica de la vida común y al marco de la mística o la ascética ortodoxa." [210]

In 1923 Barrios wrote *Páginas de un pobre diablo*, short stories about adolescents unprepared to meet the challenges of adulthood. The title story of the "pobre diablo," a young man who works in a mortuary, allows Barrios to give us his ideas on death. *Y la vida sigue* (1925) contains stories, autobiography, and his theatrical works (later collected in 1947). The two were the only works to break the long silence (rivaling that of his Chilean ancestor, Alberto Blest Gana) between *El hermano asno* (1922) and *Tamarugal* (1944).[211] Set in a mine in the nitrate fields of northern Chile, near the town of Huara, *Tamarugal* describes the struggle in the soul of a seminarist between religion and love. Barrios had experienced firsthand the miserable conditions under which the miners worked, the burning heat of the days, the piercing cold of the nights, the dust storms, the dangerous machines (one devours a man in its jaws), and the boredom, a contributing factor to some of the suicides in the area. The combination smacks of Baldomero Lillo, Emile Zola, and Juan Valera (*Pepita Jiménez*). The rich administrator of the British-owned nitrate works, Jesús Morales, falls in love with Juanita Arlegui, known as Jenny, the daughter of an office worker, and she, in turn, feels love for a young would-be priest, Javier del Campo, who comes to Tamarugal. She marries Morales, and duty triumphs over love in the seminarian's soul, as he becomes a priest. Forty years later she is a rich widow, the mother of three children, and the priest, a distinguished prelate, helps her with her extensive philanthropies. The theme of frustrated physical and spiritual love and a number of grotesque elements[212] reveal that Barrios had not changed much during his long silence; but the novel is unimpressive.

Gran señor y rajadiablos (1948), which has been called, "estilísticamente, tal vez . . . el más perfecto de cuantos ha publicado aparte *El hermano asno*, " [213] is again based on Barrios' own experiences on a large agriculture estate he had bought and through which he met a number of pioneer types and owners of other *fundos*. Barrios easily identifies with his protagonist, José Pedro

Valverde, one of the great character creations of Chilean literature whose life the author traces from birth to death. Valverde, a virile, self-reliant hacendado, a descendant of feudal nobility, is a brawling, whoring emulator of Pizarro, if not of his ancestor who accompanied the Peruvian conquistador. Valverde created an empire for himself, formed local vigilantes, resisted government taxes, yet helped defend his country. His slogan was to do unto others before they can do unto you—"Entremos pegando para que no nos peguen." Valverde commands man, nature, and himself proudly, and Barrios seems to imply that he represents Chile herself. Valverde's last words before his death are that if his son plants another vine it should be in El Fiel, "tierra inmejorable para la uva." The setting, the rodeos, the dances, the descriptions of huasos and the nineteenth-century customs create a lively and sentimental composite of Chilean history; but Barrios' apparent defense of the reactionary remnant of Chilean oligarchy and his subjectivity concerning the virile and violent Catholic protagonist of his novel, spoil the psychological effect. Barrios states that he hoped to give the impression of simplicity, to avoid any obtrusiveness of artistic style, to create "música y transparencia . . . una ficción que sirve para comunicar, no la verdad misma, sino la emoción de la verdad." [214]

Barrios' last novel, *Los hombres del hombre* (1950), treats of human jealousy and the sentiment, sensuality, and dreams of man. The protagonist, married for eleven years, finally has a son whom he names for his English godfather, Charles Moore, an intimate family friend who spent his summers with them and who later left all his millions to the godson and the parents. The husband, overwhelmed by suspicion that the Englishman may really be the father, torments himself in scenes somewhat reminiscent of *El abuelo* by Benito Pérez Galdós. The author represents the various emotions through which the protagonist goes by different facets of the latter's personality, which he divides into seven representative men, among others Fernando, the sentimental, Luis, the erotic, and Rafael, the jealous. Barrios contends that one's personality is in a constant state of becoming, and the seven men then correspond to seven different reactions (pessimistic, rational, romantic . . .) of the subconscious mind. In the dialogue (actually soliloquies), the protagonist is saved from solitude and despair through an overwhelming love for his child, his "Cabecita Des-peinada," which mutes the voices of "los hombres del hombre." Ángel Flores sees in the novel "una sutil red a la André Gide, de complicada y paradójica belleza";[215] but Alone, that sometimes caustic but honest critic, while conceding that if beautiful prose were the maximum novelistic virtue Barrios would be the best Chilean novelist, finds him deficient in invention and force. His characters, he says, "no dejan huella durable: algo les falta, anima-ción, espontaneidad; está bien, no demasiado bien . . ."[216] The truth is probably less harsh, for Barrios shows a keen eye for ob-jective observation and reflection of life which he reveals in im-pressionistic and lyrical fashion.

Víctor Domingo Silva (1882–1960), newspaperman, dramatist, poet, and essayist, was one of the most popular novelists of his day. His first novel worthy of mention, *Golondrina de invierno* (1912), is a tender idyll about a brother and sister on a ranch. Probably his best novel, it is the one most likely to endure. His most popular novel, *Palomilla Brava* (1923), first appeared in the literary supplement of *El Mercurio* as *Pepe Lucho*, a title later changed to *Papelucho*. The author, himself preferring the title *Palomilla Brava*, conceived the novel as the first part of a trilogy. He completed the second part, *El cachorro* (1937), but not the third volume. José Luis Llanquilef, known as Papelucho, is a roto from Valparaíso, the product of a good mother but of a drunken, thieving, and lazy father. Taught to read and write by a young English teacher, Alicia, he falls in love with her. In the sequel Papelucho loses his money, becomes rich once more, takes on a gringo partner, and plans to marry his schoolteacher. Unfortu-nately, he is bitten by a mad dog, and it is his son, the *cachorro*, who goes to live with her. The story of the ragamuffin's slow ascent up the ladder of success contains accurate descriptions of the northern nitrate fields and industry and a number of popular and vulgar elements. *El mestizo Alejo* (1934), about the "primer toqui chileno," and its sequel, *La criollita* (1935), are historical novels about the conquest and the Araucanian Indians, a subject which interested him, as can be seen from the title of his bio-graphical novel, *El rey de Araucania* (1936). Among his other novels, *Los árboles no dejan ver el bosque* (1948) is a good picture of life in the provinces and in the capital. In his short stories he also paints the silent and monotonous pampa and its miserable inhabitants. Silva was not one of the major literary giants, but he influenced the younger generations more than some better writers had because of his intense patriotism, his sincere defense of human dignity, his concern for social justice, and his intellectual honesty.

Rafael Maluenda (1886–1963), a member of "Los Diez," newspaperman, playwright, and director of *El Mercurio*, was much influenced by Gorki. He documents the humble lives of his protagonists in both city and country, in sordid slums and suburbs. He conceived of his novels as emotion evokers, diving for what he wanted, as one critic says, in that "océano infinito de lo humano que está constituido por el hombre y sus contingencias." [217] His story collections include *Escenas de la vida campesina* (1909), *Los ciegos* (1913), and *La Pachacha* (1914), an ironic long story about a hen who with her companions incarnates human qualities and defects. His numerous novelettes include *La señorita Ana* (1920), the confessions of a school teacher, *La cantinera de las trenzas rubias* (1925), about a blond campfollower in the war against Peru in the 1880s, and *Confesiones de una profesora* (1932). He kept writing short stories almost until his death, publishing *Colmena urbana* in 1957 (?) and what may be his best known stories, *Historias de bandidos*, in 1961, pictures of banditry whose protagonists for him are "símbolos de raza, de bravura." His two novels are *Armiño negro* (1942), about life and customs in Lima, and *Vampiro de trapo* (1958). In the first novel a high class prostitute, María Raygada de la Paz, is redeemed through her nobility of soul. Her son, longing for a father, commits suicide. The second novel is about a ventriloquist who comes to hate and envy his dummy for it prevents his enjoyment of his one true love, Carmen Barton. He finally dies of a heart attack during a performance, as the dummy returns his hate with interest. Maluenda largely emphasizes regional themes, tortured souls, the psychology of love, and the lives of people in different sections of Chile. His rotos, highly romanticized, seem unusually generous and heroic.

Januario Espinosa (1882–1946), a member of the *Generación del centenario* (along with Eduardo Barrios, Joaquín Edwards Bello, Augusto d'Halmar, and Mariano Latorre) in his best novel, *Cecilia* (1907), deals with the rural. He has also written the novelettes *Las inquietudes de Ana María* (1916) and *El juguete roto* (1927), and the short stories *La ciudad encantada* (1942). In these and in his other novels, *La vida humilde* (1914) and *Pillán* (1934), a magic story about his district of Linares, Espinosa analyses Chilean middle class life in various rural and urban settings.

Fernando Santiván (1886–   ), a newspaperman, farmer, and merchant whose real name is Fernando Santibáñez Puga, was a very close friend of Augusto d'Halmar whose half sister he married and whom he helped found the Colonia Tolstoyana. *Palpitaciones de vida* (1909) and *El bosque emprende su marcha* (1946), short story collections; *En la montaña* (1917), a novelette; *Confesiones de Enrique Samaniego* (1933) and its elaboration, *Confesiones de Santiván* (1958), literary memoirs; and *Ansia* (1910), *El crisol* (1913), *La hechizada* (1916), *Robles, Blume y cía* (1923), *Charca en la selva* (1934), *La camará* (1945), *El mulato Riquelme* (1951), and *Bárbara* (1963), novels, are his major contributions to fiction. Alone, whose judgment in this case appears not to be overly objective, says that Santiván is a man who has more heart than art, and that he writes his novels "con cualquier motivo, una palpitación interna, cálida, fácilmente agresiva, con cierto fondo de pasión turbia, donde asoman las protestas . . ." [218]

Santiván's first novel, *Ansia*, relates his own struggles against a hostile public and analyzes the lives of writers and musicians in Santiago. Most of the characters, playthings of their passions, float on the current of events "como insectos náufragos o ramillas llevadas por el viento del arroyo . . ." [219] *El crisol*, his first real success, introduces Bernabé Robles, son of a self-made hacendado, who falls in love with Adriana, the daughter of a German doctor of Santiago named Blume, once himself the owner of the hacienda. The novel contains good descriptions of school life and documents the theme of class rivalry. *La hechizada*, almost more novelette than novel, has a similar and romantic theme of a city boy's attempt to win a girl over a country rival. The rural setting impresses by its criollista veneer but is far removed from the authentic settings of writers like Latorre.[220] The theme of a true love ruined by the realization that the loved one had loved before is the kind of psychology that later became an integral part of Chilean criollo and neo-criollista novelists like Marta Brunet. *Robles, Blume y*

Cía, a sequel to *El crisol,* shows a continuing family opposition to Bernabé's marriage, his eventual success, and his gift to his factory workers in the form of a cooperative.

After trying to write two police novels, Santiván produced a new type of memoirs and articles combined which verge on fiction. The *Confesiones de Enrique Samaniego,* a reflection of Chilean letters of the twentieth century up to that time, contains revelations about Luis Orrego Luco, Pedro Prado, and Augusto d'Halmar. *Charca en la selva* takes place in a forest village on the banks of Lake Villarrica where German customs conflict with Chilean ways. *La camará,* a story of the author's agricultural experiences, is about man's struggle against a hostile nature and corrupt men who exploit the land at the expense of the tormented and hungry farm worker, who is sustained only by the loyalty and faith of his woman or *camará* (camarada).[221] *El mulato Riquelme,* whose central character is Bernardo O'Higgins, treats the youth and education (to his taking possession of the hacienda Las Canteras) of that national hero rather freely and subjectively (given the paucity of information available about O'Higgins' youth); but the novel seems authentically regional in its popular types and local customs. The author pretends he has found the mulatto's memoirs which give the details of the hero's life, including his love for Sinforosita, Riquelme's daughter. *Bárbara* (1963), a novel Santiván had written about four decades earlier but never before published, relates the adventures of Bárbara Barrales after her husband's demise in the revolution of 1891. She supports her family in the frontier town of Temico, confronting the evil forces of both man and nature.

Mariano Latorre who had known Santiván since his youth, sees a difference between his early and later novels. In the former, claims Latorre, Santiván intervened passionately, hating or defending his characters. In later works "el autor se oculta en los bastidores de su creación y no quiere mezclarse con sus personajes." [222]

Joaquín Edwards Bello (1886–1968), a major Chilean representative of the urban scene, a descendant of Andrés Bello on his mother's side and of an aristocratic family of bankers and ministers, traveled in Europe and served as correspondent for *La Nación* of Buenos Aires. Both his biography and his journalistic experience are reflected in his attacks on aristocrats, his biting satire, his rapid, tense, and careless style. His social ideas are emphatically presented, but his desire to give moral judgments on everything from whorehouses to the power of money in Chilean society affects the tight structure of his work. Somewhat indifferent himself to a tight narrative structure, which would have proved too confining for him, Edwards Bello is a good story teller who writes with warmth, color, and humanity.

Edwards Bello's first work, *El inútil* (1910), reports the by now tiresome intellectual abulia, spoiled adolescents, gambling houses, and prostitutes and attacks, in crude and personal terms, the Church and the aristocracy of his country. Indeed, the scandal caused by the publication of the novel forced Edwards Bello to leave Chile for Brazil, where he apparently led a somewhat precarious existence. The novel's protagonist, a man with a social conscience, visits the corrupt Paris and falls victim to its night life, thus changing and dulling the edge of his ideals. He leads a dissolute life and, dying finally in an uprising, thinks he is holding his girl friend's hand, in reality that of a priest. *El monstruo* (1912), an elaboration of his first novel, again has a protagonist who indulges in Parisian dissipation, but this one is saved by a return to Chile and the love of a good woman who converts him into an ex-monster. These two novels show us the worst side of Edwards Bello, his didactic inclusion of pet theories, and his constant personal intervention. Another early novel, *La tragedia del Titanic* (1912), done as a series of stories, was later elaborated and reworked, as were most of his novels, appearing under the title of *La muerte de Vanderbilt* (1922) and partly in *Cap Polonio* (1929).

La cuna de Esmeraldo (1918), begun as early as 1912, served as the prototype for what was to be his masterpiece, *El roto*, really a reworking of the earlier novel. The 1918 novel traces the adventures of a boy born in a whorehouse, La Gloria, which serves as a simulacrum of Chilean life and shows the ugliness beneath its surface. The author treats almost sentimentally the lives of a variety of picturesque characters, Esmeraldo's family and friends, his sister, Violeta, his mother, Clorinda, her friend, Ofelia, owner of the house, and assorted gamblers, pimps, and lesbians. Edwards Bello's work falls naturally into three parts. In the first he gives us a glimpse of his aesthetic theories, his ideas on criollismo, his defense of American values and literature, along with the unfortunate abulia affecting it. Here and in the prologue he stresses the beauties of the American continent, a thesis he repeats in *El nacionalismo continental* (1925), in which he underscores the need for avoiding servile imitations of European themes. The second part is the story of Esmeraldo. The third section of the novel deals with European opinion of America.

El roto (1920) strengthens its model's loose series of cuadros into a more perfectly structured if still picaresque work. Again we see the prostitutes, the low districts, the jails, and the syphilis, small-pox, and tuberculosis, all of which the author takes great pains to present graphically and with authentically documented statistics. He traces the fortunes of Esmeraldo's father, Fernando, the *garitero* or roto, the rivalries among gambling clubs, fights, en-counters with police, a rape scene, and all Chilean society from millionaires to merchants, police to pimps. He gives his grotesque scenes a natural quality so that they seem as normal as the vices, envy, superstition, and hypocrisy he says are "cosas de todos los días." A polemic occured over the author's presentation of the "roto" along with other matters; Torres-Rioseco denied that the roto offers good psychological material, accused Edwards Bello of being unjust in his attacks, and cited defects in the novel, for him essentially costumbrista, of excessive melodrama and poor tech-nique. He admitted that the work was a good sociological docu-ment but asserted that it would not survive.[223] Raúl Silva Castro, on the other hand, feels that the novel speaks its piece "con tal profundidad y dicho con tal auténtica gracia, que la novela se lee de un sorbo y el lector se queda ansiando más." [224] Whereas later Chilean novelists asserted the dignity of the roto as a hard work-ing member of his society, which often victimized him, Edwards Bello, as Arnold Chapman points out, associates the roto with crime and urbanization. The book is trail-blazing in its pictures of Santiago slums, and its author "operates under a persuasion partly drawn from Nietzsche and Darwin, both of whom he ad-mires, blended with a weak infusion of Rousseau." [225]

La muerte de Vanderbilt (1922) is complete with a masked ball, a collision with an iceberg, and heroic scenes of rescue, including that of the author and his friend. The author describes the gay holiday atmosphere and the terror and, in spite of his criticism of the opportunists of this world and his generally negative view, has some nice things to show us about humanity. Another novel of the twenties, *El chileno en Madrid* (1928), involves the search by a man for his wife and son he had abandoned years earlier. Pedro Wallace, finally discovering his son Pedrín in jail and his wife, Dolores, dying in poverty, decides to devote the rest of his life to their welfare. Edwards Bello, in his examination of the theaters, boarding houses, cafés, and the streets themselves, shows a surprising hispanophilia. *Cap Polonio* (1929), a short psychological novel about a rich Chilean and his adventure with an Argentine girl, elaborates life on board a luxury liner and attacks upper-class snobs.

Valparaíso, la ciudad del viento (1931) is an autobiographical novel of Edwards Bello's experiences at the English school there —the pupils, the escapades, vacations, professors, love affairs, and dishonest speculators. Along with a distaste for empty, vain aristocrats, he includes us in a tender recall of his childhood years. The novel was reworked (almost completely rewritten) and appeared again in 1943 under the title of *En el viejo Almendral* (a district of Valparaíso) whose narrator, Pedro Lacerda y Alderete, the author, gives us a view of the town of Quillota, his ancestral home, the role and psychology of the Chilean woman, and especially the story of Perpetua Guzmán, the family servant, her tragedy, superstition, and loyalty. Edwards Bello portrays a gallery of types: an Englishman, a Chilean aristocrat fallen on evil days, Doña Florencia, who hates Perpetua, and Florita, who, disillusioned by her husband, falls in love with the young protagonist. In his detailed study of Chilean society the author also attacks the educational system. The Valparaíso setting was again repeated in another edition, *Valparaíso Fantasmas* (1955). *Criollos en París* (1933), another of his views of Parisian night life in all its dissipation, drugs, and degradation, contains a series of complicated loves. The theme of the Spanish American in Paris has been treated also by Blest Gana, Díaz Rodríguez, Orrego Luco, Ricardo Güiraldes, and by the less well-known Martín Aldao, an almost life-long member of the Argentine colony in Paris, whose protagonist, Requema, in his novel *La vida falsa* (1933), is but a thin disguise for the author himself. Pedro Plaza, the young and aristocratic Chilean of Edwards Bello's novel, indulges his taste for whores and gambling, living off his phenomenal luck and skill.

He has a series of adventures and easy relationships with women but finally finds true love in Lucía. The plot, largely a series of intrigues, betrayals, lovers and mistresses, is quite melodramatic, but the novel gives a good picture of the shibboleths and empty values of Edwards Bello's own class abroad. Finally, *La chica del Crillón* (1935) treats of Teresa Iturrigorriaga, a society girl fallen on evil days, her subsequent rise and happiness. The by now familiar foibles of Chilean aristocrats bore one, and the humorless heroine is but a disguised Edwards Bello.[226]

Edwards Bello describes Chilean defects, vices, problems, corrupt politicians, criminals, police, bad education, alcoholism, gambling, juvenile delinquency, hypocritical and fanatical aristocrats, the generally idle rich, and a variety of other social ills. Although largely European oriented, he also seemed sincere in his belief in the need for a novel of indigenous substance. Regardless of his real understanding of the roto, it was he who introduced him as a victim of society. His novels are exciting, often incisive, and filled with "policromías voltaicas y contrastes tenebrosos; una suerte de neoimpresionismo muy personal." [227] They, however, are also obviously marred by hasty composition. He deliberately avoided painstaking stylistic revisions, for him the "rhetoric" of the elite, but in his passion and vital spirit, even in his propagandistic moments, he shares the pains and joys of all humanity. His use of extreme and even abnormal types to make his point perturbs one, but it does not damage the pace, the action, or the overall positive effect.

If Edwards Bello is the novelist of the roto, Mariano Latorre (1886–1955), the antithesis of a cosmopolitan aristocrat, is the novelist of the country and the *huaso*.[228] As he says: "Chile es el huaso. El roto no es sino una desviación urbana de ese hombre. Y constituye la reserva de Chile, porque Chile podría muy bien representarse por una huerta que tiene una mina a la espalda y una barca pescadora. . . . Porque tuve fe en ese tipo de hombre, consagré mi vida a entenderlo y pintarlo. Puede ser que mi imaginación lo haya embellecido poéticamente pero eso no importa." [229] Most of Latorre's production (largely short stories) easily earn him his title of "padre del criollismo chileno," even if many of the younger novelists, imbued with the idea of style and technique, rejected his leadership as being old-fashioned. Born in the little

town of Cobquecura, in Maule province, Latorre set about, almost
scientifically, to reveal all aspects of the Chilean countryside in
both its natural and human attributes, avoiding fantasy and emphasizing the peasant's human values sympathetically. The encyclopedic aspects of his descriptions of the sea, the cordillera,
the roads, forests, rivers, and people of his beloved country appear
to be almost "un museo de retratos y paisajes," [230] and he is the
writer of his generation who has worked "con más unidad y con-
tinuidad en las interpretaciones campesinas." [231] Mario Ferrero
has called him "el símbolo de la chilenidad, la expresión fiel de
la naturaleza, del paisaje criollo y de la psicología del hombre que
habita y complementa el carácter de ese paisaje . . . toda su obra
literaria estará orientada a dar expresión estética a la vida humilde
y directa de su terruño natal . . ." [232] Everything he wrote was
authentically national, but he used more minute details in his
early works, enlarging his concept of Chilean nature in all its
grandeur and interest in the human spirit.

Among Latorre's short stories are: *Cuentos del Maule* (1912),
Cuna de cóndores (1918), *Sus mejores cuentos* (1925), *Chilenos del
mar* (1929), *Hombres en la selva* (1933), which he labeled narraciones, *On Panta* (1935), *Hombres y zorros* (1937), *Mapu* (1942),
Viento de mallines (1944), *Chile, país de rincones* (1947), *La isla
de los pájaros* (1955). His other titles are *Zurzulita* (1920), which
he calls *relato* but which may be called a novel; *El caracol* (1952),
again a relato; *La paquera* (1958), a novel; and *Ully y otras
novelas del sur* (1923), which are really long short stories. His first
collection, *Cuentos del Maule*, gives the impression of being autobiographical. Latorre has an excellent eye for detail, and his local
color—the tavern, the houses, the robust peasant girls, the farmers
—and the local gossip make the small villages and Chilean huasos
come alive. As he admitted time and again in his essays, he deliberately tried to describe objectively, in criollo fashion, the life
of the city and the countryside, and he keeps his word in this
collection about the social transformation of a sailor society. *Cuna
de cóndores* contains impressionistic and tragic stories about sheep
ranchers in the hills. *Chilenos del mar* describes boats and fisher-
men. *Hombres y zorros* deals with mountain people, their sexual
habits and superstitions, their poverty, their living and their dying. His final collection, *La isla de los pájaros*, four stories, con-

tains an edge of bitterness not too common in previous works. His most telling story may be *On Panta*, set against the great natural backdrop of the cordillera and which relates the life of a quixotic man who hunts nonexistent mountain lions. Don Pantaleón dreams of Utopia and tries to recreate a golden age of glory and chivalry. Like his literary ancestor don Quixote he, too, is ridiculed and persecuted and, like Don Quixote, he realizes that reality and fantasy cannot exist side by side. Much as Don Quixote renounces, on his deathbed, the world of chivalry but not his ideas of good works, Pantaleón realizes the nature of his dream world when the dogs destroy his embalmed lion and with it the psychological mainspring for his existence.

Ully examines the German elements of Chilean society, relying heavily on cuadros costumbristas for effect. Set in a village on the banks of Lake Llanquihue, the novel tells of Emilio Labarga, a young painter from the city who spends his summer vacation in the house of Carlos Stolze, whose sister Ully he falls in love with. Confessing that he has a wife and child and regretfully abandoning his idyllic refuge, he returns to his family. Latorre contrasts the lazy habits of some Chileans with the industry of the Germans and the peaceful country life with the corrupt and immoral one of the city, holding out, nonetheless, a hope for future understanding between the two environments. *Zurzulita* describes the rural Chilean coast and the peasant's attachment to his land, his jealousy, his suffering during drought, as well as his happiness during holidays and when times are good. Ricardo A. Latcham, in the prologue to the 1960 edition, finds it to be a catalytic agent toward new forms, as a "obra insólita, profunda, de estilo fuerte, sólido, bien tramado." Mateo Elorduy, the new owner of the fundo of Millavoro, falls in love with the rural school teacher, Milla, the beauty from the central valley whom, in his dreams, he compares to the mountain doves or *zurzulitas*. He seduces her, and she becomes pregnant but refuses to marry him. Her love turns to indifference and even hate, and, finally, a rival, On Carmen, the village cacique and a barbaric type huaso, more primitive than criminal, has him killed. The novel contains authentic rural types and unique individuals like Samuelón, the village idiot who has a private war with one of his hands fighting the other. In analyzing the primitive psychology of the huaso, Latorre seems to say that in Chile *barbarie* will always defeat *civilización*. In *La paquera*, begun in 1916 and finished, but not published, by 1920, Latorre shows more clearly the natural world and human beings in a positive and loving light. Yet at the same time the novel exudes a cruel naturalism and harsh social satire. The title refers to the lover of a Paco or policeman. Escolástica, the protagonist, an emotionally disturbed teenager, bears the child of the director of the institution in which she is confined. The story is narrated by a young teacher in the school serving the orphanage, next to the building itself. Latorre examines adequately a variety of social problems, but one must agree with Raúl Silva Castro that the novel has structural and artistic infelicities and that it is not a "novela de primer orden." [233]

Latorre cultivated his own criollista garden and planted in it, together with a series of images projecting form and color, a variety of human actions and emotions, land and society in their interrelationships, the huaso, the roto, the city slicker, the foreigner, the priest, and the mountaineer at work and at play, at peace and at war. Latorre manages to be both authentically Chilean and universally human at the same time. He was not primarily interested in narrative plot or intricate characterization but was far more than a simple photographic eye. Alone, perhaps because of his own opposition to the concept of criollismo, accused him of lacking invention and stated that his characters lacked soul and that "nunca logran eso indefinible que Federico Gana, con un solo rasgo, les imprime. . . . [Latorre] reproduce el lenguaje y los accidentes del habla popular, punto por punto, como un copista." [234] Homero Castillo understood Latorre better. For him the artist could not be separated from his land, which "le nutre y vigoriza hasta convertirse ambas transubstanciadas en íntima comunión, en la piedra angular en que se asienta su orgullo patrio." [235]

Edgardo Garrido Merino (1888–   ), who spent most of his life in Spain, has among his novels *El hombre en la montaña* (1933), a psychological-costumbrista novel, reminiscent, in its Spanish setting, of the works of Reyles, Larreta, and d'Halmar. But the author's Spanish identification removes him perhaps from thorough consideration as a Chilean novelist.

Jenaro Prieto (1889–1946) wrote two novels, *Una muerte de*

mal criterio (1926) and *El socio* (1928). The first one is a satire about justice. A judge who has died continues to give judgment in the world beyond. Brought back to life, he decides to write a novel of his experiences, the very novel we have read. *El socio*, an expressionistic and somewhat modernist novel and a kind of Chilean *Picture of Dorian Grey*, does not conform to the pattern of either regional or psychological novel in its humorous social satire and fantasy. Julián Pardo, a frustrated businessman whose innermost thoughts we can follow, invents a mythical partner, an Englishman, Walter P. Davis, who takes on a life almost greater than that of his creator. The partner brings success to Julián, but jealousy overcomes the latter, and he dissolves the partnership. Financial ruin overtakes him, his mistress abandons him, and, going mad, he comes to believe in his own creation. He commits suicide, throwing the blame on Davis for his murder. Prieto deals with the capacity for self-deception which all of us have and suggests that fiction may be more real than reality itself.

Luis Durand (1895–1954) had a varied career as a student of agriculture, teacher, bookkeeper, administrative aid to Arturo Alessandri, and newspaper editor. He writes traditional stories of peasant life but has a sardonic and baroque overview which, together with his great sense of balance and gracefulness, saves his direct observation from monotony and excessive sentiment. His short story collections are *Tierra de pellines* (1929), *Campesinos* (1932), *Cielos del sur* (1933), and *Mi amigo Pidén* (1939). *Casa de la infancia* (1944) is a book of special stories about Traiguén and the house he lived in as a child. His longer fiction includes *Mercedes Urizar* (1934), *Piedra que rueda* (1935), *El primer hijo* (1936), *La noche en el camino* (1945), *Frontera* (1949), and *Un amor* (1957). His *Guauguau y otros amigos* (1947) is a special novel for children.

La noche en el camino is about Carmen, the daughter of Florencio Rosales, her friends, schooling, marriage, and love for the doctor who saves her son's life. *Frontera*, surely Durand's best novel, is a paean to life and a loving recall of childhood geography. He treats of peasant life and nature, especially animal life, on the southern frontier before the Guerra del Pacífico. Filled with folklore, mystery, and superstition, it relates the primitive passions one would associate with a frontier society. The protagonist, the caudillo Anselmo Mendoza, attempts to develop the virgin region. He and Isabel are symbolic projections of a Chile in the birth pangs of creating a new age. Anselmo's efforts are thwarted by his murder, but the new train which has just entered the region will finish his work. In spite of some stylistic and grammatical infelicities, the novel shows Durand's sensitivity to color, shape, and form. One can almost taste and smell the products of his land, which overflow this and his other novels, and at the same time sense their poetic essence. But if *Frontera* is a "symphonic masterpiece," [236] *Un amor*, completely divorced from the criollista tradition is a far cry from it. Written shortly before Durand's death while he was struggling against the intestinal cancer which finally destroyed him, *Un amor* has as its protagonist Juan Alsina, a middle-aged man and matrimonial failure who craves a meaningful and sincere love and a spiritual sublimation through painting, a love for which he had abandoned his law career. Aside from this novel, one may say that Durand was a functional criollista. He extracted the essence of his people and his land without forgetting the demands of plot and human characters.

José Santos González Vera (1897–1970), who won the national prize for literature in 1950, belongs to the generation of Manuel Rojas. Coming from humble origins, he held a tremendous number of different kinds of positions as apprentice tailor, antiquarian, painter, salesman, newspaperman, and editor of *Babel*, experiences which formed the material for his novels of provincial customs and tenement life. In 1954 he published *Eutrapelia*, a collection of essays on Manuel Rojas and other writers. González Vera's humor, restrained and subtle, pervades his novels, but he avoids caricature and, "spontaneous and unaffected, singularly free of malice . . . has an artless profundity that provokes thought as well as laughter." [237] He has often been compared to Azorín as a miniaturist, and, sober and delicate, he has "the virtue of being directed to minorities even though his themes go deep into the humble and dispossessed masses." [238] Another student of González Vera's works, describing his humor as one which can never wound, attributes to him the ability of placing "valores en el justo plano en que deben estar." [239] He uses ordinary words to create a simple and yet almost esoteric view of people and places, but his strange verbal combinations reinforce the portrayal of the monotony and rut of daily living.

Vidas mínimas (1923), novelettes, *Alhué* (1928), "estampas de una aldea," and *Cuando era muchacho* (1951) are González Vera's major fictional endeavors. All three, filled with ironic observations of Chilean life, are autobiographical. The first traces life in a *conventillo* of Santiago and also in Valparaíso. The two novelettes included with the first title, *El conventillo* and *Una mujer*, give us portraits of drunks, consumptives, garbage collectors, and interesting characters like superstitious old Paula and the amoral Margarita. The tenement life the author describes is what he himself lived, for, having left school at the age of thirteen and being forced to earn his living, he knew street life perfectly. His sympathy for the proletariat, of which he was a part as bootblack, messenger, and barber's apprentice, seems implied; although his approach is intellectual rather than emotional. *Alhué* has been his most popular work. Again he paints precisely the people and the Chilean streets, this time in a village with few flies in the central valley of Chile. The village has only one priest, no police, a schoolteacher, a shopkeeper, don Nazario, and his wife, but its anodyne spirit, slow and indefinite, is relieved by a dynamic change which González Vera brings to the apparently inscrutable monotony of the village to produce a kind of "mild excitement." *Cuando era muchacho*, which won the National Prize of Literature for 1950, is a kind of Bildungsroman about his childhood, adolescence, and early manhood. The reminiscences are often disconnected and fragmentary minutiae of daily life involving a passing train, an accident, a money lender, and the like, but the "estampas" are of almost photographic intensity. Again González Vera uses a variety of techniques, a special vocabulary—and aphoristic, sparkling but largely unadorned prose—to convey a somewhat more disillusioned view of life. In 1961 he wrote a collection of short narratives, anecdotes, and impressions. Many consider him to be Chile's best humorist, and few deny his grace, ingenuity, irony or his "forma de ser y de sentir los fenómenos de la vida objetiva." [240] For Alone, he is "el mejor escritor chileno, el autor nacional que me procura mayor cantidad de placer en el menor número de páginas." [241]

Manuel Rojas (1896–   ) was born in Buenos Aires, but his Chilean parents returned to Chile when he was four years old. About three years later he and his widowed mother returned to Argentina where Rojas spent most of his youth and adolescence. Most of his life story, his early readings, his association with left-wing labor groups, his meeting with the poet José Domingo Gómez Rojas, who encouraged him to become a writer, and his experiences as linotypist, director of the National Library, railroad worker, longshoreman, painter, and newspaperman and publisher are told in his novels. He fuses the experiences of reality with the imaginary until it is impossible to distinguish them from what merely has the appearance of reality. Rojas develops his real and fictional characters slowly because he believes that human dramas require a slow maturation process.

Customarily, critics divide his works into two categories, the early period in which he was a criollista, and that beginning with *Hijo de ladrón* (1951), which marked his new neorealistic period. All his work contains unusual settings and strange people. Although his novels are based on personal reminiscence, one does not receive an impression of ordinary environment. Fernando Alegría, in his discussion of the development of criollismo between 1910 and 1930, claims that many of the novelists seemed to be sidewalk photographers, superimposing the countryside on a new reality of concrete and steel without becoming truly involved in the new reality. During the last five years of the 1930s young novelists began attacking criollismo to try and discover if possible the spiritual soul of Chile and a reality to which they felt the criollistas had given the category of myth. From the first, says Alegría, Rojas' "criollismo, con ser perfecto, no era suyo, sino algo que tarde o temprano se quitaría de encima como un poncho deshilachado. . . . Manuel Rojas en el fondo no pertenecía a esa escuela . . ." [242]

Rojas himself more or less rejects the label of criollo along with the debates which arose about criollismo. He believes that a writer must write on what he knows best without classifying descriptions of land and people. In any event, he finds criollismo to be only a name for something which *all* Chilean writers, with rare exceptions, have done in writing on their land and their people. Rojas considers it natural that the early stages of Chilean fiction should consist of the description of men, customs, and traditions but not nature. He himself is not interested in man as the victim of cosmic force but rather in "un paisaje de relación entre la vida de la naturaleza y del ser humano y hasta animal que vive en él . . ." [243] This man who interests Rojas is one with universal application, and he makes no effort to describe as specific types the huaso or roto, seeing only different kinds of Chileans in a variety of tasks. Rojas, whose style is uniquely his own (he admits diverse readings from Vargas Vila and Bret Harte to William Faulkner), wishes to convey emotions rather than to provoke thought, but he has always been careful to write simply and avoid excessive metaphorical or grandiloquent language. Thus his fiction seems to consist of conversational pieces or witty, humorous, ironic, and compassionate essays. He has written short story collections: *Hombres del sur* (1926), about the workers on the Trans-Andine railroad, *El delincuente* (1929), *Travesía* (1934), *El bonete maulino* (1943), *El vaso de leche y sus mejores cuentos* (1959), and *Cuentos del sur y Diario de México* (1963). His poetry, as well as his stories, is always keenly visually-oriented.

Rojas' major novels include *La ciudad de los Césares* (1936), *Lanchas en la bahía* (1932), *Hijo de ladrón* (1951), *Mejor que el vino* (1958), *Punta de rieles* (1960), and *Sombras contra el muro* (1964). *La ciudad de los Césares* was written at the urging of don Carlos Silva Vildósola. It appeared as a folletín in *El Mercurio*, and Rojas claims that he wrote the installments while it was being published. The protagonist, an Ona Indian with his dog, is sold to Sam Cocktail, a white explorer who discovers a colony settled by survivors of a wrecked sixteenth-century ship. Rojas was later unhappy about this novel—although it has enjoyed success, especially as a textbook for American students of Spanish. *Lanchas en la bahía* describes the adolescence of Eugenio (Rojas), a young boy who becomes a night watchman, loses his position when he falls asleep, and is taken under the wing of a worker who helps him out. The same kind of situation of bitter childhood, hunger, solitude, help by a mother or father figure, and jail occur as themes in much of his work. It is a long way from *La ciudad de los Césares* about a Patagonian legendary city of gold to which an Indian guides a gold-seeking expedition.

Rojas' masterpiece, and the first fiction after a nine year silence,

Hijo de ladrón, is, states Ramón Sender, the ineffable novel of the Chilean suburbs in all its essence.[244] Rojas uses a variety of techniques (in spite of his rejection of stylistic experimentation) such as interior monologue, counterpoint, what he calls "diálogo interior," temporal and spatial experimentation, cinematic takes, and autobiographical and nostalgic recall of the first seventeen years in the life of Aniceto Hevia.[245] Through his techniques he manages to fuse the perspective of his narrator and the reader who accompanies him on what he calls his "long and confused" story, which actually covers the three days immediately following Aniceto's release from jail. Aniceto makes a pilgrimage through South America in search of a social status which he can never have because he was born the son of a thief. Drunks, thieves, and decent men, says Rojas, all end in jail because they share in common, poverty, the greatest crime of all. For him a thief is a human being like any other. Hevia, happy or sad, faces difficult life situations, including his inability to change professions. The son of a gentle jewel thief and devoted family man, Aniceto was orphaned at the age of ten when his mother died and his father was imprisoned. The police and his brothers abandon him, and he becomes a beachcomber, tramp, tailor, and finally a prisoner, unjustly accused of having robbed a jewelry store. After being released he fights to stay alive and, meeting two vagabonds, Cristián, introverted antagonist of a pitiless society, and El Filósofo, a stoic, cynical, and fatalistic painter and revolutionary, and recognizing in them his own feelings about life, sets out on a new adventure. We see poverty, suffering, and a strike—incidents drawn as fragments from the free flow of memory and filled with digressions and introspective reveries. Rojas reveals clearly his humanitarian compassion for the humble folk of the world. *Mejor que el vino*, whose title is taken from the Song of Songs, has less epic sweep than the first part of his memoirs but delves more thoroughly into certain aspects of Aniceto Hevia's life from late adolescence to middle age. Little plot and less action mark Aniceto's discovery of love and its rewards and punishments. Now a painter and working in a theater, he meditates on wife, children, mistress, and various love affairs. Aniceto—and Rojas by implication—shares the existential suffering of humanity, its pain, its joy, and above all its dreams, which must be continued if man himself is to survive. *Sombras contra el muro* completes the trilogy. Aniceto is now a secondary character among the many anarchists and crooks in Santiago and Valparaíso around 1915 who almost mechanically spend their shadow lives eating, drinking, and fornicating.

While Rojas was at Middlebury College in 1959 he revised some notes he had made in 1927 about a sexually-motivated murder by Romilio Llanca. He added these notes to material he had written two decades later on the life of Fernando Larrain Sanfuentes. This novel, *Punta de rieles*, is a weak fictional effort. Aside from the strong sexual emphasis, the author again recalls his own life experiences and reveals the moral decay of the Santiago upper classes. The stories of Llanca, wife killer, and Fernando Larrain Sanfuentes had nothing to do with each other, but Rojas, taking a page out of Faulkner's book, decided to alternate their lives and have Sanfuentes, the journalist, listen to the confession of Llanca, the carpenter. As he listens to the confession, Sanfuentes recalls from his own subconscious his own moral failures.

Rojas' generation, often called the generation of 1930, includes novelists (some of whom will be treated in the second volume) who fit no easy classification. Depending on which Chilean critics one reads, one may also find that many may be included in the peripheral generation of 1920.

Benjamín Subercaseaux (1902–), who won the national prize for literature in 1963, has written *Y al oeste limita con el mar* (1937), stories or novelettes based on his own experiences and a refined study of sexual abnormality and a view of depravity in the lives of sea captains, stevedores, and prostitutes. Subercaseaux, who studied in France but who feels strongly about the American spirit and inter-American fraternity, has also contributed volumes on his first two loves, sexual psychology, and the geography and history of Chile, the latter represented by his well-known *Chile o una loca geografía* (1940). His fiction includes the short novels *Mar amargo* (1936) and *Rahab* (1938), the latter inspired by the Biblical Joshua, and *Niño de lluvia* (1938), a kind of novelized autobiography about his medical studies and child psychology, which was later (1942) revised under the title *Daniel*. His most famous novel is *Jemmy Button* (1950), the recreation of a real nineteenth-century experience as told through two imaginary diaries. It contains interspersed English and German phrases, the author's bias against American culture as traditionally constituted, and other favorite subjects and philosophical ideas such as the struggle between civilization and barbarism, sex and its abnormalities, religion, race, and life at sea. Some Tierra del Fuego natives, captured and given exotic names by the men on board the *Beagle*, commanded by Captain Fitzroy, a British sailor who later commited suicide, are taken to London to be educated. They are eventually returned to their native land along with a missionary, Richard Matthews. The title is the name of one of the Tierra del Fuego inhabitants. Fitzroy, the civilized man, and London, the civilized world, cannot change Jemmy Button, the Indian boy of the "immutable soul," but the civilized man's failure and that of civilization may not be complete in their realization that order, wisdom, and religion do not contain all the answers to life. Subercaseaux labeled his work "simple novela de aventuras," but it is a complex study of Western culture, its condemnation, and the meaning of being human. The novel so impressed Ricardo Latcham that he stated that with its publication "la novela nacional dio un brusco salto hacia los grandes asuntos . . ." [246]

Finally, Daniel Belmar (1906–), a criollista or neocriollista, whose tenets both he and Lomboy promoted, seems more tied to the land than most of his fellow writers. He knows both city and country and shows a deep concern for social improvement and human dignity as well as with the theme of man and his relationship to nature. His novels are *Roble-huacho* (1947), about southern village life; *Oleaje* (1950), a short novel about a southern Chilean city; *Coirón* (1950), subtitled "tierra de los horizontes submergidos," which contains some autobiographical references and is one of the best regional novels of Chile; *Ciudad brumosa* (1951), a sensitive and poetic vision of the sordid in Concepción; *Desembocadura* (1953); *Sonata* (1955), "carta de una adolescente"; *Los túneles morados* (1961); and *Detrás de las máscaras* (1966), about the earthquake of 1960.

Coirón, which has been labeled a static kind of novel, is nonetheless overflowing with violence, murder, and an epic feeling for the plains. The title refers to a hard-leaved plant used in thatching huts, perhaps not inappropriate since the protagonist is the pampa in all its wild beauty and monotony. The novel resembles *Don Segundo Sombra* in its episodic relation of a trek with sheep across the pampas, a locust invasion, a grotesque and yet sad ostrich hunt, and a fight between a bull and a puma. But the human equation, universalized, is stronger in Belmar than in most of the criollistas, and he has created in the one-eyed rapist and murderer Mocho an unforgettable character. Laid in Neuquén, the novel tells of the hardships of Chilean exiles from about 1905 on as seen through the eyes of Rafael Artigas. *Sonata's* title reveals the melodic structure of the interwoven themes and the musical counterpoint between inner tension and the cruel exterior environment. All this is seen through the recollections of a fifteen-year old girl, who in her memories also recreates an absent father. In conveying man's alienation and continuing responsibility for his fellow man, Belmar adds a new note to his standard melancholy descriptive fare and evocation of a stoic and fatalistic people. *Los túneles morados*, the passages from life to death, appropriately occurs during one night and relates the lives of some bohemian students.

The Dominican Republic, which had previously produced Manuel de Jesús Galván, offered the world another good novelist in Tulio Manuel Cestero whom we have already examined under modernism. His *La sangre* (1915), "undoubtedly, one of the best novels of the period," [247] in its description of life under a tyranny falls within the category of criollista novel.

Carlos Wyld Ospina (1891–1956), a Guatemalan poet who wrote short stories such as *La tierra de las Nahuyacas* (1933) and novels, *El solar de los Gonzagos* (1924) and his best known, *La gringa* (1935), is considered by many to be a modernist writer, "uno de los escritores más prominentes del movimiento modernista en Guatemala" [248]—an acceptable classification for his poetry but not for his fiction. He himself calls *La gringa* "novela criolla" and evinces criollo concerns in his modernist-naturalistic combination. Wyld lived in Mexico, was a supporter of Victoriano Huerta, and, returning home, was a newspaperman, editor of a humor magazine, politician, and university professor. His *La tierra de las Nahuyacas* seeks to display not only the individual but the racial characteristics and spiritual order of the Guatemalan. His protagonist, Sebastian Ax, a racial archetype, is both a symbol and a man of flesh and blood. Wyld examines the effect of the Spanish conquest on the Indian's culture, religion, and superstitions and seeks to interpret the Indian's traditions, dreams, and prophecies. *El solar de los Gonzagos* resembles *Reinaldo Solar* by Rómulo Gallegos. The protagonist, the last heir of a powerful family fallen on evil days, marries for money and to start a new dynasty. *La gringa*, a kind of Guatemalan *Doña Bárbara*, describes a European girl—a tomboy who hates men—who finally dominated by a man returns to Europe. The life of Eduardo Barcos, the conqueror of sorts, and his love, Magda Peña Meich, is less important than the theme of nature versus man, the former represented by the jungle and the *matapalo*. The author includes in his picture of American life, Indian superstitions and the inevitable North American gringo.

A far greater Guatemalan novelist, Flavio Herrera (1895–   ), who combines a modernist vein, Indian mythology, and indigenista concerns, poet, short story writer, and novelist, in spite of his modernist qualities is the most realistic and regionalistic writer of his region. He treats of magic and sensuality in an almost decadent jungle setting.[249] A psychologist of the tropics, Herrera combines "los perfumes y las savias de la selva, y también las esencias del mar, para brindarnos nuevas sensaciones." [250] "El novelista guatemalteco . . . en el relato criollo," [251] the representative of "la novela criolla en Guatemala," [252] he seems clearly criollista in his themes of the moral degradation and material and spiritual suffering of the Indian and in his passionate, sensual pictures of nature and of greedy, superstitious men. Herrera's criollismo shows also in his portrayal of the gap between white and Indian culture—whose music, smells, animals and customs seem omnipresent—and his concept of machismo and the impact of tropical nature on man, especially in the struggle between civilization and barbarism. *La lente opaca* (1921) and *Cenizas* (1923) are representative short story collections. His novels are *El tigre* (1934), *La tempestad* (1935), *Siete pájaros del iris* (1936), a short work which he called "novela dramática en siete estampas," *Poniente de sirenas* (1937), which contrasts the real and oneiric worlds, and *Caos* (1949), probably his best.

El tigre is the story of civilization, the miserable Indians, and the tropical nature of Guatemala. Fernando, the tiger, kills Luis, the city man whose sensual instincts are aroused by the tropics. *La tempestad* treats of white, mestizo, and Indian relationships.

Leonarda, the mestiza, hopes to rise in station through her marriage. Frustrated by the failure of her "criollo" son, Julián, she looks forward to the day when her child will be a part of the new aristocracy. *Poniente de sirenas*, a watery version of *El tigre*, uses the sea as a natural backdrop. Delfino, victimized by the sensual sea, forgets his wife for Helen Vane as the latter abandons her husband. The lovers decide to die together in the sea. *Caos*, somewhat surrealistic and experimental but with extremely natural dialogue and a direct realism in the first half of the novel, analyzes a split personality. Adolfo, the morbid farm owner, the mysterious and evil Simón, and Luis, the solid friend interact as we examine Adolfo's youthful sexual experiences, his fears, his moral degeneration, and the man he might have become. In his novels Herrera denounces the exploitation of his people and suffers with them their tropical ills and their close identification with and love for the soil. His works are filled with symbolic feminine creations: Adela, the eternal woman; Margarita, the angelic woman; Genoveva, who suffers a sad and silent love; Leonarda, the authentic criolla; and La Troncha, the elemental, ageless woman. Beauty, love of the land, and concern for the Indian, emotionally and poetically and yet sociologically, all treated against a backdrop of natural beauty, form the principal characteristics of this most unusual novelist.

After Carrasquilla, the Colombian novelists fit no easy pattern. Efe Gómez, whose real name was Francisco Gómez Escobar (1867–1938), was primarily a short story writer of largely gloomy and anguished tales. *Mi gente* (1937), often classified as a novel, is really a skillfully combined mixture of previously published short stories. Most of these deal with poor workers in fields, jungle, and the mines and show us a humanity trapped by poverty and the fatality of life. His scenes of Antioquia are authentic, and his country folk psychologically sound; but he lacks the force of Carrasquilla. Several volumes of his stories, *Retorno, Almas rudas*, and *Guayabo negro*, were published in a posthumous edition. Antonio Álvarez Lleras (1892–1956), far better known as a dramatist, in *Ayer, nada más* (1930) wrote about Mariano Mendizábal, the psychological soul of Bogotá, the corruption which eats at the fabric of man, and about the responsibility of each man for his actions in this life. Daniel Samper Ortega (1895–1943), essayist, dramatist, and editor who qualifies as a kind of tardy modernist, wrote a half dozen novels which while not typically regional clearly express a special love for his country. Among these are *Entre la niebla* (1923), *La marquesa de Alfandoque* (1923), one of the best short novels of the first three decades, *La obsesión* (1926) and *Zoraya* (1931), subtitled "Una vida de amor y santidad," a historical novel based on the love adventures and repentance of José Solís, the eighteenth-century viceroy of Nueva Granada, which Gómez Restrepo claimed "estuvo a punto de ser en la literatura colombiana lo que *La gloria de don Ramiro* en la Argentina." [253] José Restrepo Jaramillo (1896–1945), perhaps the first psychological novelist of Colombia, treats psychoanalytic themes in *La novela de los tres* (1924) and in *David, hijo de Palestina* (1931), a novel of Freudian impact, concerned with sex and the subconscious, the story of the hopes and heroism, doubts and despair of the people of Antioquia. *Roque* (1926) is another well-known story title. In all his novels the author seeks the subconscious causes for the motivations and actions of his characters.

José Eustasio Rivera (1889–1928), Colombia's greatest criollista novelist, wrote some well-known sonnets, *Tierra de promisión* (1921), which earned him the sobriquet of "the singer of Colombian landscapes." Rivera paints the flora and fauna of his native Colombia, the color and smell of the tropics, something he was to repeat in a more violent and destructive form in his one published novel, *La vorágine* (1924), which retains its poetic force in spite of its mixture of brutal realism, passionate romanticism, love, lust, and social and psychological appurtenances. The author spent his childhood in Neiva, the capital of the department of Huila about 150 miles south of Bogotá. This was an important factor in his work, for no other panorama "habría calzado mejor al futuro del escritor. Naturaleza tropical, cansadora rutina aldeana, pleno mestizaje, codicia y aventurería, y sopor: ello se verá en sus dos únicos libros." [254] When he was eighteen Rivera went to Bogotá where he attended school and wrote poetry. After a short stint as a school superintendent and administrative officer, in 1918 he went to work at Crocue, a remote town near the Meta river, where for two years he worked as a lawyer. There he met a cattle dealer, Luis Yavarí, later a figure in his novel. In 1919 Rivera visited the Mata de Palma (the Hato Grande of his novel) and took notes on the region. He traveled the plains of Casanare and the Meta, along the Orinoco, the Río Negro, and the Casiquiare. His experiences, remembered fuzzily after a time, left him with a memory of "un mundo de color, exaltación y fuerza que le hacía sentir una extraña conmoción y una como necesidad de comunicarla a los demás." [255] In 1922, as a member of a boundary commission to settle a dispute between Venezuela and Colombia, Rivera lived in the interior near the Orinoco for several months. During this trip and on another as a member of a commission to examine petroleum affairs (he issued a strong anti-monopoly and anti-foreign report) he traveled through the rugged and varying landscape of *llano* and jungle, which he viewed as a vortex. He saw then also what an unjust society can do to human dignity.

In the *siringales*, or rubber tree groves, fortunes could be made by unscrupulous promoters who depended on a slave system of *caucheros* or peons hired to collect the crude rubber. It was the caucheros' duty to roll the rubber into balls and deliver it to specified areas on the river bank. Once a month a supply boat came by; no other contact with civilization was possible. Ironically, the jungle was probably responsible, in part, for Rivera's own death. He contracted malaria, jungle fever, and beri beri, and for a time was himself lost in the jungle. It was during his convalescence that he wrote about his experiences, and although the first part of the novel was finished by 1922 it took him a total of four bitter years of recall to sort out his impressions. He died in New York, some say of pneumonia, and of hemiplegia and malaria according to official reports. The novel, more than an autobiography, serves as a kind of epitaph, as we recall the prophetic letter of Arturo Cova that "sepan que el destino implacable me desarraigó de la prosperidad incipiente . . . para que . . . me extinguiera . . . sin dejar más que ruido y desolación." At his death, it is said, Rivera left unpublished the manuscript of another novel, *La mancha negra*.[256]

La vorágine, then, has a very real base in Rivera's own experiences. Arturo Cova is the author himself, and many of the other characters, Clemente Silva and Zoraida among others, are elaborations of real people. His stories of the cruelty of the rubber exploiters, when not obtained through actual experience or oral accounts, are taken from the documents of the operations of the

Casa Arana in the early twentieth century.²⁵⁷ The author, who pretends that the story is the manuscript written by Arturo Cova and sent to the ministry by the Colombian consul in Manaos, claims that he is carefully preserving the style and even the errors of the writer of the diary. In the epilogue we read the consul's cable, closing the Cova case with the tragic words "los devoró la selva."

As Jean Franco points out, "Rivera's one novel, *La vorágine*, can be considered in many ways: as a romantic allegory, as an urban intellectual's frightened vision of the barbarism of his country, as a novel of protest." ²⁵⁸ In part this may account for the mixed reaction the novel has received, eliciting the highest praise from novelists of the caliber of Arias Trujillo and considered "una lata" and almost worthless by another of the stature of Tomás Carrasquilla.²⁵⁹ The novel is crammed with descriptions and events and a number of unusual but representative characters. We witness gambling, crooked dealing and a corrupt judge, a cattle roundup, a stampede, a cock fight, a storm, Indians, their customs and their fighting, the legends of the jungle, a bull goring a cowboy to death, quarrels among rubber barons, slavery, and prostitution. The *llanero* comes alive before our eyes as does the regional language, whose *Yagé* (hypnotic plant), *Belduque* (small knife), *Caricari* (a falcon), *Curiara* (canoe), and a host of other words fix the American savor of the scene. Yet when we have listed these characteristics and many more, we must conclude that we have hardly touched the main aspects of the work, nature against man, man against man, man against himself, and the individual's eternal quest for self-realization. Before examining these themes, a somewhat more detailed plot analysis than usual is in order.

Arturo Cova, a romantic, immature, and impetuous poet, steals Alicia, a girl he had seduced in Bogotá but whom he does not wish to marry. After a number of difficulties they come to the plains of Casanare accompanied by a merchant trader, Rafo. They stay at La Maporita, a *fundación* (ranch) owned by Fidel Franco and his mistress, Griselda, a terribly sensual woman whose charms Cova manages to resist for a time. Narciso Barrera, a brutal but attractive labor recruiter, comes to the ranch in search of people to work in the rubber fields. Unaware of the unbelievably bad working conditions, many fall for his easy money and promises. He gives gifts to Griselda and her servant. Fidel Franco, unbewitched by the blandishments of Barrera, must nonetheless ride off with Rafo to seek money and men for the rodeo and to sell some cattle in Bogotá. Alicia intervenes on Griselda's behalf with Barrera to whom Franco's woman owes money. Cova, his jealousy aroused by an evening meeting between Alicia and Barrera, plans to kill him, but the latter escapes to Hato Grande, owned by old Zubieta. Cova seeks him there, and in a dice game Barrera wounds Cova who is nursed to health by Zubieta's mistress Clarita. Barrera recounts to Alicia and Griselda the new "love" affair of Cova. Meanwhile, Franco has closed a deal with Zubieta for the cattle, and they go off with Cova for the roundup. They learn that they are being sought by a circuit judge on a murder warrant. Returning to Hato Grande they learn that Barrera has killed and robbed Zubieta and accused Cova. Deceiving Griselda and Alicia, Barrera entices them off with him into the jungle. Cova and Franco, misinterpreting the women's actions, set out after them. Cova, a victim of neurotic seizures and recurrent nightmares, cannot easily adjust to the jungle. There they meet Helí Mesa, one of the men recruited by Barrera. He had fled the brutal and inhuman treatment of the rubber fields. All go off to the siringal of Yaguanarí, through a jungle infested with leeches and mosquitoes, to search for and free the prisoners. On the way they encounter Clemente Silva, who for sixteen years had been working the rubber fields of El Cayeno and Pezil, and he promises to help them. Silva reveals to them the horrible conditions of the rubber workers as well as his own long search for the bones of his dead son in order to give them Christian burial. He also tells them of Zoraida Ayram, a Turkish woman who is visiting El Cayeno and knows where Barrera has gone. Cova goes to see her. At the estate of El Cayeno he sees the violation of Indian girls and other atrocities committed against the Indians. After unsuccessfully attempting to foment an insurrection, he sends off a complaint to the Colombian consul at Manaos documenting the injustices he has seen. More and more depressed, at times he seems on the verge of madness. Zoraida, thinking him rich, seduces him and then falls in love with him. El Cayeno has Cova beaten but is himself murdered by Cova's friends. Cova finally catches up with Barrera and leaves him for the piranhas to eat. He and Franco are unable to free the Colombian workers who have been attacked by a contagious disease. Cova and his party go off into the jungle but outline the route they will take so that Clemente Silva may follow. Silva searches through the Yaguanarí but cannot find them. The jungle has swallowed them up.

The plot moves forward through a series of stories told by various characters like Clemente Silva or Ramiro Estévañez, who tells of the slaughter of innocent victims by Funes; but Cova is the principal narrator. The technique seems justified because the multiple narrations "le permitían a Rivera una amplificación de la visión del mundo . . . y también una flexibilidad en la ordenación y elaboración de esta visión." [260]

When one reads *La vorágine* with its jungle terrors, one immediately contrasts this tragic vision with the lovely one of William Hudson's *Green Mansions*, each beautiful in its own way. In the first part of *La vorágine*, the pleasant, peaceful plains of Casanare provide us with a beautiful vision of the high vault of starry skies, magnificent sunrises and sunsets, and occasional dark pools where alligators lurk. Even the jungle, a place of horror and death, is filled with its own beauty and mystery. But Rivera's jungle is not the poetic zoological garden of Hudson, nor indeed *Inferno verde* (1908) of Alberto Rangel (1871–1945), but a place filled with leeches, mosquitoes, and army ants, where trapped and desperate victims face a cosmic and implacably blind fate. The electric eels, man-eating fish, snakes, rot, and general destructiveness of the hostile environment symbolized by the tropical thunderstorms, evoke a corresponding almost empathic violence in the men who view the immense panorama and suffer its loneliness, hunger, fever, and terror. It is a green jail which avenges itself on man for his trespass and is itself described, though it is inhuman, in human terms as both sadistic and virginal, an anthropomorphic view in keeping with its intimate relationship to the humanity it surrounds.[261] Indeed, the jungle speaks through its human mouthpieces like Clemente Silva in what almost amounts to a jungle monologue. The trees have a magic life and primitive telluric force of their own and are indifferent to man in their freedom and mystery. The jungle, a magical and almost supernatural force, sums up in its natural conflicts "human desires frustrated by non-human powers, hostile oppression, or contrary desires; it is a story of the birth, passion, and defeat by death which is man's common fate."[262] Cova is aware of the almost mythical opposition, the cosmic force, the mystery of creation materialized in the desolation, destruction, and death which savage animals and poisonous plants reserve for intruders. He cries out, "¿ Qué hado maligno me dejó prisionero en tu cárcel verde?" As one poet has said in commenting on this novel, ". . . el artista ha creado unos personajes destinados a estrellarse contra una naturaleza terrible y a perderse en ella. . . . De este choque (del hombre civilizado con la Naturaleza salvaje), el hombre sale irremediablemente desfigurado. . . . Desaparece en la vorágine como un náufrago que viésemos desaparecer en las olas enormes, pero sin saber el momento exacto en que ha sido arrastrado al fondo oscuro."[263] As Odysseus, the king of Ithaca who wandered for ten years, Cova wanders in a place of strange myths and unknown gods toward his unknown end, an Odyssey physically real and spiritually imagined of a man in search of himself.

Peter Earle has examined what he calls the "camino oscuro" in La vorágine as a point of departure for the new Spanish American novel.[264] Another critic sees the novel as a trip to hell, the land of the dead, a kind of anthropological creation of a recurrent myth motif.[265] The diary form allows Rivera to convey the subjective emotions, the sentimental, and the mysterious which nature effects in the protagonist. Cova serves as a witness to nature's power, although as a somewhat neurotic and ineffectual dreamer he may be peripheral to the real fight of man against nature or man against his society, exemplified by the slavery, exploitation, and general cruelties of an uncivilized power structure. Ciro Alegría rejects as representative the novel's principal characters because they are neither intimately nor psychologically a part of the social problem of the rubber workers. He objects to the artificial plot structure which necessitates having Alicia to be separated from Cova so that he may be converted into "un testigo exaltado de la tragedia general, que no tiene mayor relación con su propio conflicto."[266] Yet the characters seem real enough, although Rivera abandons a few before the end of the novel. Zubieta, the astute and vicious old rancher; Clemente Silva, a living corpse, a pathetic human animal in a jungle plant world and yet the only heroic figure who dominates the jungle even though he is charmed by it; Barrera, the thieving, murdering, self-appointed, and completely callous don Juan; Zoraida, the Turkish woman from Brazil, a passionate devourer of men who, like the jungle, thrives on her victims but is easily more greedy, sensual, cold blooded, and cruel; and Arturo Cova, the cultured Bogotano whose city training is inappropriate for jungle living and whose desperate attempt to find himself ends in despair, madness, and death are all breathing, living creations. Cova is a highly manic neurotic who dreams of glory at times; at others, depressed, he suffers from hallucinations and paranoid delusions. He believes strongly in predestination and fatality. Irascible, passionate, sentimental, proud, and vain, he travels the Brazilian jungles, crossing rivers and forest paths, meeting village tribes, witnessing the degradation of the siringales, facing the jungle terrors. From the beginning we are involved in his fatality and fate, as the poet indulges himself in self-analysis and projects his fantasies, hallucinations, and nightmare terrors. Cova is a symbol of the human condition, and he is also a human being, a weak and fragile reed of a man, idealistically moved by the sight of suffering on the frontier of civilization and unable to bear the violence, terror, and grief of that life.

The romantic story of Arturo Cova and Alicia is a counterpoint for the heart-rending descriptions of life in the rubber fields. The main narrative covers a time period of seven months, but the insert stories extend that time to cover social conditions between 1905 and 1920. Rivera uses both romanticism and naturalism in his epic view of the jungle, an external and personal force against which the romantic dreamer has no chance. Cova gives us his autobiography, at times addressing himself in the second person; a variety of other characters speak in the first person. Throughout the language is rhetorical, romantic, vehemently poetic,[267] and filled with short ecstatic outbursts. The novel is in turn visionary, mystic, realistic, modernist, and melodramatic. In its chaotic and episodic structure, seemingly almost unplanned, it fuses a number of old and new literary devices in an unconventional manner, using dream projections and hallucinatory states along with a new determinism to show us man as a puppet moved by fate. In spite of its apparent lack of organization, overly grandiloquent out-

bursts, a slow plot development, and an overtly false sentimentalism, *La vorágine* will continue to be one of the major fictional
documents of the century.

Juan Marinello, in comparing *Doña Bárbara* with *Don Segundo
Sombra* and *La vorágine*, sums up the three as novels in which
Indo-hispanic America speaks out clearly. In all three he finds
"el mismo tropel de sangres voluntariosas, igual aventurerismo
machuno, idéntica confianza desmedida en el propio brazo, pareja
sospecha del vencimiento final. Ofrecen un mundo de primitivis-
mos y candores, pero no de rudezas adolescentes como en lo medieval ni de resignación cobarde ante una fatalidad civilizadora que se
repudia. Muestran un orbe contradictorio de incipiencias y has-
tíos. Dan con fidelidad profunda esa mezcla de ímpetus juveniles
y maduras desesperanzas que es propia de hombres que se saben
lejos de la meta ansiada pero que ya le conocen las grietas. Son—
América honda—, arrojo y suspicacia. Una cara mestiza, dura de
soles implacables con un ojo en ira y otro en recelo, podría
campear, síntesis eficaz, en la primera página de los tres relatos
singulares." [268]

All three novels are concerned with man versus law. Sombra
largely ignores it, Bárbara tries to circumvent it, and El Cayeno
directly confronts it. All three novels play up the supernatural,
Bárbara with her *socio*, Don Segundo with his folk tales, and Cova
in the jungle. America and American nature predominate as man
struggles against a mighty cosmic force. Rómulo Gallegos in
Doña Barbara offers a symbolic victory of good over evil and the
future over the past. Güiraldes' hero represents not only a reality
which might have been but part of a reality that is and that will
be. All three men portray in their works civilizers who fall victim
to experience in jungle, plain, or European capital, at times
triumphing, at others failing, but expressing universal and human concepts which transcend the national experience, however
authentic.

Criollista novelists, often exuberant and disordered, drew upon
their native soil and natural surroundings to present a colorful
reality of their particular society in flux, a reality at times cruel
but also warm and sensitive in its acceptance of the tragedy of
living. These novels compensate for their loose structure by often
moving and consistent portrayals of humanity in a specific locale.

Whatever the geographic or scenic background, the cordillera, the pampa, the coastal lands, the jungle, or the tenement districts of the cities, the emphasis is on the autochthonous, which may include man as a victim of external natural forces or of the political and social ones of his society. The essentially naturalistic orientation involving a malignant cosmic nature, even as artistically expressed, was to give way to other literary experiences; yet criollismo, at the very least, helped create a formidable flow of fiction, of which the best is very good indeed.

5. The Novel of the Mexican Revolution

The Mexican Revolution, according to some still going on, produced a variety of novels. As a most successful and continuing revolution, with political and social achievements of lasting duration, whatever the reservations of some Mexicans, it expressed a longing for freedom as old as mankind itself. When Benito Juárez achieved his remarkable if brief reforms, one of his faithful followers—about whom nonetheless Juárez had some doubts—was Porfirio Díaz. In 1876 Díaz took over the presidency and soon transformed it into a dictatorship he was not to relinquish until 1911. With Díaz came order, discipline, morality of a sort, and material progress (for some) but at the cost of no justice for the poor, no popular education, and no agrarian reform. The lighting system, railroads, and other trappings of modern technology cost Mexico its mineral and economic holdings, which in essence were turned over to foreign capitalists. At first some of Díaz' ministers were liberal—he came in as a liberal follower of Juárez—but he later formed a special brain trust, the *científicos*, who served as his advisers and guides. These men—Don Rosendo Pineda, José Inés Limantour, Francisco León de la Barra, among others—did not view the Indian (he could not enter the city of Mexico on certain occasions) as a contributing member of society. Technically Porfirio Díaz' regime was dedicated to the idea of self-improvement in accord with the positivistic theories of Auguste Comte (1798–1857); but positivism as a reaction against theocentric and materially impoverished conditions had come to mean an unjust social structure which viewed the Indian with scorn. Rumbles of discontent began to be heard as early as 1892, growing in intensity to a fever pitch by 1907 with the strike at Río Blanco during which many workers were killed by government troops. Díaz' greatest error may have been in granting a newspaperman named James Creelman, of *Pearson's Magazine*, an interview in 1908. Díaz stated that he was prepared to have a democratic election and allow opposition parties. Several candidates took him at his word, including General Reyes and Limantour, whom he managed to sidetrack. Among the many political parties were Bernardo Reyes' liberal one, the Anti-Reelection party, and the Anarchist group. Francisco Madero, author of a well-known work, *La sucesión presidencial en 1910* (1908), a man of personal valor who strongly opposed the reelection of Díaz, was willing to allow Díaz to finish his term but then wanted a free election for a vice-president. Díaz decreed that the compliant Ramón Corral was to be his vice-president and, jailing Madero, had himself declared reelected in October, thus breaking his promise of not seeking reelection. Madero, with the backing of the Anti-Reelection party, was nominated for the presidency with Francisco Vásquez Gómez as his running mate. Escaping the clutches of Díaz, Madero issued his manifesto of San Luis Potosí, 20 November 1910, which may be taken as one starting date for the Mexican Revolution. Revolts started in various parts of Mexico, and Emiliano Zapata, Pascual Orozco, and Francisco Villa contributed to the cause. Limantour shifted to the Maderista side. Finally, with the fall of Ciudad Juárez in May 1911, Díaz, realizing that he had lost, gave up the presidency and left the country to die in France four years later.

In October 1911 Madero was elected president. He believed in the ideals of the constitution of 1857, in political freedom, freedom of the press, public education, and agrarian reform. Madero attempted to put his idealistic program into practice, but he was too honest and naïve to rid himself of opportunists from the Díaz days. Pascual Orozco and Emiliano Zapata, the former because he thought his troops were treated unfairly and the latter because Madero failed to bring about land reform, revolted. Some intellectuals, disillusioned by the Díaz regime and positivism, became equally disenchanted with Madero. The latter's major mistake was naming Victoriano Huerta (in league with Félix Díaz, nephew of the former dictator, and Bernardo Reyes, jailed by Madero after an abortive revolt) as head of the palace guard. Huerta, aided and abetted, according to Mexican historians, by the U.S. ambassador of the time, Henry Lane Wilson, imprisoned Madero and his vice-president. The events of that week, 8 to 18 February 1913, are still known as the "ten tragic days." Huerta later murdered both men and took command of the country on 22 February 1913, a power he held until 23 July 1914.

Almost immediately uprisings began. Álvaro Obregón, a ranchero from Sonora, defeated the government troops in his area; Venustiano Carranza, governor of Coahuila, issued the Plan of Guadalupe and declared himself to be the coordinator of the constitutionalist armies; Francisco Villa, from Chihuahua, organized an informal army; and Emiliano Zapata, from the south, advanced on Mexico City. In August, Carranza, the representative of law and order to many Mexicans, much as Zapata represented the peasant and Villa popular vengeance, took over Mexico City. Carranza refused to accept the deliberations of the convention of Aguascalientes which named Eulalio Gutiérrez provisional president. Villa and Zapata assumed a tenuous control of the government, but Gutiérrez fled. Finally, Obregón retook Mexico City. Meanwhile Mexico had imprisoned some U.S. sailors, and the United States occupied Veracruz in November 1914. Carranza accepted the U.S. conditions, and Veracruz temporarily became his capital. Carranza, "el primer jefe," became president in 1917. He produced little reform and attempted to name his successor. Plutarco Calles, Álvaro Obregón, and Adolfo de la Huerta revolted, and Carranza was killed in May 1920. Zapata was assassinated in 1919; Villa, who had been defeated by Obregón, led a series of raids and was finally killed in ambush in 1923. Obregón, "El Caudillo," ruled Mexico from September of 1920, after a brief interlude under Adolfo de la Huerta, until 1924. He also was assassinated in 1928. From 1924 to 1928 Plutarco Calles, "El Líder Máximo," held power. Calles attempted a few reforms and faced serious armed Catholic revolts for his pains, but in essence he held the reins of power in Mexico until 1934 when Lázaro Cárdenas assumed the presidency. Emilio Portes Gil was provisional president from 1928 to 1930, Pascual Ortiz Rubio from 1930 to 1932, and Abelardo Rodríguez from 1932 to 1934. Cárdenas stayed on until 1940, to give way to Ávila Camacho, who, say many Mexicans, betrayed the revolution and the constitution in one form or another. Ávila Camacho was succeeded by Miguel Alemán under whose presidency the revolutionary breath became shallow to the point of extinction.

In spite of the visionary Plan de Ayala of Emiliano Zapata, which in 1911 called for land division; the constitution of 1917, which provided for a variety of humanitarian, judicial, and educational reforms; and the efforts, occasionally rewarded, of José Vasconcelos and others to establish a rural school system; these goals and a better social and economic system for the average citizen were not easily achieved. Cárdenas, almost uniquely, consistently considered the interest of his people and matched revolutionary rhetoric with radical reform. He divided the land, expropriated foreign oil interests, permitted freedom of the press, and continued the reform of the educational system. Unfortunately, later presidents did not so single-mindedly reflect the liberal and popular ideology begun by Madero and continued by Cárdenas, his ideological heir.

The above formed the raw material for the novelists of the revolution, many of whom were men who had participated as soldiers or newspapermen. The revolution itself was so vast and multifaceted that no one person has written the novel of the Mexican Revolution, although *Los de abajo* comes close. Like Azuela, many writers found it hard to realize that in spite of the betrayal of their trust, Mexican generals and politicians had not completely frustrated the people, even if land reform, independence from foreign capital, or full social and economic justice for the Indian had not been achieved. The novelists note these failures and lament the ever widening chasm between what the revolution hoped to achieve and what it actually accomplished. For many the revolution assumed impossible mythic proportions. A movement of too many generals and not enough followers, the revolution was furthered by human beings, some of whom wanted political power, some redistribution of wealth, and still others a European kind of social and political liberation. But not all is pessimistic in these novels. By concentrating on the human factor more than on social values and ideas, the novelists seek to counteract their disillusion with an implied hope of brotherhood among men. Although there were few noble heroes in the fighting, some projected an almost epic force, and for all their bloody cruelty, they often demonstrated incredible personal valor and loyalty to their fellow fighters. Since death was their constant companion and since each moment might be their last, the revolutionaries indulged more in human and physical pursuits than in philosophy. In a sense, the novel of the revolution, showing us life as it is lived, creates real human beings, "hombres con todos los vicios y las virtudes de ese destino de bestia y de ángel que llevamos siempre con nosotros." [1] Indeed, aside from an occasional noble idealist or anonymous folk hero, it is clear that more often than not these novels portray the worst side of man, his hypocrisy, greed, cruelty, and corruption, showing us frustration and failure rather than success in the social, ideological, economic, and political areas.

The novelists reflect personal ambition, class struggle, political activity, efforts at agrarian reform, the Indian and his culture, and a tortured and chaotic world—which they recreate, for the most part, without direct didacticism in spite of the social, religious, and racial problems which concerned them and their countrymen. Largely based on historical documentation and eyewitness accounts, the novels have a photographic intensity and realism, but at times they also reveal the morbid and even grotesque subjective reactions of the authors. The Mexican Revolution was a brutal, violent, bloody, and moving reality; yet many of the novels have humorous and picaresque insights into the people and their actions. Since the events were in many instances witnessed by the authors themselves, the latter use a kind of memoir form to convey their autobiographical experience and their fascination with the violence in which they were caught up. Most of the novels are fast-moving, short, lineal, episodic, choppy, and dramatic works. The novels are often regional (it might be argued that they belong in chapter 4) and *costumbrista*, but they do not limit themselves to any geographical locale. They include city and country in what seems to have been an early attempt to create a truly national literature. In retrospect, as Rosario Castellanos somewhat sadly comments, these writers give us testimony, documents, and anecdotes but, "si acaso, una o dos novelas." [2] A counterargument is that in bringing the Indian, already humanized in the paintings of Rivera, Orozco, and others, to the novel as a Mexican protagonist, the novelists of the revolution were creating the first authentic

Mexican fiction which dealt with human beings and not types. Manuel Pedro González also points out the limiting factors implicit in the novel of the revolution where "el novelista se recortó su propio horizonte artístico y le mermó posibilidades estéticas a su obra. De ahí que pronto cayera en una inevitable tautología de temas, episodios y sucedidos que en fuerza de repetirse devinieron convencionales. La novela revolucionaria acabó por caer en el pecado original de la novela mexicana anterior: el costumbrismo . . ." [3] Again, admitting the reservation, one may still say that the overriding impression left by these novels, beyond costumbrismo, is that of an intense nationalism—identity with and love for Mexico.

F. Rand Morton (*Los novelistas de la revolución mexicana*, Mexico, 1949) divides the novels as follows: (1) novels of the revolution itself; (2) novels of revolutionary ideas; (3) novels of social and revolutionary content; (4) Indianist novels; and (5) novels of the revolution remembered. Antonio Castro Leal (*La novela de la revolución mexicana*, Mexico, 1958) discusses the novels as autobiographical, episodic, epic, or of nationalist affirmation. José Luis Martínez, while conceding that the novels start about 1926, professes to find antecedents of the fiction of the Mexican Revolution in works by Rabasa, Heriberto Frías, López Portillo y Rojas, and Federico Gamboa.[4] Eugenio Chang-Rodríguez rejects altogether the label "Novel of the Mexican Revolution," because of the heterogeneous nature of the works, which included biographies, autobiographies, memoirs, and many other forms. He divides the productions into three groups, those which treat of the war, those which treat of the prerevolutionary period, and those which deal with the postrevolutionary period.[5] Similarly, Uslar Pietri distinguishes three moments in the novel of the Mexican Revolution: the objective portraits of a popular movement, as exemplified by Azuela; the vision of the revolution as a remembered past, tried by Guzmán; and the revolution as "desengaño. La actitud satírica y el relato anecdótico de su descomposición y de sus efectos demoralizantes." [6] These novels were written in a limited time period, approximately between 1928 and 1940. Later novels, with few exceptions, do not properly belong to the category of this chapter.[7]

The realistic and romantic nineteenth-century novel often had revealed a satirical, humorous, and *reformista* tendency which later combined with historical determinism, a kind of positivism, and the poetic art of the modernist novelists. The fusion of previous movements, along with an attenuated costumbrismo, insistence on a forceful natural background, an *ambiente* in which regional types such as the *huaso*, the *gaucho*, or the *zambo* act, created what we have called *criollismo*; but quite often it produced a novel that examined in naturalistic fashion the people in rural and urban environments. The tragic and catastrophic concern over the destiny of man, in all its pessimism and social degeneration, found a natural scapegoat in nature as a destructive and terror-inspiring force, one which was superior to man—who was usually portrayed as a symbolic counterforce of weaker proportions although not inevitably destroyed by his natural surroundings. Poetic and episodic narration tended toward the descriptive rather than the analytical, but novelists like Reyles and Barrios showed great insight concerning human motivations. The novelists seemed obsessed with landscape and the social problems of alienated remnants of their society such as the Indian or mestizo and voiced a continuing conviction about the triumph of civilization over barbarism. Whatever they lacked in dramatic force they replaced with vigor, color, and life. It was of this kind of novel that Manuel Pedro González was thinking when, decrying the universal praise accorded the new novels in spite of their derivative aspects, he exclaimed: "Entre 1910 y 1940, más o menos, se dieron los creadores más originales y robustos y las expresiones narrativas de mayor envergadura que hemos producido . . . Estos treinta años representan la etapa de mayor originalidad y rigor que la novela americana ha alcanzado." [8]

Perhaps, in the case of the four best known novels of the continent during the first three decades of the twentieth century, *Los de abajo*, *La vorágine*, *Don Segundo Sombra*, and *Doña Bárbara* by Mariano Azuela, José Eustasio Rivera, Ricardo Güiraldes, and Rómulo Gallegos respectively, what sets their authors apart as novelists is, paradoxically, their poetic sensibility. As poets they transmit, at times allegorically, the history of humanity, man's quarrel with himself. Within the framework of their national traditions and symbols, they treat of Everyman, his loneliness and despair, his deformation and dissimulation, using in their works the personal odyssey or journey to discover what they can about the mystery of life. Although they used a traditional form, essentially *criollista*, as we have stated, they reveal already the stirrings of a new novel, which decades later would refine their myths, superstitions, folklore, mystery, fantasy, and history in an attempt to resolve the conflicting and anguished concerns of man facing the unknown.

Mariano Azuela (1873–1952) in the period between 1908 and 1918, about twenty years before novels about the revolution and related topics were popular, wrote a series of such novels including his masterpiece, *Los de abajo*, which Torres-Rioseco called "poema épico en prosa de la revolución mexicana," [9] a view shared by Manuel Pedro González, Luis Leal, and Seymour Menton, who commented most perceptively about its epic structure.[10] In spite of the fact that Azuela's fiction has sociological and ethical bases, its poetic quality is its most distinguishing characteristic, and as Jefferson Rhea Spell says, "his technique or approach to novel writing is far closer to that of the poet than of the purely realistic or naturalistic novelist." [11]

Azuela's novels dealing with the revolution proper and the actual fighting, although most of his fiction reflects it, are *Andrés Pérez, Maderista* (1911), *Sin amor* (1912), *Los de abajo* (1916), *Los caciques* (1917), *Domitilo quiere ser diputado* (1918), *Las moscas* (1918), and *Las tribulaciones de una familia decente* (1919). At the same time, he has documented the entire history of twentieth-century Mexico in these and in earlier and later novels. Azuela is really the first twentieth-century Mexican novelist to worry about the dignity of the Mexican pueblo. This concern in turn was a generative force in the development of Mexican art—especially that of José Clemente Orozco—which in turn directly affected the novel of the revolution. Manuel Pedro González claims that Mexico has produced only two novelists of great originality, Fernández de Lizardi and Mariano Azuela. They are the two personalities who have had the greatest influence on the Mexican novel, and Azuela's name "surge siempre apareado con el de Gallegos, Rivera y Güiraldes como las cuatro más altas cimas de la novela hispanoamericana." [12]

Azuela was born in Lagos de Moreno in Jalisco. His father was a small landowner and storekeeper. Azuela studied medicine from 1892 to 1899 and, after obtaining his degree, served in a poor district, revealing early his humanitarian concerns. Luis Leal finds these medical studies and experiences to be of extreme importance in Azuela's literary creation.[13] Azuela returned to Lagos to marry his childhood sweetheart, Carmen Rivera, and they had ten children, five sons and five daughters. This may account for his novelistic stress on the good Mexican mother and the sound family man as the principal hope for his country. He was very briefly *jefe político* of Lagos in 1911 but resigned. He became a selfless adherent to the cause of Madero, whom he considered a redeemer of the poor and admired almost as a saint. When Madero was murdered in February of 1913, Azuela fought against Victoriano Huerta. During 1914 and early 1915 he was appointed director of Public Education in Jalisco when the Villa government was in power but had to flee when the government fell. Azuela served as a doctor with the forces of Julián Medina, a Villa supporter, and took part in a retreat through the hills of Jalisco, where he conceived his *Los de abajo*. Azuela later practiced medicine in Chihuahua and in October of 1915 fled to El Paso, Texas, where *Los de abajo* was first to appear. All these experiences are reflected in his works and helped condition him to what many feel is a basic pessimistic position.

Azuela believed firmly in the pueblo and thus felt deeply the betrayal of the generals whom he regarded as having frustrated the purposes of the true revolution. As a disillusioned idealist and utopian dreamer, he reiterated the negative aspects of Mexican life, the brutalities of the revolution, and the discrimination in city and country. His hatred of the political boss caused him at times to take extreme ideological positions, regarded by some as reactionary, but he was not a political activist. Along with thousands of others Azuela believed that there were two revolutions in Mexico, a permanent and ongoing one and another, that of the generals, against whom his bitterness is such that he becomes antirevolutionary although never anti-revolution. Azuela sadly comments on the thousands of opportunists who suddenly become revolutionaries after the battles have been won. Madero's government, outwardly strong and popular, was inwardly weak and unable to cope with the old ex-Porfirista opportunists accustomed to fraud and political chicanery. As Azuela says in *Cien años de novela mexicana,* "Los que tuvimos la dura experiencia de la última revolución sabemos de sobra que los que más aúllan su amor a las masas son los que espiritualmente están más alejados de ellas." [14] Azuela overreacted because of his former blind optimism in Madero's government and in the possibility of the triumph of justice over injustice, right over wrong, tolerance over intolerance, and sincerity over hypocrisy. But in spite of his disenchantment and pessimism, he always maintained a sincere desire for the betterment of his country and constantly affirmed a kind of moral integrity which will survive as long as Mexico endures. Most honest Mexicans would agree with González de Mendoza that Azuela "combatió generosa y gallardamente contra la maldad estulta y contra la injusticia," [15] even though at times it appears as though Azuela cannot see the forest for the trees.

Several Mexican esthetes who fashioned their works after the French symbolists and later along Proustian lines, feeling themselves to be the intellectual arbiters and defenders of culture, snubbed Azuela, and writers like Torres-Bodet considered him to be a kind of "curandero." Alfonso Reyes, however, recognizing Azuela's merit, proposed him for membership in the Colegio de México which Reyes had helped found. Manuel Pedro González points out the intellectual establishment's lack of acceptance of Azuela, in part because its members recognized themselves and their own shortcomings in his novels and thus tried to "frustrarlo, aniquilarlo, destruirlo, mediante la pertinaz conspiración de su silencio, silencio culpable que más parece estolidez y mimético snobismo que indiferencia despreocupada." [16]

Many of Azuela's novels resemble those of his favorite novelist, Emile Zola, at least in technique, and show people as victims of exterior forces, but his fiction is not precisely naturalistic. Azuela's son, Salvador, testifies to the profound influence of the Frenchman on his father but reiterates that in spite of Azuela's admiration for the man and the works, he avoided the doctrine of "experimental naturalism . . . scientific didacticism" and accepted rather the "lesson of vitality" of Emile Zola.[17] Paradoxically, although Azuela is more interested in environment than in character portrayal, he is excellent at dialogue but, in spite of his poetic gifts, not a master at description. It is true that very few of his characters are fully developed and many of them symbolize classes or attitudes, but he has also created some believable and even exceptional fictional persons.

María Luisa (1907), his earliest novel, which he first published as a short story in *Gil Blas Cómico* under the pseudonym of Beleño, was finished as early as 1896. A somewhat sentimental and naturalistic sketch based on a real incident, the appearance of the mistress of a friend on the dissecting table, *María Luisa* also includes discussions of alcoholism, prostitution, and tuberculosis as well as criticism of the corruption and intransigeance of provincial society. María Luisa, the idealistic if illegitimate daughter, yields to her lover. When he abandons her the inevitable result is her downfall and death. Azuela's medical studies served him well for his clinical descriptions of hospital patients in the novel.

Los fracasados (1908), which elicited almost no critical reaction at its publication, attacks ignorant officials, intriguing lawyers, and priests (Azuela was religious but anti-clerical). The protagonist, Luis Reséndez, an idealist, thinks that in rural Mexico one may live ethically but discovers that the city intrigues are the same everywhere. In spite of his disillusion Reséndez may reaffirm his lost idealism through the pursuit of a lost love and happiness with Consuelo, the daughter of a priest. Azuela laments the materialism of Mexico, the bourgeois drive for money, and the unholy alliance among corrupt politicians, clergy, and cruel landed proprietors against the interests of the poor and landless. Less melodramatic than his previous novel, in which Pancho pronounces María Luisa dead on the table without even recognizing her, *Los fracasados* is also more optimistic in the possibility of a better future. His first novel took place in Guadalajara. This one is set in Alamos, probably a fictionalized version of his own city of Lagos.

Mala yerba (1909) involves lust, superstition, folklore, jealousy, and a profound concern for the fate of the Mexican peasant. Marcela Fuentes, a sensual young lady, is the daughter of Pablo Fuentes, a servant in the house of the powerful but degenerate hacendado Don Julián Andrade. Gertrudis, the caretaker of Julián's race horses, also loves Marcela. Julián matches his position, power, and social prestige against the sensual attraction of the girl, and when he discovers that she loves Gertrudis, he has him killed. Marcela, the promiscuous girl, is a victim of the system as much as of her own psychological and moral shortcomings. She loves Gertrudis and eventually goes with him in spite of her tawdry relationship with don Julián. She is less to blame for events than is Andrade, the real *mala yerba* cluttering up the Mexican scene. Azuela attacks the hacendados, the local bosses, their inhuman treatment of the peons, and artistically shows his awareness of the tragic situation of the Mexican peasant. With *Mala yerba* "entra el agro mexicano y el feudalismo latifundista a formar parte de la temática novelística." [18] Translated into English as *Marcela, a Mexican Love Story*, it was hailed by the *New York Times* (25 September 1932, p. 7) as "a stirring tale, a breath from the heart of a people rotten at the top and storing in its Indian soul a slowly accumulating, fierce, passionate hatred on the eve of the revolution."

Andrés Pérez, Maderista (1911) is the first of his novels to deal directly and specifically with the Mexican Revolution. Andrés Pérez, a city newspaperman for *El Globo*, is trapped at a hacienda where he has been spending his vacation with his friend Antonio Reyes. Some ill-understood comments Pérez makes lead all to believe that he is a revolutionary who has come to the hacienda to hide from government persecution. More a don Juan than a revolutionary, he is carried off to the local jail. His friend, aided by his mayordomo, Vicente, organizes the peons and rescues Andrés. When an ex-colonel of the federales takes over the movement, Andrés remains to console his friend's beautiful widow. The novel shows Azuela's disillusionment at the mishandling of the principles of Madero's revolt, the potential salvation of Mexico. He attacks the press, the dictatorship of the military, and the confusion of the early movement. He comments on the poverty of the pueblo and satirizes the opportunists who, without dedication to any ideal, follow the naïve Madero for their selfish motives and manage to gain control from Madero's devoted followers who had sacrificed to bring the revolution about. The work, as John Englekirk admits, is poorly and hurriedly written, but he finds that, "ideologically, it is one of his most significant novels." [19]

Sin amor (1912), set in Azuela's home town of Lagos de Moreno, examines the great gulf between the haves and the have-nots, the evils of materialism, and the need for an ethical system and new moral values. Ana María Romero, young, sensitive, well-educated and yet not wise, marries the wealthy Ramón Torralba instead of the poor but honest Enrique Ponce. Ramón becomes a drunkard and Ana becomes as hypocritical and immoral as the family into which she had married. Enrique, the poor suitor, marries and leads a happy life. An old Mexican theme stemming from Fernández de Lizardi about poor education by parents is stressed to explain some of Ana's actions. The theme of the young and beautiful woman who rejects love for money and comes to a properly negative ending is overly arranged, but it helps show Azuela's belief that spiritual values outweigh materialistic ones and that love and marriage are prime ingredients for true happiness.

Azuela's masterpiece, *Los de abajo* (1916), did not achieve its great reputation until the fourth edition was published in 1925. When Azuela fled to El Paso in October 1915 he was completely without funds. He sold his manuscript to *El Paso del Norte*, a Spanish newspaper, which published his novel in installments in 1915. It appeared the following year in book form and again in limited editions in 1917 and 1920. Aside from intellectual opposition previously noted, political forces kept the author from being able to publish an authentic and large edition of his work. Yet by 1924 the situation had changed in Mexico. The poet Rafael López, in that year, called *Los de abajo* "the best work . . . of fiction published in Mexico in the last ten years." [20] In the same year José Corral Rigau, in *El Universal Ilustrado* of 20 November 1924, praised Azuela highly as part of a continuing debate which took place about the status of the Mexican novel. Julio Jiménez Rueda called for a virile literature. Others taking part in the debate were Federico Gamboa, José Vasconcelos, Salvador Novo, Víctor Salado Álvarez, and Francisco Monterde. Monterde, the first to acknowledge fully the merit of *Los de abajo*, supported the novel strongly against those who found it to be only a bibliographical curiosity. *El Universal* undertook to publish it, and it shortly became "the only novel of the Revolution." [21] Francisco Monterde, in the prologue to Azuela's *Obras completas*, sees *Los de abajo*, when it was finally rediscovered, as the catalytic agent for other novelists who shortly thereafter followed Azuela's trail blazing to create the "novela de la Revolución Mexicana."

The novel covers the period from the assassination of Madero to the defeat of Pancho Villa at Celaya. Demetrio Macías, a humble Indian from Zacatecas who has a wife and a child, is denounced by his enemy, the cacique of Moyahua, as being a Maderista. Abandoning his home, he is hunted by those who favor the hacendados, his dog is killed, and his hut is burned. Reacting to this injustice, Macías turns to the revolution in his private war against the federales and soon becomes the chief of a small band. He joins general Natera, becoming first a colonel and eventually a general. He returns briefly to his wife and son, and when she asks him why he is fighting, he cannot verbalize the answer. It is apparent that, like a stone rolling down hill, tugged by the force of gravity into an increasing momentum, Macías and his revolutionary band will continue to struggle. The men fight, love, and kill, but after Villa's defeat at Celaya, Demetrio and his men retreat. They are trapped and make a final stand in the same canyon where two years earlier they had won their first battle, as Demetrio awaits death, pointing his gun at the approaching enemy.

Azuela mentions social themes of earlier works, but there is, aside from the revolution itself, no center of gravity. The protagonists live intensely their individual moments, but they are not presented as complete men and are overshadowed by the primary protagonist, the revolution itself. The horrors of the fighting and the destructiveness of the revolution set off in turn the brutality of men and the triumph of the bestial over the spiritual, something burned so deeply into the mind and soul of Mexico that it has not yet freed itself fully from the effects. The rough revolutionaries burn, kill, and loot; yet they are human components of the conflagration. Azuela's portrait of humble Mexicans, with all their defective humanity exposed, is also universal.

The characters include Alberto Solís, who dies at the end of the first part of the novel, and Luis Cervantes, both deserters from the federales. Both are cynical about the revolution, but Solís, perhaps Azuela himself, believes that the revolution, beautiful in spite of its barbarity, in the end will substitute a new series of monsters for the ones being overthrown. Luis Cervantes, the complete opportunist who calls himself Demetrio's "correligionario," talks about the ideals of the revolution and the cause. He is optimistic where Solís is skeptical, perhaps because he never had the romantic dreams and illusions which Solís had maintained. The original members of the band included the skirt-chasing Güero Margarito, a man of savage and almost pathological cruelty who finds almost sensual pleasure in killing; Anastasio Montañés, who murders with less enthusiasm than his companions Pancracio and el Manteca, the former a beast who kills not only federales but a peasant brother and in the end fights to the death with Manteca; La Codorniz, thief and comic who joined the revolution for fun and loot; and Venancio, the barber, who has ambitions beyond his reach. With rare exceptions the participants are sadistic, blood-thirsty men who were able for a time to give free reign to their instincts. Valderrama, the mad poet (a fictional portrait of his friend José Becerra, a poet from Lagos), is an exception in his pure love for the revolution simply because it is a revolution, and only he deserves the full name of revolutionary.

The women of the novel include Remigia, Demetrio's resigned and brave wife; Camila, sweet and unpretentious, betrayed by Cervantes to Demetrio, for whom she comes to feel gratitude and even affection; and La Pintada, the fierce camp woman who kills Camila. Finally, Demetrio Macías, betrayed in his struggle against tyranny and for his family, also represents the Mexican pueblo, fighting for unknown and unconscious motivations. Macías has an inherent nobility which the openly lustful early companions and the later devious opportunists lack. He, nevertheless, changes also as success makes him forget, at least temporarily, the instinctive reasons for which he was fighting, reasons he understood with his marrow, blood, and bone. At novel's end he has once more become a part of the relentless forces moving him and the pueblo to their destiny.

Azuela documents in the book few of his own eyewitness accounts[22] of battles, victories, heroism, defeats, and the various idealistic, ambitious, disillusioned, and defeated men who fight for a cause or for themselves. The very fabric of revolution and revolutionaries is explored here in a simple, effortless, and popular language. Subtitled "Pictures of the revolution," the novel has a series of sober but effective descriptions of man and nature in a direct, dynamic, and unaffected prose which seems artistically perfect. Most of the novels of the Mexican Revolution portray a series of tableaux rather than exhibiting a tightly structured narrative, and *Los de abajo* is no exception as a series of *cuadros*, magnificent in themselves, "más que una novela urdida y estructurada . . ." [23] The episodes follow one another in chaotic fashion akin to the chaos and violence which sweeps man before it like a leaf in a strong wind. Though it is episodic, the novel, like the revolution, is circular, for Demetrio and his men will return to die on the same spot where they began their fight. Seymour Menton, in a convincing study, claims that by refusing to distinguish among the revolutionaries and nonrevolutionaries, identifying his characters with Indian ancestors, and by beginning in *medias res* to present the deeds of a legendary figure, Azuela was deliberately planning a work of epic structure to match the chaotic atmosphere of the revolution. He sees in *Los de abajo* a formal and mathematical structural arrangement, a topographic unity, and the use of Demetrio Macías as a unifying epic figure.[24] The novel is "well joined as a Greek ode. A story of indescribable confusion, it has the body of an inner order, an order not in the least intellectual or studied; an order that is organic." [25] Uslar Pietri, fully aware of its collective, telluric elements, its combination of direct and impressionistic narrative, considers it to be "la novela por excelencia de la revolución mexicana. Ninguna ha calado más hondo, ninguna ha dicho más con tan espontánea sencillez, ninguna la supera en equilibrio artístico y en verdad humana." [26]

Unfortunately, the lack of idealism in *Los de abajo* is augmented in following novels. Demetrio half glimpsed that he was being used by those cleverer than he and that the pueblo was the principal revolutionary victim. He was almost instinctively prepared to fight for human dignity, whatever his inarticulate status or temporary romantic aberration. The power structure, unimpressed by the primitive stoicism of men like him, blinded itself to satisfying the minimum desires of those underdogs, and the revolution did nothing to change the basic situation. *Los caciques* (1917), "novela de costumbres nacionales," is a novelette whose protagonist, Juan Viñas, saves his money for his wife and two children. Encouraged by the cacique to invest his money foolishly, he is forced to borrow and loses everything while the cacique's family, the Llanos, grow rich. Juanito and Esperanza, the children, when the revolutionaries come to town, burn down the cacique's house. This novel, which Azuela had written in 1914 and which he sold for fifty pesos,[27] shows how the ruling members of a town join the revolution, somewhat cynically, for material gain. It reveals Azuela's usual frustration and pessimistic evaluation of his country. Here the victims belong to the middle class of small merchants and shopkeepers, and Azuela concludes that idealism will lose out inevitably to the materialistic and hypocritical forces at work in Mexico. He laments the lack of morality and idealism, despairing of solving the problems of Mexico which the revolution so bravely set out to correct. In the process, however, in this novel and others, Azuela has dissected not only the revolution but also the very soul of the Mexican people.

Las moscas (1918) describes the defeat of Villa at Celaya by Carranza, analyzes the lives of some of those around Villa, and lyrically portrays the primitive glory of Villa and his tragic defeat. The novel is set on a military train bound for the north; Villa appears in the final scene at the rear door of the retreating train, which, symbolically framed against a magnificent sunset, shows the setting of his radiant power and the destruction of those who followed him. All the principal revolutionaries are here—the impulsive Villa, the stubborn organization man Carranza, and the proud and dishonest Obregón. Ostensibly the story of the Reyes Téllez family of Culiacán, the novel is even more a photographic human comedy of the *moscas*, the flies or hangers-on, interested in what they can get from any general, abandoning Villa when he can no longer help them. The opportunists switch loyalties as easily as they change hats. María Reyes Téllez and her children, a *familia decente*, are but a tiny segment of the lawyers, generals, and government employees who know when to change sides. Done in a terse dialogue of dramatic impact, the novel satirizes the bureaucrats and their intrigues and petty ambitions so cruelly that the author later regretted certain portions of his depiction.[28]

The first edition of *Las moscas* also contained a novelette, *Domitilo quiere ser diputado*, and a story, *De cómo al fin lloró Juan Pablo*. The novelette continues the theme of the success of ex-enemies of the revolution. Don Serapio, the local political boss, has survived government after government. As municipal treasurer he deceives the rich into paying a tax demanded by his good friend and companion, don Lolo, who changed his name to Xicotencatl Robespierre Cebollino to show his status in the world. The treasurer has a son, Domitilo, whom he wants to make a deputy. Again

Azuela satirizes the opportunists of Mexico, as Serapio's "vivir es adoptarse al medio" becomes the watchword of Mexicans everywhere. In the second story Juan Pablo cannot understand why nothing has changed now that the revolution has been won, for the pueblo is still enslaved, this time by new masters who are no more compassionate than the old.

Las tribulaciones de una familia decente (1918), one of Azuela's most successful novels, familiarizes us with the fortunes of the Vázquez Prado family, rich supporters of Victoriano Huerta who had fled to escape the approaching avenging forces of Carranza, Villa, and Obregón. The family, itself divided, must face the fall of a traditional way of life, and in the acceptance or rejection of new values, they reveal the ideologies involved. The young son César narrates the events of the first part, which includes his autobiography. He is a weakling and a coward who cannot understand events nor perceive their moral consequences. With his death, Azuela takes over as narrator. In the second part he shows the growing independence and manhood of Procopio, formerly dominated by his rich, spoiled, and selfish wife Agustinita. Aided and abetted by her corrupt son-in-law, Pascual, a man willing to sacrifice even his wife's virtue in order to rise in power, she sets no limits on her ambition. But Agustinita, her two lazy sons and her son-in-law represent but one side of the coin. Procopio's daughter, Lulú, helps him to reaffirm the value of honest labor. In the end Procopio has a heart attack and Pascual dies in a quarrel with some other Carrancistas. *Las tribulaciones de una familia decente* ended the cycle of novels about the Mexican Revolution. Aside from being a valuable social document, the work is also "an imaginative work of considerable power . . . in depicting the conflict between obtuse and materialistic persons who seek selfish advantage in troubled times and sensitive individuals who find the inner strength to face disaster courageously. Azuela's warmth of spirit, affection for the simple life, and moral fervor are essential ingredients of this work." [29]

Three of Azuela's following novels represent a radical departure in style, in part because of the influence of *estridentismo*, a movement fathered by Manuel Maples Arce around 1922. The novels also exhibit some of the tendencies of the vanguardists, such as Dadaism with its anti-logical experimentation, and exaggerate previous tendencies in his own work.³⁰ Azuela not only sets the stage for the novelists of the Mexican Revolution but, through his techniques, foreshadows the new Mexican novel. Regarding these three apparent attempts at "estridentismo" he states: "Considero la técnica de *La luciérnaga, La Malhora, y El desquite* como un truco de mucho efecto para ciertos lectores; pero prefiero decir las cosas con toda claridad que es más difícil que hacer trucos." ³¹ *La Malhora* (1923), based in part on his experiences of the previous two years as juryman and medical consultant, is considered by many critics to be his most artistic work. A kind of elaboration of his early novels *María Luisa* and *Mala yerba*, this one, in treating an abnormal heroine and certain aspects of the Mexican underworld, condemns the lack of concern of the courts and the materialism of doctors. La Malhora, a fifteen-year old girl abandoned by her lover, Marcelo, takes to all kinds of vice. Marcelo, now in love with La Tapatía, kills La Malhora's father and tries to kill her, too. La Malhora, only wounded and taken in by some religious ladies, temporarily becomes Altagracia but, driven by forces she cannot control, returns to a life of prostitution and sin. Azuela portrays the city dives, the "junkies," murderers, and prostitutes, miserable and unfortunate people with subhuman values. Once more his favorite thesis about woman crops up, that is, that she should be a noble and pure creature whose principal duty is to create love and a happy home, and that overwhelming physical passion can bring only tragedy. The emphasis on technique overshadows all else in the novel, "muy de acuerdo con la época de apresuramientos y de nerviosidad en que vivimos." ³²

El desquite (1925), about a woman who marries beneath her, repeats the same theme of *Sin amor*, that one may choose love or money but not both. Azuela also discourses on insanity and alcoholism. Lupe, on her mother's advice, marries Blas, a drunkard and sexual athlete. Ricardo, her husband's illegitimate brother, tries to damage her reputation so that he may inherit the money. Lupe refutes the false accusation, hastens her husband's death by encouraging his alcoholism, and is defended successfully by a former love, Martín. He marries her for her money, and she, now also an alcoholic, goes mad.

La luciérnaga (1932), set in the time of Calles, examines religious persecution and sees as the hope for new generations the idealism, devotion, heroism, and truly humble Christianity of Conchita, the loving wife. Serving as a "luciérnaga" to light the darkness, she may be a regenerative force. Dionisio leaves the province for the capital, and his brother José María remains behind. Dionisio loses everything to the thieves and opportunists of the city, but in spite of his progressive degeneration due to drugs and alcohol Conchita stands with him. She returns to the village of Cieneguilla to be with her children who need her, but when news comes that her husband is dying, she returns, against the opposition of her neighbors. José María, a thief, miser, and hypocrite, dies a miserable death also. Azuela depicts the despair of the lower classes during the religious persecution by Calles, when crime, opportunism, and injustice seemed to prevail everywhere. He exalts the primitive Christianity of Conchita, the noble wife and mother, as the only hope in an otherwise gloomy book. It is not clear, however, that the resigned and humble Conchita will be able to overcome the depravity of man.

In 1935 Azuela published two works which do not treat the contemporary scene, except by implication. *Pedro Moreno, el insurgente* is a "biografía novelada" of one of the lesser heroes of the wars of independence. The man from Jalisco, inspired by Rousseau, tells of his defense of El cerro del sombrero, his final betrayal, and the role of Javier de Mina. *Los precursores* traces the careers of three Jalisco bandits after the Mexican-U.S. War. His thesis is that the conditions of anarchy and indifference following the war that produced the bandits were identical to those following the revolution in 1910. Yet the bandits, such as Antonio Rojas, acknowledged criminals, have more right to consider themselves national heroes than the "criminals" of the twentieth century who hide their thievery beneath a respectable exterior while they pervert the very meaning of the revolution.

El camarada Pantoja (1937), one of Azuela's most directly didactic novels, is an almost vicious attack on Calles and Obregón, concerning itself with the *cristero* rebellion, Obregón's election campaign, and the vicious and stupid men who ran the government. Caterino Pantoja, influential in the workers' movement, is prodded by his wife to rise in station. By blindly following the orders of his superiors he becomes provisional governor of Zacatecas. One more revolutionary who has become rich at the expense of others, he does not blink at the exploitation, murder, and corruption of the regime against which Azuela stridently protests.

San Gabriel de Valdivias (1938) contains an attack on the abuse of authority during the Calles administration. The novel, a kind of modern *Fuenteovejuna*, tells of an unprincipled cacique who steals from the villagers, rapes their women, and is finally killed by the aroused people who flee to the hills. After the division of the land under the agrarian leader Saturnino Quintana, the village boss, conditions are worse than in the days of the Valdivias' rule. With the cristero revolt against Saturnino and his death, Gonzalo Pérez, a new leader, in turn makes new promises which he will not keep. Again Azuela shows his moral indignation, which to a greater or lesser degree marks all his later novels. The redistribution of lands solves nothing, for hacendados, agrarian reformers, and military men are all cut from the same immoral and oppressive cloth.

Regina Landa (1939), an attack on the Calles government for having misled the pueblo, is about the orphaned daughter of a general who never betrayed his trust. Disgusted with the dishonest and superficial life and a bureaucracy which stifles individual ambition and idealism, Regina resigns. Out of his bitterness and frustration at the destruction of what he thought were revolutionary goals, Azuela unjustly even attacks Lázaro Cárdenas, considered by almost everyone to be the very embodiment of the idealism of the revolution.

Avanzada (1940), set in the Cárdenas years, is again about a frustrated idealist, Adolfo, who returns to Mexico after five years in the United States. Realizing that his father, Miguel, is the victim of the traditional system of feudal bondage, Adolfo brings in modern machinery, cuts down trees, and plants new fields. His first crop is destroyed by hail, but he eventually succeeds. He defeats nature but cannot defeat the government which takes over his land. Working alongside the peons Adolfo tries to help the workers in their struggles against Communist and labor leaders but is considered a Fascist and a priest-lover and defeated in all his efforts. He and his childhood sweetheart, Margarita, leave for the coastal region of Veracruz, where, helped by an intelligent labor leader, Adolfo is for a time successful as a worker if not in his attempts at eradicating class hatred. Adolfo finally arouses the hatred of some labor men and is murdered, leaving his pregnant wife to face an uncertain Mexican future. Azuela laments that the labor unions have not improved the lot of the peasant who cannot profit from the land or understand modern technology. The novel is not so much a defense of the hacendados, as some have interpreted it, as an attack on corrupt union bosses who destroy the workers they ostensibly protect.

La nueva burguesía (1941) brings us up to the Ávila Camacho period. The suffering workers who have not benefited by political change, a fireman, a section boss, a shoemaker, and others of the working class, demonstrate that the best in man loses out to the worst (the sordid and the abnormal) humanity has to offer. When workers achieve economic well-being they have never had before, they become as materialistic and selfish as the society they have replaced. Other novels of the 1940s are La marchanta (1944), with its share of seduction and suicide, which addresses itself to the trials and tribulations of the small shopkeeper in a corrupt society; La mujer domada (1946), about a provincial girl, Serafina or Pinita, from Morelia, who seeks a literary career in Mexico City, meets some students, but, finally disillusioned, returns home, marries her childhood sweetheart, Federico, and becomes "la mujer domada"; and Sendas perdidas (1949), which returns to an earlier period of his production. Concerned with the degenerate poor of the cities and the power of sex, it was composed "con personajes y sucesos de hace más de cincuenta años cuando comenzaba a ejercer mi profesión." [33]

Azuela's fictional production is completed by two posthumously published novels, La maldición (1955) and Esa sangre (1956). The first novel is about a provincial family and its inability to adapt to Mexico City. The second novel merits special attention as a kind of continuation of Mala yerba, both as to plot and in its continuing denunciation of social defects which the revolution had not succeeded in correcting. It takes up the life of Julián Andrade after the murder of Marcela. The hacienda is now managed by Pomposo Fuentes, the former peon of the estate. Andrade, now a sick old man dreaming impossible dreams of a return to the good old days, recalls his experiences as a Villista and in Argentina where he was again involved in a murder. With the aid of his sister, Doña Refugio, he kills the local representative of the Department of Agriculture. Forgotten and ignored by everybody, Andrade achieves one last flicker of notoriety with his death and that of his sister in the drunken brawl—and with them disappear the final remnants of the old style hacendados.

In Azuela's earlier works he concentrates on social conditions and condemns the tyrannical oppression on "los de arriba." "Later, in the tragic brutality of the revolution itself, he boldly strikes at those responsible for plunging his country into a class war without any clearly defined program of social reforms; and more recently, he paints us a somber picture of post-revolution society, more corrupt and more degenerate than before, for the revolution has unleashed new forces of evil hitherto held in check through fear of a powerful centralized control." [34] In the final analysis Azuela blames all segments of society for the moral decay of Mexico. Opportunists, the city dwellers, peons, labor unions, small town politicians, caciques, city machines, and a hypocritical church share responsibility for the continuing degradation of poor folk and the injustices suffered by Indians, peasants, and the Mexican pueblo in general. Azuela could not easily accept the new status quo because new hope, having been aroused, is more bitterly abandoned. Azuela may have been overly idealistic in failing to realize the difficulty in changing men's hearts and minds. As a practicing physician he should have realized that humanity is guided by small motivations and not by large ones, but false labor leaders and self-seeking politicians, along with social and political parasites, blinded him to the positive virtues of his society.

It would be erroneous to overemphasize Azuela's pessimism. It is true, as we have seen, that he denounces the men who had betrayed the revolution through their insatiable and unforgiveable pursuit of materialistic benefits for themselves at the expense of the people from whose loins they had sprung, but he never condemned the revolution itself nor its goals. His satire and bitterness were reserved for those who had betrayed the cause. Not all of his portrayals are black, in any event, for many idealistic men and women, representing the best that Mexico has to offer, fight the good fight. Azuela apparently believes in redemption through suffering, the power of faith, and the rewards of a simple life. A frustrated idealist, he incarnates the ideas of Madero, who also dreamed of Utopia, impossible in the context of the brutal reality of human existence. Azuela brings many reasoned and intuitive insights to his works, at times sharply definitive and perceptive, at others expressing in his concern and conviction, a less than dispassionate instinctive judgment. He always moves the reader to empathy in spite of certain irrational accretions. He transmits his sense of truth and warm humanity, and if the reader on reading Azuela becomes despondent, he will certainly not be indifferent.

Aside from Azuela, probably the three major novelists of the Mexican Revolution are José Rubén Romero, Martín Luis Guzmán, and Gregorio López y Fuentes, although a dozen other novelists produced worthwhile novels. One may also include peripheral novelists like Bruno Traven and others like Miguel Lira and Francisco Rojas González, who serve as a bridge between the writers of the revolution and the early practitioners of the new novel like Agustín Yáñez and José Revueltas.

Martín Luis Guzmán (1887–   ), from Chihuahua, studied law but basically was a newspaperman and politician. A friend of Alfonso Reyes and other intellectuals, he belonged to the Ateneo de la Juventud along with Antonio Caso, José Vasconcelos, Pedro Henríquez Ureña, and Luis Urbina. Unlike Mariano Azuela or José Rubén Romero, he treats of the revolution from the point of view of "los de arriba." A Villista by persuasion, Guzmán was a delegate in 1911 to the national convention which supported Madero, and in 1913, after great difficulty and service with Obregón and Carranza, he joined the Villa forces as a soldier, something at which he was not adept. Apparently, Guzmán was not overly endowed with civic spirit either and almost never supported a losing candidate. For a time he was imprisoned by Carranza—whose portrayal in his works is understandably unflattering—and between 1915 and 1920 went into exile in Spain and in the United States. Having worked earlier on *El Imparcial* in Mexico (1908), Guzmán edited *El Gráfico* (1918) in New York. He returned to Mexico, became a deputy to Congress, worked on *El Heraldo de Méjico*, and founded *El Mundo* (1922), a Mexico City newspaper. Between 1924 and 1936 he also worked on other papers, including two important Madrid newspapers, *El Sol* and *La Voz*. Guzmán became a Spanish citizen in 1931 (under the republic he could have dual citizenship), and was an advisor to Manuel Azaña. He returned to Mexico, published *Romance* (1940–41), and became the editor of

Tiempo in 1942, thus reaffirming his close ties with the Partido Revolucionario Institucional. He was also an advisor to Camacho and wrote a number of his speeches.

Martín Luis Guzmán always had trouble identifying with the common people who made up the revolution and seems to show a decided lack of sympathy and understanding for the pueblo whose role in the revolution he almost ignores in favor of the heady politics of the leaders and generals. Perhaps for this reason, in spite of his involvement in the revolution, he seems less concerned about humanity than other writers of the time. His first works were not novels. *La querella de México* (1915), a collection of essays, explains the Mexican Revolution and Mexico's geographic reality and analyzes the Mexican spirit or lack of it. *A orillas del Hudson* (1920), a miscellany about his experiences in the United States, is dedicated to Vasconcelos. He mixes poetry and essays of various kinds on everything from politics and Wall Street through lawn tennis and Mexican literature.

When Guzmán was in Spain during his second stay, he wrote his memoirs of the revolution and sent them to Mexico City chapter by chapter. They were finally published in book form as *El águila y la serpiente* (1928), which by 1964 had gone through ten editions. The title refers to the Aztec legend concerning their gods' instructions that they were to settle on the spot where they found an eagle perched on a cactus plant, holding a serpent in its claws. They found their eagle in Tenochtitlán (cactus on a rock), and the legend became pictorially a part of the Mexican flag. The novel also symbolizes the chaos, the leadership, and the hypocrisy rampant in Mexico, for the eagle, in spite of U.S. sentimentality about it, is a bird of prey and the serpent is deceitful. This work is almost unclassifiable. Some consider it literary reporting, others a chronicle, and still others nonfiction memoirs.[35] More than a novel it is a collection of vignettes, with multiple protagonists, about the revolutionary experiences of the author and to an extent a retrospective self-justification of his own political position. It may also be considered an impersonal, impassive, and objective novel if one is kindly disposed toward Guzmán. He narrates episodes in which he took part and gives us instant and beautiful portraits of photographic intensity of revolutionary leaders but, as has been stated, shows a complete lack of understanding of the pueblo. Paradoxically, his dramatic dialogues, the exaggerations of his own contacts, and the anecdotes capture the essence of the men, the countryside, and the revolution and convey some of the heroic quality of the Mexican soul. Pancho Villa, Carranza, and Obregón live again. Even though Guzmán was a Villa supporter he does not hide that general's cruelty and immaturity. Probably the invention and the fictional elements, the intrigues, rivalries, and personalities of the time, combined with his own role, qualify this work as an autobiographical novel; yet at times Guzmán appears to be almost a society reporter giving us the activities of the local members of the Social Register instead of the uneasy military alliances of the day.

His next important novel, *La sombra del caudillo* (1929), was originally planned as part of a trilogy on various aspects of Mexican history, but the assassination of General Francisco Serrano changed his plans.[36] He reports the shady intrigues and corrupt politics, first involving Adolfo de la Huerta's uprising in 1923–24 and then the latter part of 1927 when Obregón and Calles were the men of the hour. The novel is a historical *roman à clef* about these two and their political machinations, which, according to the author, included murdering their opponents and rebel leaders like General Arnulfo Gómez and Francisco Serrano. As the author condemns the dictatorship, the cynicism, the bloody crimes and betrayals, he also presents us with the idealists of the revolution like Axkaná González, an honest man who stresses the qualities of social conscience the leaders do not have. This is the only imaginary character; all the others can be historically identified (critics differ as to the identities), and it may be argued that González (his Mayan first name and Spanish second mark him as the heir of the best in two civilizations) presents the novelist's idea of his own role. The final episode recalls the shooting of fourteen political prisoners, Serrano among them. Although some of the incidents are fictionalized and some are faithful reflections of historical events, the general tone conveys a thorough authenticity. Luis Leal identifies the Caudillo as Álvaro Obregón, Hilario Jiménez as Plutarco Elías Calles, Ignacio Aguirre as Adolfo de la Huerta (Aguirre appears to be Serrano to some degree), and Protasio Leyva as Arnulfo R. Gómez.[37] Calles' shadow, and that of Obregón, hover over everybody.

Ignacio Aguirre, young ex-general, decides to run for the presidency in opposition to the Caudillo's wishes. Too late the generous, brave but impulsive Aguirre learns the true nature of Mexican politics, as he and his men, with the exception of Axkaná, are assassinated, and Hilario Jiménez, the Caudillo's minister of the interior and handpicked candidate, fulfills his mission. *La sombra del caudillo* is one of the best political novels of Spanish America; moreover, says Manuel Pedro González, in fifty or one hundred years, when the actors of the revolution and their immediate descendants have disappeared, *El águila y la serpiente* along with Bernal Díaz' *Verdadera historia de la conquista de la Nueva España* will be the most interesting and valuable chronicles of two decisive moments in Mexican history.[38] Another well-known student of Mexican literature, José Luis Martínez, believes that both of Guzmán's novels are outstanding samples of their kind and that no other novel or revolutionary chronicle excels them in style or in "recursos narrativos, y pocas pueden ofrecer cuadros de tanta maestría y de tan poderoso dramatismo como los que figuran en ellas." [39]

Guzmán's other works include *Mina el mozo, héroe de Navarra* (1932), a biography or biographical novel of the Spanish hero who played an important role in the wars of Mexican independence. The novel traces Mina's life, education, activity against the French, his meeting with Fray Servando Teresa de Mier and Pedro Moreno, and his fight for the cause of freedom. Guzmán also planned a series of ten novels under the general heading of *Memorias de Pancho Villa*, of which five have been published and several announced as forthcoming. He obtained material for his work from the widow of Pancho Villa, Austreberta Rentería, and also from Nellie Campobello. Part chronicle and part historical novel, the work provides us with a vast and detailed historical panorama of the revolution, the cruel and bloody struggle of brutal men through whom, nevertheless, would come a new nation. It shows faith in the revolution if not in the Mexican people. Guzmán tries, with sporadic success, to reproduce the language and style of Pancho Villa, suppressing his own artistic personality, and pretending that Villa himself, a man of simple and primitive emotions, is the writer of the memoirs. In spite of Guzmán's lack of social idealism, he has conveyed the emotional drives of men in intimate and evocative pictures of the revolution. We see Villa as the outlaw in Durango, the rebel for Madero, his campaigns against Huerta, and a host of other related activities. Guzmán presents Villa as an instinctive and legendary force, perhaps the real Mexico, but one is inclined to doubt the protagonist's noble sentiment, moral force, and sense of social justice as much as one may suspect those of his creator.

Villa struggles against the forces of evil and achieves a poetic and almost mythic idealization in this strange series of volumes which combine elegant style with popular flavor. The first volume, *El hombre y sus armas* (1938), traces the life of Doroteo Arango (Pancho Villa), tells of his brothers and sisters, his outlawry, his generosity, his quarrels, his persecution by an uneven justice, his meeting with Madero, and his determination to help the Mexican poor and oppose unfeeling rascals like Pascual Orozco. The second volume, *Campos de batalla* (1939), shows the battle plans, the attack on Ciudad Juárez, Villa's honesty and charity, Carranza's intrigues, and the activities of a number of revolutionaries like Juan Medina and Natera. The author documents the defeat of Victoriano Huerta. As in his other volumes, Pancho Villa is almost a natural force, ignorant, brutal, egocentric, and yet tender. Villa, in spite of his bestiality, is a human figure, beset by lesser men, yapping hounds around a stag, and on occasion he exceeds human dimensions. *Panoramas políticos* (1939), the third volume, is about the American invasion of Veracruz, Villa's victory at Saltillo, his difficulties with the envious Carranza, the capture of Zacatecas, and his nobility in abandoning the fruits of victory to avoid a quarrel with Carranza. Martín Luis Guzmán appears here as Villa's secretary, but he again exaggerates his own role, as he was neither militarily nor spiritually an important factor in the revolution. In the fourth volume, *La causa del pobre* (1940), Huerta flees and Villa continues to dedicate himself to the cause of the poor. Obregón betrays Villa as the various factions at the convention of Aguascalientes contend for power among themselves. And so Guzmán continues what is in essence the history of the Mexican Revolution, through volume five, *Adversidades del bien* (1958). Guzmán has also published *Islas Marías* (1959), which he calls "guión para una película" and "novela y drama"; *Filadelfia, paraíso de conspiradores y otras historias noveladas* (1960), which includes material about his favorite hero, Javier Mina, more about Axkaná González, and the story of the struggles of Mexican rural teachers to aid the masses; and *Muertes históricas* (1958), biographies of Porfirio Díaz and Venustiano Carranza, among others. In his memoirs Guzmán clarifies, if nothing else, Villa's military genius. His sober almost classic narrative, while politically motivated and damaged by heavy reliance on anecdote, conveys the epic grandeur of what it means to be human.

José Rubén Romero (1890–1952), from Cotija de la Paz in Michoacán Province, which he describes so lovingly in all his novels, had something less than a bountiful youth, although his father was a politician and businessman. Perhaps this impelled Romero, later in life, to consider so highly life's physical pleasures. He spent some time in Spain and served in the diplomatic corps as ambassador to Cuba and Brazil and consul general of Mexico in Barcelona. For a time he was also a merchant and, in 1917, a representative from Michoacán to the Constitutional Convention. Romero took part in the revolution in other ways, too. He served as secretary to Dr. Silva, the governor of Michoacán, and when that worthy gentleman resigned, Romero accompanied him. Arrested and condemned to death, Romero was reprieved at the last moment.

In addition to his political, business, and revolutionary activities, Romero was also the editor of *El Universal* and wrote several volumes of verse. He is, nonetheless, primarily a narrative writer, mostly about his own life within the fictional framework of his novels. He writes poignantly about Mexico, finally free from centuries of conquest and colonization, and through his scenes of provincial and village life, defines the essence of Mexico in its strengths and weaknesses, joys and sorrows. Part of what he writes concerns happier days before the revolution changed everything, which prompted one reader to view him as an "emotional, egocentric raconteur . . . essentially a small town man of limited academic and literary culture . . . the reader finds no real analysis, no real criticism of the revolution's course and significance." [40] A fairer judgment seems to be that he does more than use the revolution as a source for anecdotal material about people he has known. In his reflection of the aspirations of his countrymen he makes clear the meaning of Madero's dream and becomes "el intérprete de la Revolución Mexicana." [41]

Romero cemented his reputation as a kind of professional comic at a Pan American conference in Havana by defining the Good Neighbor Policy as "Nosotros somos los buenos; Uds. los vecinos." This puckish sense of humor, combined with a picaresque cynicism, a sense of humanity, and tenderness and compassion for the poor, stands out in all of his novels. Romero likes to talk about himself a great deal. Through a discussion of his own quirks we learn much about his province, the revolution, and humanity in general. As with some of the criollistas in other countries, Romero, through his intensive concentration on provincial Mexico to the exclusion of cosmopolitan settings, has created human, understandable, and universal characters. His novels, although they are intensely Mexican in form and spirit, are also universal: "mérito de sus novelas . . . lo que en el campesino michoacano hay de esencial humano, de universal y permanente." [42] Romero has stated that his principal literary influence was the Portuguese novelist José María Eça de Queiroz; yet he offers a greater combination of folklore, poetry, customs, and, in general, a mixture of popular and cultured elements than the Iberian novelist.

Although he wrote a collection of short stories as early as 1915 (*Cuentos rurales*), Romero did not write his first novel until 1932. *Apuntes de un lugareño* is an autobiographical and probably quite authentic recall about historical personages he had known, his arrival at Mexico City, his newspaper, his travels, and especially a sentimental evocation of the house he lived in as a youth. Romero recalls his loving, tender father, his father's store, the family friends and the good and bad people in his village, priests and poets, criminals and madmen. The novel has a number of picaresque and grotesque scenes (a love scene on a tombstone recalls Valle-Inclán's predilections and his *esperpentos*). Romero chastises the human weaknesses he sees and presents to us, for the first time, his most famous creation, Pito Pérez, the town bum who was to appear also in *El pueblo inocente, La vida inútil de Pito Pérez, Anticipación a la muerte, Una vez fui rico,* and *Algunas cosillas de Pito Pérez que se me quedaron en el tintero*. Romero claims that when he was in Barcelona he wrote down his memories of poverty-

stricken days and trips with his father in Cotija de la Paz in order
to remember his home and not through a creative drive. By writing
his memoirs he achieved a kind of catharsis through a public self-
analysis, something he explains in *Rostros* (Mexico, 1946) and in
Hoy (11 Sept. 1948): "Al evocar estos años de mi vida, tan lejos de
mi pueblo, emocionábame profundamente, pero no me interesaba
describirlos . . ." "Mi ausencia de la patria se tradujo en un anhelo
insaciable de recordarla, y encontré la forma de dar cuerpo a mis
recuerdos, escribiendo y describiendo cuanto lleva de mí, relacionado con mi terruño, con mi provincia, con mi niñez pasada en
una casa solariega, con mi modesta juventud de romero trashu-
mante por villa y por campos de mi querido Michoacán." [43]

Desbandada (1934), which the author called a succession of
"cuadros," is a short continuation of the author's autobiography
and the story of the revolution in all its violence and suffering.
Desbandada takes place in Tacámbaro, a small town of shops,
houses, a casino called "La Fama"—where one talked of revolution
and politics—and replete with other tertulias. A group of revolutionaries arrive, but most of the people in town cannot believe that
the brutal revolutionaries really represent the revolution. Romero
cannot blame the revolution for its violence—which he views as a
passing phase—in spite of the illness of his mother, the imprisonment of his father, and the loss of the family fortune such as it
was. Inés Chávez García, a destructive sensualist and thief, rapes
all women in his path. A servant, Aurelia, dies in order to save
her own mistress. Romero hides to avoid the terror but is awed
by the chaos he sees around him when he comes out of hiding. In
a companion novel written that same year, *El pueblo inocente*,
Romero shows how the Mexican masses in the provinces cannot
understand or take advantage of the times and their concomitant
suffering as victims of continuing injustices. He shows us a gallery
of types, especially Vicente, the wise old peasant who encarnates the
best of the Mexican pueblo. Love, honor, trouble, tragedy, and
despair, combined with laughter, are the ingredients which
Romero ironically mixes with a lyrical freshness to convey his love
for the region and its people.

The first bitter note creeps into Romero's fiction in *Mi caballo,
mi perro y mi rifle* (1936). The protagonist, Julián Osorio, a weak
lad who suffers at the hands of the rich children at his school, mar-

ries an older woman whom he doesn't love, joins the revolution, and soon becomes disillusioned. When ill with fever, Osorio hears a conversation among his dog, his horse, and his rifle, symbolizing respectively the masses, the wealthy, and the evil in man's heart. He throws away his rifle, and it accidentally discharges and kills his dog, much as the evil of the revolution has helped destroy Mexico. After all the hero's suffering, including not being able to attend his mother's funeral, he finds that the system is the same and that only the chiefs are new. He feels that the revolution has defrauded those who placed their hopes in it. He has nonetheless changed through his contact with it, coming to understand a little better the vague aspirations and ideals of the pueblo. Told as a series of vignettes, the novel has its ugly moments. A man falls into a pile of excrement, a sexual excursion takes place, and an army lieutenant kills his young wife to keep her from revolutionary hands. Romero's pathological revolutionary "hero" is not likely to improve the revolution's image.

José Rubén Romero's acknowledged masterpiece, *La vida inútil de Pito Pérez* (1938), is partly based on a real person, Jesús Pérez Gaona from Michoacán, first a salesman and then a teller of tales who lived off charity and died in 1929.[44] The author states that in Michoacán and in Morelia one can still find traces of his triumphs and defeats and that "la tristeza de su vida es toda mía." [45] Pito Pérez, the third son of a large family, recalls that his saintly mother adopted an orphan with whom he had to compete, revealing these and other details to Romero. An adult dipsomaniacal vagabond, miserably dressed, and, as he himself admits, "a shadow that passed from jail to jail" and an "adventurer of the cup," Pito Pérez receives a bottle of *aguardiente* for each hour of conversation with Romero about his life. He recalls stealing from the collection box, his nickname because of his whistling, his adventures with the town druggist, a crook for whom he made snot pills and with whose wife he had an affair, his adventures with a priest, and his many love affairs. Pito stops coming to the meetings with Romero, who looks him up and finds him selling merchandise. Pito tells Romero further adventures and sadly comments on the lack of liberty and fraternity among human beings.

The author liked Pito Pérez above all his creations, finding comfort in him and identifying with him because he himself had a picaresque life as a kind of philosophical clown. Each time he felt unhappy or wounded in his self-esteem, he turned to Pito Pérez, "que no ha acabado de morir dentro de mi cerebro y lo aguzo para que no muerda a los merodeadores." [46] The series of amusing incidents in the novel do not hide the morbid background of a frustrated life. Pito finally gives up to laugh at himself and society. He is a cynical and occasionally bitter philosopher who sees the injustices commited by the rich, the lack of freedom, and the general disappearance of the world's humanitarian instincts. He cannot understand why life treats him so badly and cannot believe in a society which does not believe in him. Pito Pérez could do little of pragmatic value in Mexican life, but Romero implies that Pito may have been better than the society which rejected him. Pito is a complicated fellow: anarchistic, sensual, sentimental, sad, sincere, satirical, and anti-clerical but with a strong religious sense. He represents the oppressed Mexican people, victims of the government and of a church which preaches resignation. He is without ambition or realizable goals. Romero, through this miserable, hungry, and yet sympathetic hero, caught up by tragic events known to many Mexicans, implies that some day the Pito Pérezes of this world may come into their own as genuine revolutionary products, to the dismay and possible destruction of the smug middle class of priests, druggists, and doctors. From the anger of this humble class "surgirá un día el terremoto y entonces no quedará piedra sobre piedra."

Anticipación a la muerte (1939) resembles *La amortajada* (1938) by the Chilean novelist María Luisa Bombal. The protagonist dies and imagines events of his own burial, the funeral orations, his decaying body, and lingering spirit. As he reviews his life he realizes that if he had to do it over again he would change nothing. Through the comments of his friends and enemies Romero reconstructs the life of the revolution. Ernest R. Moore believes that this novel is Romero's most satirical and least regional and a "sincera confesión de opiniones expuesta con diversidad de tópicos, un intento de organizar una filosofía de la vida . . ." [47]

Romero wrote three novels in the 1940s. In *Una vez fui rico* (1942) he imagines he has received an unexpected inheritance. Quickly losing it, he returns once again to a simple life. Romero examines the hollow men of his society, the ministry, the gambling,

tells of a virgin's seduction, a preoccupation of Romero apparently, and portrays a grotesque scene in which the protagonist buys a
coffin for himself and then sells it. *Algunas cosillas de Pito Pérez
que se me quedaron en el tintero* (1945) obviously continues the
story of that individual. *Rosenda* (1946), possibly also autobiographical, contains Romero's one good feminine creation and is
somewhat unique in his production because of its lack of humor.
The heroine is a symbol of the Mexican soul much as the women in
Azuela's novels represent the spiritual power of country women,
their loyalty, their devotion, and their capacity to suffer. Rosenda,
the daughter of don Ruperto, is an ignorant girl of the pueblo who
is seduced and soon abandoned. Meanwhile her lover has helped
her to learn how to read, and she also learns how to write so that she
may correspond with him. The revolution breaks out, but her
lover never returns. She waits and waits and finally reads his death
notice. *Rosenda* may be Romero's best novel. It is tender, melancholy, and expresses "el amor que sintió por su tierra con el
amor de la mujer y su piadosa ternura por el pueblo." [48]

Francisco L. Urquizo (1891–   ) was a military man who
served with both Madero and Carranza and left his somewhat
shaded but realistic historical account of those tragic and pathetic
days in *Tropa vieja* (1943), a personal reminiscence about the
changes in a soldier's heart. The protagonist abandons the Díaz
regime for the revolution, gradually learns human values implicit
in war, and shows how the soldier, too, must make certain com-
promises for his conscience and his country. Antonio Castro Leal
states that "entre las novelas de la Revolución Mexicana *Tropa
vieja* ocupa un lugar excepcional porque presenta el cuadro de
los acontecimientos desde el campo de las fuerzas federales." [49] In
1967 he wrote *Fui soldado de levita de esos de caballería.*

Teodoro Torres (1891–1944), a journalist, anti-revolutionary,
conservative Catholic, wrote novels and historical works such as
Pancho Villa, una vida de romance y de tragedia (1924). He is
primarily famous for one poignant novel, the unusual *La patria
perdida* (1935). Luis Alfaro emigrates to the United States and
there meets various Mexicans who have forgotten their country
and others who, having too much invested, cannot return to
Mexico. He returns to buy a hacienda but, discovering that the old
order is gone and that he is a stranger in his own land, returns to

the United States. The novel has dramatic and lyric force and an unusual view of how the famous 1929 depression affected not only the United States but his own country. *Golondrina* (1944) shows the population loss in small villages because of the revolution and presents authentic Mexican types. Carlos González Peña, who found his 1935 novel to be vigorous, brilliant, colorful, lyrical, and human, states somewhat surprisingly and perhaps chauvinistically that it would have been "insuperada—y acaso insuperable . . . a no ser porque Torres, en plenitud y lozanía, arrebatado por la muerte, no hubiera compuesto . . . algo todavía más grande y mejor; lo que constituye su obra maestra: *Golondrina* . . ." [50]

José Mancisidor (1894–1956), from Veracruz, fought under Carranza. The best Marxist interpreter of the revolution, in spite of his often tiring denunciation of American imperialism, Mancisidor has unusual lyric force and a sincere love for Mexico and its humble citizens. His first novel, *La asonada* (1931), a Marxist view of the revolution and a propagandistic attack on imperialism and religious bigotry, forcefully expresses his fears that the revolution and the pueblo will be betrayed by its leaders. In his prologue he insists that he wants only to tell the truth, which explains why the actors of his novel lack goals, ambition, or ideals and are devoured by the very revolution they unleashed but could not understand. He is especially forceful in his condemnation of the generals who have betrayed the Mexican people for their own selfish advancement. *La ciudad roja* (1932) is a didactic proletarian novel. He published a third novel, *De una madre española* (1938), which deals with Spain, the evils of the Franco forces, and the ensuing fratricidal frenzy. *En la rosa de los vientos* (1941) is an autobiographical novel about the period between the time of Porfirio Díaz and Madero, the North American invasion of Veracruz, and a workers' strike for justice. Mancisidor tells of joining the insurgents and of his service under Captain Canteado and examines the student life, the battles, the killing, especially of a group of sleeping soldiers, and the guilt feelings which even a righteous cause cannot assuage. In 1944 he wrote a biographical novel about another war, *Miguel Hidalgo, constructor de una patria* (Hidalgo interested him so much that he wrote a biography of him in 1956). In 1953 Mancisidor published *Frontera junto al mar* and in 1956 *El alba en las simas*. The first is an epic story, replete with flashbacks, about the fight against Huerta and the struggle of Veracruz against the invasion of the United States Marines in 1914, symbolized in the strange figure of the romantic anarchist, Chespiar. The second novel, a moralizing and yet optimistic one, is about love, tragedy, and oil expropriation in his native province and an attempt to document the efforts of foreign capitalists to overthrow Cárdenas. Mancisidor wrote several other novels on similar themes. His final work, a kind of condensation of scenes already found in previous novels, gives us the memories of his early years and adolescence. The lady of the title, *Se llamaba Catalina* (1958), is his own mother. He reveals details about other members of his family, his college friends, and his sexual encounters. As for the revolution, again we see the exit of Porfirio Díaz, the North American invasion of Veracruz, and the struggle against Victoriano Huerta. But we know full well that a number of students continued to condone the cynical and the corrupt.

Gregorio López y Fuentes (1897–1967) was the son of a farmer and small store owner whose shop was frequented by Indians and muleteers. It is scenes from this country life that he later recalls in his novels. López y Fuentes was the director of *El Universal* from 1937 on. His early attempts at writing, such as the modernist poetry *La siringa de cristal* (1914), a second book of poetry, *Claros de selva* (1922), and two novels, *El vagabundo* (1922) and *El alma del poblacho* (1924), were amateurish efforts. It was only when he began to deal directly with the revolution in his fiction, something he knew first hand as a student fighter in Veracruz against the United States invasion and as a soldier under Carranza, that he obtained success. López y Fuentes concentrates on the lives of humble rural folk, their problems with the land, with the Church, and with the system. His style is often an infelicitous mixture, and his language and characterization are at times unauthentic; yet for at least one well-known critic he "corona y cierra el ciclo revolucionario." [51] More than most of his fellow writers he reflects allegorically and in a formalized manner the ideological and human commitments of Mexicans in the twentieth century.

López y Fuentes' first success, *Campamento* (1931), is a series of tableaux which takes place from one evening until the following morning in an encampment of a revolutionary column. Through this tiny view of a small section of the fighting the author manages to show us the entire revolution with its heroism, cowardice, idealism, and greed. The scenes are based on his own experience, and he often inserts verbatim conversations he overheard, tempered by the tricks of memory and the passing years. The characters, of symbolic rather than human force, show us the reactions of the ordinary soldier, the suffering of the peasants, and the price which war exacts in human misery. While rapacious opportunists steal the land, the Indian and other elements of the Mexican population sacrifice their lives for an unworthy government.

Tierra (1932), subtitled the "agrarian revolution in Mexico," is again a series of composites of various groups in the period from 1910 to 1920. We see hacienda life, the exploited peons, many robbed of their communal lands, brutal overseers, and an evil priest. The central theme is the Zapata rebellion, the hero's death and his mythification into legend. Emiliano Zapata, uneducated, primitive, ignorant, and impulsive, loves the land, inspiring the underprivileged masses with his cry of "land and liberty." Don Bernardo González, the hacendado, symbolizes all the ills of Mexico and shows the need for reform and revolution. But even the revolution will not help the peasant who will simply work for the opportunists, new masters who have managed to be on the winning side. Don Bernardo sends Antonio Hernández, a young worker, to be an army recruit. Returning, Antonio tells his fellow peons about Madero and joins Emiliano Zapata. Reactionary supporters of Porfirio Díaz, however, still manage to maintain power by adapting themselves to the new situation. Antonio dies, as does Zapata, a legend in his own time. López y Fuentes uses various dates as chapter headings, and his episodic pattern effectively reveals various facets of the struggle, even though his optimistic hope at the end of the novel cannot stem from any of the negative events he has portrayed.

Mi general (1934) exposes the ex-generals of the revolution, their reminiscences, their mediocrity, and their immorality. Many, of humble origins, had no talent for administration but obtained the standard reward of their kind (mistress and house supplied) as deputies of the official party. Dreaming idle dreams and overcome by delusions of grandeur, this particular protagonist confronts his own government; but he cannot survive in the power struggles and, losing his sinecure, is forced to return to the point of his origin.

The novel has its humorous moments, but López y Fuentes conveys his sadness at the betrayal, by a group of ruffians, of everything the revolution preached.

El indio (1935) is probably the work which has won the most positive critical acclaim for López y Fuentes. A kind of allegory of Mexico before and after the revolution, it shows three white men who, searching for gold, reach the remote and nameless mountains to which the proud but fearful Indians have fled seeking to avoid a direct and fatal confrontation with a new civilization. A white man rapes an Indian girl (López y Fuentes calls this chapter "Mestizaje") and tricks an Indian into guiding them on their search for treasure. The representative of a once proud Aztec nation, now degenerated through the contamination of the white world, is eventually crippled by the white man. When he tries to combat the "gente de razón," the law supports the whites. The secretary to the city government finds Indians insubordinate, lazy, and drunken thieves. The mayor sees them as slaves of the superior white man. The professor insists on *mestizaje* and education and on the benefits of roads and schools, projects to which the Indians are forced to pledge two days a week. The priest also demands that they build churches, thundering that an epidemic which half destroyed them was God's punishment for their lack of religious faith. So, stoically, the Indians contribute two days to the church, without pay. The highway they build is to help whites, and the Indian lands, high in the mountains, are almost untillable without tools or irrigation. The Indian youth, crippled, filled with hatred and bitterness and completely without faith, looks at the highway, the new civilized world, while his brothers, without time or energy to work their lands, lead a life of semistarvation, unable to benefit from the road, the school, or their land. López y Fuentes paints the psychology, traditions, and customs of the Indian. He also portrays other racial groups in Mexico who would respectively eliminate the Indian, keep him as slave labor, or grant him his full dignity as a fellow human being. The courage and dignity of the Indian will not suffice in Mexico to redeem him from bondage unless the white man is prepared to give him a full and equal share in his society.

Two of López y Fuentes' weakest novels, *Arrieros* (1937) and *Huasteca* (1939), rounded out his production of the thirties.

Arrieros, a first person account of a trip made by the protagonist, El Refranero, and the author as a young man, intersperses folk-loric material and a host of proverbs into the anecdotal and auto-biographical account of López y Fuentes' experience (everything from dancing to hanging) among farmers and workers. *Huasteca* documents the rise and fall of a rural family which had made some money from Veracruz oil discovered on their property. As Mexi-cans abandon agriculture for oil, the corrupt local authorities sell the country's mineral rights to foreign capitalists to the detriment of traditional Mexican values. In what is his most didactic and al-most propagandistic novel, the author reveals the incredible con-ditions under which oil workers perform their tasks, as he rails against the revolutionary leaders who made false promises which they had no intention of keeping.

Acomodaticio (1943) is a political satire on the corruption of the value system of the Mexican middle class which chooses ma-terialism over idealism. Compliant opportunists are not the only ones to blame for the situation, since the sacrifice of principles for gain, far from being something limited to generals, seems to be a human failing of the Mexican people themselves.

Los peregrinos inmóviles (1944), probably with *El indio,* López y Fuentes' best novel, resembles *Altiplano* by the Bolivian Botelho Gosálvez and *El mundo es ancho y ajeno* by the Peruvian Ciro Alegría. An Indian village, supposedly freed by the revolution, undertakes a pilgrimage to find their own glorious past, guided by their mythical longings. When the revolutionaries free them from serfdom, they are afraid to take over the land and set out on a search along the river, a kind of supernatural guide, to find their destiny. Treated like breeding animals, suffering fear, hunger, envy, hate, division, and death, wherever the Indians go they find that nothing has really changed. Marcos, the narrator, whose father started the initial exodus, sees most of his family destroyed. When fighting begins anew, it becomes obvious that the seven indigenous tribes have not solved their economic and social prob-lems, that they have never really gone anywhere, and thus have been just immobile pilgrims. López y Fuentes offers us here his most beautifully perceptive insights into the Indian, who, for the Mexican, maintains his natural and primitive values and must be the one to provide final meaning to Mexico's evolution.

López y Fuentes' final two novels, *Entresuelo* (1948) and *Milpa, potrero y monte* (1951), study the problems of Mexican families in city and country. In the first, a middle-class family lives in a Mexico City apartment between a rich family above and an extremely poor one below. Caught, as is Mexico, between these forces, the family is doomed to failure and disintegration because it has lost faith in former eternal verities it held sacred when its members lived in the country. Doña Felicitas, deserted by an indifferent son and her daughter married to a millionaire, suffers the snubs of the heirs of modern wealth. In the second novel the author makes clear in a prologue that he is not writing about one specific rural family but about "aquellas familias campesinas de México que, por la falta de garantías en algunas regiones, se refugian en las ciudades o van a desmexicanarse en las caravanas de braceros." López y Fuentes overwhelms us with the problems of the rural worker in the *milpa*, the cowboy (*potrero*) and the hunter (*montero*) in a rural society ruined by political leaders who covet what that society has gained by honest toil and against whose legal maneuvering the rural inhabitant has no chance. Don Homobono, the symbolic good farmer in the Zapata mold, dies, and the novel is largely the story of what happens to his three sons. Odilón, the oldest, works the land and sees his daughter kidnapped by a bandit gang—one supported by the city government, which uses the leader, Febronio Silva, for its own purposes. Silva steals the cattle of Oliverio, the second son. Oliverio's son, Donato, kills the bandit and is himself later killed. Honorato, Homobono's third son, loses his dog to Silva's friends. After frost, drought, and flood all three sons eventually abandon their land.

Rafael F. Muñoz (1899–   ), another newspaperman, joined the forces of Pancho Villa as a boy of fifteen. In 1916, having supported Obregón against Carranza, Muñoz had to leave Mexico for the United States for four years; with Carranza's fall from power, however, he returned to Mexico and later became Obregón's secretary. Fascinated by history and an ardent supporter of the revolution, Muñoz wrote a biography of Santa Anna and also one about his favorite historical character, Pancho Villa. Even though he admired the latter greatly, he tried to be objective about Villa's place in Mexican history. Primarily a short story writer, Muñoz has among his collections *El feroz cabecilla* (1928), whose sardonic title story is a well-known treatment of the wild exaggerations possible in wartime, *El hombre malo y otros relatos* (1930), *Si me han de matar mañana* (1934), and *Fuego en el norte* (1960).

Muñoz has produced two novels about the revolution, *Vámonos con Pancho Villa* (1931) and *Se llevaron el cañón para Bachimba* (1941). The earlier novel is almost a string of stories strung together. The protagonist, Tiburcio Maya, represents the conscience of the revolution and perhaps Mexico itself. The other five life situations of characters, like Máximo Pérez and Miguel Ángel del Toro, also serve to reveal the great power that Pancho Villa had over men and their willingness to sacrifice what most men hold dear, including even their wives and children, in order to serve with him. Included in the novel is a description of the attack on Columbus, New Mexico, the Pershing chase, the fight for Torreón and Chihuahua, and themes of justice, vengeance, and anti-Americanism. It is hard to separate fact from fiction, history from invention in this novel, for Muñoz fuses them together in a seamless narrative which contrasts sharply with the disjointed and episodic structure. Muñoz recognizes Villa's faults, but he views him as Mexico's liberating force. *Se llevaron el cañón para Bachimba* is set in the time of Madero. Antonio Abasolo, a boy of thirteen, joins the "colorados" of Pascual Orozco to fight against Madero's government. He maintains a great personal devotion to Marcos Ruiz, a general under Orozco. The boy finally returns home, changed and matured into a Mexican man. The novel has much action, some lyric force, and a variety of judgments on the revolution itself as well as on the moral implications of being a revolutionary and a man.

Xavier Icaza (1902–   ) wrote short novels or novelettes, one of which, *Panchito Chapapote*, is one of the better-known fictional works of its time. Not so well-known are *Dilema* (1921), a psychological study of the sexual and marital choice a young girl must make, and *Gente mexicana* (1924), three novelettes. *Panchito Chapapote* (1928), by far his best novel, is a semi-humorous evocation of the Mexican Revolution, an attack on Yankee imperialism and capitalistic intervention into Mexican affairs, and an analysis of the effects of a new technology on the human spirit. Panchito, a Negro, relates to a prostitute the story of his life, the discovery of oil on his land, the defeat of the Veracruz rebellion, and his loveless marriage. In what may be called a "crónica revolucionaria," the author uses a somewhat surrealistic or even at times esperpentic technique to show us Veracruz, its poetry and songs, its men and women, and its mountains and rivers.

Jorge Ferretis (1902–1962), a newspaperman and politician, points out in the introduction to *El sur quema* (1937) that he wrote didactically because he believed that fiction should serve a cause. His thesis novels and stories show his disillusion and frustration at the betrayal of the revolutionary ideals which so many died for, but his feelings are so strong that they get in the way of his art. His titles include: *Tierra caliente* (1935), about Villa's troops; three short novels or novelettes, *El sur quema* (1937), *Cuando engorda el Quijote* (1937), and *San automóvil* (1938); and two volumes of stories, *Hombres en tempestad* (1941) and *El coronel que asesinó un palomo* (1952). *El sur quema*, the lead story or novel of the three contained in the volume, is about a family who rents a room to a mestiza, the secretary of a government official. The family, eager to ascend in the world, attempts to please her, and she in turn influences one of the family boys, Humberto. In love, they go to live with her Indian mother when the minister, her father, falls from power. In *San automóvil* the spoiled rich son of a family with the only automobile in town kills an Indian. Concerned temporarily, the son recovers his aplomb and returns to his old ways and denigrating opinions about the Indian. *Cuando engorda el Quijote* is about the revolution and a worker's strike. Ángel Mallén kills a Carrancista to avenge his sister's rape and flees to the United States. He finally returns to become a labor leader. Ferretis writes satirical and at times humorous attacks on the failures of the revolution, which, he says, was "fermentada con analfabetos . . . y usufructuada por ladrones." Ferretis feels great compassion for the pueblo and the exploited classes, and much of his disillusion with the revolution stems from the poverty and misery he sees about him. The new caudillos betrayed their trust and the Mexican people, something which Ferretis could not readily forget or forgive.

Mauricio Magdaleno (1906–   ) founded a social theatrical group in Mexico and wrote dramas, scenarios, and novels. He was greatly influenced by José Vasconcelos, whom he supported against Pascual Ortiz Rubio. As did his mentor, Magdaleno also suffered a political swing to the right, in his case after a decided fling with Marxism. In his novels Magdaleno resembles Azuela superficially, and he intimates that the years of sacrifice were in vain because the revolution was never fully implemented. Among his many novels one should mention *Campo Celis* (1935), a biographical novel about Bernardo Celis, who loves the land but whose drive and ambition to become a hacendado blind him to the destruction he causes and to the victimized peasants of his society. An equally pessimistic view is that of *Concha Bretón* (1936), about an ugly woman's passionate search for love and motherhood. Although Concha herself eventually finds happiness through her son and her reconstructed lover, the lot of the Mexican middle class is an unhappy one in a cruel and dark country. *Sonata* (1941) is a panoramic view of Mexico City seen through the eyes of a student protagonist who comments on the political and intellectual chaos of the years between 1920 and 1930. *La tierra grande* (1949) takes a backward look at the revolution through a family in Tlaxcala whose lives he traces through several generations, from the great landowner fights over land and water rights to the peasant revolt and agrarian reform. The author optimistically dreams of a new Mexico in which the Indian will share in the proceeds of his land, a country in which, hate evaporated, "la tierra grande" will belong to all. *Cabello de elote* (1949) shows us a Mexican village during the Second World War and comments on the conflict between old and new ideas, the impact of foreign immigrants on Mexican life, and the attempts of a mestiza to become an accepted member of society. Magdaleno proves that he knows the capital as well as the provinces in his collection of short stories *El ardiente verano* (1954).

Magdaleno's acknowledged masterpiece, *El resplandor* (1937), talks about the isolation of the Indian in his own country and the barriers which exist between him and the white man. The Otomí Indians live resigned, hungry, miserable, and superstitious on an unproductive land. The Indians from the village of San Andrés de la Calare, the rivals of those of San Felipe, must, too, contend with the church, the police chief, and the rich landowner of the hacienda "La Brisa," whose lands once belonged to them and whose productivity they envy. To defend themselves they feel that they must learn the white man's ways. Saturnino Herrera, a mestizo brought up in San Andrés but educated elsewhere, returns as a candidate for the governorship of Hidalgo and then forgets his promises to the Indians. Abandoned to the power structure by their supposed saviour, one of their community who managed to "pass," the Indians lose all hope for the future. Aware of the cruel reality and lack of hope, "se hizo un resplandor en las conciencias inocentes y su fuego les quemaba como una hoguera." When an honest reformer attempts to help them, he finds only hopelessness and hatred for the whites. One of their oppressors wrongfully holds back grain from the starving villagers, and when they attack one of the granaries, their homes are burned, their wives and children are murdered, and more than a dozen of their leaders are hanged. Under a new Indian governor they helped to elect they are still victims of a power structure as wicked as previous ones. Only the label has changed, but "Villa Herrera," the new name of "La Brisa," is still beyond their reach, and no one recalls the "godforsaken wreck of a place called San Andrés de la Cal." The new teacher tries to strike a spark of hope, but when a new scholarship is offered, this time to the grandson of Herrera's village protector, the Indians protest vehemently, for they know that if he goes, his soul, too, will change.

Nellie Campobello (1909–1968) wrote two novels, *Cartucho* (1931) and *Las manos de mamá* (1937), both scenes of the revolution as seen through the eyes of a girl. *Cartucho*, filled with a kind of twisted and distorted imagery, contains thirty-three episodes which are impressionistic evocations of the violence and death the author saw as a child—the Carranza battles with Villa and the destruction of Mexican by Mexican. As though all emotion had been frozen by the horror of what she saw, the author relates events with an impassive objectivity which borders on cold indifference, which prompted one critic to see the novel as sadistic and "el libro más terriblemente cruel que sobre la revolución he leído . . . " [52] A book of cruel innocence, indeed, this novel is yet "una de las novelas más finas y poéticas sobre la revolución mexicana." [53] The author herself states that "las narraciones de *Cartucho*, debo aclararlo de una vez para siempre, son verdad histórica, son hechos trágicos vistos por mis ojos y de niña . . ." [54] Her second novel is also a kind of biography filled with fragmentary remembrances of mother, grandfather, the Mexican Revolution, and its effect on the little town of Jiménez.

Several novelists wrote about the cristero revolts. Plutarco Calles, on 2 July 1926, decided to enforce rigorously the separation of Church and State called for by the constitution of 1917. The clergy rebelled and Calles had the churches closed. The bishop of Mexico forbade any services as long as the law was in effect, and Catholics attempted an economic boycott. A league in defense of religious liberty was formed, a strange name in view of their exclusive Catholic position, and by the end of 1926, under the cry of "Viva Cristo Rey," several Catholic groups took up arms against the government. In January 1927 they united under René Capistrán Garza and his so-called Ejército Libertador. This posed moral and theological problems for priests, worried about the right to bear arms against a government of which they disapproved, the limits of sin, and other such matters; but these niceties were not for the majority, and a barbarous civil war developed with unbelievable cruelties on both sides.

The first cristero rebellion (1926–1929) equated hatred of the Mexican Revolution with constructive Catholicism. In 1934 the second cristero rebellion began. Although it was summarily suppressed, intransigent clergymen contrived to continue the war of attrition against the government, even though the latter had moderated its anticlerical pose. By 1938 the moderate members of the Catholic clergy and most Mexican Catholics accepted the goals of the revolution such as agrarian reform, but a few die-hard cristeros continued sporadically to resort to force.

One of the more interesting aspects of the struggle is the continuing interest in the theme in the 1960s, as exemplified by Antonio Estrada's novel, *Rescoldo* (1961) and Tomás Mojarro's *Bramadero* (1963). The earliest novel on the subject was written by a priest whose real name was David G. Ramírez (1889–1950) but who wrote under the pseudonym of Jorge Gram. In *Héctor* (1930) two priests discuss the cristero revolt, one finding it sinful for a Catholic, the other justifying that rebellion as a right and a duty. The author's conclusion is not only that absolution should be given for the fighting but that any Catholic not fighting against Calles was by definition a sinner. *Jahel* (1935) is another defense of the cristeros. Ramírez' final novel, *La guerra sintética* (1937), concerns politics and religion in 1935 as he attacks both Calles and Cárdenas and their attempts to impose what he calls a "socialistic system of education."

Another defense of the conservative view is provided by Fernando Robles (1897–   ) in *La virgen de los cristeros* (1933), originally called *Adiós, México,* an ardent attack on Calles and a defense of orthodoxy and the cristeros. The author dedicates his novel "A la memoria de mi padre asesinado por los villistas," a dedication not calculated to impress one with his objectivity, and to his mother and the rancheros of the Bajío. The hacendado he portrays is quite unusual. Pedro treats his peasants well, but agrarian reform threatens all his property. He wants to help the Catholic cause with men and money. The girl he wants to marry, a school teacher named Carmen, agrees with him, but his son, Carlos, advises him against such a move. Even though he cannot believe in the cause Carlos decides to fight for the Catholics, but he finally leaves the country. Robles later wrote *El santo que asesinó* (1936), a novelized biography of José de León Toral, Obregón's assassin; *Cuando el águila perdió sus alas* (1951), the story of the United States invasion of Mexico in 1847; and *La estrella que no quiso vivir* (1957), about a girl from the provinces who becomes a film star and sacrifices herself for her country by joining a revolutionary group. The group is defeated, and she commits suicide to preserve her virginity from the evil dictator (Calles) and persecutor of Catholics.

The opposite point of view and a condemnation of the power of tradition which not even a revolution could fully change is taken by José Guadalupe de Anda (1880–1950) in two of his novels dealing with the cristeros. *Los cristeros: La guerra santa en los Altos* (1937) tries to be objective, but the enormous cruelty, barbarity, and bloody and even depraved behavior of the priests and their followers clearly emerges. The priests steal, torture, murder, and betray their own supporters, all in the name of Christ. In the story of a rural family torn apart by the controversy, the only truly human figure is Felipe, the ex-seminary student, adrift in a world whose fanaticism has changed men into beasts, who condemns the excesses of the false defenders of Christ. Policarpo, cruel but a fanatic believer in Catholicism, is himself killed by

Vega, an uncouth, greedy, and unscrupulous priest. *Los bragados* (1942), a kind of sequel to the first novel, has some of the same characters, but now the cristeros have become out-and-out bandits who burn a government school, rape, rob, mutilate, and kill, even after the Catholic church has agreed to a peace. Juan Pistolas reflects the religious fervor of Policarpo in *Los cristeros*, but the other characters, El Pinacate and El Ruñido, are in the battle for personal gain. The aftereffects of the original movement linger on, and the heritage of hate is channeled toward attacks on peaceful villagers and civilization itself instead of against the political organization they supposedly hate. *Juan del Riel* (1943), not about the cristeros, tells the tale of railroad workers and their efforts to improve their lives. The protagonist, a rich man's son, sees the rich rob the poor. During the revolution he joins first Madero and then Villa. He has a long experience in railroading but sees that no true Mexican progress can be achieved since foreign capitalists own everything. After the revolution those in power forget about the old organizers and reward, instead, the new hangers-on. Juan del Riel, however, dies, as he has lived, taking a final trip on his railroad engine.

Jesús Goytortúa Santos (1910–   ) wrote *Pensativa* (1945), a novel which seems to adopt an intermediate position between that of Robles and Guadalupe de Anda. The author tries to show us the motivations which drove the hate-filled cristeros and how they came to represent an empty betrayal of everything that Christ stood for. No defense of tradition or theology could ever justify the barbarism to which these fighters for a cause had sunk, and, in that fight, they became far worse than the enemy they were fighting. Goytortúa also wrote *Lluvia roja* (1947) about an abortive revolt against Calles and Obregón by Adolfo de la Huerta in 1924. Enrique Montero, the "Tigre de Huasteca," shows us how man must survive in a harsh, cruel, and dog-eat-dog Mexican society where human values must give way to self-preservation. The heroine's attempt to help her fleeing lover at the end detracts from the theme.

Several writers, not precisely fitting within the classification of this chapter and yet loosely identified with it, include José Vasconcelos, Agustín Vera, Bruno Traven, the Indianists, and the Colonialists, the last named writers providing a strange little enclave of escapism from revolutionary realities. José Vasconcelos (1881–1959), not properly speaking a novelist, wrote some memoirs which are not exactly autobiography, nor essays on the political and social development of Mexico; some consider them to be novels.[55] Better known as an essayist, educator, and philosopher, Vasconcelos wrote his "novel" in five volumes: *Ulises criollo* (1935), *La tormenta* (1936), *El desastre* (1938), *El proconsulado* (1939), and *La flama* (1959). Vasconcelos gives us the whole sweep of the revolution in this story of his life, intellectual but yet as passionate and chaotic as the revolution itself; indeed, he portrays the history of Mexico in the twentieth century. He does not attempt to hide the bitterness he felt at being defrauded of the presidency of Mexico, his disgust with the regimes which perverted the ideals of the revolution, his feelings about the United States, and his love affairs. The first volume, *Ulises Criollo*, takes us to the death of Madero; *La tormenta*, "the storm," is what broke out after Madero's death, and it lasted to the end of Obregón's presidency; Vasconcelos' view of Carranza is extremely derogatory. *El desastre* is about the Calles reign from 1925 to 1929. Vasconcelos includes his own travels in Europe and America and his experience as minister of education. *El proconsulado* reveals his resentment of the United States (he had a somewhat ambivalent attitude toward it during certain parts of his life) and his belief that the United States ruled Mexico through its ambassador, the proconsul, Dwight Morrow; his campaign for the presidency and his defeat; his trip to Spain and then to Buenos Aires. *La flama*, subtitled "Los de arriba" to complement Azuela's work, ends with Vasconcelos' return to Mexico in 1939. In giving us his life story as a kind of extensive subjective soliloquy from his early moments on the Mexican-U.S. border, his experiences in law school and as district attorney, his membership in the Ateneo de la Juventud, his study of Gabino Barreda and other philosophical works, his services to education and interest in culture, he not only allows us to see Vasconcelos, the tortured human being driven by contradictory forces he could not always control, but also affords us a keen insight into the entire period of the revolution and beyond.

Vasconcelos himself expressed in *El desastre* the idea that history gives us the social process of crowds and nations, that the destiny of nations is a confused quantitative addition without differentiating or redeeming qualities and that for learning about an age no better history book can be found than its best novel. For this reason his feelings and impressions are more important than his factual material. His burning convictions and strong sense of righteousness and self-justification are everywhere apparent, and his work, part chronicle, part history, part fiery and emotional propaganda, part novel, is both an intimate account of twentieth-century Mexico and an assessment, through the Mexican experience, of humanity everywhere.

Agustín Vera (1889–1946), better known as a dramatist, wrote a period piece, *La revancha* (1930),[56] which resembles some of the realistic novels of the nineteenth century. The amalgam of romanticism and realism (love against the background of the Mexican Revolution), the multiplicity of characters, and the revenge motif place his novel somewhere between that of Portillo y Rojas, *Fuertes y débiles*, and the novels of the revolution. In general, Vera's position resembles that of Mariano Azuela. He strongly believes that the revolution and its ideals offered a step forward but also condemns its excesses. The title points up the revenge which Abundio Guerrero, the revolutionary chief, takes on Manuel, the hacendado, for the indignities practiced against his wife—including her rape by some Huerta followers. Manuel's sweetheart, Lupe, is in turn loyal to his memory. She meets Abundio and falls in love with him, but when he tells her who he is, she kills him.

Bruno Traven (1890–1969), who writes in German, Spanish, and English, handles the same themes as the novelists we have been discussing. Since he is not specifically Mexican, it may seem somewhat paradoxical to view him as the spokesman for the Mexican masses whose miserable lives he documents with compassion and artistry.[57] Born in Illinois as Traven Torsvan Croves, he became a naturalized Mexican citizen. Perhaps best known in this country as the author of *Treasure of the Sierra Madre* (1936), he treats of the Mexican Revolution in *Un puente en la selva* (1936), *La rebelión de los colgados* (1938), and *La Rosa Blanca* (1940). In his novels about the jungle and the Chiapas, whom he views as brothers, Traven clearly reveals his knowledge of the ambiente and his absolute identification with his adopted country. *Un puente en la selva* is a kind of allegory about the evils of civilization. Manuel, who had been working in the United States, gives a gift of shoes to his brother Carlosito, who is later found drowned in the river. The bridge from which he slipped and fell had no hand rails—not needed for the "natives," said the American oil company in charge of the bridge. *La rebelión de los colgados* is about debt slavery and the punishment given the Indians by hanging them from trees to be victimized by sun and insects. Cándido's wife dies along with his son; his sister is almost raped; finally the workers revolt and try to burn the files of the unholy records of their slavery. *La Rosa Blanca*, about a hacienda by that name which Traven apparently remembered from his early work in the oil fields, is owned by an Indian who loves his land. Unfortunately for him, the land is coveted by Mr. Collins of Condor Oil Company, who arranges to have Jacinto Yáñez (the Indian) killed so that he may acquire the property. In his treatment of the Indian and his relationships with the soil, Traven resembles Ciro Alegría, but his forcefulness is closer to that of Jorge Icaza and some of the Ecuadorians, as he shows us the ruthless activities of the oil company and the destruction of human values by the capitalistic system. *El general, tierra y libertad* (1966), is about the Mexican Revolution in southern Mexico.

One of the best treatments of the Indian in Mexican fiction is that of Miguel Ángel Menéndez (1905–   ) whose *Nayar* (1941) tells us about the traditions, legends, and magic of the Cora Indians in the mountains of Nayarit. The old *Canaima* and *La vorágine* theme of the impact of the tropical jungle on man appears once more. In his discussion of white, mestizo, and Indian relationships Menéndez takes us outside time into a magic world of myth and age-old superstition and shows us Indians indifferent to the white culture around them. The Cora tribe, like the Araucanians of Chile, never subjugated, live isolated in their western hills, practicing their ancient customs and beliefs. The author and a mestizo friend, Ramón Córdoba, a fugitive (he had killed a judge he found in bed with his wife), travel to the domain of the Coras and help the chief, Pedro Gervasio, against some greedy gringos. The Indians' beliefs limit but do not destroy their ability to act against their exploitation by opposing revolutionary groups. Blaming their witch doctor for part of their troubles, they decide to burn him alive. Ramón, hoping to save the Indian, asks for federal intervention, but both are killed. Poetic, dramatic, and yet simple, *Nayar*'s several "cuadros" reflect the conflicts inherent in the situation.

Other novelists have written on historical Indian themes in no way connected to the Mexican Revolution. These include Antonio Mediz (1884–1957), Andrés Henestrosa (1908–   ), Héctor P. Martínez (1906–1948), Pablo González Casanova (1889–1936), Gregorio Torres (1885–   ), and, more importantly, Ermilo Abreu Gómez (1894–   ) and Francisco Monterde (1894–   ). Among the better known titles are *Los hombres que dispersó la danza* (1929), by Andrés Henestrosa; *Canek* (1940), *Héroes mayas* (1942), *Quetzalcoatl, sueño y vigilia* (1947), and *Naufragio de indios* (1951) by Ermilo Abreu Gómez; and *Moctezuma, el de la silla de oro* (1945) and *Moctezuma II, señor del Anáhuac* (1947) by Francisco Monterde. These novels deal with the Indian during the conquest, Indian villages during the French invasion, and a variety of other historical events, often involving indigenous uprisings. At times, in their legendary and mythological aspects, they resemble slightly the later cultural composites of magic realism by Miguel Ángel Asturias and José María Arguedas.

When the Mexican Revolution started in 1910, it must be remembered, Justo Sierra was founding the National University of Mexico. A group of writers, Alfonso Reyes and Pedro Henríquez Ureña among them, presaged a cultural change as great as the political one implied by the revolution. One aspect of this cultural renovation was the appearance in the 1920s of a group of poematic and semi-surrealistic novels—to be discussed in the second volume as the definite precursors of the new Spanish American novel. About 1917 another movement began, labeled by José Luis Martínez the "moda colonialista" and involving escape from the unpleasant realities of life—"como un movimiento de huida hacia el pasado, determinado por la angustia de la Revolución." [58] Julio Jiménez Rueda agrees that it is a movement of escape to the past caused by the anguish of the revolution and that it is closely related to impressionism and modernism.[59] The novelists attempted to use affected and archaic style to create atmosphere and "looked at the past in much the way an antique hunter looks at a beautiful old table. It was a new view of the past in Mexican fiction. . . . The twentieth-century colonialistas . . . were interested in re-creating artistically a past which held for them an obsessive antiquarian charm." [60] Among the many novelists writing in this manner were Francisco Monterde, Julio Jiménez Rueda (1896–1960), Manuel Horta (1898–   ), Ermilo Abreu Gómez, Alfonso Cravioto (1884–1955), Genaro Estrada (1887–1937), and Artemio de Valle-Arizpe (1888–1961). Valle-Arizpe summed up interest in the theme as "ningún asunto tan rico en sugestiones como la historia de América virreinal, con sus cortes brillantes, su sociedad abigarrada y pintoresca, su esfuerzo por inscribir todo aquel mundo virgen en la cultura católica y occidental . . . en ella tienen cabida elementos que la historia científica desdeña, pero cuyo valor estético es extraordinario: la tradición, la anécdota . . . el folklore . . ." [61] Valle-Arizpe's novels include *Vidas milagrosas* (1921) and *La movible inquietud: En México y en otros siglos* (1948), and he has also written many traditions and legends.

Some novelists fit no easy category. Without yet writing in the new key with existential, temporal, magical, or absurd involvement, these novelists nonetheless wrote novels, with the revolution as a point of departure, involving some technical experimentation along these lines. Miguel N. Lira (1905–1961), a poet and dramatist, represents a kind of bridge between the old style novels of the revolution and the new Mexican novels from *Al filo del agua* on. Lira wrote four novels, *Donde crecen los tepozanes* (1947), *La Escondida* (1948), *Una mujer en soledad* (1956), and *Mientras la muerte llega* (1958). *La Escondida* concerns the last days of the Díaz regime and events up to the fall of Victoriano Huerta. Against this background Felipe Rojano and Máximo Tepal, two popular Maderista leaders, vie for the affections of the wife of a Díaz general whom Rojano has killed. Felipe takes her to a forest estate, "La Escondida," where she bears him a son. Máximo, unable to restrain his jealousy, kills his rival. *Una mujer en soledad* shows a murdering woman's fruitless search for herself. Miguel meets Rita on a bus and easily succumbs to her charms, which, apparently, change a lifetime of honorable behavior. After Miguel tells his story we hear of Rita's justification. The author also exposes what happens to would-be film stars in the cruel world of vices and drug traffic. *Mientras la muerte llega* recalls, as a past, the Mexican Revolution. Lira's first novel seems closest to the new type in its examination of the interrelationships between Indian and Mexican culture seeking the historical and legendary backgrounds of a *nahuatl.* Involving witchcraft, the marvelous, superstitions, and a kind of magic realism, the novel is also atemporal, set outside of time in the accepted sense, and a further development of the themes of Menéndez' *Nayar*.

Francisco Rojas González (1904–1951) wrote seven collections of short stories, among them *Cuentos de ayer y de hoy* (1946) and *El diosero* (1952). Joseph Sommers, who has written most perceptively about this diplomat, anthropologist, and novelist, considers him to be primarily a master of the short form and a man who constantly attempted to define "mexicanidad" in his examination of the revolution, of exploitation, religion, and death as factors of Mexican life, especially insofar as Indian culture is concerned.[62] He was interested in the totality of Mexico and in a penetration of its surface reality to find its joy and sorrow, victories and defeats. Rojas González is a transition writer between the novelists of the Mexican Revolution and the new school of writers. He includes his childhood memories of the Porfirio Díaz days in his short stories, many of which appeared in the liberal journal, *Crisol.* Some of his types are clearly Mexican; others have a universal quality.

Rojas González' first novel, *La negra Angustias* (1944), although it comments on the sacrifices and tragedies caused by fighting, is a psychological study of the role of a woman revolutionary who, driven by hate like her Venezuelan prototype, Doña Bárbara, whom she resembles, finds, however, a psychological niche her Venezuelan counterpart was unable to attain. Angustias Farrera is a brutal mulata who (when her mother died and her father went to prison) was raised by an old hag, doña Crescencia. Angustias, like Bárbara, has unpleasant sexual experiences. When the revolution breaks out she joins the Zapata forces with a number of soldiers under her command. Angustias avenges herself on one man by castrating him; she whips a pregnant woman who pleads for her lover's life. Eventually she falls in love with a rather effeminate and timid teacher, Manuel de la Reguera, whom she seduces. They marry and have a child. She abandons her former aggressive role for a subordinate feminine one. but her husband neglects her to sleep with a peasant girl. The treatment of a woman revolutionary is unique—aside from incidental portraits of camp followers like La Pintada in Azuela's novel—especially in its

Freudian nuances. Perhaps Rojas does not develop, as scientifically as he might have, the traumatic experiences of the heroine as they affected her sexual development nor, for that matter, the reversal of roles with a man after marriage, but the novel makes the change seem plausible to the average reader.[63] Rojas shows the intimate relation between geography and characters, their exposure to inclement weather, the hot sun, and other oppressive forces.[64] But along with indirect portraits of the revolution and the government and the psychological development, the most notable and distinctive characteristic of the plot, which often reveals psychological and tragic aspects of humanity, is "el penetrante tono de ironía omnipresente." [65]

Rojas González' second novel, *Lola Casanova* (1947), combines the Indian theme with another feminine heroine who vaguely resembles the psychological makeup of Angustias. Lola is kidnaped by Indians, falls in love with their chief, marries him, and becomes the salvation of the tribe. The author makes full use of his anthropological and sociological knowledge to show us Indian customs. Indeed, the whole novel is based on an Indian legend about a girl kidnaped and never heard of again. The customs of the Kinkaaks are expressively portrayed, but José Luis Martínez objects to the "lenguaje prosopopéyico y sembrado de alegorías y símbolos con el que hace expresarse a sus personajes indígenas." [66] Foreshadowing the preoccupations of writers like Carlos Fuentes, Rojas González seems to be saying that in miscegenation, combined with the techniques of civilization, lies the hope of his country.

Magdalena Mondragón (1913–   ), better known as a playwright, has written several novels: *Puede que l'otro año . . . novela de la Laguna* (1937), which protests the social injustice the author finds in Mexico; *Norte bárbaro* (1944); *Yo como hombre* (1944), about poverty; *Más allá existe la tierra* (1947), about the social injustices of modern Mexico but which offers hope in the union of the white Rosa and the Indian Simón whose child may not be the victim of racial and social prejudice; *El día no llega* (1950), which abandons social realism for oneiric projections, the subconscious, interior monologue, and disillusion, fear, and existential preoccupations about life; *Tenemos sed* (1956), about itinerant home builders; *Mi corazón es la tierra* (1967); and *Porque me da la gana* (1968).

As was to be expected, many novelists, without directly portraying the revolution, concentrated on costumbrista and social themes. Rosa de Castaño continued the criollista tradition in a series of novels, among them *La gaviota verde* (1935), *Rancho Estradeño* (1936), *El torrente negro* (1940), *Fruto de sangre* (1958), about the death of a witch at the hands of an Indian, and *Simiente de Quetzalcoatl* (1965). Her regionalistic and folkloric novels involve themes of social protest and portraits of exploited peons and Indian life.

Martín Gómez Palacio (1893–   ) also reflects an older realism. He contributed the naturalistic *A la una, a las dos, y a las tres* (1923); a satirical novel, *El mejor de los mundos posibles* (1927); and a more mature work, *El potro* (1940), which contains some of the modern and technical innovations of temporal and chronological juxtaposition, vaguely resembling those of William Faulkner.

Among novelists born in the twentieth century Rubén Salazar Mallén (1905–   ) draws his themes from the proletarian regions of city and country in novels such as *Camino de perfección* (1937), *Soledad* (1944), *Páramo* (1944), and *Ojo de agua* (1949), about a hated and feared cacique, Don Gabino; Alberto Bonifaz Nuño (1911–   ) published *La cruz del sureste* (1954); Jesús R. Guerrero (1911–   ) has produced bitter and compelling pictures of poverty-stricken citizens in his country, especially in *Los olvidados* (1944); and Héctor Raúl Almanza (1912–   ) attacks both his own political leaders and the United States for their exploitation of the poor Mexican farm workers in *Huelga Blanca* (1950) and exposes the deceit and the destruction of human dignity practiced by oil companies in Huasteca in *Brecha en la roca* (1955).

The novels of the Mexican Revolution blur the lines of character development and have not contributed any unique and universal personalities to fiction. In a general way the novels show the conflict between the individual's personal morality and his commitment to the sociopolitical scene. The commitment to a common cause usurps values which in other contexts they might treasure as individuals, but the characters transgress conventional boundaries in order to achieve justice. The leaders of the revolution, demanding blind allegiance of their men, seek to superimpose on their established hierarchy of values an artificial pattern of motivations and thus end by substituting one tyranny for another.

The novelists show how Pancho Villa and other movers, prepared to sacrifice all to expedite the cause, consider fellow human beings in terms of their usefulness and significance to the revolution, thus dulling an otherwise possible human compassion for the weak, the halt, and the lame.

Many of the actors of the revolution were incapable of transcending the personal aspects of their conflict or to see their problems in the perspective of collective well-being. The inability of characters and novelists as well to resolve their predicament or to escape their wretched pattern of experience through the tragic reality of the revolution—the only alternative which destiny provides—leads them to substitute sterile indignation for active involvement, not so much in the initial fighting as in the political aftermath. The novelists provide us with a spectrum of emotions ranging from chronic despair to a childlike confidence in the efficiency and magic of revolution. In contrast with later neorealists, they cannot convey the horror and compassion of the moment by humanizing abstract forms of social and economic tragedy through moving individual experience and fail to stress the human dimension over the sociological implications of the characters' behavior. The novelists' obsessive preoccupation with national events paradoxically obscures their concern for characters as people; they seem to view their creations from an exterior, superficial, and even simplistic point of view devoid both of intellectual creativity and human compassion. In their totality, nevertheless, these novels show an authentic effort at a kind of literary innovation and present us with a glowing and dramatic tapestry of historical events and the men who participated in them. We see the revolutionary fervor, the idealism, and the optimism of those men, along with their opportunism and pessimism, their great sacrifices, and the illusions and moral anguish of those who saw their fondest hopes for a new kind of world defrauded by the imperfect human beings who fell victim to their own greed and materialism at the expense of a noble idea.

Notes

CHAPTER 1

1. Irving Leonard, *Books of the Brave* (Cambridge, Ma., 1949), p. 80.
2. Ibid., pp. 81–82.
3. Henry Thomas, *Spanish and Portuguese Romances of Chivalry* (Cambridge, England, 1920) , pp. 149ff.
4. Ibid., p. 156.
5. Leonard, *Books*, pp. 138, 270.
6. Ibid., p. 325.
7. Ibid., p. 198.
8. J. Lloyd Mecham, *Church and State in Latin America* (Chapel Hill, N.C., 1966), p. 12.
9. Pedro Henríquez Ureña, *Literary Currents in Hispanic America* (Cambridge, Ma., 1945), p. 62. Pedro de Gante, member of the Franciscan order, founded the first school in Mexico in 1523. Juan de Zumárraga, bishop of Mexico, also founded schools. Indians were taught reading, writing, singing, and Christian doctrine to keep them from idleness not in keeping with the spirit of Christianity. See also Paula Alegría, *La educación en México antes y después de la conquista* (Mexico, 1936), pp. 103–4.
10. Juan Loveluck, *La novela hispanoamericana* (Santiago de Chile, 1966), p. 18.
11. Arturo Torres-Rioseco, *La novela en la América Hispana* (Santiago de Chile, 1939), p. 171.
12. Luis Alberto Sánchez, *Proceso y contenido de la novela hispano-americana* (Madrid, 1953), p. 81.
13. Fernando Alegría, *Historia de la novela hispanoamericana* (Mexico, 1966), p. 12.
14. Pedro Henríquez Ureña, "Apuntaciones sobre la novela en América," *Obra crítica de Pedro Henríquez Ureña* (Mexico, 1960), pp. 618–26.

15. Hernando Téllez, "La novela en Latinoamérica," in Loveluck, *La novela hispanoamericana*, p. 51.
16. Pedro Grases, "De la novela en América," in Loveluck, *La novela hispanoamericana*, pp. 99–105.
17. Roque Esteban Scarpa, *Lecturas americanas* (Santiago de Chile, 1948), p. 11.
18. Fernando Alegría, *Novela hispanoamericana*, p. 13.
19. Luis Alberto Sánchez, *Proceso y contenido*, p. 106. See also his study, "La novela en los cronistas," *Atenea* 104, no. 343: 108–30.
20. Edward M. Forster, *Aspects of the Novel* (New York, 1927), p. 17.
21. Camilo José Cela, *Mrs. Caldwell habla con su hijo* (Barcelona, 1958), p. 9.
22. Camilo José Cela, *Papeles de Son Armadans* 39, no. 117 (1965): 227–34.
23. Luis Alberto Sánchez, *Proceso y contenido*, p. 599.
24. Guillermo de Torre, "Perspectivas y encrucijadas de la novela contemporánea," *Revista Cubana* 31, no. 3–4 (1957): 49–70.
25. See Julio Caillet-Bois, "Bernal Díaz del Castillo o de la verdad en la historia," *Revista Iberoamericana* 25, no. 50 (1960): 199–228.
26. Irving Leonard, *Books*, p. 98, notes that on the death of Cromberger in 1540, 446 copies of *Amadís de Gaula* were part of the press inventory.
27. Otis H. Green, *Spain and the Western Tradition (The Castilian Mind in Literature from El Cid to Calderón)*, 4 vols. (Madison, Wis., 1965), 3: 34.
28. Inca Garcilaso de la Vega, *Historia General del Perú*, ed. Ángel Rosenblat (Buenos Aires, 1944), p. x.
29. Aurelio Miró Quesada, *El Inca Garcilaso* (Madrid, 1948), pp. 140–41, discusses that author's debt to romances of chivalry and the Byzantine novel on which certain episodes seem based.
30. José Durand, "Las enigmáticas fuentes de la *Florida del Inca*," *Cuadernos Hispanoamericanos* 46, no. 168 (1963): 597–609, claims that Garcilaso worked on his book from about 1567 on and that in spite of its being written as a "fantasía novelesca" it contains valuable and authentic historical material.
31. See Donald G. Castanien, "Narrative Art in *La Florida del Inca*," *Hispania* 43 (1960): 30–36.
32. Garcilaso de la Vega, *Historia del Perú*, p. xxxv "Y tal contagio de añoranzas emana de su acento que . . . el Consejo de Indias, a fines del siglo XVIII, después de la insurrección de Condorcanquí, prohibió la lectura de los *Comentarios* en el virreinato peruano y mandó recoger ocultamente los ejemplares porque . . . 'aprendían en ellos los naturales muchas cosas inconvenientes', que removían y excitaban la conciencia de la nacionalidad."
33. James Fitzmaurice Kelly, *Historia de la literatura española* (Madrid, 1916), p. 240.

34. Arturo Uslar Pietri, *Breve historia de la novela hispanoamericana* (Caracas, 1954), p. 38.

35. Enrique Anderson Imbert, *Crítica interna* (Madrid, 1960), p. 29.

36. See Daniel Samper Pizano, "El abuelo Rodríguez Freire," *Boletín Cultural y Bibliográfico* 8, no. 7 (Bogotá, 1965): 1047–53; Antonio Gómez Restrepo, *Historia de la literatura colombiana*, (Bogotá, 1956), 2: 159; Antonio Curcio Altamar, *Evolución de la novela en Colombia* (Bogotá, 1957), p. 33; Oscar Gerardo Ramos, "El carnero, libro de tendencia cuentística," *Boletín Cultural y Bibliográfico* 9, no. 11 (1966): 2178–85; and Eduardo Camacho, *Estudios sobre literatura colombiana: siglos XVI-XVII* (Bogotá, 1965), p. 47, who finds it essentially "un cruce entre la crónica y la novela."

37. Such a relation is denied by Alessandro Martinengo, "La cultura letteraria di Juan Rodríguez Freyle," *Thesaurus* 19, no. 2 (1964): 274–99.

38. Eduardo Camacho Guizado, *Estudios sobre la literatura colombiana, siglo XVI-XVII* (Bogotá, 1965), p. 49.

39. Domingo Amunátegui Solar, *Historia social de Chile* (Santiago, 1932), p. 51.

40. Enrique Anderson Imbert, *Spanish American Literature: A History* (Detroit, 1963), p. 66.

41. Luis Alberto Sánchez, *Proceso y contenido*, p. 102.

42. J. Lloyd Mecham, *Church and State*, pp. 51–52.

43. Francisco Eugenio de Santa Cruz y Espejo, *Escritos* (Quito, 1923), p. 322, refers to "nuestra ignominia, nuestro escándalo, nuestra ruina . . ."

44. Ricardo Rojas, *Obras. Literatura argentina* (Buenos Aires, 1925), 15: 1015.

45. Fernando Alegría, *Novela hispanoamericana*, p. 14.

46. Jefferson Rhea Spell, "New Light on Fernández de Lizardi and his *El Periquillo Sarniento*," *Hispania* 46 (December 1963): 753–54.

47. José Joaquín Fernández de Lizardi, *El Periquillo Sarniento* (Mexico, 1940), 2: 3.

48. For comments and comparisons of the various editions see Rhea Spell, "A Textual Comparison of the First Four Editions of *El Periquillo Sarniento*," *Hispanic Review* 31 (1963): 134–47.

49. Representative of this school of thought is the judgment of Fernando Alegría, *Novela hispanoamericana*, p. 16, "no fue un novelista por vocación sino por necesidad."

50. A number of critics have commented on this aspect of his work. See Ruth S. Lamb, "The Costumbrismo of the Pensador Mexicano and Micrós," *The Modern Language Journal* 35 (1951): 195.

51. Julio A. Leguizamón, *Historia de la literatura hispanoamericana* (Buenos Aires, 1945), 1: 377.

52. Jefferson Rhea Spell, introduction to Fernández de Lizardi, *Don Catrín de la Fachenda* (Mexico, 1944), pp. xxx-xxxi.

53. Jefferson Rhea Spell, "The Genesis of the First Mexican Novel," *Hispania* 14 (1931): 55.
54. Mariano Azuela, *Cien años de novela mexicana* (Mexico, 1947), p. 47.
55. Alfonso Reyes, "El Periquillo Sarniento y la crítica mexicana," *Obras completas* (Mexico, 1956), 4: 171.
56. Luis Alberto Sánchez, *Escritores representativos de América* (Madrid, 1963), p. 176.
57. Luis Alberto Sánchez, *Breve historia de la literatura americana* (Santiago, 1937), p. 199.
58. Mariano Azuela, *Cien años*, p. 47.
59. Jefferson Rhea Spell, in Fernández de Lizardi, *Don Catrín*, p. xxvii.
60. Carlos González Peña, *History of Mexican Literature* (Dallas, Tx., 1945), p. 182.

CHAPTER 2

1. Raimundo Lida, *Letras hispánicas* (Mexico, 1958), p. 44.
2. Alberto Zum Felde, *Índice crítico de la literatura hispanoamericana. La narrativa* (Mexico, 1959), 2: 54.
3. Arturo Uslar Pietri, *Breve historia de la novela hispanoamericana* (Caracas, 1954), p. 52.
4. Francisco Calcagno, *Diccionario biográfico cubano* (New York, 1878), p. 159.
5. Juan J. Remos, *Historia de la literatura cubana* (Havana, 1945), 2: 181, feels that "al conjuro de su imaginación fértil, de su estilo fácil, Villaverde teje con hilos de realismo crudo, una fábula romántica."
6. Manuel de la Cruz, *Obras* (Madrid, 1924), 3: 199. See also Rafael Fernández Villa-Urrutia, "Para una lectura de *Cecilia Valdés*," *Revista Cubana* 31 (1957): 31–43. He calls it "seguramente uno de los documentos políticos de mayor importancia que produjo Cuba en el pasado siglo."
7. Esteban Rodríguez Herrera, introduction to Cirilo Villaverde, *Cecilia Valdés* (Havana, 1953), p. xxxi.
8. Salvador Bueno, *Historia de la literatura cubana* (Havana, 1963), p. 178.
9. José Manuel Carbonell y Rivero, *Evolución de la cultura cubana* (Havana, 1928), 13: 4.
10. Luis Alberto Sánchez, *Proceso y contenido de la novela hispanoamericana* (Madrid, 1953), p. 137.
11. Ibid., p. 210.
12. Seymour Menton, *Historia crítica de la novela guatemalteca* (Guatemala, 1960), pp. 13–14.

13. Raúl Silva Castro, *Obras desconocidas de Rubén Darío* (Santiago de Chile, 1934), p. 186.

14. Rafael Maya, "La Manuela y el criollismo colombiano," *Boletín de la Academia Colombiana* 15 (1965): 181.

15. Marguerite Suárez-Murias, *La novela romántica en Hispanoamerica* (New York, 1963), pp. 148–49.

16. Ricardo Rojas, *Obras. Literatura argentina* (Buenos Aires, 1925), 13:937, denies that it is, in spite of its appearance, a novel,— ". . . pero también presenta aspectos de libro de viajes, de memoria, de fábula, de diálogo filosófico, de conferencia didáctica, de oratoria, de sátira, de polémica, de tratado político . . ."

17. Pedro Díaz Seijas, *Historia y antología de la literatura venezolana* (Madrid, 1955), p. 257.

18. Emilio Carilla, *El romanticismo en la América Hispana* (Madrid, 1958), p. 503.

19. Ibid., p. 42.

20. Luis Alberto Sánchez, *Historia de la literatura americana* (Santiago, 1940), p. 344, refers to this desire to express national truth as "exasperado anhelo de afirmación."

21. Enrique Anderson Imbert, "Notas sobre la novela histórica en el siglo XIX," in *La novela iberoamericana*, edited by Instituto Internacional de Literatura Iberoamericana (Albuquerque, N.M., 1952), pp. 3–24.

22. Marguerite Suarez-Murias, *La novela romántica*.

23. Amado Alonso, *Ensayo sobre la novela histórica* (Buenos Aires, 1942), p. 73.

24. Antonio Castro Leal, *La novela del México colonial* (Mexico, 1964), 1: 14.

25. Pedro Henríquez Ureña, *Literary Currents in Hispanic America*, (Cambridge, Ma., 1945), p. 118.

26. Enrique Anderson Imbert, "Notas sobre la novela," pp. 4–5.

27. John Lloyd Read, *The Mexican Historical Novel (1826–1910)*, (New York, 1939), p. 85.

28. Luis Leal, "Jicoténcal, primera novela histórica en castellano," *Revista Iberoamericana* 25, no. 49 (1960): 9–31.

29. Salvador Bueno, *Literatura cubana*, p. 140.

30. Emilio Cotarelo y Mori, *La Avellaneda y sus obras* (Madrid, 1930), p. 75, and Enrique Piñeyro, *El romanticismo en España* (Paris, 1940), p. 253, deny abolitionist intentions on her part as does Salvador Bueno, *Historia de la literatura cubana* (Havana, 1954), p. 117.

31. Helena Percas Ponseti, "Sobre la Avellaneda y su novela, *Sab*," *Revista Iberoamericana* 28, no. 54 (1962): 347–57.

32. Hugo D. Barbagelata, *La novela y el cuento en Hispanoamérica* (Montevideo, 1947), pp. 255–56.

33. José Antonio Portuondo, *Bosquejo histórico de las letras cubanas* (Havana, 1960), p. 30, does not find in her more than a "discutible

cubanidad." Alberto J. Carlos, "René, Werther y *La Nouvelle Héloise* en la primera novela de la Avellaneda," *Revista Iberoamericana* 31, no. 60 (1965): 223–38, aside from the influences mentioned in his title, finds the anguish and abolitionist and other social tendencies to be the principal strength of the novel.

34. Concha Meléndez, *La novela indianista en Hispanoamérica, 1832–1889* (Río Piedras, 1961), pp. 80–81.

35. Rafael Alberto Arrieta, *Historia de la literatura argentina* (Buenos Aires, 1958), 2: 78–79.

36. Marcelo Segall, "Las luchas de clases en las primeras décadas de la República (1810–46)," *Anales de la Universidad de Chile* 120, no. 125 (1962): 206.

37. See Mariano Morínigo, "Realidad y ficción de *El Matadero*," *Humanitas* 13, no. 18 (Universidad de Tucumán, 1965): 283–318. He sees *El matadero* as a carefully elaborated and not fragmentary work. He stresses that it is not only the first story of Argentine fiction but also the first in Spanish America to discover the concept "de configuración literaria de realidad-nación," and thus directly related to works like Miguel Ángel Asturias' *El señor presidente.*

38. Germán García, *La novela argentina* (Buenos Aires, 1952), p. 18, sees Echeverría as ". . . sin duda el primer novelista, porque *El matadero* es base pétrea en que asienta lo que vino después."

39. Roberto F. Giusti, *Lecciones de literatura argentina e hispanoamericana* (Buenos Aires, 1958), p. 405.

40. Joaquín G. Martínez, *Esteban Echeverría en la vida argentina* (Buenos Aires, 1953), p. 45. A similar view is expressed by Ernesto Morales, *Esteban Echeverría* (Buenos Aires, 1950), p. 149.

41. Myron I. Lichtblau, *The Argentine Novel in the Nineteenth Century* (New York, 1959), p. 27.

42. Arturo Giménez Pastor, *Historia de la literatura argentina* (Buenos Aires, 1945), p. 221.

43. Enrique Williams Alzaga, *La pampa en la novela argentina* (Buenos Aires, 1955), p. 121.

44. See José Ingenieros, *La evolución de las ideas argentinas,* (Buenos Aires, 1951), 2: 507, for his ideas on Vico and Herder, and José Victorino Lastarria, *Recuerdos Literarios* (Santiago, 1885), p. 89, for a description of Fidel López' activity in Chile.

45. Arturo Giménez Pastor, *Literatura argentina,* p. 226.

46. Germán García, *La novela argentina,* p. 26. "Llevó a la novela su compasión por el indio y reflejó en sus narraciones su culto de la belleza y la justicia."

47. Arturo Uslar Pietri, *Breve historia,* p. 58.

48. David Viñas, *Literatura argentina y realidad política* (Buenos Aires, 1964), p. 133.

49. Enrique Anderson Imbert, *Spanish American Literature: A History* (Detroit, 1963), p. 176; García, *La novela argentina,* p. 32, calls it

"una novela política, con una dirección y un sentido hasta de pro-paganda"; and Lichtblau, *The Argentine Novel*, pp. 46–47, feels it would be more logical to understand the work as a "novel of con-temporary affairs rather than as a historical novel."

50. Some difference of opinion exists as to the characters in the novel. Fernando Alegría, *Historia de la novela hispanoamericana* (Mexico, 1966), p. 39, finds Daniel Bello "un personaje de atractivos relieves, si no humanos, al menos literarios," the secondary figures like Rosas to be admirable, but Amalia and her lover to be pasteboard figures; Luis Alberto Sánchez, *Proceso y contenido*, p. 139, states that in this "inmortal novela" we have a portrait of the Rosas family never excelled, and Zum Felde, *Índice crítico*, p. 92, rejects the view that the characters are false or in bad taste. For him Amalia and Eduardo are representative not only of literary romanticism but of life of the time, and he finds the portrait of Rosas to match that of any litera-ture of any country.

51. Fernando Alegría, *Historia de la novela*, p. 41, agrees that the plot is of secondary importance and that the style is inflated but finds its value in its denunciation of Rosas and in its vivid dialogue. Zum Felde, *Índice crítico*, pp. 91–93, states that the novel is the culmina-tion of Argentine romanticism as the anguished cry from the depths of the soul of a generation and, in spite of its romanticism, the best treatment of the subject of tyranny, later matched in exterior realism but unequaled in its "vida interior."

52. J. Lloyd Mecham, *Church and State in Latin America* (Chapel Hill, N.C., 1966), p. 232. "Juan Manuel de Rosas . . . converted the Church into a servile instrument of the tyranny. . . . The Church allied itself with the tyranny at the start and in the end was hope-lessly subjected by it."

53. David Vela, *Literatura guatemalteca* (Guatemala, 1944), 2: 401, concurs that his greatest triumph lay in the "género costumbrista."

54. Seymour Menton, *Historia crítica*, pp. 8, 22.

55. Ibid., p. 49. Menton, nevertheless, praises it highly as "una de las mejores de todas las novelas históricas de Hispanoamérica."

56. Thomas Irving, "Las dos maneras de Pepe Milla," *Revista Univer-sidad de San Carlos* 52 (1960): 111–33, contrasts his romantic and realistic novels and finds this one "la novela más acabada de Pepe Milla y una de las mejores que se escribió en la América latina durante el siglo próximo pasado."

57. Augusto Guzmán, *La novela en Bolivia* (La Paz, 1955), p. 37.

58. Enrique Finot, *Historia de la literatura boliviana* (Mexico, 1943), p. 191, states: "El conflicto moral de los protagonistas se asemeja ex-traordinariamente al que Lamartine plantea en *Jocelyn*."

59. Mario Castro Arenas, *La novela peruana y la evolución social* (Lima, 1963), pp. 47–48.

60. Hugo D. Barbagelata, *La novela y el cuento*, p. 112.

61. John E. Englekirk and Margaret M. Ramos, *La narrativa uruguaya*, Publications in Modern Philology, 30 (Berkeley, 1967): 35.
62. Alberto Zum Felde, *Índice crítico*, p. 56.
63. Among good studies of his life are: Mario Carvajal, *Vida y Pasión de Jorge Isaacs* (Manizales, 1937); Luis Carlos Velasco Madriñán, *Jorge Isaacs, el caballero de las lágrimas* (Cali, 1942); and Max Grillo, *Vida y obra de Isaacs, Boletín de la Academia Colombiana* 2 (1937): 182–296.
64. Rubén Darío, *Obras completas* (Madrid, 1950), 3: 1139.
65. Arturo Uslar Pietri, *Breve historia*, p. 61.
66. Alberto Zum Felde, *Índice crítico*, p. 101.
67. Alfonso Reyes, "Algunas notas sobre la *María* de Jorge Isaacs," *Obras completas* (Mexico, 1955), 8: 271.
68. Augusto Arias, *Jorge Isaacs y su María* (Quito, 1937), p. 25.
69. Luis Carlos Velasco Madriñán, *Efraín y María* (Cali, Colombia, 1954), feels it was not El Paraíso but rather another home, La Rita.
70. Daniel Samper Ortega, ed., *Otros cuentistas*, Biblioteca aldeana de Colombia, no. 20 (Bogotá, 1936), p. 6.
71. Enrique Anderson Imbert, in his introduction to Isaacs, *María* (Mexico, 1951), p. 84, points out that it is occasionally stated that a passage in *María* may be the basis for Silva's famous "Nocturno."
72. Antonio Curcio Altamar, *Evolución de la novela en Colombia* (Bogotá, 1957), pp. 122–23, states that the tears of the lovers were contagious "para toda la adolescencia americana."
73. Jacob Warshaw, in the introduction to *María* (New York, 1926), p. xiv, considers Edgar Allan Poe to have been a greater influence on Isaacs than Chateaubriand.
74. Luis Carlos Velasco Madriñán, *Jorge Isaacs*, pp. 301–5. Anderson Imbert, *Crítica interna* (Madrid, 1960), p. 82, finds that whether or not María existed ". . . lo cierto es que la María de la novela, la María tal como allí aparece, no había existido nunca. Era una síntesis lírica de las experiencias de amor de Isaacs, la cifra ideal de sus primeros años . . ."
75. Alfonso Reyes, "Algunas notas," p. 271.
76. Enrique Anderson Imbert, *Crítica interna*, p. 75.
77. Fernando de la Vega, *Crítica*, Biblioteca aldeana de Colombia, no. 56 (Bogotá, 1963), p. 38. Vega states, "Creyérase por instantes que la naturaleza le disputa a la virgen protagonista el predominio de la escena en el trascurso del libro, y alcanza a vencerla." See also Oscar Gerardo Ramos, "Mujer, paisaje y ambiente en la novela, *María*," *Universidad de Antioquia*, no. 171 (1968), pp. 169–83.
78. Luis Segundo de Silvestre, *Tránsito*, Biblioteca aldeana de Colombia, no. 14 (Bogotá, 1935), p. 17.
79. Nicolás Bayona Posada, *Panorama de la literatura colombiana* (Bogotá, 1942), p. 70.
80. Gonzalo Picón Febres, *La literatura venezolana en el siglo diez y nueve* (Buenos Aires, 1947), p. 358.

81. Arturo Uslar Pietri, *Letras y hombres de Venezuela* (Caracas, 1958), p. 175.
82. Gonzalo Picón Febres, *La literatura venezolana*, p. 367. Picón states: "Pero necesario es decirlo con franqueza: el nombre interesante de don Eduardo Blanco no había de perdurar por sus novelas, sino por *Venezuela heroica.*"
83. Augusto Germán Orihuela in the prologue to Eduardo Blanco, *Zárate* (Caracas, 1956), p. x. See also Pedro Pablo Barnola, *Eduardo Blanco, creador de la novela venezolana* (Caracas, 1963).
84. Pedro Díaz-Seijas, *Historia y antología*, p. 383.
85. Julio Jiménez Rueda, *Historia de la literatura mexicana* (Mexico, 1960), p. 247.
86. Carlos González Peña, *History of Mexican Literature* (Dallas, Tx., 1945), p. 229.
87. John L. Read, *The Mexican Novel*, p. 107.
88. Ibid., p. 124.
89. Mariano Azuela, *Cien años de novela mexicana* (Mexico, 1947), p. 77.
90. J. Fernández-Arias Campoamor, *Novelistas de Méjico* (Madrid, 1952), p. 59.
91. Mariano Azuela, *Cien años*, pp. 70–71.
92. Antonio Castro Leal, prologue to *Ensalada de pollo* and *Baile de cochino* (Mexico, 1946), pp. xviff.
93. Mariano Azuela, *Cien años*, p. 103. Daniel Moreno, "El mundo real de *La linterna mágica*," *Estaciones* 3, no. 9 (1958): 22–30, differs sharply. For him "se trata de un capítulo básico para el conocimiento de la realidad mexicana de aquellas épocas y tiene también interés para desentrañar algunos aspectos de la personalidad del mexicano de todos los tiempos."
94. Castro Leal, prologue to Vicente Riva Palacio, *Martín Garatuza* (Mexico, 1945), p. viii, feels that "en Riva Palacio tiene la novela histórica uno de sus más genuinos representantes."
95. Carlos Gonzales Peña, *Mexican Literature*, p. 301.
96. Alfonso Reyes, *Obras completas* (Mexico, 1955), 1: 263.
97. José Luis Martínez, "La revista literaria *El Renacimiento*," *Cuadernos Americanos* 38 (1948): 169.
98. Marguerite Suárez-Murias, *La novela romántica*, p. 193.
99. Fernando Alegría, *Historia de la novela*, p. 60.
100. Concha Meléndez, among others, in her *La novela indianista*, considers the antecedents of the literary treatment of the Indian to begin in the works of Hernán Cortés, Bartolomé, de las Casas, Ercilla y Zúñiga, Garcilaso de la Vega (Inca), and Francisco Núñez de Pineda. Among foreign writers she cites the novels of Marmontel, Chateaubriand, and James Fenimore Cooper.
101. Concha Meléndez, *La novela indianista*, p. 95.
102. Eligio Ancona, *Los mártires del Anáhuac* in *La novela del México colonial*, ed. Antonio Castro Leal (Mexico, 1964), 1: 472.

103. Isaac J. Barrera, *La literatura ecuatoriana* (Quito, 1926), p. 106.
104. Juan León Mera, *Cumandá* (Madrid, 1891), pp. xvii–xix.
105. Juan Valera, *Cartas americanas* (Madrid, 1915), 2: 168–89.
106. Concha Meléndez, *La novela indianista*, p. 159.
107. John Reid, "Spanish American Jungle Fiction," *Quarterly Journal of Inter-American Relations* 2 (1940): 49.
108. Arturo Torres-Rioseco, "La novela de tema indígena en el Ecuador," *Modern Philology* 20 (Berkeley, 1939): 229.
109. Enrique Anderson Imbert, *Spanish American Literature*, p. 190.
110. Ángel F. Rojas, *La novela ecuatoriana* (Mexico, 1948), p. 61.
111. Juan Valera, *Cartas americanas*, p. 174.
112. Max Henríquez Ureña, *Panorama histórico de la literatura dominicana* (Río de Janeiro, 1945), p. 248.
113. José Martí, *Obras completas* (La Habana, 1936–43), 19: 207.
114. Enrique Anderson Imbert, *Crítica interna*, p. 71.
115. Pedro Henríquez Ureña, *Obra crítica* (Mexico, 1960), p. 620.
116. Enrique Anderson Imbert, *Crítica interna*, p. 64.
117. Carmen Gómez Tejera, *La novela en Puerto Rico* (Río Piedras, 1947), p. 33.
118. Raimundo Lazo, *Historia de la literatura hispanoamericana* (Mexico, 1967), p. 92.

CHAPTER 3

1. Luis Alberto Sánchez, *Proceso y contenido de la novela hispanoamericana* (Madrid, 1953), pp. 566–67.
2. Ángel Flores, "Magic Realism in Spanish American Fiction," *Hispania* 38 (1955): 187.
3. Arturo Torres-Rioseco, *Ensayos sobre literatura latinoamericana* (Berkeley, 1953), p. 93.
4. Julián Marías, *El método histórico de las generaciones* (Madrid, 1961), p. 114. See also Julius Petersen, "Las generaciones literarias," *Filosofía de la ciencia literaria*, trans. Carlos Silva (Mexico, 1906), pp. 164–88.
5. José Ortega y Gasset, *Obras. El tema de nuestro tiempo* (Madrid, 1943), 2: 834. His basic ideas are best expressed in this volume, first published in 1923, and also in *En torno a Galileo* (1933).
6. Pedro Laín Entralgo, *Las generaciones en la historia* (Madrid, 1945).
7. Leo Ulrich, *Interpretaciones hispanoamericanas* (Santiago de Cuba, 1960), p. 65. José Antonio Portuondo and José Juan Arrom have also written extensively about literary generations.
8. Fernando Alegría, *Historia de la novela hispanoamericana* (Mexico, 1966), p. 89.
9. F. Ferrándiz Alborz, "Tres precursores del nuevo realismo literario hispanoamericano," *Cuadernos Americanos* 66 (1952): 274.

10. Andrés González Blanco, *Historia de la novela en España desde el romanticismo a nuestros días* (Madrid, 1909), p. 217.
11. Samuel Lillo, *Literatura chilena* (Santiago, 1941), p. 133, states: "Antes de que aparecieran las obras de Alberto Blest Gana, puede decirse que en Chile no existió la novela."
12. Raúl Silva Castro, *Alberto Blest Gana* (Santiago de Chile, 1941), p. 121.
13. Ibid., p. 114.
14. Ibid., pp. 402–3. As does its Stendhalian model, *Martín Rivas* continues to be popular to the present. See also Silva Castro, "El centenario de Martín Rivas," *Revista Iberoamericana* 39, no. 55 (1963): 139–46.
15. In 1849 the liberals had formed a Club de la Reforma to contest the conservatives in the House of Deputies and to propagate democratic ideas and a liberal press. Among the members of the group were Benjamín Vicuña Mackenna and Santiago Arcos. When Francisco Bilbao returned to Chile in 1850 he insisted that the club members were playing games and that they should involve the poorer classes in their efforts. Arcos concurred in this opinion and together they founded the Sociedad de la Igualdad as an instrument of social and political education. It shortly changed into a center of agitation and the prime mover in opposing the candidacy of Manuel Montt. Blest Gana, even though he was not an eyewitness to these events, manages to convey some of the excitement and feeling not easily captured in the exchanges and meetings discussed in histories of the period. See *Santiago Arcos Arlegui y la Sociedad de la Igualdad: un socialista utopista chileno* (Santiago de Chile, 1942), pp. 73–208, and José Zapiola, *La Sociedad de la Igualdad y sus enemigos* (Santiago de Chile, 1902). Although the Sociedad lasted only from April to November of 1850, it was primarily the vehicle through which the pueblo managed to express itself and obviously a moving factor in the 20 April 1851 uprising which cost Rafael San Luis his life.
16. Domingo Melfi, *Estudios de literatura chilena* (Santiago de Chile, 1938), p. 34.
17. Fernando Alegría, *Novela hispanoamericana*, pp. 56–57. A different viewpoint is that of Ricardo Latcham, "Blest Gana y la novela realista," *Anales de la Universidad de Chile* 116, no. 112 (1958): 30–46.
18. Arturo Uslar Pietri, *Breve historia de la novela hispanoamericana* (Caracas, 1954), p. 72.
19. William E. Wilson, "Blest Gana's Debt to Barros Arana," *The Hispanic American Historical Review* 19 (1939): 102–5.
20. Raúl Silva Castro, *Alberto Blest Gana*, p. 473.
21. Arnold Chapman, "Observations on the *Roto* in Chilean Fiction," *Hispania* 32 (1949): 309–14, deplores generalizations about the roto, whose origin he traces. Chapman defines the roto as an un-

skilled or semiskilled city laborer and acclaims Cámara as one "of the best known fictional figures in Chile."

22. Hernán Díaz Arrieta (Alone), *Historia personal de la literatura chilena* (Santiago, 1954), p. 185.
23. Fernando Alegría, *Historia de la novela*, p. 54.
24. Mariano Latorre, *La literatura de Chile* (Buenos Aires, 1941), p. 98.
25. Hernán Díaz Arrieta, *Don Alberto Blest Gana* (Santiago de Chile, 1940), pp. 243–45.
26. The *pipiolos* were the liberals, the *pelucones*, the conservatives.
27. Unamuno states: "Al leer a *Inocencia* de Rendón se recuerda sin querer a Pereda. . . . Aquello sabe a tierra, sabe a lugar, sabe a tiempos, y sabe a humanidad." See Francisco de Paula Rendón, *Inocencia*, Biblioteca Aldeana de Colombia, no. 13 (Bogotá, 1935), p. 5.
28. Kurt Levy, in *La cultura y la literaura iberoamericanas* (Berkeley, 1957), p. 76.
29. John S. Brushwood, "The Mexican Understanding of Realism and Naturalism," *Hispania* 43 (December, 1960): 522, feels that no thoroughly realistic novel existed in Mexico before 1885.
30. Manuel Pedro González, *Trayectoria de la novela en México* (Mexico, 1951), p. 64, states: ". . . con Emilio Rabasa hace su aparición en México el realismo como una técnica o concepción nueva y distinta de la novela." Joaquina Navarro, *La novela realista mexicana* (Mexico, 1955), p. 80, agrees that "la obra de Rabasa practica por primera vez en la novela mexicana las aspiraciones y la técnica de la escuela realista."
31. Alfonso Noriega, "Conferencias dictadas en la sesión solemne en homenaje al maestro Emilio Rabasa," *El Faro*, no. 15–16 (Mexico, 1957), p. 43, calls him "hombre de una inteligencia poco común" and exalts him as a writer above Justo Sierra.
32. Manuel González Ramírez, prologue to Emilio Rabasa, *Retratos y estudios* (Mexico, 1945), p. xxi.
33. Carlos Gonzáles Peña, *History of Mexican Literature* (Dallas, Tx., 1945), p. 305.
34. Julio Jiménez Rueda, "El centenario de López Portillo," *Revista Iberoamericana* 16 (1950): 215.
35. Joaquina Navarro, *La novela realista*, p. 212.
36. Mariano Azuela, *Cien años de novela mexicana* (Mexico, 1947), p. 151.
37. Roland Grass, "José López-Portillo y Rojas y la revolución agraria en México," *Cuadernos Americanos* 146 (1966): 240–46.
38. Luis Alberto Sánchez, *Proceso y contenido*, p. 151, says that the author "intentó parafrasear a *María*."
39. Arturo Uslar Pietri, *Breve historia*, p. 76.
40. Mariano Azuela, *Cien años*, p. 132.
41. Fernando Alegría, *Historia de la novela*, p. 67.

42. Mauricio Magdaleno, "Alrededor de la novela mexicana," *El Libro y el Pueblo* 14, no. 4 (Mexico, 1941): 1.
43. Jiménez Rueda, *Antología de la prosa en México* (Mexico, 1938), p. 453.
44. Joaquina Navarro, *La novela realista*, pp. 170–71.
45. John S. Brushwood, *Mexico in its Novel* (Austin, 1966), p. 134.
46. James W. Brown, "Heriberto Frías, a Mexican Zola," *Hispania* 50 (1967): 467–71.
47. John S. Brushwood, "Heriberto Frías on Social Behaviour and Redemptive Woman," *Hispania* 45 (1962), 249–53.
48. Ernest R. Moore, "Heriberto Frías and the Novel of the Mexican Revolution," *Modern Language Forum* 27, no. 1 (1942): 12–27.
49. Adolfo Prieto, *La literatura autobiográfica argentina* (Buenos Aires, n.d.), p. 148.
50. Raimundo Lida, *Letras hispánicas* (Mexico, 1958), p. 195, admitting that it is one of the great books of Argentina, finds it "zigzagueante, el más desigual y mixto," and Ricardo Rojas, *Obras. Literatura argentina* (Buenos Aires, 1925), 15: 692, feels that as a "crónica de viaje" it lacks concision and meditation, "pero aun así, deshilvanada, ligera y redundante como es su prosa, ella descubre una vasta experiencia del mundo y un sentido profundamente humano de la vida."
51. Roberto F. Giusti, *Historia de la literatura argentina*, ed. Rafael Alberti Arrieta (Buenos Aires, 1959), p. 378.
52. Ezequiel Martínez Estrada, "*La tierra púrpura*: una novela clave," *Ficción* 5 (1957): 176–81. Luis Franco, in *Historia de la literatura argentina*, ed. Rafael Alberto Arrieta (Buenos Aires, 1959), 5: 421, claims that this novel "ha quedado como modelo vivo y para siempre de novela criolla."
53. Ricardo Rojas, *Literatura Argentina*, vol. 15, lists Cané, Mansilla, and Eduardo Wilde as "prosistas fragmentarios."
54. Juan Carlos Ghiano, *Constantes de la literatura argentina* (Buenos Aires, 1953), p. 70. See also Rodolfo A. Borello, "Los escritores del 80," *Revista de Literatura Argentina e Iberoamericana* 1 (1959): 32–46.
55. Arturo Cambours Ocampo, *Indagaciones sobre literatura argentina* (Buenos Aires, 1952), p. 76.
56. Prieto, *Autobiográfica argentina*, p. 172.
57. Alberto Zum Felde, *Índice crítico de la literatura hispanoamericana* (Mexico, 1959) 2: 168.
58. Germán García, *La novela argentina* (Buenos Aires, 1952), p. 45.
59. Arturo Giménez Pastor, *Historia de la literatura argentina* (Buenos Aires, 1945), p. 370.
60. *Quilito* (1891), based on the Stock Market crash of 1890, resembles Zola's *L'Argent* (1891), but Theodore Anderson, *Carlos María Ocantos, Argentine Novelist* (New Haven, 1934), p. 86, denies such influence.

61. Myron I. Lichtblau, *The Argentine Novel in the Nineteenth Century* (New York, 1959), p. 185.

62. Raimundo Lazo, *La literatura cubana* (Mexico, 1956), p. 158, states that "la pintura del ambiente, animada y veraz, vale más que la estructura y el movimiento de la trama"; Juan J. Remos, on the other hand, in *Proceso histórico de las letras cubanas*, (Madrid, 1958), p. 202, considers *Leonela* to be superior to *Cecilia Valdés* in style but "no así en ese admirable dominio de la descripción."

63. Ángel Valbuena Briones, *Literatura hispanoamericana* (Barcelona, 1967), p. 277, states categorically that "Eduardo Acevedo Díaz inició el naturalismo en la Banda Oriental. Estructuró su obra con una sólida base informativa, presentando un análisis psicológico de tendencia determinista."

64. Fernando Alegría, *Historia de la novela*, p. 204.

65. Alberto Zum Felde, *La narrativa en Hispanoamérica* (Madrid, 1964), p. 56, calls him the father of the historical novel, which, he says, in Uruguay substituted for the epic poem his country never achieved.

66. Domingo A. Caillava, *Historia de la literatura gauchesca en el Uruguay, 1810–1940* (Montevideo, 1945), pp. 71–72.

67. Alberto Zum Felde, *Proceso intelectual del Uruguay y crítica de su literatura* (Montevideo, 1941), p. 176.

68. Alberto Zum Felde, *Índice crítico*, p. 123, states: "En la novela de Acevedo Díaz comienza a sentirse ya esa realidad telúrica del Continente, si bien el acento de su obra cae mayormente sobre los caracteres humanos, y de éstos, sobre los valores."

69. F. Ferrándiz Alborz, "Tres precursores del nuevo realismo literario hispanoamericano," *Cuadernos Americanos* 66 (1952): 277.

70. Alberto Zum Felde, *Proceso intelectual*, p. 280.

71. Alberto Lasplaces in Carlos Reyles, *Historia sintética de la literatura uruguaya* (Montevideo, 1931), p. 13.

72. Hugo D. Barbagelata, *La novela y el cuento en Hispanoamérica* (Montevideo, 1947), p. 113, calls it ". . . algo así como la introducción de su epopeya nacional en prosa."

73. Alberto Lasplaces, in Reyles, *Historia sintética*, pp. 23–24.

74. Alberto Zum Felde, *Índice crítico*, p. 112.

75. Ibid., p. 115.

76. Alejandro Andrade Coello, *Motivos nacionales* (Quito, 1927), p. 148.

77. Manuel J. Calle in Luis A. Martínez, *A la costa* (Quito, 1946), p. xix.

78. Enrique Gil Gilbert in Martínez, *A la costa*, p. xxii.

79. Alejandro Coello Andrade, *Motivos nacionales*, p. 106.

80. F. Ferrándiz Alborz, "Notas literarias," *América* 2 (1936): 76.

81. Luis Alberto Sánchez, *Proceso y contenido*, p. 258, seems to imply that *feísmo* is indispensable.

82. Arturo Uslar Pietri and Julián Padrón, *Antología del cuento mo-*

derno venezolano (1895–1935), Biblioteca Venezolana de Cultura (Caracas, 1940), 1: 4.

83. Álvaro Yunque (Arístides Gandolfi Herrero), *La literatura social en la Argentina* (Buenos Aires, 1941), p. 192, approves of Cambaceres' liberal positions and insists that "con Eugenio Cambaceres puede decirse que aparece la novela en la Argentina."

84. Phyllis Powers Beck, "Eugenio Cambaceres: The Vortex of Controversy," *Hispania* 46 (1963), 755–59.

85. Ricardo Rojas, *La literatura argentina*, 15: 637.

86. Ricardo Rojas in Eugenio Cambaceres, *Sin rumbo* (Buenos Aires, 1917), pp. 7–8.

87. Myron I. Lichtblau, *The Argentine Novel*, p. 166, calls *Sin rumbo* "the most noteworthy work of Argentine naturalistic fiction in the 19th century." Ghiano, *Testimonio de la novela argentina* (Buenos Aires, 1956), p. 54, considers *Sin rumbo* to be "una de las más desesperanzadas novelas naturalistas de América."

88. Alberto Zum Felde, *Índice crítico*, p. 188.

89. Enrique Williams Alzaga, *La pampa en la novela argentina*, (Buenos Aires, 1955), p. 150.

90. Enrique Anderson Imbert, *Spanish American Literature: A History* (Detroit, 1963), p. 226.

91. Phyllis Powers Beck, "Eugenio Cambaceres," p. 755.

92. Fermín Estrella Gutiérrez and Emilio Suárez Calimaño, *Historia de la literatura argentina* (Buenos Aires, 1941), p. 289.

93. F. J. Solero, "Eugenio Cambaceres y la novela argentina," *Ficción* 3 (1957): 109.

94. Myron I. Lichtblau, *The Argentine Novel*, pp. 150–51.

95. Ricardo Rojas, *La literatura argentina*, p. 680.

96. Augusto Tamayo Vargas, *Apuntes para un estudio de la literatura peruana* (Lima, 1947), p. 223, claims Mercedes Cabello is the true initiator of the Peruvian realistic novel.

97. Mercedes Cabello de Carbonera, *La novela moderna* (Lima, 1948), p. 21. Although she was a naturalist she stated: ". . . la escuela naturalista los [corazones] ha dañado por carencia de ideales, por atrofia del sentimiento y supresión completa del ser moral."

98. Luis Alberto Sánchez, *La literatura del Perú* (Buenos Aires, 1943), p. 126.

99. Enrique A. Laguerre, "El arte de novelar en Zeno Gandía," *Asomante* 4 (1955): 52, sees them as "tipos de alguna condición social y apenas se conocen como seres normales."

100. José M. Colina, "La naturaleza en *La Charca*," *Asomante* 5 (1949): 53.

101. Manrique Cabrera, "Manuel Zeno Gandía: Poeta del novelario isleño," *Asomante* 4 (1955): 26.

102. Cesáreo Rosa-Nieves, *Historia panorámica de la literatura puertorriqueña* (1963), 1: 721.

103. Hugo D. Barbagelata, *La novela y el cuento*, p. 123.

104. Vicente Salaverri, *Florilegio de prosistas uruguayos* (Buenos Aires, 1918), p. 207.
105. Carlos Roxlo, *Historia de la literatura uruguaya* (Montevideo, 1915), 6: 88.
106. Domingo A. Caillava, *Literatura gauchesca*, p. 199.
107. Javier de Viana, *Autobiografía. Sobre el recado* (Montevideo, 1940), p. 14.
108. Alberto Zum Felde, *Proceso intelectual del Uruguay* (Montevideo, 1930), p. 194.
109. John E. Englekirk and Margaret M. Ramos, *La narrativa uruguaya*, Publications in Modern Philology, no. 3 (Berkeley, 1967), p. 67.
110. Federico Gamboa, *Impresiones y recuerdos* (Mexico, 1893), p. 267.
111. Manuel Pedro González, *Trayectoria*, p. 72.
112. Robert J. Niess, "Federico Gamboa: The Novelist as Autobiographer," *Hispanic Review* 13 (1945): 346–47.
113. Mariano Azuela, *Cien años*, p. 190.
114. Joaquina Navarro, *La novela realista*, p. 307.
115. Donald F. Brown, "A Chilean Germinal. Zola and Baldomero Lillo," *Modern Language Notes* 65 (January 1950): 47.
116. José Santos Gonzáles Vera, introduction to Baldomero Lillo, *Sub Sole* (Santiago, 1931), p. 19.
117. Ruth Sedgwick, "El mensaje social de Baldomero Lillo," *Memorias del Segundo Congreso Internacional de Catedráticos de Literatura Iberoamericano* (August 1940), p. 43.
118. See Miguel de Carrión, *La esfinge* (Havana, 1961), p. 7.
119. Juan J. Remos, *Proceso histórico de las letras cubanas* (Madrid, 1958), p. 270.
120. Juan J. Remos, *Tendencia de la narración imaginativa en Cuba* (Havana, 1935), p. 174.
121. Salvador Bueno, *Historia de la literatura cubana* (Havana, 1963), p. 356, states that Castellanos was "apegado a las fórmulas modernistas . . . su obra está colocada bajo el signo del naturalismo francés. . . . Es posiblemente el primer narrador cubano que se libera del realismo español decimonónico." In *Medio siglo de literatura cubana* (Havana, 1953), p. 76, Bueno states: "*La conjura* . . . de indudable estirpe modernista."
122. Estrella Soto Morejón, "Jesús Castellanos," *Revista de la Universidad de la Habana* 26, no. 158 (1962): 257–70, believes he is a Balzac-type realist or a naturalist in the Maupassant manner.
123. Max Henríquez Ureña, "Jesús Castellanos: su vida y su obra," in Jesús Castellanos, *Colección póstuma* (Havana, 1914), 1: 48.
124. Luis Monguió, "Reflexiones sobre un aspecto de la novela hispano-americana actual," *La novela iberoamericana* (Albuquerque, N.M., 1951), p. 96.
125. Alfredo A. Roggiano, "El modernismo y la novela en la América Hispana," *La novela iberoamericana*, p. 43.
126. Luis Alberto Sánchez, *Proceso y contenido*, p. 58.

127. Federico de Onís, introducción to *Antología de la poesía española e hispanoamericana, 1882–1932* (Madrid, 1934).
128. Ned Davison, *The Concept of Modernism in Hispanic Criticism,* (Boulder, Co., 1966), p. 47.
129. Martí himself referred in a derogatory fashion to his novel as "de poco valor." See Andrés Iduarte, *Martí, escritor* (Mexico, 1945), pp. 108, 207–10.
130. Max Henríquez Ureña, *Breve historia del modernismo* (Mexico, 1954), p. 286.
131. Arturo Uslar Pietri, *Breve historia,* p. 85.
132. Max Heníquez Ureña, *Modernismo,* p. 214, contends that "entre los modernistas sería difícil encontrar otro que hubiera empleado mayor número de palabras nuevas."
133. Jorge Max Rohde, *Ángel de Estrada* (Buenos Aires, 1924), p. 82.
134. Enrique Larreta, *Páginas escogidas* (Buenos Aires, 1942), p. 100.
135. Max Henríquez Ureña, *Modernismo,* p. 211.
136. Amado Alonso, *Ensayo sobre la novela histórica. El modernismo en La gloria de don Ramiro* (Buenos Aires, 1942), p. 181.
137. Arturo Berenguer Carísomo, *Los valores eternos en la obra de Enrique Larreta* (Buenos Aires, 1946), p. 36.
138. Ibid., p. 73.
139. See the introduction to Enrique Larreta, *Obras completas* (Buenos Aires, 1959).
140. Ibid., "Palabras preliminares," p. 12.
141. Arturo Uslar Pietri, *Breve historia,* p. 86.
142. André Jansen, "*La gloria de don Ramiro* de Enrique Rodríguez Larreta," *Cuadernos Hispanoamericanos,* no. 128–29 (1960), p. 175.
143. Cristóbal de Castro, "Páginas hispanoamericanas," *Nuevo Mundo* (24 September 1915).
144. Enrique Anderson Imbert, *Spanish American Literature,* p. 301.
145. Enrique de Gandía, "Palabras preliminares," in Larreta, *Obras completas,* p. 15.
146. Ángel Valbuena Briones, *Literatura hispanoamericana* (Barcelona, 1967), 3: 300.
147. Juan Carlos Ghiano, *Testimonio de la novela argentina* (Buenos Aires, 1956), p. 28.
148. Hugo D. Barbagelata, *La novela y el cuento,* p. 79.
149. Arturo Berenguer, "Las dos últimas novelas de Enrique Larreta," *Cuadernos Hispanoamericanos,* no. 75 (1956), p. 331.
150. Arturo Torres-Rioseco, *Novelistas contemporáneos de América* (Santiago de Chile, 1939), p. 377, calls him ". . . uno de los grandes estilistas modernos de lengua castellana. Al lado de Rodó y de Valle Inclán es uno de los escritores que maneja la prosa con más elegancia."
151. Dilwynn F. Ratcliff, *Venezuelan Prose Fiction* (New York, 1933), p. 187.

152. Henry Holland, "Manuel Díaz Rodríguez. Estilista del modernismo," *Hispania* 39 (1956): 281–86.
153. Luis Monguió, "Manuel Rodríguez y el conflicto entre lo práctico y lo ideal," *Revista Iberoamericana* 11, no. 2 (1946): 49–54.
154. Raúl Agudo Freytes, "El anacronismo literario de Díaz Rodríguez," *Revista Nacional de Cultura* 9, no. 67 (1948): 147–52.
155. Fernando Alegría, *Historia de la novela*, p. 123.
156. Julio Planchart, *Temas críticos* (Caracas, 1948), p. 16, calls it "una linda novela bucólica de rústicos del valle de Caracas que ennoblece el criollismo." See also Edoardo Crema, "Armonía de tendencias en *Peregrina*," *Revista Nacional de Cultura* 21, no. 136 (1959): 86–106.
157. Hernán Díaz Arrieta, *Los cuatro grandes de la literatura chilena* (Santiago, 1963), pp. 20, 36.
158. Julio Arriagada and Hugo Goldsack, "Augusto d'Halmar," *Tres ensayos esenciales y una antología* (Santiago de Chile, 1963), p. 7.
159. Fernando Alegría, *Historia de la novela*, p. 132.
160. Mario Ferrero, *Premios nacionales de literatura* (Santiago de Chile, 1965), 1: 1.
161. Hernán Díaz Arrieta, *Historia personal*, p. 15.
162. Domingo Melfi, *Literatura chilena*, p. 70.
163. John M. Fein, *Modernism in Chilean Literature. The Second Period* (Durham, N.C., 1965), p. 24.
164. Mario Ferrero, *Premios nacionales*, p. 13.
165. Julio Orlandi Araya, *Augusto d'Halmar* (Santiago de Chile, 1959), p. 17.
166. John M. Fein, *Modernism in Chilean Literature*, p. 36.
167. Fernando Alegría, *Historia de la novela*, p. 136.
168. Raúl Silva Castro, *Pedro Prado, vida y obra* (New York, 1959), pp. 48–49.
169. Arturo Torres-Rioseco, "Las novelas de Pedro Prado," *Atenea*, no. 389 (1960), pp. 220.
170. Julio Arriagada Augier and Hugo Goldsack, "Pedro Prado, un clásico de América," *Atenea*, no. 323 (1952), p. 319.
171. Raúl Silva Castro, *Panorama literario de Chile* (Santiago, 1961), p. 131.
172. Arturo Torres-Rioseco, "Notas sobre el desarrollo de la literatura hispanoamericana desde 1916," *Hispania* 50 (1967): 958.
173. Hugo D. Barbagelata, *La novela y el cuento*, p. 268, believes that ". . . el regionalismo, lo autóctono no atrae a Hernández Catá."
174. Salvador Bueno, *Literatura cubana*, p. 365.
175. José Antonio Ramos, "Alfonso Hernández Catá," *Revista de la Universidad de la Habana* 23 (1947): 81–89.
176. Max Henríquez Ureña, *Panorama histórico de la literatura cubana* (New York, 1963), 2: 339.
177. Miguel Ángel de la Torre, *Prosas varias* (Havana, 1966), p. 327.
178. Juan Loveluck, "*De sobremesa*, novela desconocida del modernismo," *Revista Iberoamericana* 31, no. 59 (1965): 17–32, believes

that no other modernist novel "nos trasmite tan fielmente . . . el enrarecido intelectualismo imperante en el fin de siglo exquisito y problemático." The novel gives us the psychology of an artist and the aesthetics and cosmopolitanism of an age.

179. Arturo Pagés Larraya, "Macedonio Fernández, un payador," *Cuadernos Hispanoamericanos,* no. 166 (1963), p. 139.

180. Joaquín Balaguer, *Historia de la literatura dominicana* (Santo Domingo, 1955), p. 289.

181. Gerald Wade, "Introduction to the Colombian Novel," *Hispania* 30 (1947): 475.

182. Manuel Ugarte, *Escritores iberoamericanos de 1900* (Santiago de Chile, 1942), p. 231.

183. Javier Arango Ferrer, *La literatura de Colombia* (Buenos Aires, 1940), p. 84.

184. Rafael Maya, "Crónica sobre Vargas Vila," *Boletín Cultural y Bibliográfico* 6, no. 1 (1965): 1656–62. This number contains several articles on Vargas Vila.

185. Alberto Zum Felde, *Índice crítico,* p. 384.

186. Earl M. Aldrich, Jr., *The Modern Short Story in Peru* (Madison, Wi., 1966), p. 25.

CHAPTER 4

1. Salvador Bueno, *Historia de la literatura cubana* (Havana, 1963), p. 5. See also Ricardo Latcham, "Historia del criollismo," *Anales de la Universidad de Chile* 113, no. 94 (1954): 5–22. Latcham points out that Garcilaso attributed the term to the Negro—"nombre que lo inventaron los negros."

2. José Juan Arrom, "Criollo: definición y matices de un concepto," *Hispania* 34 (1951): 172–76.

3. Luis Alberto Sánchez, *Proceso y contenido de la novela hispanoamericana* (Madrid, 1953), p. 284.

4. Ibid., p. 228.

5. Arturo Torres-Rioseco, "La novela criolla: El mester de gauchería," *Revista Hispánica Moderna* 4 (1937): 1.

6. Arturo Uslar Pietri, *Breve historia de la novela hispanoamericana* (Caracas, 1954), p. 82.

7. Guillermo de Torre, *Claves de la literatura hispanoamericana* (Madrid, 1959), p. 27.

8. Pedro Henríquez Ureña, *Obra crítica* (Mexico, 1960), p. 248.

9. Alberto Zum Felde, *Índice crítico de la literatura hispanoamericana* (Mexico, 1959), 2: 8–9.

10. Mariano Latorre, "Algunas preguntas que no me han hecho sobre el criollismo," *Anales de la Universidad de Chile* 113, no. 100 (1955): 74.

11. Manuel Vega, "En torno al criollismo," *Anales de la Universidad de Chile* 113, no. 93 (1954): 23–33.

12. Pedro Grases, "De la novela en América," in Juan Loveluck, *La novela hispanoamericana* (Santiago de Chile, 1963), pp. 100–102.

13. Arturo Torres-Rioseco, in Loveluck, *La novela hispanoamericana,* pp. 109–12.

14. Enrique Anderson Imbert, "Discusión sobre la novela en América," in Loveluck, *La novela hispanoamericana,* pp. 115–19.

15. Milton Rossel, "Significación y contenido del criollismo," *Atenea,* no. 358 (1955), pp. 9–28.

16. A good discussion of the development of the American criollo spirit may be found in Uslar Pietri, "Lo criollo en la literatura," an appendix to *Breve historia,* pp. 155–72, or in *Las nubes* (Santiago de Chile, 1956), where he finds that "lo mestizo" is "la fuente de la novedad americana."

17. Homero Castillo, "Mariano Latorre y el criollismo," *Hispania* 39 (1956): 438.

18. See Uslar Pietri's essay, *Las nubes,* previously mentioned, for an elaboration of these points.

19. Dillwyn F. Ratcliff, *Venezuelan Prose Fiction* (New York, 1933), p. 78.

20. Hugo D. Barbagelata, *La novela y el cuento en Hispanoamérica* (Montevideo, 1947), pp. 178–79.

21. Rafael Angarita Arvelo, *Historia y crítica de la novela en Venezuela* (Berlin, 1938), p. 37.

22. Julio Planchart, *Temas críticos* (Caracas, 1948), pp. 8–9.

23. Pedro Díaz-Seijas, *Historia y antología de la literatura venezolana* (Madrid, 1955), p. 459.

24. Arturo Uslar Pietri, *Letras y hombres de Venezuela* (Caracas, 1958), pp. 256–57.

25. Mariano Picón-Salas, *Formación y proceso de la literatura venezolana* (Caracas, 1943), p. 162.

26. Kurt Levy, *Vida y obras de Tomás Carrasquilla* (Medellín, 1958), p. 238.

27. Julio Cejador y Frauca in Federico de Onís, *España en América* (Madrid, 1955), p. 637.

28. John E. Englekirk, *An Outline History of Spanish American Literature* (New York, 1965), p. 98, sees him as a costumbrista writer of loosely connected sketches of provincial customs and landscape.

29. Kurt Levy, *Tomás Carrasquilla,* p. 247.

30. Federico de Onís, *España en America,* p. 644.

31. Carlos García Prada, *Letras hispanoamericanas,* 2da serie (Madrid, 1963), p. 122.

32. Carlos García Prada, *Estudios hispanoamericanos* (Mexico, 1945), p. 255.

33. Carlos García Prada, *Letras,* p. 141.

34. Kurt Levy, *Tomás Carrasquilla*, pp. 209–22, has a good analysis of the language of that author.

35. Ibid., p. 136.

36. "Nada de lo que he publicado —fuera de *Salve Regina*— me parece bueno . . .", *Novelas por D. Tomás Carrasquilla*, Biblioteca aldeana de Colombia no. 12 (Bogotá, 1935), p. 13.

37. Rubén Arango H., *Mi literatura* (Medellín, 1949), p. 118.

38. *Novelas por D. Tomás Carrasquilla*, pp. 11–12.

39. Horacio Bejarano Díaz, "Tomás Carrasquilla: Novelista del pueblo antioqueño," *Universidad de Antioquia*, no. 122 (1955), p. 44, states: "A nuestro juicio, es esta la novela menos popular . . . por su índole especial . . ."

40. Enrique C. de la Casa, *La novela antioqueña* (Mexico, 1942), p. 48.

41. Carlos García Prada, introduction to Tomás Carrasquilla, *Seis cuentos* (Mexico, 1959), p. 17.

42. Carmelo M. Bonet, "Una semblanza de Roberto J. Payró," *Boletín de la Academia Argentina de Letras* 32, no. 123–24 (1967): 235–54.

43. Arturo Uslar Pietri, *Breve historia*, p. 95.

44. Álvaro Yunque, *La literatura social en la Argentina* (Buenos Aires, 1941), 1: 198.

45. Juan Pablo Echagüe, *Vida literaria* (Buenos Aires, 1941), p. 140.

46. Germán García, *La novela argentina* (Buenos Aires, 1952), p. 113.

47. Miguel Ángel Calcagno, "Introducción a un estudio de la novela rioplatense," *Revista Iberoamericana de Literatura* 4, no. 4 (1962): 15.

48. Germán García, *Roberto J. Payró, testimonio de una vida y realidad de una literatura* (Buenos Aires, 1961), p. 95.

49. Alberto Zum Felde, *Índice crítico*, p. 177.

50. Antonio Gómez Restrepo, prologue to *Lo irremediable*, Biblioteca aldeana de Colombia, no. 95 (Bogotá, 1936), p. 9.

51. Hernán Díaz Arrieta, *Historia personal de la literatura chilena* (Santiago, 1954), p. 245.

52. Domingo Melfi, *Estudios de literatura chilena* (Santiago de Chile, 1938), p. 103.

53. Lautaro Yankas, "El paisaje y la gente de Chile en la obra de Federico Gana," *Cuadernos Hispanoamericanos*, no. 208 (1967), pp. 147–48.

54. Fernando Alegría, *Historia de la novela hispanoamericana* (Mexico, 1966), p. 106.

55. Domingo Melfi, *Literatura chilena*, p. 11, affirms: "En realidad el tipo de novela *Casa Grande* no ha tenido hasta hoy continuadores en la literatura chilena."

56. Ibid., p. 170. Melfi calls *Casa Grande* "el primer documento serio para el estudio de nuestra sociedad —provocó la más sorda tempestad que libro alguno haya provocado en Chile." Salvador Reyes, "Apuntes sobre la novela y el cuento en Chile," *Cuadernos Hispanoamericanos*, no. 22 (1951), p. 68, finds it to depict in the patriarchal

ambient of the family a "mentalidad, formada por un largo pasado agrícola, no ... mellada por la vida ciudadana."

57. Gilberto González y Contreras, *Radiografía y disección de Rufino Blanco Fombona* (Havana, 1944), p. 79.
58. Arturo Uslar Pietri, *Letras y hombres*, p. 261.
59. Pedro Díaz-Seijas, *Historia y antología*, p. 466, calls him "el creador del criollismo en la literatura venezolana." Max Henríquez Ureña, *Breve historia del modernismo* (Mexico, 1954), p. 287, claims that "si no fue el iniciador del criollismo, sí fue el que le dio mayor dignidad literaria."
60. Alberto Zum Felde, *Índice crítico*, p. 330.
61. Enrique Anderson Imbert, *Spanish American Literature: A History* (Detroit, 1963), p. 404.
62. Humberto Cuenca, "Hacia una interpretación de la obra de José Rafael Pocaterra," *Cultura Universitaria*, no. 48–49 (Caracas, 1955), pp. 95–103.
63. Arturo Uslar Pietri, *Letras y hombres*, p. 156.
64. Mariano Picón-Salas, *Literatura venezolana* (Caracas, 1948), p. 193.
65. Julio Planchart, *Temas críticos*, p. 19.
66. For a discussion of Gallegos and *La Alborada* see Julio Rosales, "Evocación de La Alborada," *Revista Nacional de Cultura* 21, no. 135 (1959): 6–18.
67. Lowell Dunham, *Rómulo Gallegos, vida y obra* (Mexico, 1957), p. 29.
68. Felipe Massiani, *El hombre y la naturaleza venezolana en Rómulo Gallegos* (Caracas, 1943), p. 153.
69. Julio Planchart, *Temas críticos*, p. 21.
70. John E. Englekirk, "Doña Bárbara, Legend of the Llano," *Hispania* 31 (1948): 259–70.
71. Jorge Añez, *De La vorágine a Doña Bárbara* (Bogotá, 1944), pp. 18–19.
72. Mariano Picón-Salas, *Literatura venezolana*, p. 197.
73. Jorge Añez, *De La vorágine*, p. 22.
74. Lowell Dunham, *Rómulo Gallegos*, pp. 222ff.
75. Ibid., p. 227.
76. John E. Englekirk, "Doña Bárbara," pp. 259–70.
77. José Antonio Pérez Regalado, *Doña Bárbara y La catira* (Valencia, 1960), p. 20.
78. Raúl Ramos Calles, *Los personajes de Rómulo Gallegos a través del psicoanálisis* (Caracas, 1947), examines the Oedipus complex, the Electra complex, the Cain-Abel syndrome and similar themes in a number of Gallegos' works. Thus Bárbara is the mother figure, Santos kills his father when he removes the lance, and Marisela is a mother figure. Santos also serves as Marisela's father figure and thus Bárbara's lover. One can read penis envy, castration, homosexuality, and the like into many things, but this study tends to show the characters' human qualities and weaknesses.

79. Arturo Torres-Rioseco, *Novelistas contemporáneos de América* (Santiago de Chile, 1939), p. 97.
80. Guillermo Kaul, "Tres intérpretes del paisaje hispanoamericano," *Cuadernos Hispanoamericanos*, no. 10 (1949), p. 201.
81. Mariano Picón-Salas, *Formación y proceso* (1940), p. 219.
82. Ulrich Leo, *Estudios filológicos sobre letras venezolanas* (Caracas, 1942), p. 46.
83. Donald G. Castanien, "Introspective Techniques in Doña Bárbara," *Hispania* 51 (1958): 282–88.
84. Ben Frederic Carruthers, "Gallegos' Doña Bárbara: The Llanos Personified," *The Pan American* (January 1950), p. 19.
85. Mariano Picón-Salas, *A veinte años de Doña Bárbara* (Mexico, 1959), p. 8.
86. José Rivas Rivas, "Santos Luzardo—A Character in Doña Bárbara," *Revista Nacional de Cultura* (March-April 1958), pp. 23–42.
87. Freyda Schultz de Montovani, "Doña Bárbara y la América de Rómulo Gallegos," *Sur*, no. 230 (Buenos Aires, 1954), pp. 79–96.
88. Orlando Araujo, *Lengua y creación en la obra de Rómulo Gallegos* (Buenos Aires, 1955), p. 24.
89. Andrés Iduarte, *Veinte años con Rómulo Gallegos* (Mexico, 1954), p. 13.
90. Lowell Dunham, *Rómulo Gallegos*, p. 237.
91. Ciro Alegría, "Notas sobre el personaje en la novela hispanoamericana," in *La novela iberoamericana*, edited by Instituto Internacional de Literatura Iberoamericana (Albuquerque, 1952), p. 56.
92. Lowell Dunham, *Rómulo Gallegos*, pp. 31–50.
93. Ángel Valbuena Briones, *Literatura hispanoamericana* (Barcelona, 1962), p. 356.
94. Alberto Zum Felde, *Índice crítico*, p. 232.
95. Ulrich Leo, *Rómulo Gallegos, estudio sobre el arte de novelar* (Mexico, 1954), pp. 59–109. The critic believes, however, that *Sobre la misma tierra*, his next novel, is truly fiction and not a disguised essay.
96. Lowell Dunham, *Rómulo Gallegos*, p. 283.
97. Arturo Uslar Pietri, *Letras y hombres*, p. 14.
98. Dmitry Merejkowski, "Dostoevski, precursor de la revolución rusa," *Nosotros* 39 (1921): 145–67, 292–317.
99. Representative are George O. Schanzer, "Parallels Between Spanish American and Russian Novelistic Themes," *Hispania* (1952): 42–48; Sánchez, *América, novela sin novelistas* (Santiago, 1939), p. 159; and Max Daireaux, "La novela rusa y la literatura hispanoamericana," *Nosotros* 71 (1927): 24.
100. José Carlos Mariátegui, "Nacionalismo e indigenismo en la literatura americana." *La Pluma* 1 (1927): 24.
101. John E. Englekirk and Margaret M. Ramos, *La narrativa uruguaya*, Publications in Modern Philology, no. 3 (Berkeley, 1967), p. 65, while placing the beginning of "narrativa de tema criollo" around

1920, consider Reyles to be "dentro del doble marco psicológico y esteticista . . . ha de figurar siempre entre los grandes cultivadores de la novela criolla en América."

102. George O. Schanzer, "La literatura rusa en el Uruguay," *Revista Iberoamericana* 17, no. 34 (1951–52): 361–73, points out the great influence in Uruguay of Russian literature.

103. Alberto Zum Felde, *Índice crítico*, p. 360.

104. Arturo Torres-Rioseco, *Novelistas contemporáneos*, p. 313.

105. Max Henríquez Ureña, *Del modernismo*, p. 229.

106. Edward Larocque Tinker, "The Cult of the Gaucho and the Creation of a Literature," *Proceedings of the American Antiquarian Society* 57 (1947): 341.

107. Ángel Valbuena Briones, *Literatura hispanoamericana*, p. 280.

108. Luisa Luisi, "The Literature of Uruguay in the Year of Its Constitutional Centenary," *Bulletin of the Pan American Union* 64 (1930): 673. Strangely enough she hardly mentions the caudillo in her extended analysis of this novel in *Nosotros* 41 (1922): 451–68. Víctor Pérez Petit, "El Terruño," *Nosotros* 25 (1917): 471–99, finds the characters admirably drawn and Mamagela to be the equal of the best characters of European master novelists.

109. Álvaro Guillot Múñoz, "Estudio sobre Carlos Reyles," in Carlos Reyes, ed., *Historia sintética de la literatura uruguaya* (Montevideo, 1931), p. 40.

110. Jorge Mañach, "La literatura de hoy, Carlos Reyles," *Revista Hispánica Moderna* 5 (1939): 18.

111. Arturo Torres-Rioseco, *Novelistas contemporáneos*, p. 343.

112. Ángel Valbuena Briones, *Literatura hispanoamericana*, pp. 286–87.

113. Arturo Torres-Rioseco, *Novelistas contemporáneos*, pp. 338–44.

114. Martha Allen, "Personalidad literaria de Carlos Reyles," *Revista Iberoamericana* 13, no. 25 (1947): 91–115.

115. Emir Rodríguez Monegal, "Horacio Quiroga: una perspectiva," *Ficción*, no. 5 (1957), pp. 99–112. Anderson Imbert, in his *History*, p. 299, feels Quiroga "remained faithful to his initial esthetics . . ."

116. Seymour Menton, *El cuento hispanoamericano* (Mexico, 1964), 2: 15.

117. Emir Rodríguez Monegal, *Objetividad de Horacio Quiroga*, (Montevideo, 1950), p. 12.

118. José Enrique Etcheverry, *Horacio Quiroga y la creación artística* (Montevideo, 1957), p. 11.

119. John F. Garganigo, "Gaucho Tierra y Don Segundo Sombra," *Revista Hispánica Moderna* 32 (1966): 198–205.

120. John E. Englekirk and Ramos, *La narrativa uruguaya*, p. 84.

121. Arturo Sergio Venca, "Panorama de la actual narrativa uruguaya," *Ficción* 5 (1957): 120–26.

122. Luisa Luisi, "The Literature of Uruguay," p. 675.

123. Alberto Lasplaces, *Antología del cuento uruguayo* (Montevideo, 1943), 2: 70.

124. Mario Benedetti, *Literatura uruguaya: siglo XX* (Buenos Aires, 1963), pp. 41ff.
125. Rafael Alberto Arrieta, *Historia de la literatura argentina* (Buenos Aires, 1959), 4: 144.
126. Estela Canto, "Benito Lynch o la inocencia," *Sur* 21, no. 215–16 (Buenos Aires, 1952): 109–13.
127. Arturo Torres-Rioseco, *Novelistas contemporáneos*, p. 162.
128. Marshall R. Nason, "Benito Lynch, otro Hudson," *Revista Iberoamericana* 23, no. 45 (1958): 65–82.
129. Julio Caillet-Bois, *La novela rural de Benito Lynch* (La Plata, 1960), p. 11.
130. Roberto F. Giusti, "Benito Lynch," *Nosotros* 48 (1924): 92–102, comments on her tenderness and love and finds her to be "la amante ejemplar," a view shared by many later critics.
131. Arturo Torres-Rioseco, *Novelistas contemporáneos*, p. 200.
132. Germán García, *La novela argentina*, p. 151.
133. See David Viñas, "Benito Lynch y la Pampa cercada," *Cultura Universitaria* 56 (Caracas, 1954): 40–55.
134. Juan Pinto, *Panorama de la literatura argentina contemporánea* (Buenos Aires, 1941), p. 16.
135. Gustavo Martínez Zuviría, *El Kahal* (Santiago de Chile, 1934), p. 19. Another of his anti-semitic texts is *Oro* (1935).
136. As quoted by César Tiempo, "Alberto Gerchunoff," *Hispania* 35 (1952): 37.
137. Sara Jaroslavsky de Lowy, *Alberto Gerchunoff: Vida y obra* (New York, 1957), pp. 26–27.
138. Mateo Booz, *Gente del litoral* (Buenos Aires, 1944), preface.
139. Laura Milano, *Mateo Booz* (Santa Fe, 1964), p. 9.
140. Guillermo de Torre, *Tres conceptos de la literatura hispanoamericana* (Buenos Aires, 1963), pp. 115–24.
141. Guillermo Ara, *Ricardo Güiraldes* (Buenos Aires, 1961), p. 17.
142. Federico de Onís, "Originalidad de la literatura hispanoamericana," *España en América* (Madrid, 1955), p. 127.
143. Ricardo Güiraldes, "De mi hemorragia," *Proa* (July 1925), pp. 35–41.
144. Juan Carlos Ghiano, *Constantes de la literatura argentina* (Buenos Aires, 1953), p. 87, n. 3.
145. Guillermo Ara, *Ricardo Güiraldes*, p. 186.
146. Guillermo de Torre, *Tres conceptos*, p. 122.
147. Barbagelata, *La novela y el cuento*, p. 86.
148. See also Giovanni Previtali and Pablo Max Ynefraín, "El verdadero Don Segundo en *Don Segundo Sombra* de Ricardo Güiraldes," *Revista Iberoamericana* 29, no. 56 (1963): 317–20.
149. For a further exploration of some of these points see Ofelia Kovacci, *La pampa a través de Ricardo Güiraldes* (Buenos Aires, 1961), pp. 99, 142–43.
150. Hugo Rodríguez-Alcalá, *Ensayos críticos* (Mexico, 1958), p. 133.

151. See Garganigo, "Gaucho Tierra y Don Segundo Sombra," p. 203, and García, *La novela argentina*, p. 140.

152. Eunice J. Gates, "The Imagery of Don Segundo Sombra," *Hispanic Review* 16 (1948): 33–49. See also Juan Collantes de Terán, "En torno al simbolismo e impresionismo en Don Segundo Sombra," *Estudios Americanos* 13, no. 64 (1957): 17–39.

153. G. H. Weiss, "Techniques in the Works of Ricardo Güiraldes," *Hispania* 43 (1960), 353–58.

154. Hugo Rodríguez Alcalá, "Lo real y lo ideal en Don Segundo Sombra," *Revista Hispánica Moderna* 32 (1966): 191–97.

155. Edwin S. Morby, "Es Don Segundo Sombra novela picaresca?," *Revista Iberoamericana* 1, no. 2 (1939): 375–79.

156. Fernando Alegría, *Historia de la novela*, pp. 187–88.

157. Juan Carlos Ghiano, *Constantes*, p. 106.

158. A number of articles have appeared about the structure of the novel, among others those of Donald Fabián, "La acción novelesca de Don Segundo Sombra," *Revista Iberoamericana* 23, no. 45 (1958): 147–53, and Giovanni Battista de Cesare, "Sobre la estructura y los protagonistas de Don Segundo Sombra," *Thesaurus* 19 (1964): 558–65.

159. The boy admits that the stories "introduced a radical change in my life," and Ramón Xirau, "Ciclo y vida de Don Segundo Sombra," *Cuadernos Americanos* 116 (1961): 245, sees in them a teaching technique for explaining the world and the conduct of man.

160. Thomas B. Irving, "Myth and Reality in Don Segundo Sombra," *Hispania* 40 (1957): 44–48.

161. Germán García, *La novela argentina*, p. 138.

162. John F. Garganigo, "Gaucho Tierra y Don Segundo Sombra," pp. 190–205.

163. Hugo Rodríguez Alcalá, "Lo real y lo ideal," pp. 191–97.

164. Arturo Torres-Rioseco, *The Epic of Latin American Literature* (New York, 1942), p. 164.

165. Ciro Alegría, "Notas sobre el personaje," p. 51.

166. Guillermo Ara, *Ricardo Güiraldes*, p. 231.

167. Rafael Alberto Arrieta, *Historia de la literatura argentina*, p. 135.

168. Irma Cuna, "Símbolos de Don Segundo Sombra," *Revue de Littérature Comparée* 36 (1962): 408.

169. Bernardo Gicovate, "Notes on Don Segundo Sombra. The Education of Fabio Cáceres," *Hispania* 34 (1951): 366–68.

170. G. H. Weiss, "Argentina, the Ideal of Ricardo Güiraldes," *Hispania* 41 (1958): 149–53.

171. Jefferson Rhea Spell, *Contemporary Spanish American Fiction* (Chapel Hill, 1944), pp. 203–4.

172. Jorge Luis Borges. "Sobre Don Segundo Sombra," *Sur*, no. 217–18 (Buenos Aires, 1952), p. 9.

173. Aristóbulo Echegaray, *Don Segundo Sombra. Reminiscencia infantil de Ricardo Güiraldes* (Buenos Aires, 1954), pp. 10, 47.

174. Arturo Torres-Rioseco, *Ensayos sobre literatura latinoamericana* (Berkeley, 1953), p. 120, calls it "la mejor novela americana." Peter G. Earle, "El sentido poético de *Don Segundo Sombra*," *Revista Hispánica Moderna* 26 (1960): 126–32, denies that it is a "good" novel and states that Güiraldes superficially complies with novelistic techniques in order to write what is essentially poetry and the outstanding example of "elementalismo y refinamiento," a rare form of poetry.

175. Luis Alberto Sánchez, "Manuel González Prada, poeta indigenista," in Manuel González Prada, *Baladas peruanas* (Santiago de Chile, 1935).

176. Jorge Mañach, "Manuel González Prada y su obra," *Revista Hispánica Moderna* 4, no. 1 (1937): 17.

177. Augusto Guzmán, *La novela en Bolivia* (La Paz, 1955), p. 75.

178. For a good discussion of the reaction to Arguedas' thesis, see Mary Plevich, "El origen de Arguedismo," *Universidad de Antioquia*, no. 134 (1958), pp. 407–14.

179. See Miguel de Unamuno, *Contra eso y aquello* (Buenos Aires, 1945), pp. 34–41, and *Mi religión y otros ensayos breves* (Buenos Aires, 1945), pp. 43–50.

180. Fernando Díez de Medina, *Literatura boliviana* (Madrid, 1954), p. 278.

181. Mario T. Soria, *Armando Chirveches A., novelista boliviano* (Hiram, Oh., 1962), pp. 71–72.

182. Alberto Zum Felde, *Índice crítico*, p. 195.

183. José Antonio Galaos, "Manuel Gálvez, novelista cronista de Buenos Aires," *Cuadernos Hispanoamericanos*, no. 170 (1964), p. 344.

184. In his *Amigos y maestros de mi juventud* (Buenos Aires, 1944), Gálvez shows the background for some of his novels and reveals how painstakingly he prepared himself to be a writer of fiction. His dedication to his calling also shows in *El novelista y las novelas* (Buenos Aires, 1959).

185. Mireya Jaimes Freyre, "Gálvez y su laberinto," *Revista Iberoamericana* 18, no. 36 (1952–53): 315–37, believes Gálvez painted his own soul rather than an objective Argentine reality.

186. Germán García, *La novela argentina*, p. 125.

187. Jefferson Rhea Spell, *Contemporary Fiction*, p. 63.

188. Otis H. Green, "Manuel Gálvez, Gabriel Quiroga, and *La maestra normal*," *Hispanic Review* 11 (1944): 221–52. See also "Manuel Gálvez, Gabriel Quiroga, and *El mal metafísico*," *Hispanic Review* 11 (1944): 314–27.

189. See the prologue to Eduardo Barrios, *Un perdido* (Santiago de Chile, 1958), p. 7.

190. Manuel Gálvez, *En el mundo de los seres ficticios* (Buenos Aires, 1961), p. 68.

191. Manuel García Blanco, "El escritor argentino Manuel Gálvez y Unamuno," *Cuadernos Hispanoamericanos*, no. 53 (1954), p. 184.

192. Manuel Orgaz, "Conversación con Manuel Gálvez," *Cuadernos Hispanoamericanos*, no. 160 (1962), p. 117.

193. Myron I. Lichtblau, "The Recent Novels of Manuel Gálvez," *Hispania* 42 (1959): 502.

194. See Guillermo Cotto-Thorner, "Manuel Gálvez y su trilogía de la guerra del Paraguay," *Revista Iberoamericana* 16, no. 31 (1950): 77–89. For a devastating criticism of *Los caminos de la muerte* see José Bianco, "Los caminos de la muerte," *Nosotros* 61 (1928): 99–105.

195. Manuel Gálvez, *Entre la novela y la historia* (Buenos Aires, 1962), 3: 35.

196. Cotto-Thorner, "Manuel Gálvez y su trilogía," p. 87.

197. Henry Alfred Holmes, "Una trilogía de Manuel Gálvez: Escenas de la guerra del Paraguay," *Revista Hispánica Moderna* 3 (1937): 210.

198. The quality of Barrios' psychology from a scientific point of view has generated much discussion. See Ángel Manuel Vásquez-Bigi, "Los tres planos de la creación artística de Eduardo Barrios," *Revista Iberoamericana* 29, no. 55 (1963): 125–37.

199. Jaime Peralta, "La novelística de Eduardo Barrios," *Cuadernos Hispanoamericanos*, no. 173 (1964), p. 362.

200. Hernán Díaz Arrieta, *Panorama de la literatura chilena durante el siglo XX* (Santiago, 1931), p. 80.

201. Arturo Torres-Rioseco, *Novelistas contemporáneos*, p. 249.

202. Raúl Silva Castro, "Eduardo Barrios (1884–1963)," *Revista Iberoamericana* 30, no. 58 (1964): 243–46.

203. Eduardo Barrios, *Y la vida sigue* (Buenos Aires, 1925), p. 86.

204. Milton Rossel, "Eduardo Barrios, el hombre y su obra," in Eduardo Barrios, *Obras completas* (Santiago, 1962), 1: 14.

205. Arturo Torres-Rioseco, *Novelistas contemporáneos*, p. 226.

206. Arnold Chapman, "The *Perdido* as a Type in Some Spanish-American Novels," *PMLA* 70 (1955): 23.

207. Ned J. Davison, "Conflict and Identity in *El Hermano Asno*," *Hispania* 42 (1959): 498–501.

208. See Luisa Luisi, *A través de libros y de autores* (Buenos Aires, 1925), p. 210, for elaboration of this point.

209. A. M. Vázquez-Bigi, "Los conflictos psíquicos y religiosos de *El Hermano Asno*," *Cuadernos Hispanoamericanos*, no. 220 (1968), pp. 120–45, raises the possibility that Barrios, in presenting a caricature, might also have shown that it was Lázaro who really attempted to violate María, that he, too, suffered from mental instability, and his punishment at the end was fully justified. Vázquez-Bigi feels that the ambiguity was deliberately created by Barrios.

210. Carlos Hamilton, "La novelística de Eduardo Barrios," *Cuadernos Americanos* 85 (1956): 285.

211. He himself sees nothing strange about the unproductive interval, stating that he wrote again when he felt the need. See Eduardo Barrios, *Los hombres del hombre* (Santiago de Chile, 1950), p. 28.

212. See Jerry L. Benbow, "Grotesque Elements in Eduardo Barrios," *Hispania* 51 (1968): 86.
213. José Antonio Galaos, "Eduardo Barrios, novelista autobiográfico," *Cuadernos Hispanoamericanos*, no. 168 (1963), p. 173.
214. Eduardo Barriso, *Obras completas* (Santiago de Chile, 1962), 1: 28.
215. Ángel Flores, *Historia y antología del cuento y la novela en Hispanoamérica* (New York, 1959), p. 321.
216. Hernán Díaz Arrieta, *Historia personal*, pp. 232–33.
217. Luis Alberto Sánchez, "Rafael Maluenda, novelista de almas," *Revista Nacional de Cultura* 5, no. 38 (1943): 58–68.
218. Hernán Díaz Arrieta, *Historia personal*, p. 309.
219. Emilio Vaisse (Omer Emeth), *Estudios críticos de literatura chilena* (Santiago, 1961), 2: 370.
220. Hugo Montes and Julio Orlandi, *Historia de la literatura chilena* (Santiago, 1955), p. 221.
221. Mario Ferrero, *Premios nacionales de literatura* (Santiago de Chile, 1965), p. 194, claims the novel "está a la altura de las mejores novelas realistas que se hayan escrito en América."
222. Mariano Latorre, "Fernando Santiván, el hombre, el escritor," *Cuadernos Hispanoamericanos*, no. 49 (1954), pp. 83, 85.
223. Arturo Torres-Rioseco, *Novelistas contemporáneos*, p. 285.
224. Raúl Silva Castro, *Panorama de la novela chilena* (Mexico, 1955), p. 154.
225. Arnold Chapman, "Observations on the *Roto* in Chilean Fiction," *Hispania* 32 (1949): 312. See also Carlos Seura Salvo, "Tipos chilenos en la novela y en el cuento nacional," *Anales de la Universidad de Chile* 95, no. 25–26 (1937): 41–50.
226. Mariano Latorre, *La literatura en Chile* (Buenos Aires, 1941), p 82.
227. Lautaro Yankas, "Cuentistas y novelistas del mar chileno," *Cuadernos Hispanoamericanos*, no. 123 (1960), p. 311.
228. For a good discussion on the huaso in Chile see Tomás Lago, *El Huaso* (Santiago, 1953). Lautaro Yankas, "Dimensión y estilo de Mariano Latorre," *Cuadernos Hispanoamericanos*, no. 221 (1968), pp. 430–39, believes that Latorre's protagonist is *el medio* rather than *el hombre*. He comments on the musical and plastic qualities of the prose and on Latorre's naturalism.
229. See Domingo Melfi y Mariano Latorre, "Letras chilenas: dos discursos," *Atenea* 156 (June 1938): 340–48, for this and other expressions of Latorre's love for the land and identification with the Chilean *ambiente*.
230. Omer Emeth, *Estudios críticos de literatura chilena* (Santiago, 1940), p. 325.
231. Magda Arce, "Mariano Latorre, novelista chileno contemporáneo," *Revista Iberoamericana* 5, no. 10, (1942): 359.
232. Mario Ferrero, *Premios nacionales*, p. 79.

233. Raúl Silva Castro, "Mariano Latorre y su novela, *La paquera*," *Revista Iberoamericana* 24, no. 48 (1959): 297–306.
234. Hernán Díaz Arrieta, *Historia personal*, pp. 253–54.
235. Homero Castillo, "Mariano Latorre," *Hispania* 37 (1954): 315.
236. Raúl Silva Castro, *Panorama*, p. 180.
237. Donald F. Fogelquist, "The Humorous Genius of José Santos González Vera," *Hispania* 36 (1953): 314–18.
238. Enrique Anderson Imbert, *Spanish American Literature*, p. 409.
239. Amanda Labarca H., "En torno a González Vera," *Repertorio Americano* (15 March 1952), p. 238.
240. Mario Ferrero, *Premios nacionales*, p. 66.
241. Hernán Díaz Arrieta in Mario Ferrero, *Premios nacionales*, p. 42.
242. Fernando Alegría, *Historia de la novela*, pp. 210–12.
243. Manuel Rojas, *Obras completas* (Santiago de Chile, 1961), pp. 33–34.
244. Ramón Sender, "Sobre la novela rapsódica y la urbe," *Revista Iberoamericana* 17, no. 34 (1951–52): 269–83.
245. Manuel Rojas, in his *Obras completas*, p. 29, states that he follows the same process here as the mind follows—thinking, remembering, wandering, without being subjected to fixed norms, "y sin respeto al orden cronológico, o sea: nunca me propuse, conscientemente, tener un estilo ni construir una técnica."
246. Ricardo Latcham, "Novela chilena actual: Las viejas generaciones," in Juan Loveluck, *La novela hispanoamericana*, p. 329.
247. Enrique Anderson Imbert, *Spanish American Literature*, p. 305.
248. Martin E. Ericson, "Escritores modernistas de Guatemala," *Revista Iberoamericana* 6, no. 12 (1943): 479–91.
249. R. Amílcar Echeverría, *Antología de prosistas guatemaltecos* (Guatemala, 1957), p. 289.
250. Ruth Lamb, *Antología del cuento guatemalteco* (Mexico, 1959), p. 46.
251. Ricardo Estrada, *Flavio Herrera y su novela* (Guatemala, 1960), p. 8.
252. Seymour Menton, *Historia crítica de la novela guatemalteca* (Guatemala, 1960), p. 172.
253. Javier Arango Ferrer, *La literatura de Colombia* (Buenos Aires, 1940), p. 83.
254. Luis Alberto Sánchez, *Escritores representativos de América* (Madrid, 1963), 3: 143.
255. Eduardo Neale-Silva, *Horizonte humano. Vida de José Eustasio Rivera* (Madison, 1960), p. 222. Neale-Silva also comments on the origins of the novel in "The Factual Bases of *La vorágine*," *PMLA* 54 (1939): 316–31.
256. See the prologue by David Rivera in José Eustasio Rivera, *Obras completas* (Medellín, Colombia, 1963), p. 19.
257. Jorge Añez, *De La vorágine a Doña Bárbara* (Bogotá, 1944), pp. 153–63.

258. Jean Franco, *The Modern Culture of Latin America: Society and the Artist* (New York, 1967), p. 86.
259. Eduardo Neale-Silva, *Horizonte humano*, p. 367.
260. Joan R. Green, "La estructura del narrador y el modo narrativo de *La vorágine*," *Cuadernos Hispanoamericanos*, no. 205 (1967), p. 107.
261. For a more complete discussion of this point see W. E. Bull, "Nature and Anthropomorphism in *La vorágine*," *Romanic Review* 39 (1948): 307–18.
262. Suzanne K. Langer, *Philosophy in a New Key* (New York, 1951), p. 153.
263. José Ángel Valente, "La naturaleza y el hombre en *La vorágine* de José Eustasio Rivera," *Cuadernos Hispanoamericanos* 24, no. 67 (1955): 102–8.
264. Peter Earle, "Camino oscuro. La novela hispanoamericana contemporánea," *Cuadernos Americanos* 152 (1967): 204–22.
265. Leónidas Morales, "*La vorágine*: Un viaje al país de los muertos," *Anales de la Universidad de Chile* 122, no. 134 (1965): 148–70.
266. Ciro Alegría, "Notas sobre el personaje," p. 55.
267. Edmundo de Chasca, "El lirismo de *La vorágine*," *Revista Iberoamericana* 13, no. 25 (1948): 73–90, comments at length on its lyrical style and form, which consists of epic, popular, romantic, and pathetic elements. He finds its best pages to be "la visión poética más poderosa de la naturaleza tropical que se haya escrito . . . acaso en cualquier idioma." See also Otto Olivera, "El romanticismo de José Eustasio Rivera," *Revista Iberoamericana* 18, no. 35 (1952–53): 41–61.
268. Juan Marinello, "Tres novelas ejemplares," *Sur* 6, no. 16 (1936): 59–75.

CHAPTER 5

1. Luis Arturo Castellanos, "La novela de la revolución mexicana," *Universidad* 73 (Santa Fe, Argentina, 1967): 64.
2. Rosario Castellanos, "La novela mexicana contemporánea y su valor testimonial," *Hispania* 57 (1964): 223.
3. Manuel Pedro González, *Trayectoria de la novela en México* (Mexico, 1951), p. 107.
4. José Luis Martínez, *Literatura mexicana: siglo XX* (Mexico, 1949), pp. 39–40.
5. Eugenio Chang-Rodríguez, "La novela de la revolución mexicana y su clasificación," *Hispania* 42 (1959): 527–35.
6. Arturo Uslar Pietri, *Breve historia de la novela hispanoamericana* (Caracas, 1954), p. 132.
7. Manuel Pedro González, *Trayectoria*, p. 95.

8. Manuel Pedro González, *Ensayos críticos* (Caracas, 1963), p. 100.
9. Arturo Torres-Rioseco, *Novelistas contemporáneos de América* (Santiago de Chile, 1939), p. 16.
10. Seymour Menton, "La estructura épica de *Los de abajo* y un prólogo especulativo," *Hispania* 50 (1967): 1001–11.
11. Jefferson Rhea Spell, *Contemporary Spanish American Fiction* (Chapel Hill, 1944), p. 100.
12. Manuel Pedro González, *Trayectoria*, pp. 11–12.
13. Luis Leal, "Mariano Azuela, novelista médico," *Revista Hispánica Moderna* 28 (1962): 295–303.
14. Mariano Azuela, *Cien años de novela mexicana* (Mexico, 1947), p. 13.
15. J. M. González de Mendoza, "Mariano Azuela y lo mexicano," *Cuadernos Americanos* 63 (1952): 285.
16. Manuel Pedro González, *Trayectoria*, p. 166.
17. Frances Kellam Hendricks and Beatrice Berler, trans., *Mariano Azuela. Two novels of the Mexican Revolution* (San Antonio, 1963), p. ix.
18. Manuel Pedro González, *Trayectoria*, p. 133.
19. Mariano Azuela, *Los de abajo*, ed. John E. Englekirk (New York, 1939), p. xviii.
20. Mariano Azuela, *Obras completas* (Mexico, 1958), 3: 1174.
21. See John E. Englekirk, "The Discovery of *Los de Abajo*," *Hispania* (1938): 51–62.
22. Mariano Azuela, "Azares de mi novela, *Los de abajo*," *Universidad de México* 1, no. 2 (1946): 2, states: "Por lo demás, la mayor parte de los sucesos referidos en la novela no fueron presenciados por mí, sino constituidos o reconstruidos con retazos de visiones de gente y acontecimientos." He acknowledges, nonetheless, that many of his characters are based on real people he knew.
23. John S. Brushwood and José Garcidueñas, *Breve historia de la novela mexicana* (Mexico, 1959), p. 97.
24. Seymour Menton, "La estructura épica," pp. 1001–11.
25. Waldo Frank, "The Mexican Invasion," *The New Republic* (23 October 1929), p. 276.
26. Arturo Uslar Pietri, *Breve historia*, p. 112.
27. Mariano Azuela, *Obras completas*, 3: 1076.
28. Ibid., p. 1091.
29. Mariano Azuela, *Las tribulaciones de una familia decente*, ed. Frances Kellam Hendricks and Beatrice Berler (New York, 1966), p. 26.
30. Jefferson Rhea Spell, *Contemporary Fiction*, p. 88.
31. Bernard Dulsey, "Azuela Revisited," in Letters to the Editor, *Hispania* 35 (1952): 332.
32. Hugo D. Barbagelata, *La novela y el cuento en Hispanoamérica* (Montevideo, 1947), pp. 244–45.
33. Mariano Azuela, *Obras completas*, 3: 1044.

34. Mariano Azuela, *Los de abajo*, pp. xiv-xv.

35. Helen Phipps Hauck, "Las obras novelescas de Martín Luiz Guzmán," *Revista Iberoamericana* 3, no. 5 (1941): 139–57, explains why it is *not*, in her opinion, a novel.

36. F. Rand Morton, *Los novelistas de la revolución mexicana* (Mexico, 1949), p. 422.

37. Luis Leal, *"La sombra del caudillo*, roman a clef," *Modern Language Journal* 36 (1952): 16–21.

38. Manuel Pedro González, *Trayectoria*, pp. 206–8.

39. Martínez, *Literatura mexicana*, p. 43.

40. R. Anthony Castagnaro, "Rubén Romero and the Novel of the Mexican Revolution," *Hispania* 36 (1953): 300–304.

41. Raúl Arreola Cortés, "José Rubén Romero, vida y obra," *Revista Hispánica Moderna* 12, no. 1–2 (1946): 14, 17.

42. Manuel Pedro González, *Trayectoria*, pp. 225–26.

43. See Alejandro Arratia, "Tres novelas de José Rubén Romero," *La Nueva Democracia* (April 1958), pp. 92–97; William O. Cord, "José Rubén Romero: The Writer as Seen by Himself," *Hispania* 44 (1961): 431–37; Cord, *José Rubén Romero* (Mexico, 1963), p. 29.

44. William O. Cord, "The Writer as Seen by Himself," p. 434.

45. José Rubén Romero, *Obras completas*, (Mexico, 1957), p. 76.

46. José Rubén Romero, "Fecha y fichas de un pobre diablo," *Cuadernos Americanos* 22, (1945): 254.

47. Ernest R. Moore, *Novelistas de la revolución mexicana* (Havana, 1940), p. 43.

48. Fernando Alegría, *Historia de la novela hispanoamericana* (Mexico, 1966), p. 157.

49. Antonio Castro Leal, *La novela de la Revolución Mexicana* (Madrid, 1960), 2: 363.

50. Carlos González Peña, *Historia de la literatura mexicana* (Mexico, 1958), p. 415.

51. Alberto Zum Felde, *Índice crítico de la literatura hispanoamericana* (Mexico, 1959), 2: 306.

52. Manuel Pedro González. *Trayectoria*, p. 289.

53. Juan Uribe Echeverría, "La novela de la revolución mexicana y la novela hispanoamericana actual," *Anales de la Universidad de Chile* 93, no. 20 (Santiago, 1935): 61.

54. Nellie Campobello, *Mis libros*, (Mexico, 1960), p. 17.

55. Manuel Pedro González, *Trayectoria*, p. 277. See also Gabriella de Beer, *José Vasconcelos and His World* (New York, 1966), p. 51, who claims that *Ulises Criollo* "is generally considered one of the major novels of the Revolution."

56. Manuel Pedro González has a good study of this novel, "Una novela desconocida," *Cuadernos Americanos* 54 (1950): 290–97.

57. Luis Alberto Sánchez, *Proceso y contenido de la novela hispanoamericana* (Madrid, 1953), p. 527, calls Traven *"el* novelista de la Revolución Mexicana, aunque no sea un mexicano de nacimiento

ni de idioma."

58. José Luis Martínez, *Literatura mexicana*, p. 18.
59. Julio Jiménez Rueda, *Historia de la literatura mexicana* (Mexico, 1960), p. 327.
60. John S. Brushwood, *Mexico in its Novel* (Austin, Tx., 1966), p. 186.
61. Artemio de Valle-Arizpe, *Obras completas* (Mexico, 1959), 1: 21.
62. See Joseph Sommers, *Francisco Rojas González, exponente literario del nacionalismo mexicano* (Xalapa, Mexico, 1966).
63. Mary Ann Lowe, *Francisco Rojas González, novelista* (Mexico, 1957), and Joseph Sommers, "La génesis literaria en Francisco Rojas González," *Revista Iberoamericana* 29, no. 56, (1963): 299–309, claim that in an interview with Fernando Benítez, the author admitted knowing a Remedios Farrera on whom he based the protagonist. This was later confirmed by Rojas' widow and Benítez in articles on the matter.
64. Ruth Stanton Lamb, "Francisco Rojas González," *Modern Language Forum* 31 (March-June 1946): 1.
65. Joseph Sommers, "La negra Angustias," *La Palabra y el Hombre* 10, no. 40 (1966): 637–52.
66. José Luis Martínez, *Literatura mexicana*, p. 244.

Bibliography

Histories of literature, both general and specific, sociological, philosophical, psychological, and historical texts, and short book reviews do not as a rule appear in this bibliography. Where possible, entries on authors active in various genres have been limited to their fictional output.

GENERAL WORKS ON THE SPANISH AMERICAN NOVEL

Agüero, Luis. "Saldo y promesa." *Casa de las Américas* 4, no. 22 (1964): 60–69.

Alegría, Ciro. "Notas sobre el personaje en la novela hispanoamericana." In *La novela iberoamericana*, edited by Instituto Internacional de Literatura Iberoamericana, pp. 49–58. Albuquerque, 1952.

Alegría, Fernando. *Breve historia de la novela hispanoamericana.* Mexico, 1966.

Alegría, Fernando. *Las fronteras del realismo.* Santiago, 1962.

Alegría, Fernando. "Una clasificación de la novela hispanoamericana contemporánea. In *La novela iberoamericana*, edited by Instituto Internacional de Literatura Iberoamericana, pp. 61–75. Albuquerque, 1952.

Alonso, Amado. *Ensayo sobre la novela histórica.* Buenos Aires, 1942.

Amorós, Andrés. *Introducción a la novela contemporánea.* Salamanca, 1966.

Anderson Imbert, Enrique. "Discusión sobre la novela en América." In *Estudios sobre escritores en América.* Buenos Aires, 1954. Also included in this work are discussions of Padre Las Casas, Hernán Cortés, Bernal Díaz del Castillo, Jorge Isaacs, Manuel de Jesús Galván, and the historical novel.

Anderson Imbert, Enrique. "La novela en América Latina." *Cuadernos,* no. 89 (Paris, 1964), pp. 7–13.

Anderson Imbert, Enrique. "Notas sobre la novela histórica en el siglo XIX." In *La novela iberoamericana,* edited by Instituto Internacional de Literatura Iberoamericana, pp. 3–24. Albuquerque, 1952. Included is a "Catálogo de novelas históricas."

Andrade Coello, Alejandro. "Algo sobre la novela en la América del Sur." *Revista Instituto Mejía,* no. 32 (Quito, 1936), pp. 1–18.

Arrom, José Juan. "Criollo: Definición y matices de un concepto." *Hispania* 34 (1951): 172–76.

Arrom, José Juan. *Esquema generacional de las letras hispanoamericanas.* Bogotá, 1963.

Baker, Armand F. "El tiempo en la novela hispanoamericana." Ph.D. dissertation, University of Iowa, 1968.

Barbagelata, Hugo D. *La novela y el cuento en Hispanoamérica.* Montevideo, 1947.

Bellini, Giuseppe. *La protesta nel romanzo ispanoamericano del novecento.* Milano, 1957.

Borges, Jorge Luis. "El arte narrativo y la mágica." *Sur* 2, no. 5 (Buenos Aires, 1932): 172–79.

Bueno, Salvador. *La letra como testigo.* Santa Clara, Cuba, 1957.

Caballero Calderón, Eduardo. "Hispanoamerica en sus novelistas." *Cuadernos Hispanoamericanos,* no. 64 (1955), pp. 45–58.

Caballero Calderón, Eduardo. "La novela y la soledad." *Cuadernos* no. 70 (Paris, 1963), pp. 26–28.

Cambours Ocampo, Arturo. *El problema de las generaciones literarias.* Buenos Aires, 1963.

Carpentier, Alejo. *Tientos y diferencias.* Mexico, 1967.

Carrilla, Emilio. *El romanticismo en la América Hispana.* Madrid, 1958.

Carrión, Benjamín. "La novela regional." *Cuadernos,* no. 19 (Paris, 1956), pp. 111–24.

Carsuzán, María E. *La creación en la prosa de España e Hispanoamérica.* Buenos Aires, 1955.

Ceuto, M. I. *La novela hispanoamericana.* Santiago, 1934.

Chang-Rodríguez, Eugenio. "Variaciones sobre el indigenismo." *La Nueva Democracia* 36, no. 1 (1956): 96–111.

Chapman, Arnold. "The *Perdido* as a Type in Some Spanish-American Novels." *PMLA* 70 (1955): 19–36.

Clulow, Alfredo. "La novela en América." *Nosotros* 47 (1924): 66–74.

Coloquio de la novela hispanoamericana. Mexico, 1967. Participants: Ivan Shulman, Manuel Pedro González, Juan Loveluck, and Fernando Alegría.

Cometta Manzoni, Aida. *El indio en la novela de América.* Buenos Aires, 1949.

Cortázar, Julio. "Situación de la novela." *Cuadernos Americanos* 52 (1950): 223–43.

Coulthard, G. R. "El mito indígena en la literatura hispanoamericana contemporánea." *Cuadernos Americanos* 156 (1968): 164–73.

Coulthard, G. R. "Spanish American Novel: 1940–1965." *Caribbean Quarterly* 12, no. 4 (1967): 3–29.

Crow, John A. "A Critical Appraisal of the Contemporary Spanish American Novel." *Hispania* 24 (1951): 155–64.

Cruz, Salvador de la. *La novela iberoamericana actual.* Mexico, 1956.

Cruz, Salvador de la. *Nuevos novelistas iberoamericanos.* Mexico, 1955.

Daireaux, Max. "La novela rusa y la literatura hispanoamericana." *Nosotros* 71 (1931): 23–29.

Davison, Ned J. *The Concept of Modernism in Hispanic Criticism.* Boulder, Co., 1966.

Earle, Peter. "Camino oscuro. La novela hispanoamericana contemporánea." *Cuadernos Americanos* 152 (1967): 204–22.

Esquenazi-Mayo, Roberto. "Marginal Notes on the Twentieth-Century Spanish American Novel." *Prairie Schooner* 39 (1964): 126–31.

Flores, Ángel. *Historia y antología del cuento y la novela en Hispanoamerica.* New York, 1959.

Flores, Ángel. "Magical Realism in Spanish American Fiction." *Hispania* 38 (1955): 187–92.

Fornet, Ambrosio. "La nueva narrativa y sus antecedentes." *Casa de las Américas* 4, no. 22 (1964): 3–10.

Fox, Hugh. "The Novelist as Filter. Naturalism in Latin America." *Southwest Review* 5, no. 53 (1968): 258–65.

Franco, Jean. *The Modern Culture of Latin America: Society and the Artist.* New York, 1967.

Franklin, Albert B. "La realidad americana en la novela hispanoamericana." *Hispania* 22 (1939): 373–80.

Fuentes, Carlos. "La situación del escritor en América Latina." *Mundo Nuevo,* no. 1 (July 1966), pp. 5–21.

Galaos, José Antonio. "Hispanoamérica a través de sus novelas." *Cuadernos Hispanoamericanos,* no. 143 (1961), pp. 241–49.

Gallegos, Gerardo. "¿Dónde están los personajes de la novela indohispanoamericana?" *Universidad de Antioquia,* no. 29 (June 1939), pp. 85–88.

Gándara, Carmen. "América, la sin memoria. Vicisitudes de la novela." *Sur,* no. 198 (1951), pp. 9–24.

González, Manuel Pedro. "Crisis de la novela en América." *Revista Nacional de Cultura* 24, no. 150 (1962): 50–69.

González, Manuel Pedro. "La novela en América." *Humanismo* 5, no. 138 (1956): 64–84.

González y Contreras, Gilberto. "Aclaraciones a la novela social americana." *Revista Iberoamericana* 6, no. 12 (1943): 403–18.

Grases, Pedro. "De la novela en América." *Bitácora,* no. 4 (Caracas, 1943), pp. 63–67.

Grases, Pedro. *La primera versión castellana de Atala.* Caracas, 1955. A study of Atala's influence on Latin American romanticism.

Harss, Luis and Dohmann, Barbara. *Into the Mainstream.* New York, 1967.

Henríquez Ureña, Max. *Breve historia del modernismo*. Mexico, 1954.

Henríquez Ureña, Max. "Influencias francesas en la novela de la América española." In *La novela hispanoamericana*, edited by Juan Loveluck, pp. 145–52. Santiago de Chile, 1966.

Henríquez Ureña, Pedro. "Apuntaciones sobre la novela en América." *Humanidades* 15 (La Plata, 1927): 133–46.

Hogan, Margarita Blondet. "Picaresque Literature in Spanish America." Ph.D. dissertation, Columbia University, 1953.

Iglesias, Ignacio. "Novelas y novelistas de hoy." *Mundo Nuevo*, no. 28 (1968), pp. 84–88.

Kayser, Wolfgang. "Orígenes y crisis de la novela moderna." *Cultura Universitaria*, no. 47 (Caracas, 1955), pp. 5–50.

Kite, Ralph B. "Socialist Realism in the Spanish American Novel." Ph.D. dissertation, University of New Mexico, 1968.

Kline, Walter D. "The Use of Novelistic Elements in Some Spanish-American Prose Works of the Seventeenth and Eighteenth Centuries." Ph.D. dissertation, University of Michigan, 1957.

Latcham, Ricardo. *Antología del cuento hispanoamericano contemporáneo, 1910–1956*. Santiago, 1958.

Latcham, Ricardo. "La querella del criollismo." *Bolívar*, no. 54 (1957), pp. 565–93.

Latcham, Ricardo. "Perspectivas de la literatura hispanoamericana contemporánea." *Atenea*, no. 380–81 (1958), pp. 305–36.

Latcham, Ricardo et al. *El criollismo*. Santiago, 1956.

Latorre, Mariano. "Algunas preguntas que no me han hecho sobre el criollismo." *Anales de la Universidad de Chile*, no. 100 (1955), pp. 73–80.

Leal, Luis. "El realismo mágico en la literatura hispanoamericana." *Cuadernos Americanos*, 153 (1967): 230–35.

Leal, Luis. "Trends in the Development of the Spanish American Novel." *Emory University Quarterly* 13 (1957): 27–34.

Leonard, Irving, *Books of the Brave* (Cambridge, Ma., 1949).

Leonard, Irving. "Don Quijote and the Book Trade in Lima, 1606." *Hispanic Review* 8 (1940): 265–304.

Leonard, Irving. *Romances of Chivalry in the Spanish Indies*. California Publications in Modern Philology, vol. 16, Berkeley, 1933.

Lindo, Hugo. "La novela actual." *El Libro y el Pueblo* (Mexico, March-April 1958), pp. 14–21.

Llerena, Mario. "Función del paisaje en la novela hispanoamericana." *Hispania* 32 (1949): 499–504.

López Núñez, Carlos. "Visión sociológica de la novela americana." *Estudios Americanos* 5, no. 18 (1953): 261–77.

Loveluck, Juan. ed. *La novela hispanoamericana*. Santiago de Chile, 1966.

Loveluck, Juan. "Una revisión de la novela hispanoamericana." *Atenea*, no. 163 (1966), pp. 139–48.

Manzor, Antonio. *Antología del cuento hispanoamericano*. Santiago de Chile, 1940.

Martí, Jorge L. "Consideraciones sobre la novela indianista." *Torre*, no. 58 (1967), pp. 186–201.

Meléndez, Concha. *La novela indianista en Hispanoamérica, 1832–1889*. Río Piedras, 1961.

Mendilow, Adam A. *Time and the Novel*. London, 1952.

Menton, Seymour. *El cuento hispanoamericano*. 2 vols. Mexico, 1964.

Menton, Seymour. "In Search of a Nation: The Twentieth-Century Spanish American Novel." *Hispania* 38 (1955): 432–42.

Monguió, Luis. "A Decade of Spanish American Prose Writing." *Hispania* 40 (1957): 287–89.

Monguió, Luis. "Reflexiones sobre un aspecto de la novela hispanoamericana actual." In *La novela iberoamericana*, edited by Instituto International de Literatura Iberoamericana, pp. 91–104. Albuquerque, 1952.

Montenegro, Ernesto. "Aspectos del criollismo en América." *Anales de la Universidad de Chile* 114, no. 102 (1956): 51–62.

Monterde, Francisco. *Novelistas hispanoamericanos*. Mexico, 1943.

Morínigo, Mariano. "El contorno natural en la novela de la tierra." *Humanitas* 3, no. 7 (Tucumán, Argentina, 1957): 13–20.

Morley, Silvanus G. "La novela del cow-boy y la del gaucho." *Revista Iberoamericana* 7, no. 14 (1944): 225–70.

Norris, Robert. "El novelista latinoamericano frente a la realidad indígena contemporánea." *Casa de la Cultura Ecuatoriana* 14, no. 24 (1966): 175–211.

"Notas para un panorama de la novela en América Latina." *Revista Nacional de Cultura* 29, no. 80 (1967): 76–113.

Ocampo, Victoria. *"Sur." Revista Hispánica Moderna* 12 (1946): 44–54.

Olza Zubirí, Jesús. "Novelistas contemporáneos hispanoamericanos." *Estudios Centroamericanos* 21, no. 219 (San Salvador, 1966): 215–18.

Onís, José de. *Los Estados Unidos vistos por escritores hispanoamericanos*. Madrid, 1956.

Ospina, Uriel. *Problemas y perspectivas de la novela americana*. Bogotá, 1964.

Pagés Larraya, Antonio. "Tradición y renovación en la novela hispanoamericana." *Mundo Nuevo*, no. 34 (1969), pp. 76–82.

Palacios, Alfredo I. "Civilización y barbarie: Dualismo simplista inaceptable." *Cuadernos Americanos* 105 (1959): pp. 162–212.

Pereda Valdés, Ildefonso. "El negro en la literatura iberoamericana." *Cuadernos*, no. 19 (Paris, 1956), pp. 104–10.

Phillips, Allen W. "El arte y el artista en algunas novelas modernistas." *Revista Hispánica Moderna* 34, no. 3–4 (1968): 757–75.

Pineda, Salvador. "América, novela de antología." *Cuadernos*, no. 16 (Paris, 1955), pp. 7–73.

Pla, Roger. "El problema actual de la novela." *Universidad*, no. 19 (Santa Fe, Argentina, 1946), pp. 155–79.

Portuondo, José Antonio. "El rasgo predominante en la novela hispanoamericana." In *La novela iberoamericana*, edited by Instituto Internacional de Literatura Iberoamericana, pp. 79–87. Albuquerque, 1952.

Prenz, Juan Octavio. "La temática de la novela hispanoamericana." *Filoloski Pregled*, no. 3–4 (Belgrade, 1964), pp. 89–101.

Rama, Ángel. "Diez problemas para el novelista latinoamericano." *Casa de las Américas* 4, no. 26 (1964): 3–43.

Reid, John T. "Spanish American Jungle Fiction." *The Inter-American Quarterly* 2, no. 1 (1940): 48–58.

Reyles, Carlos. "El nuevo sentido de la narración gauchesca." In *Historia Sintética de la Literatura Uruguaya*, vol. 3. Montevideo, 1931.

Rodríguez Monegal, Emir. "Los nuevos novelistas." *Mundo Nuevo*, no. 17 (1967), pp. 19–24.

Rodríguez Monegal, Emir. *Narradores de esta América*. Montevideo, 1961.

Roggiano, Alfredo A. "El modernismo y la novela en la América Hispana." In *La novela iberoamericana*, edited by Instituto Internacional de Literatura Iberoamericana, pp. 24–45. Albuquerque, 1952.

Rossel, Milton. "Significación y contenido del criollismo." *Atenea*, no. 358 (1955), pp. 9–28.

Rumazo González, Alfonso. "Teoría de los pactos en la novela nueva americana." *Cuadernos Hispanoamericanos*, no. 209 (1967), pp. 406–12.

Sábato, Ernesto. *El escritor y sus fantasmas*. Madrid, 1964.

Sábato, Ernesto. *Hombres y engranajes*. Buenos Aires, 1951.

Sábato, Ernesto. "Realidad y realismo en la literatura de nuestro tiempo." *Cuadernos Hispanoamericanos*, no. 178 (1964), pp. 5–20.

Salazar Bondy, Sebastián. "La evolución del llamado indigenismo." *Sur*, 293 (Buenos Aires, 1965), pp. 44–50.

Salgado, María A. "La nueva prosa modernista." *Thesaurus*, no. 22 (1967), pp. 81–94.

Sánchez, Luis Alberto. *América: novela sin novelistas*. Santiago, 1940.

Sánchez, Luis Alberto. "El indianismo literario: ¿Tendencia original o imitiva?" *Revista Nacional de Cultura* 22, no. 138 (1959–60): 107–17.

Sánchez, Luis Alberto. "La novela en los cronistas." *Atenea*, no. 343 (1954), pp. 108–30.

Sánchez, Luis Alberto. *Proceso y contenido de la novela hispanoamericana*. Madrid, 1953.

Sarduy, Severo. "Las estructuras de la narración." *Mundo Nuevo*, no. 2 (1966), pp. 15–26.

Saz, Agustín del. *La novela hispanoamericana*. Barcelona, 1954.

Schanzer, George O. "Parallels Between Spanish American and Russian Novelistic Themes." *Hispania* 35 (1952): 42–48.

Schulman, Ivan A. "La novela hispanoamericana y la nueva técnica." *Universidad de Antioquia*, no. 171 (1968), pp. 75–94.

Sommers, Joseph. "The Indian-Oriented Novel in Latin America; New

Spirit, New Forms, New Scope." *Journal of Inter-American Studies* 6 (1964): 149–166.

Sorel, Andrés. "La nueva novela latinoamericana: I, Uruguay, Bolivia, Chile." *Cuadernos Hispanoamericanos*, no. 191 (1965), pp. 221–54.

Sorel, Andrés. "La nueva novela latinoamericana: II, Costa Rica y Perú." *Cuadernos Hispanoamericanos*, no. 201 (1966), pp. 705–26.

Sosa López, Emilio. *La novela y el hombre*. Córdoba, Argentina, 1958.

Soto-Ruiz, Luis. "El tema del pirata en la novela histórica hispanoamericana." Ph.D. dissertation, University of Michigan, 1959.

Spell, Jefferson Rhea. *Contemporary Spanish American Fiction*. Chapel Hill, N.C., 1944.

Suárez-Murias, Marguerite. *La novela romántica en Hispanoamérica*. New York, 1963.

Téllez, Hernando. "La novela en Latinoamérica." In *La novela hispanoamericana*, edited by Juan Loveluck, pp. 47–54. Santiago de Chile, 1966.

Tilles, Solomon. "Some Examples of 'Zeitgeist' in the Spanish-American Novel." *Romance Notes* 7 (1965): 25–29.

Tinker, Edward Larocque. "The Cult of the Gaucho and the Creation of Literature." In *Proceedings of the American Antiquarian Society*, no. 57 (1947), pp. 309–48.

Torre, Antonio M. de la. "Naturalism and the Spanish American Novel." *Books Abroad* 26 (1952): 147–50.

Torre, Guillermo de. "Para una polémica sobre la nueva novela." *Mundo Nuevo*, no. 34 (1969), pp. 83–85.

Torre, Guillermo de. "Perspectivas y encrucijadas de la novela contemporánea." *Revista Cubana* 31, no. 3–4 (1957): 49–70.

Torres-Rioseco, Arturo. "De la novela en América." In *La novela hispanoamericana*, edited by Juan Loveluck, pp. 109–12. Santiago, 1966.

Torres-Rioseco, Arturo. "El modernismo y la crítica." *Hispania* 12 (1929): 357–64.

Torres-Rioseco, Arturo. "El nuevo estilo en la novela." *Revista Iberoamericana* 3, no. 5 (1941): 75–83.

Torres-Rioseco, Arturo. "La ciudad en la novela." *Estudios Americanos* 13 (Seville, 1957): 276–83.

Torres-Rioseco, Arturo. "La dictadura, tema novelístico." *Revista Iberoamericana* 24, no. 48 (1959): 307–10.

Torres-Rioseco, Arturo. "La novela criolla: El mester de gauchería." *Revista Hispánica Moderna* 4 (1938): 1–6.

Torres-Rioseco, Arturo. *La novela en la América Hispana*. Berkeley, 1939.

Torres-Rioseco, Arturo. "La renovación de la prosa y la novela." *Memoria del Primer Congreso de . . . Literatura Iberoamericana*, pp. 35–44. Mexico, 1938.

Torres-Rioseco, Arturo. "Notas sobre el desarrollo de la literatura hispano-americana desde 1916." *Hispania* 50 (1967): 955–62.

Torres-Rioseco, Arturo. *Novelistas contemporáneos de América.* Santiago de Chile, 1939.

Torres-Rioseco, Arturo. "Novelistas contemporáneos de América." *Papeles de Son Armadans* 28 (1963): 125–44.

Torres-Rioseco, Arturo. "Nuevas tendencias en la novela." *Revista Iberoamericana* 1, no. 1 (1939): 91–94.

Torres-Rioseco, Arturo. "Social Trends in the Latin American Novel." *The Quarterly Journal of Inter-American Relations* 1 (1939): 76–80.

Undarraga, Antonio de. "Crisis en la novela latinoamericana." *Cuadernos,* no. 80 (Paris, 1963), pp. 62–65.

Uribe Echeverría, Juan. *La narración literaria.* Santiago, 1959.

Uslar Pietri, Arturo. *Breve historia de la novela hispanoamericana.* Caracas, 1954.

Vega, Manuel et al. *El criollismo.* Santiago de Chile, 1956.

Verdevoye, Paul. "Aspects sociologiques du roman hispano-americain contemporain." *Cahiers d'histoire mondiale* 8, no. 2 (Neuchatel, 1964): 356–61.

Verdugo, Iber H. "Perspectivas de la actual novela hispanoamericana." *Mundo Nuevo,* no. 28 (1968), pp. 75–83.

Vidal, Hernán. "Mutaciones de la tradición mimética en la novela de espacio hispanoamericana de comienzos del sigo XX." Ph.D. dissertation, University of Iowa, 1968.

Wade, Gerald E. and Archer, William H. "The Indianista Novel Since 1889." *Hispania* 33 (1950): 211–20.

Wolfe, Bertram D. "The Novel in Latin America." *The Antioch Review* 3 (1943): 191–208.

Yates, Donald A. "The Spanish American Detective Story." *Modern Language Journal* 40 (1956): 228–32.

Zum Felde, Alberto. *Índice crítico de la literatura hispanoamericana,* vol. 2, *La Narrativa.* Mexico, 1959.

Zum Felde, Alberto. *La narrativa en Hispanoamérica.* Madrid, 1964.

ARGENTINA—GENERAL WORKS

Aita, Antonio. "Algunos aspectos de la novela argentina." *Nosotros* 64 (April, 1929): 5–21.

Barcia, Primero. "The Argentine Novel of Artistic Design." Ph.D. dissertation, University of Southern California, 1951.

Becco, Horacio J. *Cuentistas argentinos.* Buenos Aires, 1961.

Beck, Vera F. "Las heroínas en la novelística argentina." *Revista Hispánica Moderna* 10 (1944): 231–50.

Blanco Amor, José. "La novela argentina de hoy y el país real." *Cuadernos*

Hispanoamericanos, no. 205 (1967), pp. 134–43.

Bonet, Carmelo M. "Buenos Aires, su gente, sus barrios, sus novelistas." *Ficción,* no. 40 (1962), pp. 43–56.

Bonet, Carmelo M. *Gente de novela.* Buenos Aires, 1939.

Borello, Rodolfo A. "Los escritores del 80." *Revista de Literatura Argentina e Iberoamericana* 1 (1959): 32–46.

Brughetti, Romualdo. "Una nueva generación literaria argentina (1940–1952)." *Cuadernos Americanos* 63 (1952): 261–81.

Bullrich, Silvina. "La inquietud de Buenos Aires en la novela contemporánea argentina." *Nosotros,* 4, no. 41 (1939): 341–57.

Carter, Erwin D. Jr. "Magical Realism in Contemporary Argentine Fiction." Ph.D. dissertation, University of Southern California, 1966.

Castagnino, Raúl E. "Otros caminos de la estilística: las formas de relieve por vía tipográfica en la técnica de algunos novelistas contemporáneos argentinos." *Humanidades* 36 (1960): 123–48.

Dellepiane, Ángela B. "La novela argentina desde 1950 a 1965." *Revista Iberoamericana,* no. 66 (1968), pp. 237–82.

Díaz-Plaja, Guillermo. "Meditación sobre lo argentino en la novela." *BAAL* 19 (1950): 177–209.

García, Germán. *La novela argentina.* Buenos Aires, 1952.

Ghiano, Juan Carlos. "Rasgos de la novela argentina." *Ficción,* no. 6 (1957), pp. 117–23.

Ghiano, Juan Carlos. *Testimonio de la novela argentina.* Buenos Aires, 1956.

Lichtblau, Myron I., *The Argentine Novel in the Nineteenth Century.* New York, 1959.

Loprete, Carlos Alberto. *La literatura modernista en la Argentina.* Buenos Aires, 1955.

Mastroangelo, Carlos. *El cuento argentino.* Buenos Aires, 1963.

Moya, Ismael. *Orígenes del teatro y de la novela argentinos.* Buenos Aires, 1925.

Nichols, Madaline W. *The Gaucho, Cattle Hunter, Cavalryman. Ideal of Romance.* Durham, N.C., 1942.

(La) novela argentina. *Contorno,* no. 5–6 (Buenos Aires, 1955), 62 pp.

Pagés Larraya, Antonio. *Cuentos de nuestra tierra.* Buenos Aires, 1952.

Pagés Larraya, Antonio. "Tendencias de la novela romántica argentina." *Atenea,* no. 379 (1956), pp. 208–20.

Pesante, Edgardo. "El cuento en la literatura argentina." *Universidad,* no. 76 (Santa Fe, Argentina, 1968), pp. 195–218.

Portantiero, Juan Carlos. *Realismo y realidad en la narrativa argentina.* Buenos Aires, 1961.

Valbuena Briones, Ángel J. "Evolución de la narración argentina de temas hasta *Don Segundo Sombra.*" *Revista Nacional* 4, no. 221 (Montevideo, 1959): 327–54.

Walsh, Rodolfo. *Antología del cuento extraño.* Buenos Aires, 1956.

Williams Alzaga, Enrique. *La pampa en la novela argentina.* Buenos Aires, 1955.

Yates, Donald A. "The Argentine Detective Story." Ph.D. dissertation, University of Michigan, 1961.

ARGENTINA—AUTHORS

Cambaceres, Eugenio

Beck, Phyllis Powers. "Eugenio Cambaceres: The Vortex of Controversy." *Hispania* 56 (1963): 755–59.

Melian Lafinur, Luis. "Sobre *Música sentimental,* silbido de un vago de Eugenio Cambaceres." *Anales del Ateneo del Uruguay* 7 (1953): 387–400.

Solero, F. J. "Eugenio Cambaceres y la novela argentina." *Ficción,* no. 3 (1957), pp. 105–24.

Cané, Miguel (hijo)

Sáenz Hayes, Ricardo. *Miguel Cané (hijo) y su tiempo.* Buenos Aires, 1955.

Correa, Miguel Ángel (Mateo Booz)

Milano, Laura. *Mateo Booz.* Rosario, Argentina, 1964.

Echeverría, Esteban

Bogliolo, Rómulo. *Las ideas democráticas y socialistas de Esteban Echeverría.* Buenos Aires, 1937.

Furt, Jorge M. *Echeverría.* Buenos Aires, 1938.

García Merou, Martín. *Ensayo sobre Echeverría.* Buenos Aires, 1944.

Ghiano, Juan Carlos. *"El matadero" de Echeverría y el costumbrismo.* Buenos Aires, 1968.

Halperin Donghi, Tulio. *Esteban Echeverría.* Buenos Aires, 1952.

Martínez, Joaquín. *Esteban Echeverría en la vida argentina.* Buenos Aires, 1953.

Morales, Ernesto. *Esteban Echeverría.* Buenos Aires, 1950.

Morínigo, Mariano. "Realidad y ficción de *El Matadero." Humanitas* 13, no. 18 (Universidad de Tucumán, 1965): 283–318.

Rojas Paz, Pablo. *Echeverría, el pastor de soledades.* Buenos Aires, 1951.

Estrada, Ángel de

Homenaje. *Nosotros* 46, no. 177 (1924): 237–81.

Rohde, Jorge Max. *Ángel de Estrada.* Buenos Aires, 1924.

Fernández, Macedonio

Jurado, Alicia. "Aproximación a Macedonio Fernández." *Ficción,* no. 7 (1957), pp. 65–79.

Pagés Larraya, Arturo. "Macedonio Fernández, un payador." *Cuadernos Hispanoamericanos,* no. 166 (1963), pp. 133–46.

Rodríguez Monegal, Emir. "Macedonio Fernández, Borges y el ultraísmo." *Número* 4, no. 19 (Montevideo, 1952): 172–83.

Gálvez, Manuel

Anzoátegui, Ignacio B. *Manuel Gálvez.* Buenos Aires, 1961.

Bianco, José. "Los caminos de la muerte." *Nosotros* 61 (1928): 99–105.

Cotto-Thorner, Guillermo. "Manuel Gálvez y su trilogía uruguaya." *Revista Iberoamericana* 16, no. 31 (1950): 79–89.

Desinano, Norma B. "Gálvez y la novela histórica: El ciclo Rosista." *Duquesne Hispanic Review* 2 (1963): 179–90.

Galaos, José Antonio. "Manuel Gálvez: novelista cronista de Buenos Aires." *Cuadernos Hispanoamericanos,* no. 170 (1964), pp. 344–55.

Gálvez, Manuel. *El novelista y la novela.* Buenos Aires, 1959.

Gálvez Manuel. *En el mundo de los seres ficticios.* Buenos Aires, 1961.

Gálvez Manuel. *Entre la novela y la historia.* 3 vols. Buenos Aires, 1962.

García Blanco, Manuel. "El escritor argentino Manuel Gálvez y Unamuno." *Cuadernos Hispanoamericanos,* no. 53 (1954), pp. 182–98.

González, Manuel Pedro. "*Hombres en soledad* de Manuel Gálvez." *Revista Iberoamericana* 2, no. 4 (1940): 419–25.

Green, Otis H. "Gálvez's *La sombra del convento* and its Relation to *El Diario de Gabriel Quiroga.*" *Hispanic Review* 12 (1945): 196–210.

Green, Otis H. "Manuel Gálvez' Gabriel Quiroga and *El mal metafísico.*" *Hispanic Review* 11 (1944): 314–27.

Green, Otis H. "Manuel Gálvez' Gabriel Quiroga and *La maestra normal,*" *Hispanic Review* 11 (1944): 221–52.

Holmes, Henry A. "Una trilogía de Manuel Gálvez: *Escenas de la guerra del Paraguay.*" *Revista Hispánica Moderna* 3 (1937): 201–12.

Jaimes Freyre, Mireyra. "Gálvez y su laberinto." *Revista Iberoamericana* 18, no. 36 (1952–53): 315–37.

Jitrick, Noé. "Los desplazamientos de la culpa en las obras 'sociales' de Manuel Gálvez." *Duquesne Hispanic Review* 2 (1963): 143–66.

Lichtblau, Myron I. "The Recent Novels of Manuel Gálvez." *Hispania* 42 (1959): 502–5.

Mastronardi, Carlos. "Gálvez y el estilo barroco." *Sur,* no. 245 (1957), pp. 104–7.

Messimore, Hazel M. "City Life in Some Novels of Manuel Gálvez." *Hispania* 32 (1949): 460–66.

Olivari, Nicolás and Stanchina, Lorenzo. *Manuel Gálvez, ensayo sobre su obra.* Buenos Aires, 1924.

Onega, Gladys S. "Gálvez: *La maestra normal.*" *Duquesne Hispanic Review* 2 (1963): 129–41.

Prieto, Adlolfo. "Gálvez: *El mal metafísico,*" *Duquesne Hispanic Review* 2 (1963): 119–28.

Stevens, Leonard E. "Feminine Protagonists in Manuel Gálvez' novel." Ph.D. dissertation, University of Indiana, 1964.

364   *Bibliography*

Torres-Rioseco, Arturo. "Manuel Gálvez." *Nosotros* 3 (1938): 411–26.
Turner, Esther H. "Hispanism in the Life of Manuel Gálvez." Ph.D. dissertation, University of Washington, 1958.
Turner, Esther H. "The Religious Element in the Work of Manuel Gálvez." *Hispania* 46 (1963): 519–24.

Gerchunoff, Alberto

Blondet, Olga. "Alberto Gerchunoff: bibliografía." *Revista Hispánica Moderna* 23 (1957): 257–59.
Homenaje. *Davar*, no. 31–33 (Buenos Aires, 1951).
Jaroslavsky de Lowy, Sara. "Alberto Gerchunoff. Vida y obras." *Revista Hispánica Moderna* 23 (1957): 205–57.
Labrador Ruiz, Enrique. "Gerchunoff." *Cultura* 10 (San Salvador, 1956): 77–79.
Longo, Iris E. "Presencia de Gerchunoff en la narrativa argentina." *Universidad*, no. 72 (Santa Fe, Argentina, 1967), pp. 47–66.
Tiempo, César. "Alberto Gerchunoff, vida y mundo." *Hispania* 35 (1952): 37–41.

Gorriti, Juana Manuela

Chaca, Dionisio. *Historia de Juana Manuela Gorriti*. Buenos Aires, 1940.
Sosa, Francisco. "Juana Manuela Gorriti." *Revista Nacional* 16 (Buenos Aires, 1892): 351–60.

Groussac, Paul

Canter, Juan. "*Fruto vedado*." *Nosotros* 68 (1930): 359–79.
Ferrero, Alfonso de la. "Paul Groussac." *Nosotros* 65 (1929): 9–15.
González, Juan B. "Groussac, novelista." *Nosotros* 65 (1929): 132–47.

Güiraldes, Ricardo

Alonso, Amado. "Un problema estilístico en *Don Segundo Sombra*." *Materia y forma en poesía*. Madrid, 1955.
Ara, Guillermo. "Lo mítico y lo místico en Güiraldes." *Cuadernos Americanos* 122 (1962): 241–54.
Ara, Guillermo. *Ricardo Güiraldes*. Buenos Aires, 1961.
Battistesa, Ángel. "Güiraldes y Laforgue." *Nosotros* 7, no. 71 (1942: 149–70.
Becco, Horacio J. *Don Segundo Sombra y su vocabulario*. Buenos Aires, 1952.
Boj, Silverio. *Ubicación de Don Segundo Sombra y otros ensayos*. Tucumán, 1940.
Borges, Jorge Luis. "Sobre *Don Segundo Sombra*." *Sur*, no. 217–18 (1952), pp. 9–11.
Caracciolo, Enrique. "Otro enfoque de *Don Segundo Sombra*." *Papeles de Son Armadans* 39, no. 116 (1965): 123–39.
Chapman, Arnold. "Pampas and Big Woods: Heroic Initiation in Güiraldes and Faulkner." *Comparative Literature* 40 (1959): 61–77.

Collantes de Terán, Juan. "En torno al simbolismo e impresionismo en *Don Segundo Sombra.*" *Estudios Americanos* 13, no. 64 (1957): 17–39.

Collantes de Terán, Juan. "*Rosaura* en el estilo literario de Ricardo Güiraldes." *Revista de Literatura* 14 (1958): 198–209.

Colombo, Ismael. *Ricardo Güiraldes, el poeta de la pampa, 1886–1927.* Buenos Aires, 1952.

Cuña, Irma. "Símbolos de *Don Segundo Sombra.*" *Révue de Littérature Comparée* 36 (1962): 404–37.

Cúneo, Dardo. "La crisis argentina del '30 en Güiraldes . . ." *Cuadernos Americanos* 140 (1965): 158–75.

Da Cal, Ernesto G. "*Don Segundo Sombra,* teoría y símbolo del gaucho." *Cuadernos Americanos* 41 (1948): 245–59.

Earle, Peter G. "El sentido poético de *Don Segundo Sombra.*" *Revista Hispánica Moderna* 26 (1960): 126–32.

Etchegaray, Aristóbulo. *Don Segundo Sombra, reminiscencia infantil de Ricardo Güiraldes.* Buenos Aires, 1955.

Fernández Hutter, Julián. *El alma errante de Don Segundo Sombra.* Santa Fe, Argentina, 1945.

Gates, Eunice J. "The Imagery of *Don Segundo Sombra.*" *Hispanic Review* 16 (1948): 33–49.

Ghiano, Juan Carlos. "La lección de don Segundo Sombra," *Torre* 9, no. 34 (1961): 95–114.

Ghiano, Juan Carlos. *Ricardo Güiraldes.* Buenos Aires, 1966.

Gicovate, Bernardo. "Notes on *Don Segundo Sombra:* The Education of Fabio Cáceres." *Hispania* 34 (1951): 366–68.

González, Juan B. "Un libro significativo: *Don Segundo Sombra.*" *Nosotros* 54 (1926): 377–85.

Irving, T. B. "Myth and Reality in *Don Segundo Sombra.*" *Hispania* 40 (1957): 44–48.

Kovacci, Ofelia. *La pampa a través de Ricardo Güiraldes.* Buenos Aires, 1961.

Leguizamón, María Luisa C. de. "Ricardo Güiraldes y algunos aspectos de su obra." *Cuadernos Americanos* 69 (1953): 278–90.

Liberal, José R. *Don Segundo Sombra de Ricardo Güiraldes.* Buenos Aires, 1946.

Lugones, Leopoldo. "*Don Segundo Sombra.*" *Atenea,* no. 96 (1933), pp. 319–25.

Morby, Edwin S. "¿Es *Don Segundo Sombra* novela picaresca?" *Revista Iberoamericana* 1, no. 2 (1939): 375–80.

Neyra, Joaquín. *El mito gaucho en Don Segundo Sombra.* Bahía Blanca, 1952.

Pagés Larraya, Antonio. "*Don Segundo Sombra* y el retorno." *Cuadernos Hispanoamericanos,* no. 152–53 (1962), pp. 275–85.

Pastoriza de Etchebarne, Dora. *Elementos románticos en las novelas de Ricardo Güiraldes.* Buenos Aires, 1957.

Previtali, Giovanni. *Ricardo Güiraldes and Don Segundo Sombra*. New York, 1963.

Previtali, Giovanni. *Ricardo Güiraldes, biografía y crítica*. Mexico, 1965.

Previtali, Giovanni and Ynsfraín, Pablo Max. "El verdadero Don Segundo Sombra en *Don Segundo Sombra* de Ricardo Güiraldes." *Revista Iberoamericana* 29, no. 56 (1963): 317–20.

Rodríguez, María del Carmen. *El paisaje en Don Segundo Sombra y otros ensayos*. Paraná, 1950.

Rodríguez Alcalá, Hugo. "A los cuarenta años de *Don Segundo Sombra*." *Cuadernos Americanos* 151 (1967): 224–55.

Rodríguez Alcalá, Hugo. "Lo real y lo ideal en *Don Segundo Sombra*." *Revista Hispánica Moderna* 32 (1966): 191–97.

Rust, Zell O. "The Prose Style of Ricardo Güiraldes." Ph.D. dissertation, University of Southern California, 1957.

Smith, Herbert B. *Don Segundo Sombra: su influencia en la argentinidad*. La Plata, 1946.

Torres-Rioseco, Arturo. "The Twenty-Five Year Anniversary of *Don Segundo Sombra*." *New Mexico Quarterly* 21 (1951): 274–88.

Weiss, Harry. "Ricardo Güiraldes, argentino (1886–1927)." Ph.D. dissertation, University of Syracuse, 1955.

Weiss, Harry. "Techniques in the Works of Ricardo Güiraldes." *Hispania* 47 (1960): 353–58.

Weiss, Harry. "The Spirituality of Ricardo Güiraldes." *Symposium* 10 (1956): 231–42.

Xirau, Ramón. "Ciclo y vida de *Don Segundo Sombra*." *Cuadernos Americanos* 116 (1961): 240–46.

Hudson, Guillermo Enrique

Ara, Guillermo. *G. E. Hudson: el paisaje pampeano y su expresión*. Buenos Aires, 1954.

Franco, Luis. *Hudson a caballo*. Buenos Aires, 1956.

Martínez Estrada, Ezequiel. *El mundo maravilloso de Guillermo Enrique Hudson*. Mexico, 1952.

Martínez Estrada, Ezequiel. *"La tierra púrpura:* una novela clave." *Ficción*, no. 5 (1957), pp. 176–81.

Mendoza, Angélica. "Guillermo Enrique Hudson (1841–1922)." *Revista Hispánica Moderna* 10 (1944): 193–222.

Urbanski, Edmund S. "Two Novels of the Amazon." *Americas* 17 (March 1965): 33–38.

Velázquez, Luis Horacio. *Guillermo Enrique Hudson*. Buenos Aires, 1963.

Larreta, Enrique

Aldao, Martín. *El caso de La gloria de don Ramiro*. Buenos Aires, 1943.

Alonso, Amado. *Ensayo sobre la novela histórica. El modernismo en La gloria de don Ramiro*. Buenos Aires, 1942.

Berenguer Carísomo, Arturo. "Las dos últimas novelas de Enrique Larreta." *Cuadernos Hispanoamericanos*, no. 75 (1956), pp. 327–40.

Berenguer Carísomo, Arturo. *Los valores eternos en la obra de Enrique Larreta*. Buenos Aires, 1946.

Bonet, Carmelo M. "Enrique Larreta: visión panorámica de su obra." *Boletín de la Academia Argentina de Letras* 31, no. 121 (1966): 419–49.

Davison, Ned. "Remarks on the Form of *La gloria de don Ramiro*." *Romance Notes* 3 (1961): 17–22.

Jansen, André. "El cincuentenario de una gran novela: La crítica ante *La gloria de don Ramiro*." *Revista Hispánica Moderna* 25 (1959): 199–206.

Jansen, André. "*La gloria de don Ramiro* de Enrique Rodríguez Larreta." *Cuadernos Hispanoamericanos*, no. 128–29 (1960), pp. 175–89.

Lida, Raimundo. "La técnica del relato en *La gloria de don Ramiro*." In *Cursos y Conferencias*, pp. 225–47. Buenos Aires, 1935.

Scrimaglio, Marta. "Larreta, Modernismo y barroco." *Boletín de Literatura Hispánica*, no. 4 (Rosario, Argentina, 1962), pp. 19–38.

Sullivan, J. *El caso de La gloria de don Ramiro*. Buenos Aires, 1914.

López, Vicente Fidel

Cané, Miguel. "Sobre *La novia del hereje* o La inquisición de Lima." *Revista de Buenos Aires* 2 (December 1885): 624–52.

Rodó, José Enrique. "Sobre *La loca de la guardia* de Vicente Fidel López." *Revista Nacional de Literatura* 3 (1897): 22–25.

Lynch, Benito

Caillet-Bois, Julio. *La novela rural de Benito Lynch*. La Plata, 1960.

Canto, Estela. "Benito Lynch o la inocencia." *Sur*, no. 215–16 (1952), pp. 109–13.

Davis, Jack E. "The Americanismos in *El inglés de los güesos*." *Hispania* 33 (1950): 333–37.

Defant Durán, Alba. "Los muchachos en la obra de Lynch." *Humanitas* 7, no. 11 (Tucumán, 1960): 167–72.

Gates, Eunice Joiner. "Charles Darwin and Benito Lynch's *El inglés de los güesos*." *Hispania* 44 (1961): 250–53.

Giusti, Roberto F. "Benito Lynch." *Nosotros* 48, no. 184 (1924): 92–102.

González, J. B. "El novelista Benito Lynch." *Nosotros* 69, no. 25 (1930): 252–67.

Head, Gerald L. "Characterization in the Works of Benito Lynch." Ph.D. dissertation, U.C.L.A., 1964.

Leslie, John K. "Símiles campestres en la obra de Benito Lynch." *Revista Iberoamericana* 17, no. 34 (1951–52): 331–38.

Nason, Marshall R. "¿Benito Lynch otro Hudson?" *Revista Iberoamericana* 23, no. 45 (1957): 65–82.

Nason, Marshall R. "En torno al estilo de Benito Lynch." *Revista de la Universidad*, no. 13 (La Plata, 1961), pp. 141–57.

Owre, J. Riis. "Los animales en las obras de Benito Lynch." *Revista Iberoamericana* 3, no. 6 (1941): 357–69.

Ray, Gordon B. "The Artistic Novel and Benito Lynch." *Papers of the Michigan Academy of Science, Arts and Letters* 37 (1951): 465–69.
Saloma, Roberto. *Benito Lynch.* Buenos Aires, 1959.
Viñas, David. "Benito Lynch y la pampa cercada." *Cultura Universitaria* 46 (Caracas, 1954): 40–53.

Mansilla, Lucio V.

Irazusta, Julio. "Lucio V. Mansilla." *Sur*, no. 40 (1938), pp. 44–54.
Lanuza, J. L. *Lucio V. Mansilla.* Buenos Aires, 1967.
Popolizio, Enrique. *Vida de Lucio V. Mansilla.* Buenos Aires, 1954.

Martínez Zuviría, Gustavo (Hugo Wast)

Bernáldez, José María "Hugo Wast." *Razón y Fe* 166 (1938): 33–44.
Burgos, Fausto. "Dos novelas de Hugo Wast." *Boletín de la Academia Argentina de Letras* 11, no. 44 (1943): 819–26.
Coester, Alfred. "Bibliografía de 'Hugo Wast,' " *Hispania* 16 (1933): 187–88.
Echague, Juan Pablo. "Hugo Wast, romancier argentin." *Revue de l'Amérique Latine* (Paris, 1 February 1929), pp. 108–12.
Sedgewick, Ruth. "Hugo Wast, Argentina's Most Popular Novelist." *Hispanic American Historical Review* 9 (February 1929): 116–26.

Miró, José (Julián Martel)

Lewald, H. Ernest. "Society and *La Bolsa* in the Argentine Novel." *Hispania* 43 (1960): 198–200.

Ocantos, Carlos María

Anderson, Theodore. *Carlos María Ocantos, Argentine Novelist.* New Haven, 1934.

Payró, Roberto J.

Anderson Imbert, Enrique. *Tres novelas de Payró.* Tucumán, 1942.
Bonet, Carmelo M. "Una semblanza de Roberto J. Payró." *Boletín de la Academia Argentina de Letras* 32, no. 123–24 (1967): 235–54.
Fernández de Vidal, Stella María. *Bibliografía de Roberto J. Payró.* Buenos Aires, 1962.
García, Germán. *Roberto J. Payro. Testimonio de una vida y realidad de una literatura.* Buenos Aires, 1961.
Giusti, Roberto F. "Homenaje." *Crítica y Polémica.* 2a. serie. Buenos Aires, 1924, pp. 9–36.
Homenaje a Payró. *Nosotros*, 22, no. 228 (1928).
Larra, Raúl. *Payró: el hombre, la obra.* Buenos Aires, 1938.
Larra, Raúl. *Payró, el novelista de la democracia.* Buenos Aires, 1952.

Wilde, Eduardo

Echague, Juan Pablo. "Eduardo Wilde y su obra." *Boletín de la Academia Argentina de Letras* 13, no. 47 (1964): 271–91.

Escardó, Florencio. *Ensayo sobre Eduardo Wilde*. Buenos Aires, 1943.
Ponce, Aníbal. *Eduardo Wilde*. Buenos Aires, 1916.

BOLIVIA–GENERAL WORKS

Arana, Oswaldo. "El hombre en la novela de la guerra del Chaco." *Journal of Inter-American Studies* 6 (1964): 347–65.
Arana, Oswaldo. "La novela de la guerra del Chaco: Bolivia y Paraguay." Ph.D. dissertation, University of Colorado, 1964.
Botelho Gosálvez, Raúl. "La novela en Bolivia." *Cuadernos Americanos* 112 (1960): 266–81.
Calcagno, Miguel Ángel. "Introducción al estudio de la novela indigenista boliviana." *Revista Iberoamericana de Literatura* 1, no. 1 (Montevideo, 1959): 21–34.
Guzmán, Augusto. *La novela en Bolivia, 1847–1954*. La Paz, 1955.
Jones, Willis Knapp. "Literature of the Chaco War." *Hispania* 21 (1938): 33–46.
Rodrigo, Saturnino. *Antología de cuentistas bolivianos contemporáneos*. Buenos Aires, 1942.
Soriano Badani, Armando, ed. *El cuento boliviano, 1900–1936*. Buenos Aires, 1964.
Ulibarrí, George Sarracino. "The Gamonal in Selected Contemporary Novels of Social Protest in Peru, Bolivia, and Ecuador." Ph.D. dissertation, State University of Iowa, 1952.

BOLIVIA–AUTHORS

Aguirre, Nataniel

"A la memoria de Nataniel Aguirre en el centenario de su nacimiento." *Revista Jurídica* (Cochabamba, December 1943), pp. 1–27.
Díaz Machicao, P. *Nataniel Aguirre*. Buenos Aires, 1945.
Homenaje. *Kollasuyo* (October 1943), pp. 181–244.
Sánchez, Luis Alberto. "*Juan de la Rosa* (Es la mejor novela americana del siglo XIX)." *Kollasuyo* (August 1942), pp. 97–101.
Taborga, C. G. "La vida y obra de Nataniel Aguirre." *Kollasuyo* (May-June 1944), pp. 195–211.

Arguedas, Alcides

Alvarado, Julio Clarobscuro de. "Alcides Arguedas." *Revista de la Sociedad de Escritores de Chile* 2, no. 5 (1946): 17–34.
Bellini, Giuseppe. "Alcides Arguedas en la novela moderna." *Revista Hispánica Moderna* 26, no. 3–4 (1960): 133–35.
Díez de Medina, Fernando. "Alcides Arguedas: el hombre y el escritor."

Bolívar, no. 19 (Bogotá, 1953), pp. 805–08.

Lacosta, Francisco C. "El indigenismo literario de Alcides Arguedas." *Cultura Boliviana,* no. 2 (Universidad Técnica de Oruro, 1965), pp. 4–5, 18.

Moretie, Yerko. "*Raza de bronce.*" *Atenea,* no. 304 (October 1950), pp. 131–40.

Otero, Gustavo Adolfo. "Temperamento, cultura y obra de Alcides Arguedas." *Casa de la Cultura Ecuatoriana* 2, no. 4 (1947): 164–93.

Plevich, Mary. "Alcides Arguedas: Contemporary Bolivian Writer." Ph.D. dissertation, Columbia University, 1957.

Plevich, Mary. "El origen del Arguedismo." *Universidad de Antioquia,* no. 134 (1958), pp. 407–14.

Vilela de Villar, Hugo. *Alcides Arguedas y otros nombres en la literatura de Bolivia.* Buenos Aires, 1945, pp. 13–31.

Vaca Guzmán, Santiago

Valda, Ángel C. "El Dr. Santiago Vaca Guzmán," *Boletín de la Sociedad Geográfica* no. 333–36 (1937), pp. 39–44.

CHILE—GENERAL WORKS

Antología del cuento chileno. Santiago de Chile, 1963.

Castillo, Homero. *El criollismo en la novelística chilena.* Mexico, 1962.

Cerruto, Oscar. "Panorama de la novela chilena." *Nosotros* 5, no. 21 (1937): 393–407.

Chapman, Arnold. "Observations on the Roto in Chilean Fiction." *Hispania* 32 (1949): 309–14.

Chapman, Arnold. "Perspectiva de la novela de la ciudad en Chile." In *La novela iberoamericana,* edited by Instituto Internacional de Literatura Iberoamericana, pp. 193–212. Albuquerque, 1952.

Chinchón, Oswaldo. "The Sea as a Motif in Fictional Literature of Chile." Ph.D. dissertation, University of Virginia, 1967.

Espinosa, Januario. "El pueblo chico en la novela chilena." *Atenea* (April 1935), pp. 5–13.

Fein, John M. *Modernism in Chilean Literature. The Second Period.* Durham, N.C., 1965.

Ferrero, Mario. "La prosa chilena del medio siglo." *Atenea,* no. 386 (1960), 50 pp.

Godoy, Juan. "Breve ensayo sobre el roto." *Atenea,* no. 163 (1939), pp. 33–40.

Goic, Cedomil. "Bibliografía de la novela chilena del siglo XX." *Boletín del Instituto de Filología de la Universidad de Chile* 14 (1961): 51–168.

Goic, Cedomil. *La novela chilena.* Santiago de Chile, 1968.

Goic, Cedomil. "La novela chilena actual." *Anales de la Universidad de Chile* 118, no. 119 (1960): 250–58.

Guerrero, Leoncio. "La novela reciente en Chile." *Journal of Interamerican Studies*, no. 3 (1963), pp. 379–95.

Guzmán, Nicomedes. *Nuevos cuentistas chilenos.* Santiago, 1941.

Homenaje de la Universidad de Concepción al sesquicentenario de la independencia de Chile. *Cien años de la novela chilena.* Concepción, 1961.

Illanes Adaro, Graciela. "La naturaleza de Chile en su aspecto típico y regional a través de sus escritores." *Anales de la Universidad de Chile* 98, no. 39–40 (1940): 80–226.

Latcham, Ricardo A. "Literatura imaginativa y novela feminina en Chile." *Estudios Americanos*, no. 48 (Seville, 1955): pp. 337–49.

Latcham, Ricardo A. "Novela chilena actual: las viejas generaciones." *Estudios Americanos*, no. 42 (Seville, 1955), pp. 219–34.

Latcham, Ricardo A. "Novelistas chilenos de la generación del 40." *Estudios Americanos*, no. 45 (Seville, 1955): 643–73.

Latorre, Mariano. *Antología de cuentistas chilenos.* Santiago, 1938.

León Echaiz, René. *Interpretación histórica del huaso chileno.* Santiago de Chile, 1955.

Loveluck, Juan. *El cuento chileno, 1864–1920.* Buenos Aires, 1964.

Montecinos, Manuel. *El mar en la literatura chilena.* Santiago, 1959.

Moseley, William W. "An Introduction to the Chilean Historical Novel." *Hispania* 43 (1960): 338–42.

Moseley, William W. "Origins of the Historical Novel in Chile." *Hispania* 41 (1958): 274–77.

Ornstein, Jacob. "Breve panorama de la novela chilena reciente." *Revista Iberoamericana* 18, no. 36 (1951–52): 339–44.

Pereira Salas, Eugenio. "Notas sobre la novela histórica acerca de Chile." *Atenea* no. 291–92 (1949), pp. 278–96.

Ramírez, Adolfo. "The Chilean Novel of Social Protest." Ph.D. dissertation, University of Wisconsin, 1956.

Ramírez Jones, Julia. *Los precursores de la novela en Chile.* Santiago, 1923.

Reyes, Salvador. "Apuntes sobre la novela y el cuento en Chile." *Cuadernos Hispanoamericanos*, no. 22 (1951), pp. 67–74.

Santana, Francisco. *La biografía novelada en Chile.* Santiago, 1953.

Santana, Francisco. *La nueva generación de prosistas chilenos.* Santiago de Chile, 1949.

Seura Salvo, Carlos. "Tipos chilenos en la novela y en el cuento nacional." *Anales de la Universidad de Chile* 95, no. 25–26 (1937): 41–50.

Silva Castro, Raúl. "Centenario de la novela chilena." *Cuadernos*, no. 12 (Paris, 1955), pp. 65–69.

Silva Castro, Raúl. *Creadores chilenos de personajes novelescos.* Santiago de Chile, 1953.

Silva Castro, Raúl. *Historia crítica de la novela chilena.* Madrid, 1960.

Silva Castro, Raúl. "Nuevos talentos para la novela chilena." *Ficción,* no. 23 (1960), pp. 78–81.

Silva Castro, Raúl. *Panorama de la novela chilena, 1843–1953.* Mexico, 1955.

Silva Castro, Raúl and Castillo, Homero. *Historia bibliográfica de la novela chilena.* Mexico, 1961.

Teitelboim, Volodia. "La generación del 38 en busca de la realidad chilena." *Atenea,* no. 380–81 (1958), pp. 106–31.

Torres, Aldo. "El adolescente en la novela chilena." *Cuadernos Hispanoamericanos,* no. 124 (1960), pp. 80–93.

Torres-Rioseco, Arturo. "Nuevas consideraciones sobre la novela chilena." *Papeles de Son Armadans* 33 (1964): 7–16.

Valenzuela, Víctor M. "A New Generation of Chilean Novelists and Short Story Writers." *Hispania* 37 (1954): 440–42.

Yankas, Lautaro. "Cuentistas y novelistas del mar chileno." *Cuadernos Hispanoamericanos,* no. 123 (1960), pp. 307–16.

Zamudio, José. *La novela histórica en Chile.* Santiago, 1949.

CHILE—AUTHORS

Barrios, Eduardo

Barrios, Eduardo. *Y la vida sigue.* Buenos Aires, 1925.

Benbow, Jerry L. "Grotesque elements in Eduardo Barrios." *Hispania* 51 (1968): 86–91.

Cotto-Thorner, Guillermo. "Eduardo Barrios: novelista del sentimiento." *Hispania* 34 (1951): 271–72.

Davison, Ned J. "Conflict and Identity in *El hermano asno.*" *Hispania* 42 (1959): 498–501.

Davison, Ned J. "The Significance of *Del natural* in the Fiction of Eduardo Barrios." *Hispania* 44 (1961): 27–33.

Decker, Donald M. "Eduardo Barrios talks about his novels." *Hispania* 5, (1962): 254–58.

Fogelquist, Donald F. "Eduardo Barrios en su etapa actual." *Revista Iberoamericana* 18, no. 35 (1952): 13–25.

Fogelquist, Donald F. "Una visita a Eduardo Barrios." *Cuadernos Americanos* 116 (1961): 234–39.

Galaos, José Antonio. "Eduardo Barrios, novelista autobiográfico." *Cuadernos Hispanoamericanos,* no. 166 (1963), pp. 160–74.

Gálvez, Manuel. Prologue to Eduardo Barrios, *Un perdido.* Santiago de Chile, 1958.

Hamilton, Carlos D. "La novelística de Eduardo Barrios." *Cuadernos Americanos* 85 (1956): 280–92.

Lozano, Carlos. "Paralelismos entre Flaubert y Eduardo Barrios." *Revista Iberoamericana* 24 (1959): 265–96.

Monguió, Luis. "Sobre un milagro en Meléndez, Palma y Barrios." *Revista Hispánica Moderna* 22 (1956): 1–11.

Peralta, Jaime. "La novelística de Eduardo Barrios." *Cuadernos Hispanoamericanos*, no. 173 (1964), pp. 357–67.

Ramírez, Manuel D. "Some Notes on the Prose Style of Eduardo Barrios." *Romance Notes* 9 (1967): 40–48.

Rossel, Milton. "El hombre y su psique en las novelas de Eduardo Barrios." Separata de la revista *Atenea*, no. 389 (1956), 62 pp.

Rossel, Milton. "Un novelista psicológico." *Atenea*, no. 82 (1940), pp. 5–16.

Salaverri, Vicente A. "Las grandes novelas americanas: *Un perdido* de Eduardo Barrios." *Nosotros* 16 (1922): 81–89.

Silva Castro, Raúl. "Eduardo Barrios (1884–1963)." *Revista Iberoamericana* 30, no. 58 (1964): 243–46.

Silva Castro, Raúl. "La obra novelesca de Eduardo Barrios." *Cuadernos*, no. 78 (Paris, 1963), pp. 76–82.

Vázquez-Bigi, Ángel M. "El tipo sicológico en Eduardo Barrios y correspondencias en las letras europeas." *Revista Iberoamericana* 24 (1959): 265–96.

Vázquez-Bigi, Ángel M. "La verdad sicológica en Eduardo Barrios," Ph.D. dissertation, University of Minnesota, 1962.

Vázquez-Bigi, Ángel M. "Los conflictos psíquicos y religiosos de *El hermano asno*," *Cuadernos Hispanoamericanos*, no. 220 (1968), pp. 120–45.

Vázquez-Bigi, Ángel M. "Los tres planos de la creación artística de Eduardo Barrios." *Revista Iberoamericana* 29, no. 55 (1963): 125–37.

Vidal, Hernán. "El modo narrativo en *El hermano asno* de Eduardo Barrios." *Revista Hispánica Moderna* 33 (1967): 241–49.

Blest Gana, Alberto

Astorquiza, Eliodoro. "Don Alberto Blest Gana." *Revista Chilena* 34 (August 1920): 345–70.

Díaz Arrieta, Hernán. *Don Alberto Blest Gana, biografía y crítica.* Santiago, 1940.

Donoso, Armando. "Alberto Blest Gana." *Revista Chilena* 37 (November 1920): 208–13.

Fuenzalida Grandón, Alejandro. "Algo sobre Blest Gana y su arte de novelar." *Anales de la Universidad de Chile* 90 (1932): 187–242.

Huneeus, Roberto. *Don Alberto Blest Gana y la novela histórica.* Paris, 1897.

Latcham, Ricardo A. "Blest Gana y la novela realista." *Anales de la Universidad de Chile* 96, no. 112 (1958): 30–46.

Latorre, Mariano. "El pueblo chileno en las novelas de Blest Gana." *Atenea* (August 1933), pp. 180–97.

Miller, F. D. *La sociedad chilena coetánea como se ve a través de las principales novelas de Alberto Blest Gana.* Mexico, 1949.

Phillips, Walter T. "Chilean Customs in the Novels of Alberto Blest Gana." Ph.D. dissertation, University of Southern California, 1943.

Pool, A. M. *La influencia francesa en tres novelistas iberoamericanos del siglo XIX.* Mexico, 1950.

Silva Castro, Raúl. *Alberto Blest Gana, 1830–1920.* Santiago de Chile, 1955.

Silva Castro, Raúl. *Blest Gana y su novela Durante la reconquista.* Monograph. Santiago, 1934.

Silva Castro, Raúl. "El centenario de Martín Rivas." *Revista Iberoamericana* 29, no. 55 (1963): 139–46.

Silva Castro, Raúl. "La obra novelística del chileno Alberto Blest Gana." *Cuadernos Hispanoamericanos,* no. 89 (1957), pp. 324–46.

Silva Castro, Raúl. "Las novelas de don Alberto Blest Gana," *Revista Hispánica Moderna* 23, no. 3–4 (July-October 1957): 292–304.

Wilson, W. C. E. "The Historical Element in the Novels of Alberto Blest Gana," Ph.D. dissertation, University of Washington, 1931.

Wilson, W. C. E. "Blest Gana's Debt to Barros Arana." *The Hispanic American Historical Review* 19 (1939): 102–5.

D'Halmar, Augusto (See Thomson, Augusto)

Durand, Luis

Decker, Donald M. "Bibliografía de y sobre Luis Durand." *Revista Iberoamericana* 30 no. 58 (1964): 313–17.

Homenaje a Luis Durand. *Atenea,* no. 353 (1954).

Huerta, E. "El cuento chileno y Luis Durand." *Atenea,* no. 279–80 (1948), pp. 27–33.

Pagés Larraya, Antonio. "Luis Durand, escritor viviente." *Atenea,* no. 358 (1955), pp. 41–46.

Sánchez, Luis Alberto. "Para una antología de Luis Durand." *Atenea,* no. 353–54 (1954), pp. 69–106.

Edwards Bello, Joaquín

Coll, Edna. *Chile y los chilenos en las novelas de Joaquín Edwards Bello.* Havana, 1947.

Orlandi, Julio. "Trayectoria de Joaquín Edwards Bello." *Cien años de la novela chilena.* Concepción, 1961, pp. 153–68.

Ramírez, Alejandro y Orlandi, Julio. *Joaquín Edwards Bello.* Santiago de Chile, 1959.

Silva Castro, Raúl. "Joaquín Edwards Bello y Daniel de la Vega, prosistas chilenos." *Revista Hispánica Moderna* 24 (1968): 791–98.

Stanford, G. Alonzo. "Joaquín Edwards Bello and his *En el viejo Almendral.*" *Hispania* 27 (1944): 446–52.

Urbistondo, Vicente. "Manifestaciones naturalistas en la novela chilena: D'Halmar, Orrego Luco y Edwards Bello." Ph.D. dissertation, University of California, 1964.

Gana, Federico

Castillo, Homero. "Federico Gana, maestro del relato criollista." *Cuadernos Americanos* 140 (1965): 235–45.

Montenegro, Ernesto. "El encantamiento de Federico Gana." *Cuadernos Americanos* 108 (1960): 260–77.

Yankas, Lautaro. "El paisaje y la gente de Chile en la obra de Federico Gana." *Cuadernos Hispanoamericanos*, no. 208 (1967), pp. 147–53.

González Vera, José Santos

Alegría, Fernando. "Gonzalez Vera: El humorismo de la imprecisión." *Humanitas*, no. 3 (Monterrey, Mexico, 1962), pp. 259–67.

Castillo, Homero. "Ambiente y personajes en dos obras de José Santos González Vera." *Hispano*, no. 11 (1964), pp. 53–61.

Castillo, Homero. "Dos momentos de la literatura chilena." *La Nueva Democracia* 40, no. 1 (1960): 73–77.

Castillo, Homero. "José Santos González Vera: Perspectiva de una realidad urbana." *Symposium* 14, no. 4 (1960): 282–88.

Espinoza, Enrique. "El humorismo de González Vera." *Atenea*, no. 370 (1955), pp. 95–108.

Fogelquist, Donald F. "The Humorous Genius of José Santos González Vera." *Hispania* 36 (1953): 314–18.

Ljungstedt, Ester. *Un prosista chileno: José Santos González Vera*. Madrid, 1965.

Lastarria, José Victorino

Castillo, Homero. "*El mendigo*: Primer relato novelesco de Chile." *Quaderni Ibero-Americani*, no. 27 (1961), pp. 158–64.

Donoso, Armando. *Don José Victorino Lastarria: recuerdos de medio siglo*. Santiago, 1917.

Fuenzalida Grandón, Alejandro. *Lastarria y su tiempo, 1817–1888*. 2 vols. Santiago, 1911.

Zañartu, Sady. *Lastarria, el hombre solo*. Santiago, 1938.

Latorre, Mariano

Alegría, Fernando. "Mariano Latorre y *On Panta*." *Atenea* (November 1935), pp. 332–46.

Arce, Magda. *Mariano Latorre*. New York, 1955.

Arce, Magda. "Mariano Latorre, novelista chileno contemporáneo." *Revista Iberoamericana* 5, nos. 9–10 (1942): 121–30; (1942): 359–81; 6, nos. 11–12 (1943): 101–19; (1943): 303–34.

Castillo, Homero. "El relato urbano en el criollismo de Mariano Latorre." *Asomante* 17, no. 3 (1961): 48–54.

Castillo, Homero. "Mariano Latorre, orígenes de una vocación." *Cuadernos Americanos* 109 (1960): 228–37.

Castillo, Homero. "Mariano Latorre y el criollismo." *Hispania* 39 (1956): 438–45.

Castillo, Homero. "Proyecciones de la crítica y la obra de Mariano Latorre." *Cien años de la novela chilena*, pp. 80–89. Concepción, 1961.

Castillo, Homero. "Tributo a Mariano Latorre." *Revista Iberoamericana* 22, no. 43 (1956): 83–94.

Espinosa, Januario. "Mariano Latorre, Chile's Foremost Regional Writer." *Chile* (New York, March 1930), pp. 114–39.

Fuensalida, Héctor. "Mariano Latorre: Reportaje póstumo." *Anales de la Universidad de Chile* 114, no. 101 (1956): 23–28.

Guanse, Domenec. "La obra literaria de Mariano Latorre." *Atenea*, no. 232 (1944), pp. 4–17.

Homenaje issue of *Atenea*, no. 370 (1955–56). It contains articles on Latorre by Milton Rossel, Ricardo A. Latcham, Raúl Silva Castro, Juan Uribe Echeverría, Luis Merino Reyes, Leoncio Guerrero, Enrique Labrador Ruiz, Juan Godoy, Homero Castillo, Vicente Mengod, Marco A. Bontá, Aldo Torres, Waldo Vila, Cedomil Goic, Lisolette Schwarzenberg, and Ricardo Benavides.

Huerta, Eleazar. "Creación y estilo en las novelas de Mariano Latorre." In Mariano Latorre, *La isla de los pájaros* (Santiago de Chile, 1955).

Perry, B. D. "*Hombres y zorros*," *Atenea*, no. 155 (1938), pp. 282–89.

Pinilla, Norberto. "Mariano Latorre: Introducción." *Revista Hispánica Moderna* 9 (1943): 17–21.

Ramírez, Alejandro y Orlandi, Julio. *Mariano Latorre*. Santiago de Chile, 1959.

Santana, Francisco. *Mariano Latorre*. Santiago, 1956.

Silva Castro, Raúl. "Mariano Latorre y su novela, *La paquera*." *Revista Iberoamericana* 24, no. 48 (1959): 297–306.

Yankas, Lautaro. "Dimensión y estilo de Mariano Latorre." *Cuadernos Hispanoamericanos*, no. 221 (1968), pp. 430–39.

Lillo, Baldomero

Brown, Donald F. "A Chilean Germinal: Zola and Baldomero Lillo." *Modern Language Journal* 65 (1950): 47–51.

Sedgwick, Ruth. "Baldomero Lillo y Emile Zola." *Revista Iberoamericana* (February 1944), pp. 321–28.

Sedgwick, Ruth. "El mensaje social de Baldomero Lillo." In *Memorias del segundo congreso internacional de catedráticos de literatura iberoamericana*, pp. 35–44. Berkeley, 1940.

Maluenda, Rafael

Castillo, Homero. "Sentido humano de Rafael Maluenda." *La Nueva Democracia* 51, no. 3 (1961): 12–15.

Oyarzún, Luis. "Rafael Maluenda." *Mapocho* 4, no. 11 (1965): 189–96.

Sánchez, Luis Alberto. "Rafael Maluenda, novelista de almas." *Revista Nacional de Cultura* 5, no. 38 (1943): 58–68.

Silva Castro, Raúl. "Rafael Maluenda y su última novela." *Revista Hispánica Moderna* 25 (1959): 311–13.

Orrego Luco, Luis

Chapman, G. Arnold. "Don Luis Orrego Luco y la vida en Chile." *Atenea,* no. 278 (1948), pp. 211–32.

Melfi, Domingo. "La novela *Casa Grande* y la transformación de la sociedad chilena." *Anales de la Universidad de Chile,* no. 106–7 (1948–49), pp. 239–57.

Melfi, Domingo. "Luis Orrego Luco, novelista." *Cien años de novela chilena,* pp. 123–40. Concepción, 1961.

Vaisse, Emilio. "*Casa Grande.*" *Anales de la Universidad de Chile,* no. 106 (1948–49), pp. 225–38.

Prado, Pedro

Arriagada Augier, Julio y Goldsack, Hugo. "Pedro Prado, un clásico de América." Separata de la revista *Atenea,* no. 321–24 (1952), 107 pp.

Benge, Frances. "Bergson y Prado." *Cuadernos Americanos* 147 (1966): 116–23.

Brandau, Valentín. *Elogio de Pedro Prado.* Santiago, 1953.

Donoso, Armando. "Pedro Prado." *Nosotros* 22, no. 84 (1916): 22–54.

Montenegro, Ernesto. "La sonrisa de Pedro Prado." *Revista Iberoamericana* 18, no. 35 (1952–53): 93–104.

Morales, Ernesto. "Alsino." *Nosotros* 37, no. 143 (1921): 499–506.

Silva Castro, Raúl. "Pedro Prado, Premio Nacional de Literatura." Separata de la revista *Occidente* (June 1949), 15 pp.

Silva Castro, Raúl. "Pedro Prado: Vida y obra." *Revista Hispánica Moderna* 26 (1960): 1–80.

Torres-Rioseco, Arturo. "Las novelas de Pedro Prado." *Atenea,* no. 389 (1960), pp. 219–30.

Prieto, Jenaro

Espinosa, Januario. "Jenaro Prieto—Humorist." *Chile* (New York, December 1930), pp. 190–207.

Rojas, Manuel

Alegría, Fernando. "Manuel Rojas: Trascendentalismo en la novela chilena." *Cuadernos Americanos* 103 (1959): 244–58.

Espinosa, Enrique. "Notas sobre Manuel Rojas." *Atenea,* no. 346–47 (1954), pp. 108–21.

Larrieu, Norman Cortés. "*Hijo de ladrón* de Manuel Rojas." *Anales de la Universidad de Chile* 118, no. 120 (1960): 193–202.

Lichtblau, Myron I. "Los últimos capítulos de *Hijo de ladrón.*" *Revista Hispánica Moderna* 34 (1968): 707–13.

Sender, Ramón J. "Sobre la novela rapsódica y la urbe." *Revista Iberoamericana* 17, no. 34 (1951–52): 269–83.

Silva Castro, Raúl. "Manuel Rojas y sus cuentos." *Revista Hispánica Moderna* 27 (1951): 323–28.

Santiván, Fernando

Latorre, Mariano. "Fernando Santiván, el hombre, el escritor." *Cuadernos Hispanoamericanos*, no. 49 (1954), pp. 77–86.

Subercaseaux, Benjamín

Goic, Cedomil. "*Jemmy Button*, novela per Benjamín Subercaseaux." *Atenea*, no. 312 (1951), pp. 497–501.

Osses, Mario, "*Jemmy Button*, de Benjamín Subercaseaux," *Atenea*, no. 311 (1951), pp. 323–35.

Thomson, Augusto

Arriagada, Julio and Goldsack, Hugo. "*Augusto D'Halmar*," *Tres ensayos esenciales y una antología*. Santiago, 1963.

Bourgeois, Louis Clarence, III. "Augusto d'Halmar, Chilean Novelist and Storyteller." Ph.D. dissertation, University of California, 1964.

Díaz Arrieta, Hernán. "Augusto D'Halmar." In *Cien años de la novela chilena*, pp. 56–79. Concepción, 1961.

Homenaje a Augusto d'Halmar. *Revista de Educación*, no. 55 (Santiago de Chile, June 1950), 96 pp.

Labarca Garat, Gustavo. "Semblanza de Augusto D'Halmar." *Atenea*, no. 298 (1950), pp. 21–29.

Orlandi Araya, Julio. *Augusto d'Halmar*. Santiago, 1959.

Ramírez, Alejandro and Orlandi, Julio. *Augusto d'Halmar*. Colección Premios Nacionales de Literatura. Santiago, 1959.

Smith, George Ernest. "Augusto Thompson d'Halmar, Fantasist." Ph.D. dissertation, University of Indiana, 1959.

Smith, George Ernest. "Bibliografía de las obras de Augusto d'Halmar." *Revista Iberoamericana* 28, no. 53 (1962): 365–82.

COLOMBIA—GENERAL WORKS

Airó, Clemente. "El presente de la novela y su desarrollo en Colombia." *Espiral*, no. 96 (Bogotá, 1965), pp. 3–16.

Bejarano Díaz, Horacio. "La novela en Antioquia." *Universidad Pontificia Bolivariana* 26 (1964): 267–85.

Bronx, Humberto. *Veinte años de novela colombiana*. Medellín, 1966.

Casa, Enrique. *La novela antioqueña*. Mexico, 1942.

Cortázar, Roberto. *La novela en Colombia*. Bogotá, 1908.

Curcio Altamar, Antonio. *Evolución de la novela en Colombia*. Bogotá, 1957.

Englekirk, John E. and Gerald E. Wade. "Bibliografía de la novela colombiana." *Revista Iberoamericana* 15, no. 30 (1950): 309–411.

González, José Ignacio. "La novela y el cuento en Antioquia." *El Pueblo Antioqueño*. Medallin, 1942, pp. 329–48.

Keller, Jean P. "El indígena y la tierra en cuatro novelas recientes de Colombia." *Revista Iberoamericana* 17, no. 34 (1951–52): 301–13.

Latcham, Ricardo A. "Perspectivas de la novela colombiana actual." *Atenea*, no. 248 (1946), pp. 200–235.

Luque Valderrama, Lucía. *La novela femenina en Colombia*. Bogotá, 1954.

Maya, Rafael. "La novela y el criollismo colombiano." *Boletín de la Academia Colombiana* 15, no. 58 (1965): 181–91.

McGrady, Donald. "Adiciones a la bibliografía de la novela colombiana: 1856–1962." *Thesaurus* 20 (1965): 120–37.

McGrady, Donald. *La novela histórica en Colombia, 1844–1959*. Bogotá, 1962.

Pachón Padilla, Eduardo. *Antología del cuento colombiano*. Bogotá, 1959.

Rivas Moreno, Gerardo. *Cuentistas colombianos*. Cali, 1966.

Wade, Gerald E. "An introduction to the Colombian Novel." *Hispania* 30 (1947): 467–83.

Wade, Gerald E. and Englekirk, John E. "Introducción a la novela colombiana." *Revista Iberoamericana* 15, no. 30 (1949–50): 231–51.

COLOMBIA–AUTHORS

Acosta de Samper, Soledad

Otero Muñoz, Gustavo. "Doña Soledad Acosta de Samper." *Boletín de Historia y Antigüedades* (Bogotá, April 1933), pp. 169–75.

Carrasquilla, Tomás

Bejarano Díaz, Horacio. "Tomás Carrasquilla, novelista del pueblo antioqueño." *Universidad de Antioquia*, no. 122 (1955), pp. 400–422.

Blanco, Julio Enrique. "Carrasquilla en cuanto novelista." *Universidad de Antioquia*, no. 160 (1965), pp. 85–101.

Cadavid Restrepo, Tomás. "Tomás Carrasquilla." *Anuario de la Academia Colombiana* 8 (1940–41): 487–503.

Cadavid Uribe, Gonzalo. "El mundo novelesco de Tomás Carrasquilla." *Universidad de Antioquia*, no. 131 (1957), pp. 473–508.

Cadavid Uribe, Gonzalo. "La paremiología en las obras de Carrasquilla." *Universidad Pontificia Bolivariana* 25 (1961): 83–129.

Casa, Enrique C. de la *Apuntes bibliográficos sobre el maestro Carrasquilla*. Mexico, 1944.

Casa, Enrique C. de la. *La universalidad de Tomás Carrasquilla*. Mexico, 1944.

García Prada, Carlos. "Tomás Carrasquilla, clásico antioqueño." *Revista Iberoamericana* 24, no. 47 (1959): 9–28.

García Valencia, Abel. "Tomás Carrasquilla y la literatura antioqueña." *Universidad Pontificia Bolivariana* 22 (1957): 135–45.

Gutiérrez, Benigno A. *Glosas al volumen de las obras completas de Tomás Carrasquilla.* Medellín, 1952.

Homenaje a Tomás Carrasquilla. *Revista de las Indias* 1, no. 1 (1936): 12–24.

Levy, Kurt L. "New Light on Tomás Carrasquilla." *PMLA* 68 (1953): 65–74.

Levy, Kurt L. "Sobre el maestro Tomás Carrasquilla." *Universidad de Antioquia,* no. 109 (1952), pp. 61–65.

Levy, Kurt L. *Vida y obras de Tomás Carrasquilla.* Medellín, 1958.

Maya, Rafael. "Tomás Carrasquilla." *Bolívar,* no. 16 (Bogotá, 1953), pp. 231–35.

Mejía Duque, Jaime. "Obra y mensaje de don Tomás Carrasquilla." *Bolívar,* no. 33 (Bogotá, 1954), pp. 356–85.

Montoya, José. "Tomás Carrasquilla." *El Montañés* 1, no. 3 (Medellín, 1897): 105–12.

Onís, Federico de. "Prólogo." In *Obras completas de Tomás Carrasquilla,* pp. xi–xxv. Madrid, 1952.

Zalamea, Jorge. "Tomás Carrasquilla y la literatura colombiana." *Revista Hispánica Moderna* 14 (1948): 358–67.

Díaz, Eugenio

Camacho Roldán, Salvador. "*Manuela,* novela de costumbres colombianas, por Eugenio Díaz." *Estudios.* Bogotá, 1936, pp. 67–92.

Maya, Rafael. "La *Manuela* y el criollismo colombiano." *Boletín de la Academia Colombiana* 15, no. 54 (1965).

Gómez Escobar, Francisco

Levy, Kurt L. "Ecos de Schopenhauer en Efe Gómez." *Memoria del X Congreso del Instituto Internacional de Literatura Iberoamericana,* pp. 131–40. Mexico, 1965.

Isaacs, Jorge

Arias, Augusto. *Jorge Isaacs y su María.* Quito, 1937.

Bermejo, V. *Jorge Isaacs.* Arequipa, 1937.

Brown, Donald F. "Chateaubriand and the Story of Feliciana in Jorge Isaacs' *María*." *Modern Language Notes* 62 (1947): 326–29.

Carvajal, Mario. *Vida y pasión de Jorge Isaacs.* Manizales, 1937.

Embeita, María J. "El tema del amor imposible en *María* de Jorge Isaacs." *Revista Iberoamericana* 32, no. 61 (1966): 109–12.

Grillo, Max. *Vida y obra de Isaacs, Boletín de la Academia Colombiana* 2 (1937): 182–296.

López Michelsen, A. "Ensayo sobre la influencia semítica en *María*." *Revista de las Indias* 20, no. 62 (1944): 5–10.

Mateus Becerra, Hernán. "¿Quién era la verdadera María?" *El Tiempo.* Bogotá, 3 May 1953.
McGrady, Donald. "Las fuentes de *María* de Isaacs." *Hispano,* no. 24 (1966), pp. 43–54.
Naranjo M., Enrique. "Alrededor de *María*." *Revista Iberoamericana* 5, no. 9 (1942): 103–8.
Olivera, Otto. "*María*, tema predilecto de Isaacs." *Symposium* 14 (1960): 7–25.
Ramos, Oscar Gerardo. "Mujer, paisaje y ambiente en la novela *María*." *Universidad de Antioquia,* no. 171 (1968), pp. 169–83.
Reyes, Alfonso. "Algunas notas sobre la *María* de Jorge Isaacs." *Obras completas.* Mexico, 1955. 8: 271–73.
Sánchez Montenegro, Víctor. "Jorge Isaacs y 'El Mosaico.'" *Bolívar,* no. 19 (Bogotá, 1953), pp. 669–800.
Stein, E. *Jorge Isaacs, su vida, su época y su obra.* Mexico, 1951.
Velasco Madriñán, Luis Carlos. *Efraín y María.* Cali, 1954.
Velasco Madriñán, Luis Carlos. *Jorge Isaacs, el caballero de las lágrimas.* Cali, 1942.
Warshaw, Jacob. "Jorge Isaacs' Library: New Light on Two *María* Problems." *The Romanic Review* 32 (1941): 389–98.

Marroquín, José Manuel

Martínez Silva, Carlos. "Sobre *Amores y leyes* de José Manuel Marroquín." *Reportorio Colombiano* 19 (1896): 214–25.
Martínez Silva, Carlos. "Sobre *El Moro* de José Manuel Marroquín." *Repertorio Colombiano* 16 (1893): 81–96.
Roab, Sister Mary Ricarda. "José Manuel Marroquín. A Study of His Works." Ph.D. dissertation, St. Louis University, 1965.
Samper, José María. "José Manuel Marroquín." *Repertorio Colombiano* 5 (1879): 321–30.

Marroquín, Lorenzo

McGrady, Donald. "Sobre una alusión literaria en la novela *Pax*." *Revista Iberoamericana* 29, no. 55 (1963): 147–56.
Suárez, Marco Fidel. *Análisis gramatical de Pax.* Bogotá, 1926.

Palacios, Eustaquio

Martín, John L. "*El Alférez Real*: Another Novel of the Cauca Valley." *Hispania* 24 (1941): 193–96.
Scarpetta, Oswaldo. "*El Alférez Real*." *Boletín de la Academia de Historia del Valle del Cuenca* 28, no. 118 (Cali, 1960): 627–33.

Rendón, Francisco de Paula

García Valencia, Abel. "Francisco de Paula Rendón." *Universidad Pontificia Bolivariana* 20, no. 73 (1955): 279–81.

Moreno, Magda. *Síntesis biográfica y anecdótica de Don Francisco Paula Rendón*. Medellín, 1955.

Zuluaga, Hernando Agurear. "Rendón y la novela costumbrista." *Universidad de Antioquia*, no. 122 (1955), pp. 453–62.

Rivera, José Eustasio

Añez, Jorge. *De La vorágine a Doña Bárbara*. Bogotá, 1944.

Bull, William E. "Nature and Anthropomorphism in *La vorágine*." *The Romanic Review* 39 (1948): 307–18.

Callan, Richard J. "*La vorágine*: A Touchstone of Character." *Romance Notes* 3 (1961): 13–16.

Chasca, Edmundo de. "El lirismo de *La vorágine*." *Revista Iberoamericana* 13, no. 25 (1948): 73–90.

David, Elba R. "El pictorialismo tropical de *La vorágine* y *El viaje* de Alexander von Humboldt." *Hispania* 47 (1964): 36–40.

Green, Joan R. "La estructura del narrador y el modo narrativo de *La vorágine*." *Cuadernos Hispanoamericanos*, no. 205 (1967), pp. 101–7.

James, E. K. "José Eustasio Rivera." *Atenea*, no. 54 (1929), pp. 394–401.

Marinello, Juan. "Tres novelas ejemplares." *Sur*, no. 16 (1936), pp. 59–75.

Meléndez, Concha. "Tres novelas de la naturaleza americana: *Don Segundo Sombra, La vorágine, Doña Bárbara*." *Cultura Venezolana* 43, no. 116 (1931): 138–49.

Morales, Leonidas. "*La vorágine*: Un viaje al país de los muertos." *Anales de la Universidad de Chile* 122, no. 134 (1965): 148–70.

Neale-Silva, Eduardo. *Horizonte humano. Vida de José Eustasio Rivera*. Madison, Wi., 1960.

Neale-Silva, Eduardo. "Rivera, polemista." *Revista Iberoamericana* 14, no. 28 (1948): 213–50.

Neale-Silva, Eduardo. "The Factual Bases of *La vorágine*." *PMLA* 54 (1939): 316–31.

Olivera, Otto. "El romanticismo de José Eustasio Rivera." *Revista Iberoamericana* 17, no. 35 (1952–53): 41–59.

Ramos, Oscar G. "Clemente Silva, héroe de *La vorágine*." *Boletín Cultural y Bibliográfico* 10 (Bogotá, 1967): 568–83.

Valbuena-Briones, A. "El arte de José Eustasio Rivera." *Thesaurus* 17 (1961): 129–39.

Valente, José Ángel. "La naturaleza y el hombre en *La vorágine* de José Eustasio Rivera." *Cuadernos Hispanoamericanos*, no. 67 (1955), pp. 102–8.

Wyld Ospina, Carlos. "*La vorágine*." *Repertorio Americano* 13 (1926): 181–83.

Rodríguez Freyle, Juan

Martinengo, Alessandro. "La cultura letteraria di Juan Rodríguez Freyle." *Boletín Instituto Caro y Cuervo* 19, no. 2 (1964): 274–99.

Ramos, Oscar Gerardo. "*El carnero*, libro de tendencia cuentística." *Boletín Cultural y Bibliográfico* 9, no. 2 (1966), 2178–85.
Samper Pizano, Daniel. "El abuelo Rodríguez Freire." *Boletín Cultural y Bibliográfico* 8, no. 7 (Bogotá, 1965): 1047–53.

Samper, José María

Ferero, Manuel José. "Don José María Samper." *Revista de América* (Bogotá, July 1945): 138–43.

Silva, José Asunción

Loveluck, Juan. "*De sobremesa*, novela desconocida del Modernismo." *Revista Iberoamericana* 31, no. 59 (1965): 17–32.

Vargas Vila, José María

Andrade Coello, Alejandro. *Vargas Vila, ojeada crítica de su obra.* Quito, 1912.
Besseiro, Victorio Luis. *Un hombre libre: Vargas Vila, su vida y su obra.* Buenos Aires, 1924.
Giordano, Alberto. *Vargas Vila, su vida y su pensamiento.* Buenos Aires, 1946.
Maya, Rafael. "Crónica sobre Vargas Vila." *Boletín Cultural y Bibliográfico* 7, no. 1 (Bogotá, 1965): 1655–62.
Vargas, José E. "Vargas Vila, el desconocido." *El Libro y el Pueblo* 6, no. 102 (Mexico, 1968): 19–23.

COSTA RICA—GENERAL WORKS

Castro Rawson, Margarita. *El costumbrismo en Costa Rica.* San José, 1967.
Menton, Seymour. *El cuento costarricense.* Lawrence, Ka., 1964.
Núñez, Francisco María. *Itinerario de la novela costarricense.* San José, 1947.
Solera, Rodrigo. "La novela costarricense." Ph.D. dissertation, University of Kansas, 1964.
Tejada, Francisco Elías de. "Novela y poesía centroamericana." *Estudios Americanos* 11, no. 53 (1956): 133–39.
Thompson, Miriam Henrietta. "Twentieth-Century Yankee Imperialism in the Prose Fiction of Middle America." Ph.D. dissertation, Tulane University, 1955.

CUBA—GENERAL WORKS

Boydston, Jo Ann H. "The Cuban Novel: A Study of its Range and

Characteristics." Ph.D. dissertation, Columbia University, 1950.

Bueno, Salvador. *Antología del cuento en Cuba*. La Habana, 1953.

Bueno, Salvador. "Los temas de la novela cubana." *Asomante* 16, no. 4 (1960): 39–48.

Coulthard, G. R. *Race and Colour in Caribbean Literature*. London, 1962.

Espinosa, Ciro. *Indagación y crítica; novelistas cubanos*. La Habana, 1940.

Fornet, Ambrosio. *Antología del cuento cubano contemporáneo*. Mexico, 1967.

García Vega, Lorenzo. *Antología de la novela en Cuba*. La Habana, 1960.

Ibarzábal, Federico de *Cuentos contemporáneos*. La Habana, 1937.

Llerena, Mario. "Función del personaje en la novela cubana." *Revista Hispánica Moderna* 16 (1950): 113–22.

Marquina, Rafael. "Los caminos de la novela cubana contemporánea." *Revista Cubana* 12 (April-June 1938): 68–90.

Norman, Isabel H. "La novela romántica en las Antillas." Ph.D. dissertation, Yale University, 1966.

Portuondo, José Antonio. *Cuentos cubanos contemporáneos*. Mexico, 1946.

Remos, Juan J. *Tendencia de la narración imaginativa en Cuba*. La Habana, 1935.

Salazar y Roig, S. "La novela en Cuba." *Anales de la Academia Nacional de Artes y Letras* 16 (1934–35): 8–37.

Torriente, Loló de la. "Los caminos de la novela cubana." *Cuadernos Americanos* 69 (1953): 243–62.

Unión de Escritores y Artistas Cubanos. *Nuevos cuentos cubanos*. La Habana, 1964.

CUBA—AUTHORS

Betancourt, José Victoriano

Hernández Travieso, Antonio. "Genio y figura de José Victoriano Betancourt." *La Nueva Democracia*, no. 30 (October 1950), pp. 48–51.

Castellanos, Jesús

Henríquez Ureña, Max. "Jesús Castellanos, su vida y su obra." In *Colección póstuma de las obras de Jesús Castellanos*, vol. 1. La Habana, 1914.

Morejón, Estrella Soto. "Jesús Castellanos." *Revista de la Universidad de la Habana* 26, no. 158 (1962): 257–70.

Gómez de Avellaneda, Gertrudis

Bravo Villasante, Carmen. *Una vida romántica: Avellaneda*. Barcelona, 1967.

Carlos, Alberto. "René, Werther y *La Nouvelle Héloise* en la primera novela de la Avellaneda." *Revista Iberoamericana* 31, no. 60 (1965): 223–38.

Cotarelo y Mori, Emilio. *La Avellaneda y sus obras.* Madrid, 1930.

Kelly, Edith. "Bibliografía de la Avellaneda." *Revista Bimestre Cubana* 35 (1935): 107–39, 261–95.

Kelly, Edith. "La Avellaneda's *Sab* and the Political Situation in Cuba." *The Americas* 1 (Washington, 1945): 303–16.

Marquina, Rafael. *Gertrudis Gómez de Avellaneda.* La Habana, 1939.

Percas Ponseti, Helena. "Sobre la Avellaneda y su novela, *Sab.*" *Revista Iberoamericana* 28, no. 54 (1961): 347–57.

Heredia, Nicolás

Collado López, Olga. "Nicolás Heredia—Vida y obra." *Revista de la Biblioteca Nacional de la Habana* 5, no. 3 (1954): 103–97.

Remos, Juan J. "La personalidad de Nicolás Heredia y su obra polémica." *Boletín de la Academia Cubana de la Lengua* 4, no. 3–4 (1955): 199–218.

Hernández Catá, Alfonso

Balseiro, José. "Revisión de Hernández-Catá." In *La novela iberoamericana*, edited by Instituto Nacional de Literatura Iberoamericana, pp. 107–22. Albuquerque, 1952.

Ramos, José Antonio. "Alfonso Hernandez Catá." *Revista de la Universidad de la Habana* 23 (1947): 81–89.

Martí, José

Anderson Imbert, Enrique. "Comienzos del modernismo en la novela." *Nueva Revista de Filología Hispánica* 7 (1954): 515–25.

Anderson Imbert, Enrique. "La prosa poética de José Martí. A propósito de *Amistad funesta.*" In *Estudios sobre escritores de América*, pp. 125–65. Buenos Aires, 1954.

García Espinosa, Juan M. "En torno a la novela del Apóstol." *Revista de la Universidad de la Habana*, no. 171 (1965), pp. 7–99.

Iduarte, Andrés. *Martí escritor.* Mexico, 1945.

Iñigo Madrigal, Luis. "Martí, novelista." In *Lengua, Literatura, Folklore*, pp. 233–43. Santiago de Chile, 1967.

Villaverde, Cirilo

Cruz Manuel de la. "Cirilo Villaverde." In *Cromitos Cubanos*, pp. 189–211. Havana, 1892.

Fernández de la Vega, Oscar. "La nueva traducción de *Cecilia Valdes.*" *Revista Interamericana de Bibliografía* 14 (1964): 415–22.

Fernández Villaurrutia, Rafael. "Para una lectura de *Cecilia Valdés.*" *Revista Cubana* 31, no. 1 (1957): 31–43.

Nunn, Marshall. "La primera novela cubana." *América* 39, no. 1 (1953): 30–34.

Nunn, Marsall. "Las obras menores de Cirilo Villaverde." *Revista Iberoamericana* 14 (1948): 255–61.

Nunn, Marshall. "Some Notes on the Cuban Novel *Cecilia Valdés*." *Bulletin of Spanish Studies* 24 (1947): 184–86.

Santovenia, Emeterio S. *Cirilo Villaverde*. La Habana, 1911.

Santovenia, Emeterio S. *Personajes y paisajes de Villaverde*. Havana, 1955.

Tejera, Diego Vicente. "Juicio crítico sobre *Cecilia*." *Revista Cubana* 4 (1882): 534–41.

Torriente, Loló de la. "Cirilo Villaverde y la novela cubana." *Revista de la Universidad de la Habana* 15 (July-December 1950): 179–94.

Torriente, Loló de la. *La Habana de Cecilia Valdés*. La Habana, 1946.

Varona, Enrique José. "Sobre *Dos amores*." *Revista Cubana* 7 (1888): 84–92.

Ximeno, Manuel de. "Papeletas bibliográficas de Cirilo Villaverde." *Revista de la Biblioteca Nacional* 4, no. 2 (Havana, 1953): 133–53.

Young, Robert J. *La novela costumbrista de Cirilo Villaverde*. Mexico, 1949.

DOMINICAN REPUBLIC–GENERAL WORKS

Tena, Jorge. "Notas acerca del cuento y la novela en la República Dominicana." *Espiral*, no. 84 (1962), pp. 40–53.

Valledeperes, Manuel. "Evolución de la novela en la República Dominicana." *Cuadernos Hispanoamericanos*, no. 206 (1967), pp. 311–25.

DOMINICAN REPUBLIC–AUTHORS

Cestero, Tulio M.

Villaespesa, Francisco. "A propósito de Tulio M. Cestero." *Revista Dominicana de Cultura* 2, no. 3 (Santo Domingo, 1956): 24–29.

Galván, Manuel de Jesús

Anderson Imbert, Enrique. "El telar de una novela histórica: *Enriquillo*, de Galván." *Revista Iberoamericana* 15, no. 30 (1950): 213–29.

Cestero, Manuel F. "*Enriquillo*." *Cuba Contemporánea* 13 (April 1917): 316–37.

Cestero, Manuel, F. "*Enriquillo* de Manuel de Jesús Galván." *Cuba Contemporánea* 21 (1919): 365–408.

García Godoy, F. "Enriquillo." *Cuba Contemporánea* 17 (1918): 311–13.

Meléndez, Concha. "El *Enriquillo* de Manuel de Jesús Galván. La tradición indianista en Santo Domingo." *Hispania* (1934): 97–112.

ECUADOR—GENERAL WORKS

Allison, Wayne L. "A Thematic Analysis of the Contemporary Ecuadorian Novel." Ph.D. dissertation, University of New Mexico, 1965.

Arias, Augusto. "Apunte acerca de la novela en el Ecuador." *Mensaje de la Biblioteca Nacional,* no. 3 (1936), pp. 78–85.

Carrión, Benjamín. "La novela ecuatoriana." *Cuadernos Americanos* 50 (1950): 261–74.

Crooks, Esther J. "Contemporary Ecuador in the Novel and Short Story." *Hispania* 23 (1940): 85–88.

Da Silva, Zenia Sacks. "The Contemporary Ecuadorian Novel." Ph.D. dissertation, New York University, 1955.

Ferrándiz Alborz, F. "Los precursores." *América* 11 (1936): 70–81.

Franklin, Albert B. "Ecuador's Novelists at Work." *Inter-American Quarterly* 2 (1940): 29–41.

Guerrero, Jorge. "Cinco modernos cuentistas del Ecuador." *Revista de las Indias* (February 1943), pp. 358–68.

Icaza, Jorge. "Relato espíritu unificador en la generación del año 30." *Revista Iberoamericana* 33 (1966): 211–17.

Latorre, Mariano. "El criollismo tardío del Pacífico." *Atenea* 12, no. 124 (1935): 134–36.

McNeil, Mary L. "Costumbrismo in the Social Novel of the Central Andean Region." Ph.D. dissertation, State University of Iowa, 1952.

Ribadeneira M., Edmundo. *La moderna novela ecuatoriana.* Quito, 1958.

Rojas, Ángel F. *La novela ecuatoriana.* Mexico, 1948.

Rumazo González, Alfonso. "La generación de escritores ecuatorianos de principios del siglo veinte." *Revista Nacional de Cultura* 20, no. 130 (1958): 56–71.

Schwartz, Kessel. "Henri Barbusse and the Ecuadorian Novel." *Romance Notes* 1 (1959): 33–35.

Schwartz, Kessel. "Russian Literature in Contemporary Ecuadorian Fiction." *Kentucky Foreign Language Quarterly* 3, no. 3 (1956): 141–45.

Schwartz, Kessel. "The Contemporary Novel of Ecuador." Ph.D. dissertation, Columbia University, 1953.

Siegel, Reuben. "The Group of Guayaquil. A Study in Contemporary Ecuadorian Fiction." Ph.D. dissertation, University of Wisconsin, 1951.

Uscátegui, Emilio. "Novela y novelistas del Ecuador." *Americas,* no. 6 (Washington, 1964), pp. 29–34.

Vásconez Hurtado, G. "La novela indigenista en el Ecuador." *Primeras Jornadas de Lengua y Literatura Hispanoamericanas* 10, no. 1 (Salamanca, 1956): 467–78.

Viteri, Atanasio. "El cuento ecuatoriano moderno." *América* 10 (1935): 223–38.

ECUADOR—AUTHORS

Andrade, Roberto

Lloret Bastidas, Antonio. "Roberto Andrade, el atormentado por la libertad." *Revista del Nucelus del Azuay de la Casa de la Cultura Ecuatoriana* 5 (Cuenca, 1953): 83–127.

Bustamante, José Rafael

Gangotena y Jijón, Cristóbal de. "Bustamante." *Boletín de la Academia Nacional de Historia* (Quito, July-December 1943), pp. 207–20.
Zaldumbide, Gonzalo. "La novela de nuestras serranías." *América* 24, no. 90–92 (1948): 32–34.

Calle, Manuel J.

Andrade y Arizaga, Ignacio. *El príncipe del periodismo en el Ecuador, don Manuel de Jesús Calle.* Cuenca, 1939.
Reyes, Oscar Efrén. *La vida y la obra de Manuel J. Calle.* Quito, 1930.

Campos, José Antonio

Huerta Montalvo, Francisco. "Don José Antonio Campos, abuelo espiritual de la novela vernácula ecuatoriana." *Revista del Colegio Nacional Vicente Rocafuerte* (Guayaquil, December 1958), pp. 85–94.
Rolando, Carlos A. "Notas bibliográficas: Don José Antonio Campos." *Libros y Bibliotecas*, no. 3 (Guayaquil, September 1939), 73 pp.

Martínez, Luis A.

Arias, Augusto. "Cincuentenario de la novela precursora *A la costa.*" *Universidad de Antioquia*, no. 120 (1955), pp. 49–57.
Benites, Leopoldo. "*A la costa* de Luis A. Martínez, novela de tiempo histórico." *Letras del Ecuador* (May 1948), pp. 3–4, 14.
Ferrándiz Alborz, F. "Tres precursores del nuevo realismo literario hispanoamericano." *Cuadernos Americanos* 66 (1952): 267–84.

Mera, Juan León

Andrade Coello, Alejandro. "Juan León Mera, precursor del americanismo literario." *Revista de América* (Bogotá, January 1949), pp. 78–96.
Arias, Augusto. "Evocación de Mera." *América* (Quito, June-August 1952), pp. 421–40.
Arias, Augusto. Prologue to *Cumandá*. In *Clásicos Ecuatorianos*, vol. 16. Quito, 1948.
Borja, Luis F. *Juan León Mera. Breves apuntes críticos.* Quito, 1932.
Crespo Toral, Remigio. "Juan León Mera, maestro de la cultura nacional." In *Memoria de la Academia Ecuatoriana*, Entrega XIII. June 1933.
Guevara, Darío C. *Juan León Mera.* Quito, 1941.

EL SALVADOR–GENERAL WORKS

Barba Salinas, Manuel. *Antología del cuento salvadoreño, 1880–1955*. San Salvador, 1959.
Lindo, Hugo. "Una generación de cuentistas salvadoreños." *Atenea*, no. 369 (1956), pp. 297–306.

GUATEMALA–GENERAL WORKS

Amílcar Echeverría, R. *Antología de prosistas guatemaltecos*. Guatemala, 1957.
Ciruti, Joan E. "The Guatemalan Novel: A Critical Bibliography." Ph.D. dissertation, Tulane University, 1959.
Ericson, Martin E. "Escritores modernistas de Guatemala." *Revista Iberoamericana* 6, no. 12 (1943): 479–91.
Lamb, Ruth. *Antología del cuento guatemalteco*. Mexico, 1959.
Menton, Seymour. *Historia crítica de la novela guatemalteca*. Guatemala, 1960.
Menton, Seymour. "Sobre influencias en la novela guatemalteca." *Revista Iberoamericana* 25, no. 50 (1960): 309–15.
Pellino, Michael W. "Guatemalan Narrative of the Nineteenth Century." Ph.D. dissertation, University of Cincinatti, 1959.

GUATEMALA–AUTHORS

Gómez Carrillo, Enrique

Cáceres, Zoila Aurora. *Mi vida con Enrique Gómez Carrillo*. Madrid, 1929.
Cárdenas, R. F. "Gómez Carrillo, príncipe de la crónica." *Síntesis*, no. 2 (San Salvador, 1955), pp. 75–79.
Donis de Dardans, Hersilia. "The Life and Works of Enrique Gómez Carrillo." Ph.D. dissertation, University of Pittsburg, 1936.
Mendoza, Juan Manuel. *Enrique Gómez Carrillo: estudio crítico biográfico; su vida, su obra y su época*. 2 vols. Guatemala, 1940.
Sánchez, Luis Alberto. "Enrique Gómez Carrillo y el modernismo." *Revista de las Indias* 36, no. 112 (1950): 11–26.

Herrera, Flavio

Estrada, Ricardo. *Flavio Herrera, su novela*. Guatemala, 1960.

Irisarri, Antonio José de

Feliú Cruz, Guillermo. "Los últimos años de un polemista—Don Antonio José de Irisarri—1864–1868." *La Información* (Santiago, July 1929), pp. 191–205.

Montaner, Ricardo. "Don Antonio José Irisarri." *Atenea* (July 1933), pp. 38–61.

Silva Castro, Raúl. "Antonio José de Irisarri." *Anales de la Universidad de Chile* 109, no. 83–84 (1951): 5–25.

Milla, José

Irving, Thomas. "Las dos maneras de Pepe Milla." *Universidad de San Carlos*, no. 52 (1960), pp. 111–33.

Johnston, Marjorie C. "José Milla, retratista de costumbres guatemaltecas." *Hispania* 32 (1949): 449–52.

Martin, John L. "Las obras literarias de José Milla." *Universidad de San Carlos*, no. 11–12 (1947), pp. 7–25; (July-September 1947), pp. 33–38.

Sánchez, Luis Alberto. "José Milla y Vidaurre, el sosegado." *Atenea*, no. 323 (1952), pp. 254–68.

Wyld Ospina, Carlos

Ordóñez Arguello, Alberto. "Guatemala y Wyld Ospina." *Revista de Guatemala* (September 1946), pp. 107–25.

MEXICO—GENERAL WORKS

Arjona, Doris King and Vázquez Arjona, Carlos. "Nacionalismo en la novela mexicana." *Revue Hispanique* 81 (1933): 440–55.

Azuela, Mariano. *Cien años de novela mexicana.* Mexico, 1947.

Baer, Bárbara. "Aspectos de la revolución en la novela contemporánea de Mexico." *Universidad de San Francisco Xavier* 14 (1946): 51–131.

Besler, Beatrice. "The Mexican Revolution as Reflected in the Novel." *Hispania* 47 (1964): 41–46.

Bisbal Siller, María T. *Los novelistas y la ciudad de México, 1810–1910.* Mexico, 1963.

Brushwood, J. S. "La novela mexicana frente al porfirismo." *Historia Mexicana* 7 (1957): 368–405.

Brushwood, J. S. *Mexico in its Novel.* Austin, 1966.

Brushwood, J. S. "The Mexican Understanding of Realism and Naturalism." *Hispania* 43 (1960): 521–28.

Brushwood, J. S. *The Romantic Novel in Mexico.* Columbia, Mo., 1954.

Brushwood, J. S. and Garciadueñas, José. *Breve historia de la novela mexicana.* Mexico, 1959.

Carballo, Emmanuel. *Cuentistas mexicanos modernos.* Mexico, 1956.

Carballo, Emmanuel. "Del costumbrismo al realismo crítico." *Casa de las Américas* 3, no. 19 (1963): 3–19.

Carballo, Emmanuel. "La prosa narrativa en México." *Casa de las Américas* 5, no. 28 (1965): 3–17.

Carter, Boyd. "The Mexican Novel at Mid-Century." *Prairie Schooner* 28 (1954–55): 143–56.

Castellanos, Luis Arturo. "La novela de la Revolución Mexicana." *Cuadernos Hispanoamericanos* 62 (1965): 123–46.

Castellanos, Rosario. "La novela mexicana contemporánea y su valor testimonial." *Hispania* 47 (1964): 223–30.

Castro Leal, Antonio. *La novela de la Revolución Mexicana*. Madrid, 1960.

Castro Leal, Antonio. *La novela del México colonial*, vol. 1. Mexico, 1964.

Chang-Rodríguez, Eugenio. "La novela de la Revolución Mexicana y su clasificación." *Hispania* 42 (1959): 527–35.

Chávarri, Raúl. "La novela moderna mexicana." *Cuadernos Hispanoamericanos* 58, no. 173 (1964): 367–79.

Coll, Edna. *Injerto de temas en las novelistas mexicanas contemporáneas*. Palencia, 1964.

Delgado, Jaime. "La novela mexicana de la revolución." *Cuadernos Hispanoamericanos* no. 61 (1955), pp. 75–86.

Fernández-Arias Campoamor, J. *Novelistas de Méjico*. Madrid, 1952.

Gamboa, Federico. *La novela mexicana*. Mexico, 1914.

González, Manuel Pedro. *Trayectoria de la novela en México*. Mexico, 1951.

Hernández, Julia. *Novelistas y cuentistas de la revolución*. Mexico, 1965.

Iguiniz, Juan B. *Bibliografía de novelistas mejicanos*. Mexico, 1926.

Jiménez Rueda, Julio. *Antología de la prosa en México*. Mexico, 1938.

Larrinaga, Miguel Alonso. "Cinco novelas mexicanas de la escuela realista del siglo XIX." *Cuadrante* 2, no. 1–2 (1953): 5–12.

Leal, Luis. *Breve historia del cuento mexicano*. Mexico, 1956.

Maggipinto, Francis Xavier. "Naturalism in the Mexican Novel." Ph.D. dissertation, Stanford University, 1953.

Martínez, José Luis. *Problemas literarios [Novela mexicana]*. Mexico, 1955.

McManus, Beryl J. M. "La técnica del nuevo realismo en la novela mexicana de la revolución." In *Memoria del Cuarto Congreso del Instituto Internacional de Literatura Iberoamericana*, pp. 313–33. Havana, 1949.

Meinhardt, Warren Lee. "The Mexican Indianist Novel: 1910–1960." Ph.D. dissertation, University of California at Berkeley, 1965.

Moore, Ernesto. *Bibliografía de novelistas de la Revolución Mejicana*. Mexico, 1941.

Moore, Ernesto. *Novelistas de la revolución mexicana*. Havana, 1940.

Morton, F. Rand. *Los novelistas de la revolución mexicana*. Mexico, 1949.

Navarro, Joaquina. *La novela realista mexicana*. Mexico, 1955.

Portuondo, José Antonio. "Trayectoria de la novela en México." *Cuadernos Americanos* 61 (1952): 285–89.

Read, John Lloyd. *The Mexican Historical Novel, 1826–1910*. New York, 1939.

Reyes Nevares, Salvador. "La novela de la revolución mexicana." *Mundo Nuevo*, no. 32 (1969), pp. 4–9.

Rodríguez Chucharro, César. "La novela indigenista mexicana." In *Estudios Literarios*, pp. 93–150. Mexico, 1963.

Rojas Garcidueñas, José. "La novela en la Nueva España." *Anales del Instituto de Investigaciones Estéticas*, no. 3 (1962), pp. 57–78.

Seymour, Arthur R. "The Mexican *novela de costumbres*." *Hispania* 8 (1925): 283–89.

Stanton, Ellen R. "La novela de la revolución mexicana: Estudio relacionado con el movimiento literario y social." Ph.D. dissertation, University of Southern California, 1943.

Torriente, Loló de la. "Apuntes para un ensayo sobre la novela mexicana." *Revista de la Universidad de la Habana*, no. 40–42 (1942), pp. 49–83.

Tyre, Carlos and Annemarie. "El medio a través de la novela mexicana." *Memoria del Primer Congreso . . . de Literatura Iberoamericana* (Mexico, 1938), pp. 85–91.

Uribe Echeverría, Juan. "La novela de la revolución mexicana y la novela hispanoamericana actual." *Anales de la Universidad de Chile* 93, no. 20 (Santiago, 1935): 5–95.

Warner, Ralph E. *Historia de la novela mexicana en el siglo XIX*. Mexico, 1953.

Wheeler, Howard T. "The Mexican Novel as a Reflection of the National Problems of Mexico." Ph.D. dissertation, Stanford, 1935.

MEXICO—AUTHORS

Abreu Gómez, Ermilo

Abreu Gómez, Ermilo. "De mi vida literaria y algo más." *Cuadernos Americanos* 112 (1959): 260–73.

Altamirano, Ignacio Manuel

Alba, José de. "Semblanza de Ignacio Manuel Altamirano." *Cuadernos*, no. 86 (Paris, 1964), pp. 86–88.

Carrell, Thelma R. "The Role of Ignacio Manuel Altamirano in El Renacimiento." Ph.D. dissertation, University of Illinois, 1953.

Nacci, Chris N. "El enderezamiento del carácter varonil en las obras de Altamirano." *Kentucky Foreign Language Quarterly* 10 (1963): 157–61.

Warner, Ralph E. *Bibliografía de Ignacio Manuel Altamirano*. Mexico, 1955.

Azuela, Mariano

Azuela, Mariano. "Azares de mi novela, *Los de abajo*." *Universidad de México* 1, no. 25 (1946).

Azuela Arriaga, María. *Mariano Azuela, novelista de la revolución mexicana.* Mexico, 1955.

Cotto-Thorner, G. "Mariano Azuela, el poeta en el novelista." *La Nueva Democracia* 31, no. 4 (1951): 76–83.

Dulsey, Bernard M. "Azuela Revisited." *Hispania* 35 (1952): 331–32.

Englekirk, John E. "The Discovery of *Los de abajo.*" *Hispania* 18 (1935): 53–62.

Englekirk, John E. and Kiddle, Lawrence B. Introduction to text edition of *Los de abajo.* New York, 1939.

González, Manuel Pedro. "Bibliografía del novelista Mariano Azuela." *Revista Bimestre Cubana* 48 (July-August 1941): 50–72.

González de Mendoza, J. M. "Mariano Azuela y lo mexicano." *Cuadernos Americanos* 63 (1952): 282–85.

Hendricks, Frances K. and Berler, Beatrice. Introduction to *Two Novels of the Mexican Revolution.* San Antonio, 1963.

Kercheville, Francis M. "El liberalismo en América." *Revista Iberoamericana* 3, no. 6 (1941): 381–98.

Leal, Luis. *Mariano Azuela, vida y obra.* Buenos Aires, 1967.

Leal, Luis. "Mariano Azuela, novelista médico." *Revista Hispánica Moderna* 28 (1962): 295–303.

Menton, Seymour. "La estructura épica de *Los de abajo* y un prólogo especulativo." *Hispania* 50 (1967): 1001–11.

Monterde, Francisco. "En torno a *Los de abajo* del doctor Mariano Azuela." *Filosofía y Letras* (University of Mexico) 23 (1952): 265–69.

Moore, Ernest R. "Novelists of the Mexican Revolution: Mariano Azuela." *Mexican Life* 16, no. 8 (1940): 21–24, 52–61.

Nemtzow, Mary. "*Esa sangre*, una novela inédita del doctor Mariano Azuela." *Revista Iberoamericana* 19, no. 37 (1954): 65–70.

Rama, Ángel. "El perspectivismo social en la novela de Mariano Azuela." *Revista Iberoamericana de Literatura* 1, no. 1 (Montevideo, 1966): 63–94.

Sánchez, Luis Alberto. "Mariano Azuela." *Revista Nacional de Cultura* 24, no. 151–52 (1961–62): 117–27.

Spell, Jefferson Rhea. "Mexican Society of the Twentieth Century as Portrayed by Mariano Azuela." *Inter-American Intellectual Exchange* (Institute of Latin American Studies: University of Texas), pp. 49–61.

Torres-Rioseco, Arturo. "Mariano Azuela." *Revista Cubana* 11 (1938): 44–72.

Woolsey, A. W. "Los protagonistas de algunas novelas de Mariano Azuela." *Hispania* 23 (1940): 341–48.

Balbuena, Bernardo de

Van Horne, John. *Bernardo de Balbuena, Biografía y Crítica.* Guadalajara, Mexico, 1940.

Bramón, Francisco

Benwell, Frank Paul. "Francisco Bramón's *El triunfo de la Virgen.*" *The Americas,* no. 11 (1954), pp. 51–55.

Campo, Ángel de (Micrós)

Fernández del Castillo, A. *Micrós: Ángel de Campo, el drama de su vida.* Mexico, 1946.
Lamb, Ruth S. "The Costumbrismo of the Pensador Mexicano and Micrós." *The Modern Language Journal* 35 (1951): 193–98.
Magdaleno, Mauricio. "El sentido de lo mexicano en Micrós." *El Libro y el Pueblo* (November 1953), pp. 404–10.

Campobello, Nellie

Campobello, Nellie. *Mis libros.* Mexico, 1960.
Moore, Ernest R. "Novelists of the Mexican Revolution: Nellie Campobello." *Mexican Life* 17 (1941): 21–22.

Cuéllar, José Tomás

Peñalosa, Joaquín A. "La literatura mejicana según José Tomás Cuéllar." *Estilo,* no. 25 (January-March 1953), pp. 13–17.

Delgado, Rafael

Allemand, P. F. "Rafael Delgado, costumbrista mexicano." *Museo Nacional de Arqueología, Historia y Etnología* 24 (1931–33): 147–236.
Bickley, James G. *The Life and Works of Rafael Delgado.* Berkeley, 1935.
Caffarel Peralta, Pedro. "Rafael Delgado, novelista." *Universidad Veracruzana* 3, no. 1 (1954): 40–52.
Homenaje a Delgado. *Universidad Veracruzana* 2, no. 3 (1953).
Jiménez Rueda, Julio. "El centenario de don Rafael Delgado." *Revista de Filosofía y Letras* (University of Mexico) 24 (1952): 175–81.
Moore, Ernest and Bickley, James. "Rafael Delgado, Notas bibliográficas y críticas." *Revista Iberoamericana* 6, no. 11 (1943): 155–202.
Salado Álvarez, Vicente. "Máscaras. Rafael Delgado." *Revista Moderna* 6, no. 1 (1908): 241–43.
Torres Manzó, C. "Perfil y esencia de Rafael Delgado." *Cuadernos Americanos* 70 (1953): 247–61.

Díaz Covarrubias, Juan

Brushwood, John S. "Juan Díaz Covarrubias: Mexico's Martyr Novelist." *The Americas* 10 (1958): 301–6.
Spell, Jefferson Rhea. "Juan Díaz Covarrubias, a Mexican Romantic." *Hispania* 16 (1932): 327–44.

Díaz del Castillo, Bernal

Caillet-Bois, Julio. "Bernal Díaz de Castillo o de la verdad en la historia." *Revista Iberoamericana* 25, no. 50 (1960): 199–228.

Fernández de Lizardi, José Joaquín

Davis, Jack Emory. "Estudio lexicográfico de *El Periquillo Sarniento*." Ph.D. dissertation, Tulane, 1956.

Godoy, Bernabé. *Corrientes culturales que definen al Periquillo.* Guadalajara, 1938.

Godoy, Bernabé. "Lo permanente y lo transitorio en el *Periquillo*." *Et Caetera* (January-June 1951), pp. 1–22.

González Obregón, D. L. *José Joaquín Fernández de Lizardi.* Mexico, 1888.

Knowlton, Jr., Edgar C. "China and the Philippines in *El Periquillo Sarniento*," *Hispanic Review* 31 (1963): 336–47.

Lozano, Carlos. "*El Periquillo Sarniento* y la *Histoire de Gil Blas de Santillana.*" *Revista Iberoamericana* 20, no. 40 (1955): 263–74.

Monterde, Francisco. "Fernández de Lizardi, novelista." *Cultura Mexicana* 5 (1946): 119–27.

Moore, Ernest. "La desconocida segunda edición del *Peregrino*." *Revista de Literatura Mexicana* 1 (1940): 307–17.

Moore, Ernest. "Una bibliografía descriptiva. *El Periquillo Sarniento* de José Joaquín Fernández de Lizardi." *Revista Iberoamericana* 10 (1945): 383–403.

Reyes, Alfonso. "*El Periquillo Sarniento* y la crítica mexicana." *Revue Hispanique* 38 (1916): 232–42.

Reynolds, Winston A. "The Clergy in the Novels of Fernández de Lizardi." *Modern Language Forum* 40 (1955): 105–12.

Solomón, Noel. "La crítica del sistema colonial de la Nueva España en *El Periquillo Sarniento*." *Cuadernos Americanos* 138 (1965): 167–79.

Spell, Jefferson Rhea. "A Textual Comparison of the First Four Editions of *El Periquillo Sarniento*." *Hispanic Review* 31 (1963): 134–47.

Spell, Jefferson Rhea. "New Light on Fernández de Lizardi and his *El Periquillo Sarniento*." *Hispania* 46 (1963): 753–54.

Spell, Jefferson Rhea. "The Genesis of the First Mexican Novel." *Hispania* 14 (1931): 53–58.

Spell, Jefferson Rhea. "The Historical and Social Background of *El Periquillo Sarniento*." *Hispanic American Historical Review* 34 (1956): 447–70.

Spell, Jefferson Rhea. "The Intellectual Background of Lizardi as Reflected in *El Periquillo Sarniento*." *PMLA* 71 (1956): 414–32.

Spell, Jefferson Rhea. *The Life and Works of José Joaquín Fernández de Lizardi.* Philadelphia, 1931.

Ferretis, Jorge

Holden, Paul H. "The Creative Writings of Jorge Ferretis: Ideology and Style." Ph.D. dissertation, University of Southern California, 1966.

Martínez Cáceres, Arturo. "Jorge Ferretis." *Oraciones*, Suplemento, no. 71 (5 May 1963).

Frías, Heriberto

Brown, James W. "Heriberto Frías, a Mexican Zola." *Hispania* 50 (1967): 467–71.

Brushwood, John S. "Heriberto Frías on Social Behaviour and Redemptive Woman." *Hispania* 46 (1962): 249–53.

Moore, Ernest A. "Heriberto Frías and the Novel of the Mexican Revolution." *Modern Language Forum* 27, no. 1 (1942): 12–27.

Gamboa, Federico

Butler, Charles William. "Federico Gamboa, Novelist of Transition." Ph.D. dissertation, University of Colorado, 1955.

Campos, Jorge. "El naturalismo mexicano: Federico Gamboa." *Insula* 20, no. 228–29 (1965): 21.

Carreño, A. M. "Federico Gamboa." *Abside* 2, no. 12 (1938): 18–38.

González-Peña, Carlos. "Las bodas de oro de un novelista." *Letras Mexicanas* 2, no. 10 (1936): 6–7.

Jiménez Rueda, Julio. "Federico Gamboa." *Revista Iberoamericana* 1, no. 2 (1939): 361–63.

Latcham, Ricardo A. "En el centenario de Federico Gamboa." *Revista Nacional* 9 (1964): 594–96.

Menton, Seymour. "The Life and Works of Federico Gamboa." Ph.D. dissertation, New York University, 1952.

Moore, Ernest. "Bibliografía de obras y crítica de Federico Gamboa, 1864–1939." *Revista Iberoamericana* 2, no. 3 (1940): 271–79.

Moore, Ernest. "Federico Gamboa, Diplomat and Novelist." *Books Abroad* 14 (1940): 364–67.

Niess, Robert J. "Federico Gamboa: the Novelist as Autobiographer." *Hispanic Review* 13 (1945): 346–51.

Niess, Robert J. "Zola's *L'Oeuvre* and *Reconquista* of Gamboa." *PMLA* 61 (1946): 577–83.

Rosenberg, S. L. M. "El naturalismo en México y don Federico Gamboa." *Bulletin Hispanique* 36 (1934): 472–87.

Theobald, J. O. "Naturalism in the Works of Federico Gamboa." *University of Arizona Bulletin* 4, no. 5 (1933): 47–48.

Woolsey, A. W. "Some of the Social Problems Considered by Federico Gamboa." *The Modern Language Journal* 34 (1950): 294–97.

Goytortúa Santos, Jesús

Kolb, Glen L. "Dos novelas y un solo argumento." *Hispania* 46 (1963): 84–85.

Guzmán, Martín Luis

Abreu Gómez, Ermilo. "Bibliografía de Martín Luis Guzmán." *Revista Interamericana de Bibliografía* 9 (1959): 136–43.

Hauck, Helen P. "Las obras novelescas de Martín Luis Guzmán." *Revista Iberoamericana* 3, no. 5 (1941): 139–57.

Leal, Luis. "*La sombra del caudillo,* roman à clef." *Modern Language Journal* 36 (1952): 16–21.

Stanton, Ruth. "Martín Luis Guzmán's Place in Modern Mexican Literature." *Hispania* 26 (1943): 136–38.

Inclán, Luis G.

Novo, Salvador. "El coronel Astucia y los hermanos de la hoja o los charros contrabandistas." *México en el Arte* (September 1948).

Paredes, Americo. "Luis Inclán: First of the Cowboy Writers." *American Quarterly* 12 (1960): 55–70.

Jiménez Rueda, Julio

Monterde, Francisco. "Julio Jiménez Rueda." *Revista de la Universidad de Yucatán* 2, no. 9 (1960): 43–46.

Valle, Rafael Heliodoro. "Diálogo con Julio Jiménez Rueda." *Universidad de Méjico* (September 1947), pp. 5–7.

López Portillo y Rojas, José

Furness, Edna S. "The Literary Theories of José López Portillo y Rojas." Ph.D. dissertation, University of Colorado, 1940.

Grass, Roland. "José López-Portillo y Rojas y la revolución agraria en México." *Cuadernos Americanos* 146 (1966): 240–46.

Jiménez Rueda, Julio. "El centenario de López Portillo." *Revista Iberoamericana* 16, no. 32 (1950–51): 215–17.

Spell, Lota M. "An Early Novel by López Portillo." *Library Chronicle of the University of Texas* 8, no. 1 (1965): 3–8.

López y Fuentes, Gregorio

Armitage, Richard H. "The Problem of Modern Mexico in the Novels of López y Fuentes." Ph.D. dissertation, Ohio State University, 1946.

González, Manuel Pedro. "Apostillas en torno a dos novelas mexicanas recientes." *Revista Iberoamericana* 1, no. 2 (1939): 321–33.

Mate, Hubert E. "Social Aspects of Novels of López y Fuentes and Ciro Alegría." *Hispania* 39 (1956): 287–92.

McKegney, James Cuthbert. "Female Characters in the Novels of José Rubén Romero and Gregorio López y Fuentes." Ph.D. dissertation, University of Washington, 1959.

Menton, Seymour. *Las novelas de Gregorio López y Fuentes.* Mexico, 1949.

Moore, Ernest. "López y Fuentes, Novelist of the Mexican Revolution." *The Spanish Review* 4, no. 1 (1937): 23–31.

Magdaleno, Mauricio

Cruz, Salvador de la. "Nuevos novelistas iberoamericanos." *El Libro y el Pueblo* 17, no. 15 (1955): 5–75.

Lacosta, Francisco C. "Notas sobre un tema indigenista: Mauricio Magdaleno, *El resplandor.*" *Duquesne Hispanic Review* 1 (1962): 37–40.

Ratchford, Joanne C. "Recurring Themes and Views in the Major Works of Mauricio Magdaleno." Ph.D. dissertation, University of Virginia, 1968.

Stanton, Ruth. "The Realism of Mauricio Magdaleno." *Hispania* 22 (1939): 345–53.

Muñoz, Rafael

Puga, Mario. "El escritor y su tiempo." *Universidad de México* 10, no. 2 (1955): 16–18.

Ochoa, Antonio de

Moore, Ernest R. "La primera novela histórica mexicana." *Revista de Literatura Mexicana* 1 (1940): 370–78.

Payno, Manuel

Knapp, Jr., Fran A. "Some Historical Values in a Famous Mexican Novel." *The Americas* 11 (1959): 131–39.

Ortiz Vidales, Salvador. *Los bandidos en la literatura mexicana.* Mexico, 1949.

Spell, Jefferson Rhea. "The Literary Works of Manuel Payno." *Hispania* 12 (1929): 347–56.

Rabasa, Emilio

Guillén y Castañón, E. *Vida y obra literaria de Emilio Rabasa.* Mexico, 1947.

Noriega, Alfonso. "Conferencias dictadas en la sesión solemne en homenaje al maestro Emilio Rabasa." *El Faro,* no. 15–16 (January-June 1957).

Riva Palacio, Vicente

Díaz de Ovando, Clementina. "Un gran literato liberal — Vicente Riva Palacio." *Anales del Instituto de Investigaciones Estéticas* 7, no. 27 (1958): 47–62.

Leal, Luis. "Dos cuentos olvidados de Vicente Riva Palacio." *Anales del Instituto de Investigaciones Estéticas* 7, no. 27 (1958): 63–70.

Leal, Luis. "Vicente Riva Palacio, cuentista." *Revista Iberoamericana* 22, no. 44 (1957): 301–9.

Millán, María del Carmen. "Tres novelistas de la reforma." *La Palabra y el Hombre* 4 (1957): 53–63.

Slavens, Marjorie R. "Mexican Identity in the Prose Works of Vicente Riva Palacio." Ph.D. dissertation, St. Louis University, 1968.

Rodríguez Beltrán, Cayetano

Díaz de Ovando, Clementina. "Dos novelistas veracruzanos." *Anales del Instituto de Investigaciones Estéticas* 5, no. 20 (1952): 45–68.

Rojas González, Francisco

Lowe, Mary Ann. *Francisco Rojas González, novelista.* Mexico, 1957.

Menton, Seymour. "*La negra Angustias,* una *Doña Bárbara* mexicana." *Revista Iberoamericana* 19, no. 38 (1954): 299–308.

Sommers, Joseph. *Francisco Rojas González, exponente literario del nacionalismo mexicano.* Xalapa, 1966.

Sommers, Joseph. "La génesis literaria en Francisco Rojas González." *Revista Iberoamericana* 29, no. 56 (1963): 299–309.

Sommers, Joseph. "*La negra Angustias.*" *La Palabra y el Hombre* 10, no. 40 (1966): 637–52.

Romero, José Rubén

Alba, Pedro de. *Rubén Romero y sus novelas populares.* Barcelona, 1936.

Arratia, Alejandro. "Tres novelas de José Rubén Romero." *La Nueva Democracia* 38, no. 2 (1958): 92–97.

Arreola Cortés, Raúl. "José Rubén Romero, vida y obra." *Revista Hispánica Moderna* 12 (1946): 7–34.

Castagnaro, R. Anthony. "Rubén Romero and the Novel of the Mexican Revolution." *Hispania* 36 (1953): 300–304.

Cord, William O. *José Rubén Romero, cuentos y poesías inéditas.* Mexico, 1963.

Cord, William O. "José Rubén Romero: The Voice of Mexico." Ph.D. dissertation, University of Colorado, 1961.

Cord, William O. "José Rubén Romero: The Writer as Seen by Himself." *Hispania* 44 (1961): 431–37.

Cord, William O. "José Rubén Romero's Image of Mexico." *Hispania* 45 (1962): 612–20.

Eoff, Sherman. "Tragedy of the Unwanted Person in Three Versions: Pablos de Segovia, Pito Pérez, Pascual Duarte." *Hispania* 39 (1956): 190–96.

González y Contreras, G. *Rubén Romero, el hombre que supo ver.* Havana, 1940.

Iduarte, Andrés. "José Rubén Romero: Retrato." *Revista Hispánica Moderna* 12 (1946): 1–6.

Lafarga, Gastón. *La evolución literaria de Rubén Romero.* Paris, 1938.

MacKegney, James C. "Some Non-Fictional Aspects of *La vida inútil de Pito Pérez.*" *Romance Notes* 6 (1964): 26–29.

Moore, Ernest R. "José Rubén Romero: Bibliografía." *Revista Hispánica Moderna* 12 (1946): 35–40.

Phillips, Ewart E. "The Genesis of Pito Pérez." *Hispania* 47 (1964): 698–702.

Romero, José Rubén. "Fecha y fichas de un pobre diablo." *Cuadernos Americanos* 22 (1945): 244–58.

Stanton, Ruth. "José Rubén Romero, costumbrista of Michoacán." *Hispania* 24 (1941): 423–28.

Vasconcelos, José

Cotto-Thorner, Guillermo. "Germen novelístico en Vasconcelos." *La Nueva Democracia* 36 (1956): 32–35.

PANAMA—GENERAL WORKS

Miró, Rodrigo. *El cuento en Panamá.* Panama, 1950.

PARAGUAY—GENERAL WORKS

Calcagno, Miguel Ángel. "Introducción a un estudio de la novela rioplatense." *Revista Iberoamericana de Literatura* 4, no. 4 (1962).

Pla, Josefina. "La narrativa en el Paraguay de 1900 a la fecha." *Cuadernos Hispanoamericanos* 77, no. 231 (1969): 641–54.

Pla, Josefina and Pérez-Maricevich, Francisco. "Narrativa paraguaya." *Cuadernos Americanos* 159 (1968): 181–96.

PERU—GENERAL WORKS

Aldrich, Jr., Earl M. *The Modern Short Story in Peru.* Madison, Wisconsin, 1966.

Arias-Larreta, Abraham. "Definición del indigenismo peruano." *La Nueva Democracia* 36, no. 3 (1956): 36–42.

Arias-Larreta, Abraham. "Presencia y actitud del nativo en la novela peruana." *América* (July 1954), pp. 14–26.

Cabello de Carbonera, Mercedes. *La novela moderna.* Lima, 1948.

Castro Arenas, Mario. *La novela peruana y la evolución social.* Lima, 1965.

Castro Arenas, Mario. "La nueva novela peruana." *Cuadernos Hispanoamericanos,* no. 138 (1961), pp. 307–29.

Cortés, Louis Joseph. "The Social Novel of Peru, 1920–1952." Ph.D. dissertation, University of Colorado, 1957.

Escobar, Alberto. "El cuento peruano." *Estudios Americanos* 9, no. 43 (1955): 289–312.

Escobar, Alberto. *El cuento peruano, 1825–1925.* Buenos Aires, 1964.

Escobar, Alberto. *La narración en el Perú.* Lima, 1960.

Goodrich, Diane R. "Peruvian Novels of the Nineteenth Century." Ph.D. dissertation, Indiana University, 1966.

Lora Risco, Alejandro. "Fronteras universales de la novela peruana." *Atenea* 156 (1968): 135–51.

Montero, Manuel. "Literatura narrativa en el Perú." *Estudios Americanos* 14 (1957): 41–49.
Nemtzow, M. "Acotaciones al costumbrismo peruano." *Revista Iberoamericana* 15, no. 29 (1949): 45–62.
Oviedo, José Miguel. *Narradores peruanos [Antología].* Caracas, 1968.
Simmons, Ozzie G. "The Criollo Outlook in the Mestizo Culture of Coastal Peru." *American Anthropologist,* no. 57 (1955), pp. 107–15.

PERU—AUTHORS

Carrió de la Vandera, Alonso

Bataillon, Marcel. "Introducción a Concolorcorvo y su itinerario de Buenos Aires a Lima," *Cuadernos Americanos* 111 (1960): 197–216.
Mazzara, Richard A. "Some Picaresque Elements in Concolorcorvo's *El lazarillo de ciegos caminantes.*" *Hispania* 44 (1961): 323–27.
Tamayo-Vargas, Augusto. "Concolorcorvo ¿sería Fray Calixto San Joseph Tupac Inga?" *Revista Iberoamericana* 24, no. 48 (1959): 333–56.

Cisneros, Luis Benjamin

Tovar, Enrique. "Luis Benjamín Cisneros." *Mercurio Peruano* (January 1943), pp. 30–35.

García Calderón, Ventura

Barbagelata, Hugo D. "Ventura García Calderón." *Revista Nacional* 4, no. 202 (1959): 584–86.
Delgado, Luis Humberto. *Ventura García Calderón.* Lima, 1947.
Gómez de la Serna, Ramón. *Ventura García Calderón.* Geneva, 1946.

Garcilaso de la Vega, Inca

Castanien, Donald G. *El Inca Garcilaso de la Vega.* New York, 1969.
Castanien, Donald G. "Narrative Art in *La Florida del Inca.*" *Hispania* 43 (1960): 30–36.
Durand, José. "Las enigmáticas fuentes de *La Florida del Inca.*" *Cuadernos Hispanoamericanos,* no. 168 (1963), pp. 597–609.
Miró Quesada, Aurelio. *El Inca Garcilaso.* Madrid, 1948.

Matto de Turner, Clorinda

Crouse, Ruth Compton. "Clorinda Matto de Turner: An Analysis of Her Role in Peruvian Literature." Ph.D. dissertation, Florida State University, 1964.
McIntosh, C. B. "*Aves sin nido,* and the Beginning of Indianismo." Ph.D. dissertation, University of Virginia, 1932.

Palma y Román, Angélica

Warren, Virgil A. "Angélica Palma y Román (1883–1935)." *Hispania* 22 (1939): 295–302.

Palma, Clemente

Warren, Virgil A. "La obra de Clemente Palma." *Revista Iberoamericana* 2 (1940): 161–71.
Wiesse, María. "Semblanza de Clemente Palma." *Hora del hombre* (Lima, 1946), pp. 17–22.

Palma, Ricardo

Adán, Martín. "Palma." *Mercurio Peruano* 25, no. 191 (1943): 39–49.
Nemtzow, M. "Motivos de ironía y sátira de Ricardo Palma." *Memoria del Cuarto Congreso* (April 1949), pp. 293–312.
Pereda Valdés, Ildefonso. "Valor folklórico y estilístico de las *Tradiciones Peruanas*." *Memoria del Segundo Congreso* (August 1940), pp. 339–57.
Remos, Juan J. "El alma del Perú en las *Tradiciones Peruanas*." *Revista Cubana* (January-December 1946), pp. 72–89.
Sánchez, Luis Alberto. *Don Ricardo Palma y Lima*. Lima, 1927.
Thomas, Ruth S. "Las fuentes de las *Tradiciones Peruanas*." *Revista Iberoamericana* 2, no. 4 (1940): 461–69.
Umphrey, George W. "Ricardo Palma, tradicionalista." *Hispania* 7 (1924): 147–56.
Xammar, L. F. "Elementos románticos y anti-románticos de Ricardo Palma." *Revista Iberoamericana* 4, no. 7 (1941): 95–107.

PUERTO RICO—GENERAL WORKS

Arroyo, Anita. "La novela en Puerto Rico." *Revista del Instituto de Cultura Puertorriqueña* 25 (July-September 1965): 48–54.
Babín, María Teresa. "Expresión de Puerto Rico en la literatura contemporánea." *Revista Iberoamericana* 22, no. 44 (1957): 353–58.
Cabrera, F. Manrique. "Notas sobre la novela puertorriqueña de los últimos 25 años." *Asomante* 11, no. 4 (1955): 20–25.
Gómez Tejera, Carmen. *La novela en Puerto Rico*. University of Puerto Rico, 1947.
Laguerre, Enrique A. *Antología de cuentos puertorriqueños*. Mexico, 1966.
Márquez, René. *Cuentos puertorriqueños de hoy*. San Juan, 1959.
Márquez, René. "La función del escritor puertorriqueño en el momento actual." *Cuadernos Americanos* 127 (1963): 55–63.

Meléndez, Concha. "La literatura de ficción en Puerto Rico (1955–1963)." *Asomante*, no. 3 (1964), pp. 7–23.

Suárez-Murias, Marguerite. "Los iniciadores de la novela en Puerto Rico." *Asomante* 18, no. 3 (1962): 43–48.

PUERTO RICO—AUTHORS

Zeno Gandía, Manuel

Barrera, Héctor. "*La charca*: Osario de vivos o generación de fantasmas." *Asomante* 11, no. 4 (1955): 59–64.

Cabrera, F. Manrique. "Manuel Zeno Gandía: poeta del novelar isleño." *Asomante* 11, no. 4 (1955): 19–47.

Colina, José M. "La naturaleza en *La charca*." *Asomante* 5, no. 2 (1949): 50–59.

Galaos, José Antonio. "Zeno Gandía y sus crónicas de un mundo enfermo." *Cuadernos Hispanoamericanos*, no. 177 (1964), pp. 415–20.

Laguerre, Enrique. "El arte de novelar de Zeno Gandía." *Asomante* 11, no. 4 (1955): 48–58.

Olivera, Otto. "Los cuentos de Zeno Gandía." *Symposium* 16, no. 3 (1962): 221–24.

Quiñones, Samuel R. "El novelista de Puerto Rico: Manuel Zeno Gandía." *Ateneo Puertorriqueño* 1, no. 1 (1935): 8–34.

Rosa-Nieves, Cesáreo. "Presencia de Manuel Zeno Gandía." *Asomante* 11, no. 4 (1955): 54–58.

URUGUAY—GENERAL WORKS

Caillava, Domingo. *La literatura gauchesca en el Uruguay*. Montevideo, 1921.

Englekirk, John E. and Ramos, Margaret M. *La narrativa uruguaya*. Publications in Modern Philology, vol. 30. Berkeley, 1967.

García, Serafín J. *Panorama del cuento nativista del Uruguay*. Montevideo, 1943.

Garganigo, John F. *El perfil del gaucho en algunas novelas de Argentina y Uruguay*. Montevideo, 1966.

Lasplaces, Alberto. *Antología del cuento uruguayo*. 2 vols. Montevideo, 1943.

Salaverri, Vicente. *Florilegio de prosistas uruguayos*. Buenos Aires, 1918.

Visca, Arturo Sergio. "Panorama de la actual narrativa uruguaya." *Ficción*, no. 5 (1957), pp. 120–26.

URUGUAY—AUTHORS

Acevedo Díaz, Eduardo

Acevedo Díaz (hijo), Eduardo. *La vida de batalla de Eduardo Acevedo Díaz*. Buenos Aires, 1941.

Darío, Rubén. "La novela en América: Eduardo Acevedo Díaz." *Revista Nacional*, no. 146 (1951), pp. 175–78.

Etcheverry, José Enrique. "Historia, nacionalismo y tradición en la novela de Eduardo Acevedo Díaz." In *La novela iberoamericana*, edited by Instituto Internacional de Literatura Iberoamericana, pp. 155–65. Albuquerque, 1952.

Figueroa, Pedro Pablo. "Un novelista oriental, Eduardo Acevedo Díaz." *El Cojo Ilustrado* 5 (1896): 706–7, 733–73.

Ibáñez, Roberto. "La novela de Eduardo Acevedo Díaz." *Revista de la Facultad de Humanidades y Ciencias* 10 (1953): 69–85.

Martínez Vigil, Carlos. "Eduardo Acevedo Díaz." *Vida Moderna* 3, no. 1 (1902): 5–60.

Pereira Rodríguez, José. "*El combate de la tapera* de Eduardo Acevedo Díaz." *Revista Nacional*, no. 221 (1964), pp. 454–64.

Pérez Petit, Víctor. "Eduardo Acevedo Díaz." *Revista Nacional* (January 1938), pp. 41–64.

Rodríguez Monegal, Emir. *Eduardo Acevedo Díaz*. Montevideo, 1963.

Torres Ginart, Luis. "Eduardo Acevedo Díaz o la tragedia de la personalidad." *Revista Nacional* (December 1938), pp. 397–412.

Montiel Ballesteros, Adolfo

Delgado, José María. "Los escritores que culminan: Adolfo Montiel Ballesteros." *Revista Nacional*, no. 107 (1947), pp. 267–86.

Garet Mas, Julio. "La etapa europea de Montiel Ballesteros." *Revista Nacional*, no. 227 (1966), pp. 103–14.

Garganigo, John F. "*Gaucho Tierra* y *Don Segundo Sombra*: Dos idealizaciones gauchescas." *Revista Hispánica Moderna* 32 (1966): 198–205.

Santandren Morales, Ema. "Montiel Ballesteros y su fábula." *Revista Americana de Buenos Aires* (September-October 1940), pp. 3–14.

Morosoli, Juan José

Visca, Arturo Sergio. *Tres narradores uruguayos: Reyles, Viana, Morosoli*. Montevideo, 1962.

Quiroga, Horacio

Boule-Christanflour, A. "Una historia de locos: *Los perseguidos* de Horacio Quiroga." *Mundo Nuevo*, no. 8 (1967), pp. 51–57.

Carrera, Gustavo Luis. "Aspectos del tema de la selva en Rómulo Gallegos y Horacio Quiroga." *Revista Nacional de Cultura* 20, no. 127 (1958): 12–20.

Crow, John A. "La locura de Horacio Quiroga." *Revista Iberoamericana* 1, no. 1 (1939): 33–45.

Crow, John A. "Vida y obra de Horacio Quiroga." In *Horacio Quiroga— Sus mejores cuentos*, pp. ix-lii. Mexico, 1943.

Delgado, José María and Alberto Brignole. *Vida y obra de Horacio Quiroga*. Montevideo, 1939.

Englekirk, John E. "La influencia de Poe en Quiroga." *Número* 1 (1949): 323–39.

Etcheverry, José Enrique. *Horacio Quiroga y la creación artística*. Montevideo, 1957.

Flores, Ángel. "Latin American Writers: Horacio Quiroga." *Panorama*, no. 25 (1944), pp. 18–23.

Floripe, Rodolfo O. "Horacio Quiroga: Novelistic Materials and Techniques." Ph.D. dissertation, University of Wisconsin, 1951.

González, Juan B. "Horacio Quiroga, novelista y cuentista." *Nosotros* 67, no. 228 (1930): 26–41.

Orgambide, Pedro G. *Horacio Quiroga, el hombre y su obra*. Buenos Aires, 1954.

Ray, Gordon B. "Infancia, niñez y adolescencia en la obra de Horacio Quiroga." *Revista Iberoamericana* 18, no. 36 (1953): 273–314.

Rodríguez Monegal, Emir. "Cincuentenario de *Los arrecifes de coral*." *Número* 3, no. 15–17 (1951): 298–343.

Rodríguez Monegal, Emir. "Horacio Quiroga: una perspectiva." *Ficción*, no. 5 (1957), pp. 99–112.

Rodríguez Monegal, Emir. *Objetividad de Horacio Quiroga*. Montevideo, 1950.

Rodríguez Monegal, Emir. "Una historia perversa." *Mundo Nuevo*, no. 8 (1967), pp. 57–60.

Speratti Pinero, Emma Susana. "Hacia la cronología de Horacio Quiroga." *Nueva Revista de Filología Hispánica* 9 (October-December 1955): 367–82.

Reyles, Carlos

Allen, Martha. "La personalidad literaria de Carlos Reyles." *Revista Iberoamericana* 13, no. 25 (1947): 91–115.

Bateson, Howard L. "French Influences in the Work of Carlos Reyles, Uruguayan Novelist." Ph.D. dissertation, University of Illinois, 1943.

Bonet, Carmelo M. "Aproximación a Carlos Reyles." *Cursos y Conferencias* 46, no. 269 (1955): 110–47.

González, Hipólito. "Carlos Reyles." *Boletín del Instituto de Filología de la Universidad de Chile* 22, no. 6 (1965): 5–223.

Homenaje. *La Cruz del Sur* (Montevideo, April–May 1931).

Llerena Acevedo de Blixen, Josefina. *Reyles*. Montevideo, 1943.

Lucero, A. L. "*La raza de Caín*." *Revista de Derecho, Historia y Letras* 8 (1901): 570–77.

Luisi, Luisa. "Escritores uruguayos." *Nosotros* 41, no. 158 (1922): 292–320; no. 159: 451–83.
Mañach, Jorge. "Carlos Reyles." *Revista Hispánica Moderna* 5 (1939): 18–20.
Mattiace, Vincenza A. "Carlos Reyles and his Social Consciousness of the Uruguayan Scene." Ph.D. dissertation, New York University, 1958.
Maule, Mary-Eleanor. "Modernismo in Two Spanish American Novelists: Carlos Reyles and Pedro Prado." Ph.D. dissertation, University of Wisconsin, 1957.
Menafra, Luis Alberto. *Carlos Reyles.* Montevideo, 1957.
Morby, Edwin S. "Una batalla entre antiguos y modernos." *Revista Iberoamericana* 4, no. 7 (1941): 119–43.
Pérez Petit, Víctor. "*El embrujo de Sevilla* de Carlos Reyles." *Nosotros* 46 (1938): 526–40.
Pérez Petit, Víctor. "*El Terruño.*" *Nosotros* 25 (1917): 471–99.
Sisto, D. T. "Character Analysis in the Works of Carlos Reyles." Ph.D. dissertation, University of Iowa, 1952.
Suárez Calimaño, E. "*El gaucho Florido.*" *Nosotros* 78 (1933): 209–24.
Torres-Rioseco, Arturo. "Carlos Reyles." *Revista Iberoamericana* 1, no. 2 (1939): 47–72; no. 2 (1939): 339–51.

Viana, Javier de

Donahue, Frances. "El mundo uruguayo de Javier de Viana." *Revista Interamericana de Bibliografía,* no. 6 (1966), pp. 403–10.
Freire, T. J. *Javier de Viana.* Montevideo, 1957.
González Arrete, B. "Vida de un gran cuentista campero, Don Javier de Viana." *Pampa Argentina* (November 1947), pp. 3–5.
Mata, Ramiro. "El gaucho en Javier de Viana." *Revista Nacional,* no. 141 (1950), pp. 410–26.
Pereda Valdés, Ildefonso. "El campo uruguayo a través de tres grandes novelistas: Acevedo Díaz, Javier de Viana y Carlos Reyles." *Journal of Inter-American Studies* 8 (1966): 535–40.
Redmond, Emily. "Javier de Viana, the Man and his Work." Ph.D. dissertation, University of Pittsburg, 1940.

Zavala Muniz, Justino

Ferrándiz Alborz, F. "Justino Zavala Muniz en la nueva literatura hispanoamericana," *Cuadernos Hispanoamericanos,* no. 93 (1957), pp. 245–58.
Velasco Aragón, Luis. "Justino Zavala Muniz y su *Crónica.*" *Revista Universitaria* 40, no. 100 (1951): 259–66.

VENEZUELA—GENERAL WORKS

Angarita Arvelo, Rafael. *Historia y crítica de la novela en Venezuela.* Berlin, 1938.

Bibliografía de la novela venezolana. Centro de Estudios Literarios, Universidad Central de Venezuela, 1963.

Díaz Seijas, Pedro. *Orientaciones y tendencias de la novela venezolana.* Caracas, 1949.

Freilich de Segal, Alicia. "El niño en el cuento venezolano." *Revista Nacional de Cultura* 24, no. 153 (1962): 126–63.

Izaguirre, Rodolfo. "Venezuela y el tiempo de su novela." *Revista Nacional de Cultura* 24, no. 148 (1961): 202–7.

Mancera Galletti, A. *Quienes narran y cuentan en Venezuela.* Mexico, 1958.

Meneses, Guillermo. *Caracas en la novela venezolana.* Caracas, 1966.

Meneses, Guillermo. "Veinte y cinco años de la novela venezolana." *Revista Nacional de Cultura* 25, no. 161 (1963): 207–24.

Planchart, Julio. "Reflexiones sobre novelas venezolanas." *Cultura Venezolana* 9, no. 77 (1926): 158–89.

Ratcliff, D. F. *Venezuelan Prose Fiction.* New York, 1933.

Venegas Filardo, Pascual. *Novelas y novelistas de Venezuela.* Caracas, 1955.

Yepes Boscán, G. *La novela indianista en Venezuela.* Maracaibo, 1965.

VENEZUELA—AUTHORS

Blanco, Eduardo

Barnola, Pedro Pablo. *Eduardo Blanco, creador de la novela venezolana.* Caracas, 1963.

Blanco Fombona, Rufino

Arroyo Álvarez, Eduardo. "El polifacetismo de Rufino Blanco Fombona." *Revista Nacional de Cultura* 16, no. 101 (1953): 76–78.

Barón Castro, Rodolfo. "Rufino Blanco-Fombona." *Revista de Indias* 6 (1945): 373–83.

Benítez, Justo Pastor. "Blanco Fombona." *América* 45 (1954): 18–30.

Cansinos Assens, Rafael. "Rufino Blanco Fombona." *Ars* 9 (1958): 26–37.

Carmona Nenclares, F., ed. *Rufino Blanco Fombona, su vida y su obra.* Caracas, 1944.

Carmona Nenclares, F., ed. *Vida y literatura de Rufino Blanco-Fombona.* Madrid, 1928.

Cestero, Tulio Manuel. "Rufino Blanco Fombona." *Cuadernos Americanos* 25 (1946): 269–81.

Coll, Pedro Emilio. "Lectura sobre Rufino Blanco-Fombona." *Boletín de la Academia Venezolana Correspondiente de la Española* (January-March 1945), pp. 119–31.

Fabbiani Ruiz, José. "Los cuentos de Blanco Fombona." *Revista Nacional de Cultura* 12, no. 83–84 (1950): 35–41.

Fombona Pachano, Jacinto. "Rufino Blanco Fombona." *Boletín de la Academia Venezolana* (April-June 1945), pp. 150–54.

Gallegos Valdés, Luis. "Rufino Blanco Fombona, 1874–1944." *Revista del Ministerio de Cultura* (San Salvador, September-December 1947), pp. 175–84.

González y Contreras, Gilberto. *Radiografía y disección de Rufino Blanco Fombona*. Havana, 1944.

Lazo, Raimundo. "Rufino Blanco Fombona." *Revista Cubana* (January-December 1944), pp. 144–56.

MacDonald, H. B. *Rufino Blanco Fombona: su vida, su obra y su actitud para con los Estados Unidos*. New York, 1925.

Monticone, C. R. *Rufino Blanco Fombona: The Man and His Work*. Pittsburg, 1931.

Ríos, Berthy. "*La bella y la fiera*." *Revista de la Universidad de Zulia* 4, no. 17 (1962): 91–101.

Rodríguez Fabregat (hijo), Enrique. "Presencia de Rufino Blanco Fombona." *Revista Nacional* (March 1945), pp. 447–53.

Rodríguez Mendoza, E. "Blanco Fombona." *Bitácora* (June 1943), pp. 36–57.

Yépez, Luis. "Evocación de Rufino Blanco Fombona." *Revista Nacional de Cultura* 21, no. 136 (1959): 6–15.

Coll, Pedro Emilio

Fabbiani Ruiz, José. "La obra narrativa de Pedro Emilio Coll." *Revista Nacional de Cultura* 11, no. 80 (1950): 41–45.

González Paredas, Ramón. "La prosa de Pedro Emilio Coll." *Bitácora* (August-September 1943), pp. 83–90.

Homenaje a Pedro Emilio Coll. *Cultura Universitaria* (May-June 1947).

Díaz Rodríguez, Manuel

Agudo Freytes, Raúl. "El anacronismo literario de Díaz Rodríguez." *Revista Nacional de Cultura* 9, no. 67 (1948): 147–56.

Bonilla, Manuel Antonio. "Manuel Díaz Rodríguez." *Boletín de la Academia Venezolana Correspondiente a la Española* (April-June 1945), pp. 256–61.

Correa, Luis. *Manuel Díaz Rodríguez en "Terra Patrum."* Caracas, 1941.

Crema, Edoardo. "Armonía de tendencias en *Peregrina*." *Revista Nacional de Cultura* 21, no. 136 (1959): 89–106.

Dunham, Lowell. "Manuel Díaz Rodríguez, maestro del estilo." *Boletín de la Academia Venezolana Correspondiente de la Española* (January-June 1949), pp. 1–103.

Dunham, Lowell. *Manuel Díaz Rodríguez, vida y obra*. Mexico, 1959.

Holland, Henry. "Manuel Díaz Rodríguez. Estilista del modernismo." *Hispania* 39 (1956): 281–86.

Monguió, Luis. "Manuel Díaz Rodríguez y el conflicto entre lo práctico y lo ideal." *Revista Iberoamericana* 11, no. 2 (1946): 49–54.

Moreno García, Alberto. *Manuel Díaz Rodríguez o la belleza como imperativo*. Bogotá, 1957.

Gallegos, Rómulo

Allen, Richard F. "Social and Political Thought in the Early Narrative of Rómulo Gallegos." Ph.D. dissertation, University of Maryland, 1961.

Araujo, Orlando. "El folklore en Rómulo Gallegos." *Archivos Venezolanos de Folklore* 1, no. 2 (1952): 323–51.

Araujo, Orlando. *Lengua y creación en Rómulo Gallegos.* Buenos Aires, 1955.

Araujo, Orlando. "Sentido y vigencia en la obra de Gallegos." *Revista Nacional de Cultura* 24, no. 153 (1962): 34–51.

Arciniegas, Germán, "Novela y verdad en Rómulo Gallegos." *Cuadernos Americanos* 76 (1954): 37–43.

Carvajal de Arocha, Mercedes (Lucila Palacios). "Una interpretación de la novela de Rómulo Gallegos." *Revista Nacional* no. 164 (1963), pp. 21–31.

Castanien, Donald G. "Introspective Techniques in *Doña Bárbara.*" *Hispania* 41 (1958): 282–88.

Consalvi, Simón A. *Rómulo Gallegos, el hombre y su escenario.* Caracas, 1964.

Díaz Seijas, Pedro. *Rómulo Gallegos: realidad y símbolo.* Caracas, 1965.

Dunham, Lowell. "Rómulo Gallegos: creador de la literatura nacional venezolana." *Revista Nacional de Cultura* 26, no. 164 (1964): 32–38.

Dunham, Lowell. *Rómulo Gallegos, vida y obra.* Mexico, 1957.

Durand, René L. F. "El cuarto de siglo de *Doña Bárbara.*" *Cultura Universitaria,* no. 45 (1954), pp. 5–17.

Englekirk, John E. "*Doña Bárbara,* Legend of the Llano." *Hispania* 31 (1948): 259–70.

González, Manuel Pedro. "A propósito de *Doña Bárbara.*" *Bulletin of Spanish Studies* 7, no. 28 (1930): 162–67.

Gramcko, Ida. "La mujer en la obra de Gallegos." *Revista Shell* 9, no. 37 (1960): 33–40.

Homenaje de *Cuadernos Americanos* 77 (1954): 75–155.

Hyde, Jeannine E. "The Function of Symbol in the Novels of Rómulo Gallegos." Ph.D. dissertation, University of Oklahoma, 1964.

Iduarte, Andrés. "Rómulo Gallegos, novelista de América." *Humanismo* 3, no. 22 (1954): 49–63.

Iduarte, Andrés. *Veinte años con Rómulo Gallegos.* Mexico, 1954.

Johnson, Jr., Ernest A. "The Meaning of *civilización* and *barbarie* in *Doña Bárbara.*" *Hispania* 39 (1956): 456–61.

Kolb, Glen L. "Aspectos estructurales de *Doña Bárbara.*" *Revista Iberoamericana* 28, no. 53 (1962): 131–40.

Landa, Rubén. "La personalidad moral de Gallegos." *Cuadernos Americanos* 115 (1961): 61–93.

Leo, Ulrich. "*Doña Bárbara,* obra de arte." *Revista Nacional de Cultura* 2, no. 17 (April 1940): 21–50.

Leo, Ulrich. *Rómulo Gallegos, estudio sobre el arte de novelar.* Mexico, 1954.

Leo, Ulrich. *"Sobre la misma tierra* — Apuntes al estilo de la novela-película." *Revista Nacional de Cultura* 7, no. 52 (1945): 55–74, 75–91.

Liscano, Juan. *Rómulo Gallegos y su tiempo.* Caracas, 1961.

Loveluck, Juan. "Los veinticinco años de *Doña Bárbara*." *Atenea*, no. 359 (1955), pp. 153–74.

Magdaleno, Mauricio. "Imágenes políticas de Rómulo Gallegos." *Cuadernos Americanos* 60 (1951): 234–59.

Massiani, Felipe. *El hombre y la naturaleza venezolana en Rómulo Gallegos.* Caracas, 1943.

Morínigo, Mariana. "Civilización y barbarie en *Facundo* y *Doña Bárbara*." *Revista Nacional de Cultura* 25, no. 161 (1963): 91–117.

Morón, Guillermo. "Sobre Rómulo Gallegos. Noticias para extranjeros." *Revista Bolívar* 11, no. 50 (1958): 221–73.

Pardo Tovar, Andrés. "Rómulo Gallegos, novelista de América." *Revista de las Indias*, época 2, no. 66–67 (June-July 1944), pp. 165–88.

Peralta, Jaime. "Una aproximación a la idea de América en Rómulo Gallegos." *Cuadernos Hispanoamericanos*, no. 178 (1964), pp. 136–45.

Pérez Díaz, Lucila. "Evolución progresiva de un protagonista de Rómulo Gallegos." *Revista Nacional de Cultura* 7, no. 53 (1945): 13–22.

Picón-Salas, Mariano. "A veinte años de *Doña Bárbara*." In *Obras selectas*, pp. 169–76. Madrid, 1953.

Piper, Anson. "El Yanqui en las novelas de Rómulo Gallegos." *Hispania* 33 (1950): 338–41.

Ramos Calles, Raúl. *Los personajes de Rómulo Gallegos a través del psicoanálisis.* Caracas, 1947.

Rosales, Julio. "Evocación de *La Alborada*." *Revista Nacional de Cultura* 21, no. 135 (1959): 6–18.

Ross, Waldo. "La soledad en la obra de Rómulo Gallegos." *Revista Nacional de Cultura* 24, no. 148 (1961): 28–45.

Ross, Waldo. "Meditación sobre el mundo de Juan Solito." *Revista Nacional de Cultura* 25, no. 156–57 (1962): 57–72.

Schultze de Montovani, Freyda. "*Doña Bárbara* y la América de Rómulo Gallegos." *Sur* 33, no. 230 (1954): 79–96.

Selva, Mauricio de la. "Alrededor de Rómulo Gallegos." *Cuadernos Americanos* 89 (1956): 256–69.

Valbuena-Briones, Ángel. "La idea política en la novela de Gallegos." *Atenea*, no. 403 (1964), pp. 84–93.

Vila Selma, José. *Procedimientos y técnicas en Rómulo Gallegos.* Seville, 1954.

Welsh, Louise. "The Emergence of Rómulo Gallegos as a Novelist and Social Critic." *Hispania* 40 (1957): 444–49.

Mendoza, Daniel

Crema, Edoardo. "Daniel Mendoza, el Aristofanesco." *Revista Nacional de Cultura* 10, no. 71 (1948): 34–41.

Picón Febres, Gonzalo

Barnola, Pedro Pablo. "Gonzalo Picón Febres." *Boletín de la Academia Venezolana de la Lengua* 28, no. 106–8 (1960): 59–72.

Cuesta y Cuesta, Alfonso. "Gonzalo Picón Febres." *El Farol* 23, no. 198 (1962): 28–32.

Pocaterra, José Rafael

Cuenca, Humberto. "Hacia una interpretación de la obra de José Rafael Pocaterra." *Cultura Universitaria,* no. 48–49 (1955), pp. 95–103.

Díaz Sánchez, Ramón. "Tres ciudades iluminadas por un novelista venezolano." *Revista Nacional de Cultura* 14, no. 98 (1953): 7–21.

Fabbiani Ruiz, J. "El drama de lo grotesco." In *Cuentos y cuentistas,* pp. 53–57. Caracas, 1951.

Fabbiani Ruiz, J. "Realismo grotesco y realismo lírico." *El Farol* (December 1947), pp. 22–23.

Medina, José Ramón. "José Rafael Pocaterra." *El Farol* 23, no. 199 (1962): 27–29.

Tejera, María Josefina. "Lo grotesco, forma de crítica en José Rafael Pocaterra." *Revista Nacional de Cultura* 29, no. 186 (1968): 75–91.

Romero García, Manuel Vicente

Capriles, Carlos L. "*Peonía,* alrededor de una polémica." *Revista Nacional de Cultura* 2, no. 21 (1940): 43–54.

Díaz, Alirio. "Nuestra música tradicional popular en *Peonía.*" *Cultura Universitaria* 92 (July-September 1966): 25–45.

Planchart, Julio. "Una defensa más y *Peonía.*" *Revista Nacional de Cultura* 11, no. 8 (1940): 13–36.

Index of Authors

Index of Titles